WALTHER EICHRODT

THEOLOGY OF THE OLD TESTAMENT

VOLUME ONE

THE OLD TESTAMENT LIBRARY

WALTHER EICHRODT

THEOLOGY
OF THE
OLD TESTAMENT

VOLUME ONE

Translated by
J. A. BAKER

The Westminster Press
Philadelphia

Library of Congress Catalog Card No. X 61–11867

TYPESET IN GREAT BRITAIN
PRINTED IN THE UNITED STATES OF AMERICA

14   15

*This edition in the English language
is dedicated to the
Society for Old Testament Study
and to the
Society of Biblical Literature and Exegesis
with the gratitude of the author
for honorary membership of
these British and American learned bodies*

CONTENTS

From the PREFACE TO THE FIRST EDITION

THE spiritual situation in general and that of theology in particular is impressing ever more peremptorily on everyone concerned with Old Testament studies the need for a new essay in OT theology. There are quite enough historical descriptions of Israelite and Judaistic religion: but by contrast only the most rudimentary attempts have been made to present the religion of which the records are to be found in the Old Testament as a self-contained entity exhibiting, despite ever-changing historical conditions, a constant basic tendency and character. It is precisely such a presentation, however, which has today become quite indispensable in the face both of the deep issues raised by the comparative study of religions and of the current impassioned analyses of the Christian religion and its relation to its Israelite past. Indeed, to anyone who is in any way acquainted with the problems involved the whole difficulty of the project is so strongly contemporary, that a doubt whether the question can be solved with the means at present at our disposal must seem only too well justified. The author of the present work has, therefore, entered on his task not light-heartedly but only under the strongest pressure from very diverse quarters. The experience which he has been able to gain in working over the material during repeated courses of lectures has indeed been encouraging: but in addition what has helped him to persevere in his work is the conviction that it is better at least to hazard an attempt to master a problem which has become too insistent to ignore—and thereby, perhaps, to provide a stimulus for better solutions—than to leave the whole matter undisturbed. He is fully aware that in doing so he has departed from the usual procedure, not only in the arrangement of the material, but even more in the effort to determine which questions are fundamental to the faith of the OT. This will be especially noticeable with regard to the significance of the Covenant, its institutions in Law and Cult, and its instruments of expression in Prophecy and Priesthood. But this approach will seem a disadvantage only to those who cannot see how miserably inadequate at just these points is the usual theology—one which thinks that the essence of OT religion can be displayed in the bloodless abstraction of 'ethical monotheism', simply because it cannot free itself from the values of a rationalistic individualism and the structure-patterns of developmental theories. It is, therefore, the author's hope that this first part of the *Theology of the Old Testament*, which aims at clarifying the most important fundamental questions, may be of some service to many who in the controversy about the OT are looking for new lines along which to direct their thoughts.

W. EICHRODT

Basel
July 1933

PREFACE TO THE FIFTH REVISED EDITION

SINCE the appearance of the First Edition of the present work there has been a very happy revival of theological work on the Old Testament, and such work has now won back its rightful place in academic studies in a field where the religio-historical approach for a long time held wellnigh undisputed sway. In 1933 it was still necessary to fight for recognition of the fact that a new conception of the OT system of faith in its particular quality of revelation was needed at all; today this has penetrated even the academic world. We are still, however, in the thick of the argument over the nature, method and purpose of an objective exposition and balanced presentation of the message of the OT; and the discussion is still far from coming to any agreed results. It seemed imperative to the author, therefore, to retain the basic lay-out and exposition of his material, in order that in the present conflict of opinions the approach to the problem confronting us which he personally advocated should be given a hearing in its strongest form. This means, in the first place, a conscious insistence on treating OT theology as a historical question and the rejection of all attempts, however enticing, to draw it into the domain of the normative sciences, as has been proposed, for example, by F. Baumgärtel ('Erwägungen zur Darstellung der Theologie des Alten Testaments', *TLZ* 76, 1951, pp. 257 ff.). That this has nothing to do with 'historicism', but rather with a new concept of the essential nature of true historical study, ought to be clear enough from the first chapter of this book; and this impression will be confirmed by the fact that a fundamental opposition to that understanding of the OT which characterizes the developmental theory is maintained throughout the work. Secondly, in the face of all objections, the 'covenant' has been retained as the central concept, by which to illuminate the structural unity and the unchanging basic tendency of the message of the OT. For it is in this concept that Israel's fundamental conviction of its special relationship with God is concentrated. The decisive consideration on this point is neither the presence nor absence of the

13

actual term *bᵉrīt*, as certain all too naïve critics seem to imagine (for a discussion of the avoidance of the word by many of the prophets, cf. e.g. pp. 51 f.), but the fact that every expression of the OT which is determinative for its faith rests on the explicit or implicit assumption that a free act of God, consummated in history, has raised Israel to the rank of the People of God, in whom the nature and will of God are to be revealed. The word 'covenant', therefore, is so to speak a convenient symbol for an assurance much wider in scope and controlling the formation of the national faith at its deepest level, without which Israel would not be Israel. As an epitome of the dealings of God in history the 'covenant' is not a doctrinal concept, with the help of which a complete corpus of dogma can be worked out, but the characteristic *description of a living process*, which was begun at a particular time and at a particular place, in order to reveal a divine reality unique in the whole history of religion. Reference to this living process in every single paragraph of this work will not escape the attentive reader.

But this is not to say that the scientific understanding of the witness of the OT may only take the form of repeating the OT's own account of its history. Something of this sort, allowing for deliberate overemphasis, seems to have been the aim of G. Ernest Wright in his short programmatic work, *God Who Acts: Biblical Theology as Recital* (1952: cf. my own review in *JBL* 73, 1954, pp. 240 ff.) and G. von Rad comes very close to the same position in his 'Typologische Auslegung des Alten Testaments' (*EvTh* 12, 1952/53, pp. 17 ff., reprinted in *Vergegenwärtigung, Aufsätze zur Auslegung des Alten Testaments*, 1955, pp. 47 ff.). This emphasis on the objective historical facts and events in the OT message at the expense of the testimony of faith to the divine revelation, which is advocated by both writers, has grown out of an understandable aversion from the misuse of the OT in the construction of dogmatic systems of doctrine. It comes, however, hazardously near to an uncontrolled and arbitrary attestation of God in individual facts of history, which can then only acquire real significance for faith in two ways; either by an extremely exaggerated 'salvation-history' approach, or by typological metamorphosis as 'prefiguring' the NT Christ-event. This is not, of course, to suggest that such a conclusion accurately describes the ultimate purpose of these particular efforts at securing the unity of the biblical faith. Nevertheless, it seems necessary to us to emphasize that the withdrawal from all 'conceptualism' with regard to the activity of

God in history ought never to involve isolating this activity in such a way as to ignore the testimony of faith evoked in response to it from the OT community. It is rather that the latter affords the only legitimate commentary on that activity. It is the interior overmastering of the human spirit by God's personal invasion, which in the first place brings to life the OT understanding of history. Here is to be found the decisive inward event, without which all external facts must become myth. Therefore the activity of God in the OT salvation-history can only be presented and expressed in words in combination with the response of the People of God to the historical event sent to them. It is from this involvement with a binding will of God that clearly defined expressions of faith spring, forming a testimony to God's nature and purpose which achieves perfect clarity only in the NT. If, however, there is to be any talk either of a unity of the biblical faith, or of any living meaning of the OT for Christians, then this state of affairs must be able to commend itself intuitively as self-evident—and in that case clearly defined concepts cannot be dispensed with anyway.

For this reason it is not a 'self-contained dogmatic totality, but a real God becoming manifest in history' (pp. 502 f.) to which the Scriptures of the OT bear witness. To enable this testimony to be heard once more, and by this means once more to make practicable the long obstructed path from the Old Testament to the New, is the reason for undertaking the theology of the OT—is, at any rate, the goal which all the expositions in this book are striving to reach. To this end the citation of the OT evidence in the notes has been made as thorough as possible: similarly, the index has been newly revised and corrected. The reshaping of whole sections was only undertaken where the burning issues of contemporary OT studies compelled it, namely in the matters of the Kingship of Yahweh and its expression in the cult, and of cult prophecy. The book has, however, been improved or clarified in a good many particular points, and especial note has been taken of the most important theological literature, though naturally only a selection of contributions to periodicals could be cited. To strive for absolute completeness—a goal which is hardly feasible now that in this 'ecumenical age' the boundaries have been pushed back far beyond the area of the German language—was no part of the author's intention. He must be content with the hope that no really serious gaps have been left.

In conclusion it is the author's prayer that this new edition of the first volume (which should be followed in the foreseeable future by volumes 2 and 3) may meet with a friendly reception and, like the earlier editions, be of service beyond all confessional frontiers, both in the sphere of academic study and in the practical ministry of the pastor and missionary, to the glory of God and the happiness of the reader.

W. EICHRODT

Basel
February 1957

PREFACE TO THE ENGLISH EDITION

IT IS a great joy to the writer to be able at last to make Part One of his *Theology of the Old Testament* available to English-speaking readers; and he would like to acknowledge his great debt of gratitude to the SCM Press and to the Westminster Press for sharing the risk of this undertaking. Likewise his heartfelt thanks go to the translator, who has accomplished his arduous task with great competence and insight. In this new revision the work has remained true to its original programme as defined in the Preface to the first edition. This was 'to present the religion of which the records are to be found in the Old Testament as *a self-contained entity exhibiting, despite ever-changing historical conditions, a constant basic tendency and character.*' The main concern was then, and is still, to arrive at a new understanding of the religious world of the OT precisely in respect of its *religious* quality, an aspect which for too long had been buried either under the schematizations imposed by 'development' theories or under the bloodless abstractions of a rationalist individualism. This meant deliberately striking away from the well-worn paths, not only in the arrangement of the material, but even more in deciding what questions really were fundamental to the religious life of the OT; above all in assessing the significance of the covenant, of its terms in law and cultus, and of the men who were its instruments in prophetism and priesthood. The concept of the covenant was given this central position in the religious thinking of the OT so that, by working outward from it, the structural unity of the OT message might be made more readily visible.

Notwithstanding many alterations in detail, and in spite of the fact that many objectors were prepared to see in it no more than an artificial construction, this overall orientation of the work has been deliberately retained. For the concept of the covenant enshrines Israel's most fundamental conviction, namely its sense of a unique relationship with God. The crucial point is not—as an all too naïve criticism sometimes seems to think—the occurrence or absence of the

Hebrew word *b'rit*,[1] but the fact that all the crucial statements of faith in the OT rest on the assumption, explicit or not, that a free act of God in history raised Israel to the unique dignity of the People of God, in whom his nature and purpose were to be made manifest. The actual term 'covenant' is, therefore, so to speak, only the code-word for a much more far-reaching certainty, which formed the very deepest layer of the foundations of Israel's faith, and without which indeed Israel would not have been Israel at all. As epitomizing God's action in history 'covenant' is not a dogmatic concept with the help of which a 'corpus of doctrine' can be evolved, but the *typical description of a living process*, which began at a particular time and place, and which was designed to make manifest a divine reality quite unique in the whole history of religion. The references to this living process in every single chapter of this work will not escape the attentive reader.

Even today this fundamental orientation, argued for in the following pages, needs stressing as much as ever. It is true that in the last decades theological work on the OT has revived in a most satisfactory way, and regained its proper place in academic studies. A whole series of treatments of the subject, such as those of Procksch, Vriezen and Jacob, to mention only a few, have in their different ways, but on the basis of a similar assessment of the contemporary theological situation, striven toward a common goal. But we are still in the thick of the argument about the nature, methods and purpose of an objective exposition and correct presentation of the OT message. Above all, the *OT Theology* of G. von Rad,[2] now completed with the publication in 1960 of the second volume, gives evidence of a highly interesting reappraisal of the problem here confronting OT studies, and one that will doubtless evoke lively discussion. Whether the route explored by its author—a path significantly different from the one trodden in the present work—can lead us to a solution of the questions still outstanding, or at least make a decisive contribution thereto, will call for the most careful consideration.[3] In any event, however, the attempt which we have made in these pages to unfold the content of the faith of the OT may perhaps be permitted to

[1] On the avoidance of this term in many of the prophets, cf. ch. II. 2. II.
[2] *Theologie des Alten Testaments.* Vol. I: *Die Theologie der geschichtlichen Überlieferungen Israels*, 1957. Vol. II: *Die Theologie der prophetischen Überlieferung Israels*, 1960.
[3] A discussion of the most important points of disagreement between von Rad and myself in the assessment of the present state of the problem will be found in the Excursus on 'The Problem of OT Theology' in the Appendix to this book.

stand as a pointer to a problem of OT Theology which remains urgent, and which must be solved if we are to understand the place of the OT in the Canon and, therefore, as a standard of faith for the Christian congregation.

WALTHER EICHRODT

Münchenstein
Basel
December 1960

TRANSLATOR'S PREFACE

T HE English version of the present work has taken the lion's share of what spare time the translator has been able to salvage from work in parish and university during the past four to five years. On reading the result he is aware acutely of defects in the style, which is still in many places too leaden-footed to make enjoyable reading. But to correct this fault right through a book of such size would have meant a delay unjustified by any probability of improvement, and a taxing of the publishers' already generous patience; it is only to be hoped, therefore, that students will not be put off by any superficial difficulties of this kind. For the intimate knowledge that can only come from rendering into a new language has deepened the translator's own conviction that this is incomparably the greatest book in its field— a work in which burning faith and scientific precision combine to give the reader a living experience of that 'new reality of God' of which it so often speaks, and which is the unique possession of the Old Testament.

The translator's deep gratitude is due to Professor Eichrodt and his daughter who have checked the *accuracy* of the entire MS. That it is a faithful rendering the reader can therefore be sure; more than that let him be charitable and not require!

J OHN B AKER

Corpus Christi College
Oxford
May 1961

ABBREVIATIONS

AAG   Altassyrische Gesetze (see p. 74 n. 1)
ANEP   J. B. Pritchard, *The Ancient Near East in Pictures*, 1954
ANET   J. B. Pritchard, *Ancient Near Eastern Texts relating to the Old Testament*[2], 1955
AOB   H. Gressmann, *Altorientalische Bilder zum AT*[2], 1927
AOT   H. Gressmann, *Altorientalische Texte zum AT*[2], 1926
AT   Alte Testament, alttestamentliche
BWANT   Beiträge zur Wissenschaft vom Alten und Neuen Testament, ed. A. Alt and G. Kittel
BZAW   Beihefte zur *ZAW*
CH   Codex Hammurabi
ET   English translation
EvTh   *Evangelische Theologie*
EVV   English versions
HG   Hethitische Gesetze (see p. 74 n. 1)
HRE   J. J. Herzog, *Realenzyklopädie für protestantische Theologie und Kirche*[3], ed. A. Hauck
JBL   *Journal of Biblical Literature*
JTS   *Journal of Theological Studies*
N.F.   Neue Folge
NKZ   *Neue Kirchliche Zeitschrift*
OTS   *Oudtestamentische Studiën*
RB   *Revue Biblique*
RGG   *Die Religion in Geschichte und Gegenwart*, 2nd edn, ed. H. Gunkel and L. Tscharnack, 1927–31; 3rd edn, ed. K. Galling, 1956 ff.
TLZ   *Theologische Literaturzeitung*
TWNT   *Theologische Wörterbuch zum Neuen Testament*, ed. G. Kittel, 1933 ff.

ZAW   *Zeitschrift für die alttestamentliche Wissenschaft*
ZNW   *Zeitschrift für die neutestamentliche Wissenschaft*

Biblical references are according to the chapters and verses of the Hebrew Bible. (Where these differ from EVV, they are noted in the margin of the RV and RSV.)

I

OLD TESTAMENT THEOLOGY:
THE PROBLEM AND THE METHOD

AMONG ALL THE PROBLEMS known to OT studies, one of the most far-reaching in its importance is that of the theology of the OT: for its concern is to construct *a complete picture of the OT realm of belief*, in other words to comprehend in all its uniqueness and immensity what is, strictly speaking, the proper object of OT study. The tasks of this science are very various in character, but this is the crown of them all; and to this, therefore, the other disciplines involved are ancillary.

But though the domain of OT theology proper is comparatively restricted, yet it is closely linked both to the prolific variety of pagan religions and to the exclusive realm of NT belief. Thus it exhibits a *double aspect*.

On the one side it faces on to the *comparative study of religions*. To adapt a well-known dictum of Harnack [1] (which he coined in opposition to the thesis of Max Müller that 'The man who knows only one religion knows none') one might say, 'The man who knows the religion of the OT knows many.' For in the course of its long history it has not only firmly consolidated its own unique contribution, but also, by a process of absorption and rejection, has forged links with the most varied forms of paganism. Hence the study of it can become at the same time a course in the comparative study of religions. *No presentation of OT theology can properly be made without constant reference to its connections with the whole world of Near Eastern religion.* Indeed it is in its commanding such a wide panorama of the rich domain of man's

[1] *Die Aufgabe der theologischen Fakultäten und die allgemeine Religionsgeschichte,* 1901, p. 10.

25

religious activity that many will prefer to see the special significance of the faith of the OT.

And yet there is this *second aspect*, looking on towards the New Testament. Anyone who studies the historical development of the OT finds that throughout there is a powerful and purposive movement which forces itself on his attention. It is true that there are also times when the religion seems to become static, to harden into a rigid system; but every time this occurs the forward drive breaks through once more, reaching out to a higher form of life and making everything that has gone before seem inadequate and incomplete. This movement does not come to rest until the manifestation of Christ, in whom the noblest powers of the OT find their fulfilment. Negative evidence in support of this statement is afforded by the torso-like appearance of Judaism in separation from Christianity.

The affinity with the NT is not, however, exhausted by a bare historical connection, such as might afford material for the historian's examination but no more. It rather confronts us with an essential characteristic, which must be taken into account if the OT is to be understood. Moreover this is an impression which is confirmed over and over again when we enter the unique spiritual realm of the NT. For in the encounter with the Christ of the Gospels there is the assertion of a mighty living reality as inseparably bound up with the OT past as pointing forward into the future. *That which binds together indivisibly the two realms of the Old and New Testaments—different in externals though they may be—is the irruption of the Kingship of God into this world and its establishment here.* This is the unitive fact because it rests on the action of one and the same God in each case; that God who in promise and performance, in Gospel and Law, pursues one and the selfsame great purpose, the building of his Kingdom. This is why the central message of the NT leads us back to the testimony of God in the old covenant.

But in addition to this historical movement from the Old Testament to the New there is a current of life flowing in the reverse direction from the New Testament to the Old. This reverse relationship also elucidates the full significance of the realm of OT thought. Only where this two-way relationship between the Old and New Testaments is understood do we find a correct definition of the problem of OT theology and of the method by which it is possible to solve it.

Hence to our general aim of obtaining a comprehensive picture of the realm of OT belief we must add a second and closely related purpose—*to see that this comprehensive picture does justice to the essential relationship with the NT* and does not merely ignore it. Naturally this does not mean that the language of the OT must be artificially screwed up to the pitch of the New in order that both Testaments may be on the same spiritual plane. To seek to do this would merely betray a very poor idea of the difference between a process in real life and a process in logical thought. It was just at this point that the old orthodoxy, in spite of having a sound idea of the correct course, had the misfortune to lose its grasp of the living reality and to slip back into the procedures of logical demonstration, thereby concealing rather than clarifying the actual relation between the Old and New Testaments. The reaction to this was rationalism with its root-and-branch rejection of the OT.

This then is the problem that confronts us. In expounding the realm of OT thought and belief we must never lose sight of the fact that the OT religion, ineffaceably individual though it may be, can yet be grasped in this essential uniqueness only when it is seen as completed in Christ. None other than B. Stade, well known for the radical nature of his criticism, emphasized this 'homogeneity and similarity of the Old and New Testament revelations' in his own theology of the OT; and he saw in this fact the premiss from which this branch of OT studies could be proved to be a necessary part of Christian theology. [1]

The more clearly the shape of this problem is seen, the more apparent it becomes that it is not to be solved along the lines which OT studies have so far taken, namely the consideration of the process of historical development only. It is not just a matter of describing the all-round expansion of OT religion, or the phases through which it passed, but of determining to what extent—as B. Stade remarked —it ties up with the NT revelation and is analogous to it. But this can only be done by taking a cross-section of the realm of OT thought, thus making possible both a comprehensive survey and a sifting of what is essential from what is not. In this way both the total structure of the system and the basic principles on which it rests can be exposed to view. In other words we have to undertake a *systematic examination* with objective classification and rational arrangement of the varied material. This does not in any way imply that the historical method

[1]*Biblische Theologie des Alten Testaments*, 1905, p. 15.

of investigation is worthless, nor that it should be set aside. We ought rather to build deliberately on its conclusions and make use of its procedures. Nevertheless developmental analysis must be replaced by systematic synthesis, if we are to make more progress toward an interpretation of the outstanding religious phenomena of the OT in their deepest significance. [1]

A glance at the history of our particular discipline will abundantly confirm that this method, deriving as it does from the nature of the material, is the proper one. As we have already stated, rationalism tore to shreds the inadequate attempts of orthodoxy to demonstrate the inner coherence of the Old and New Testaments by the collation of proof-texts and an extensive system of typology. [2] It proved that it was impossible to reduce the whole realm of OT thought, conditioned as it is by such an immense variety of ages and individuals, to a handbook of dogmatic instruction without doing violence to it. Rationalism itself, however, was quite unable to offer any substitute; for in its delight in critical analysis it lost its feeling for the vital synthesis in the OT and could only see the differing teachings of individual biblical writers. [3]

Into the meaningless confusion of *disjecta membra*, into which the OT on such a view degenerated, the new approach to history which began to flower with the age of romanticism brought a unifying principle. It dismissed once for all the 'intellectualist' approach, which looked only for doctrine, and sought by an all-inclusive survey to grasp the totality of religious life in all its richness of expression. Furthermore it brought this unexpected expansion of the field of study under control with the magic formula of 'historical develop-ment', allowing all the individual elements to be arranged in one historical process and thus enabling the meaning of the whole to be demonstrated in its final achievement.

This method of treatment, which began with Herder [4] and de

---

[1] I have given the main outlines of the relationship between this task and the dogmatic religious presentation, properly so called, of OT religion in my lecture, 'Hat die alttestamentliche Theologie noch selbständige Be-deutung innerhalb der alttestamentlichen Wissenschaft?', *ZAW* 47, 1929, pp. 83 ff.

[2] It is not possible to take into consideration in this work such exceptional cases as G. Calixt and J. Cocceius.

[3] Cf. C. F. Ammon, *Biblische Theologie*, 1792; G. L. Bauer, *Theologie des Alten Testaments*, 1796, and others.

[4] *The Spirit of Hebrew Poetry, Letters on Theology, The Oldest Documents of the Human Race*, etc.

Wette,[1] reached its high-water mark with Wellhausen[2] and his school, and for decades diverted work on OT theology into historical channels. Of what avail was it that a Beck[3] or a Hofmann[4] should attempt, about the middle of the last century, to develop a system of biblical doctrine? By making use of the OT for this purpose they were indeed standing up for its vital importance for the Christian faith, but they made no headway against the rising stream of historical investigation—to say nothing of the fact that the dogmatic system to which they harnessed the thought of the OT was seriously defective.

All the more deserving of notice, therefore, are three men who in the second half of the nineteenth century, right in the thick of the triumphal progress of historical criticism, attempted to expound the essential content of the OT in systematic form, while at the same time giving full consideration to the newly emergent problems connected with it. These were G. F. Oehler,[5] A. Dillmann,[6] and H. Schultz.[7] All three took account of the new movement by prefacing their exposition with a historical summary of OT religion. They then went on, however, to contend earnestly for a systematic correlation of the elements which had so far been examined only as they occurred in the course of the historical process. It was unfortunate that the two first-named works did not appear until after the deaths of their authors and so were already at the time of their publication no longer defensible in many details.[8] Nevertheless, repeated new editions witness to their having met a pressing need. Even today they still provide the most thorough treatment of the realm of OT belief from the systematic standpoint; and even though since that time research has brought to light much new relevant material and has introduced different ways of framing the problems, so materially altering the total picture, one can turn to them again and again. It is significant that for twenty-five years after the last edition of Schultz's *Theology* no one ventured on a further attempt to provide an exposition of this kind in the realm of OT belief. The historical approach had triumphed on every side.

[1]*Beiträge zur Geschichte des Alten Testaments*, 1806–7; *Biblische Dogmatik*, 1813, 3rd edn, 1831.
[2]*Prolegomena to the History of Israel*, ET, 1885; originally 1878; *History of Israel*, ET, 1894; *Die israelitisch-jüdische Religion*, 1906 (Kultur der Gegenwart 1, 4).
[3]*Die christliche Lehrwissenschaft nach den biblischen Urkunden*, 1841.
[4]*Der Schriftbeweis*, 1852–55.
[5]*Theologie des Alten Testaments*, 1873; 3rd edn, 1891.
[6]*Handbuch der alttestamentlichen Theologie*, ed. R. Kittel, 1895.
[7]*Old Testament Theology*: ET in 2 vols., 2nd edn, 1898; 5th German edn, 1896.
[8]This applies also to the less important OT Theology of E. Riehm, 1889.

To say this is of course not to attempt to deny that this method accomplished an immense amount for the historical understanding of OT religion. It is impossible even to conceive of a historical picture that does not make use of its findings, and to that extent not one of us can help being in its debt. For this very reason, however, the method had a particularly fatal influence both on OT theology and on the understanding of the OT in every other aspect, because it fostered the idea that once the historical problems were clarified everything had been done. The essential inner coherence of the Old and New Testaments was reduced, so to speak, to a thin thread of historical connection and causal sequence between the two, with the result that an external causality—not even susceptible in every case of secure demonstration—was substituted for a homogeneity that was real because it rested on the similar content of their experience of life. How appallingly this impoverished the conception of the relationship of the two Testaments strikes one at once; but it is also clear that the OT itself, if valued only as the historical foundation or forerunner of the New, was bound to lose its own specific value as revelation, even though from the historical angle it might be assessed as highly as ever. One consequence of this is the fact that the OT has completely lost any effective place in the structure of Christian doctrine. Indeed, in the circumstances, it sometimes seems more from academic politeness than from any real conviction of its indispensability that it is so seldom denied all value as canonical Scripture [1]—a step which would enable the whole subject to be transferred from the sphere of theology to that of the comparative study of religions.

That OT theologians for their part were content to put up with this development, and thought that the value of the OT could be safeguarded even along these lines, can only be understood if we remember that the full flood of historicism, which overflowed every academic discipline, had blinded them to the fact that historical investigation, for all its glittering achievements, could yet offer no serious substitute for the concept of the essential coherence of the Old and New Testaments. The little still left to OT theology to do, viz., the historical presentation of the Israelite and Judaistic religion, was quite insufficient to conceal, even with the help of the magic word 'development', how serious the loss had been. There was no longer any unity to be found in the OT, only a collection of detached periods which were simply the reflections of as many different

[1]Harnack (*Marcion*, 1921, pp. 247 ff.) was one notable exception.

religions. In such circumstances it was only a logical development that the designation 'OT Theology', which had formerly had quite a different connotation, should frequently be abandoned and the title 'the History of Israelite Religion' substituted for it.[1] Even where scholars still clung to the old name,[2] they were neither desirous nor capable of offering anything more than an exposition of the historical process.

When, therefore, in 1922 E. König ventured to publish a Theology of the OT which attempted to take its title seriously, it was a real act of courage which deserves to be recorded. It is true that to some extent a hybrid form is still noticeable in the book. The historical-developmental method of examination, carrying over from the opening historical section into the systematic part, never allows the synthesis its rightful scope. Furthermore, the recalcitrant material is forced into a Procrustes' bed, because it has been made to fit a dogmatic arrangement foreign to the subject. Nevertheless, that the author had rightly sensed the need of the contemporary situation was proved by the grateful reception accorded to his work.

It is high time that the tyranny of historicism in OT studies was broken and the proper approach to our task re-discovered. This is no new problem, certainly, but it is one that needs to be solved anew in every epoch of knowledge—*the problem of how to understand the realm of OT belief in its structural unity and how, by examining on the one hand its religious environment and on the other its essential coherence with the NT, to illuminate its profoundest meaning.*[3] Only so shall we succeed in winning back for OT studies in general and for OT theology in particular that place in Christian theology which at present has been surrendered to the comparative study of religions.

We are not for one moment trying to make light of the difficulties that stand in the way of this undertaking. It is a fact that the unique

[1]So R. Smend in his widely-used *Lehrbuch der alttestamentlichen Religionsgeschichte*[2], 1899; F. Giesebrecht, *Grundzüge der israelitischen Religionsgeschichte*, 1904; K. Marti, *Geschichte der israelitischen Religion*[5], 1907; K. Budde, *Die Religion des Volkes Israel bis zur Verbannung*[3], 1912; E. König, *Geschichte der alttestamentlichen Religion*[2], 1915; R. Kittel, *The Religion of the People of Israel*, ET, 1925; G. Hölscher, *Geschichte der israelitischen und jüdischen Religion*, 1922.

[2]B. Stade, *Biblische Theologie des Alten Testaments*, E. Kautzsch, *Biblische Theologie des Alten Testaments*, 1911. So also A. Kuenen, *De godsdienst van Israel*, 1869 ff., and the work of the same name by B. D. Eerdmans, 1930.

[3]In this connection cf. the examination by R. Kittel of the importance of OT theology in his essay, 'Die Zukunft der alttestamentlichen Wissenschaft', *ZAW* 39, 1921, pp. 94 ff.

quality of Israelite religion obstinately resists all efforts to subject it completely to systematic treatment. For if there is one feature that it exhibits more than any other religion, it is an abundance of creative religious personalities, who are closely involved in the historical experiences of the people. In any religion where this is not so the main content of the thought is usually present at its foundation and changes but little in the course of time, being rather worn away and levelled down than made more profound or fashioned afresh. In the OT, however, we find both a stock of spiritual values firmly established at the outset and also an incessant process of growth which is continually enriching the religion by drawing into its sphere new content from without. At the same time the internal shape of the religion becomes increasingly well-defined. It is *this prominence of the personal and historical factors* in Israelite religion which constitutes a constant temptation to the writer to resort to an exposition along the historical line of development.

But though such a motive may be justifiable, it should not be overriding. A picture of the historical development of Israelite religion can equally well be conveyed by means of a History of Israel, so long as the religious life is allowed that place in the work which its close contact and interaction with the political history merits. It is true that to this extent OT theology presupposes the history of Israel. Nevertheless, in so far as the spiritual history of Israel has brought about a drastic remodelling of many religious ideas, the right way to make allowance for this is *to have the historical principle operating side by side with the systematic in a complementary role.* In treating individual religious concepts the major elements of their historical background must be taken into account. Only so can we hope to do justice to the great unitive tendency that runs through the whole religious history of Israel and makes it with all its variety a self-consistent entity.

One thing, however, must be guarded against and that is any *arrangement of the whole body of material* which derives not from the laws of its own nature but from some dogmatic scheme. It is impossible to use a system which has been developed on a basis quite different from that of the realm of OT thought to arrive at the OT belief about God. All that results is a grave danger of intruding alien ideas and of barring the way to understanding.

It has often been observed that the OT contains very little actual 'doctrine'. Nowhere are formal 'instructions' about the Being of God or his attributes delivered to the Israelite. His knowledge of God comes to him from the realities of his own life. He learns about the nature of God by reasoning *a posteriori* from the standards and usages of Law and Cult, which rule his personal life with divine authority, from the events of history and their interpretation by his spiritual leaders, in short, from his daily experience of the rule of God. By this means he comprehends the divine essence much more accurately than he would from any number of abstract concepts. The result is that the formation of such concepts in the OT lags far behind, while the same spiritual values which they are normally the means of conveying to us are yet uncompromisingly real and effective.

In deciding, therefore, on our procedure for the treatment of the realm of OT thought, we must avoid all schemes which derive from Christian dogmatics—such, for example, as 'Theology—Anthropology—Soteriology', *'ordo salutis'* and so on. Instead we must plot our course as best we can along the lines of the OT's own dialectic. This speaks of a revelation of the God of the People, who in his rule proves himself to be also the God of the World and the God of the Individual. We are therefore presented with three principal categories, within which to study the special nature of the Israelite faith in God: *God and the People, God and the World* and *God and Man.* [1]

[1] I owe this pregnant formulation of the three major categories to the outline by O. Procksch, which formed the basis of his university lectures on OT theology and which has provided me with many stimulating ideas. The division of the material here suggested had already been anticipated by H. Schultz in the arrangement of the second part of his *OT Theology*, except that in a way characteristic of him he treated Hope separately in a special section.

Since the first edition of this work several expositions of the faith of the OT have appeared, which likewise accept as their controlling concepts the ones here developed. Pre-eminent is the monumental work of O. Procksch (*Theologie des Alten Testaments*, 1950) which formed the crowning achievement of the extremely productive life of this scholar, but which he unfortunately did not live to see in print. By prefacing the systematic treatment with a historical sketch he sought to relieve the former of the burden of historical problems and so free himself to take a cross-section of the OT message and arrange it according to the same basic plan as we have adopted. Next there is the fine work of T. C. Vriezen (*Hoofdlijnen der Theologie van het Oude Testament*, 1949, 2nd edn, 1954; ET, *An Outline of Old Testament Theology*, 1958), which seeks in the first part to elucidate the problem 'Knowledge and Faith, History and Revelation' in order in the second to be able to expound the central elements of the witness to God found in the OT. Here the concept which controls the arrangement is that of the new God-given community relationship, and by this means a vital comprehension is achieved both of the inner unity of the OT and of its overall pointing to Christ. E. Jacob (*Théologie de l'Ancien Testament*, 1956; ET, *Theology of the Old Testament*, 1958) has aimed at a systematic synthesis of the essential content of OT theology in the framework of God's activity as Creator of the world and man and as Lord of history. A prefatory section on the Being of God, and a shorter concluding section on Sin, Death and the End enable him to incorporate those themes which could not otherwise be fitted into the pattern.

By contrast, E. Sellin (*Theologie des Alten Testaments*, 1933, 2nd edn, 1936) and L. Köhler (*Theologie des Alten Testaments*, 1936, 2nd edn, 1949; ET, *Old Testament Theology*, 1957) follow the old dogmatic outline with its strongly didactic arrangement. The former attempts to illuminate the historical connections of the later didactically developed section by a parallel account of the history of Israelite and Jewish religion. The latter is concerned to present in a more eclectic manner only those ideas, thoughts and concepts of the OT which are theologically important, and can therefore be content with the old dogmatic division into Theology, Anthropology and Soteriology, for in his view a christologically determined inner unity of the OT can only be shattered by bringing in historical differentiations.

G. von Rad (*Theologie des Alten Testaments*, vol. I, 1957) has attempted to solve this problem of the relationship of history to theology along new lines. He abandons the idea that the OT message must be related to historical facts such as may be established by the methods of the critical historian, and in its place expounds as the proper object of OT theology Israel's recital of her history from the standpoint of faith—a recital in his view both completely subjective and confessional in character. Hence what emerges as a 'theology of Israel's historical traditions' is the reproduction of the theological concepts and kerygmatic schemes of the various OT history-writers; and it is the differentiation between them, worked out with precision, which presents us with constantly fresh aspects of Israel's understanding of herself as the people of God. The resultant picture is that of a diversified collection of testimonies; any structurally unified religious totality, as with the work of L. Köhler, has quite disappeared, nor is it even possible to grasp the organic link between the Old Testament and the reality that comes with the New. The last chapter, although only loosely connected to what has gone before, offers a sensitive treatment of the Psalm and Wisdom literature; the theology of prophetism is reserved for the second volume.

A. Lods (*La Religion d'Israel*, vol. 2, 1935–9) and M. Buber ('Het Geloof van Israel', in *De Godsdiensten der Wereld*, ed. G. van der Leeuw, vol. I, 2nd edn, 1948, pp. 168–307) still adhere to the method of presentation by a continuous historical narrative.

For the Anglo-Saxon reader the following works may also be mentioned:

N. H. Snaith (*The Distinctive Ideas of the Old Testament*, 1944) and H. H. Rowley (*The Faith of Israel*, 1956) provide outstanding surveys of the world of OT belief, dealing concisely with the principal problems of importance for the message of the OT.

O. J. Baab (*The Theology of the Old Testament*, 1949) seeks to present in systematic cross-section, in a manner akin to that of L. Köhler, a selection of those religious ideas which seem to him to be the most truly important for our own approach to the OT. His study contains much that is of value, but it is equally unsuccessful in covering the whole scope of OT religion. This is particularly apparent in the fact that, apart from the history of ideas, it is not possible to pay sufficient attention to the life of the Israelite community in law and cultus. Even less satisfactory is the psychologizing and rationalizing attempt to demonstrate that the faith of the OT, as a *reasonable* faith, answers to the needs of the human spirit. As the logical corollary of this any idea that the theology of the OT should be fundamentally controlled by the faith of the NT—an idea inevitably prominent, for example, in the concepts of prediction and fulfilment—is naturally rejected.

W. F. Albright's comprehensive archaeological study (*Archaeology and the Religion of Israel*[2], 1946) forms a welcome supplement to his important work, *From the Stone Age to Christianity*[2], 1946, in which the author has set the faith of the OT in the whole vast perspective of the history of the ancient Near East.

These afford us some hope of guarding ourselves against pale and abstract theorizing and of seizing instead something of the living immediacy of the Israelite faith in God, even when treating it in a theoretical manner. However that may be, one quite unexpected advantage accrues right at the start. We have by-passed the argument over *how much material is relevant to the exposition of Israelite religion*; may this be confined to the OT documents, or ought it also to draw on the extra-canonical Scriptures of Judaism? Although there can be no vital objection to bringing within the scope of our study the ways in which later Judaism worked over and appropriated the realm of OT thought, yet we cannot help being aware that the fact that Jesus and the whole NT make almost exclusive use of the OT canon and thereby accord it a special significance for all their thinking is no superficial coincidence. The plain fact of the matter is that within these limits is to be found the major and most valuable part of those thoughts and ideas which gave the faith of Israel its character. The theology of later Judaism, therefore, enters into consideration only in so far as it may have given a particular turn to the development of many OT conceptions and so have affected the influence of the Old Testament on the New. The more detailed historical study of the realm of belief of later Judaism is a subject which must be referred respectively to the history of Israel and the history of NT times.

II

THE COVENANT RELATIONSHIP

I. THE MEANING OF THE COVENANT CONCEPT

THE CONCEPT IN WHICH Israelite thought gave definitive expression to the binding of the people to God and by means of which they established firmly from the start the particularity of their knowledge of him was the covenant. That the basis of the relationship with God can be regarded as embodied in a covenant from Mosaic times has of course been sharply contested. [1] Nevertheless, it can be demonstrated that the covenant-union between Yahweh and Israel is an original element in all sources, despite their being in part in very fragmentary form. Indeed this is still true even of those passages where the word *bᵉrit* has disappeared altogether. [2] The whole course of early Israelite history, in which the religious sense of solidarity is bound up with the Sinai tradition, affords further evidence of this. [3] Moreover, in the post-Mosaic era, wherever the relationship with God has the character of a relationship of grace, that is to say, it is founded on a primal act in history, maintained on definite conditions and protected by a powerful divine Guardian, then even where the covenant is not explicitly mentioned the spiritual

---

[1]The principal exponent of this view was R. Kraetzschmar, who in his work *Die Bundesvorstellung im AT*, 1896, argued that the idea of the covenant first appeared as a result of the work of the major prophets. Such a conclusion was only the natural consequence of his contention that the early religion of Israel was a nature religion. Similarly B. Stade designates Jeremiah as the first prophet to conceive of Israel's relationship with Yahweh as a *bᵉrit* (*Biblische Theologie des AT*, p. 234).

[2]Cf. Ex. 24.9–11 (J₁); 24.3–8 (E); 34.10, 27 (J₂). H. Gressmann (*Mose und seine Zeit*, 1913, pp. 183 ff.) has demonstrated this particularly happily for the narrative of the divine meal on the mountain.

[3]Judg. 5.4 f., 9, 23; 6.13; 11.16; I Sam. 2.27; 4.8; 10.18; 15.6; Ex. 15.1 ff., 21; Num. 23.22; 24.8.

premisses of a covenant relationship with God are manifestly present. [1] Finally, the use of the covenant concept in secular life argues that the religious *b'rīt* too was always regarded as a bilateral relationship; for even though the burden is most unequally distributed between the two contracting parties, this makes no difference to the fact that the relationship is still essentially two-sided. [2] The idea that in ancient Israel the *b'rīt* was always and only thought of as Yahweh's pledging of himself, to which human effort was required to make no kind of response (Kraetzschmar), can therefore be proved to be erroneous. [3] The safest starting-point for the critical examination of Israel's relationship with God is still the plain impression given by the OT itself that Moses, taking over a concept of long standing in secular life, based the worship of Yahweh on a covenant agreement. This, however, makes the task of defining clearly the theological meaning of the covenant concept all the more important.

(a) First of all it must be noted that the establishment of a covenant through the work of Moses especially emphasizes one basic element in the whole Israelite experience of God, namely *the factual nature of the divine revelation.* God's disclosure of himself is not grasped speculatively, not expounded in the form of a lesson; it is as he breaks in on the life of his people in his dealings with them and moulds them according to his will that he grants them knowledge of his being. This interpretation of the covenant is indicated by the whole historical process leading up to it. The foundation of an enduring covenant order appears as the purpose and consummation of the

[1]Cf. the exhaustive discussion in E. Sellin, *Beiträge zur israelitischen und jüdischen Religionsgeschichte*, I, 1896, pp. 15 ff. Also P. Volz, *Mose*[1], 1907, pp. 28 ff.; *Mose und sein Werk*[2], 1932, pp. 108 ff.

[2]Gen. 21.23; 26.29; Josh. 9.1 ff.; I Sam. 11.1; 20.1 ff.; I Kings 20.34; Ezek. 17.18 etc.

[3]Cf. J. P. Valeton, 'Bedeutung und Stellung des Worts *b'rīt* im Priesterkodex usf.', *ZAW* 12, 1892, pp. 1 ff., 224 ff.; 13, 1893, pp. 245 ff. This statement is in no way dependent on whatever may be the root meaning of the word, which is etymologically uncertain. According to Valeton and Kautzsch this is 'cutting', with reference to the sacrificial ceremony; according to Kraetzschmar and Karge 'fettering', with reference to the binding of the free will of the partners in the contract; according to Hempel (art. 'Bund', *RGG*[2] I, col. 1360) 'eating' or 'meal' with reference to the ceremony necessary to seal the covenant; in *RGG*[3] I, col. 1514, all attempt at derivation is abandoned. The various types of covenant-making both within and outside the OT (cf. Hempel, *op. cit.*; M. Noth, 'Das alttestamentliche Bundschliessen im Lichte eines Maritextes' in *Gesammelte Studien zum AT*, 1957, pp. 149 ff.; J. E. Mendenhall, *Law and Covenant in Israel and the Ancient Near East*, 1955) leave no doubt of the reciprocity of the Israelite covenant relationship.

mighty deliverance from Egypt; the power, the ready assistance, the faithfulness of Yahweh experienced thus far are offered to the people for their permanent enjoyment, while at the same time their behaviour is subjected to definite standards. Moreover, because this demonstration of the will of Yahweh appears as a concrete fact of history, as a covenant expressed in the forms of actual events, it lays quite unmistakable emphasis on the practical relationship of living founded on these events, and causes the formation of religious concepts to be left to the natural advance of spiritual knowledge.

(b) Strong pressure in this direction is in any case already to be found in the immediate circumstances of the divine covenant. First *a clear divine will* becomes discernible, which can be depended upon and to which appeal can be made. The covenant knows not only of a demand, but also of a promise: 'You shall be my people and I will be your God.' In this way it provides life with a goal and history with a meaning. Because of this the fear that constantly haunts the pagan world, the fear of arbitrariness and caprice in the Godhead, is excluded. With this God men know exactly where they stand; *an atmosphere of trust and security* is created, in which they find both the strength for a willing surrender to the will of God and joyful courage to grapple with the problems of life. [1]

Such an account can, of course, only be fully valid on one assumption, namely that the concrete content of the covenant order warrants and confirms the deductions that may be made from its formal character. Only if we recognize that the simple laws of ancient Israel, infused with a deep feeling for righteousness, which are to be found in the Decalogue and the 'Book of the Covenant', do to some extent constitute the basis of the actual Mosaic covenant contract, [2]

---

[1]This statement is, of course, not to be controverted by reference to certain inexplicable divine acts of punishment, such as those in II Sam. 6.6 ff.; 24.1, for the point about these events is precisely that they are the exceptions which fail to shake the certainty of God's fundamental attitude to his people. On the subject of the value attached to resignation in the face of the inexplicable dealings of God cf. ch. VII. 5, pp. 259 ff.; 6, pp. 276 f. Of that uncertainty concerning the divine will which is so eloquently expressed in the famous 'royal lament' of the Babylonian Job (cf. Ungnad, *Religion der Babylonier und Assyrier*, 1921, p. 228) Israel knows nothing.

[2]Estimates of what the extent may actually be vary considerably according to the importance attached to the orally transmitted paradigms ('Normen') or to the fixing of a basic text in writing. Those who consider, in opposition to the view taken here, that generally speaking nothing can be known of the terms of the Mosaic covenant are bound to regard statements about the direction of the divine will as no more than conjecture, inevitably lacking any real force: so e.g., Kautzsch, *Biblische Theologie des AT*, pp. 66 ff.

can we get beyond the realm of mere possibilities and attractive suppositions, and see in the establishment of a moral and social order by one all-ruling divine will the basis not only of the strongly unified character of the Israelite view of the world, but also of its robust affirmation of life, two marks that distinguish it clearly from the fissile and pessimistic tendencies of paganism. (Cf. further discussion of this point in ch. III: 'The Institutions of the Covenant'.)

(c) The content of the will of God thus defined in the covenant also shows its formative power by the way in which it makes the human party to the covenant aware of his unique position. For participation in the divine covenant impressed a special character on the loose tribal coalition, in which Israel awoke to historical self-awareness. It is no tightly closed national community giving religious expression to national feeling in the worship of Yahweh. That which unites the tribes to one another and makes them a unified people with a strong sense of solidarity is the will of God. It is in the name of Yahweh and in the covenant sanctioned by him that the tribes find the unifying bond, which proves a match even for the centrifugal tendencies of tribal egoism and creates from highly diversified elements a whole with a common law, a common cultus and a common historical consciousness. It is small wonder that in a nation which was built up on this foundation it was the idea of the divine Lord of the Covenant which exercised a dominating influence. The concerns of the nation as a whole derived their power to bind together the individual component parts solely from the idea of the authoritative divine will, as this was expressed in the covenant and thus subordinated the entire national life to its own purposes.[1] It is striking that this association draws no clear line to exclude the stranger, but is continually absorbing outsiders into itself.[2] Moreover, the decisive requirement for admission is not natural kinship but readiness to submit oneself to the will of the divine Lord of the Covenant and to vow oneself to this particular God. The size of a nation which grows

[1]P. Volz speaks of a 'Yahweh league' (Mose[1], pp. 94, 99), M. Weber of the Israelite 'confederacy' (Gesammelte Aufsätze zur Religionssoziologie, III: Das antike Judentum, 1921, passim) and E. Sellin sees Moses as the founder of an esoteric religion within a nation already fully formed (Geschichte des israelitisch-jüdischen Volkes I, 1924, pp. 85, 93 f.)

[2]From the time of the Exodus from Egypt onwards new elements were continually entering the tribal covenant union. Sometimes these were Hebrew—the Joshua covenant of Josh. 24 refers to such a case—sometimes foreign, especially among the southern tribes which had not been into Egypt. This explains why the twelve tribes are enumerated differently in Judg. 5; Gen. 49; and Deut. 33.

up in this way is not determined by purely natural factors. It does not receive the law of its being from blood and soil. It is a historically determined divine creation, a 'psychical totality',[1] which acquires cohesion and character from an inward order and strength. The *foedus iniquum* of the Sinai covenant, therefore, in fact created a domain with an overlord and subjects; henceforward the idea of the *Kingdom of God* is in the air. At present, however, it is not this concept, formed by analogy from political life, which is of major importance, but the more purely religious descriptions which define the peculiar position of the covenant people. The body of human partners in the covenant, when it comes together in obedience to the call of God,[2] is described as *qāhāl* and *'ēdāh*, 'assembly' and 'congregation'—titles which probably spring from the life of those ancient religious confederations best known to us in the Greek form of the 'amphictyony'.[3] A more general description, which shows no connection with specifically cultic concerns, is *'am (hā)'·lōhīm*[4] or *'am yhwh*,[5] that is to say, a people possessing unity in their situation as clients of a common God.[6] In the opinion of many the term Israel, as a name binding together the confederation of tribes and meaning 'God rules', would also have had a predominantly sacral-religious and not political connotation.[7]

[1]Thus N. A. Dahl in his profound examination of the 'church-consciousness' of primitive Christianity, *Das Volk Gottes*, 1941, p. 4, with reference to J. Pedersen, *Israel, its Life and Culture*, I–II, 1926, p. 475.

[2]*Qāhāl*: Gen. 49.6; Num. 16.33; 22.4; Micah 2.5; Deut. 5.19; 9.10; 10.4; 18.16; 23.2–9; I Kings 8.14, and frequently in the P stratum. *'Ēdāh* only in the latter, e.g. Ex. 12.3, 19, 47; 16.1 f.; 34.31; Lev. 4.13; 8.3–5; Num. 1.18 etc.: this is certainly a specifically cultic description, the age of which cannot be exactly established. Cf. L. Rost, *Die Vorstufen von Kirche und Synagoge im Alten Testament* (BWANT IV 24), 1938.

[3]Cf. A. Alt, 'Israel', *RGG²*, III, cols. 437 ff. For more precise information cf. M. Noth, *Das System der zwölf Stämme Israels*, 1930. This comparison should not lead us to underestimate the unique power of the divine will, which reaches out beyond the existence of a number of individual tribes to unite them in an *'am yhwh*.

[4]Judg. 20.2; II Sam. 14.13, *et al.*

[5]Judg. 5.11; I Sam. 2.24, *et al.*

[6]In later times the expressions *'am qādōš*, 'holy people' and *'am s·gullā* or *nah·lā*, 'peculiar people' were preferred: cf. ch. IX, 2, III, p. 452. Quite unique and extremely difficult to date, though probably elohistic, is the designation *mamleket kōh·nīm w·gōy qādōš*, Ex. 19.6. On the whole subject cf. further ch. III, pp. 90 f.

[7]Cf. Sachsse, *Die Bedeutung des Namens Israel*, 1922; P. Volz, *Mose und sein Werk²*, 1932, pp. 88 f.; M. Buber, *Moses*, 1952, p. 134; E. Auerbach, *Moses*, 1953, p. 213. A different view is taken by S. A. Danell in his extended treatment: *Studies in the Name Israel in the OT*, 1946. He regards this rendering as only a later explanation of the name and attempts to show that Israel was originally a divine name of a similar kind to *Ješurun* and *'Ašer*.

This means, however, that the existence of the nation could not become an end in itself. From the start it had to remain subordinate to a higher purpose, an overriding conception, the achievement of the nation's religious destiny. Even though this may on many occasions have coincided with the requirements of national existence, for example in war, yet it was recognized as being of a higher order than any considerations of expediency, because it was based entirely on the will of the jealous God who demanded obedience. It was for this reason that the expression of the new relationship with God in the form of a covenant between God and the people proved itself ideally suited to effecting an organic involvement of the new faith with the very existence of the nation, without bringing that faith into a false dependence on the people's own will to power and survival. *There is no question of a national religion in the accepted sense of these words,* for no nation, properly speaking, is yet in existence. Since, nevertheless, this religion operates as the strongest possible driving-force toward existence as a nation, it is therefore not felt to be something organically unrelated to the life of the people.

(d) Already implied in this, however, is the conclusion that faith in the covenant God assumes the existence of a remarkably *interior attitude to history.* Just as this faith was founded in the first place on a fact of history, from which it is continually rekindled,[1] so history provides the field in which it is worked out in practice. It experiences the divine will in the formation of the people's social life; it encounters the divine activity in the fortunes of the nation. In this way history acquires a value which it does not possess in the religions of the ancient civilizations. It is true that the ancient East recognized the action of the deity in isolated events and experienced these as judgment or succour;[2] but it never occurred to them to identify the nerve of the historical process as the purposeful activity of God or to integrate the whole by subordinating it to a single great religious conception. Their view of the divine activity was too firmly imprisoned in the thought-forms of their Nature mythology. In Israel,

---

[1]A. Weiser (*Glaube und Geschichte im AT*, 1931, pp. 70 ff.) pertinently calls attention to the role of cult and tradition in mediating the lasting effect of this historical event.

[2]Of countless instances perhaps outstanding are (a) the way in which the Cyrus cylinder (*AOT*, pp. 368 ff.; *ANET*, pp. 315 f.) gives the sacrilegious edicts of Nabonidus as the reason for his overthrow, and (b) the ascription of the victory of the Egyptians over the Hittites near Kadesh to the assistance of Amon in the inscription of Ramses II (A. Erman, *Die Literatur der Ägypter*, 1923, pp. 329 ff.).

on the other hand, the knowledge of the covenant God and his act of redemption aroused the capacity to understand and to present the historical process, at first only in the limited framework of the national destiny but later also universally, as the effect of a divine will—and even to press the Nature myth itself into the working out of this conception (the linking up of Creation and History!). [1] How deeply this attitude to history was rooted in the fundamental events of the Mosaic era is shown by the part which the deliverance from Egypt and the occupation of the Holy Land play as a sort of paradigm of the divine succour, not only in the historical books, but also in the prophets and the law. [2] Hence it is the ideas of election and the covenant and, closely associated with them, the divine lawgiving which become the decisive motifs of the Israelite view of history. [3]

(e) With this basic relationship between religion and the nation came also *certain safeguards against an identification of religion with the national interest* against the day when the consciousness of nationhood should awake to full strength and acquire a sphere of influence of its own.

In the first place *any understanding of God's involvement with his people in terms of popular Nature religion was rejected*. The covenant agreement excluded the idea, which prevailed widely and was disseminated among Israel's neighbours as well, that between the national God and his worshippers there existed a bond inherent in the order of Nature,

[1]Cf. M. Noth, 'Die Historisierung des Mythus' (*Christentum und Wissenschaft*, 1928, pp. 265 ff., 301 ff.).

[2]A complete list of references would be out of the question, but by way of example the following may be cited: Num. 23.22; 24.8; Judg. 5.4 f.; 6.13; I Sam. 4.8; II Kings 17.7; Ex. 15.13, 21; Amos 2.10; 9.7; Hos. 12.10; 13.4; Jer. 2.6; 3.19; 16.14; 32.21 ff.; Micah 6.4; Deut. 4.34; 6.12; 26.9. The frequent allusions in the Psalms should also be remembered.

[3]Cf. Hos. 2.17, 21; 9.10; 11.1 ff.; 13.5; Jer. 2.1 ff.; Micah 6.1 ff. Note also: the significance of the divine election for the kingdom, I Sam. 8–10, *et al.*; the election of Jerusalem in the Deuteronomic literature, the election of the patriarchs in the Genesis narratives, the consolation found in the thought of election in Deutero-Isaiah; also, the covenant concept in the patriarchal narratives, in the Deuteronomic histories, in the imagery of the marriage covenant between Yahweh and Israel in Hosea and Jeremiah, in the description of the golden age of salvation in Jeremiah, Ezekiel and Deutero-Isaiah; finally, the place of the law in the Deuteronomic and Priestly views of history. In this connection cf. A. Weiser, *op. cit.*, pp. 52 ff.; also H. H. Rowley, *The Biblical Doctrine of Election*, 1950, and Th. C. Vriezen, *Die Erwählung Israels nach dem Alten Testament*, 1953. While the latter ascribes the first explicit appearance of the election concept to the Deuteronomists and distinguishes it from the covenant concept, G. E. Wright, *The Old Testament against its Environment*, 1950, would prefer to regard the covenant as the concrete expression of the election concept.

whether this were a kind of blood relationship, or a link between the God and the country which created an indissoluble association between himself and the inhabitants. [1] This type of popular religion, in which the divinity displays only the higher aspect of the national self-consciousness, the national 'genius', or the *mysterium* of the forces of Nature peculiar to a particular country, was overcome principally by the concept of the covenant. Israel's religion is thus stamped as a 'religion of election', using this phrase to mean that it is the divine election which makes it the exact opposite of the nature religions.

The fact that ideas from primitive religion appear to have had some effect on the covenant ritual in no way alters this essential character of Israel's faith. It may, for instance, be adduced that the sprinkling of the blood on the altar and on the people in the covenant sacrifice as related in Ex. 24.6, 8 falls in the class of mystery rites for renewing the life of the community, such as are known from many primitive usages; and the covenant meal on the mount of God described in Ex. 24.9–11 lends further weight to such considerations. But a comparison with primitive 'covenant rituals', in which the object is the mediation of mysterious 'power', only serves to bring out more clearly the distinctive character of the Israelite covenant concept. To begin with it is an invariable mark of these rites that they have to be continually repeated, since their effect lasts only for a time. *The Israelite covenant sacrifice cannot be repeated,* but creates the covenant relationship for all time at its first performance. [2] Secondly, the primitive rituals are effective simply by virtue of being correctly carried out; they are automatic. *They lack the moral basis and orientation,* which are of the essence of the Israelite covenant ritual. Finally—and closely connected with the foregoing—the primitive rituals are not directed at the establishment of *a personal communion between God and man.* They are fulfilled in the totally impersonal transference of

[1] The former seems to be closer to the idea of the people's connection with their deity which obtained among the tribes on the borders of Palestine, e.g., the Moabites, cf. Num. 21.29; the latter seems to be more characteristic of the original inhabitants of Canaan, cf. II Kings 17.24 ff. and below ch. V. 3. ii, pp. 200 ff.

[2] Joshua's covenant ceremony (Josh. 8.30 ff.; 24) exhibits different forms and is occasioned by a new intake of tribes hitherto not included in the Yahweh covenant. The sacrificial practice as a whole, however, is never a completion or renewal of the making of the covenant, but the exercise of a prerogative resting on the fact that the covenant has been made. So also, M. Buber, *Königtum Gottes*, 1932, pp. 114 f. and p. 232 n. 23, as against Bin Gorion, *Sinai und Garizim*, 1926, pp. 363 ff.

'power', thus creating no relationship between person and person, but regarding the divinity primarily as a substance marvellously endowed with such power and fullness of life. In the making of the Israelite covenant that which defines the newly established relationship is the idea of lordship, with its utterly personal character; and while this does not exclude the ideas of participation in life and power, yet it admits them only in the form of a gift accorded by sovereign authority. One indication of decisive importance in this respect is the fact that the covenant is not concluded by the performance of a wordless action, having its value in itself, but is accompanied by the word as the expression of the divine will.

This clear dissociation from any naturalistic idea of the relationship with the divinity is buttressed by yet another consequence of the covenant concept, namely that *this is something on which God has entered freely and which he on his side may dissolve at any time*. Any compulsive linking of God to his people is thus utterly denied. He existed long before the nation, he is by nature independent of their existence and can abandon them whenever they refuse to be conformed to his will.

The covenant concept also includes, though less explicitly, the defence against another danger, that of *legalistic distortion of the relationship* defined in this way, by which the attempt is made to degrade it to the level of an agreement based on mutual service between two partners of equal status. God's voluntary initiation of the covenant relationship in history constantly serves to remind men that the character of the Sinai covenant is utterly different from that of human contracts, for as a gift of God's grace it lays the stress on his right to dispose all things as he wills. If this reminder is to be made effective, however, it is of the greatest importance that *the sovereignty of the personal God* should make itself felt so powerfully in human consciousness that it comes naturally to men to bow in fear and trembling before this gracious Being. Only so can all thought of a mercenary relationship between God and man, in which all that matters is external observance of the stipulated conditions, be precluded. There can be no doubt that in the setting up of the covenant the idea of sovereignty is dominant throughout. It is the manifestation of power with which Yahweh preludes the actual covenant-making which gives the Yahweh worship of the Mosaic period this character of trembling prostration before the jealous God, who will admit no derogation from his majesty. The terrifying power of the God, who will turn his weapons of leprosy, serpent and plague [1] (cf. Ex. 4.1–7; Num. 21.6 ff.; 11.33 f.) even against his own people, leaves men in no doubt that the covenant he has created is no safe bulwark, behind which they can make cunning use of the divine power to prosecute their own interests. The covenant lays claim to the whole man and calls him to a surrender with no reservations.

2. THE HISTORY OF THE COVENANT CONCEPT

The more significant the factors we have mentioned may be for the total understanding of the covenant, the more deleterious must be the effect on the covenant relationship in practice of any encroachment on their rightful position. It is therefore no wonder that in the whole long process of adjusting the Mosaic religion to the environment of Canaanite religion and culture it is round this crucial issue that the struggle fluctuates to and fro, now assimilating, now rejecting, striving in part toward distortion, in part toward new understanding and sharper definition of the covenant concept. A glance at the history of the concept is therefore indispensable if it is to be properly understood.

1. *The jeopardizing of the Yahweh covenant*

It can be shown that the process of assimilation which threatened the religion of Yahweh in Canaan developed in three main ways, each of which contributed to the endangering of the original meaning of the divine covenant. These were approximation to the Canaanite idea of God, one-sided development of the cultic aspect of religion and the according of a false independence to the national power.

(a) *Acquaintance with the benefactor deities of Canaan* influenced the popular picture of Yahweh by perverting the connection between the god and the worshipper into the mere communication of divine vitality. As a result naturalistic conceptions of communion with the divine power by means of ritual entry into the sphere of the 'holy' and sensory experience of the overmastering impact of that power in ecstatic exaltation became all-important. In comparison with this mysterious life-force not only did the moral will of the divinity recede in importance but also the essential feeling for the distance of God

[1]Cf. the interesting comparison in Böhl, *Exodus*, 1928, p. 184, cf. p. 105. See also below ch. VII. 6, pp. 278 f.

from all humankind. The gulf set between God and man by his terrifying majesty was levelled out of existence by the emphasis laid on their psycho-physical relatedness and community. The sense of distance was kept alive only by occasional motiveless outbreaks of anger. Hence the former importance of the idea of sovereignty came to be questioned. The god of the bull-image, of wine, of cultic sexual lust cannot possess the absolute power to ordain of him who is exalted over Nature. [1] This involves the weakening, if not the loss, of one indispensable presupposition of the covenant concept and opens the door to the misinterpretation and misuse of the covenant for the purpose of harnessing God to human requirements.

Closely associated with this is the thought of the god as restricted to the borders of the land and so more strongly bound to the people. Wherever an attempt is made to conceive of the divine power in the mystery of the life of Nature, then this power will also become involved in the localization of natural phenomena and be pictured and thought of as the steward of the blessings peculiar to one particular country. The consequence for the concept of the covenant is that the dependence of the covenant on moral conditions is glossed over, since it is part of the very nature of a benefactor deity that he must distribute his gifts to the inhabitants of his land. It is his one essential function, without which he cannot even be imagined to exist. There are, of course, certain conditions even in his case on which alone his favour can be earned, but these do not guarantee the divinity any existence independently of his land and people; they simply correspond to his role as protector of the natural and national life. It is therefore in the deity's own interests not to overdo his demands, but to suit them to men's natural requirements. A divine will which can set itself in opposition to the national existence of the people, which might even in certain circumstances sacrifice the people to the fulfilment of its demands, thus becomes incomprehensible. The covenant becomes an expression of the fact that God and the people have been thrown together and that neither can well survive without the other.

(b) This transformation of the covenant relationship into a locally limited community relation deriving from the necessities of the nature of the god himself received fatal reinforcement from *the one-sided development of the cultic aspect of religion* in conformity with Canaanite

---

[1] These effects of the assimilation of the faith of Yahweh to the Canaanite idea of God have been best described for us in the polemic of the prophets, Hosea and Jeremiah in particular.

and general Near Eastern custom. Political consolidation was accompanied by a growth in the importance of the great sanctuaries and their priesthoods which favoured an enhancing and entrenching of the outward apparatus of religion that had the strongest influence on religious thought and behaviour. The natural momentum of a richly developed cultic practice concentrated all the reality of religion into the sphere of outward performance, the meritorious works of sacrifices, festivals, pilgrimages, fasting and so on. As a result the social and moral aspects of the divine demands were allowed to recede from men's attention. The danger thus became acute that the cultus would be degraded to the level of an *opus operatum* and that it would be valued simply in proportion to the magnificence with which it was carried out. The far-reaching changes in the state of Israelite culture in the eighth and seventh centuries together with the social divisions they introduced did not a little to increase this danger, as is shown by the picture which the prophets draw for us of the piety of their nation—all the typical features of religious mass-movements, omitting nothing of their darker side. As far as the covenant was concerned this meant the externalization of man's relation to God, its transformation into a religion of '*Do ut des*' in which the divine gift is bound to reciprocate human performance. This legalistic distortion of the covenant relationship into a commercial arrangement between parties of equal status before the law rendered all intercourse with the deity lifeless and trained men in an irreverent calculation of divine obligations, which made any attitude of trustful surrender impossible. In this way the religious values originally mediated by the covenant were falsified and the covenant concept itself became nothing more than a protective cover for irreligious self-seeking.

(c) This aberration was furthered by the failure to arrive at any satisfactory *adjustment between the national power consolidated in the state and the will of God with its absolute demands*. At quite an early stage self-conscious despotism, established on the basis of new and stronger forms of political life, came into conflict with the social foundations of the Yahweh covenant. [1] Partly under the pressure of circumstances, partly in imitation of Canaanite and other foreign models, the charismatic kingship, which had at first met with resistance, more and more deliberately took the road toward a hereditary tyranny; and even if it did not succeed in reaching that goal until quite late,

[1]Cf. Abimelech, Judg. 9; Saul, I Sam. 15; see also ch. IX. 2, 'The King'.

yet the strong tendency in that direction made it impossible to avoid sharper and sharper clashes with the champions of the will of Yahweh. This state of conflict, at one time more open, at another more underground, was significant for the development of religious thought because of the religious basis of the monarchical pretensions. For by his use of the title 'Son of God' the king arrogated to his position as ruler, which had been acquired by ordinary natural succession, whether as a member of the dynasty or as leader of the army, the prerogative of supreme religious functionary, a prerogative which could only properly be justified if the candidate for the throne were charismatically selected. By thus disguising his egoistic-dynastic or imperialistic aims he enlisted the support of the covenant God in the most emphatic way for the institution of the nation as such and caused Yahweh to appear as the natural ally of the national greatness and power. The transference of the title of King to Yahweh, and the Enthronement Festival with its regular renewal of the divine Kingship on earth, could not but give further impetus to this train of thought; for now that the relation of the people to their king was projected on to that of the people to their God, the latter connection also appeared as something simply 'given' and not as founded in the first place by a special act of condescending grace. Henceforward the covenant also is no longer regarded as an inconceivable gift of grace from a God who is supreme over all earthly power, and who in this way gives his sovereign decrees to his people, but as a more or less modified version of a natural relationship between two partners dependent on one another. Consequently any criticism of the national life from the standpoint of religion is largely crippled and the climate made favourable to the equation of the will of God with the national interest. The whole attitude of the people in the time of the prophets [1] —and also the spirit of many of the patriarchal narratives while they were current in popular oral tradition and had not yet received the internal correction of emphasis which their present arrangement has given them—bear witness to this dissolving of the precautions against the naturalistic conception of God which were part of the concept of the covenant.

When, however, the original concept of the covenant was thus imperilled by assimilation to Canaanite ways of thought, the spiritual representatives of the true Yahwist understanding were compelled to take fresh stock of their position.

[1] Cf. Amos 9.10b; Hos. 8.2; Micah 2.6 f.; 3.11; Jer. 14.9, 21.

II. *The re-fashioning of the covenant concept*

(a) Reference must first be made to an enlargement and elucidation of the covenant concept which is to be found in *the earlier narratives of the Pentateuch* and which is of the greatest consequence. The Yahwist and Elohist strata exhibit, partly by explicit statement, partly in the general manner of their presentation of the patriarchal history, a remarkable retrojection of the covenant concept into the earliest period of the national life. In this way they base Israel's consciousness of her election on the fortunes of the patriarchs.

No doubt the basic assumptions necessary for such an interpretation were already present in the material itself, for the story tells of a religiously determined migration of the people's ancestors from Mesopotamia to Canaan and of the individual character of their worship of God. Nevertheless, the breaks and lacunae within the tradition and the distinctive stamp given to the patriarchal story in each of the Pentateuchal writers show clearly that the total conception which controls their picture of the patriarchal age received its characteristic form from an idea of God created by the establishment of the Mosaic covenant. J_1 presents the story of the divine election as a series of blessings, by which a pre-eminent position as a nation and the possession of the land are reserved to the posterity of Abraham;[1] J_2 indicates this same unique position of Abraham and his descendants[2] in a narrative which works up from the expiatory sacrifice of Noah to a climax in the covenant sacrifice of Abraham, the unique execution of which recalls that of the covenant-making on Sinai;[3] and finally E presents us with a series of divine testings which, when undergone in faith and obedience, effect the separation of the patriarchs from their heathen environment.[4] The deepest meaning of these early traditions taken as a whole is that Israel's consciousness of election was based on the divine choice of the Fathers.

It may be asked what grounds there are for thus extending to the patriarchs the historical basis of Israel's covenant relationship and making it to some extent a rival of the Mosaic covenant,[5] as a result

[1]Gen. 9.25 ff.; 12.1 ff.; 25.23; 32.29; 49.
[2]Gen. 8.20 ff.; 15.7 ff.; 26.24; 27.29a; 28.13 ff.
[3]Cf. O. Procksch, *Die Genesis* [2], [3], 1924, pp. 110 f.
[4]Gen. 15.1 ff.; 22.16–18; 26.2–5; 27.27, 29b; 28.10 ff.; 30.10 f.; 35.1 ff.; 48.15 f., 20.
[5]It is to the great credit of K. Galling to have seen and formulated clearly the problem inherent in the dual form of the election tradition in his work, *Die Erwählungstraditionen Israels*, 1928.

of which in many circles, for example the prophets, there is complete silence concerning it. It would be a mistake to look for an explanation in purely political terms, [1] an attempt to hold up the ideal of 'Pan-Israel' to a people whom the division of the kingdom into two hostile camps had put in need of recall to their God-given vocation. It is better to begin by taking into account seriously the formative effect which the covenant concept itself exerted on history. It was the inner dynamic of this concept which submitted the unco-ordinated traditions of the early period, adulterated by alien ingredients, to the idea of purposeful divine election, thus integrating them into a systematic sequence of events and enabling the national history in its entirety to be understood as the work of Yahweh.

On the other hand the tendency to provide a reflective commentary on the past must not be underestimated. The experience of the startling rise of Israelite power under David and Solomon drove men to seek a satisfactory explanation of Israel's position among the nations by linking up its history with that of the world at large. It was in the story of the patriarchs that the unique divine vocation could best be made manifest, by which Yahweh, from the most unpromising beginnings, had created for himself a people whose existence was from the start based on his own wondrous acts. Here too Israel's claim to supremacy found a basis in the universal pattern; the God of the Fathers is also the Creator, who makes his choice and carries out his plan for Israel as Lord of the human race.

Hence the working out of the covenant and election concepts in the patriarchal history provides the counterpoise both to misconceptions of a narrow-minded, particularist kind and to naturalistic distortions of the covenant relationship. The God of the covenant is also the God of the whole world and his designs comprehend far more than just Israel. The aggrandizement of the people is the unmerited effect of the mighty blessings in the promises made to the Fathers and as such urges men to humility. The example of the Fathers also shows that election must have its response from the human side, an attitude of humble obedience and unconditional trust which must be maintained throughout severe testing. Such a living interpretation of the covenant relationship, which was to undergo further development of

[1]So Galling, op. cit. The difficulties lie principally in the late dating of the Yahwist and in the idea of a Judaean, who would have had to surrender the claims made for Jerusalem (cf. Gen. 49.8–12!), transmitting the vision of Pan-Israel under the hegemony of Ephraim.

the greatest importance in Deuteronomy and P, undoubtedly put powerful religious forces into the field against the tendency to rigorize belief in election into legalistic formulas and lifeless dogma. These forces continue to prove their strength in the straitened circumstances of the exilic and post-exilic periods; and after the Mosaic covenant had been broken their account of the patriarchs reinforces trust in a wholly unmerited covenant grace. [1]

(b) It remains, none the less, a surprising phenomenon that throughout the period when *the classical prophets* were drastically criticizing the popular religion of Israel, the covenant concept should recede into the background. It is certainly an exaggeration to consider, as Kraetzschmar did, that generally speaking the prophets before Jeremiah knew nothing of a covenant relationship of God with Israel. It is after all a fact that Hosea speaks twice of the *b˓rit* that Israel has broken (6.7; 8.1). Nevertheless it is worth noting that even for him the emphasis is not on the covenant concept, but that he makes use of other categories to describe the religious relationship. Amos, Isaiah and Micah all present it as an accepted fact that Israel's relationship with Yahweh is based on the latter's own free decision and inconceivable grace; it is only necessary to recall such passages as Amos 3.2, where the prophet is quite definitely expressing the proud conviction of the nation as a whole, when he speaks of Yahweh's favour in choosing Israel above all other nations. But this makes it only the more astonishing that in precisely such passages as these, where to us the word 'covenant' suggests itself at once, the prophets never use it.

There is perhaps some justification in this remarkable fact for Kraetzschmar's radical attempt at a solution. It is, however, quite out of the question to suppose that any further progress in this problem can be made simply with the scalpel of literary criticism. We must take into consideration the whole position of the prophets *vis-à-vis* the spiritual stock-in-trade of their nation; and when this is done, the factor of decisive significance is seen to be that these reforming spirits have set themselves to oppose every instance of dead externalism in religious practice and mechanical routine in religious thought. What confronted them was an insistence on statutes and ordinances, on settled custom and usage, on the precisely organized performance of duties toward God, and a corresponding reckoning on Yahweh's automatic performance in return. An Amos inveighs strenuously

[1] Isa. 41.8 ff.; 51.2; Neh. 9.6 ff.; Ps. 105.7 ff.; Micah 7.18 ff.

against the unwearying processions and pilgrimages to famous sanctuaries and the sumptuous Temple worship;[1] a Hosea castigates the priests for making money out of the people's sense of sin and for getting fat on their offerings;[2] an Isaiah stigmatizes the eager frequenting of the Temple and the magnificent prayers there offered as the 'commandment of men'.[3] In all of them the stress is on the personal note in the relationship to Yahweh; it is because they find this lacking that they insist with all the force and passion at their command on the ideas of honesty, of love, of surrender. Correspondingly they present Yahweh's acts as the operations of a fully personal love and loyalty, which courts the trust of the people with living warmth of feeling and looks for a response that is spontaneous and from the heart.[4] In this struggle to eradicate all thought of an *opus operatum* the concept of the covenant could not help them; for, as we noticed earlier, the weakness inherent in it which made it a potential danger to religious life was precisely its legal character, because of which it was liable to become the seedbed of a parasitic '*Do ut des*' religion.

When, therefore, the prophets come to speak of the founding of Israel's supremacy, it is not hard to see why they make no reference to the Sinai covenant, but instead call to mind the deliverance from Egypt. In no other way could they have illuminated more clearly the gracious favour of Yahweh, or guarded against the false perversion of his activity into an obligatory performance by the covenant deity. It should also be noted that in Isaiah it is the idea of the sovereignty of Yahweh, on which he likes to lay such stress, which takes the place of the covenant concept; for the latter, as we have already seen, leads directly to the thought of God's dominion.

(c) From the Josianic reform onward the position is quite different. In *the Deuteronomic Law* and the great body of writings which grew up under the influence of its major themes we suddenly find the concept of the *berit* employed with a quite special emphasis and partiality. We certainly do not contend that the concept had up to this time fallen into oblivion; rather, it had been cherished only in certain circles, those to whom the cultivation of the Torah was entrusted, cf. Deut. 33.9. But its popularity under Josiah is manifestly due to a new total spiritual situation, which arose as a result of the prophetic

---

[1]Amos 4.4 f.; 5.5 f., 21 ff.; 8.10, 14.
[2]Hos. 4.8 f.; cf. also 4.14 f.; 5.1 f., 6; 7.14; 8.11 ff.; 9.1 ff.
[3]Isa. 1.11 ff.; 29.13.
[4]Hos. 6.4 ff.; 7.13 f.; 9.10; 11.1 ff.; Isa. 1.2 f.; 5.1 ff.; 7.9, 13; 9.12; 22.8, 11 ff.; Jer. 2.1 ff ; 3.19 ff.; 5.1 ff. etc.

activity. The attempt is made to carry out a thorough reform of the whole national life and this gives new life to the old concept of the divine covenant. With the discovery of the Book of the Covenant (*sēper habbᵉrît*, II Kings 23.2) the epoch of Manasseh was branded as an iniquitous breach of the covenant; and the new covenant, which King Josiah now made by engaging to keep the law, was at the same time a symbol of a return to the old divine covenant. It is hardly to be wondered at that the narrators of the history of the nation should now view the past as well in the light of this concept, when their purpose was to set before the eyes of the people the faithfulness of their God and the unfaithfulness of man.

They had learnt from Isaiah to regard history as a process governed by a divine plan, which had prepared it in the long distant past and was now guiding it toward its goal. While, however, Isaiah had contemplated the history of the whole human race, the men of the reformation were concerned primarily with *the history of Israel*, which they undertook to record didactically for the benefit of their nation. In this project the concept of the covenant offered them the most impressive image by which to convey the systematic and beneficent character of God's activity. The covenant with Abraham and the covenant at Sinai appeared as two interrelated events which, when regarded as prologue and fulfilment, gave the history of Israel its distinctive stamp of one guided by God. Indeed it seems that isolated writers of this school added yet another covenant in the land of Moab to form the third in the series, so that 'the whole structure of the religious relationship now rested on these three covenants as on three massive pillars'.[1] At any rate, Deut. 26.17–19; 28.69; 29.8, 11, 13, 20 point in this direction. This approach provided an excellent method of presenting Israel's past in the form of 'salvation history' and thus of making clear at the same time both the continuity of the divine favour and the full seriousness of men's own carelessness and offence. The extensive use which Jeremiah and Ezekiel, in strong contrast to their prophetic predecessors, make of the covenant concept gives some idea of the power with which this conception laid hold on the spirits of the age.

At the same time *a slight shift in the concept of the bᵉrît* can be detected in the Deuteronomic writings. The term is still used, certainly, to designate the once-for-all establishment of the covenant in history,[2]

[1] Kraetzschmar, *Die Bundesvorstellung im AT*, p. 138.
[2] Cf. Deut. 5.2 ff.

but it often appears as well in the sense of a constantly enduring relationship;[1] indeed it can even be used of the obligations of this relationship, the conditions of the covenant. This is already implicit in the fact that *ṣiwwāh bᵉrit* is now frequently used in place of *kārat bᵉrit*.[2] Deut. 4.13, 23 understands by *bᵉrit* simply the Decalogue; and even the Tables of the Law can be described in short as *habbᵉrit* (I Kings 8.21). Hence the legal basis of the covenant is brought into especial prominence; *ḥukkīm, miṣwōt, mišpāṭīm* are the terms used to denote its content.[3] Correspondingly, on the human side, the stress is on the 'keeping' (*šāmar*) of the covenant, Deut. 29.8; I Kings 11.11; and conversely there are warnings against 'transgressing' or 'breaking' the covenant ('*br; hpr; m's; 'zb; škḥ*).[4]

A consequence of this shift in the concept is that *the principal emphasis falls on the legal character*, the element of 'ordained once for all', in the relationship created by God. In the prophets it was the free action of divine love that was the more prominent feature; that love which manifests itself in ever fresh demonstrations of grace and faithfulness and which is constantly re-establishing and re-fashioning at a deeper level the relationship which man's sin has destroyed. Among the men of the Deuteronomic reform the love of Yahweh is seen in the creation of a new total situation of enduring and reliable stability and security; it is love, so to speak, objectified and made available for man's enjoyment in the form of the covenant relationship. This objectification of the divine activity of love is brought out most strongly when it is credited with eternal durability. Man cannot annul the covenant; if he breaks it, this only means that he is violating its conditions. The majesty of divine love shows itself in this, that God alone has the power to dissolve the relationship, yet never makes use of it.[5] Hence Yahweh's glorious Name now becomes *šōmēr habbᵉrit wᵉhaḥesed*='He which keepeth covenant and mercy' (Deut. 7.9, 12; I Kings 8.23; Neh. 1.5; 9.32; Dan. 9.4).

That there were advantages and disadvantages to this abstract conception of the relationship with God is obvious. The teaching of

---

[1]This is the reason for the absence of any precise historical reference of the term *bᵉrit* in such passages as Deut. 17.2; 31.16, 20; Josh. 7.11, 15; 23.16; Judg. 2.1, 20, etc.

[2]Cf. Deut. 4.13; Josh. 7.11; 23.16; Judg. 2.20; I Kings 11.11.

[3]Deut. 26.17; I Kings 11.11; II Kings 17.15.

[4]Deut. 17.2; Josh. 7.11, 15; 23.16; Judg. 2.20; II Kings 18.12; Deut. 31.16, 20; Deut. 29.24; II Kings 17.15; Deut. 4.23, 31 etc.

[5]Cf. Deut. 4.31; Judg. 2.1.

Deuteronomy conveyed to the people a striking and easily understood complex of ideas in which the loving condescension and unwearied faithfulness of God were closely linked with the obligations and performances expected from men in their turn. There was the strongest emphasis on the superiority which Israel, as the possessor of a divine covenant, enjoyed over all other peoples; but at the same time humility and seriousness were inculcated, humility at the thought of their own unworthiness and seriousness in the duty of perfectly fulfilling their covenant obligations. The dangers that threatened from Canaanite ideas of God were thus successfully averted.

This conception, however, was of less value against the misinterpretation of the covenant in a nationalist or cultic sense. It is to a certain extent understandable that a good many critics should talk of a 'falling away from the heights of the prophetic knowledge of God'. In the one-sided over-valuation of the concept of the *b'rit*, in the Deuteronomic sense, particularism and the uncomprehending rejection of the heathen *can* without doubt find a weapon ready to their hand. Indeed the Deuteronomic school did in practice set the nations outside the covenant and taught that this should be regarded as a specifically Israelite privilege. Yet this is really only a description of the actual historical situation and does not envisage an absolute exclusion of the heathen as a matter of principle. As far as the historical work which fell to the Deuteronomic school is concerned, the only possible course for them was to set about equipping their own people as thoroughly as they could for the religious task assigned to them; and in the concept of the *b'rit* they found a most useful means to this end and one capable of taking the thought of the prophets into its system.

On the other hand, once the *b'rit* has become the all-embracing symbol for expressing the religious relationship and is no longer qualified by other images, then the danger of perverting the covenant order into a relationship of cultic performance is ever present. In Deuteronomy, however, this danger is as yet not acute. God is not simply seen as the founder of the *b'rit*; he is in addition both the divine Lord, in whose presence there can be no haggling or bargaining, but only absolute obedience, and also the Father who loves his son Israel and does not confront him merely as the stern judge to whom he must render account. As long as the covenant is still regarded as a proof of Yahweh's love as this seeks to awaken the responsive confidence and love of men, there is an effective precaution against its abuse as a purely legalistic institution, in which a religious relationship rooted in the heart is apt to come off very much worse than the exact observance of mutual rights and duties.

(d) Incomparably deeper is the mark made on history by the new understanding of the covenant concept which we find in *the Priestly stratum of the Pentateuch*. That which strikes the reader most of all is the tendency to sharp definition, to exact formulation and systematic use of the concept—characteristics which in other connections also are distinctive of the priestly writings, using that term in the strict sense. Thus P avoids using the word *b⁻rît* in a secular context and restricts it entirely to the 'salvation history', so that it becomes an exclusively religious concept. By precise terminology it is given a unique character different from that of any secular *b⁻rît*. For the Yahwist it was still quite natural to use the expression *krt brt* of Yahweh, thus presenting him as a contracting party after the human model; by contrast P says of Yahweh, *hēqîm b⁻rît* or *nātan b⁻rît*, he 'establishes' or 'grants' the covenant. [1] The fact that the covenant can only be bestowed as a gift of grace—the implication of this change of language—strikingly conveys the sublimity of the divine covenant-maker. For the same reason the covenant he concludes is a *b⁻rît 'ōlām*, one valid for *all* ages; for he is incapable of making his grant of salvation dependent on the behaviour of men, but maintains it for all time by virtue of his eternal steadfastness. [2] Finally, the solemn conclusion of Yahweh's covenant with Israel takes place at the Abraham covenant only, and the events at Sinai are not given the status of an independent covenant-making, but only of a renewal and re-fashioning of the earlier one with Abraham.

This might be ascribed to nothing more than a penchant for systematization with no real bearing on the content of the term *b⁻rît*, for Deuteronomy, Jeremiah and Ezekiel had also declared that Israel's relationship with God was based on God's oath to the patriarchs. Yet there is more to it than that. The point is that the divine covenant which is the decisive one for Israel's history is concluded *before* the giving of the detailed ceremonial law. The right condition of the human parties to the covenant does not depend on any particular performances, but simply on the living of life before

[1] *hēqîm:* Gen. 6.18; 9.9, 11, 17; 17.7, 19, 21; Ex. 6.4; Lev. 26.9, etc. *nātan:* Gen. 9.12; 17.2; Num. 25.12.
[2] Gen. 9.16; 17.7, 13, 19; Ex. 31.16; Lev. 24.8; Num. 18.19; 25.13.

the face of God and in his presence—the sort of life described in the expression in use for the pious of nations other than Israel as well, 'to walk with God': *hithallēk 'et–(lipnē–) hā'·lōhīm*. Here is the expression of a strong sense of the essentially religious character of the *b·rīt*; its goal is not the performances of men, but the creation of a real community between God and man. [1] Hence there are no special cultic practices attached to the covenant with Abraham; for even circumcision is not to be regarded as such, but as a sign of the covenant, [2] neglect of which results in exclusion from the covenant community. Human performance, therefore, acts more as a means by which man obtains the use of, or enters into the enjoyment of the gift granted to him.

It is from this that the refusal to employ the concept of the covenant to describe the revelation at Sinai derives its profoundest significance. If the cultus, there introduced for the first time, does no more than indicate the appropriation by the whole nation of the covenant with Abraham, then no more than circumcision can it possess the character of a human performance, by which man on his side makes the covenant effective; rather it has that of a sacrament, in which God unfolds himself to man in community. By this means the idea of the covenant as a legal relationship with mutual duties and performances precisely laid down is done away, and the concept of a relationship of grace is put in its place. It is when seen in this light that the expressions which P employs to speak of the granting and establishing of the covenant reveal their special purpose. They leave no room any more for the idea of a bilateral compact or engagement, but only for that of an institution created by divine omnipotence. This finally brought to full development a particular aspect of the covenant concept, which had been present from the very first, but which had hitherto been defenceless against legalistic misinterpretation—the only protection coming from an element outside the complex of ideas associated with the covenant, namely the idea of sovereignty. This development now made impossible any abuse of the covenant law to satisfy selfish human desires.

In addition P attempted to exclude the danger of abuse of the covenant concept in a particularistic sense. P is indeed the only Israelite writer to tell of a divine covenant with the human race before Abraham. The narrative of the covenant with Noah, Gen. 9, certainly

[1] Gen. 17.7, 8, 19.
[2] Gen. 17.11.

came down to him from an ancient tradition, as many early elements in it prove, but the fact that he in particular was the one to adopt it and to fit it into his narrative as he does, shows the universalist character of his faith. According to him not only Israel, but the whole of humanity stands to God in a *b˓rît* relationship, and theirs too is a *b˓rît* possessing eternal validity. Thus P has 'stretched out a mighty panorama of the course of history as this is seen from the vantage-point of the covenant concept' (Kraetzschmar); the relationship of God to men has been realized, as it were, 'in two concentric circles', [1] the Noah covenant for the whole human race and the Abraham covenant for Israel alone. In these two forms the relationship of God to men remains eternally constant. As in his contemplation of nature, so in his examination of history, the dominant note in P is his feeling for the statutory, the consistent, the eternally binding, corresponding to his towering vision of the transcendent, eternal God. As a result, however, P seems to have lost any idea that this relationship with God might one day be brought to higher perfection. For the heathen to enter into closer union with God is only envisaged as possible in terms of their entry into Israel in a manner precisely similar to that in which the slaves and foreign-born among Abraham's household were adopted by circumcision into the community of El Shaddai. It is true that a renewal and perfecting of the Abraham covenant is not thereby excluded, but Israel's privileged position is at all events firmly safeguarded. The truth in this view is to be found in the saying from St John's Gospel: 'Salvation is from the Jews' (4.22).

In such an understanding of the divine work of salvation, determined by the cast of thought peculiar to the priestly school and yet not disowning the prophetic influence, it is no wonder that P should give central significance to the concept of the *b˓rît*. In it is summed up the whole of religion and in such a way that all the emphasis lies on God's activity in communicating himself. 'I will be your God' (cf. Gen. 17.7b)—that is the supreme message of the covenant for P, as it is for Jer. 31.31 ff. For P *b˓rît* is the ideal term 'to express the concept of a religion of revelation', [2] based entirely on God's promise and holding fast, in spite of the fact that time and place must necessarily limit its realization, to the universality of the divine saving plan.

(e) The understanding of the covenant concept in *the prophets from the start of the seventh century onwards* develops along quite different lines.

[1] So Procksch, *Genesis*[2], p. 518.
[2] Procksch, *op. cit.*, p. 519.

During the first period of his activity *Jeremiah* makes no explicit reference to the *bᵉrit*.[1] After the Josianic reform,[2] however, he does accord it more significance and, while still not giving it a central position, yet uses it as one favourite method of conveying his prophetic message. Just as it is God's condescending grace that is thrown into striking relief by the covenant-making at the time of the Exodus from Egypt, so it is ingratitude that sums up the breaking of that covenant by the people. On this fact rests the firm conviction of the prophet that judgment is inevitable.[3] Nevertheless, the old idea of the *bᵉrit* as an act consummated in history by which a covenant is established is retained throughout; what the prophet does not do is to expand the concept into that of an ever-enduring covenant relationship and deepen it into a comprehensive description of the divine revelation. Instead, the images of real significance, when God's attitude to Israel is spoken of, are the ancient ones of marriage, of the father-son relationship and of the divine role of shepherd.[4] The pastorally-minded prophet saw too clearly the deficiencies of the original Sinai covenant and of its renewal under Josiah for it to be able to speak to him with eternal meaning. It is a sign of penetrating criticism as well as of a high evaluation, when he contrasts with the old covenant the new covenant of the age of salvation, in which God establishes a new and inward relationship of men to himself by transforming their hearts.[5] It is possible to find here a point of contact with P, inasmuch as the perfect divine community is manifested in the form of a *bᵉrit* which thereby loses completely the character of a relation based on reciprocal performance. But in Jeremiah all the emphasis is on God's fresh creative activity and the position of greatest prominence is reserved for the relationship of the individual heart to God; in place of an unchanging statutory order he stresses God's redemptive work. This emphasis on the personal element in man's communion with God and the fact that the prophets, with their eyes wholly fixed on the new age, were incorruptible in their criticism of the existing order gave a somewhat different stamp to the conception of the covenant.

Ezekiel also belongs to this tradition—indeed it is possible to speak of a clear dependence on Jeremiah, a dependence combined with an equally clear avoidance of the priestly ways of thought. For him too

[1] Cf. chs. 2–6.
[2] Cf. ch. 11.
[3] 7.23 ff.; 11.3 ff.; 14.21; 22.9; 8.7; 9.12 ff.
[4] 13.27; 31.3 f., 32; 3.19; 31.9, 20; 13.17, 20; 23.1, 3, *et al.*
[5] 31.31 ff.

the b⁻rīt still means only the one established in the past at Sinai;[1] and the breaking of this covenant plays a part in his scheme as a weighty indictment of the faithless nation.[2] It certainly cannot be argued, however, that his whole way of thinking is dominated by the covenant concept; in ch. 16, for example, where it is fairly strongly emphasized, yet the image of marriage runs throughout, parallel to it and independent of it. In the great historical survey of ch. 20 the concept of the b⁻rīt is most strikingly completely absent from the account of Yahweh's acts of revelation; in its place appear constantly repeated allusions to the self-communication of the divine Being in the name Yahweh: 'ᵃnī yhwh.[3] It is just as striking that, both here and in 36.20 ff., Israel is to be spared from the judgment of wrath not as a consequence of the indestructibility of the divine b⁻rīt, but because of God's jealousy for the honour of his Name.[4] It is quite clear that the main interest of the prophet is in Yahweh's personal dealings and the institutional as such fades into the background (cf. pp. 51 f. above). At the same time it is true to the genius of prophecy that, when the positive significance of the covenant concept does become prominent for the first time, it is in connection with eschatology. When Israel is restored to nationhood under her shepherd David, then Yahweh will conclude a covenant of peace with her, which will last for ever and will set up an enduring relationship of grace between God and his people.[5] The contrast with the Sinai covenant is here clear enough. For Ezekiel as for others the sense of standing amid the break-up of the old and the building of the new was much too strong to permit him to except any existing institution from the annihilating judgment and to use it as an indestructible basis for the salvation to come. All that survives the destruction of state and Temple is the God who is jealous for the honour of his Name; and it is solely in his knowledge of this God that the prophet sees a guarantee of the new

---

[1]The breaking up of the single covenant-making into several revelations at different times suggested by Kraetzschmar (*op. cit.*, p. 164) rests on a misunderstanding.

[2]Ezek. 16.8, 59 ff.; 20.37 (the text is uncertain at this point).

[3]It may be true that this phrase 'ᵃnī yhwh links up with the Sinai Decalogue and so is a reference to the Sinai covenant, but this only underlines the avoidance of the actual term b⁻rīt connected with it in the tradition. What Kraetzschmar proposes here is pure conjecture.

[4]Kraetzschmar (p. 166) reads into this an incorporation of the ancient prophetic concept of holiness into that of the covenant; but this depends entirely on his use of the dubious passage 16.60 ff.—on which see below.

[5]Ezek. 34.25; 37.26.

covenant. The point of contact with the priestly ways of thinking is limited, as in Jeremiah, to this: that the *b⁐rît* of the future is seen as a relationship of pure grace. However, through the close association of the covenant with the new David, it follows that the new order of things acquires in addition a fairly strong character of rigid legal establishment. [1]

The prophetic interpretation of the covenant concept attains its greatest profundity in *Deutero-Isaiah*. In common with earlier prophecy he has nothing to say about the particular covenant at Sinai, but speaks instead of the deliverance from Egypt, [2] in which Yahweh formed his people for himself. [3] He does, however, present the ideal conditions of the time of the End, in which the divine plan of salvation for Israel is realized, as a *b⁐rît*. [4] In order to link this with the dealings of God in the past, he uses as his guiding motif the thought of the election of Abraham [5] and of the divine faithfulness, which brings to completion the work begun in olden time. [6] It is by the ever constant nature of the divine activity, miraculously transcending normal reality, that faith is kindled, not by a single historical institution like the Sinai covenant which derives from this activity. The prophet even invites his hearers to forget former blessings, in order to accept with the more ecstatic rejoicing the unheard-of revelation of salvation now standing at their very doors; [7] similarly, the old covenant is to be completely overshadowed by the eternal covenant of peace, which Yahweh is about to conclude with his people. After a miraculous wandering in the wilderness he will settle them in their homeland, transforming it into a paradise, and therein establish his dominion anew.

This manifestation of the *b⁐rît* in the last times is, however, no

---

[1] A closer affinity to P could only be assumed, if the section 16.60–63 could definitely be attributed to Ezekiel. Here the old covenant is presented as the basis of the new, quite in the P manner, and the continuity of God's covenant care for his people is emphasized by the use of the term *hēqīm*, with its 'meaning oscillating between "establish" and "maintain" ' (Kraetzschmar). But the fact that this is manifestly a modification of the usual prophetic line rather seems to argue that in this section, which is in any case a later addition, we are dealing not with a rounding off of Ezekiel's thought, but with a revision of it in accordance with the thought of the priestly school, such as we find in other parts of the book.

[2] Isa. 43.16 f.; 51.9 f.; 52.4.

[3] Isa. 44.21, 24.

[4] Isa. 54.10; 55.3; 61.8.

[5] Isa. 41.8 f.; 51.2.

[6] Isa. 42.6, 21; 46.3 f.

[7] Isa. 43.18; 54.4.

isolated act of a ritual character, no new constitution or organization, but something embodied in the life of a human person, the Servant of God, who is defined as the mediator of the covenant to the nation. [1] In him the divine will for the community is revealed as one of vicarious suffering, by which the covenant people with their messianic ruler are united in an indissoluble community and reconciled with God. At the same time, by this gathering of the people round a king, raised to sovereignty from suffering, God's own purpose of absolute lordship receives unqualified acceptance. The first intimations of this association of the covenant concept with the messianic hope have already appeared in Ezekiel, [2] but it is in Deutero-Isaiah that it is first found as a full organic unity; and by this means the inmost concern of prophetism—to free the *b'rīt* from objective, impersonal habits of thought and to lift it into the sphere of personal and moral life—is brought to complete fulfilment.

If in this respect Deutero-Isaiah can be regarded as the perfecter of Jeremiah's thought, yet on a second important point he goes beyond Jeremiah. He uses this fusion of the messianic element with the covenant concept to link the latter at the same time with the idea of universalism. Yahweh's decree of salvation realized in the Servant of God also embraces the nations of the earth. Indeed it is precisely in his role as covenant-mediator that the *'ebed* is to be the 'light of the Gentiles' and Yahweh's law is to shine out from the newly created people of God over the whole world, bringing the nations into voluntary subjection to the divine order revealed in it. [3] It is true that a certain position of superiority is still reserved to Israel in the appropriation of the covenant blessings; and in this we can still see the formative consequences of the history of the Sinai covenant. Nevertheless, the heathen become, if not full citizens, at any rate settlers in the Kingdom of God [4]—indeed they have a certain right to a share in Yahweh's salvation, for they long after his *mišpāṭ*, his ordinance of justice for the whole earth, and wait for his *ṣ'dākā*, the redeeming work befitting his position as God of the universe. [5]

In this way the *b'rīt* conception was completely assimilated by the

---

[1] Isa. 42.6; 49.8.
[2] Ezek. 34.24 f.; 37.25 f.
[3] Isa. 42.1, 4; 49.6; 55.3–5. The last-named passage shows that, even outside the sections relating to the Servant of God, the new covenant still retains its messianic character. The closest parallel in other prophetic writers is Isa. 2.2–4.
[4] Isa. 55.3 ff.; 60.5 ff.; 61.5 f.
[5] On this point 45.22; 51.5 should be added to the passages already cited.

thought of the prophets. As distinct from the covenant relationship in P, which is rooted in the present situation, in Jeremiah, Ezekiel and Deutero-Isaiah it has become a description of the great good lying in the future, and the Sinai covenant is for them but the shadow cast by the coming consummation. This projecting of a central element of Israelite religion into the 'Not yet' cuts away the ground from under the feet of pious souls in their attempts to 'make themselves tabernacles' and rest in some stage that earthly history has already attained. It is not that the past and the present are to be counted as nothing worth; the very description of what is to come as *b᷂rit* bears witness to the essential affinity between the divine revelation hitherto and that which is still in the future. But God's supreme work of redemption for Israel, his self-disclosure to the community in a covenant, is something that will only unveil its ultimate meaning in a community relationship beyond any earthly horizon, in an order where the depth of personal life, the strength of the national life and the breadth of the life of the whole human race are each and all renewed by the divine presence and so fulfil the purpose of their creation. This means, however, that in the *b᷂rit* man is brought into close contact with the workings of God; and this takes from him all earthly security and places the goal of his existence in a future that is guaranteed by the divine promise alone.

(f) *The post-exilic period* adhered more closely to Deuteronomy and P in its understanding of the covenant concept. In addition to the historical making of the covenant[1] it saw in the *b᷂rit* the actual relationship currently existing between God and Israel and the rights and duties deriving from that. The latter especially came into prominence once more; *b᷂rit* as a term epitomizing the covenant regulations occurs frequently in the Psalms. [2] Occasionally the word is given the even more general sense of 'cultus' or 'religion', the element of obligation being in the forefront. [3] The thought of God's activity as Creator and Giver in the *b᷂rit*, which with the prophets—and even in P as well—was definitely primary, is here manifestly disappearing from the concept and giving way to a more formalistic conception of religious right behaviour and its standards. So soon, however, as *b᷂rit* becomes the term for a system of precepts, then it to a great

[1]For the Abraham covenant, cf. Ps. 105.8, 10; for the covenant with Noah, Isa. 24.5.
[2]Pss. 25.10, 14; 44.18; 50.16; 78.10, 37; 103.18.
[3]Dan. 9.27; Zech. 9.11.

extent reverts to legalistic definitions of the religious relationship instead of remaining a dominant concept of living religion. The violent calls to God to think of his covenant obligations and to deal with the congregation according to their piety and uprightness, as we find them in Pss. 44; 74; 79 etc., exhibit the unhappy consequences of this restricted understanding.

It is the same line of anthropocentric thinking which finally results in the term *b'rit* being used to denote the human possessors and guardians of the covenant, the Jewish congregation. [1]

Meanwhile the interpretation of the covenant relationship as a relation of grace, lived out in the contemporary situation, as P had presented it, was still widely accepted. This is demonstrated by many of the expressions of the piety of the Psalms, [2] but also in particular by the usage of Chronicles, in which a distinctive extension of the priestly point of view can be discerned. The Chronicler recognizes many historical instances of the making of a covenant, such as a covenant with David and other later ones, all of which aim at a purification and renewal of the religion of the Fathers. [3] But the covenant-makings which initiate Israel's state of election, the covenants with Abraham and at Sinai, are just the ones he does not mention; he even avoids referring to them in those places where they are suggested to him by his model. [4] By this device he manages to extricate the saving relationship of Israel from any historical basis or limitation and stamps it instead as something existing from eternity, an element in God's universal design which is constant from the beginning. The genealogical lists in the Chronicler's work, covering the whole course of history up to David, constitute, by their very monotony, 'a profound expression of the knowledge of a saving relationship between God and his people which is unchanged from the very beginning'. [5]

It was this exaltation of God's *b'rit* with Israel into a timeless entity, which won greater respect than really befitted their importance for many covenant-makings that hitherto had been very much in the background. Most important of these is *the David covenant*, which in Chronicles forms a basic element of the writer's theological outline of

---

[1]Dan. 11.22, 28, 30, 32; Ps. 74.20; Prov. 2.17; Mal. 2.10, 14 (?); 3.1 (the *mal'āk* of the covenant = the guardian angel of the congregation).

[2]Pss. 106.45; 111.5, 9.

[3]II Chron. 15.12; 23.3, 16; 29.10; 34.31.

[4]II Chron. 6.11 compared with I Kings 8.21; and II Chron. 34.31 f. compared with II Kings 23.3.

[5]Cf. von Rad, *Das Geschichtsbild des chronistischen Werkes*, 1930, p. 66.

history;[1] however, it also plays such a prominent part in passages of a liturgical or prophetic character from the post-exilic period, that it must patently have been dear to the faith long before the Chronicler. [2] We have no means of throwing light on the history of this idea in detail, but it is permissible to conjecture, on the basis of certain reliable pieces of evidence from the monarchical period such as II Sam. 23.5 and Ps. 132, that the Davidic dynasty very early based its claims to suzerainty on a special covenant with Yahweh. The association of the messianic expectation with the house of David soon naturalized this idea as a vital part of Israel's faith and in times of oppression this afforded a welcome focus for hope. In conjunction with the theme of the 'sure mercies of David' [3] it also reinforced faith in the irrefragable character of the divine promise of salvation; and because the David covenant was from the beginning strictly a relationship of grace, it could much more easily be integrated with the prophetic hope of salvation than could the Sinai covenant.

Less important is *the Levi covenant* which, like the covenant with David, connects the constancy of the divine purpose of salvation with a particular act of election in the past. In this case the need to legitimize definite priestly claims also plays a part. [4] However, the experience of the Jewish congregation that a priesthood conscious of the dignity of its calling was essential to a full communal life raises the divine promise to Levi out of its private and limited context and makes it yet another instance of the concern of the covenant God for his whole people. [5]

In conclusion, the LXX translation gave a special colouring to the OT concept of the covenant. Here the Hebrew *berit* is rendered by the Greek διαθήκη, although, as is well known, a more exact correspondence would require συνθήκη, the term in fact used by Aquila and Symmachus. The word διαθήκη comes from Hellenistic civil law and, in addition to the general sense of 'statute' or 'ordinance', denotes in particular the final instructions of a testator. It is from the overtones of this latter meaning that the concept acquires its own special note of solemnity; and a further consequence is that the thought of the primacy of God, the covenant as the solemn,

[1] II Chron. 7.18; 13.5; 21.7, *et al.*
[2] Jer. 33.14-26; Ps. 89.4, 29, 35, 40; Isa. 55.3.
[3] Isa. 55.3; Ps. 89.2, 3, 50 (49); Ps. 132.11.
[4] Num. 25.13; 18.19.
[5] Mal. 2.4, 5, 8; Jer. 33.18 ff.; Neh. 13.29.

unbreakable expression and confirmation of his will, is more strongly preserved than by the term συνθήκη.

Nevertheless, the bilateral character proper to the Hebrew *b'rit* is not entirely lacking in the Greek idiom. The 'definite one-sided character which we are inclined to stress from analogy with our present-day juristic conceptions is not always associated' with the Greek διαθήκη, 'but, side by side with unilateral testamentary dispositions there exist others having the nature of settled agreements —an oscillation which is to be explained by the derivation of testaments in Greece from the *donatio inter vivos*'.[1] The last will of the testator binds both himself and his heirs. The recipients of the testament are bound on their part to carry out the appointed terms. Thus the divine 'injunction' of the διαθήκη is aimed at a fresh ordering of man's relationship to God; and this 'testamentary' connotation comes through most clearly in the Epistle to the Hebrews, where the bestowal of the inheritance as wholly a gift of grace is given especial prominence by the fact that the death of Christ is an indispensable prerequisite and by the eternal duration of the divine settlement. At the same time the element of human obligation has not just disappeared; and to that extent it is true that the LXX rendering is not a misunderstanding, intruding a complete transformation of sense. Nevertheless, the term διαθήκη does place the emphasis differently from our word 'covenant' and the Hebrew *b'rit* and cannot, therefore, simply be subsumed under the concept 'covenant'.

(g) In any case, as the history of the concept has shown, the rendering 'covenant' for the Hebrew *b'rit* can itself only be regarded, when all is said and done, as a makeshift. One cannot help being aware that the term has to cover two lines of thought along which the meaning has developed. The first runs from 'covenant' through 'covenant relationship', 'covenant precept' and 'legal system' to 'religion', 'cultus' and 'covenant people'; the other from 'covenant' through the divine act of 'establishment', 'the relationship of grace' and 'revelation' to the 'order of redemption', the 'decree of salvation' and the final 'consummation of all things'. These two lines of development, in relation to which P's dual conception must always occupy a key position, represent two divergent understandings of the covenant, which, though in opposition to one another, can yet only in conjunction render the whole content of that divine activity covered by the term *b'rit*. A very similar picture is presented by the

[1]Lohmeyer, *Diatheke*, 1913, p. 40.

concept of the Kingdom of God in the NT, where the controversy whether this referred to a present or a future entity remained for a long time undecided. The beginnings of a solution came with the realization that the assertion of the present reality of the Kingdom and the promise of its coming were only two sides of the one concept. It is the same with the *berit*. The unique, inimitable richness of the divine activity to which it relates is demonstrated precisely in this, that it is quite impossible to dispense either with the present legal order of the link between God and man or with its progressive development and eschatological fulfilment. It is in this conjunction of opposites that the unique character of the relationship with God mediated by the OT is preserved.

Yet another opposition, however, constitutes a vital factor in the history of the convenant concept; and that is the opposition between this concept deriving from the realm of law and those definitions of man's relationship with God which have grown out of the natural conditions of human life. In this connection it has already been pointed out that the concept of the covenant excludes any involvement of the divinity with the nation which is naturalistic and therefore inherently indissoluble. On the other hand certain descriptions of this involvement do tend in this direction, e.g., those of the Father and Son, the Ruler and his People, the one image being taken from family, the other from political life. Both descriptions were widely used in heathen nations. We hear incidentally in the OT of Chemosh, the god of the Moabites, for example, that his worshippers were described as his sons and daughters, Num. 21.29. It is also only natural that among almost all civilized peoples the deity should be thought of under the title of King, with which the symbol of the Shepherd may also be associated. The trouble is, however, in all such cases, that the thought is never far away that the deity on his side is in a certain sense dependent on the worshippers so closely linked to him; for what would a father be without sons? or a king without a people? Even though he may occasionally turn against them in anger, yet it is in his own interests to preserve his people from annihilation and in all circumstances to protect them from their enemies.

The concept of the *berit* denies this particular aspect of the images derived from Nature all validity for the description of the relationship between God and the people; and yet the descriptions themselves are not thereby excluded, but rather are used with living force in Israel from the first. The ancient folk-story of Ex. 4.22 f. is already aware that Israel is Yahweh's first-born son. Isaiah takes up this image in the complaint: 'I have nourished and brought up sons [1] and they have rebelled against me, saith Yahweh' (Isa. 1.2). Indeed the prophets imported new analogies—Hosea that of marriage, Jeremiah that of betrothal, Ezekiel that of the foundling, Deutero-Isaiah that of the mother who cannot forget her child (49.15) and that of the gō'ēl, i.e., the relative who has the duty of redeeming a man who has been enslaved for debt (Isa. 43.1, et al.). Moreover, all the prophets employ the images of the ruler and the shepherd of his flock as a matter of course. The use of these analogies weighs all the more heavily, when we find them in precisely those prophets who neglect the concept of the bᵉrît.

Two points must be noticed. First, the prophets themselves by their style of speaking avoid any misuse of these images. Isaiah speaks of sons whom God has nourished. Nevertheless, by leaving the plural indefinite—'sons', not 'my sons'—it is implied that we are concerned with sons taken over voluntarily, in fact with adopted children. The term giddēl in the same passage recalls Israel's history since the entry into Canaan and thus once more looks back over the free demonstration of divine grace that has marked the days from Egypt onward. It is just the same with the extended parable of the foundling, Ezek. 16. Hosea's likening Israel to Yahweh's wife avoids misusing the symbolism by envisaging the dissolution of the marriage because of the wife's adultery; in this way attention is focused particularly on the unmerited mercy of God who is even prepared to take back the wife he has justly repudiated. Deutero-Isaiah handles the naturalistic relations of love and kinship with the greatest freedom in order to demonstrate the never-wearying love of God; but he is at the same time the prophet who knows how to portray most impressively of all the sublimity of the God of the universe and so never allows the condescension in the love to be overlooked.

The second point is that the prophets quite plainly feel such comparisons to be necessary in order to characterize correctly Yahweh's essential disposition. The concept of the covenant never proved adequate to the outpouring of the riches of their vision of God. In a one-sided portrayal of Yahweh as the founder of the covenant the idea of God could easily become inflexible. To this tendency the naturalistic ideas of God's relationship to men provide

[1] EVV 'children' (Tr.).

an indispensable corrective, without which the picture of God would become impoverished. These two expressions of Yahweh's self-communication—at first sight so contradictory—prove in the event to require and complete each other. If the idea of the establishing of the covenant especially illuminates God's truth and faithfulness, yet the imagery of the Father, the Husband, the Redeemer, the Shepherd enable us to understand a little better his goodness, long-suffering and love. Hence Israel is made aware from the beginning that Yahweh is never the hard 'creditor', relentlessly exacting the conditions of his covenant, but that his claim to honour rests on the fact that he owns the title *'erek 'appayim* (Ex. 34.6) with as much right as he bears the name of *'ēl qannā*.

It may indeed be true that the composite picture, this insight into the inner coherence of two at first sight divergent manifestations of the divine will, was not to be found, at any rate in this form, in ancient Israel. But even though these two aspects of the divine activity might be considered independently, no one doubted the reality of both. It may, perhaps, also be permissible to observe at this point, that it was given to Israel to experience the demands and the graciousness of God with equal directness. Herein lies the significance of the fact that these differing descriptions of man's relationship with God, on the one hand the covenant, on the other the symbols of sonship, marriage, kinship and lordship, exist side by side.

IIII

THE COVENANT STATUTES

ALL THE SOURCES are in agreement that the inauguration of the divine covenant involved a fresh ordering of the legal side of the nation's life under the authority of the covenant God. Moreover, anyone who has realized that the life work of Moses was not merely the deliverance of the enslaved nationals from Egypt, but also the welding them into a single people of Yahweh is forced to recognize that this tradition is correct. It needs no special demonstration that religious enthusiasm alone was not enough to overcome the centrifugal tendencies of the individual tribes for long; the strong unifying bond of a common system of law was indispensable. Throughout all the centuries that followed men lived by this consciousness that their law rested on the revealed will of the covenant God.

Opinions, however, diverge all the more violently, when it comes to establishing the content of the Mosaic law. The dominant view for a long time was that the reorganization of the law could not possibly involve more than purely oral instruction and jurisdiction by Moses himself; that likewise oral transmission sufficed for a long period thereafter; and that only centuries after the settlement in Canaan would this have been replaced by a written codification. [1] This opinion was based on a belief that the Hebrew tribes were at a primitive stage of civilization; since this belief has had to be corrected in the light of our greater knowledge of the ancient East, serious consideration has had to be given once more to the possibility of a written codification of the law in the time of Moses, and either *the*

---

[1] The outstanding exponent of this view was, of course, Wellhausen, *Prolegomena to the History of Israel*, p. 342.

Decalogue of Ex. 20[1] alone or the Decalogue and *the Book of the Covenant*[2] (Ex. 20–23) together have been derived from Moses himself. In this connection the form-critical examination of the law, with its distinction between casuistical and apodeictic or categorical forms of law, has opened up entirely new possibilities for our understanding of the nature of legal tradition. It has brought out clearly that, in addition to the casuistical form, the relationship of which to the general tradition of ancient Near Eastern law has long been recognized, we are dealing in Israel with a genuinely new formation —law expressed in short, categorical commandment-sayings, mostly in rhythmical form.[3] The close association of this law with the cult festival as the scene of its promulgation and, therefore, with the idea of the fulfilling of the pure will of Yahweh only emphasizes more strongly that the Israelite legal system is primarily rooted in the activity of the founder of the religion; for it is this conception of the burning exclusiveness of the will of Yahweh which formed the heart of the Mosaic teaching about God. Even the legal system of the ancient Near East, which was originally quite independent of the Yahweh faith, and which found its way into Israel in the form of casuistical law, was seized upon by this out-and-out religious conception embodied in the apodeictic law. Once it had thus been drawn into the sacral sphere, it was launched on a process of transformation, the beginnings of which may be detected in the complex appearance presented by the Book of the Covenant. There is thus concrete evidence in support of the contention, inherently probable in itself, that no nation lives by general axioms and principles, but only by particular institutions and ordinances, in which these prin-

---

[1]So Kittel, *Geschichte des Volkes Israel*[5] I, 1923, pp. 383 ff.; H. Gressmann, *Mose und seine Zeit*, pp. 473 ff.; H. Schmidt, 'Mose und der Dekalog,' in *Eucharisterion* (Essays presented to Hermann Gunkel), 1923, pp. 78 ff.; P. Volz, *Mose*[2], pp. 20 ff.; *et al.* It is not possible in such a work as this to go more closely into the literary problems and the reader is therefore referred to the literature mentioned.

[2]Cf. E. Sellin, Introduction to the Old Testament, ET 1923, pp. 40 ff.; B. D. Eerdmans, *De Godsdienst van Israel* I, pp. 40 ff. R. Kittel would prefer to connect this with Joshua's covenant-making in Shechem (Josh. 24.25) and to explain it as a collation of the various definite pieces of legislation then available, in which the legal material handed down from Moses was combined with Canaanite law (*Great Men and Movements in Israel*, ET, 1929, pp. 314 ff.).

[3]This field was opened up by the work of A. Alt, *Die Ursprünge des israelitischen Rechts*, 1934. An attempt to carry the understanding of the law further along the lines laid down by Alt was made by K. H. Rabast in his work, *Das apodiktische Recht im Deuteronomium und im Heiligkeitsgesetz*, 1948.

ciples have been given solid expression. [1] Historically, therefore, the soundest opinion would seem to be that which derives these ancient collections of laws ultimately from Moses himself—always remembering that in the course of a long period of transmission they cannot have escaped a good deal of interference and alteration of one kind and another. [2] However, even in circles where the idea of a written transmission of the Mosaic legal settlement is regarded with scepticism, there is another fact which cannot be ignored. In the legal tradition both of the period of the Judges and of the Monarchy there is a force at work of a distinctive character, inseparably connected with that powerful impetus to renewal which came with the establishment of the religion.

The Shechemite Twelve Commandments, which have been handed down to us in Deut. 27.15–26, may well come from the period of the Judges. [3]

The second major work of law in the Pentateuch, the Book of Deuteronomy, may be looked at in two ways. In its present form it is a product of the later monarchy, to be exact of the seventh century. Both its language and the content of its thought betray the influence of the prophetic preaching, and it may therefore be used as evidence for the legal ideas of this period. The law-material in it, however, shows that it goes back to a far earlier age. When the basic stratum of the book is cleared of later supplements and commentaries, it is seen to know nothing of the centralization of the cultus and, in its relationship to the laws of the Book of the Covenant and the older Priestly regulations, to bear a most primitive character. [4] Hence this

[1]Stressed with particular force by M. Noth, Das System der zwölf Stämme Israels, pp. 62 ff.

[2]H. Cazelles, Etudes sur le Code de l'Alliance, 1946, has urged that the provenance of the Book of the Covenant is to be found in the Mosaic period at the time when the tribes east of the Jordan were becoming settled. Ex. 34.10–26 constitute neither a Decalogue nor a Dodecalogue, but simply the fragmentary relics of the yahwistic legal tradition, which has its parallels in the Elohistic Decalogue and the Book of the Covenant.

[3]Cf. E. Sellin, op. cit., p. 44; H. Gressmann, Schriften des AT II, 1, 1914, pp. 235 ff.; S. Mowinckel, Psalmenstudien V, 1924, pp. 97 ff.

[4]Attempts to establish with certainty the provenance of the ancient material in Deuteronomy are to be found in: K. Steuernagel, Einleitung ins Alte Testament, 1912, pp. 176 ff.; J. Hempel, Die Schichten des Deuteronomiums, 1914, pp. 253 ff.; M. Löhr, Das Deuteronomium, 1925; R. Kittel, Gesch. des Volkes Israel[4], 1916, I, pp. 289 ff.; A. Jirku, Das weltliche Recht Israels, 1927. On the question of the centralization of the cultus, about which widely divergent views are still held, cf. M. Kegel, Die Kultusreformation des Josia, 1919; T. Oestreicher, Das deuteronomische Grundgesetz, 1923; G. Holscher, 'Komposition und Ursprung des Deuteronomiums' (in ZAW

collection can to some extent be adduced as evidence for the most
ancient popular conception of the Law of Yahweh. [1]

It is the *Priestly Law* which places the greatest obstacles in the way
of its use for our present purpose. Here the explanatory additions of
the post-exilic period have expanded to such an extent, that it has
become extremely difficult to separate the pre-exilic concept of the
law from the post-exilic. Yet, on the other hand, it is quite certain
once again, that the basic stratum of this law goes right back to the
beginnings of the nation's history and confirms the tradition that
Moses regulated its cultic life as well. [2] In the traditions relating to the
place where God is to be served, in the precepts concerning sacrifices
and purity, and in the ordering of festivals, P has preserved ancient
material, worked over to a greater or less degree, which affords a
valuable source of knowledge for the importance of cultic legislation
in the earliest stages of Israelite religion. Since, however, this legal
material received its distinctive stamp in the eighth or seventh century, it can be adduced alongside Deuteronomy as a source of
information on the sacred law in the monarchical period; though,
when doing so, it is constantly necessary to bear the post-exilic
redaction in mind.

Even the briefest survey of the Israelite legal tradition cannot but
impress on us that, when dealing with the sacred law, we are not
concerned with a rigid entity, fixed once for all, but with the formation

---

40, 1922, pp. 161 ff.); W. Stärk, *Das Problem des Deuteronomiums*, 1925. The older
position is maintained by: H. Gressmann ('Josia und das Deuteronomium', *ZAW*
42, 1924, pp. 313 ff.); K. Budde ('Das Deuteronomium und die Reform König
Josias', *ZAW* 44, 1926, pp. 177 ff.); W. Baumgartner ('Der Kampf um das
Deuteronomium', *Theol. Rundschau*, N.F.I, 1929, pp. 7 ff.); E. König ('Deuteronomische Hauptfragen', *ZAW* 48, 1930, pp. 43 ff.).

[1] In his last pronouncement on the question Kittel (*Great Men and Movements in
Israel*, pp. 319 ff.) would prefer to place the book found in the time of King Josiah
at an earlier stage close to the Book of the Covenant and to claim it as legislation
originally obtaining among a small circle of Judaean origin. A. C. Welch ('On the
method of celebrating Passover', *ZAW* 45, 1927, pp. 24 ff.) assumes that the Passover regulations in Deut. 16 preserve an older cult law from Northern Israel. The
Northern Israelite provenance of the Deuteronomic traditions is argued by: von
Rad (*Studies in Deuteronomy*, ET, 1953, p. 68) and A. Alt ('Die Heimat des
Deuteronomiums', in *Kleine Schriften zur Geschichte des Volkes Israel* II, 1953,
pp. 250 ff.).

[2] Cf. B. D. Eerdmans, *Alttestamentliche Studien* IV, 1912, and *De Godsdienst van
Israel* I, pp. 40 ff., 56 ff., 108 ff., 131 ff.; R. Kittel, *Geschichte des Volkes Israel*[4] I,
pp. 317 ff., and *Great Men and Movements in Israel*, pp. 325 ff.; M. Löhr, *Das Ritual
von Lev. 16*, 1925, and *Das Raücheropfer im Alten Testament*, 1927; E. Sellin, *op. cit.*,
pp. 81 ff.

and development of social and cultic ordinances which correspond to actual historical situations and in which differing trends are
striving to prevail. It is, therefore, all the more important to ask
what are the abiding basic principles by which the Israelite law is to
be distinguished from those national laws of the ancient East known
to us from other sources. [1] There can be no question of engaging here
in a detailed and thoroughgoing comparison of Israelite law with
these other collections of laws. We must be content to throw into
relief the most important divergences, which will serve as pointers to
the unique character of Israelite law. It is assumed to be a well-known
fact that this law includes a considerable proportion of material
common to Oriental law in general. For convenience sacred and
secular law will be dealt with separately; but it should always be
remembered that in Israel this distinction was never carried through.
Jus and *fas* always derived their validity from being inseparable parts
of the one holy law.

A. THE SECULAR LAW

I. ITS DISTINCTIVE CHARACTER

1. If we are seeking to define the distinctive character of the
Mosaic law when contrasted with the corresponding laws of other
ancient peoples, then attention must first be drawn to *the emphasis*

[1]Of such national laws the following are extant today: 1. The Babylonian law
of the time of King Hammurabi, c. 1700 BC, in the so-called Code of Hammurabi
(CH); 2. A collection of ancient Assyrian laws (AAG), apparently preserved in a
private list going back to c. 1100 BC; 3. Hittite laws (HG) from the State archives
of Boghaz-keui, belonging to the period c. 1300 BC. In addition there are fragments
of Sumerian and Neo-Babylonian law, such as the legal documents from Nuzu.
These laws are most conveniently accessible in the collection edited by H.
Gressmann, *Altorientalische Texte und Bilder*[2] I, 1926. Cf. also W. Eilers, *Die
Gesetzesstele Chammurabis*, 1932 (Der alte Orient 31, fasc. 3/4); H. Ehelolf, *Ein
altassyrisches Rechtsbuch*, 1922 (Mitteilungen aus der vorderasiatischen Abteilung
der Staatl. Museen zu Berlin, fasc. 1); H. Zimmern and J. Friedrich, *Hethitische
Gesetze*, 1922 (Der alte Orient 32, fasc. 2); C. H. Gordon, 'Parallèles Nouziens aux
lois et coutumes de l'Ancien Testament' (in *RB* 44, 1935, pp. 34 ff.). On the collections of early Babylonian laws before Hammurabi, viz., the Code of Urnammu
(c. 2080 BC), the legal reforms of Eshnunna (c. 1850 BC) and the slightly later
laws of Lipit-Ishtar, cf.: E. Szlechter, 'Le Code d'Ur-Nammu' in *Revue d'Assyriologie*
49, 1955, pp. 169 ff.; S. N. Kramer, 'Urnammu Law Code' in *Orientalia*, N.S. 23,
1954, pp. 40 ff.; F. R. Krauss, 'Neue Rechtsurkunden der altbabylonischen Zeit.
Bemerkungen zu Ur- Excavation Texts 5' in *Welt des Orients*, II. 2, 1955, pp. 120 ff.;
A. Götze, 'The Laws of Eshnunna' in *Annual of the American Schools of Oriental
Research* 31, 1956; Steele, 'The Code of Lipit-Ishtar', *American Journal of Archaeology*
52, 1948, pp. 425 ff. A selection from these texts may be found in J. B. Pritchard,
Ancient Near Eastern Texts relating to the Old Testament[2], 1955.

with which the entire law is referred to God. Not only the cultic law, but the secular law derives its validity from being a direct command of Yahweh; any breach of it is an outrage against Yahweh himself. The law thus acquires a majesty, which removes it from the sphere of human arbitrariness and relativism and bases it firmly on the metaphysical.

It is certainly true that in pagan religions the law is also invested with the authority of the national god. The Code of Hammurabi,[1] for instance, is explicitly referred, both at the beginning and the end, to the will of Shamash. The king is represented as his deputy. Yet it is precisely in this feature that the difference between this law and that of Israel becomes properly clear. For the mention of the god is restricted to the introductory and closing formulas. In the law itself the deity is silent and the human lawgiver takes the centre of the stage; the Code is expressly described at the beginning and the end as the king's own work. In Israel, by contrast, the mutual involvement of religion, law and morality is still experienced with vivid immediacy. Every breach of the law is seen as an offence against God. In every instance it is the divine lawgiver who lays down the law, and the human mediator comes after him. That is why one does not speak of the Law of Moses,[2] but of the Law of Yahweh. In the Decalogue this central divine reference is clearly seen not only in the fact that the very first commandments describe our duties toward God, but perhaps even more in the fact that here we have a selection and collation of ten commandments representing the whole wide field of *pietas* and *probitas*. It is just this manifest concentration on the religious ordering of the national life as its indispensable foundation, which indicates a spiritual achievement without parallel in the ancient East, and one made possible only by a disciplined determination to relate the whole of life to the one all-ruling will of God. The same religious atmosphere, however, inbreathes the whole of the Book of the Covenant and witnesses to the raising of ancient Semitic law to an entirely new level.[3] Furthermore, indicating as this does a

---

[1]Cf. above, p. 74 n. 1.

[2]This description first occurs with any frequency in the Deuteronomic circle, cf. Josh. 22.2; 23.6; I Kings 2.3; II Kings 14.6; 23.25; but thereafter becomes firmly established in Judaism. Nevertheless, the more precise expression *hattōrā b'yad-mōše* is still found in Chronicles, cf. II Chron. 33.8; 34.14; 35.6.

[3]As Jepsen has shown in his exhaustive examination, (*Untersuchungen zum Bundesbuch*, 1927), the working-over of pre-Mosaic law to be found in the Book of the Covenant can also be detected by the changes in the stylistic forms. It is a striking fact, that in the passages regarded by him on the basis of their stylistic

prophetic nature in the author, it gives us an indubitable right to argue *a posteriori* from the unique character of this law to the religious awareness that stands behind it. In this sense the OT tradition is absolutely right, when it says that Moses received the law on Sinai from God himself; for the contemplation of the divine Being must have exercised a decisive influence on its formation.

2. What sort of a divine will then is expressed in this law? The special character of the Decalogue at once gives us a lead in answering this question. The uniqueness of the Decalogue does not consist to any great extent in the intrinsic worth of its moral precepts. The prohibition of murder, adultery and theft, and the inculcation of respect for parents, comprise no more than the elementary bases of communal human life, such as are to be found at quite primitive levels. Indeed, without them any kind of social organization would scarcely be possible. The prohibitions against bearing false witness and against coveting the property of one's neighbour do of course presuppose more developed cultural conditions; but they include nothing remarkable, nothing which would not have been regarded as an offence both in Babylonia and in Egypt and, indeed, in Canaan, influenced as it was so strongly by both those countries. [1] The really remarkable feature of the Decalogue is rather *the definite connection of the moral precepts with the basic religious commands*. It is the expression of a conviction that moral action is inseparably bound up with the worship of God. This means, however, that the God whose help man

---

characteristics as genuinely Israelite—though certainly not exclusively in these—the distinctive religious and moral tone of the Israelite law-giving is most prominent; cf. Ex. 21.6, 12–17, 23b–27, 31; 22.9–12, 17–19. The formulation of the law in weighty prohibitions or in lapidary definitions of those crimes that are capital offences accords extremely well with the Mosaic preaching of the mighty Will of God. I have already explained elsewhere (*Theologie der Gegenwart*, 1928, pp. 253 ff.) why I cannot wholly accept Jepsen's conclusions concerning the authorship and dating of the law. Jirku's methodological principle—'If Moses had in fact bequeathed to his people a codified law, then he would certainly have composed and promulgated these laws in a single homogeneous style' (*op. cit.*, p. 52)—seems to me to take too little account of the fact that Moses, for the very reason that he had to reorganize traditional law in accordance with the revelation vouchsafed to him personally, may very well have made use of various stylistic forms. Whether, with the means now at our disposal, we can ever succeed in restoring the original form of the Book of the Covenant and in disentangling its various components with certainty, seems to me, in view of the complexity of the situation, extremely doubtful. In this connection, cf. also the above-mentioned study of A. Alt.

[1] Cf. the Egyptian Book of the Dead, ch. 125: 'The Confession before the Judges of the Dead' (*AOT*, pp. 9 ff.; *ANET*, pp. 34 ff.) and the Babylonian Shurpu series of adjurations (*AOT*, pp. 324 f.).

craves regards obedience to the moral standards as equally important with the exclusive worship of himself; and consequently his whole will and purpose is directed to that which is morally good. The same state of affairs can be discerned in the Book of the Covenant also. Compared with the *mišpāṭim*, the fundamental commands of the civil law, the cultic *d·bārim* in chs. 22 and 23 occupy a relatively small space. This primer of the nation's law places the just fashioning of social life in the forefront throughout as the main content of the divine will.

3. As regards the content of this legal regulation of life it is most significant that we find no trace of *juristic casuistry*. While in the Code of Hammurabi—and to an even greater extent in the Hittite and Assyrian laws—juristic technique is much more highly developed and there is a striving after as plentiful a distinction and classification of the various cases as possible, Israelite law on the whole contents itself with applying a few basic dicta fairly freely over and over again. These dicta are, however, inculcated as the divine will and thus impressed on the heart and conscience. Application to individual concrete instances is then left in many cases to a healthy feeling for justice. Even in the later books of the law things have not progressed much beyond this stage. This is not to be ascribed *solely* to backward cultural development, though this is of course partly responsible, but also to a sound judgment on the necessity of a living feeling for law, without which the most exhaustive legal regulations must remain ineffective. The law that God wills is something simple and clear— not a system which is too complex ever to be grasped as a whole and in which life is therefore bound to be suffocated.

4. In this way great confidence is exhibited in the strength of moral standards once these have been vitally appropriated; and this confidence, in its turn, must rest on the experience of a powerful moral will of God. Similarly, by the principal points on which it differs from the Code of Hammurabi, the Book of the Covenant bears witness to the real growth of *a deepened moral sensibility* out of the religious vitality that pulses through it. This can be seen first in the fact that *a higher value is placed on human life* than on any materialistic values. The death penalty is abolished for offences against property, whereas in Babylonian law it is used quite unsparingly.[1] The slave is

---

[1]CH, § 6–11; 15 f.; 19; 22. E. Ring (*Israels Rechtsleben im Licht der neuentdeckten assyrischen und hethitischen Gesetzesurkunden*, 1926, pp. 60 ff.) makes some remarkably pertinent observations on the difference in outlook dominating the question of

given protection against inhuman abuse; [1] he is not merely a thing, as he is in the whole of the rest of the ancient world, [2] but a human being as well! In fatal accidents where the party responsible is only indirectly culpable, as also in the case of deaths caused by the goring of an animal, the penalty is never to be exacted from the children of the guilty party on the principle of indirect talion, [3] though this is frequently the practice in Babylonia. [4]

A further very noteworthy characteristic of Israelite law is *the abolition of gross brutality* in the punishment of the guilty. Not only is the rule 'one crime, one punishment' accepted, whereas the Assyrian law, for example, provides for a wide range of physical and monetary penalties, [5] but there is an absence of those pernicious bodily mutilations so general elsewhere, such as the cutting off of the hands, [6] the cropping of the nose or ears, the plucking out of the tongue, branding, cutting off the breasts. In the Code of Hammurabi such mutilations are not at all uncommon; while in the Assyrian law from the

---

protection of property in Israel and in the great civilizations respectively. In Israel it is a matter of preserving possessions in the interests of the family and the tribe; in Assyria of guarding property as the basis of the resources of a civilized state.

[1] Ex. 21.20, 26 f.

[2] Even the otherwise extremely humane Hittite Law is no exception in this respect, as Ring seems to imagine (*op. cit.*, p. 143).

[3] On the basis of this explanation of Ex. 21.31 (first propounded as far as I know by D. H. Müller, *Die Gesetze Hammurabis*, 1903, pp. 165 ff., and never refuted) it seems certain that in the Book of the Covenant, though without a great deal of palaver, the principle is already firmly established, that children are not to be punished in the place of their parents. This principle is not found in so many words until Deut. 24.16, for which reason it has mostly been regarded as an expression of the refined sensibility of the seventh century. Seeing, however, that we know of this same principle from § 2 of AAG and from a Hittite inscription of the fifteenth century B.C. (cf. Puukko, 'Die altassyrischen und hethitischen Gesetze und das Alte Testament' in *Studia Orientalia* I, 1925, pp. 125 ff., and my review in *Theologie der Gegenwart*, 1926, pp. 238 ff.) and at the same time learn that it was by no means obeyed in every case (§§ 49 and 54 of AAG, for example, seem still to presuppose indirect talion), there would seem to be no need any longer to ignore the ruling of the Book of the Covenant in this connection. If the behaviour of King Amaziah in II Kings 14.6 is stressed as being especially praiseworthy, this is not because we have here one of the earliest applications of this principle, but because of its extension to cover a case of high treason, which would normally have been much more severely dealt with.

[4] In the case of the death of hostages from ill-treatment, § 116; of brawls resulting in a miscarriage, § 210; of housebreaking, § 230.

[5] AAG, §§ 7; 18–21; 40; 44.

[6] The single exception occurs in Deut. 25.11 f., significantly in the case of an act felt to be especially shameless.

period c. 1100 b.c., that is to say some hundred years after Moses, [1]
they are multiplied in the most repulsive manner. There is evidence
here of a genuinely noble humanity and a deepened feeling for equity
as traits of Israelite law. This can hardly be explained except in terms
of the knowledge of God—that God who created man after his own
image and therefore protects him, even when he is liable to punishment, because of the value and the right to life that pertain to him as
a human being.

This humanitarian spirit loses nothing of its uniqueness, when it is
compared with the spirit of the Hittite law. In this code, which
appeared c. 1250 b.c., apparently as a result of a royal reform of the
existing law, there is indeed a relaxation of the old severe code of
punishment, but to such a degree that the inviolable bases of moral
retribution are badly shaken. Murder, for example, is no longer in
any instance punishable by death. [2] That this 'humanitarianism', on
the other hand, is quite uncontrolled by any coherent principle, is
demonstrated by the fact that the death penalty is retained for slaves
in cases where the free man escapes with a fine, [3] and also by the
acceptance of punishment by mutilation. [4] In Israel the relaxation of
penalties proceeds from a clear change in the fundamental estimate
of the crime, and can therefore be combined with an unrelenting
severity and the recognition of absolute standards.

There is a third characteristic of the utmost significance for the
Israelite sense of law, and that is *the rejection of any class-distinction in the
administration of justice.* We hear nothing of any special law for the
priesthood or the aristocracy. The isolated alien, who cannot enforce
his rights with the help of a powerful clan, is of equal standing with
the Israelite in the eyes of the law. There is express warning against
oppressing those without economic resources, the widow and the
orphan. [5] It is true that the distinction between free and slave is still
maintained, but even the slave is afforded the protection of the law:
severe maltreatment gives the victim the right to emancipation;
manslaughter incurs heavy penalties. [6] By contrast, we find in the
Code of Hammurabi, as in the other ancient codes of law, explicit

[1]CH, §§ 127; 192–195; 205; 218; 226; 253; 282. AAG, §§ 4; 5; 8; 9; 15; 20;
24; 40.
[2]I. 1–5.
[3]II. 55.
[4]I. 96, 100.
[5]Ex. 22.20 f.
[6]Ex. 21.26 f., 20.

class legislation, which distinguishes sharply not only between members of the Court, priests, government officials, free men and slaves, but even between individual callings. It is clearly symptomatic of this difference in outlook that in the Code of Hammurabi the law relating to slaves comes at the end, whereas in the Book of the Covenant it has been moved to the beginning.

5. Finally, attention should be drawn to the heightening of the moral sense in that most personal of all the spheres of morality, the relations between the sexes. Admittedly it is just on this subject that an important part of the Book of the Covenant has been lost to us, for there is quite obviously a gaping lacuna after Ex. 22.17, where the marriage law must at one time have stood. It is possible, however, to attempt a reconstruction of it by comparing the conditions in pre-Mosaic and post-Mosaic times on the basis of the picture in the historical books. By so doing it can be established that in this department also a decisive change must have taken place in the Mosaic period. In earlier times marriage to two sisters simultaneously, or the raising of a handmaid to the status of a wife, was accepted without question, as the stories of Jacob and Abraham show.[1] This custom, which is based on Babylonian law,[2] no longer obtains in the post-Mosaic period; on this point, therefore, legislation must obviously have modified the traditional ancient Semitic law of marriage.[3] The refinement of feeling for the value of marriage which is perceptible here may be traced also in the injunction against selling one's wife —or even a woman who was only a slave taken as a concubine—into slavery for some offence;[4] in Babylonia in similar circumstances this was the husband's right.[5]

It is true that even so we are still a long way from a complete solution of the problems of marriage; a good deal of the mentality typical of the ancient world still remains. In particular it is important

---

[1]Gen. 21 and 16. It is hardly legitimate to regard the details of this narrative simply as witnessing to the customs of the post-Mosaic period, when that period affords us no evidence whatsoever of such a usage in law.

[2]The most striking examples of such legal customs have been found in the contracts of the town of Nuzu to the S.E. of Nineveh from the fourteenth and fifteenth centuries B.C.; cf. C. H. Gordon, 'Parallèles Nouziens . . .', RB 44, 1935, pp. 34 ff., and 'Biblical Customs and the Nuzu Tablets', The Biblical Archaeologist 3, 1940, pp. 1 ff.; also, H. H. Rowley, 'Recent Discovery and the Patriarchal Age', in The Servant of the Lord, 1952, pp. 299 ff.

[3]As e.g. in the direction of Lev. 18.18.

[4]Ex. 21.7 f.; cf. Deut. 21.14.

[5]CH, §§ 117; 119.

to recognize that in Babylonia the wife had many rights of which Israelite legislation appears to know nothing. Thus dissoluteness on the part of the husband entitled her to take the initiative in breaking up the marriage partnership. [1] Further, she is given the right in the marriage contract to refuse to give security for debts contracted by the husband before marriage. [2] There is also no reference in Israelite law to legal provision for the divorced wife or the widow, such as is envisaged by the Code of Hammurabi. [3] This extension of the rights of the wife is simply one expression of that general superiority of Babylonia to Israel in the external details of civilization which is well known to us from many other examples. In general, it may indeed be said, that wherever a highly developed culture dissolves, or merely loosens, the cement of family and clan, then intensified legal protection for the individual normally becomes necessary. The Israelite kingdoms, however, were for the greater part of their existence peasant, agricultural states; once trade and large landed property came to play a more important part in their life, they soon fell to destruction. In such simpler conditions the strength of the family and clan affords the individual a powerful support, which takes the place of many legal measures. A typical example of this is the answer of the Shunammite woman to Elisha, when the prophet offered to use his influence with the king on her behalf: 'I dwell among mine own people,' [4] i.e., I need no protection, the fellow-members of my clan are sufficient protection for me. If this great importance of the clan right into the monarchical period is borne in mind, then the absence of these Babylonian-type legal stipulations in Israel becomes easier to understand. In Israel the wife still had sufficient backing in her family. However, the one piece of Israelite divorce law which we possess, Deut. 24.1 ff., concerning the age of which it is hardly possible to arrive at any definite conclusion, does at least show that in the course of time steps were taken to limit the caprice of the husband in the matter of divorce, by requiring him first to demonstrate the presence in his wife of an '*erwā*, a 'disgraceful' or 'scandalous' thing.

[1] CH, § 142.
[2] CH, § 151.
[3] CH, §§ 137–140; 171; 172: cf. also AAG, § 46. In the divorce law of the Jewish military colony of Elephantine, however, there is the stipulation that on divorce the wife should be allowed to take with her everything which she brought at the time of the marriage (cf. A. Cowley, *Aramaic Papyri of the Fifth Century* B.C. 1923, p. 44, no. 15 = Assuan G.).
[4] II Kings 4.13; reading '*ammī*.

In Babylonian law this is not required. [1] Furthermore, the prohibition of the remarriage of a divorced wife to her first husband, assuming that in the meantime she had married another man and then been released from that also either by death or divorce, is dictated by the same general intention, and affords another example of new points of view prevailing over the old. Moreover, evidence of a lofty conception of marriage even in the earliest period is to be found in the attitude of the Yahwistic Creation narrative. Here the wife is presented as a help meet for the man, equal to him in status. The bold prophetic comparison of the relationship of Yahweh with his people to a marriage equally testifies to the placing of the highest value on the institution.

A consideration of Lev. 20 points in the same direction. The terminology of this section of the Priestly Code so strikingly recalls the Book of the Covenant, that it is hard to resist the impression that we are here confronted with a part of the material missing from that book. The passage deals with the penalties for unchastity and it is to be noted that these offences are on the whole more severely punished in Israel than in Babylonia. Indeed, in the former the death penalty is the general rule, while in the latter a fine or banishment may be substituted. [2] Moreover, in Israelite law we find no legal protection for prostitution, such as is afforded by the Code of Hammurabi. [3] In Deut. 23.18 cultic impurity is expressly forbidden. This austerity of moral outlook, in the narrowest sense of the word 'moral', is especially striking when we compare it with the unbelievable laxity brazenly displayed in the Hittite law. [4]

By the very fact that it was its inward involvement with religion which enabled Israel to achieve an altogether higher sense of the meaning of law, such as we seek in vain among other peoples, it may readily be concluded that here we are confronted with the fact of the moral personality of God. If such a strengthening and refinement of the moral sense proceeds from the worship of Yahweh, then this God must be conceived as the power of goodness and the pattern of all human righteousness. He is exalted far above the role of a mere protector of prescriptive rights.

[1]CH, §§ 137–140.
[2]CH, §§ 154–158.
[3]CH, §§ 108–111; 127; 178–184.
[4]HG, I. 37; II. 73–76, 80 f., 85 f.

2. SOME CRUCIAL PHASES IN THE DEVELOPMENT OF THE LAW

The historical sources do not make it possible to give a coherent presentation of the development of the law in Israel, for the way in which their account is set out is governed by considerations which have nothing to do with pure juristic knowledge. Nevertheless, some firm indications may be derived from the more narrative portions taken in conjunction with the strictly legal tradition, and these are of importance for the evaluation of the legal aspect of Israel's life.

1. It is impossible to do more than mention cursorily how vital it is for our understanding of the period of Israel's settlement in Canaan to assume that the associated tribes were able to enter the strange country with a law of their own. The history of Israel in the time of the Judges becomes extremely hard to comprehend, indeed, almost a complete enigma, if the incoming migrants be supposed to have possessed nothing but an orally transmitted prescriptive law of a primitive kind. However great a role one assigns to religious enthusiasm during the war of conquest and afterwards in individual military incidents, its force would not have been sufficient to overcome the problems of everyday life involved in the gradual process of acclimatization to a totally new cultural environment. At every turn history shows us primitive conquering peoples who make the change to living in a highly civilized area surrendering more or less rapidly to the indigenous spiritual and legal life. It was so, for example, in the case of the Germans who invaded Italy, or of the Arab hordes which swamped the East Roman civilization. Islam is a very good example of how in such circumstances the spiritual outlook of the conquerors as a whole can be slowly transformed, until eventually something quite different is created out of the original religion.

Such reflections as these make clear the weakness of any survey, which does not take the unique character of ancient Israelite law seriously into account. To regard the Israelites as primitive nomads invading the advanced civilization of Canaan involves explaining the force with which their individuality developed either on the basis of their Yahwist enthusiasm or of their robuster character as a people or of some mysterious thing called 'vitality'. None of these theories, however, can make this approach satisfactory, because it contradicts the facts of the national life in the period of the Judges, as these are portrayed for us in the ancient narratives. What we see there is a drastic disintegration, which dangerously weakened the nation's cohesion and led to indifference in face of matters of common moment, to widespread adherence to Canaanite customs, and even to syncretistic phenomena in the sphere of religion. In the light of such evidence, therefore, the Canaanite influence on Israelite national consciousness has often been regarded as decisive and an Israel posited at the beginning of the monarchical period which has been completely changed from the one that had migrated to the country some two hundred years earlier. This new Israel had been wholly assimilated to the Canaanite pattern and had forgotten its own best traditions. Yet against such a background as this figures like Samuel, Nathan and Elijah cannot but become totally incomprehensible. They emerge rather like ghosts, pleading for Mosaic ideas in a world utterly alien to them, a world which had long ago thrown away the inheritance of the Mosaic period. But these men are pictured in the Old Testament tradition as solid, individual figures, drawn from real life and with firm roots in the spiritual life of their people. Their activities imply that they have a broad basis of thought and faith in common with their contemporaries. Such considerations prove that there must be a false assumption concealed in the kind of description of the Canaanization of Israel to which we alluded. This false assumption is precisely that of undervaluing Israel's own living pattern of law at the time of the Entry. If Moses is to be credited with no more than merely oral instruction in, and promulgation of, the law—and that in any case limited to the Decalogue—then there cannot possibly be any solid reason for a comparatively strong Israelite resistance to the character of Canaan. Only a Mosaic law-giving can explain the remarkable force and persistence of the true personality of Israel, in spite of all the cases of adaptation and receptive borrowing in their new home. [1]

2. From the time of the Entry the individual local community becomes the special instrument for the administration of Israelite law. The citizens possessing full civil and political rights in each place handle the business of making legal pronouncements within their own circle. They are convened as a judicial body as occasion demands and deal with any case that is pending in public session in the gate, giving their decision on the spot. [2] It is obvious that such an

---

[1] In this connection cf. also the remarks on the subject of charismatic leaders in ch. VIII below.

[2] Cf. Ruth 4.1 ff.; Jer. 26. The importance of the judicial body has been very well described by L. Köhler (*Die hebräische Rechtsgemeinde*, 1931). Nevertheless, the significance of the priesthood and the monarchy for the development of the law seems to me to have been underestimated in his treatment.

emphasis on the separate life of each particular Palestinian community, fostered by the sense of independence which marked the Israelite tribes, was bound to lead to differences in the formation of the law and in the administration of its pronouncements. This is confirmed by the fact that within our present OT books of law we can establish the existence of various ancient collections. [1] It is, therefore, significant that *the transmission and elaboration of the law* were not left to the individual community, but *were influenced from the great cultic centres* and guided in a definite direction.

This was possible because of *the close and constant involvement of law and religion*. Some idea of the nature of this connection is given us by *the formulas of cursing* in Deut. 27.15 ff. The close parallel these afford to the stipulations of the Book of the Covenant and the Decalogue prove that in them the Israelite law has discovered a new and distinctive form of expression. The evildoer who has escaped detection is delivered up to the Deity by means of a solemn cursing at the holy place. In spite of the literary problems presented by the explanatory framework of the Shechemite Twelve Commandments, [2] there are no conclusive grounds for rejecting the assumption that we are here dealing with a formulary, going back to a very early period, which was used at the covenant festivals held at Shechem to commemorate the covenant made in the time of Joshua. [3] This cursing of the transgressor at a sanctuary which was a place of pilgrimage serving a considerable area constituted a reinforcement of the divine law at the hands of the actual congregation, which could not help but impress on the memory of the people over and over again the great basic principles of the legal pronouncements and thus have a strong directive effect throughout a wide circle. Since similar usages were probably to be found at other great sanctuaries, the significance of the cultus for the formation of the law becomes obvious.

The same considerations apply to *the priestly liturgies*, in which the visitor to the sanctuary was instructed in the conditions of his admission to the holy place. It may be that the formulas which we find in

[1] Ex. 34.10 ff.; Lev. 18 f. and the sources of the Book of Deuteronomy are examples of just such locally differentiated versions of the Mosaic law; they derive, however, not from the individual judicial bodies, but from their common cultic centres at a great sanctuary. A. C. Welch (*ZAW* 45, 1927, pp. 24 ff.) argues convincingly for a similar situation underlying the double recension of the regulations for the Passover festival in Ex. 12 f.

[2] Cf. S. Mowinckel, *Psalmenstudien* V, pp. 75 ff.; E. Sellin, *Gilgal*, 1917.

[3] Cf. Jepsen, *Untersuchungen zum Bundesbuch*, pp. 82 ff.; A. Alt, 'Altisraelitisches Recht', *Forschungen und Fortschritte*, 1933, pp. 217 f.

Ps. 15 and Ps. 24.3–6, and, in prophetic guise, in Isa. 33.14–16, are not among the oldest specimens of this genre. The practice itself, however, is primitive, for it arises from an extremely practical need of the pilgrim. [1] The content of such formulas, with their echoes of the Decalogue and the major religious prescriptions related to it, bear witness to the significance of divine worship for the sacred law and its inculcation.

In addition there is the fact that *the great cultic festivals* not only provided an opportunity for holding the principal markets and fairs, [2] but also for the settlement of all kinds of cases and legal business. [3] That this was so might be conjectured from the presence of similar features in the life of other peoples; but there are grounds for such a view in the Old Testament tradition as well. An outstanding example is the description of Samuel's activity as a judge during the great annual festivals at the sanctuaries of Ephraim and Benjamin; and in the same way his sons are installed as judges at the famous pilgrim shrine of Beersheba. [4] If the assumption that in the period of the Judges the Israelite amphictyony already had officers empowered to decide difficult causes of contention is sound, [5] then Samuel's office must be regarded as a permanent arrangement. It is possible that the introductory speeches in Deuteronomy ought to be regarded as a product of this practice of proclaiming the law to the extensive circle represented by the crowds who gathered at the cultic centre [6]—at any rate, in so far as they exhibit a developed stage of an originally much shorter exhortation by the judge, urging obedience to the law of God, as this came into being under the influence of the prophetic preaching toward the end of the eighth century.

[1]Cf. Gunkel, *Die Psalmen, übersetzt und erklärt*, 1926, pp. 47 f.

[2]Cf. Deut. 33.18 f. The role of Mecca in this respect, even before the time of Mohammed, is well known. The same practice is also attested for Egypt and Greece.

[3]Kadesh, the cultic centre for the surrounding nomad tribes long before the time of Israel, was originally called *'ēn mišpāṭ*, 'well of judgment' (Gen. 14.7). The famous sanctuary of Dan at the source of the Jordan similarly indicates by its name that the practice of proclaiming the law was carried on there.

[4]I Sam. 7.16; 8.1 ff.

[5]So M. Noth, *Das System der zwölf Stämme Israels*, pp. 97 ff., 151 ff.

[6]According to the interesting conjecture of A. Klostermann, *Der Pentateuch*, N.F., 1907, pp. 184 ff. Whether there was in Israel the office of a 'reciter of law', similar to that of the Icelandic lögsaga, as Klostermann assumes (*op. cit.* pp. 348 ff.), cannot be determined from the OT indications. A. Alt (*op. cit.*) suggests that the office of the so-called 'lesser judges' may have been of this kind: Judg. 10.1 ff.; 12.8 ff.

There can be no question but that in this close association of the cult with the expansion and application of the traditional law the priests took a prominent part. It is true that we hear little of the specifically judicial activity of the priests. In practice the administration of the law lay largely in the hands of the laity, especially the elders. [1] But to suppose that the *juristic functions of the priesthood* were limited to the occasional casting of oracles for the purpose of conveying some divine decision, or to an equally occasional participation in the judicial body in their capacity as citizens, patently does not fit the facts. To the priests—especially at the great sanctuaries—fell the vital tasks of assisting in the settlement of difficult cases and of compiling and elaborating the law. It is impossible to conceive of anyone other than a priest as author of the cursing formulas and liturgies referred to above; and a priest is the man most likely to be responsible for the local collections of laws. [2] This is, moreover, absolutely confirmed by the terms in which the role of Levi is characterized in Deut. 33.9 ff. Admittedly, we know nothing of the division of judicial responsibility between priests and laymen, and the influence of the priesthood may have varied with the importance of the upholders of the priestly position. [3] The evidence adduced, however, allows us to conclude with certainty that their assistance was of the most material importance to the whole process of legal development, and that it was because of this that the religious character of the law was preserved.

As far as the general attitude to the sacred law is concerned, it is significant that men felt themselves fairly free *vis-à-vis* the actual letter of the law. There was no sense that any particular formulation was binding as such, or had inviolable force; rather, the individual commandments were shaped according to the special needs and circumstances of the sanctuary in question and its surrounding district. [4] The transmission of the law is throughout a living thing, capable of adaptation to changing conditions. For this reason, however, the responsibility of those in control of the legal tradition is all

[1]Cf. I Kings 21.8; Deut. 19.12.
[2]Cf. p. 85 n. 1 above and the prophetic polemic in Jer. 8.8.
[3]The gradual predominance of the Levites at the great sanctuaries meant in any case a strengthening of the influence of Yahwist ideas on the law. Cf. ch. IX. 1, pp. 395 ff. below.
[4]This is made abundantly clear by a comparison either of the short basic laws such as the Decalogue and the Shechemite Twelve Commandments, or of the older collections such as the Book of the Covenant, Ex. 34, Lev. 18 f. and the sources of Deuteronomy.

the greater; and the violent clashes of the prophets with the priesthood were occasioned not least by the accusation that the latter were neglecting their duty as guardians of the law in favour of a lucrative trade in sacrifices.

3. The monarchical period brings with it a considerable enrichment of the law. With the *monarchy* a new social factor was introduced into the life of the nation and this required particular bases in law for its development. The *b 'rit*, on which according to II Sam. 5.3 the royal power rested, could not but involve both a limitation of the rights of those in whom power had hitherto been vested in favour of the royal authority and also the conferring of new rights on the king. Hence we hear of a 'law of the king',[1] which is said to have been already drawn up by Samuel and deposited in the sanctuary before Yahweh. Although the details given in the account are not feasible as history,[2] it may be, nevertheless, that a perfectly sound tradition has found expression in this form, recalling that a new law of the kingship invaded the legal framework then existing and partly displaced it. The reigns of Saul and David give the impression that this adjustment between the monarchy and the old laws of the nation was not accomplished without friction. To begin with, the requirement of a standing army, indispensable for a monarchy, seriously disturbed the prevailing balance of power to the disadvantage of the upholders of the power of the tribe, and was bound to lead to internal tensions.[3] Another typical example is the autocratic attitude of the king toward the ancient law of the 'ban'.[4] The crisis of the Absalom rebellion indicated clearly what threatened the king, should the people—with or without good reason—find the conduct of the new institution unsatisfactory .Both the rebellion of Jeroboam against Solomon and the secession of the Northern tribes under Rehoboam enable one to realize how strongly national feeling reacted against any attempt by the king to enlarge his prerogatives by despotic means.

The whole course of Israelite history, therefore, shows that the structure of Israel's national law was so firmly established that the

---

[1] I Sam. 8.9; 10.25.

[2] It has long been recognized that the account in I Sam. 8.11 ff. does not contain a 'law of the kingdom', properly speaking, but a sharp criticism of the absolutist monarchy. Anything that can be said, therefore, about the actual content of the royal *b 'rit* must necessarily be conjecture.

[3] Cf. A. Alt, *Die Staatenbildung der Israeliten in Palästina*, 1930, pp. 34 ff.

[4] I Sam. 15.

monarchy was quite unable to disrupt it. This remained true even when, as in Judah, the monarchy was successful in achieving its dynastic aims and, by means of high taxation, a standing army and a bureaucracy, was able to extort a considerable measure of power. This can be seen especially clearly in the administration of the law. The king definitely claimed to be recognized as the final court of appeal in legal disputes; and the cases of Absalom[1] and Jotham[2] indicate the high value of this function. However, the judgment of the elders continued side by side with that of the king;[3] when it is a question of decreeing important laws of state, the elders have a share in the decision[4] and, in certain circumstances, the assembly of the people as well.[5] Similarly, in spite of heedless encroachments by the monarchy, they would not allow their share in the election of the king to be taken away from them;[6] indeed, in Judah the position is reached where a Supreme Judge is appointed in addition to the king.[7]

In the same way, flagrant breaches of the national law on the part of the king himself bring about severe internal crises, as a result of which sooner or later the earlier situation is restored. The judicial murder of Naboth aroused the unappeasable hostility of considerable sections of the people against the House of Omri; Isaiah raised his voice against the abuse of the law-giving authority by the monarchy under Ahaz;[8] the despotism of a Manasseh, established with the help of Assyrian military power, was brought to an end in bloody revolution, as soon as Assyrian pressure was removed;[9] Jeremiah hurled his threatenings against the tyranny of Jehoiakim.[10] In the

[1]II Sam. 15.1 ff.; cf. also II Sam. 14.4–11.
[2]II Kings 15.5.
[3]I Kings 21.8; Deut. 19.12; 16.18; it is doubtful whether the last-named passage refers to *judges and officials chosen by the people*, thus indicating an innovation, as Galling considers (*Die Erwählungstraditionen Israels*, p. 40).
[4]I Kings 20.7 f.; II Kings 23.1;   [5]II Kings 11.14, 18; 23.3.
[6]Elders: II Sam. 5.3; I Kings 12.6; people: I Sam. 11.15; II Sam. 5.1; I Kings 12.4; 16.16; II Kings 21.23 f.; 23.30.
[7]Deut. 17.9, according to Galling's interpretation (*op. cit.*, p. 41). M. Noth, *Die Gesetze im Pentateuch, ihre Voraussetzungen und ihr Sinn*, 1940, has emphatically pointed out the remarkable fact that, although the collections of laws in the OT come from the period of the monarchy, they are not presented in the form of royal law, but avoid all reference to the interests and requirements of the state and assume as their underlying social structure the ancient sacral union of the Twelve Tribes.
[8]Isa. 10.1 ff.
[9]II Kings 21.23 f.
[10]Jer. 22.13 ff.

Deuteronomic law relating to the king[1] the popular demand for definite and absolute limits to the royal power finds unmistakable expression. The fact that the Josianic reform, in which the state religion and state law are newly consolidated by the co-operation of king and people, comes at the close of the history of Israel as an independent nation shows the indestructible strength of the Israelite sense of law, which never tolerated an exaltation of the law of the monarchy over that of the people. An arrangement which was taken for granted in all other Oriental states was in Israel decisively rejected, for the manifest reason that it contradicted the general feeling for justice.[2] The fact that the law of the people was rooted in the will of their God created a solidarity on which the lust for power of the kings was always doomed to shatter. Once more it is made clear what moral force was released by Israel's religious faith, which united all members of the nation as 'brothers'[3] and, therefore, how firmly entrenched in the nation must have been the experience of Yahweh as morally good. It may safely be said, that the national conscience of Israel had reached a higher degree of sensitiveness and refinement and reacted more sharply against any breach of the law than that of other peoples. This is confirmed by the emergence of the prophets and the response which their battle-cry awoke in the hearts of the nation.

4. It was not, however, solely in defensive action that the Israelite feeling for justice expressed itself; it was also able to *act creatively* in many directions. That this was so is attested first and foremost by the unique *Lawbook of Deuteronomy*.

If justice is to be done to this work, it is important to begin by noting its external form. It is clear that we are dealing neither with a proper *Codex iuris*, concerned with juristic formulations and the

[1]Deut. 17.14–20. For our present purposes the question whether this section is to be associated with the 'Josianic constitution', as Galling (*op. cit.*, pp. 58 f.) believes, or whether, with other more recent scholars, it should be regarded as a later insertion, can be left out of account.

[2]E. Junge (*Der Wiederaufbau des Heerwesens des Reiches Juda unter Josia*, 1937) and G. von Rad (*Studies in Deuteronomy* and *Der heilige Krieg im alten Israel*, 1951, pp. 68 ff.) have demonstrated, though from different angles, that what occurred in the Josianic reform was an attempt at a political restoration in a determined effort to get back to the arrangements of the pre-monarchical tribal confederation. On the unique evolution of the idea of the state concealed in this archaic disguise cf. W. Eichrodt, 'Religionsgeschichte Israels' (*Historia Mundi* II, pp. 425 ff.).

[3]This designation of the individual Israelites is a favourite term in Deuteronomy, but does not occur in the Book of the Covenant.

fixing of penalties, nor with a mere collection of laws, in which old and new definitions are set down side by side, but with a *book of legal instruction*, marked throughout by a parenetic tone. Its language is not that of the law, but that of the heart and conscience. This characteristic is most strongly expressed in the introductory sermons; but it is also a constant and prominent feature of the laws proper. [1] It is this formal characteristic which gives the book its unique 'personality' and a unity of conception which runs through all the various sections despite the disorder and incompleteness of the legal material contained in them. Those who speak to us in the pages of Deuteronomy are men who know that a national law can never attain its goal so long as it remains a system reluctantly endured and effective only by compulsion; it must be founded on the inward assent of the people.

But if this law in its outward form and in its sense of purpose is a unified entity, this rests ultimately on the fact that its legal content is interpreted throughout with a single mind. The promoters of this work of legal instruction are convinced that Israel's law is a precious possession, which must find willing, nay enthusiastic, acceptance, because its regulations express the life-giving will of the covenant God, on which the very existence of the people ultimately depends. [2] It is as a result of this unified basic conception that the lawgiver succeeds in establishing *an inner unity between the cultic and the politico-social ordinances*, which is not to be found in the simple juxtaposition of these items in the Book of the Covenant. On the beneficent purposes of God, which embrace the chosen people in its entirety and know of no distinctions of class or position, is founded an unconditional solidarity of all the members of the nation, which bestows on each individual a right to the divine blessing. This not only ensures the fulfilment of the most elementary requirements of the law [3] and makes possible the building up of a just and reliable judicial machinery, [4] but takes under its especial care precisely those who are under-privileged, the slave, the foreigner, the poor, the prisoner of

---

[1]This must always be a strong argument against the common assumption that what we have in Deuteronomy is a basic code of law for the state. We ought rather to think of a handbook of popular instruction based on the law of the state; cf. my remarks in *NKZ* 32, 1921, pp. 71 ff.

[2]Deut. 4.1, 6–8.

[3]The lawgiver has no need to go into details on the matter of how to deal with murder, theft, etc., obviously because he can assume that these things are already well known.

[4]Deut. 16.18 ff.; 17.8 ff.; 19.15 ff.

war, the woman. [1] Moreover, since the festivals at the sanctuary with their joyful sacrificial meals are described as opportunities for demonstrating sentiments of brotherhood, and the Sabbath and the sabbatical year, the firstfruits and the tithes, are all closely linked with social and ethical responsibilities, [2] man's duties toward God and his neighbour are indissolubly fused and his social consciousness is directly rooted in his religion. The implications of this for the concept of the state may be seen in the 'law of the king' (Deut. 17.14–20). Here is a passionate denunciation of the dynastically-minded war-*politik*, of foreign influence on the direction of the national life resulting from the contracting of marriages with the royal houses of other lands, of the heedless exploitation of the national sources of revenue in the interests of a luxurious court. The ideal king is portrayed as 'the ruler who is truly conscious of his social responsibilities' [3] (Galling), who subordinates his own power to the law of the land. Deuteronomy is, therefore, not concerned with refinements of technical, juristic formulation, nor with a casuistic expansion of the law; indeed, there is hardly any new legal material, properly speaking. The concern is rather with education in the feeling for justice, with the direction of attention by means of examples to that spirit which must inform any just organization of the people's life.

As a consequence, however, of this fundamental religious temper, which we have already noted as of significance for the Mosaic law, there grew up an understanding of *the total ordering of the people's life as a revelation of the saving will of God*. The course of Israel's history brought no secularization of the civil law, but its conscious incorporation into the context of the divine will on which the whole existence of the people depended. *Even the state is a part of the divine reality.* This belief, however, was not expressed, as it was elsewhere in the ancient East, in the divine kingship and the state cultus, with all its complicated apparatus of sacrifices, divination and priestly hierarchy, but in the subjection of the entire national life to the ordinances of the divine covenant, which gave every individual an equal share in God's blessing of man's earthly existence. [4]

There can be no doubt that this meant the abandonment of a

[1]Deut. 15; 21.10 ff.; 22.1 ff.; 23.16 f., 20 ff.; 24.
[2]Deut. 12.12, 18 f.; 16.11 f., 14; 5.12 ff.; 15; 26.1–11, 12 f.; 14.27 ff.
[3]German 'Sozialherrscher' (Tr.).
[4]Cf. G. von Rad, *Das Gottesvolk im Deuteronomium*, 1929, pp. 37 ff.

formalist attitude to the law. It is no longer a question of simply carrying out certain external regulations, assisted by the power of the state; the law has been drawn into the sphere of operation of the spiritual and moral life, where external compulsion must be replaced by personal moral decision. Nevertheless, the Deuteronomic law-giver is marked off from all exponents of merely sentimental, utopian theories of the state by his clear awareness that the kind of national character he proclaims is not possible on the basis of some pragmatic rationalism, but must be the expression of a faith determined by the reality of the covenant God. Behind the state, as its only support and guarantee, stands the congregation. Nothing less than this is implied by his declaration that *the primary commandment is that of love for God*. This alone can point the way to a just observance of God's ordinances. [1] One might be tempted to think that to make this love the subject of a command is no better than a lawyer's caricature of the love of God, which can never be extorted from man by a legal imperative. But this would only be a just assessment if what we were dealing with in Deuteronomy were a basic code of state law of a formal and juristic character, and not a popular work of legal *instruction*, which goes beyond mere statement of the law. It is genuine preaching, the teaching of religion. Furthermore, because it is this kind of work with which we are concerned, the thought of the teacher of the law can be defined in this way: that each individual ruling is only to be understood rightly as the will of God, in so far as it is comprehended as the detailed expression of an overall injunc-tion of love, by which God claims man for his own—not just in this or that particular obligation, but in man's whole personal being, 'with all his heart and all his soul and all his strength'. In fact, what is usually foisted on to Deuteronomy as its fundamental error and made the principal ground for reproach is the one thing with which the book will have nothing to do—the perverting of complete self-surrender, such as the prophets demand, into an external legalism. On the contrary, it teaches that all these laws, which can be so easily taken in a legalistic sense as individual casuistic definitions quite unrelated to one another, are to be understood as the applica-tion and practice in particular concrete situations of the primary command of love; for it is in such situations that the Israelite is incorporated as a member of his people. The law is a practical guide for the man who wishes to set God up as the supreme director of his

[1]Deut. 6.5; cf. 10.12; 11.13, 22; 19.9; 30.16.

whole being. Conversely, it is as a result of this relating of a multitude of separate commandments to one great commandment, that the material accumulated in the Deuteronomic collection gives the impression not of a striving after casuistic completeness, but rather of the unfolding with the help of examples of what it means to behave in accordance with the righteous fear of God. Moreover, any legalistic misunderstanding of the command to love God is countered by the great stress laid on the demonstration of God's love for man. Long before there was any human action in response, this love chose the people for God's own possession and gave them the law as a token of their special position of favour. To obey the law thus becomes man's response of love to the divine act of election. [1]

The form 'Thou shalt' in the command to love God, therefore, constitutes nothing more than the conscious employment of legal idiom in order to drive home this basic claim of God which is greater than all law. It emphasizes in a way impossible to ignore the appeal of the divine Lord directed at the will and decision of the individual person. Because the Israelite finds the proper scope for his piety not in emotion, but in moral testing, the demands of the law can never be considered as something foreign to his love for God. That is why Jesus was able to use the same form of words, 'Thou shalt', to express the ultimate decision demanded of him by God.

What the Deuteronomic lawgiver did for the organization of the law in terms of man's relation to God, *the civil law of the Priestly Code* accomplished for the mass of the law's social requirements in terms of his relation to his neighbour. We see here in operation something which was a particular characteristic of Israelite law from the very beginning, the close connection between legal prescription and moral exhortation. It is the latter which reaches beyond the formal letter of the law and demands that which cannot be guaranteed by any law, the readiness to help one's brother, the fellow-countryman who is suffering or has fallen into want. Lev. 19 lays down this 'fundamental social and ethical law of the Yahweh religion' [2] not only in a new formulation, enjoining all to reverence the elderly, but by giving it its normative and all-embracing expression in the concept of love: 'Thou shalt love thy neighbour as thyself.' [3] Once

[1]Deut. 4.5–8, 37; 7.6 ff.; 10.14 ff.; 23.6.
[2]Hempel, *Gott und Mensch im Alten Testament*, 1926, p. 18 n. 1.
[3]Lev. 19.18; cf. 19.34.

more we find, framed in legal phraseology, a maxim[1] which jettisons the idea of the law as a rigid definition of the limits of human social relations and assigns it instead the role of a guide, giving detailed, concrete directions for a far higher level of moral life, removing from the exclusive domination of man's lust for power and egoistic self-interest all those matters with which the law is concerned and infusing them with its own spirit. The fact that the concept of love is of limited application and operates only toward the *rēaʿ* and the *gēr*, the fellow-countryman and the resident alien, should not conceal from us the implicit recognition that 'a man must be regarded as a human being rather than as a person coming under the law's jurisdiction'.[2] The limitation arises from the sober realism of the nation's law, which aligns the social responsibility of the individual Israelite in accordance with his actual situation, living among his own people, and is not interested in giving a cosmopolitan turn to its own prescriptions.[3] The seriousness with which the demand of love was taken in practice may be seen clearly enough in Ex. 23.4 f., where a later interpolation into the Book of the Covenant extends the rendering of assistance even to one's enemy.[4] Such a requirement overthrows the very essence of particularism, as does also the proverbial wisdom-saying about giving food and drink to one's enemy in his need.[5] It is true that comparable maxims are known to the humane temper of the wisdom literature of the ancient East in general.[6] It is also true, on the other side, that hatred toward one's enemy remained the natural reaction for the typical representative of Old Testament piety.[7] But the fact that we can cite instances in

[1]For this reason Quell calls it bluntly a paradox (*TWNT* I, 1933, p. 24; ET, *Love* (Bible Key Words 1), 1949, p. 7).

[2]Quell, *op. cit.*, p. 26 (ET, p. 9).

[3]Cf. E. Stauffer's fine delineation of this idea of love as 'always defined in terms of a . . . concrete situation': 'The cosmopolitan Greek loves all the world; the patriotic Israelite his neighbour; the impulse working centrifugally in the one and centripetally in the other' (*Love*, p. 33; *TWNT* I, p. 39).

[4]The parallel passage Deut. 22.1–4, which accentuates the unconditional obligation by its designation of the fellow-countryman as 'brother', certainly does nothing to moderate this demand.

[5]Prov. 25.21.

[6]Cf. the fine passage in the Assyrian Wisdom sayings: 'Deal not wickedly with thine adversary; whoever does evil to thee, he should be requited with good; let righteousness be thy return to thine enemy . . .' (*AOT*, p. 292; cf. *ANET*, p. 426) and in general W. Baumgartner, *Israelitische und altorientalische Weisheit*, 1933.

[7]Cf. in addition to II Sam. 19.7, the plentiful evidence of the Psalms: 5.11; 35.5 ff.; 41.11; 54.7; 58.11 f.; 109, etc.

support of both sides, [1] and that practice often fell far short of theory, should not prevent us from rightly assessing the full import of this reduction of all social relations to the one norm of love. It demonstrates to us that the development of Israelite law is constantly moving toward the point at which the very essence of law as such will have to be overthrown and a complete self-denial and surrender, rooted in the divine act of redemption, be substituted for it. But in the whole history of ancient law this is the sole instance of such a phenomenon.

The Priestly law, however, has also preserved for us a valuable quantity of relatively detailed legislation. Reference has already been made to its marriage laws (cf. pp. 80 ff. above). *The land laws of Lev. 25* also demonstrate how forcefully the efforts to protect the freedom and independence of the small man, which were a notable feature of Deuteronomy, were backed up in priestly circles. Here the law of redemption sets bounds which refuse any one person unrestricted rights over his landed property. According to this law the sale of land is not to be regarded as an absolute transfer of property rights in perpetuity; the seller (or his nearest relatives) has the right of compulsory re-purchase of the land on repayment of the original purchase price less a certain sum in consideration of the purchasers' usufruct of the property. The only exception to this right of re-purchase relates to houses in walled towns, in the case of which the right expires at the end of one year. The earliest instance of the operation of this law to be found in the Old Testament occurs in Jeremiah. [2] Since, however, the institution can be attested for ancient Babylonia, [3] there can be no objection to assuming that it was already operative in Israel as well at a much earlier date—an assumption strengthened by the fact that the basis of the law is clearly the high value attaching to family and clan in the early period. Another reason for regarding this land law as of ancient origin is the principle on which, for P, it is based; namely that the ownership of the whole land is vested in Yahweh alone, and that the Israelites are but strangers and sojourners upon it. For the prophets count on the general acceptance of this principle in their condemnation of the speculations in land of the commercial classes as an offence against Yahweh. [4]

The significance of these regulations lies in the fact that by blocking

---

[1]Cf. the Joseph story and David's conduct in I Sam. 24.18 ff.; 26.23 f.
[2]Jer. 32.8 ff.
[3]Cf. B. Meissner, *Beiträge zum altbabylonischen Privatrecht*, 1893, pp. 40 ff.
[4]Micah 2.1 ff., 9 f.; Amos 2.6 f.; 5.11; Isa. 5.8 ff.

speculation in landed property they make it easier for that peasant class which springs from the soil to preserve its independence. The law concerning the so-called 'year of Jubilee' or 'year of the trumpet-blast' in Lev. 25.8 ff. goes a great deal further in this direction. According to this law, in every fiftieth year 'Ye shall . . . proclaim liberty throughout the land unto all the inhabitants thereof . . . and ye shall return every man unto his possession and ye shall return every man unto his family' (25.10). In these circumstances any outright sale of land was excluded, any such sale being in effect only the sale of the produce of the land until the next year of Jubilee. What has really happened is that sale of lease is substituted for freehold tenure.

There is no means of telling whether this law was ever enforced, or whether it remained simply an ideal requirement. [1] The struggle of the prophets against the great landowners suggests that, in their day at any rate, no such regulation was of general application. The remission of all outstanding debts imposed by Nehemiah was clearly an extraordinary measure to meet a particular emergency. [2] In either case the fact remains that the basic idea of this law constitutes a consistent and energetic attempt to guarantee the independence and liberty of each individual Israelite. In contrast to the dominance of the *latifundia* system, which was accepted in the great civilized empires of the ancient East almost as if it were an immutable law of nature, and which may be seen at its most blatant in Babylonia and Egypt, we find here an independence of thought, which is not content to surrender economic development to the section of the nation with capital resources for its own private profit, but attempts to keep it on healthier lines. The lawgiver 'wished to ensure to every member of the nation free access to the natural source of all production, the land, without at the same time reducing the individual to the status of a tenant, dependent on the governing authority of the moment, or taking from him the liberty to manage his own affairs and enjoy the fruits of his own labours'. [3] These efforts, based as they were on religious conviction, bring home to us once more how firm was the understanding of the will of God as implying an even-handed justice, and how determined was the attempt to introduce this understanding into the nation's law.

[1] A. Jirku, 'Das israelitische Jobeljahr' (*Reinhold-Seeberg-Festschrift*, 1929, vol. II, pp. 169 ff.) argues for an early dating of the basic principle of this regulation. A different view is taken by H. Schmidt, *Das Bodenrecht im Verfassungsentwurf des Esra*, 1932.
[2] Neh. 5.1 ff.
[3] A. Damaschke, *Geschichte der Nationalökonomie* [13], 1922, vol. I, p. 7.

IV

THE COVENANT STATUTES

B. THE CULTUS

I. THE SIGNIFICANCE OF THE CULTUS FOR RELIGION IN GENERAL

IN THE PRESENT CONTEXT the term 'cultus' should be taken to mean the expression of religious experience in concrete external actions performed within the congregation or community, preferably by officially appointed exponents and in set forms.[1] This assumes that, in contrast to the immediate human experience in which it is rooted, the cultus is secondary. For the personal and spontaneous feelings of piety it inevitably entails a certain limitation and constraint; in the first place material, because of the stress on sacred places, seasons and rites, secondly sociological, because the determining factor is the community as a whole. These two considerations, however, must not be taken to suggest that in the cultus we are dealing with a concern which is not truly religious, or that the aim of the cultus is something fundamentally different from spiritual intercourse with God, some sort of common life based on material or sociological factors and on an altogether inferior plane. The cultus is no mere epiphenomenon, but a genuine expression of a living religion, seeking to penetrate the whole of human life; for it makes not only the spiritual and personal, but also the physical side of life into an agent and medium of its activities.

The truth of this may be seen, first of all, in the fact that *the cult considered simply as a means of expression* is concerned to help the very living stuff of religion to achieve a physical existence true to its real

[1]We have here adopted the definition of cultus put forward by G. Quell, as distinct from certain other conceptions (*Das kultische Problem der Psalmen*, 1926, pp. 18 ff.)

98

meaning. It is because 'all belief strives toward Incarnation'[1] that the physical phenomenon can become the means of expressing a spiritual reality. For the men of the ancient world the outward form possessed a symbolic significance, totally different from the significance it has in the eyes of modern western man. Intercourse with God was to be carried on not simply through direct personal communion, but through such bodily actions as kneeling and prostration in prayer, through sacred dances and antiphonal singing, through the marking off the sacred enclosure from the common ground, through the vesting of the priests and the preparation of the sacrifice, through the solemn silence which accompanied the offering of the holy gift before God, and through the clouds ascending from the altar of incense. All these visible things were soaked with symbolic meaning; and for that reason they signify not an unimportant or secondary, but a necessary and essential activity of religious experience.[2]

It is not, therefore, fair to the real meaning of the cultus to distinguish it from properly religious behaviour, as if the latter were a striving for unmediated communion with God, and the former nothing but a machinery for the efficacious promotion of piety[3]— a method of providing the religious life with crutches, when it no longer has any power of movement in itself. It means that a side-effect of cultic activity is made without proper thought into its primary object. The two modes of relationship are not to be distinguished in terms of any difference in their spheres of interest: they share a common goal. The difference lies rather in this, that they find their fulfilment in separate areas of human life; the one in the emotional life of the spirit in the individual, the other in man's physical and corporate social life. The mutual relations of these two aspects of religious practice depend entirely on the way in which these two areas interact—on which gains the ascendancy and makes the other subservient to it.

The cultus is, however, not only the inwardly necessary expression of spiritual realities by means of the physical, but also *the medium by which divine power is presented* to men for their participation. Such a conception rests on the deep conviction of the ancient world, that

[1]W. Stählin, *Vom Sinn des Leibes*, 1930, p. 105.
[2]This is not to deny that these forms can be emptied of their inner meaning and degenerate into mere trappings; but this should not be confused with the different question of what was the original significance of the cultus.
[3]Cf. G. Quell, *op. cit.*, p. 58.

the deity gives himself to men not merely through the subjective channels of the conscious mind, but also uses the body as a means of access by which he may effectuate weal or woe.[1] Because the physical and spiritual sides of human life have not as yet been violently dissociated, but man is still taken seriously in his totality as a psychosomatic being, his sensory life also plays its part in his relationship with God. In the outward actions of the cult the power of the divine blessing is communicated to the actual mode of man's existence. The sacred action becomes a sacrament.[2]

It becomes apparent, therefore, that the cultus implies a social and material integration of religious feeling as the manifestation of the divine activity. This activity seeks to make the individual its own only through the medium of the community and brings home to men, through the 'Here and Now' of the cultic action, that the divine condescension is incompatible with any element of arbitrary action on the part of man. It is true, therefore, that the cultus involves a straitening of man's intercourse with God, and hence of individual piety. But straitening is not suppression; it is rather the way in which, by setting bounds to the human spirit in its constant striving to transcend all bounds and by bringing it into subjection to divinely ordered reality, man is impressed with a deep sense of his own creatureliness—a sense which a purely self-determined piety will always seek to throw off as a burdensome restriction.

The relationship of this sacramental cultus to the spiritual intercourse of the individual with God will, in its turn, depend on the answer to the question, in which of these areas do the divine operations

[1]This understanding of human life as a totality even in the sphere of religion has become completely foreign to present-day man owing to the effects of Greek Neoplatonist thought: hence the inability to conceive the cultic life, even of OT religion, as anything but a relic of heathenism, having no positive relation to the real essence of this religion; hence also the tendency to criticize the level of religion at any given time from the standpoint of the unexpressed ideal of a religion completely free from cultic elements.

[2]G. Quell (*op. cit.*, p. 45 n. 2) is quite right to reject the use of the word 'sacramental' to describe those magical processes of primitive religion by which the sacred material, impregnated with power, is brought to bear on human beings, and to employ instead the term 'sacrificial'. For the decisive element in the sacrament is the activity of the Holy One; and this is something that can only be effectively realized in theistic forms of religion. Nor is it really possible to derive the sacramental from the magical process as the product of a simple sequence in time. The transposition, which can frequently be observed, by which a purely dynamistic process becomes an act of the divine will can only be explained by taking very definite account of that creative power which stems from the inmost depths of a theistic faith (cf. also Bertholet, art. 'Kultus', *RGG*² III, p. 1371).

have their full and decisive effect? It is possible to define a great variety of forms in which this relationship might be found. The extremes, however, between which it must lie, may be described as follows: on the one hand there is the complete penetration and exposition of the cultus by the spoken word, in which is established the supremacy of the individual person's spiritual relation to God over the sacramental experience of God; on the other hand there is a wordless worship, knowing only δρώμενα, acts quite without interpretation, true 'mysteries', according supreme importance to that reality which can be apprehended through the senses. In the majority of cases, the truth will lie somewhere between these two extremes.

Even if, however, the cultus proves indispensable to genuine religion, because it springs from the heart of its essential nature, it should not be forgotten that an ideal relationship of the sort here envisaged is hardly ever realized perfectly in practice. This results in part from the intractable and equivocal nature of material media, which can never be shaped to represent or interpret exactly the spiritual content underlying them. But perhaps still more is it due to the inability of the physical, once it has received a particular form, to keep pace with the transformations of the spiritual life within it and to adapt itself to that life with complete flexibility. Cultus adheres with extraordinary tenacity to the form it has evolved in the course of history, even when its content has been radically altered. It finds itself, therefore, only partially able to fulfil its true function, and indeed may become a very real drag on the full development of the content entrusted to it. Hence it is that in every living religion the harmonious co-operation of cultus and religious experience is constantly being shattered by their inherent mutual opposition. The spectator is compelled to recognize that the cultus cannot be assumed, without qualification, to be an accurate embodiment of the religious life of its period, and that the degree of correspondence between the two is a variable quantity which has to be taken into account in his assessment to the best of his ability.

2. THE SIGNIFICANCE OF THE CULTUS IN THE RELIGION OF ISRAEL

A fact of decisive importance for any estimate of the position of the cultus in Israelite religion is that it does not represent a completely new production, but is recognizably an inheritance from the distant past. Nor does such a statement refer solely to that relationship of historical continuity in which the Mosaic establishment stands to the preceding periods. It is concerned equally with the general function of all cultic activity—that of giving expression to the fundamental religious feelings of worship, trust, gratitude and submission, which play their part in all the higher religions. It is hardly to be wondered at, therefore, if the comparative history of religions is able to present us with a long list of items in which the usages of the Israelite cultus correspond to those of the heathen world, and can point to far-reaching similarities both in outward practice and in the accompanying conception of divine worship. The picture of the early period which saw Israelite cultic practice as a direct revelation from God, full of new and original information about the relationship between the terrestrial and divine worlds, and which regarded all related phenomena in heathenism as distorted or counterfeit versions of Israelite customs, is no longer tenable. For this very reason, however, it is an all the more urgent task to investigate whether, and in what way, the faith of Yahweh made itself felt in the characteristic development of the cultus. Moreover, this involves considering not only what cultic acts were rejected or excluded, but also what meaning was attached to those ordinances which were retained or invented. For this purpose it is of less value to aim at a comprehensive catalogue of the material, such as the archaeologist provides, than to examine the most important cultic concepts.

1. *Sacred Sites*[1]

The religion of the Old Testament shares with every other the belief that the deity reveals himself at particular places and that, therefore, worship is not to be offered at any spot which may happen to be convenient, but only at these sites in particular. This belief is the expression of an entire dependence on the will of God, whose manifestations cannot be compelled, but who reserves to himself the right to decide where men are to call upon him. Hence, in the time of Israel's wanderings, apart from the Ark of God or the sacred Tent, it is only on Sinai, the Mount of God, or at the sacred spring of Kadesh that men can draw near to God. After the Occupation,

---

[1]Cf. A. von Gall, *Altisraelitische Kultstätten*, 1898; G. Westphal, *Jahves Wohnstätten*, 1908; K. Möhlenbrink, *Der Tempel Salomos*, 1932; W. Zimmerli, *Geschichte und Tradition von Beerseba im Alten Testament* (Göttingen Dissertations, 1932).

there are the various greater and lesser sanctuaries of Canaan; of these the tribal sanctuaries, the sites like Shiloh and Mizpah at which the shrines of the period of wandering were permanently established, and later the royal sanctuaries attained to particular importance. All these, however, are ultimately superseded by the Temple of Zion, which after the Exile becomes the dominating centre of Jewish religion.

The more emphatically a religion becomes tied to the sacred sites, the more dangerous are their inevitable effects on the idea of God and on his worship. The holy place, especially when it is also thought of as the dwelling-place of the divinity, leads to the localization of the Godhead and the limitation of his sphere of influence. Indeed, where it is a question of a number of rival cultic sites, the result is sometimes the disintegration of the divine Being into minor deities. Moreover, the cultus itself, when too much importance is attached to the precise place at which sacrifice is to be offered, tends very easily to ascribe all value and efficacy to its own procedure and so to have a prejudicial effect on the personal element in worship. Finally, this development constitutes the most serious of all obstacles to a religion's ever outgrowing the purely particularist stage.

How did the religion of Yahweh behave in the face of these dangers? From the outset there was a constant tension between the advantages of a real presence of the divinity at the sacred sites and the vivid realization that Yahweh's nature was totally incompatible with his sensible limitation to any one spot. It is possible, therefore, to observe from the first an effort to establish the character of the sacred localities as places not where Yahweh dwells, but where he manifests himself. It is in a special and quite inconceivable manifestation that Yahweh makes himself visible to Moses on the Mount of God. [1] He comes down on to Sinai in order to conclude the covenant with his people. [2] The Ark, which—though the divine throne—remains unoccupied, together with the regalia of the rod of God and the sacred lot, [3] bear witness to the invisibility of the divine Lord, whose presence as Leader during the migration or in war is only assured to the eye of faith and is, moreover, described only in oblique terms as the presence of his *pānīm*. [4] The sacred Tent marks the

[1] Ex. 3.1 ff.
[2] Ex. 19.11, 18, 20.
[3] Num. 10.35 f.; Ex. 4.17; 17.9, 15 f.; Num. 21.8 f.; Deut. 33.8: cf. also pp. 86 f., 90 ff. above.
[4] Ex. 33.14 f.

meeting-place between Yahweh and Moses, where, appearing from time to time in the cloud, he makes known his will to the captain of his people. [1] Even the Canaanite sanctuaries are traced back to particular appearances of Yahweh—a device which establishes them as places where he reveals himself, not where he dwells. [2] Furthermore, a belief in his manifestation of his presence at these sites [3] is held simultaneously with an equally strong belief in Sinai as his favourite site, [4] and, at all periods, it is accepted as a matter of course that God's dwelling-place is in Heaven. [5] These varying conceptions, which even in the prophets are occasionally to be found side by side, with no attempt at harmonization, [6] afford impressive grounds for thinking that the dynamic of the divine nature was far too powerful to admit of his being restricted to any one locality—nay, that it demanded that such contradictory expressions should stand side by side. Another indication in the same direction is the belief that, although the cultic worship of Yahweh is possible only at definite places within the land of his holy inheritance, [7] yet he will hear the prayer of his worshippers in every place and be at hand to succour them. [8]

The longer this conception was subjected to the influences of the world of Canaanite religion, however, the more it was called in question. In the popular religion of Canaan, although the idea of the God of Heaven was by no means foreign to it, the Baal was the principal figure, conceived as the divine landlord of his particular area, within which he bestowed the blessings of Nature on his

[1]Ex. 33.7–11: cf. pp. 107 f.; 112 ff. below.
[2]Gen. 12.7 (Shechem); Gen. 13.18; cf. 18 (Hebron); Gen. 26.23 ff. (Beersheba); Gen. 28.10 ff. (Bethel); Gen. 32.2 f. (Mahanaim); Gen. 32.22 ff. (Peniel); Josh. 5.13–15 (Gilgal or Gerizim: cf. 8.30); Judg. 6.24 (Ophrah); II Sam. 24.16, 18 ff. (Zion); Gen. 31.49 (Mizpah in Gilead); Josh. 4.20 ff. (Gilgal).
[3]The distinction between a temple where the deity manifests himself and one where he dwells is recognized also in Babylonia and Assyria: cf. W. Andrae, *Das Gotteshaus und die Urformen des Bauens im Alten Orient*, 1930, pp. 15 ff. K. Möhlenbrink (*op. cit.*) believes that a close affinity can be demonstrated between the Solomonic Temple and the Assyrian sacral buildings.
[4]Judg. 5.1 ff.; I Kings 19.8 ff.; for Sinai as the Mount of God, cf. Ex. 3.1; 4.27; 18.5; 33.3–6.
[5]Gen. 11.5; 18.21; 21.17; 22.11; 24.7; 28.12; Ex. 19.11, 18, 20; 20.22; Pss. 18.7; 2.4; Isa. 31.4; Micah 1.2; Deut. 4.36; 26.15 etc.
[6]An especially conspicuous feature of Isaiah: cf. 1.12; 6; 8.18; 31.9; also 18.4; 31.4: for further instances cf. Jer. 7.14 and 23.24; Ps. 20.3 and 7.
[7]Gen. 4.14; I Sam. 26.19; II Sam. 15.8; II Kings 5.15 ff.; Hos. 3.4; 9.3 f., 15; Jer. 16.13; Deut. 28.36.
[8]Gen. 24.12; Judg. 16.28; I Sam. 27.1 ff.; 30.23, 26; II Sam. 15.8.

worshippers. Here the constant presence of the god was as much taken for granted as the unceasing existence of the forces of Nature in which that presence was manifested; and from this it followed that the god was firmly settled in the sanctuary dedicated to him. This is confirmed by the importance for the Canaanite cult sites of the sacred springs, trees and stones, and of the temple building, the existence of which in Shechem has been proved by excavation, and which can be assumed for all the major towns. After the Occupation this conception of God's dwelling in the midst of his people, and of his being inseparably connected with the holy places, made great headway in Israel as well. It is true that the erection in Shiloh of a permanent temple building, thought of as God's dwelling, where a light burned continually[1] and where an oracle could always be obtained by incubation,[2] followed as it was by the erection of similar buildings in Jerusalem, Bethel, Dan, Samaria, Ophrah and Mizpah, was felt by the Yahwist zealots to be a destructive innovation and was disowned out of hand. They rightly saw in this the irruption of the usages of Canaan, Phoenicia and Egypt.[3] Slowly, however, even this foreign element was assimilated. The taking over of the Canaanite *bāmōt* 'on every high hill and under every green tree'[4] gradually became the prevalent and readily accepted practice. With it went a process of localizing and limiting the covenant God, which bound him indissolubly to land and people and occasionally even disintegrated him into different local deities.[5] The effects of this wave of Canaanite influence may also be seen in the veneration of the Ark of God, which at times presupposes a connection of Yahweh with the cult-object so close that it almost amounts to identification.[6]

[1] I Sam. 3.3.

[2] I Sam. 3.2 ff.; cf. 21.8; I Kings 3.5. Cf. also E. L. Ehrlich, *Der Traum im Alten Testament* (BZAW 73), 1953, pp. 13 ff.

[3] II Sam. 7.5 ff.; cf. Elijah's pilgrimage to Horeb, I Kings 19.8 ff. Later even the prophets speak of Yahweh's 'house', cf. Isa. 1.12; Jer. 7.10, or alternatively, his *māqōm*, Jer. 7.12. In the Law Yahweh's abiding at the place of the cult is quite unreflectingly taken for granted: cf. Ex. 23.15; 34.20.

[4] Deut. 12.2; I Kings 14.23; II Kings 16.4; Jer. 2.20; 3.6, 13; 17.2; Ezek. 20.28. For mention of the sacred trees, cf. Gen. 12.6; 13.18; 21.33; 35.4; Judg. 9.37; Hos. 4.13; Deut. 12.2: sacred stones, e.g., Gen. 28.18; 31.45 ff.; Ex. 24.4; Josh. 4.9, 20–24; Hos. 10.1: for the command of the law to overthrow them, cf. Ex. 23.24; 34.13; Deut. 12.3; 16.22. For an instance of the sacred stone under the holy tree, cf. Josh. 24.26. For the sacred pole, cf. Judg. 6.28; I Kings 14.23; II Kings 10.26; 17.10; 23.6, etc.

[5] I Sam. 1.3 (the Yahweh of Shiloh); II Sam. 15.7 (the Yahweh of Hebron). Deut. 6.4 may possibly be a polemic against this development.

[6] I Sam. 3.10; 4.7.

Nevertheless, the Yahwist faith did not suffer this invasion of Canaanite ideas without resistance. There was a violent reaction, which in the end emerged triumphant. Not only was there the opposition of the older prophetic circles and of certain sects such as that of the Rechabites; [1] the great prophets also directed their weighty attacks precisely against that presumption which saw the temples as guarantees in stone of the divine presence, [2] and against the arrogant certainty which went with it that in the day of necessity Yahweh's assistance could not possibly be withheld. It was their proclamation of the transcendence of God which helped to set his presence at the holy place in the right perspective as an act of gracious condescension for the purpose of self-revelation.

Others, however, by purposeful theological treatment went further and even managed to incorporate the new approach safely into their system of religious thought. On the one hand there is the Deuteronomic school, which preserved the reality of the divine presence at the holy place by substituting for the heathen conception of God's personal dwelling that of the dwelling of his Name. [3] In this way they succeeded in integrating the truth that the God who is exalted above all heavens reveals himself in an unconditioned act of power with the satisfaction of man's deep desire for a God who is in very deed close to him. By passing the sacred Tent over in silence and reducing the function of the Ark to that of a casket for the safe keeping of the Tables of the Law they further demonstrated a radical policy of dissociating the sacred objects from the self-revelation of the living God—a policy which accords perfectly with the puritan tendencies of the Deuteronomic circle. On the other hand, though not so drastic as the Deuteronomic reaction, the theological work of the Priestly writings was perhaps even more influential; for they succeeded in welding into one impressive whole all the ordinances hallowed by tradition. In their description of the Tabernacle, Ark and Tent became fused in an indivisible unity; [4] and although the conception of Yahweh's dwelling as such continued to be employed, yet it was made unmistakably clear by the narratives of Yahweh's appearances

[1]This sect carried the puritanism of their Yahweh worship even to the point of refusing to live in permanent houses.

[2]Amos 9.1 ff.; Micah 3.11 f.; Jer. 7.4, 12 ff.; 26.9; Ezek. 8–11.

[3]Deut. 12.5, 21; 14.23 f.; 16.2, 6, 11; 26.2; II Sam. 7.13; I Kings 8.16, 18 f., 29; 9.3, 7; 11.36; 14.21, etc.; Jer. 7.12.

[4]Ex. 25 ff.

in the sanctuary,[1] that the transcendent God was present only from time to time in special revelations, and even then veiled in his *kābōd*. Apart from these special manifestations Yahweh's dwelling in the sanctuary can only be understood in a qualified sense. The cultic setting, being a copy of the heavenly sanctuary, creates as it were an image of the divine presence,[2] a pledge that God is in an especial relation with this particular place on the earth, so that the cultic activities are carried out 'before the face of Yahweh', *lipnē yhwh*.

It is fully accordant with this conception, that even the prophets should retain a belief in the future importance of Jerusalem, understood as a place where God reveals himself. It is from Jerusalem that the knowledge of the true God is to spread;[3] and in worshipping him at this place the new unity of all peoples in submission to the God of Israel is to find its symbolic expression.[4]

Thus it was that in Israel the holy place finally became the means whereby the concrete historicity of the revelation could be most strongly emphasized. In the teeth of all purely human notions it was established at this one place and remained there; and from there it sought to reach out to all peoples. Loyalty to the holy place was thus to be equated with loyalty to the expression of the will of God in history; and this was to continue to be so, until the day in which the concrete historical fact of the revelation itself decreed its own independence of any holy place—when it reached its fulfilment in a Man who could say of himself: 'One greater than the Temple is here!'[5]

II. Sacred Objects

Our concern here is not with the cultic furniture of the sacred site, with such items as the altar, the *maṣṣēbā*, the candlestick, the shewbread, the altar of incense and so on, but only with those objects which were held in a special way to guarantee the effective presence of Yahweh. These are the Ark, the sacred Tent, the rod of God and the sacred lot.

(a) In determining *the significance of the Ark* the overwhelmingly probable assumption from which to start is that it represents the

[1]Ex. 40.34 f.; Num. 9.15 ff.; 10.11; Lev. 9.23 f.; Num. 14.10; 16.19 ff.; 17.7 ff.; 20.6.
[2]Ex. 25.9, 40; I Chron. 28.19; cf. ch. IX. 1. II (d), p. 423 below.
[3]Isa. 2.2–4; Micah 4.1–3; Isa. 52.9 f.
[4]Isa. 19.23; Zech. 8.3, 22 f.; Isa. 56.7; 60.10 ff.; Zech. 14.5–9, 16 ff.
[5]Matt. 12.6.

'unoccupied throne of the deity', [1] a class of sacred objects of which instances are to be found outside Israel. [2] Such an assumption renders quite superfluous conjectures that it represents a shrine containing stone fetishes, [3] or an image of the divinity in the form of a bull. [4] Quite apart from the fact that the evidence for such theories is very weak, they contradict the other indications of the Israelite picture of God. Moreover, the information, first found in Deuteronomy and P, that the Tables of the Law were kept in the Ark, [5] can easily be combined with the throne conception, since the custom of depositing contracts and deeds at the feet of the divinity is well known from Asia Minor and Egypt, [6] and the ancient thrones of God frequently took the form of a chest. [7]

That the Ark of Yahweh can possibly be a shrine of the Mosaic period is frequently disputed; the making of it is more usually assumed to derive from Canaanite models. [8] Indeed there is a certain difficulty in the fact that the oldest sources seem to know nothing of it. On the other hand such an ancient piece of evidence as Num. 10.35 f., [9] together with the undoubted suitability of the Ark as a

[1] First explicitly stated by Reichel, *Vorhellenische Götterkulte*, 1897, and J. Meinhold, *Die Lade Jahves*, 1900. The thesis was established with great care by M. Dibelius, *Die Lade Jahves*, 1906. The most significant passages in the OT bearing witness to this conception are Num. 10.35 f.; I Sam. 3.3, 10; 4.4, 7; II Sam. 6.2; II Kings 19.14 f.; Jer. 3.16 f.; Ezek. 43.7.

[2] In addition to the Greek examples adduced by Dibelius (*op. cit.*, pp. 65 ff.) it is now possible to cite two Phoenician thrones of Astarte, flanked to right and left by two winged beings, which were discovered during the French excavations in Syria: cf. Clermont-Ganneau, *Comptes rendus de l'Académie des Inscriptions*, 1907; Ronzevalle, *Mélanges de la faculté orientale* III, 2, pp. 753 ff., and *Syria* V, 1924, plate XXXII (quoted by von Rad, 'Zelt und Lade', *NKZ* 42, 1931, p. 484). Cf. also the Throne of the Cherubim, on which Ishtar sits, from the rock relief of Maltaya, *AOB*, plate CXXXV; *ANEP*, fig. 537. For the cherubim represented on the ivory plaques from Samaria, cf. *Palestine Exploration Fund, Quarterly Statement*, 1932/33.

[3] E. Meyer, *Die Israeliten, und ihre Nachbarstämme*, 1906, p. 214.

[4] H. Gressmann, *Die Lade Jahves und der Allerheiligste des Salomonischen Tempels*, 1920.

[5] Deut. 10.1 ff.; Ex. 25.16, 21.

[6] Cf. J. Herrmann, 'Ägyptische Analogien zum Funde des Deuteronomiums', *ZAW* 28, 1908, pp. 299 ff. Also A. Jirku, *Altorientalischer Kommentar zum Alten Testament*, 1923, pp. 184 f.

[7] Cf. e.g. *AOB*, plate CXXIX, fig. 322: Throne of the Sun-god, c. 870 B.C. The fact that the term *'arōn*, 'chest', is applied to the Ark is not therefore a point against the 'throne' theory.

[8] Cf. H. Gressmann, *Die Lade Jahves*, pp. 67 ff.

[9] In spite of the fact that this passage is defectively integrated with the context, it is hardly possible to excise it from the complex of the Wilderness narratives. The linking-up of the differing accounts of 10.29 ff. by means of the implied question, who is to be Israel's guide, is quite in accordance with the methods of other

portable shrine, [1] argues strongly for its existence during the period of Israel's wandering in the wilderness. The golden plate covering the Ark, which was called the *kapporet* and plays so great a part in P, may well belong to the later equipment of the sanctuary. [2] In view of the fact that redactional activity has exercised its most drastic effects on precisely those traditions which relate to Sinai, it might be wise not to lay too much weight on the absence of any account of the origins of the Ark in the older sources.

(b) A more serious objection might be raised to an early provenance of the Ark, were the concept of God which it attests in real and unresolvable contradiction with that symbolized by *the sacred Tent*. The evidence for the latter as a shrine of the Mosaic period is good, [3] and therefore, in opposition to the theory which once held the field, [4] it is not to be regarded merely as a covering for the Ark— of no importance in itself—but as a shrine in its own right. [5] The constructive element in the P 'Tabernacle' tradition is not the invention of the Tent shrine, but the unbreakable association established between the Tent and the Ark. Both the name of this shrine and the accounts of the uses to which it was put make its function clear. As *'ōhel mō'ēd*, 'the Tent of Meeting', [6] it serves as a place where

redactional elements. There is nothing unusual in the fact that the shrine of the wanderings should also be the palladium in war.

[1] Cf. R. Kittel, *Geschichte des Volkes Israel*[4], I, p. 570: J. Morgenstern, *The Ark, the Ephod and the Tent of Meeting*, 1945.

[2] Ex. 25.17 ff. According to Torczyner, *Die Bundeslade und die Anfänge der Religion Israels*, 1922, pp. 23 ff., this is to be understood as an image and embodiment of the storm-cloud, within which Yahweh moves—an interpretation which would fit in very well with the Priestly symbolic terminology of the heavenly 'original' and its 'copy'. The Cherubim who spread their wings in protection over the Ark must be regarded as the addition of a later period, which, as von Rad conjectures, may derive from Egyptian influence. Originally they may have been the beasts on which the throne was borne—whence the ancient name of Yahweh, 'Him that sitteth upon the cherubim', I Sam. 4.4; II Sam. 6.2. Whether the vision of the *merkābā* in Ezek. 1, which has in its turn undergone later revision, can be used to reconstruct the Ark, as H. Schmidt ('Kerubenthron und Lade', *Eucharisterion* I, 1923, pp. 120 ff.) and Torczyner would like to do, is at least extremely doubtful.

[3] Ex. 33.7-11.

[4] E.g. Wellhausen, *Prolegomena*, p. 37.

[5] First established in detail by E. Sellin, 'Das Zelt Jahves', *Alttest. Studien Kittel dargebracht*, 1913, pp. 168 ff. For Arabian evidence relating to sacred tents, cf. R. Hartmann, 'Zelt und Lade', *ZAW* 37, 1917-18, pp. 216 ff.

[6] This name occurs in E: Ex. 33.7 ff.; Num. 11.11 ff.; 12.4; Deut. 31.14; and in P: Ex. 27.21; 28.43; 29.10 f.; Lev. 1.1, 3 etc. Usually explained as from *nō'ad*, 'to come together with', Ex. 25.22; 29.42 f. etc. Other designations used in P include: *'ōhel hā'ēdūt*, Num. 9.15; 17.22 f.; 18.2: *miškān hā'ēdūt*, Ex. 38.21; Num. 1.50, 53; 10.11: *hammiškān*, Ex. 26.1; Num. 9.15, 18 ff. etc.

Yahweh can meet with Moses. The deity is not present indiscriminately in all places, but appears in the cloud at the door of the Tent, either for the purpose of granting to the man who calls upon him the answer to his prayer,[1] or, in the case of contention among the congregation, to hold his court and to pass judgment.[2] It is, therefore, explicitly the transcendent God[3] who here manifests himself and directly inspires his envoy without the use of any machinery of mediation: 'And the Lord spake unto Moses face to face, as a man speaketh unto his friend.'[4]

The view here presented is unquestionably in a certain tension with that symbolized by the Ark. The Tent gives characteristic expression to a strong feeling for the unapproachableness of God and for the fact that his self-communication is an act of condescension, which is not at the beck and call of man. The Ark on the other hand, as the throne of the invisible God, emphasizes by contrast his nearness and his abiding in the midst of his people. Nevertheless, one has only to note that the functions of the two sacred objects are totally different to realize that this is not a case of an irreconcilable opposition. In the case of the Tent the concern is with guidance in the internal affairs of the people through the giving of oracles: the Ark is the medium through which the deity leads his people in their wanderings and in war.[5]

[1]Ex. 33.7 (E); 29.42 f.; 30.6, 36; Num. 7.89; 17.19 (P).
[2]Num. 11.14 ff.; 12.5; 14.10, 26 ff.; 16.19 ff.; 20.6 ff.
[3]Too much importance should not be attached to the position of the Tent outside the camp, for on this point Ex. 33.7 ff. is itself full of contradictions. Indeed, vv. 8 and 10 assume that the Tent stands in the centre of the camp (as Holzinger, *Exodus*, 1900, p. 109, remarked long ago), which may well be the original version. Similarly, a statement like that of Ex. 33.5, which only makes sense within the context of the Elohistic tradition, cannot be produced to disprove the existence of a belief in Yahweh's succouring presence.
[4]Ex. 33.11; Num. 12.8. On the basis of these passages M. Haran ('The Tent of Meeting', *Tarbiz* 25, 1955, pp. 11–20, cf. *ZAW* 67, 1955, p. 280) would regard the *'ōhel mō'ēd* not primarily as a sanctuary, but as a medium of prophetic inspiration.
[5]Num. 10.33, 35; cf. I Sam. 4.3 ff.; II Sam. 11.11; in P the function of guiding the people in their journeyings is transferred to the cloud which stands over the Tent: Num. 9.15 ff. and 10.11 f.—a later attempt at harmonization. A. Musil (*The Manners and Customs of the Rwala Bedouins*, 1928, pp. 571 ff., and earlier, *Die Kultur* 11, 1910, pp. 8 f.) has recorded an interesting religio-historical analogy to this migratory shrine. This is the empty camel-saddle among the Rwala tribes east of the Jordan, which has come down from the tribal patriarch and serves as the visible focus of unity for all the related bedouin. As the place to which Allah especially delights to resort it is offered up before him every year, with the result that his guidance is secured for the movements of the tribe and his presence affords the most powerful assistance when battle is fierce.

This combination of a belief in the self-communication of God in isolated acts[1] and in his constant presence in power amid all the perils of the journey in the wilderness is perfectly understandable in the light of the actual situation of the people between Sinai and Canaan.[2] The fact that the Mosaic religion takes into its system, in terms of its two principal shrines, the latent tension between the immanent and the transcendent God only goes to show that it is not controlled by some concept of deity which is the product of logical construction, but by the living reality of God with all its contradictions. In the same way, only at a higher level, this reality is experienced by the prophets, but also finds expression in the priestly regulation of life.

With the separation of the two shrines in Canaan[3] there arose an emphasis on the constant presence of Yahweh in the midst of his people as the divine Lord enthroned at the holy place, which was one-sided and therefore succumbed to Canaanite influences. It is true that the occasional loss of the Ark provided a counterpoise to too grossly materialistic a conception of the divine presence, and the terrifying experiences of the punishments imposed by divine justice kept at bay that false confidence which might arise from a belief in the secure possession of the national God in one's midst. Moreover, with the activity of the seers and the rise of the *nābī'* and of the charismatic kingship there was a strong development along the lines associated with the sacred Tent, which kept alive a sense of the independent action of the distant God through those who were endowed with his spirit. With the disappearance of the Ark into the darkened sanctum of the Temple on Zion the ideas which it represented were

[1]It should not be forgotten, that the very nature of an oracle as a word from God delivered on a single occasion undoubtedly favours the disintegration of the divine presence into individual strongly differentiated instances.

[2]Moreover, with the laying up of the basic covenant documents at the feet of the enthroned divinity, the transition has already begun from a covenant God who is arbitrary and incalculable to one who rules in accordance with fixed principles. In addition, the Jahwist narrator already shows signs of the endeavour to modify the presence of the enthroned God into the idea of the presence of his *pānīm*, his countenance—a term which designates one of the forms in which the transcendent God manifests himself, his representative, so to speak, on earth: Ex. 33.14 f.; Num. 10.33 (J₂).

[3]After the Entry of the Israelites into Canaan the Ark appears at Shiloh and eventually, after varied fortunes, arrives at Jerusalem (cf. I Sam. 4–6; II Sam. 6): the sacred Tent, according to I Chron. 21.29 f.; II Chron. 1.3, found a home on the Yahwist high place at Gibeon—a piece of information which, in spite of its only occurring in a late source, possesses a high degree of intrinsic probability.

transferred to the sacred site, which thus became the citadel of the imageless Yahweh-worship. These now underwent a strong process of sublimation. On the one hand they were associated with the prophetic conception of the universal God;[1] on the other, through the priestly theological concepts of the šēm and the kābōd, the Name and the Glory of Yahweh, and through their identification with the tradition of the sacred Tent, they acquired a new significance.[2] In time the earthly object to which these ideas were attached, the Ark itself, lost its importance, and its final disappearance, like that of the sacred Tent, occasioned no great distress.[3] The fundamental principle, however, of which these two shrines were the focus, the concept of the distant God who yet condescends to be really present in the midst of his people and enables them to participate in the divine life, lives on in the symbolic language of the New Testament, which uses the image of the 'tabernacling' to tell of the dwelling of the eternal God among men.[4]

(c) To the complex of ideas associated with the Ark belong also *the rod of God* and the oracle of the sacred lot. As regards the former, the serpent miracles which are reported in connection with it[5] and the description in Num. 21.4 ff. of how it was set up[6] suggest a 'snake-staff', that is to say, a rod round which the figure of a serpent was entwined.[7] The close connection of the rod with Yahweh derives firstly from its having come from Yahweh as his gift,[8] secondly from its being laid up 'before Yahweh',[9] and finally from the part which it played during the battle in Rephidim.[10] The altar erected there received the name 'Yahweh my banner'.[11] The victory is thought of as the work of Yahweh, effectively present in the rod; to him also sacrifice is offered, probably in the form of the placing of

[1]Isa. 6; Ezek. 1.
[2]Cf. above pp. 106 f.
[3]Jer. 3.16.
[4]John 1.14; Heb. 8.2; 9.11; Rev. 7.15; 15.5; 21.3.
[5]Ex. 4.2 ff.; 7.8 ff.
[6]We are here dealing with the Elohistic account of the serpent staff, where its importance as the rod of the leader is suppressed or omitted altogether, while prominence is given to its role as an apotropaic sacred object.
[7]For the religio-historical parallels, cf. H. Gressmann, *Mose und seine Zeit*, pp. 159 ff., 453 ff.
[8]Ex. 4.17.
[9]Num. 20.9.
[10]Ex. 17.8 ff.
[11]Ex. 17.15.

the rod upon the altar.[1] This is, therefore, not an instance of fetishism. We are here dealing with an appanage of the invisible deity who fights alongside his people; with a physical means of representing the presence of the god which is comparable to the Ark and which symbolizes both the victory of Yahweh over the hostile powers and his authority over the serpent demons, who are the instruments of his judgment. The serpent staff apparently plays no part in the later period. A passing notice of its destruction by Hezekiah[2] suggests that it was preserved at Jerusalem, where incense was offered to it as a relic of the Mosaic era. The prophetic epoch had no idea what to make of such a symbol.

(d) With the symbols of Yahweh's presence and the sites at which he revealed himself goes the one technical means of inquiring the will of God, *the sacred lot of Urim and Thummim.* In Deut. 33.8 it is mentioned as the special prerogative of Levi; but the earliest sources nowhere record its use by Moses. Only P includes it in the equipment of the High Priest as ordained by Moses.[3] Probably the oracle by lot was already in the possession of the Kadesh priesthood and Moses allowed it to remain.

In outward form it was in fact the simplest kind of lot or arrow oracle, allowing of only two possible answers to the question put to it. An idea of how it was used can best be obtained from the procedure described in I Sam. 14.41 ff. According to which little stick jumped out when the container of the lots was shaken the answer of the deity was taken to be 'Yes' or 'No'.[4] Closely related to the lot was the ephod—according to the most probable interpretation a priestly garment, on to which was sewn a pocket for holding the lots.[5] It is true that the ephod is not mentioned in the Moses sagas

---

[1]In this role the rod recalls the standards of the Egyptians, Assyrians and many other peoples, which were also decorated with the emblem of the god and cultically venerated.

[2]II Kings 18.4: Gressmann argues convincingly for the connection of Nehushtan with the rod of Moses (*op. cit.*, p. 458).

[3]Ex. 28.15 ff.

[4]Hence also the name, Urim and Thummim, the easiest interpretation of which is 'light' and 'truth'. There may, however, also be some connection with the first and last letters of the alphabet, aleph and tau, which were possibly scratched on the sticks, or with the light ('*ūrīm*) and dark colour of the two lots.

[5]Lotz, *HRE* V, pp. 402ff., and XXIII, pp. 425 ff. and E. Sellin, 'Das israelitische Ephod', *Oriental. Studien für Nöldeke*, 1906, pp. 699 ff., take it to be an apron for holding the oracle. However, H. Thiersch, *Ependytes und Ephod* (Geisteswiss. Forschungen, ed. W. Mitscherlich, 8) 1936, after a thorough survey of the classical and Oriental archaeological evidence, regards it as the garment of the god, and

either; nevertheless, wherever the Urim and Thummim occur, the ephod should probably be assumed as well, seeing that P attributes this too to the Mosaic period.[1] The relationship of this oracle to those attested among the Arabs[2] suggests that the Yahweh priesthood had adopted a more ancient usage and enlisted it in the service of Yahweh. It is a significant indication of the spirit of the Yahweh religion that it should never have absorbed into its system any but this, the simplest technical device for inquiring the will of God. Because of this the control of the priest over the divine decisions, which is bound up with the development of a science of divination incomprehensible to the layman, was prevented for all time.[3]

Frequently mentioned in the early period of Israel's history,[4] it was mostly employed by priests, though on occasion by laity also.[5] It is odd that it could become the central object of a sanctuary, thus acquiring independent importance,[6] but this fits in quite well with the dispersal of the Mosaic sacred objects after the Occupation. So long as the Ark, the rod of God and the oracle of the sacred lot were kept together at a central sanctuary, they could serve as symbols of the idea of the divine Lordship and be subordinated to it. Their dispersal led to a false independence of the individual sacred object; and being now regarded as holy in itself, it attracted a superstitious veneration even more easily. It is worth noting, that after the transference of the Ark to the royal sanctuary on Zion nothing more is heard of the oracle of the sacred lot.[7] It sinks into insignificance,

---

then of his earthly representative. He assumes that the name was later transferred to an image of the god, but this remains improbable, and reference to the Ras Shamra epic (*Syria* 15, 1934, p. 305) is held by K. Galling (*Biblische Reallexikon*, 1937, art. 'Kultgerät') to exclude it altogether.

[1]Ex. 28.6 ff.: P, however, distinguishes the ephod as an apron from the *ḥōšen mišpāṭ*, the pocket (Ex. 28.15 ff.) in which the Urim and Thummim were kept (Ex. 28.30).

[2]Cf. J. Wellhausen, *Reste arabischen Heidentums*, 1887, pp. 126 ff.; F. Buhl, *Das Leben Muhammeds*, 1930, p. 81.

[3]Cf. ch. IX, 1. 1, p. 396 below.

[4]I Sam. 14.18 (emended); 23.9; 30.7. Passages such as II Sam. 2.1 f.; 5.19 also seem to refer to this.

[5]Judg. 18.5.

[6]Judg. 8.24 ff.; 17.5: possibly also in the case of the house of Eli in Nob, I Sam. 22.13.

[7]In association with the ephod, Josh. 7.14 ff. and I Sam. 10.17 ff. seem to assume yet another sacred lot, about which nothing is known in more detail. II Sam. 5.23 f.; Hos. 4.12; Gen. 12.6; Deut. 11.30; Judg. 9.37 appear to be references to a kind of tree-oracle found in Canaan. Num. 17.1 ff. (MT 17.17 ff.) suggests a special oracular use of rods. *Tᵉrāpīm* are conjectured by some to have been masks

becoming merely an item of the priestly regalia; and is finally reserved for the High Priest and used for various incidental cultic occasions. [1]

(e) Alien from primitive Yahwism, and introduced into the Yahweh cultus predominantly as a result of Canaanite influence, were *the maṣṣēbāh, the Ashera and the bull image*. It is true that the practice of erecting a memorial stone to mark the site of a holy place or a grave is of very ancient derivation, as can be proved from the customs of many other peoples. Nevertheless, its frequent and distinctively cultic employment, not merely as a means of indicating a sacred site, but as itself a sacred object, seems to be specifically Canaanite. The description of the stone as *bēt'ēl*, the seat of the god, the name Βαιτυλος for a Phoenician deity (Philo of Byblus) and the conception of the sacred stones as λίθοι ἔμψυχοι (*ibid.*) are all relevant pointers to this Canaanite-Phoenician origin. [2] The basis of this evaluation is less likely to be a belief that some daemon or divinity is dwelling in the stone, [3] than a transference to this particular object of the divine power effective at the holy place as a whole. In this way the stone itself becomes a medium of power. Several practices make this clear, in particular that of setting up stone columns on the altar; in addition, the Phoenician sanctuaries were equipped with two massive temple columns, and the Carthaginian with these and many smaller ones as well, while the Canaanite *bāmōt* were characterized by whole rows of stone pillars. Hence the rites of libation and anointing are not so much offerings [4] as consecratory acts designed to strengthen and augment the 'holy' power; [5] likewise, the kissing and caressing of the stones serve to transfer this

worn over the face for the purpose of obtaining oracles, but according to others the name is a derogatory term for the images of household gods ('the decaying ones'). In any case they are not to be attributed to Moses (as against H. Gressmann, *op. cit.*, p. 246), but were from the start thought of in Israel as a foreign, probably Aramaic importation, and were held in derision (cf. Gen. 31.19 ff.; Judg. 17.5 ff.; I Sam. 19.13, 16). None of these technical devices for enquiring the will of God attained to any great importance and they were ousted by the divine word mediated through human persons. Cf. below p. 302.

[1]E.g., in the selection of the scapegoat, Lev. 16.8.

[2]Cf. W. von Baudissin, 'Malsteine bei den alten Hebräern', *HRE* XII, pp. 130 ff.: G. Beer, *Steinverehrung bei den Israeliten*, 1921.

[3]This at one time widespread view was connected with the over-estimation of the importance of animism which was then the dominant theory.

[4]Gen. 28.18; 31.13; 35.14; I Kings 1.9.

[5]Cf. below, pp. 133 f. This indicates that the customary explanation advanced for the Bethel story in Gen. 28.10 ff. is mistaken.

power to human beings. On this basis it is easy enough to understand the adoption of these sacred stones even in the more elevated cultus of sky- or star-deities—a feature which it is difficult to explain in terms of some improbable admixture of animistic concepts. The ideas associated with a belief in *mana* are much easier to incorporate into theism than those connected with animism, especially where, as in Canaan, theism is in essence a divinization of nature. Moreover, even the use of the *maṣṣēbāh* in the Yahweh cult—an element which has long been admitted as incontrovertible—can be understood in this way. Thanks to the flexibility of the *mana*-concept, it was possible to combine this practice with all kinds of ideas, some more refined and spiritual, others more coarse and crude, without prejudicing their common reference to the one Yahweh. The interpretation of the stones as memorials of Yahweh's self-manifestations [1] was able to subsist side by side with the popular conception that they were receptacles of holy power and signs of God's abiding presence. The latter view was dangerously prone to the temptation to seek to control the divine holiness by sacrificial rites, and to the closely associated misunderstanding of Yahweh as a locally limited Nature deity. Hence the condemnation of the sacred pillars in the course of the cultic reforms of both Hezekiah and Josiah [2] signifies the rejection both of those mystical ideas which degraded sacrifice to something magical and of the naturalistic conceptions of God.

By contrast with the pillars, the sacred poles, called *Asheras*, were always thought of in Israelite religion as incompatible with the nature of Yahweh and resisted accordingly. [3] The explanation of this attitude, so different from the unembarrassed moderation shown in the case of the sacred stones, is the sense, never completely lost, that the pole, which symbolized the goddess Asherah, a West Syrian deity identical with the Assyrian Ishtar, meant opening the door to the unequivocally sensual and sexual character of the vegetation deities and introducing the element of bisexuality into the concept of God. Hence every revival of the sense of what the worship

[1] Gen. 28.18 ff.; Ex. 24.4; Josh. 4.6; 24.26 f.; I Sam. 7.12; II Sam. 20.8.

[2] II Kings 18.4; 23.14; Deut. 12.3 ff.; 16.22; cf. Ex. 23.24; 34.12; Lev. 26.1. For the prophetic polemic cf. Hos. 3.4; 10.1 f.; Micah 5.12; Jer. 2.27.

[3] I Kings 14.15, 23; 16.33; II Kings 13.6; 17.10; 21.3, 7. For the cult regarded as the worship of the goddess Asherah cf. Judg. 3.7; I Kings 15.13; 18.19; II Kings 21.3; 23.4. The many statuettes of the naked female deity discovered in the course of excavations, and notices such as Jer. 7.18; 44.17 ff. show how deeply rooted the cult had become during the syncretistic period, especially among the womenfolk. For illustrations cf. *AOB*, plates CXVIII—CXXI; *ANEP*, pp. 161 f.

of Yahweh really involved was accompanied by the destruction of this symbol;[1] and the detailed requirements of the laws of the Deuteronomic era explicitly make it an obligation to do so.[2]

Another symbol which was adopted, though equally one derived from a heathen environment, was much more tolerantly regarded—namely, *the bull image* introduced by Jeroboam I at the royal sanctuaries of Bethel and Dan.[3] As with the sacred objects mentioned earlier, this innovation was not an instance of a true image of Yahweh, but only a symbolic indication of the divine presence. The bull, which was associated with several deities in Western Asia as a sacred animal,[4] stood in an especially close relationship to the storm god Hadad; when the god was represented in human form, it served as a podium,[5] but it is also found on its own as a symbol of the deity.[6] Yahweh is thought of as invisibly present and is expressly described as the god who brought the people up out of Egypt, as Jeroboam's words indicate. There is a clear parallel with the Ark in Jerusalem, except, however, that this particular divine symbol defines Yahweh's nature one-sidedly as a vegetation deity and teaches men to see his manifestations in the destructive and creative forces of Nature. The superstitious veneration of this image involved an increasingly materialistic conception of God, which was fiercely resisted by Hosea;[7] and the school of thought which produced the Deuteronomic reform characterized the erection of the image as the 'sin of Jeroboam', which branded as sinful not only himself but the whole Northern kingdom.[8]

[1]Judg. 6.25 ff.; I Kings 15.13; II Kings 18.4; 23.6, 15.
[2]Deut. 7.5; 12.3; 16.21; Ex. 34.13.
[3]I Kings 12.28. W. F. Albright, *From the Stone Age to Christianity*[2], 1946, pp. 229 f., also interprets it as a divine symbol. Cf. further J. Hempel, *Gott und Mensch im Alten Testament*[2], 1936, pp. 265 f. and O. Eissfeldt, *ZAW* 58, 1940–41, pp. 199 ff.
[4]Associated with Ra in Egypt and with Tešup in Asia Minor, but also with special bull-gods invoked in oaths at the making of treaties; so also in Babylonia where, however, the bull is supremely the symbol of the storm-god Ramman, as it is of Hadad in Syria. Cf. the extraordinarily careful and voluminous collection of the Near Eastern material in L. Malten, 'Der Stier im Kult und mythischen Bild', *Jahrbuch des Deutschen Archaeolog. Instituts* 43, 1928–29, pp. 90 ff.; also M. von Oppenheim, *Tell Halâf*, 1931, pp. 104–115, 210; K. Galling, *Biblisches Reallexikon*, 1937, art. 'Götterbild', cols. 202 ff. and 219 f.; E. Otto, *Beiträge zur Geschichte der Stierkulte in Ägypten*, 1938.
[5]Cf. *AOB*, figs. 143 f. (a victory stele of Esarhaddon) and fig. 335 (the rock-relief of Maltaya); cf. *ANEP*, figs. 447 and 537.
[6]E.g. on a boundary stone, *AOB*, fig. 317; *ANEP*, fig. 521.
[7]Hos. 8.4–6; 10.5 f.; 13.2.
[8]I Kings 12.30; 14.9; 15.34; 16.31, etc.

(f) The bull image is yet another witness to the existence in Israel of a vivid awareness that Yahweh could not be pictorially represented; and this is confirmed by the well-established fact, that there is no evidence in the Old Testament of there ever having been a true *image of Yahweh* to which no objection was raised.[1] The images of God which are mentioned here and there[2] seem to have been in the first place heathen idols, which did not in fact take the place of Yahweh,[3] but were incorporated into his cultus either as subordinate or as co-equal deities. Be that as it may, the intermingling of these heathen practices with the worship of Yahweh was bound in many cases to lead to an inability on the part of the ordinary man to distinguish properly between an image of Yahweh and the images of other gods. Together with the attributes and the cultic practices associated with the Baals their images also were transferred to Yahweh.[4] The carved images in Gilgal[5] and the carved and molten images in the house of Micah the Ephraimite[6] will, therefore, be examples of Yahweh images, even if perhaps of secondary importance.

The spiritual leaders of Israel, however, always made a firm stand against this adoption of heathen image-worship, regarding it as an innovation which contradicted the essence of the Yahweh religion. The fundamental laws of the earliest period had from the outset proscribed the worship of images,[7] and this prohibition was inculcated again and again,[8] being kept alive by the prophetic polemic (see n. 2 below). Such local aberrations as emerge from time to time are quite insufficient to throw doubt on the combative attitude

[1]As has been proved by H. Th. Obbink, 'Jahvebilder', *ZAW* 47, 1929, pp. 264 ff.; K. H. Bernhardt, *Gott und Bild. Ein Beitrag zur Begründung und Deutung des Bilderverbots im AT*, 1956; H. Schrade, *Der verborgene Gott. Gottesbild und Gottesvorstellung im alten Israel und im alten Orient*, 1949.

[2]Hos. 2.4 ff.; 8.4–6; 11.2; Jer. 8.19; Isa. 48.5.

[3]Guthe, *Der Prophet Hosea*, p. 2 (in Kautzsch-Bertholet, *Die Heilige Schrift des AT⁴* II, 1923) is absolutely right on this point; even when acting in this way, Israel has no intention of rejecting Yahweh.

[4]In this connection, Obbink (*op. cit.*, p. 273) seems to be too optimistic, when he assumes that the mass of the people were always able to distinguish on this point between the Yahwist and the alien cults.

[5]Judg. 3.19.

[6]Judg. 17.4; according to one conjecture, which it would seem impossible to prove, the ephod of the priests of Nob (I Sam. 21.10) and of Gideon (Judg. 8.27) should be regarded as a substitute for an original Elohim-image: cf. E. Sellin, *Geschichte des isr.-jüd. Volkes* I, pp. 134 f.

[7]Ex. 20.4; Deut. 27.15.

[8]Deut. 4.16; 5.8; Lev. 26.1.

of genuine Yahwism. Moreover, even if it is not permissible without qualification to say that the erection of an image of the deity always means that the image and the god are identified, yet the veneration of images implies a tendency to make the concept of God a materialistic one; and it was only the fact that this was thoroughly understood which averted a very serious threat to the spiritual character of Israel's religious faith.

This was not merely a case of the retention of the ancient and sacred usage of the primitive period in opposition to the cultic practice of a more advanced civilization; it was a spiritual attitude rooted in the very heart of the Yahwist faith. This is proved by the way in which all the remaining divine symbols originally in use were gradually stripped of their importance, whereas in the later stages of the religions of the great civilizations such symbols were endlessly multiplied. It is all the more remarkable that this eradication of the last outlets for the effort of primitive religious feeling to make the deity sensibly present should be accompanied by no weakening of interest in the real presence of God at the sanctuary, or in his readiness to hear, to forgive and to bless. The whole emphasis, however, falls on the personal spiritual intercourse of man with God; the line of development runs clearly and logically from the sacrificial to the sacramental form of cultus.

III. *Sacred Seasons*

The belief in sacred seasons also reveals the effect on Israelite religion of extremely ancient religious traditions, which had to be adopted by and assimilated into the worship of Yahweh. Thus not only the observance of particular days of the moon, especially the new moon, [1] but also the keeping of definite festival seasons such as the Passover certainly derive from the pre-Yahwist period. It is a characteristic feature in these cases that the cultic community was originally formed not of the congregation of the people as a whole, but from the smaller circle of the family or clan. [2] The settlement in Canaan may well have resulted in the introduction of Canaanite

---

[1] I Sam. 20.5 f.; II Kings 4.23; Amos 8.4 f.; Ezek. 45.18 f.; 46.1 ff.; Num. 28.11 ff.; 29.1 ff. The fixing of the Feast of Tabernacles at the full moon of the autumnal equinox (Lev. 23.34) and of the Passover at the full moon of the first month of spring (Ex. 12.6) suggest that the day of the full moon was also significant. The Sabbath seems originally to have stood in some relation to the phases of the moon: cf. below.

[2] I Sam. 20.6; Ex. 12.3 f., 21.

nature festivals to take their place beside the feasts of pre-Mosaic provenance. Such were the feasts of corn-harvest, of fruit-gathering, and vintage, the adoption of which was made easier by their approximation to or amalgamation with ancient Israelite festivals. In addition the *maṣṣōt* and New Year festivals and the Sabbath are more or less closely related to pre-Yahwist or Canaanite practices. In this department also the religion of Yahweh had to come to terms with heathen notions and rites.

The significant features of the heathen festivals are the extent to which they are rooted in the life of Nature, and their association with the belief in spirits and in *mana*. These characteristics find expression in primitive apotropaic rites and in magical practices, designed to ensure both that ordinary life shall be flooded with divine power and that these very powers themselves shall be made even stronger; in the development of proper mysteries, which frequently come to be limited in a particularist way to definite classes and groups; and finally, in an extensive system of carefully selected sacred days.

(a) As far as *the Nature festivals* are concerned, the emphasis which these lay on the involvement of human life with its basis in Nature, with the generation and abundance, the growth and maturation of plant and animal life, is deliberately retained. Thus, on the occasion of the Passover, there is the offering of the firstborn. At the *maṣṣōt* festival[1] the solemn partaking of the first of the new corn, together with precautions against any admixture of the previous year's harvest[2] and the dedication of the 'first sheaf',[3] commemorates the renewed assurance of the necessities of existence. At the Feast of Weeks,[4] after the completion of the corn harvest, thanksgiving as in duty bound is offered to the Lord of the harvest, and his gracious presence is celebrated with the presentation of the firstfruit loaves,[5] sacrifices and feasting.[6] At the autumn festival[7] the joy reaches its climax; the festal booths are pitched,[8] the tithes are handed over,[9]

[1]*ḥag hammaṣṣōt*, Ex. 23.15.
[2]The avoidance of leaven is also to be explained in this way: Ex. 12.15, 18 f.; 13.6 f.; 23.15; 34.18; Deut. 16.3 f.; Lev. 23.6.
[3]Lev. 23.10 f.
[4]*ḥag šābū'ōt* or *ḥag bikkūrē qᵉṣīr ḥiṭṭīm*, Ex. 34.22.
[5]Lev. 23.17.
[6]Deut. 16.9 ff.
[7]*ḥag hā'āsīp*, 'vintage festival', Ex. 23.16; 34.22.
[8]Neh. 8.15 ff.; Lev. 23.39 ff.
[9]Deut. 14.22 ff.; 26.12 ff.; Amos 4.4.

the vigils of the feast are kept,[1] and those sacrifices due in fulfilment of the year's vows are offered. In all this the life of the farmer is consecrated as the sphere of God's blessing, whereby in the gifts of Nature the divine landowner allows men to taste of his power and abundance.

This association of the natural with the divine was not to be despised; but it was very easy, under the influence of the Baal religion, for association to become amalgamation of the two spheres, and for men to imagine that they could lay hold on God in the processes of Nature and so become one with him. In this attitude were rooted the orgiastic practices of the agricultural cults; and the tendency was strengthened by the ancient magical belief that by mimicking the natural processes, from the giving of light and water right through to the *hieros gamos*, new vitality could be given to the mysterious forces of life. When, however, these practices invaded the life of Israel, they were rejected on principle, and a tenacious struggle to exclude them was undertaken again and again by the spiritual leaders of the nation, so that the worship of Yahweh was able to preserve its fundamental distinctiveness from the Nature religions. The absence of any cultic occasion devoted to lamenting the dying vegetation, such as played a great part in the Syrian-Babylonian cult of Adonis-Tammuz, is a significant pointer to the way in which Yahwism subordinated Nature to the will of the divine Lord as this was manifested in the history of his people. Where such a lamentation-rite does occur,[2] it is clearly a foreign importation conducted in the actual name of the heathen deity.[3]

The unique character of Yahweh worship is demonstrated, however, not only by what it rejected, but by the new elements which it incorporated into the cycle of Nature festivals. The old agricultural feasts were given a series of new motivations, deriving their content from the historical revelation of the covenant God. This was achieved either by the amalgamation of these feasts with other Yahweh feasts observed at about the same time of year, or by a more external

[1]Especially well attested for later Judaism; cf. Sukka 5.4 in Mishnah: Seder Mo'ed. Isa. 30.29 suggests the same custom in earlier times.

[2]Ezek. 8.14 f.; cf. Isa. 17.10 f.

[3]The acceptance of such a lamentation-rite as an original component of the Passover festival (T. H. Gaster, *Passover, its History and Traditions*, 1949) is nowhere supported by the OT tradition, and can only be reconstructed by analogy from the practice of foreign nations.

association with the memory of some historical event. [1] Thus the Passover attracted to itself the *maṣṣōt* festival, which had originally been quite independent, and associated both feasts with the same theme of the escape from Egypt, thus connecting them with the basic act of redemption of the national God. In the regulations for the feast as we have them this process of amalgamation is already complete; though in the strongly arable economy of Northern Israel the name *ḥag hammaṣṣōt*, [2] and in Judah, which was predominantly settled by herdsmen, the name *ḥag happesaḥ* [3] respectively were used for the composite festival. However, that both feasts for a long time continued to exist side by side, with one or the other being preferred in different parts of the country, is suggested by the fact that in Deuteronomy and P the regulations for the *maṣṣōt* festival were apparently first incorporated as a postscript to the Passover feast. [4]

Just as the unleavened bread was fashioned into a memorial symbol of the escape from Egypt, in the same way the vintage festival was given a historical motivation by being associated with the *Feast of Booths* or *Tabernacles*. [5] It is difficult to see in the latter an old harvest custom, namely that of living in light booths out of doors during the vintage, turned to cultic use. [6] It is much more likely to be a practice of nomad life retained in civilization, [7] thus bringing the custom of living in tents into close relation with the God of the sacred Tent. [8] In all probability, however, this feast of

[1]Whether the general tendency of the Priestly Code to fix these harvest festivals on a particular day of the month should be regarded as an attempt to dissociate them from their basis in the cycle of Nature is doubtful. In view of the great differences in climate between the various areas of Palestine the fixing of a compromise date for the celebrations at the local sanctuaries was inevitable even earlier than the time of the Code.

[2]Ex. 23.15; cf. 13.3 ff.; 34.18: that the customs of Passover were incorporated into this festival seems to be indicated by Ex. 23.18; 34.25.

[3]Deut. 16.1 f., 5 f.; Ex. 34.25.

[4]Deut. 16.3 f., 8; Lev. 23.5 ff.; Num. 28.16 ff.; Ex. 12.15 ff. It may be wondered whether Ex. 34.18 also owes its existence to later redaction.

[5]*ḥag hassukkōt*, Deut. 16.13; Lev. 23.34, 40 ff.; cf. Neh. 8.15 ff.

[6]The Canaanite vintage festival *hillūlīm* (Judg. 9.27) exhibits different customs, carousals in the temple connected with sacrificial meals.

[7]The same kind of thing can be seen today at the feast of the *nebi Rubīn* at the stream of the same name north of Jaffa, where for a few weeks every year, round a shrine which at other times is quite deserted, a giant city of tents springs up. Similar instances are the *nebi Musa* festival in the wilderness of Judaea, and the Christian Marian festival at the Tomb of Mary in the Kidron valley.

[8]Cf. P. Volz, *Das Neujahrsfest Jahwes*, 1912, pp. 20 ff. H. J. Kraus has confirmed this thesis in a new investigation, and brought out its significance for the history of the Israelite cultus (*Gottesdienst in Israel. Studien zur Geschichte des Laubhüttenfestes*,

tents is also an ancient New Year festival,[1] celebrating the advent of Yahweh into the midst of his people, and the blessing on the new year which men looked to him to provide. Although admittedly the evidence for them is late, the nocturnal ceremony of the feast of lights and the ceremonial pouring of water are surely of extreme antiquity, and suggest ancient fertility rites aimed at securing the prayed-for renewal of the forces of Nature.

The heart of the Law, however, is the commemoration of the Wilderness wanderings, with their climax in the conclusion of the Sinai covenant. Form-critical examination of the Sinai pericope (Ex. 19–24), of the narrative of the Joshua covenant (Josh. 24) and of the Book of Deuteronomy has revealed as the underlying pattern of all three the schema of a festival of covenant renewal. The constants in this schema are a historical presentation of the events at Sinai, followed by a recital of the law, a promise of blessing and the conclusion of a covenant; and the purpose was to renew the source and basis of the life of the federation of the Twelve Tribes by means of a regular cultic representation of its origin.[2] This festival, repeated at intervals (originally perhaps only every seven years; cf. Deut. 31.9–13) manifestly constituted the central celebration in the cultus of the Israelite amphictyony. It kept alive the realization that the covenant was rooted in history and bound up with a new ordering of life, and resisted any attempt to dissolve the covenant concept in the timelessness of myth. The association with the Nature-determined harvest festival of Canaanite provenance, which for a long time maintained its separate existence, though celebrated at approximately the same season, thus brought into being the principal feast of the year, to which was given the name *heḥāg*, the feast *par excellence*, and in the process linked the Nature festival firmly to salvation history.

(b) The Feast of Tabernacles underwent a remarkable development in the monarchical period, when it was enriched by new and

---

1954, pp. 25 ff.). The refutation put forward by E. Kutsch (*Das Herbstfest in Israel*, Diss. Mainz, 1955; art. 'Feste und Feiern, II: In Israel', *RGG*³ II, col. 916) is at present unconvincing.

[1] Cf. P. Volz, *op. cit.*; S. Mowinckel, *Psalmenstudien* II, 1922; H. Schmidt, *Die Thronfahrt Jahves*, 1927; J. M. Th. Böhl, *Nieuwjaarsfeest en Koningsdag in Babylon en in Israel*, 1927; W. Caspari, 'Der Herr ist König', *Christentum und Wissenschaft*, 1928, pp. 23 ff.

[2] Cf. A. Alt, *Die Ursprünge des israelitischen Rechts*; G. von Rad, *Das formgeschichtliche Problem des Hexateuchs*, 1938, and *Studies in Deuteronomy*. Also H. J. Kraus, *Gottesdienst in Israel*, 1954.

important action in the form of *the Enthronement festival* of the king.
As II Sam. 6, the *hieros logos* of the sanctuary on Zion, when considered in connection with I Kings 8 and Ps. 132, makes clear,
David's translation of the old amphictyonic sacred object of the
Ark to Jerusalem provided the occasion for a royal Feast of Tabernacles, the theme of which was the close association of the election
of Jerusalem as the city of God with the election of the king from the
House of David. The solemn assembly of the nation, the festal
procession built up round the sacred Ark and the king with his
retinue, the entry into the city of David, the offering of the royal
sacrifice at the sanctuary, the proclamation of the covenant with the
House of David, the election of the holy mount of Jerusalem as God's
dwelling-place, and finally the dispensing of Yahweh's blessing
through the mediation of the king must have constituted the main
dramatic action of the celebration. [1] By means of this festival, which
is certainly to be attributed to David himself, the kingdom was
incorporated into the sacred tradition of the Yahweh amphictyony,
and the yearly proclamation of the monarchy as a gift of the covenant will of Yahweh came to occupy a central position in the cultic
experience of the covenant people.

There can be no doubt that this was also the setting for the
enthronement of each new member of the Davidic dynasty. The
New Year festival, at which the renewal of Yahweh's benediction for
the coming year was experienced in the solemnities of the cult,
supplied the accession of the new monarch and the annual feast of
his enthronement with the most effective of all frameworks. It had
already served the same purpose in Babylonia; and there are good
grounds for assuming that with the addition of the Enthronement
festival to the ancient New Year festival of Israel many elements of
the corresponding festival in the neighbouring heathen empires—
possibly mediated by the tradition of the Canaanite city-monarchy

[1] For the reconstruction of this royal festival on Zion we are indebted to the
penetrating study of H. J. Kraus (*Die Königsherrschaft Gottes im Alten Testament*,
1951). Unfortunately his thesis is needlessly encumbered by his use of II Sam. 7,
which cannot be justified on literary-critical grounds, in that it entails the assertion
that the proclamation of a divine covenant with the Davidic dynasty was part of
David's original festival. In actual fact this particular version, according to which
David was legitimated by the very fact of carrying out his cultic innovation, is by
no means the only one. There are two ancient parallel versions in II Sam. 24, to
which should be added the prophecies quoted in I Sam. 25.30; II Sam. 3.18; 5.2.
It was only after the redaction of the Books of Samuel that Nathan's speech acquired
its favoured position, and became the standard version in the eyes of posterity.

of Jerusalem—also found their way into Israel. Royal psalms such as Pss. 2; 45; 72; 110 present features of the court-style and the king-mythology of the ancient East which could only have percolated into Israel from her heathen environment. The adoption formula, which designates the king as the son of the god (Ps. 2.7), the image of the breaking of the potter's vessel, which seems to derive from Egyptian usage (Ps. 2.9), the practice of addressing the king as *'elōhīm* (Ps. 45.7), the proclamation of the boundaries of his world-wide domain (Ps. 72.8) and the king's taking the place of honour at the right hand of the deity on the throne of God (Ps. 110.1) stand out as some of the especially striking instances. [1] The Temple which Solomon built in the foreign style, with its increasing wealth of cultic apparatus, must also have favoured such an assimilation of the Israelite royal festival to those which had long been established in the countries round about. This does not imply that the whole cultic and mythical basis of the monarchy, as found in the heathen world, was transferred lock, stock and barrel to the Israelite institution. [2] Nevertheless the king was approximated to the deity in a way hitherto unheard-of in Israel, and this brought with it the temptation to use cultic apotheosis to enlarge the royal power and authority and to disarm popular criticism.

It was possible, however, for all this to come about only at the price of suppressing the original content of the Feast of Booths. The procession of the king to the sanctuary, which had first been thought of simply as a dazzling preliminary, pushed its way more and more to the centre of the stage, relegating the rest of the action of the festival to the shadows, in order that all the limelight might fall on the person of the God-elected ruler. This emphasis on the holiness of the king guaranteed by the cultic action certainly fitted in easily with the ideas of the priesthood, which always tended to revolve round

[1] For further details cf. the commentaries.

[2] This assumption, which was first maintained by Mowinckel in order to account for the related features in the ancient Eastern material, was carried to extravagant lengths by English and Scandinavian scholars (cf. the relevant literature, p. 437 n.2 below). It goes, however, far beyond the limits of possible proof, and fails to do justice to the clear subordination of those elements of the king-myth which were taken over to the idea that the king is commissioned by the sovereign covenant God. On the subject of the cry *Yahweh mālāk*, which is used as evidence for the existence of a festival in Israel analogous to the Babylonian Enthronement festival, D. Michel has shown ('Studien zu den Thronbesteigungspsalmen', *Vetus Testamentum* 6, 1956, pp. 40 ff.) that an act of enthronement is precisely what cannot be deduced from this slogan; it signifies rather the acclamation of subjects, possibly even a proclamation of Yahweh's kingly status to the outside world.

the descent of the divine life into the earthly sphere. Furthermore it meant that the sanctuary gained in splendour and importance, so that opposition to the new customs was hardly to be expected from the priesthood of the Temple on Zion. It is clear, however, that the prophetic assessment of this institution was bound to be very different; and this will have to be considered at a later stage.

Was the ceremony of *the enthronement of the god*, which played such an important part in the New Year festival at the sanctuaries of the great empires, also inseparably associated in Israel with this enthronement of the king? The well-attested fact that the procession at the royal festival on Zion included a procession of the sacred Ark, the throne of the invisible God, certainly suggests a simultaneous enthronement of Yahweh, [1] and inclines one to give an affirmative answer to this question. This is all the more likely in view of the fact that the evidence of the Babylonian New Year festival and of the Egyptian Enthronement festival, [2] with which in the opinion of many scholars the cultic practices presupposed by the Ugaritic texts are in full agreement, [3] seems to require an analogous interpretation of the so-called 'Enthronement' psalms. [4] Nevertheless this thesis on the one hand takes too little account of the material actually to be derived from the Old Testament itself, and on the other too greatly exaggerates the unity to be found in the various cultic acts as described in the ancient Eastern evidence, [5] for it to be accepted as a definitive solution of the question.

One of the principal items of evidence to be considered is the *hieros logos* of the festival recorded in II Sam. 6 and I Kings 8, and

[1]H. J. Kraus takes too little account of this in what is otherwise a most useful critique (*Gottesdienst in Israel*). The procession of the Ark indubitably does suggest 'a *point de départ* for affirming the existence of a festival at which Yahweh was enthroned' (*op. cit.*, p. 101).

[2]Cf. H. Zimmern, *Das babylonische Neujahrsfest*, 1926; K. Sethe, *Dramatische Texte zu altägyptischen Mysterienspielen*, vol. II: *Der dramatische Ramesseumpapyrus, ein Spiel zur Thronbesteigung des Königs*, 1928. Also, Jean de Savignac, 'Essai d'interprétation du Psaume CX à l'aide de la littérature égyptienne' (*OTS* 9, 1951, pp. 107 ff.).

[3]Notably the work of I. Engnell (*Studies in Divine Kingship in the Ancient Near East*, 1945) has attempted to interpret the texts on these lines.

[4]The passages in question are principally Pss. 24.6 ff.; 47; 93; 96 f.; 99. The claim that these belonged to this festival was first advanced by S. Mowinckel in his standard work, *Das Thronbesteigungsfest Jahves, Psalmenstudien* II, 1922. A defence of his thesis against various objections can be found in the essay, *Zum israelitischen Neujahrsfest und zur Deutung der Thronbesteigungspsalmen*, 1952.

[5]Cf. H. Frankfort, *The Problem of Similarity in Ancient Near Eastern Religions*, 1951, and *Kingship and the Gods*, 1948.

the cultic presentation of this, as it may be at any rate partly preserved in Pss. 132 and 24.7–9. These texts suggest that Yahweh's
procession to the throne during the royal festival on Zion is aimed
not at the enthronement of the God, but at the election of Zion and
the establishing of the king. It is the divine entry in state, the visitation of the people by their God, which is represented on this occasion
and experienced as a reality in the cult. But this renewed assumption
of the supreme lordship by Yahweh was actualized in the cult in the
central actions of the associated Feast of Booths, as these have been
described above, and therefore did not require to be presented in
the mythological forms of the ancient East, the strong connection of
which with the act of creation by the king-God before the dawn of
history and with the mystery of death and resurrection was foreign
to the thought of pre-exilic Israel.

A change seems to have set in, when the break-up of the kingdom
deprived the royal festival on Zion of its principal importance;
while, during the Exile, the kingship of Yahweh found its most
eloquent exponent in Deutero-Isaiah. In the liberation and restoration of Israel, and in the redemption of the Gentiles that went with
it, the prophet saw the God of Israel, who hitherto had withdrawn
himself from his people in his anger, entering anew and in reality
upon his supreme dominion; and in this certainty that a turning-
point in history was imminent he summoned the nation to the singing
of a new song(42.10) that should spread abroad the gospel of God
the King. To this end he made use of many of the forms of the
Babylonian festival of Marduk the King, though transposing them
in terms of his own eschatological expectation. Thus, for example,
he adopted the imagery of the triumphal procession of the God
along the richly decorated processional way, and the traditional cry
of the festival, which with the substitution of Yahweh for Marduk
now ran: 'Yahweh is become King!' (52.7–10). The exaggerated
expectations of salvation, which as a result of this preaching dominated the post-exilic community, had in their turn to be provided
with cultic expression. Consequently at the principal Yahweh
festival God was hailed as King on his return in triumph to Zion,
and the setting-up of his world-wide dominion was presented in the
cultic solemnities as already a reality. The so-called 'Enthronement'
psalms, 47; 93; 96 f.; 99, may be regarded as part of the liturgical
accompaniment to this festival. Their use substituted the enthronement of the heavenly King for that of the earthly monarch and

brought about a decisive change in what had hitherto been the character of the feast. The *outward* sign of this change is to be found in the moving of the date of the festival to the first day of the seventh month, Tishri, thus ensuring that even after the transition to the use of the Babylonian calendar, which placed the beginning of the year in the spring, this season was retained for the religious celebration of the New Year and, indeed, invested with new splendour as a result of the feast of Yahweh's enthronement. [1] The *inward* transformation of the festival is symbolized by the attribution to the king-God of the cosmic functions of universal Creator, Judge and Consummator. These now took their rightful place in the cultic celebration and firmly established the universalism of the prophets in the life of the congregation, yet without the essentially historical reference of the attributions being questioned for a moment. In this way the new Enthronement festival, despite considerable dependence on the corresponding Babylonian feast, preserved its unique character and left no room for the corruption of its content by unrestricted mythologizing.

How long the festival continued in this form it is impossible to say. It is not unlikely that the promulgation of the Law by Ezra in 444 may have changed its character in the direction of a glorification of the Law and a repression of the eschatological expectation, a change which would be consonant with the victory of the Priestly interpretation of the Yahweh covenant in the Jewish community. [2] A strong note of penitence even seems to have taken the place of the originally joyous atmosphere, [3] and to have made the festival a kind of preparation for the great Day of Atonement. The nucleus of the celebrations, however, the old Feast of Booths, together with its traditional date in the middle of the month, retained the spirit of jubilation and enthusiasm proper to it in virtue of its significance as a feast of covenant renewal.

The *Feast of Weeks* was linked up with the history of the nation at a much later date than the other agricultural festivals; and it is not until roughly A.D. 100 that we have evidence of its interpretation as a commemoration of the giving of the Law on Sinai.

[1] If Neh. 8.2 and the tradition of the Mishnah are taken into account, this view, which is also that of H. J. Kraus (*Gottesdienst in Israel*, p. 102), would seem to be correct, as against that of N. H. Snaith (*The Jewish New Year Festival: its Origins and Development*, 1947, p. 206).
[2] Cf. H. J. Kraus, *op. cit.*, p. 108.
[3] Cf. N. H. Snaith, *op. cit.*, p. 205.

This linking-up of the life of Nature with the events of history was one factor which gave new meaning to the agricultural feasts; but at the same time their primitive associations with the belief in spirits and in 'power', which were still very much a vital part of many of the festivals, were also given a new interpretation with their incorporation into the religion of Yahweh, and this checked any continuing active influence which they might have had on the shaping of the feasts. This is especially true of the *Passover*, [1] the only great festival to be explicitly mentioned in the stories of the Exodus. The blood-ritual characteristic of this festival, its close connection with the spring full moon, its sacrificial animal, the lamb, its character as a family celebration, which it managed to preserve in the teeth of the great Temple feasts, [2] all make it probable that the ultimate origins of the festival are to be found in an ancient ritual of the Hebrew herdsmen even before the time of Moses. The primary objects of this ritual would have been expiation and protection from evil spirits; the offering of the firstborn of the herds may also have been associated with this at an early stage. [3] The festival may have been adopted into the religion of Yahweh in the time of Moses, when the name, the original meaning of which can hardly be established with any certainty, [4] came to be referred to the forbearance of Yahweh in 'passing over' the Israelites, when he visited the Egyptians to afflict them. [5] In this way the festival became an effective proclamation of the redeeming grace of the covenant God, teaching men to venerate in mingled joy and awe both Yahweh's fundamental act of deliverance and his terrifying judgment. [6]

[1] *ḥag happesaḥ*, Ex. 34.25.
[2] The attempt of the Deuteronomic law to turn the feast of Passover into a public Temple festival (Deut. 16.1 f., 5 ff.; cf. II Kings 23.21 ff.) failed in its object, as even P retains the old usage (Ex. 12.3–14). In the post-exilic period, however, it was the normal practice to slay the Passover lambs in the Temple court (II Chron. 30.17; 35.5 ff., 11).
[3] Cf. the detailed account of similar rituals among other peoples in P. Volz, *Die biblischen Altertümer*, 1914, p. 102.
[4] *psḥ* is sometimes explained in terms of the 'passage' of the full moon through the zenith of its orbit, and sometimes in terms of a cultic 'limping' dance.
[5] Ex. 12.21–27 (J); Ex. 12.1, 3–14 (P).
[6] If the theory of Elhorst ('Die deuteronomischen Jahresfeste', *ZAW* 42, 1924, pp. 136 ff.) that originally the Passover was the only annual festival mentioned in Deuteronomy, is correct, this would indicate the high religious value set on this festival by the puritan reformers. Cf. further H. Guthe, 'Das Passahfest nach Dtn 16', *Baudissin-Festschrift*, 1918, pp. 217 ff., and 'Zum Passah der jüdischen Religionsgemeinde', *Theologische Studien und Kritiken* 96, 1925, pp. 144 ff.; N. M. Nicolsky, 'Pascha im Kult des jerusalemischen Tempels', *ZAW* 45, 1927, pp. 171 ff., 241 ff.

(c) Just as the Passover was the solemn spring festival of expiation, so in the autumn, which in ancient times marked the beginning of the year, came *the great Day of Atonement*. [1] An analysis of the ordinances of the feast [2] reveals a fusion of various rituals: these comprise an ancient ceremony of expiation connected with the sacred Tent, by which the ritual transgressions of the congregation were effaced and the focus of which was the rite of the scapegoat for Azazel, [3] and also an expiatory action before the Ark and the altar, involving the multiple sprinkling of blood. [4] Both go back to very early times and are alike in describing ceremonies strictly confined to the priesthood—a feature which is quite sufficient to explain the silence of the older codes on the subject of this festival. [5] The Priestly Code, in accordance with its practice of amalgamating the traditions of the Tent and of the Ark, now combined both these ancient elements; and also added an incense ritual. [6] The rich and complex act of atonement thus created was now given special significance by making the congregation active participants, [7] with the result that the Day of Atonement now became the great day of repentance and the medium through which the whole nation expressed its need of reconciliation, the tremendous consummation of that concept of atonement which dominated the whole sacrificial law. [8] It is extremely significant for any study of the laws relating to festivals in

[1]Lev. 16. *yōm hakkippūrīm*, Lev. 23.27; 25.9.

[2]Cf. Landersdorfer, *Studien zum bibl. Versöhnungstag*, 1924; M. Löhr, *Das Ritual von Lev. 16*, 1925; G. von Rad, *Die Priesterschrift im Hexateuch*, 1934, pp. 85 ff.; R. Rendtorff, *Die Gesetze in der Priesterschrift*, 1954, pp. 59 ff.

[3]According to Löhr, contained in Lev. 16.2–10, 21, 23 f., 26.

[4]Contained in Lev. 16.11b, 14a, 15a, 16, 17a, 18 f.

[5]The dating on the tenth day of the seventh month, that is to say, five days before the autumn full moon, with which the year originally began (Lev. 16.29; 23.27 ff.), fits in with the fact that, when the reckoning is in lunar months, five intercalary days have to be inserted into the solar year. The transference of the New Year to the first day of the seventh month (Lev. 23.24 ff.; Num. 29.1 ff.; Ezek. 45.18–20) is certainly connected with the elimination of the old New Year festival in favour of the autumn festival. Cf. Benzinger, *Hebräische Archäologie*[3], 1927, p. 386 n. 4.

[6]Lev. 16.12 f.

[7]Lev. 16.29 ff.

[8]Whether this had already come about before the Exile, or whether it only happened as a result of the post-exilic additions to the Priestly Code, it is hard to say. The usual argument adduced to prove post-Ezranic provenance, namely that the account in Neh. 9.1 ff., which is dealing with the period from the first to the fifteenth day of Tishri, makes no mention of a Day of Atonement, is not absolutely decisive: cf. G. Hölscher, *Geschichte der isr.-jüd. Religion*, 1922, p. 146 n. 5; E. König, *Theologie des AT*, p. 267.

the Old Testament that the Day of Atonement should have been brought out of its isolation as a purely priestly ceremony in this way. The majority of the religions of the great civilizations were concerned to develop mystery rites, mediating a special way of redemption not available to the mass of mankind and conferring on the central object of the religion the character of an impenetrable secret. So little is this tendency observable in Israel, that on the contrary even rites which might seem to have been specifically designed for such a purpose are deliberately incorporated into the cultic activity of the whole congregation and brought into the broad daylight of public participation. It is also in keeping with this concern that everything should be done openly, that there is no trace at any point of particularist attempts to confine the rite to certain age-groups or guilds. The congregation of Yahweh includes the family and all its members; neither age nor sex bestow any special privileges. Even the woman is under obligation to take part in the cultus [1] and is made equally responsible with the man for maintaining its purity. [2] Not until the development of the stricter observance of later Judaism do we find a partial exclusion of women. [3]

(d) The tendencies of the religion of Yahweh in the matter of the cult can be seen most clearly in the case of the Day of Yahweh *par excellence*, the *Sabbath*. [4] One has only to compare it with the Baby-

[1]In the case of the Passover, Ex. 12.3 f.; of the Sabbath, II Kings 4.22 f.; Ex. 20.9 f.; 34.21; of the autumn festival, I Sam. 1.3 ff.; Deut. 16.14; with reference to other occasions, Deut. 14.26; 15.20; 16.11.

[2]Deut. 13.7; 17.2, 5; 29.17; Lev. 20.27; II Chron. 15.13; Josh. 8.35; Neh. 8.2 f. Cf. further M. Löhr, *Die Stellung des Weibes zu Jahvereligion und Kult*, 1908, pp. 42 ff.

[3]The fact that according to ancient custom the woman was not able to carry out any sacrificial rites seems to be due partly to the position of the paterfamilias and partly to the more frequent ritual uncleanness of the woman. The dominance of men in the cultic affairs of the congregation (Ex. 23.17; 34.23; Deut. 16.16) is similarly connected with the position of the heads of families as the normal representatives of their houses. Women, however, still had their place in worship at the sanctuary and as singers even in the Judaistic period (Ex. 38.8; I Sam. 2.22; Neh. 7.67; Ezra 2.65: cf. Ex. 15.20). Cf. further, M. Löhr, *op. cit.*, pp. 49 ff.

[4]Various reasons have been advanced for refusing to accept the Sabbath as belonging to the oldest regulations of Yahweh worship. First, it has been objected that a day of rest is only conceivable in an agricultural setting (so Stade, *Biblische Theologie*, p. 177, *et al.*). Secondly, others have thought that it was originally a day of the full moon (a view particularly associated with Meinhold, *Sabbath und Woche im AT*, 1905; 'Die Entstehung des Sabbaths' *ZAW* 29, 1909, pp. 81 ff.). Thirdly, the existence of a moon-day called *šapattu* or *šabattu* in Babylonia has suggested to others, that Israel could only have acquired the Sabbath at the earliest via the Canaanites after the Occupation (so Friedrich Delitzsch, *Babel und Bibel*[5], 1905, p. 65; *Die grosse Täuschung* I, 1920, pp. 99 f.; Eissfeldt, 'Feste und Feiern in

lonian days of the moon, which were regarded as days of ill omen, for its distinctive character to become at once apparent. For, however likely it may be that it was originally connected with the phases of the moon, it was at some stage dissociated from them, as is shown by the fact that the seven-day week marked out by it was maintained throughout the year without reference to the lunar month. The same fact proves conclusively that the Sabbath had become quite independent of the practice of carefully selecting particular days, which was so closely bound up with the heathen worship of the heavenly bodies; the way to a belief in sacred days and days of ill omen, which bulks so large in the heathen festi-

Israel', *RGG*[2] II, col. 553). In reply, it has been pointed out with justification, that even in the life of the herdsman and wandering shepherd there are a number of tasks which can be omitted on particular days (cf. F. Buhl, 'Gottesdienstliche Zeiten im AT', *HRE* VII, p. 23; R. Kittel, *Geschichte des Volkes Israel*[5, 6] I, 1923, pp. 446 f.) quite apart from the fact that Israel was never a purely nomadic people. The interpretation of the Sabbath as a day of the full moon runs into insuperable difficulties, because it offers no satisfactory explanation either of the changeover from being a day of the full moon to being the seventh day or of the ancient evidence testifying to the particular importance of the seventh day (cf. esp. K. Budde, 'Sabbath und Woche', *Die Christliche Welt* 43, 1929, pp. 202 ff., 265 ff.; also *ZAW* 48, 1930, pp. 121 ff., 138 ff.). There may possibly be a connection with the Babylonian *šapattu*, but it is by no means clear; for apart from the one point of a general correspondence to the phases of the moon, which is anyway much looser in the case of the Israelite seventh day than in that of the Babylonian *šapattu*, detailed comparison reveals fundamental differences. First, it is not certain whether the name *šapattu* was applied to all the appointed days of the moon, since it is only attested for the fifteenth day of the month. In any case, the moon festival-days observed on fixed days of the month (the first, seventh, fifteenth and twenty-eighth) were something quite different from the Israelite sabbath, which was the last day of a seven-day week running uninterruptedly right through the year, without reference to the beginning of each month. Finally, in Babylonia the 'seventh' days (i.e., the seventh, fourteenth, nineteenth, twenty-first and twenty-eighth of the month) had the character of a *dies nefastus* (Bab. *ûmu limnu*) on which special care had to be taken, the king in particular having to submit to all kinds of precautionary measures (e.g., not to mount his chariot, not to offer sacrifice, etc.). Of a general intermission of work there is no mention whatsoever. Only on the fifteenth day was work suspended in Babylonia; and far from this being due to the joyful, festal character of the day, it was obviously actuated by quite different motives, namely that on this particular day there was no luck to be had, and it was necessary to pacify the gods (whence the name *ûm nuḫ libbi*: 'day of pacification of the heart') and to appease their anger by a kind of day of penitence and prayer. Even therefore if the name Sabbath is not Israelite, the thing which it denotes is only to be found in Israel. Translations of the Babylonian inscriptions relating to the seventh days are given in Zimmern, *Die Keilinschriften und das AT*[3], 1903, p. 593; Hehn, *Siebenzahl und Sabbat*, 1907, p. 106; Delitzsch, *Babel und Bibel*[5], p. 64; *AOT*, p. 329; B. Landsberger, *Der kultische Kalender der Babylonier und Assyrer*, 1915, p. 120.

vals,[1] is effectively blocked. This is finally made quite explicit, when the Sabbath is extolled as the will of the sovereign Creator God at the foundation of the world;[2] and from thenceforward the consecration of this day to Yahweh is combined with the pious act of abstaining from work.[3] The keeping holy of the seventh day forms an emphatic reminder that God is the Lord of Time, and that no business, however pressing, must be allowed to keep men from regularly seeking his fellowship; but the joyful character of the day of rest also brings home to the worshipper that his God is a kindly Master, who does not lay on men a yoke too heavy to bear.[4] This aspect of the Sabbath may not perhaps at first have been the most prominent, but it came to be felt with increasing force;[5] indeed, the fact that this day was explained in terms of the rest of God himself after the work of Creation, proves that it was regarded as a source of blessing of universal significance, and bears witness to the enthusiasm with which the pious Israelite rejoiced in this day of rest as an act of devotion. It was not until in later Judaism a religion of harsh observances had replaced the religion of the Old Testament that the Sabbath changed from a blessing to a burdensome duty.

IV. *Sacred Actions*

(*a*) *Consecration and Purity Rites:* There is a whole field of religious ritual common to Israel and every other religion of the ancient world, which emerges with special clarity. The Old Testament

[1]Typical examples are the important role of unlucky days in the Babylonian omen-literature, the fixing of Greek agricultural festivals on the last day of the waxing moon, and the dating of similar feasts in ancient Rome as far as possible on an odd day of the month.

[2]Ex. 20.11; Gen. 2.2 f.

[3]Even as early as Amos 8.4 f.; II Kings 4.23; Ex. 23.12; 34.21. That from the time of the Exile onward the Sabbath should have acquired importance as a sign by which the pious Jew was known in a heathen environment is only natural; this certainly cannot be cited as evidence against its early introduction (cf. Isa. 56.2 ff.; Ezek. 20.12 ff.; Neh. 13.15 ff.).

[4]Cf. the injunction that the day of rest shall be observed even at the busiest time of the year, Ex. 34.21; according to Isa. 1.13 it was the practice to visit the Temple on this day, and it was also customary to choose it for making enquiries of a man of God, II Kings 4.23. Because the Sabbath rest had this far-reaching effect on daily life, it is perfectly understandable that this day and no other should have been included in the basic law of the Decalogue.

[5]Especially emphasized in Deuteronomy (5.12 ff., cf. Ex. 23.12) but already known to Hosea (2.13), the Sabbath joy is later mentioned in Isa. 58.13. For the importance of the Sabbath in Israelite thought, cf. E. Jenni, *Die theologische Begründung des Sabbatgebotes im Alten Testament* (Theologische Studien, ed. K. Barth, No. 46), 1956.

contains a great mass of prescriptions on the subject of cleanness and uncleanness, of rites for the recovery of cleanness once lost or for acquiring special holiness. The comparative study of religion has supplied us with an overwhelming quantity of material, which has been successfully used to throw light on the ultimate origins of such customs in primitive tabu-beliefs. [1] But in this context more than in any other it is necessary to keep in mind the proverb, 'The same thing done by two different people is not the same thing.' The ultimate task of the comparative study of religion must be to establish what the religion of Yahweh made of the material which it inherited.

(1) It is possible to mention a number of individual commandments which have undergone no noticeable alteration or change of meaning as a result of their adoption by the Yahweh religion, in particular, fertility rites arising from the old beliefs in 'power', such as the prohibition against seething the kid in its mother's milk, and so on. [2] It should not be forgotten, however, that in the majority of cases a special significance is given to these customs, namely their value as ammunition for the exclusivist Yahweh-worshippers in their fight against all beliefs associated with 'power' or spirits. Everything which has to do with alien gods or their cultus is condemned as unclean, and debars from the cult of Yahweh; and the fact that this proscription is backed by the whole weight of the ancient tabu-belief makes the dividing-line clear and absolute. Foreign land and foreign food are therefore unclean. [3] The use of many animals for food is forbidden for the reason that they figure in alien cults or magic rites; such are the pig, which was an ancient Canaanite domestic and sacrificial animal, and mice, serpents and hares, which were regarded in magical belief as especially effective media of

[1]Cf. especially J. Döller, Die Reinheits- und Speisegesetze des AT in religionsgeschichtlicher Beleuchtung, 1917.

[2]Ex. 34.26; 23.19; Deut. 14.21. The underlying idea is to avoid mingling the life of the mother with that of her young, since this would result in destroying the beneficent effects of the life-force. Similar presuppositions explain the prohibitions of Lev. 19.19; 22.28; Deut. 22.6 f., 9–11. Cf. A. Wendel, Das Opfer in der altisraelitischen Religion, 1927, p. 172. A. Bertholet ('Über den Ursprung des Totemismus', Festgabe für J. Kaften, 1920, p. 12) offers a different explanation of the prohibition against sowing a field with two kinds of seed; the purpose is to prevent a superstitious practice which sought by sowing heterogeneous things to interest several different demonic powers in the one field and so to ensure good growth. This would be a matter of strengthening the 'power' by the addition of a variety of potent elements.

[3]Amos 7.17; Ezek. 4.13; Hos. 9.3.

demonic power.[1] Again, it is well known that the processes of the sexual life and the practices connected with the dead were a happy hunting-ground for magical and spiritist beliefs, so that the refusal of the Yahweh religion to have anything to do with such customs is perfectly understandable.[2] The close association of the Canaanite deities with generation and birth and of the Egyptian with the cult of the dead may have helped to intensify these regulations; and similar motives may have operated in the prohibition of mutilation and tattooing.[3] The outspoken repugnance to the consumption of blood[4] is not simply to be explained by horror at the idea of absorbing an alien kind of life, for the latter attitude is to be found elsewhere side by side with acceptance of the practice of consuming the blood; rather is it connected with the rejection of heathen customs which made the drinking of blood a part of the cult of certain animals or a means of inducing ecstatic prophecy or of orgiastic communion with the deity.[5]

Nevertheless it would be wrong to regard this as the sole basis of the purity regulations in the religion of Yahweh. Thus, for example, the defiling effect of leprosy[6] derives not so much from any association with evil spirits[7] as from the appalling consequences of the disease. Because this was feared as contagious, it led to the exclusion of the afflicted person from human society and branded him as someone smitten by the wrath of God.[8] It is obvious that anyone cut off in this way from the congregation of Yahweh was bound to

[1]Cf. the lists of clean and unclean animals, Lev. 11.1 ff.; Deut. 14.3–21; also Gen. 7.2. Lack of information prevents us in many cases from knowing exactly why a particular animal was prohibited. The effect of later systematization on the lists has naturally been to enlarge the class of forbidden animals. On this point cf. R. de Vaux, 'Les sacrifices de porcs en Palestine et dans l'ancien Orient' in *Eissfeldt Festschrift*, 1958, pp. 250 ff. On the part played by asses, dogs, snakes, mice and beetles in Babylonian religion and superstition cf. M. Jastrow, *Die Religion Babyloniens und Assyriens* II, 1912, pp. 775 ff.

[2]Lev. 12; 15; 21.1–5; Num. 19.11 ff.; I Sam. 21.5; 20.26 give us some idea of the antiquity of these regulations. That death was regarded as defiling because it was a consequence of the Fall (so e.g. E. König, *Theologie*, p. 272) cannot be proved from the OT.

[3]Deut. 23.2; 14.1; Lev. 19.27 f.; 21.5; cf. Deut. 22.5.

[4]Gen. 9.4; I Sam. 14.32 ff.; Lev. 19.26.

[5]Cf. Chantepie de la Saussaye, *Lehrbuch der Religionsgeschichte*[4], 1925, I, pp. 37, 54; II, p. 514. Cf. also the dismembering and eating of living animals as found in certain local practices in Islam; cf. K. Budde, *Die altisraelitische Religion*[3], 1912, p. 136, n. 26, and W. R. Smith, *The Religion of the Semites*[3], 1927, pp. 338 f.

[6]Lev. 13 f.

[7]So Benzinger, *Archäologie*[3], p. 397.

[8]Hence the expression *nega'*, 'blow', for leprosy; Lev. 13.2 f., *et al.*

be considered unclean. Moreover, men's natural preference for the complete and normal and their revulsion from its opposite should not be left out of account. Just as no animal can be accepted for sacrifice, if it is in any way defective, so no one called to the office of a priest must exhibit any bodily blemish.[1] Similarly in many cases disgust at the appearance and habits of certain animals will have led to their rejection as unclean.

The great variety of means of purification mentioned in the Law was needed in order to cope with the large number of possible occasions of defilement. In slight cases it was sufficient to wash with pure water,[2] but for more serious defilement special methods of purification were provided, for use under the supervision of the priest,[3] among which may be included anointing with oil.[4]

(2) Because in Israel all these diverse conceptions of purity and rites of purification are unified by their common relation to Yahweh and to the establishment of a holy people, they acquire a much deeper ideal significance than they possessed in isolation, when they concerned many different deities or were still completely dominated by the belief in demons. The strong emphasis on the demands of the divine will ensures that the older motives of purely mechanical removal of objective impurity are bound to recede in importance; and their place in the forefront of men's minds is taken by the idea of establishing a way of life pleasing to God with the help of those means provided by God himself. Hence what is recognized as being the most valuable effect of *tabu*-regulations in all religions, namely that they help men to grasp the idea of an absolute standard,[5] is brought about in Israel on a higher plane. For here the norm resides in the all-controlling concept of Yahweh himself and has as its goal the setting up of a personal relationship with God.[6] By contrast in other religions, owing to the heterogeneous and haphazard character of the *tabu* relations and the lack of any unified controlling concept, this development is constantly being jeopardized.

[1]Lev. 21.17 ff.
[2]Lev. 11.24 f., 28, 32, 40; 15.5 ff., 16–18, 21 f.
[3]Lev. 14.4, 49; Num. 19.6.
[4]Lev. 14.17 f.
[5]Cf. esp. W. Hauer, *Die Religionen* I, 1923, pp. 151 ff.
[6]This finds expression also in the association of purificatory ceremonies with particular sacrifices; thus the purification of lepers is accompanied by guilt, sin and burnt offerings (Lev. 14.10 ff.), of a Nazirite by guilt and sin offerings (Num. 6.9 ff.), and that of a woman after childbirth by burnt and sin offerings (Lev. 12.6 ff.).

Hence even the increasing rationalization of life which inevitably accompanies the rise of any civilization was unable to uproot or enfeeble the obligatory nature of these commandments in Israel, but resulted only in a transformation of their original meaning. Hand in hand therefore with the sporadic systematizing attempts [1] to substitute for the old motives, which have manifestly fallen into oblivion, some sort of classification on rational principles, we find a close association between Levitical purity and moral behaviour, conceived as a means of bringing the congregation into a state pleasing to God. Both in the Deuteronomic and Priestly law [2] ritual purity frequently appears as a symbol and outward expression of moral perfection. The usage of the word qadoš makes this especially clear. Not only is the meaning of the division between sacred and profane clarified, in that the decisive element in the concept of holiness is shown to be that of belonging to God—not that of separation, which is secondary [3]—but holiness itself, from being a relational concept, becomes a condition, a personal quality. The man who belongs to God must possess a particular kind of nature, which by comprising at once outward and inward, ritual and moral purity will correspond to the nature of the holy God. [4]

In the same way the organization of the theocracy in the latter part of the Book of Ezekiel is based on the assumption of a nation converted by Yahweh and taken into a new covenant; and many of the Psalms also make use of ritual actions in a purely metaphorical manner as symbols of interior processes. [5] This close involvement of outward and inward, in virtue of which the performance of the ritual testifies to an inner detachment from all conduct opposed to the divine will, makes of the ceremonial law a form enabling the nation both to live and to be seen to live in holiness. It is inseparable from the nation's spiritual stature; it grows up with it and gives it a protective husk, which even after the collapse of the state and nation as such makes it capable of independent existence within a heathen environment.

[1] E.g., Deut. 14.3–21; Lev. 11.1–23.
[2] Especially in the so-called Holiness Code, Lev. 17–26. In Deuteronomy cf. 21.6, where hand-washing has become such a symbol.
[3] Num. 16.5: 'In the morning will Yahweh make known who is his, and who (therefore) is holy.' The priests are here called holy, because they stand in an especially close relationship to God.
[4] Cf. Lev. 19.2: 'Ye shall be holy, for I, Yahweh your God, am holy,' and the whole Holiness Code, Lev. 17–26.
[5] Ps. 51.9, the sprinkling with hyssop and the sacred washing: Ps. 141.2, the offering of incense and the evening sacrifice.

(3) This is particularly noticeable in the case of the rite of *circumcision*. This puberty rite, which is found all over the world as an act whereby the young husband is consecrated and the fertility of the marriage guaranteed, [1] was in Israel at an early stage transferred to the time of infancy [2]—a feature which may possibly be connected with the abolition of child sacrifice. [3] In any case the rite had a religious significance from the very first and was understood as an act of dedication witnessing to the fact that the person belonged to the people of Yahweh, [4] even though it was not an official practice of the cult. This symbolic significance was recognized in Judah by the seventh century. [5] It remained for the Priestly legislation to give the private act of dedication the status of an official symbol of the covenant, and so to bestow upon it a new meaning within the framework of the covenant system. [6] As the terms 'uncircumcised' and

[1] The analogous descriptions and practices regulating the stage at which the produce of the fruit tree may first be enjoyed are decisive on this point. The tree must remain three years 'uncut' or 'uncircumcised', i.e., ungathered; in the fourth year the fruit is brought to Yahweh as a thank-offering—the tree being as it were circumcised; in the fifth year the fruit can be enjoyed (Lev. 19.23 f.). Just as the fruitfulness of the field must be bought from the divine owner, so a man at his wedding so to speak presents an offering to the Lord of human fruitfulness in the form of circumcision, the blood of which has atoning power. For the distribution and meaning of the custom, cf. A. E. Jensen, *Beschneidung und Reifezeremonien bei den Naturvölkern*, 1933.

[2] The relevant narrative (Ex. 4.24–26) seeks to explain the transference of circumcision from the husband to the child, i.e. the displacement of adult circumcision by child circumcision, by the story of Zipporah's action. But the change can be dated much earlier; it is possible that various usages were in competition in Mosaic Israel. Gen. 34.22 ff. and 17.10 ff. point to circumcision in pre-Mosaic times; and in the latter passage the fact that the practice was common to Arabs, Edomites, Moabites and Ammonites as well is explained by their all being descendants of Abraham. On Ex. 4.24 ff. cf. J. Hehn, 'Der "Blutsbräutigam"', *ZAW* 50, 1932, pp. 1 ff.; H. Junker, 'Der Blutbräutigam', *Alttest. Studien F. Nötscher gewidmet*, 1950.

[3] So Kuenen, *De Godsdienst van Israel* I, p. 238. The fixing of circumcision on the eighth day after birth (Lev. 12.3) is markedly divergent from Egyptian and Arab practice, and when taken in conjunction with Ex. 22.28 points very strongly to such a connection.

[4] Cf. Josh. 5.2 ff. and the use of '*ārēl*, 'uncircumcised', as a term of abuse for the Philistines (Judg. 14.3; 15.18; I Sam. 17.26 etc.). Jer. 4.4; 9.24 f. also throw light on the religious value of circumcision.

[5] Jer. 4.4; 9.24 f.; 6.10; Deut. 10.16; 30.6; Lev. 26.41; Ex. 6.12.

[6] Gen. 17. The older substratum of the present version, which can be detected in vv. 1–6, 9–11a, 14, 16b, 22 and 26, shows that this idea is of great antiquity: cf. K. Steuernagel, 'Bemerkungen zu Gen. 17', *Beiträge zur alttest. Wissenschaft K. Budde überreicht*, 1920, pp. 172 ff. The special emphasis laid on the rite is best understood not in the context of the Exile, but much earlier, in the seventh century, as a reaction against the flooding of Judah with Assyrian and Babylonian religious customs—especially since circumcision was not normally practised in Mesopotamia.

'unclean' became more and more closely identified,[1] so circumcision came to signify the removal of uncleanness, and at the same time adoption into the community of the people of God with the obligation of keeping its sacred statutes. In this way a practice of originally only limited importance became a symbol of the purified people of God and summed up in itself all the fundamental convictions of Israel's election.

(4) By contrast, one dedicatory rite, which had at first been of the very greatest importance, gradually became meaningless, namely, *the custom of the ban in war.* The annihilation of the enemy, together with his women and children, his cattle and his possessions—a practice known to have obtained among other peoples[2]—was also a traditional custom in Israel. It cannot, however, be explained either as a sacrificial or as an oblatory act.[3] It is part of the discipline laid on the warrior, by which he renounces something in thanksgiving to the deity present in the camp. This means that the enemy is regarded as holy or dedicated, and so no longer available for human possession;[4] the renunciation is irrevocable. There can be no doubt that the strict form of the ban[5] must have done away with the waging of war simply from lust of conquest or booty, seeing that even the victor might be visited with the ban, if guilty of transgressing it[6]—a punishment which did in fact befall Yahweh's people themselves.[7]

The introduction of this custom of war into the worship of Yahweh was linked with the Mosaic demand for unqualified devotion to the

[1]Isa. 52.1; Ezek. 44.7.
[2]The most notable instance is that of the Stele of Mesa, King of Moab (*AOT*, pp. 440 ff.; *ANET*, pp. 320 f.) but the custom is also found among Arabs, Indians and Germanic tribes: cf. F. Schwally, *Semitische Kriegsaltertümer* I, 1901, pp. 35 ff.
[3]This interpretation is ruled out by the fact that the human beings are killed, not burnt, and the booty not consecrated, but burnt or utterly destroyed. That the ban was a solemn vow does not suggest that it was understood as a sacrifice, only that it was a duty of special importance; moreover, it was not required on every occasion when war was waged. The occasional description of the ban as *kālil*, whole burnt offering (Deut. 13.17), is to be understood metaphorically.
[4]In this respect *heḥ'rim* is equivalent in meaning to *hiqdīš*; cf. Jer. 12.3. J. Pedersen sees one of the sources of this custom in the fear of alien spiritual power, which permeates the persons and possessions of the enemy and can only be made harmless by consecration to Yahweh (*Israel, its Life and Culture*, III–IV, 1940, pp. 27 ff.).
[5]Cf. e.g., Josh. 6.17 ff.; 8.24–26, 28; Judg. 20.48; 21.10 ff.; I Sam. 15; 22.11 ff.; Deut. 13.16 f.; 20.16 ff.; possibly also II Kings 6.21 and II Chron. 25.12 f.
[6]Cf. Josh. 7.1 ff.
[7]Judg. 20.48; 21.10 ff.

cause of God. The fact that it was the wrath of Yahweh himself raging in the slaughter of battle made even the giving up of the enemy to annihilation an act of worship. It is significant, however, that the ideas of judgment and requital are also introduced. It is because the Canaanites are ripe for judgment [1] and the Amalekites are cruel plunderers, [2] or because the idolatry of their enemies might become an occasion of stumbling to Israel, [3] that they are delivered to destruction. Thus the ban becomes the execution of Yahweh's sentence, and by means of it he takes vengeance on his enemies; [4] to deliver up to the ban and to punish are the same thing. [5] Hence even here the rite undergoes a change of meaning based on the nature of the covenant God.

Nevertheless, the practice could not last, but was considerably modified with the passage of time; cattle and booty, [6] even women and children, [7] were excepted from the ban, and it was possible for the male prisoners to be dedicated to the service of the sanctuary. [8] On the whole Israel tended to show clemency in the waging of war, and the Israelite kings had the reputation of being merciful. [9] Slaughter out of sheer lust for blood, which often features so repulsively in the Assyrian inscriptions, [10] is unknown. Similarly there is nowhere any mention of the raping of women by Israelite warriors, and fruit trees were protected by the laws of war. [11] In the later period of the monarchy the custom of the ban seems to have disappeared; it was already disregarded in the time of Ahab, [12] which would seem to suggest quite clearly that no sense of obligation any longer attached to it. The men of the Deuteronomic reform made an attempt to revive the ancient custom as part of their return to the regulations of the ancient Yahweh amphictyony; but the end of the

[1] Cf. Gen. 15.16; Lev. 18.25, 28; and the generally unfavourable opinion of the Canaanites, Gen. 9.22; 19.5.
[2] I Sam. 15.2, 33.
[3] Deut. 7; Num. 31.
[4] Jer. 50.13 f., 15; Micah 4.13.
[5] Ex. 22.19; cf. Saul's punishment of the priests of Nob, I Sam. 22.11 ff.
[6] Deut. 2.34 f.; 3.6 f.; Josh. 8.2, 27; 11.14.
[7] Deut. 20.13 ff.; Num. 31.7 ff.
[8] Josh. 9.23; cf. Lev. 27.28 ff.
[9] I Kings 20.31.
[10] The inscriptions of Sennacherib are especially noted for this.
[11] Deut. 20.19 f.
[12] I Kings 20.35 ff.

state also put an end for ever to the institution of the holy war.[1]

(b) *Sacrificial Worship*

Any attempt to discover the religious ideas underlying the sacrificial worship of Israel must always bear in mind two things. First, the Old Testament nowhere gives us a direct exposition of the meaning of this worship; it is possible to arrive at various conclusions *a posteriori*, but never with more than a certain degree of probability. The certainty with which judgments are at times expressed on this point and on the subject of the whole pattern of development of the idea of sacrifice[2] is usually in inverse proportion to what the available evidence will bear. Secondly, the gaps in the Old Testament tradition cannot simply be filled in from the comparative study of religion, on the tacit assumption that everything must have happened in Israel exactly as it did everywhere else—even indeed, that the ideas of sacrifice which can be shown to have existed elsewhere must also, wherever possible, be discovered *in toto* in the Israelite cultus. If anywhere, then particularly in the field of sacrificial worship it is vital not to lose sight of the connection with the fundamental controlling concepts of Israelite religion.[3]

A systematic enumeration of the various types of sacrifice under the heads of nomenclature, material and manner of performance is outside the scope of the present study; the reader is referred to the relevant sections of the works on biblical archaeology, the articles in the encyclopaedias and the *Theologie des Alten Testaments* of E. König (edn. 3 & 4, 1923, pp. 87 ff.). Here we shall simply deal with the meaning and significance of sacrifice.

(1) The comparative study of religions indicates as the most important fundamental ideas of the sacrificial cultus those of *feeding*, the offering of gifts, sacral communion and atonement. The most

[1] Cf. G. von Rad, *Der heitige Krieg im alten Israel*, 1951, where an attempt is made to expound the significance of this institution for the religious message of the prophets. Cf. further H. Kruse, *Ethos Victoriae in Vetere Testamento*, 1951, which gives a detailed survey of the literature, and H. Junker, 'Der alttest. Bann gegen heidnische Völker als moraltheologisches und offenbarungsgeschichtliches Problem', *Trierer Theologische Zeitschrift* 56, 1947, pp. 74 ff.

[2] So e.g., W. R. Smith, *The Religion of the Semites*, who tries to derive everything from the sacred communion meal, and S. R. Curtiss, *Ursemitische Religion im Volksleben des heutigen Orient*, 1903, who sees as the determining factor the substitutionary death of the sacred animal. Even A. Wendel's work, *Das Opfer in der altisraelitischen Religion*, 1927, is not free from this kind of subjectivism: cf. e.g. pp. 44 ff., 53 ff.

[3] A good survey is to be found in H. H. Rowley, *The Meaning of Sacrifice in the Old Testament*, 1950.

primitive attitude is certainly that which sees the sacrifice as the means by which the deity is provided with nourishment and renewed strength. Whether this conception takes cruder or more refined forms—that is to say, whether it envisages an actual consumption of food like that of human beings, or the absorption of the invisible virtue present in the food, or merely the enjoyment of the savour of the burnt offering—is really immaterial. In any case the deity is regarded as dependent on what men do, and consequently the sacrifice is valued as the most effective means of influencing the divine power in human interests. That this is bound to imperil both God's exaltedness and the attitude of awe with which men ought to bow before him is obvious. Conversely, wherever the picture of God acquires more spiritual traits, this conception usually tends to recede or even to disappear altogether.

An examination of the ritual and language of Israelite sacrifice with this in mind reveals unmistakable traces of this conception. The materials of sacrifice, being all edible, inevitably suggest the idea of nourishment. Salt and oil respectively are used to make the meat and meal offerings tasty; and the meat is sometimes boiled before being offered. [1] The subsidiary offerings of food and wine at the time of the solemn sacrifice of animals recall the drink and side-dishes which go with the main meat course. If these customs are to be explained by the idea of feeding, then equally the practice of placing loaves, the *leḥem pānīm*, which is renewed at regular intervals, [2] in the presence of the deity (a usage common also in Babylonia) points to the concept of the god's absorbing the essential life-giving virtue of the offering. The same may be true of the occasional practice of simply setting out the prepared food at an appointed spot. [3] Finally, the enjoyment of the essence of the offering in the smell is expressed in the description of the sacrifice as a 'savour of pacification', which disposes the deity to a friendly attitude. [4]

This situation, however, is extraordinarily instructive as to the danger of twisting the meaning of the evidence under pressure from the analogous material furnished by the comparative study of religion. For in fact all this proves no more than that, as regards material

[1]Cf. Judg. 6.19 f.; I Sam. 2.13.
[2]I Sam. 21.7; I Kings 7.48; Ex. 25.30 etc.
[3]Judg. 6.19 f. in Ophrah; cf. 13.19.
[4]Gen. 8.21; Lev. 1.9, 13, 17; 26.31; Ezek. 6.13; 16.19; 20.28.

and ritual, the Israelite sacrifice *ultimately derives* from the conception of the feeding of the deity. But it is extremely doubtful whether this conception was still a *living* reality in Israel. The value of linguistic usage as proof is in the last resort decisively rebutted by the automatic employment of the old terminology in even the very latest writings, by which time the ideas that underlay the actual wording were quite certainly dead. This applies not only to such phraseology as that of God 'smelling the savour of pacification',[1] but also to the description of the sacrifice as God's food, *leḥem ' ᵉlōhīm*, which is to be found in Ezekiel and Malachi as well as in the Priestly Code.[2] These instances perfectly exemplify the persistence of cultic terminology even when the ideas corresponding to it have been changed out of all recognition, and provide a salutary warning against drawing hasty conclusions about the ancient period. In actual fact a too literal interpretation of Gen. 8.21 is in diametrical opposition to the conception of God found elsewhere in the Yahwist writer; and it should be noted that Judg. 13.16 expressly rejects the idea that the angel of Yahweh might be able to absorb food as incompatible with the nature of a heavenly being.[3] Quite apart, however, from particular instances, the whole tenor of ancient Israel's belief in Yahweh is irreconcilable with the idea that God is fed by the sacrifice, bound up as this is with God's dependence on man. The central concept of the covenant asserts no less than that Yahweh already existed and had proved his power, before ever Israel sacrificed to him.[4]

Even the at first illuminating evidence of the material and ritual of the sacrifice loses a great deal of its force, once it is realized that the sacred action itself may have undergone a change of meaning, even though its original component elements may have been tenaciously retained. This is a commonplace of the comparative study of religion; one has only to think of the transformation in the meaning of those magical rites associated with sacrifice to the deity, as, for example, in the case of the Roman feast of the Robigalia or of the purificatory rites which formed part of the worship of Apollo. Similar assumptions must also be made for the Yahweh cult. Here

[1]Cf. previous note.
[2]Lev. 21.6, 8, 17; 22.25; Ezek. 44.7; Mal. 1.7.
[3]To treat meals and sacrifices on a level, as the feeding of men and gods respectively, is simply to misunderstand the whole subject (A. Wendel, *op. cit.*, p. 4).
[4]Rightly pointed out by M. Weber, *Religionssoziologie* III, p. 145.

the offering of food and drink reminds men that God is the sole giver of life and nurture; and it is for this reason that their gifts to him take the form of the necessities of life. Nevertheless, it is worth noting that milk and milk-products, although the principal food of a cattle-raising society, are never mentioned as ingredients of Israelite sacrifice. That God takes the offering to himself by fire can be adequately explained by the nature of Yahweh, who prefers to manifest himself through the form of fire. [1] The idea of God smelling the sweet savour of the offering, however, serves to express the belief that he has heeded the sacrifice and is graciously pleased to accept it.

Nevertheless, even if the idea of providing food for God must be regarded as alien to Yahwism, this is not to say that it did not constantly attempt to insinuate itself into the Israelite cultus. These attempts were certainly assisted by the influence of Canaanite cult practices, a clear example of which is that of the wine-libation. The picture of Abraham showing hospitality to God (Gen. 18.5)—a piece of popular story-telling originally of Canaanite provenance— proves that the idea of God's eating food must have been very much alive, even if it has been diluted by the Yahwist into a story of a meal given to angels unawares. Those stories of the Judges which are genuinely Israelite will have nothing to do with this conception; [2] nevertheless, despite the fact that it does not seem to have caused concern to the pre-exilic prophets, it still has to be explicitly attacked at a fairly late date. [3] Hence it would seem that the idea of God's feeding on the sacrifice should be included among those coarser conceptions of heathenism which from time to time sought to drag the image of Yahweh down into their own sphere of influence.

(2) Frequently associated with the idea of feeding, but in fact to be distinguished from it as an independent sacrificial category, is *the conception of sacrifice as a gift to the deity*. Just as an inferior brings a present to his superior, or a client to his patron, or a vassal to his lord, as the normal expression of his subjection and fealty, so the pious worshipper makes an offering to his God. Naturally only something valuable, the surrender of which involves an act of renunciation on the part of the giver, is suitable for such an offering. Hence food—and that only at its best—accords admirably with this idea of a gift, because it is essential to life; indeed, it might be

[1]So also A. Wendel, *op. cit.*, p. 49.
[2]Judg. 6.19 f.; 13.16.
[3]Ps. 50.12 f.; Isa. 40.16 ff.

sufficient by itself, though in fact precious things of all kinds can be offered to the deity. The normal term for such a sacrifice is *minḥā* (Gen. 4.3 ff.; I Sam. 2.17, *et al.*). The whole gamut of human motives, however, very easily comes to be combined with this simple basic idea of a gift; according to the disposition of the giver and the character of the recipient the offering may be accompanied by the feeling of total self-surrender or by a mistrustful appeasement of the deity, by confident intercession or calculating self-interest. It is easy to overlook the wide range of possible subjective attitudes left to the offerer, and also to forget that for man in the ancient world a concrete form of expression for his feelings was an absolute necessity. Modern man's sentimental disparagement of the cultus constantly leads him to assume as a matter of course that the motives behind it must have been of the lowest. Such an assumption has already been disproved in the case of primitive peoples, [1] and it is equally unfair to the more developed cultus of the higher religions.

If, however, we are to distinguish between voluntary and obligatory gifts on the basis of the occasion which prompts the offering, there would seem to be some justification for an adverse judgment at any rate in the case of the frequent and general practice of *the vow* (*neder*). The conditional promise of a gift evinces only too easily the characteristics of precaution and mistrust, which try to make sure of performance on God's side before giving up anything of their own; a good example of this is afforded by the precise balancing of requests and promises in Jacob's vow at Bethel. [2] In this instance, however, it is necessary to take into account the element of studied character-drawing on the part of the narrator, and to remember that on the other side of the picture a completely different outlook is exhibited in the vow of Hannah. [3] Here the vow is the expression of a deep inward trustfulness, which is revealed in her 'pouring out of her soul' before God and is completely certain of being heard. It would seem then, that a real element in the vow is the spontaneous conviction that God's gifts require from men not merely words, but deeds of gratitude, and that for the person praying to make his readiness for such an act explicit is to express a right attitude of mind and to show a real

---

[1] Cf. W. Schmidt, *Der Ursprung der Gottesidee* I, 1912; II, 1929; III, 1931; F. Heiler, *Das Gebet*⁴, 1921, pp. 71 ff.

[2] Gen. 28.20 ff. The passage loses something of its repetitiousness, if conflation of two sources can be assumed: cf. Procksch, *Die Genesis*², ³, *ad loc*. A different view is expressed by von Rad, *Genesis*, ET, 1961, p. 281.

[3] I Sam. 1.10 f.

awareness of God's graciousness in answering his prayer. If in addition it is remembered that the vow is the exact opposite of any attempt to exert compulsion by means of magic, and equally incompatible with any idea of threats as to what one will do if one's request is not manifestly granted—a feature to be found in Islam [1]— we may be on our guard against assuming that the frequent occurrence of the vow [2] is a sign that Israelite religion was on a low plane. Moreover, the prayers which accompanied the votive offering, examples of which are preserved in Pss. 107 and 116, with their solemn acknowledgment of the divine assistance, testify to a living faith which is not to be despised. Again the fact that, as the case of Absalom shows, [3] the personal piety which found expression in the vow did not regard the effective working of its God as restricted to within the borders of his inheritance is striking evidence of a large and forceful confidence in God which, despite its essential connection with the cult, could transcend a mere particularistic narrowness. Thus it is that no direct attack on this aspect of piety is to be found in the prophets; [4] and the Law is content to emphasize the need for conscientiousness in the practice of the vow and to lay down definite regulations for the performance of this traditional religious custom, [5] which kept its place down to the very latest times. [6]

A similar role to that of the more prominent vow is that of *the petitionary sacrifice*, which was offered at the time when the supplication was made with the purpose of adding to its force. To this category belong the sacrifices made by the king before going out to

[1]Cf. the excellent investigation of A. Wendel, *Das freie Laiengebet im vorexilischen Israel*, 1932, pp. 118 ff.; also H. Seeger, *Die Triebkräfte des religiosen Lebens in Israel und Babylon*, 1923, p. 38.

[2]Cf. also Num. 21.2; Judg. 11.30; I Sam. 1.21; Pss. 61.6, 9; 22.26.

[3]II Sam. 15.8.

[4]Hos. 14.3; Jer. 44.25; Isa. 19.21; Nahum 2.1; Mal. 1.14 all maintain a neutral attitude to the vow.

[5]Deut. 23.19 ff.; Lev. 22.21 f.; 27.2 ff.; Num. 30.2 ff.

[6]The Psalms testify to the continued existence of the custom in post-exilic times (Pss. 22.26; 65.2; 66.13; 76.12; 116.18) though it is also possible to detect occasionally a spiritualizing of the vow (Pss. 50.14; 61.9; Jonah 2.10). At the same time, however, voices are raised which see a danger for the pious in what was obviously a very prevalent habit of making vows lightly and seek to warn men against it (Prov. 20.25; Eccl. 5.1, 4; 8.2; Ecclus. 18.22 f.). This constituted a 'turning-point in the history of the vow' (A. Wendel, *Das israelitisch-jüdische Gelübde*, 1931, p. 31), which thereafter gradually became secularized and was often nothing more than an emphatic form of assertion. For this reason the lawyers of Judaism became increasingly hostile to it (cf. A. Wendel, *op. cit.*, pp. 41 ff.), though without actually condemning it root and branch.

battle[1] and at the beginning of his reign.[2] In this case the accepted practice seems to have been to consume the victim completely in the fire, whence the fact that this type of sacrifice was usually referred to by the name '*ōlā*, 'burnt offering', or *kālīl*, 'whole burnt offering'.

In addition, however, the completely voluntary offering, *n‹dābā*, and the sacrifice presented as a token of gratitude for some act of divine assistance, *tōdā*, were also customary in Israel.[3] Together with the vow they are mentioned in the Priestly system as the three classes of 'peace offering', *zebaḥ š‹lāmīm*.[4] The *n‹dābā* is an example of a free act of homage, which voices man's humble recognition of and submission to his divine Lord,[5] and was a common practice on the occasion of the regular visits to the sanctuary at the time of the great annual festivals.[6] The *tōdā* springs spontaneously from man's need to give public and material expression to his gratitude for some deliverance or marvellous benefit, a purpose to which the customary methods of sacrifice by burning or immolation could fittingly be applied.[7] The ideas which actuated these sacrificial rites are the very ones to be found in the hymns and thanksgivings of the Psalter, which may indeed for the most part have been composed for just these occasions and which form some of the most beautiful expressions of Old Testament piety.

Finally, under the heading of freewill offerings, must be mentioned *dedicatory gifts to the sanctuary*. These were set up as trophies or memorials[8] or as tokens of gratitude and adoration offered to the deity, and took the form of weapons, money and treasure,[9] cultic objects,[10] or even simple pillars.[11] It was also possible to dedicate

[1]Ps. 20; cf. I Sam. 7.9; 13.9.
[2]I Kings 3.4.
[3]Already assumed by the time of Amos 4.5.
[4]Lev. 7.12 ff. These sharp distinctions in terminology seem only to have become established in the schematic treatment of the Priestly Code. Before that there was partial overlapping as in the case of the vow and the thank-offering, cf. Pss. 50.14; 56.13. In the opinion of many scholars *šelem* as a sacrifice ought to be distinguished from *zebaḥ*; so E. König, *Theologie*[3, 4], p. 287; G. Hölscher, *Geschichte der israelitischen und jüdischen Religion*, p. 77.
[5]Micah 6.6.
[6]Ex. 23.15; 34.20.
[7]Gen. 46.1; II Sam. 6.13, 17; Jer. 17.26; 33.11; Pss. 50.14; 56.13; 107.22; 116.17.
[8]I Sam. 21.10; Ex. 16.33.
[9]I Sam. 21.10; II Sam. 8.11; I Kings 10.16 f.; 14.26; 15.15; II Kings 12.19; 16.8.
[10]Ex. 17.15; Josh. 22.10; Judg. 6.24; 8.24 ff.; 17.3; I Sam. 14.35.
[11]I Sam. 7.12.

human beings to the service of the sanctuary. [1] Nevertheless, the unique character of the Yahweh religion in this latter connection stands out at two points: it knows nothing of human sacrifice, and utterly condemns consecration to cultic prostitution.

That *human sacrifice* was practised in pre-Israelite Canaan has been demonstrated unmistakably by excavation. Sometimes this was a building sacrifice, as in the case of the skeletons discovered in the foundations of walls and towers at Gezer, Taanach and Megiddo; other instances are of child sacrifice—very probably the offering of the firstborn—as has been proved by the bodies of large numbers of children found buried in great barrel-shaped jars at the sites already mentioned and at Lachish. [2] Human sacrifice seems also to have been practised at times of especial crisis, for example, in war. [3]

In Israel human sacrifice was expressly forbidden by the Law, [4] though this fact gives no indication how far back this particular insight may go. The unqualified form in which the demand for the giving of the firstborn to Yahweh is expressed in the Book of the Covenant [5] has led some to conclude that it was the practice in ancient Israel to sacrifice the firstborn child. Two facts, however, argue against this conclusion. First, even outside Israel the sacrifice of the firstborn was not the invariable custom, but something extraordinary; secondly, one of the constant themes of the Old Testament is that of rejoicing at the birth of the firstborn son, rejoicing which is given eloquent expression so early as the Blessing of Jacob (Gen. 49.3). It is also worthwhile pointing out the nonsensical nature of the idea—supported, incidentally, by no evidence in any source—that there could possibly have been a regular practice of sacrificing firstborn children in Israel, when this would have resulted in the 'extermination of the greater part of the nation's potential manpower'. [6]

[1] I Sam. 1.11, 22; Lev. 27.1–8. On the subject of the Nazirite vow cf. ch. VIII. 3, pp. 303 ff. below.

[2] Cf. P. Volz, *Die biblischen Altertümer*, pp. 178 ff.; Benzinger, *Hebr. Archäologie*³, p. 360; R. Kittel, *Geschichte des Volkes Israel*⁴ I, pp. 172, 204 f.; H. Vincent, *Canaan d'après l'exploration récente*, 1907, pp. 188 ff.

[3] Attested for the Moabites, II Kings 3.27; also known to have been practised among the Phoenicians. Cf. von Baudissin, art. 'Moloch', *HRE* XIII, pp. 269 ff.; R. Dussaud, *Les origines cananéennes du sacrifice israélite*, 1921, pp. 163 ff.; G. Contenau, *La civilisation phénicienne*, 1926, pp. 137 ff.

[4] Deut. 12.31; 18.10; Lev. 18.21; 20.2–5.

[5] Ex. 22.28; in the parallel passage, 34.20, the permission to redeem has become an order.

[6] So M. Buber, *Königtum Gottes*², 1936, p. 219, in a careful examination of the thesis put forward by Eissfeldt (cf. p. 149 n. 8 below).

Wherever the divine demand covers *all* firstborn sons (Ex. 13.2; 22.28), it is commuted and presupposes the principle of substitution. Least of all can we appeal to a prophet of the Exile, Ezekiel, to throw doubt on this conclusion. In one place [1] he says that Yahweh, as a punishment for his people's idolatry, gave them statutes and judgments which were bound to lead to their destruction; by means of their child sacrifices, he polluted them and filled them with desolation. This passage is in fact evidence for nothing more than the idea, put forward by others of the prophets beside Ezekiel, that because of the sin of the nation even that which had originally been given them as a blessing was turned into a curse. Thus it was that the preaching of the prophets and the signs which they wrought often only increased the people's hardness of heart [2]—in fact their inherent propensity to falsehood actually resulted in the substitution of a false prophecy for the true. [3] In exactly the same way the laconic demand in the Law for the dedication of all the firstborn sons of men was twisted in the minds of a people alienated from God to mean that Yahweh desired child sacrifice. The fact that this horrible custom was widespread in Judah in the eighth and seventh centuries [4] is clearly connected with the renascence of ancient Canaanite heathenism and the influx of foreign cult practices which marked this period. Phoenician influence may be indicated by the particular connection of this offering with the *Melek*, [5] who had his special place of sacrifice for this purpose in the valley of Ben-Hinnom; for both the practice and this title of the god were native to Phoenicia. [6] Naturally, however, in the popular mind the 'King' simply meant Yahweh, as can be seen from Isa. 30.33, where the annihilation of the Assyrian is ironically compared to the *melek*-sacrifice in the valley of Hinnom. [7] The fact that in Punic inscriptions the word *mōlek* can be shown to be the name of a particular kind of sacrifice does not really affect the issue. [8] For even if this

[1] Ezek. 20.25 f.
[2] Isa. 6.9 f.
[3] Isa. 30.10 f.; Micah 2.11; Jer. 5.31; Ezek. 13.10 f.
[4] II Kings 16.3; 21.6; 23.10; Jer. 2.34; 3.24; 7.31; 32.35; Micah 6.6 f.; Deut. 12.30 f.; 18.10.
[5] Changed to Molek (Moloch) during the pointing of the text.
[6] Cf. von Baudissin, art. 'Moloch', *HRE* XIII, pp. 275 ff., 281 ff., 289, and *Kyrios* III, 1929, pp. 101 ff.; H. Cazelles, art. 'Moloch' in *Dictionnaire de la Bible*, Suppl. V, cols. 1337–46.
[7] Cf. p. 196 below.
[8] Cf. O. Eissfeldt, *Molk als Opferbegriff im Punischen und Hebräischen und das Ende des Gottes Moloch* (Beiträge zur Geschichte des Altertums, Heft 3), 1935.

terminology is adopted for many Old Testament passages, thus changing the rendering of Lev. 18.21 and similar regulations to read: 'Thou shalt not give any of thy seed to consecrate them as a sacrifice,' the use of such a technical term from Phoenician-Punic sacrificial language would only confirm that this was a case of a type of offering borrowed from Phoenicia, which was in no way native to Israel, but had been imported for reasons clearly connected with the historical situation of the later monarchy.[1] But the very possibility of such a rendering must remain uncertain, since in every instance about which there can be no doubt the dative with the verbs 'to consecrate' and 'to give up' denotes the recipient of the gift and not the type of offering.[2] Furthermore, such a phrase as that in Lev. 20.5, 'to go whoring after Molech', obviously implies that the object is either a personal being or the image of a god, which makes it even more certain that in the other passages from the Law the recipient of the sacrifice is meant. This was, of course, not a special god Moloch,[3] but Yahweh himself, whose epithet Melek was changed into Molech by those who pointed the text. In this their motive may have been, by making use of the Phoenician term Molk, to indicate the foreign origin of this sacrificial rite,[4] but the additional possibility that the change was made to suggest the assonantal bōšet cannot be excluded.

If, however, by the time of the ancient Israelite law there was no longer any need to forbid human sacrifice, but its avoidance could be taken for granted, then the narrative of Gen. 22 may be right, when it dates the rejection of this widespread cultic practice back to pre-Mosaic times. The significance of the story is that, without surrendering the affirmation that God is entitled to the most drastic sacrifices on the part of his worshippers, it yet teaches that the divine will is kindly and life-giving, and elevates the substitution of an animal for a human victim to the status of an invariable rule.

Where, nevertheless, human sacrifice is still mentioned in the Old Testament, it is clearly a case of the revival of a long suppressed

---

[1]Cf. W. von Soden, *TLZ* 61, 1936, cols. 45 f., and M. Buber, *op. cit.*, pp. 212 f.; it is therefore impossible to agree with Eissfeldt, when he thinks that this Molek sacrifice can be shown to be a legitimate part of the Israelite cultus down to the time of Deuteronomy.

[2]Deut. 12.31; II Kings 17.31; Ezek. 16.20 f.; 23.37; Ps. 106.37 f.; this point has been strikingly emphasized by M. Buber, *op. cit.*, pp. 211 f.

[3]On this point Eissfeldt is completely correct.

[4]The explanation favoured by Buber (*op. cit.*, p. 224).

practice in extraordinary circumstances. But whether it be under the pressure of war during the barbaric period of the Judges, [1] or from dread of the possible sinister consequences of a curse at the rebuilding of a town that had once been under the ban, [2] it is always an exceptional phenomenon having no connection with the official cult of Yahweh. The killing of Agag by Samuel [3] and the exposing of the sons of Saul on the Yahweh high place at Gibeon after their execution [4] have as little to do with sacrifice as has the ban in war. [5]

As we have seen, the certainty that the will of the covenant God was life-giving and beneficent led, in spite of passing deviations, to the permanent exclusion of cultic suicide. In the same way the clear distinction drawn between the will of this divine Lord and the blind life-force in Nature barred from his worship the practice of self-prostitution. The *sacrifice of chastity* by both men and women took the form either of selling oneself on a single occasion at the beginning of married life, or of permanent prostitution at the sanctuary. In either case it has its roots in magical practices designed to ensure increased fertility by means of sympathetic magic at the demonistic level, either by securing from the divinity through the *hieros gamos* a share in the divine power, or, apotropaically, by buying off the jealous malevolence of the demon. In this context the deity is worshipped principally as the mysterious life-force in Nature, and it is the worship characteristic of an agricultural civilization which is the normal setting for such customs. This sacrifice is to be found firmly entrenched throughout the Near East, being especially important in Babylonia, where it is dealt with in legislation. [6] The *qādēš* and *qᵉdēšā*, the 'consecrated' male prostitute and hierodule in the worship of the Baal and of the Asherah or Baalat are peculiar to Canaan.

These cultic practices, arising as they do from magical and orgiastic tendencies, are of their very nature foreign to the religion of Yahweh. The absence of any sexual differentiation within the being of the covenant God [7] and the fierce reaction against all the shamelessness which went with natural unaffectedness in the treatment of the

[1] Judg. 11.34–40, Jephthah's sacrifice. Cf. the careful study of W. Baumgartner, 'Jephtas Gelübde', *Archiv für Religionswissenschaft* 18, 1915, pp. 240 ff.
[2] I Kings 16.34, where we are probably meant to understand a building sacrifice.
[3] I Sam. 15.33.
[4] II Sam. 21.
[5] Cf. the remarks on this subject, pp. 139 f. above.
[6] Cf. the Code of Hammurabi, §§ 178–182, 187.
[7] Cf. ch. VI. 3, p. 223, below.

sexual processes [1] have already indicated that in the sphere of religious thinking, both ritual and moral, Israel's sensibilities instinctively resisted the whole sexual-orgiastic complex which was bound up with magic and the divinization of Nature and which was such an important feature of their heathen environment. Behind this attitude lies their awareness of the exalted nature of the covenant God, who is open to no kind of coercion and holds sway over the natural order as its true Lord. Hence time and again the introduction of cultic prostitution at the Yahweh sanctuaries produces a violent reaction on the part of the king and the lawgiver. [2] The Melkart cult imported under Ahab is summed up by Jehu as simply whoredom and witchcraft; [3] and the indiscriminate way in which the cult of Baal and the cult of Yahweh, where this has been assimilated to Canaanite models, are both described as 'harlotry' [4] is also due to this opposition, which was given further powerful expression by the polemic of the prophets. [5]

In addition to the freewill offering another very ancient class of sacrifices in which the idea of the gift predominates is that of *tribute regularly paid to the deity*. The outstanding example of this is *the offering of the firstfruits*, which is to be found even among very primitive tribes. [6] The motive may be either to obtain God's blessing and sanctification of all one's property, or else to acknowledge that God is the real owner of all things, and only allows men to enjoy the fruits of the earth in return for a regular tribute. Thus in Israel the firstborn of the cattle and the firstfruits of the land (corn, olive and wine) were offered. [7] Those animals that had not already been sacrificed on the eighth day after their birth at a local cultic site [8] might be used for the sacrificial meal, and the Feast of the Passover in the spring seems

[1]It is the sexual perversions in particular which are branded in the OT as *nᵉbālā* (Gen. 34.7; Deut. 22.21; Judg. 19.23 f.; 20.6, 10; II Sam. 13.12; Jer. 29.23), and it was on this point especially that Israel was aware of being different from the Canaanites (Gen. 9.22 ff.; 19.5; 20.11; 38.9 f.; Lev. 18.3, 24 ff.; 20.23). Attention should also be drawn to the strong feeling against any form of physical nudity (Gen. 9.22 ff.; Ex. 20.26) and the fact that the word 'nakedness' could be used to denote any illicit sexual union (Lev. 18). Cf. further, M. Weber, *Religionssoziologie* III, pp. 202 ff.
[2]I Kings 15.12; 22.46; Deut. 23.18 f.; Lev. 19.29.
[3]II Kings 9.22.
[4]Hos. 1 f.; Jer. 3.1 ff.; Ezek. 16 and 23.
[5]Amos 2.7; Hos. 4.13 f.; Jer. 5.7; 13.27; 23.10, 14; Micah 1.7.
[6]Cf. W. Schmidt, *Der Ursprung der Gottesidee* I, pp. 165 f.; II, p. 473, pp. 858 f., 895; III, pp. 125 f., 281, 288 f., 368, 534 f.
[7]*bikkūrīm* and *rē'šīt*, Ex. 23.16, 19; 34.26; Deut. 15.19 ff.; 18.4; Lev. 19.23–25; Num. 15.18 ff.; 18.13; II Kings 4.42; Neh. 10.38.
[8]Ex. 22.29.

very likely to have been the principal occasion associated with this offering; [1] for the presentation of the firstfruits the three great agricultural festivals were considered especially suitable. [2] The human firstborn was redeemed. [3] Deut. 26.1 ff. has preserved for us the prayer which accompanied the presentation of the firstfruits; in it the profound significance of these tributes at the sanctuary is given pure and beautiful expression; they are Israel's recognition of the duty of thankfulness for the gracious gift of the land at the hands of their divine Lord.

Just as the offering of the firstfruits was the accepted method of sanctifying the produce of the harvest, so the *tithe* constituted the proper tribute payable to the divine owner of the land. Sometimes, in exceptional circumstances, the tithe seems to have been a voluntary act; [4] and even the king might lay claim to it. [5] Nevertheless it is also of great antiquity as a standard cultic practice, and must be carefully distinguished from the offering of the firstfruits. [6] In view of the fact that the presentation of the tithe was celebrated with a sacrificial meal, after the priest had received his share, [7] the sacrificial character of this offering, which was normally presented at the autumn harvest festival, is very marked. Since, however, the divine Lord at the same time entertained his worshippers with the gifts which they had dedicated to him, the festival carried with it no oppressive feeling that this was a burdensome exaction, but rather called to mind the goodness of the God who had granted the fruits of the earth, and who required that those who had received them should pass them on to their poorer fellows. Deuteronomy is especially concerned to make these cultic occasions into opportunities for the expression of the brotherly solidarity of all the members of the nation. To this end it instructs that the tithes of every third year shall be given direct to the needy, and emphasizes the holiness attaching to this act by means of a solemn confession to be made at the sanctuary. [8] It was only as a result

[1]So G. Beer, *Pesachim*, 1912, p. 12: cf. Ex. 13; 34.19 ff.; Num. 3.13.
[2]Lev. 23.9 f., 15 ff.
[3]Cf. above, pp. 148 f.
[4]Gen. 14.20; 28.22.
[5]I Sam. 8.15, 17.
[6]Ex. 22.28; Amos 4.4; Deut. 14.22 ff.; 26.12 ff.; Num. 18.21 ff. For the individual references cf. O. Eissfeldt, *Erstlinge und Zehnten im AT*, 1917.
[7]Deut. 12.17 f. The emphasis on rejoicing and feasting in Deuteronomy, which in any case always tries to bring out the happy side of worship, should not be taken to imply the exclusive use of the tithes for this purpose; the claim of the priests to a portion of the tithe was taken for granted from the very first.
[8]Deut. 14.28 f.; 26.12 ff.

of the Exile that the tithe lost its sacrificial character, and became simply a tax paid to the cultic personnel.[1] The idea of regular homage and tribute consequently came to be transferred more and more to the daily morning and evening sacrifices in the Temple,[2] later given the name *tāmīd*,[3] at which a lamb was presented as a burnt offering on behalf of the congregation. The participation of every single member of the congregation in this sacrifice, which became the central act of the cultus, was brought out by the levying of a poll-tax of half a shekel.[4] The forerunner of this arrangement was undoubtedly the regular royal sacrifice, which symbolized the king's permanent relationship to God.[5]

(3) Sacrifice, however, represents not only the gifts of man to God, but also the gifts of God to man. It is *the concept of sacral communion* which makes the sacrifice into a true sacrament. On the primitive level the belief in a magical power residing in the sacrificial victim leads men to regard the sacrificial meal as the most intimate possible means of contact with the power of the god;[6] but at the same time this signifies a strengthening of the deity himself, either as a result of the sacrifice alone, or of the allocation of certain portions of the victim to the deity as his share of the feast, and this strengthening is designed to bring about the active participation of the deity in the rite.

That such ideas had their effect even on the higher religions is incontestable, although they underwent considerable modification, wherever the deity acquired more strongly personal characteristics. They may have been the origin of many of the features of the sacrificial cultus, the selection of certain kinds of animals for the victims and the exclusion of others, the tradition of family sacrifices which persisted even within the framework of the larger cultic community,[7] the manipulations of the blood of the victim which were so popular,

---

[1]Num. 18.21 ff.; Mal. 3.8, 10; Neh. 10.38 ff.; 13.5, 10 ff.
[2]II Kings 3.20; I Kings 18.29.
[3]Ex. 29.38 ff.; Num. 28.3 ff.
[4]Ex. 30.11 ff.
[5]II Kings 16.15.
[6]Cf. e.g., A. Bertholet, 'Zum Verständnis des alttest. Opfergedankens' (*JBL* 49, 1930, pp. 230 ff.); W. R. Smith, *The Religion of the Semites*, pp. 213 ff., though the latter is too one-sided in its stress on totemism. Totemism is just one particular form of this belief, not its only form: as A. Wendel also seems to hold in *Das Opfer in der altisraelitischen Religion*, pp. 82 ff. On the other hand the provision of food for the dead has, at any rate in the first place, nothing to do with the idea of communion.
[7]Cf. I Sam. 20.6, 29.

the habit of making oneself completely befuddled with wine and narcotics, even perhaps the technical language of sacrifice. [1]

It would, however, be one-sided to take only these origins into account. Equally important is the primitive conception of the life of each individual as a closed sphere of influence, in which not only outward and inward, body and soul, but also clothes and weapons, words and names, possessions and actions, in short everything by which the individual affects his environment is permeated with the same living power and issues from the same living personality. [2] All one's relations with one's neighbour involve the mutual exchange of elements from these personal spheres of influence, and so can have the most drastic consequences for those concerned; and it is for this reason that the very closest association with one's kith and kin and the hostile avoidance of any sort of contact with one's enemy form a basic maxim of common prudence. In such a context a gift and the acceptance of a gift denote a real transference of power from one system of personal life to another; a word can exert a compelling force; and most of all, the act of eating together signifies participation in a common source of life, and common contact with the power of a particular object creates an intimate association and fellowship which cannot be broken without the most serious consequences.

It is an accepted fact that this primitive conception of life has had a most decided effect on the relationships of all civilized peoples. Its influence can be seen in the cult, among other things, in the high value set on sacred objects, and in the great effectiveness ascribed to words, especially names; and not the least important of these instances is the idea of sacral communion. It thus throws new light on the power of the sacrifice to create a bond of fellowship. Because the deity and his worshippers enter the same system of living power, indicated by the victim or the victim's blood, they are united by the strongest possible bond; or, to put it another way, by himself partaking of the gifts which have been dedicated to God and so now belong to him man receives a share in the divine life. It is easy to see how

[1] Cf. the parallel Latin phrases *deos extis mactare* and *deis hostiam mactare* (Pfister, art. 'Kultus' in Pauly, *Realenzyklopädie des klassischen Altertums* XI, 2, 1922).
[2] On the following points cf. V. Grönbech, 'Die Germanen', in Chantepie de la Saussaye, *Lehrbuch der Religionsgeschichte*[4], II, pp. 559 ff. and J. Pedersen, *Israel* I–II, pp. 99 ff. and *Der Eid bei den Semiten*, 1914, pp. 22 ff. (The phrases 'closed sphere of influence', 'personal spheres of influence' are an attempt to render in English—without success—the German '[geschlossener] Lebensraum': Tr.)

adaptable such ideas can be, and how they might function quite differently according as the deity is conceived more as an impersonal force or more as a personal will. It is as well to bear in mind this possibility of the sublimation of these primitive conceptions when they are employed in the Israelite cult, or in any higher religion.

The presence of this concept of fellowship through the sacrifice, if not of this concept alone, may be safely assumed in every case where an offering to Yahweh is combined with a feast of which the offerer partakes, even if there is no explicit reference to the concept in any particular case. It is the *zebaḥ*, the slaughtered sacrifice or offering, rather than the '*ōlā*, the burnt offering, which normally features in this rite of sacral communion. [1] This can be seen most clearly from the sacrifices offered on the occasion of a covenant festival. At such a festival the common meal denotes physical entry into a new association, a fact that emerges with especial emphasis from the account of the feast of the seventy elders on Sinai in the presence of the covenant God. [2] Similarly, the initiatory sacrifices offered by the kings at their accession serve to establish a special connection between Yahweh and his anointed, and at the same time between Yahweh and the people, who have concluded a *bᵉrīt* with their king and sealed it with a common meal. [3] The bringing of the Ark to Zion and the consecration of the Temple, occasions on which communion with Yahweh and his actual presence are particularly desired, also provide an opportunity for this sacral communion through the *zebaḥ*. [4] Again, the sacrifices offered at the beginning of a war, [5] the sacrificial meal at the offering of the firstfruits, and the annual sacrifices at the autumn festival at the very least must have contained this idea of the setting up of a communion relationship. In all these instances the entry of the deity into the sacral fellowship was symbolized by the sprinkling of the blood of the victim and the burning of the fat portions on the altar. [6]

[1]Dussaud (*op. cit.*, p. 17) designates the *zebaḥ* a 'communion sacrifice'. The association of the term with the verbs *hēbī'* and *higgīš*, however, shows that in the historical period, probably as a result of involvement with other ideas of sacrifice as well, notably that of the gift, this particular character of the *zebaḥ* was not always sensed very clearly. Cf. L. Rost, 'Erwägungen zum israelitischen Brandopfer' in *Eissfeldt Festschrift*, 1958, pp. 177 ff.

[2]Ex. 24.9–11 (J₁). V. 2 proves that the sacrifice in question was offered by Moses. For a parallel in the case of the concluding of a covenant between human partners, cf. Gen. 31.44 ff.

[3]I Sam. 11.15; II Sam. 15.12; I Kings 1.9; 3.15.

[4]II Sam. 6.17; I Kings 8.63.

[5]Ps. 20; I Sam. 13.8 ff.

[6]II Kings 16.13; Lev. 3.

Even older seems to be the practice, mentioned on only one occasion, that of the covenant sacrifice on Sinai,[1] of sprinkling not only the altar but also the offerers with the blood, and by means of this 'blood of the covenant' bringing the sacramental relationship into being.[2]

The special character which the communion with the deity mediated in this way acquired in Israel can only be rightly defined by reference to the nation's unique conception of God. This sacred meal is certainly concerned with the real presence of the deity and that personal union with him from which all life and strength derive. But right from the start, with the making of the covenant on Sinai, which had been prepared for by the redemption from Egypt and which was given its specific content in the stipulations of the Decalogue, the confirmation of this union in the covenant sacrifice led not to a physical and magical conception of the divine presence, but to a personal and moral fellowship with a divine Lord whose will shaped and regulated afresh the life of his people. Moreover, the consuming holiness of his nature constantly breaking into human life further excludes any thought of presuming on the bond of blood-brotherhood. In the face of this God there is no room either for the divinization of human nature through consecratory rites, such as was promised by the mystery cults, or for any ideas that the elements and ritual of the sacrifice were endued with the power of automatically ensuring blessing. The power of the sacral communion mediated by the sacrifice rests rather on God's declaration that he is prepared to enter into a special relationship with his people and to give them a share in his own life. The communion sacrifice becomes a sacrament, in which the blessing pronounced by the priest,[3] the hymn sung to the glory of God,[4] the casting of oracles and the promulgation of law carried out in conjunction with the ritual,[5] all recall men to the

[1]Ex. 24.5–8 (E).

[2]That this and no other must have been the purpose of sprinkling the people is confirmed by the ancient Arabian practices which accompanied the making of covenants between human parties, in which the partners dipped their hands in a bowl filled with the blood of an animal: cf. W. R. Smith, *op. cit.*, pp. 314 f.; J. Wellhausen, *Reste des arabischen Heidentums*[2], 1897, p. 128. The application of blood to human beings in the cases of the consecration of priests (Ex. 29.20 f.) and the purification of lepers (Lev. 14.5–7) is not relevant in this connection, having quite a different significance, namely that of dedication and cleansing.

[3]Cf. I Sam. 9.13.

[4]Pss. 67; 81.2 ff.; 95.1 ff.; 100; 114; the prophetic polemic refers to this practice, Amos 5.23; 6.5; Hos. 9.1 ff.

[5]Cf. Pss. 20.7; 50.5 ff.; 81.6 ff.; 95.8 ff.; Isa. 28.7b.

exalted power of their divine Lord and Judge, whose fellowship they are experiencing in the celebration. Of course such celebrations sometimes incurred the dangers which threaten all liturgical acts, and from which even the Christian Communion rites have not always been exempt—externalism, abuse as a means to human self-interest, lowering of moral standards.[1] But we have no right to use such phenomena as a guide to the normal and authentic interpretation of Israelite sacrificial ceremonies, and to write off the chastened rejoicing and holy enthusiasm, which are attested by the exhortations of the Deuteronomic lawgiver,[2] by the sympathetic attitude of such a man as Isaiah to the Temple services,[3] and by many of the Psalms,[4] as rare exceptions. The persistent struggle against the introduction of orgiastic practices which finally resulted in their complete expulsion from the cult proves that jealous champions of the ideal of true Yahweh worship were to be found even in the worst times.

(4) The fourth basic category of sacrificial concepts is closely connected with the most important elements in the creed of a religion of redemption. This is *the idea of atonement or expiation.* It is, however, precisely in this field also that the strongest links with the primitive undercurrents of religion are most clearly visible and that the ambiguity of all cultic acts makes it especially difficult to form a judgment. For the prevalence of the most ancient purification ceremonies and apotropaic and cathartic rites in the field of atonement sacrifices emerges incontestably from any examination of the material. This primitive inheritance includes such features as ancient lustration rites associated with the belief in 'power' and which once were regarded as having mechanical magical effects, a wide variety of uses of blood as the principal medium of power for the purpose of purifying or consecrating both men and things,[5] the preparation of special water for purification by the use of power-loaded materials such as the ashes of a sacrificial victim,[6] the transference of uncleanness and sin, conceived as something material, by means of the laying-

---

[1]I Sam. 1.13; Ex. 32.6; Isa. 22.13; 28.7 f.; Amos 2.8; Hos. 8.13; 9.1.
[2]Deut. 12.7, 12, 18; 14.26; 16.11, 14, 15; 26.11; 27.7.
[3]We are given some insight into this by the call-vision which he experienced in the Temple (Isa. 6) and by his promise of a feast of rejoicing when Assyria shall have been overcome (Isa. 30.29).
[4]Pss. 26.6 ff.; 27.1–6; 42 f.; 81; 84; 95; 122 etc. Cf. also the beautiful picture of Ecclus. 50.
[5]Ex. 24.6, 8; Lev. 8.23; 14.5–7, 14; 16.14–19; Ezek. 43.19 f.; 45.18 f. Cf. also A. Bertholet, *op. cit.*, pp. 222 ff.
[6]Lev. 14.5–7; Num. 19, cf. 8.7.

on of hands or dipping, [1] and precautions against any contact between the materials needed for making atonement, impregnated as they were with power, and the things of everyday life. [2] Among the objects used in these expiatory sacrifices are prominent various well-known media of sympathetic magic. Examples that may be quoted are the use of golden plague-spots and golden mice to drive away the plague, [3] the offering of a golden locust for similar deliverance from the locust-swarms, [4] and the sacrificing of red dogs to avert rust on the corn. [5]

In the theistic religions this world of demonistic practices is invaded by a deity who is conceived as a person and brings to life a whole series of new ideas to oppose the magical and mechanistic conceptions of lustration. Just as the concept of sin develops from one of *tabu*-uncleanness or demonic possession to that of an offence against a divine person, so the procuring of atonement comes to be thought of, sometimes more, sometimes less explicitly, as a transaction between two persons. Gifts are brought to the angry God to express man's recognition of his complete dependence and subjection and his desire to make good the harm he has done. Because, in a sense, God has been deprived of something, a substitute for that must be produced and his good pleasure aroused toward both gift and giver. The formulas of magic and incantation, which formerly constituted the liturgical texts, are now replaced by prayer and the confession of sin. We are here dealing with two quite different systems of concepts, two types of action which are qualitatively distinct and which cannot be derived the one from the other or interpreted as the stages of a linear development in time; they correspond to experiences which are different in kind, about the possibility or impossibility of which in any particular period of civilization no completely satisfactory opinion can ever be formed on the basis of purely scientific investigation.

The picture of cultic atonement in the theistic religions is complicated by the fact that its forms are frequently borrowed from the ancient magical lustration rites or have been combined with them in a peculiar amalgam. The material of the expiatory offering and the ritual of its presentation may very well derive from that other system of ideas, and yet have undergone a change of meaning. Sickness or

[1]Lev. 16.21; 14.6 f.
[2]Ex. 12.10; 23.18; 34.25; Lev. 6.11, 20 f.; 7.6, 15 ff.; 8.31 f. etc.
[3]I Sam. 6.4.
[4]Cf. *AOB*, plate CXXXIV, fig. 334; *ANEP*, fig. 535.
[5]In the Roman festival of the Robigalia; cf. Chantepie, vol. II, pp. 426 f.

other natural calamities may no longer be magicked away by the preparation of expiatory objects, but such objects may still be offered to make atonement. Purificatory rites involving exorcism, laying-on of hands, and scrupulous separation from all contact with the profane now become means to the highest possible degree of unqualified inward dedication to the deity.

The more definite this transformation of meaning becomes, the more explicit is the recognition of the personal characteristics of God; and in the faith of Israel this is achieved to a unique extent. The stress here is laid on the divine demands in worship and law, in custom and morality. The divine 'Thou shalt' drives home the fact of a God whose personal will is present to control all human conduct. Hence both sin and expiation acquire a special character in the light of man's personal relation with God.

Two effects of this may be seen in the expiatory sacrifices of Israel. The first is that atonement is made to the wrath of God by self-humiliation and reparation; the second that the sinner is transferred from a state of defilement to one of purity. The former clearly derives from the ideas of atonement proper to theism; the latter belongs to the primitive system of thought and has only subsequently been assimilated. Consequently these two conceptions of atonement differ in value.

That even in the earliest period the personal relation to God is the more important element can be seen from the fact that the expiatory offering may take the form of a simple oblation and no more,[1] though care is taken to make the gift as valuable as possible in order to emphasize the attitude of humble renunciation.[2] Since, however, the object is to win back the favour of an angry God, the sacrifice is normally accompanied by prayer and confession of sin[3] and exerts no kind of compulsive effect. Reconciliation remains the gift of God's independent majesty,[4] which explains why there are offences which cannot be expiated by sacrifice.[5]

[1] I Sam. 3.14; 26.19.
[2] Micah 6.6–8.
[3] I Sam. 7.5 f.; Lev. 5.5; 16.21; Num. 5.7; Jer. 3.25, cf. 2.35; Job 42.8; cf. also Josh. 7.19 f. The fact that the prayers accompanying the atonement sacrifice are not very frequently mentioned can hardly mean that repentance, sorrow and confession of sin were not generally taken for granted as the subjective conditions of forgiveness: cf. II Sam. 12.13; I Kings 21.27 ff.; Joel 2.12–14; Pss. 25.7; 32.5; 38.19; 41.5; 51.6 ff.; 65.4; 130.3 f.; Lam. 3.40 ff., etc.
[4] Ex. 32.33 f.; 33.19.
[5] I Sam. 3.14; 15.24 ff.

This personal element in the offering of sacrifice was strengthened by the influence of legal practice. A breach of trust between human beings involved the payment of compensation. The same obligation toward God was expressed in *the guilt offering* or *sacrifice of reparation* (*'āšām*).[1] Moreover, the proper legal compensation had to be made either direct to the injured fellow-citizen, or to the sanctuary at the same time as the sacrifice; and this would seem to suggest that the meaning of the guilt offering lay rather less in what was actually done —since the penalty was in any case not graduated in proportion to the seriousness of the offence, nor could it be increased of one's own freewill—than in the confession which the sacrifice symbolized and in the act of self-humiliation.

In addition to the guilt offering the Priestly Code mentions *the sin offering* (*ḥaṭṭā't*),[2] which may be an ancient designation of the expiatory sacrifice.[3] The lack of any reference to it in many passages where this might have been expected[4] may simply be due to the differences in usage at the various local sanctuaries. Its incorporation into the system of the Priestly Code seems in any case to have occurred fairly late; the fact that its applicability is restricted simply to the inadvertent transgression of some commandment[5] certainly suggests a limitation of its sphere of effectiveness which was not originally characteristic of this sacrifice.[6] The ideas of confession and supplication

---

[1]Lev. 5.14 ff.; 7.1 ff.; 19.20–22; Ezek. 40.39. The theory that *'āšām* originally denoted a fine of money paid to the sanctuary, which was later replaced by a sacrifice, does not follow from II Kings 12.17, nor does it fit in with the normal pattern of development which can be assumed from other cases, by which offerings in kind come to be commuted into money payments (cf. also B. Stade, *Bibl. Theologie des AT*, pp. 165 f., and E. König, *Geschichte der alttestamentlichen Religion*[3,4], 1923, pp. 274 f.). Hos. 4.8 affords no evidence to the contrary.
[2]Lev. 4; 5.1–13; Num. 15.22 ff.; not to mention Ezek. 45.17, 18 ff.
[3]II Kings 12.17; perhaps also Hos. 4.8.
[4]Deut. 12; I Sam. 3.14; Lev. 22.14.
[5]Lev. 4.2; 5.1 ff.; Num. 15.22, 30 f.; Ezek. 45.20.
[6]Num. 17.6–13 already shows a change in the conception of the atoning power of sacrifice. However, in view of the fact that the transgressions mentioned in Lev. 5.20 ff.; 19.20–22 (disclaiming knowledge of trust money or lost property, perjury, extortion) can hardly be regarded as unintentional sins or sins of inadvertence, it may be that the meaning customarily ascribed to the term *bišgāgā*, 'unwittingly', ought to be abandoned for the more general sense 'in human frailty', reserving the opposite phrase *b*yād rāmā*, 'with a high hand', not so much for deliberate offences as for open apostasy and impenitent contempt for the Law. The difference between the two kinds could be tested by the person's willingness to confess his sin and his effort to make reparation. Nevertheless, the actual interpretation to be found in the text at 4.13 f.; 22 f.; 5.1–10 argues for the narrower conception and may possibly be due to the struggle of the post-exilic congregation against the

in conjunction with the expiatory offering may also have played their part here, but the details of the picture give the principal importance to those of purification and dedication. This is indicated by the complicated manipulation of the blood,[1] the making of 'atonement' for inanimate objects such as the altar, the covering of the Ark and the doorposts of the Temple,[2] the use of the sin and guilt offerings explicitly as consecratory sacrifices,[3] and the idea of making atonement by transferring the sin to an animal.[4]

The commonest of all expressions for 'making atonement', *kipper*,[5] also points in the same direction, if the original meaning of this term may be defined as 'to wipe away' on the basis of the Babylonian and Assyrian parallels. Here the fundamental conception of sin is of a material impurity, and the blood, as a holy substance endowed with miraculous power, is expected to remove the stain of sin quite automatically. Thus the cultic act designated in Babylonian by the term *kuppuru* is concerned with purification, healing and exorcism.[6] Since, however, the derivation based on the Arabic, giving the meaning 'to cover', seems equally possible, it may well be that the idea is that of covering one's guilt from the eyes of the offended party by means of reparation, which would by contrast emphasize the personal character of the act of atonement.[7]

---

unreliable elements in their midst. The threat of the death penalty for gross sins, normally by stoning (cf. the list of these offences in E. König, *Theol. des AT*[3, 4], pp. 294 f.), presupposes the regular course of law, with the discovery of the crime, laying of an accusation, etc., and hardly envisages voluntary confession. That the latter alters the situation is clear from a comparison of Lev. 5.20 ff. with the penalties stipulated in the Book of the Covenant, Ex. 21.37; 22.3 ff.; but it is naturally impossible to say to what extent this applied in the case of other offences. It is interesting to note that in later Judaism the view was put forward, that even transgressions which could incur judicial execution were expiated by the scapegoat on the Day of Atonement (Shebuoth 1.6). The latest attempt to limit the effect of the atoning sacrifice to sins of weakness (D. Schötz, *Schuld- und Sündopfer im AT*, 1930, pp. 44 f.) is unsatisfactory.

[1]In addition to the pouring out of the blood at the foot of the altar, there is the smearing on the horns of the altar of burnt offering (Lev. 4.25, 30), or of the altar of incense (Lev. 4.7, 18) and the sevenfold sprinkling by the veil of the holy place (Lev. 4.6, 17).

[2]Lev. 8.15; 16.14–19; Ezek. 43.19 f.; 45.18 f.

[3]Ex. 29; Lev. 8.14 ff. at the installation of the priest; Lev. 14.12 ff. at the purification of the leper; Num. 6.9 ff. at the purification of the Nazirite.

[4]Lev. 16.21.

[5]A penetrating examination of the usage and meaning of this word may be found in J. Herrmann, *Die Idee der Sühne im AT*, 1905.

[6]By contrast such blood-ritual plays no part in Babylonian sacrifice.

[7]In favour of this derivation there is also the construction of *kipper* with *'al*,

Those expiatory sacrifices which were *regularly* offered also exhibit the connection with the ancient consecratory and purificatory rites. Thus *the slaying of the Passover lamb* and the smearing of its blood on the lintel and the door-posts of the house are examples of apotropaic expiation rituals of immense antiquity, with which every spring the purification of the house was effected and the increase of the flocks assured, and which have been and still are used for similar purposes among many other peoples.[1] Equally, *the sacrifices of the great Day of Atonement* in the autumn bear witness to the ancient ideas of purifying and consecrating even inanimate objects through the sacred medium of the blood of the sacrifice.[2]

These primitive lustration concepts must, however, in so far as they held their place in the cultic system of expiation, have undergone an essential change of significance as a result of their connection with the divine Lord to whom atonement had to be made. First of all great stress was laid on the institution of the atonement rituals by God himself. It is well-known that the Priestly Code attaches great importance to the fact that God himself has created and enjoined the means of propitiation, and bases its conviction of their effectiveness on this divine origin. This is not just a post-exilic theory, but represents the Israelite counterpart to the claim put forward by the Babylonian priesthood, that they received their methods of propitiation from Ea

which may be used to express either the covering of the sin (Jer. 18.23; Ps. 79.9) or the face of the offended party (Gen. 32.21). Since, however, the only meaning which can be established with certainty is the technical cultic one of 'make atonement, pardon', the physical connotation of the stem must remain obscure. In the cult law the subject of *kipper* is the priest, in the language of the prophets God himself.

[1] E.g., among the Egyptians, Germans, Athenians and present-day inhabitants of Palestine: cf. P. Volz, *Die biblischen Altertümer*, p. 102. On the subject of the Passover festival cf. above p. 129. The attempt of D. Schötz (*op. cit.*, pp. 82 f.) to explain the smearing with the blood on the basis of the covenant concept certainly does not succeed in reproducing the original significance of the rite, but only a development in the meaning which occurred later in Israel.

[2] Lev. 16.14–19. That the idea of the life-force in the blood plays some part in the sprinkling of the blood at the holy place, so that by this means the sacred area is 'loaded with power', is confirmed by the correspondence between the atoning rites used in this context and those employed at the initial consecration of the sanctuary (Ex. 29.36 f.; Lev. 8.15; Ezek. 43.18 ff.). Similarly, the special attention shown to the horns of the altar, in the form of smearing them with blood, is also designed to make them objects of power, with the effect of reinforcing the holiness of the places where sacrifice is offered, and for this reason (not because they are the 'throne of the deity') endowing them with apotropaic-cathartic significance (cf. atonement made for one guilty of manslaughter). It is clear that the rituals of the Day of Atonement go back to the most ancient times. Cf. above pp. 130 f.

or from his son Marduk, the Chief Magician of the gods, and that this was what guaranteed their operation.[1] While, however, in Babylonia a whole host of gods and demons demanded to be propitiated, in Israel this mutual conflict of divine powers has disappeared. Yahweh is concerned for the propitiation of himself alone, and this means that the element of magic and sorcery has to give way to the personal element which seeks the submission and obedience of men. Atonement does not depend on the frequency of the offerings or the ingenious agglomeration of the most effective possible rites, but on the obedient performance of what the covenant God himself has ordained for the maintenance of his covenant. This also eliminates the idea that there is something especially meritorious in the act of sacrifice,[2] for the apparatus of sacrifice is itself a gift graciously vouchsafed by the covenant God in order to give men the opportunity for confession and reparation.

The result of this direction of attention to the God who has created the cultic processes of atonement is that the individual rites have had their meaning transformed at many points. Thus the meaning of the smearing and sprinkling with blood is now brought under the aspect of oblation, which implies the presenting to God only of the most valuable offering, namely the life of the animal—a point of view which is carried to its logical conclusion in the Priestly Code.[3] The graduated scheme for the application of the blood on the Day of Atonement, which comprises sprinkling the altar, smearing its horns, sprinkling seven times by the inner veil, smearing the horns of the altar of incense, sprinkling the whole of the holy place and sprinkling the blood on the mercy-seat and in front of it seven times, is to be understood as an ascending scale of actions by which the offering is brought as close as possible to the Deity. The transference of the sin to the scapegoat, or of the impurity of the leper to the bird, symbolizes that it is completely done away.[4] The

---

[1]Cf. O. Weber, *Die Literatur der Babylonier und Assyrer*, 1907, pp. 150, 158 ff.; B. Meissner, *Babylonien und Assyrien* II, 1925, pp. 64 ff.

[2]The means of atonement never therefore come to be thought of in a commercial or calculating way, which might try to strike a balance between guilt and expiation, as has in fact happened in the legalist religions of Islam and Parseeism.

[3]Both the laying-on of hands by the offerer (see below) and the waving and heaving of the sacrifice by the priest to symbolize its surrender (Lev. 7.30; 9.21; 10.15; 14.12, 24; 23.11, 20; Num. 5.25; 6.20) help to define the offering as a gift.

[4]For a different interpretation of the ceremony with the bird in the case of the leper, cf. D. Schötz, *op. cit.*, p. 70, where it is suggested that this is symbolic of the giving back of life to the man.

belief in demons thus loses its religious power; Azazel now stands
for the sphere of the unclean outside the limits of the theocracy—a
comparable conception to which may be found in Zech. 5.6 ff.

The attempt has been made to explain the atoning power of
blood in particular in terms of a correspondence between the life
of the victim that is offered and that of the offerer; and this conception, though all the evidence for it is late, may well be of considerable
antiquity. [1] The connection, however, between the sinner and the
expiatory sacrifice is comparatively loose, and does not justify us in
saying that the idea of making atonement by an oblation of great
value is completely replaced by a strict concept of *satisfactio vicaria*. [2]
The substitutionary value of the victim is restricted to the quite
general principle that, if man were to omit the prescribed form of
expiation, he would *irrevocably* fall under the just and annihilating
wrath of God, and that therefore to this extent it is true to say that
by means of the offering of the *nepeš* in the blood atonement is
effected *'al-n^epāšōt* of the sinners. Similarly the resting or placing
of the hands of the offerer upon the victim, the *s^emīkā*, means no
more than that the close relation between the offerer and the victim
ought to take the form of a readiness on the part of the offerer to

[1]It is certainly present in the case of the redemption of a human being by the
offering of an animal, Ex. 34.20; I Sam. 14.45. There might possibly be a connection with the idea of a substitutionary sacrifice in a secondary manner, in so far as
the living animal victim with its limbs and blood passes from being an *equivalent*
to being a *correspondence* to the sinner; and this all the more when the atoning
sacrifice availed not merely for sins of inadvertence, but also for more serious
transgressions. In Babylonia the substitution of an animal victim for the human
being played some part in the healing of the sick by exorcism (cf. O. Weber,
op. cit., pp. 169, 175) and in the cursing of perjurers (B. Meissner, *op. cit.*, vol. I,
p. 140). Here the animal was used limb by limb as a substitute or stand-in to
represent the guilty person: e.g., 'Take a sucking pig; place it on the head of the
sick person; remove its heart and lay it on the heart of the sick person; with its
blood sprinkle the sides of the sick-bed; cut up the pig limb by limb and distribute
them on the sick person! . . . offer the pig as a substitute for him, its flesh in place
of his flesh, its blood in place of his blood, and may the gods accept it' (O. Weber,
op. cit., p. 175).

[2]The principal arguments against accepting a substitutionary interpretation of
the sacrificial death of the slaughtered animal may be briefly summarized as
follows: (1) If the victim were regarded as laden with sin and guilt, it would be
counted unclean; but in fact it is considered exceptionally holy. (2) The principal
action ought to be the slaying of the victim as the execution of the death penalty,
and it ought to be performed by the priest and not by the offerer. (3) In the case of
satisfactio vicaria it would be quite impossible for the sacrifice to be commuted to a
meal offering. (4) The offences atoned for by the sacrifice are, at any rate in the
present text of the Priestly Code, none of them sins worthy of death. (On the question of the ritual of the laying-on of hands, cf. the remarks immediately following.)

surrender that which belongs to him. [1] It may have been that the frequency of particular substitution in the Babylonian rituals of cursing and exorcism hindered the adoption of this idea in Israel. Nevertheless, the idea remains, that sin is not forgiven as a matter of course, but as a result of the offering of a pure and innocent life as expiation for the guilt-laden life of the offerer; and this forms a deep and impressive lesson on the seriousness of sin. However, the absence of any theory of atonement properly so-called made it possible for expiation through the cult to be based all the more firmly on the free and gracious ordinance of the covenant God, and emphasized that the decisive requirement was that of trusting obedience on the part of the offerer.

The unique character of the Israelite conception of atonement stands out all the more clearly when it is compared with the Babylonian ideas. Mention has already been made of the magical effect ascribed to the Babylonian rites and formulas of expiation, and this becomes especially clear when it is remembered that the confession of sin actually forms part of the ritual of exorcism and has *ex opere operato* efficacy. [2] This is closely bound up with an outlook which, under the influence of belief in demons, sees sin not as a state of personal guilt, but as one in which a person is overpowered and enchanted by evil spirits. Hence every expiatory rite must conclude with an expulsion of the demons. In Israel every sin is a case of an offence against the will of Yahweh, and therefore every act of atonement must be directed at him and at the regaining of his good pleasure. For this reason all such rites have their place in the proper cultus, which will have nothing to do with exorcism. By the same token the equal importance attached to moral and cultic transgressions in Israel is nevertheless not accompanied by the tormenting uncertainty noticeable in Babylonia; for while in the latter cultic

[1]To this extent it is correct to compare this with the Roman legal practice of *manumissio*, the release of a part of one's own property, even though the intention of the Israelite offerer to ensure by means of the sacrifice that he will obtain for his own person the gift he requires, and thus to establish an explicit relation between himself and the coming sacrificial action, cannot be left out of account. Why there can be no question of a transference of the sin and impurity of the offerer to the victim has been explained in the previous note. The fact that such a transference obtains in the case of the scapegoat is no proof that it must obtain in all other cases, for the simple reason that the scapegoat is not a sacrificial victim. Cf. Kautzsch, *Bibl. Theologie des AT*, pp. 344 f.; E. König, *Theologie des AT*, pp. 290 f.; Benzinger, *Archäologie*[3], p. 371; Matthes, 'Der Sühnegedanke bei den Sündopfern', *ZAW* 23, 1903, pp. 97 ff.

[2]Cf. especially the *locus classicus* of the Šurpu exorcism texts, *AOT*, pp. 324 f.

impurity was attributed to the demons, who might insinuate themselves at any point, in Israel it was the result of well-known and invariable causes, against which it was possible to take precautions.[1] This also meant that in Israel the priests never acquired the inflated importance, which they did possess in Babylonia, of being indispensable experts in a technique of atonement with which it was impossible for anyone else to be fully acquainted. In all these respects the personal character of Israel's relationship with God succeeded in prevailing over all other influences.

The stress thus laid on the personal element in atonement derived strong support from the belief in *the atoning efficacy of intercession*. That the prophets and other devout persons could plead for their people, and that through their prayers atonement could be made for the nation's transgressions, was a general conviction,[2] even though in each case the decision whether or not to grant the request remained the prerogative of Yahweh's sovereign will.[3] If account is also taken of the fact that the idea of substitution in the relationship of king and people, by which the actions of the one might be credited to the other,[4] was taken over from legal custom into the religious life, then it will be seen that the idea of cultic atonement was constantly being limited and interpreted in terms of a purely personal intercourse of the faithful with their God.

This fact should be remembered equally when considering *the systematic development of the concept of atonement in the Priestly Code* and the rejection of sacrifice as a sufficient means of expiation in the case of the prophets and psalmists. On the one hand, the fact that as a result of the prophetic preaching Israel's sense of sin became stronger and deeper, and that in the Priestly Code and still more in the postscripts to Ezekiel (45.15 ff.) the whole sacrificial system was subordinated to the idea of atonement does not necessarily imply that the theory of expiation had become completely materialistic. Rather did it give sacrificial worship the character of an obedient humility in the presence of God, in whose eyes no man is pure, and made it

---

[1]Cf. on this point Seeger, *Die Triebkräfte des religiösen Lebens in Israel und Babylon*, 1923, pp. 95 f.

[2]Gen. 18.23 ff.; Ex. 32.11–14, 32; I Sam. 12.23; Amos 7.2, 5; Jer. 7.16; 11.14; 14.11; 15.1, 11; Ezek. 13.5; 14.14; 22.30.

[3]This is the fundamental point of difference from the intercessors endowed with power whom we find in other religions.

[4]II Sam. 24.17; Hos. 1.4; I Kings 8.25; 11.34 ff.; 14.16; II Kings 8.19; 20.6; 22.20; Jer. 23.6; Isa. 53; IV Macc. 6.28 f.

the token of the graciousness with which he admits man to his fellowship and which makes any idea of merit quite untenable. On the other hand, *the protest of the prophets against the abuse of sacrifice* by regarding it as an act with intrinsic value not only safeguarded God's sovereign right to forgive even where no sacrifice was offered, but made it clear that the rightful status of the cult as the machinery of divine grace could only obtain within the framework of the covenant relationship; and it was the irreparable breach of this relationship by the sin of the nation which they for their part were bound to proclaim. [1] Moreover, the rejection of sacrifices in favour of a right attitude of heart in many of the Psalms [2] constitutes a claim, based on personal experience of the God who both punishes and forgives sins, to the right to dispense with sacrifices, wherever their essential meaning, spiritual intercourse with God, has been overpoweringly experienced in prayer. Partly this springs from an opposition to the tendency of the sacrificial system to make the forgiveness of sins a mechanical process; [3] but another motive present is to protest against the lavish indulgence in sacrifice of those who were rich in this world's goods.

A new turn of some importance was given to the practice of sacrificial atonement *in post-exilic Judaism*. The ground for this had been prepared by the regulation of sacrificial worship in P. Here atonement had been made the purpose of all sacrifice, though admittedly without basing the efficacy of the latter on anything other than the absolute will of God, who had prescribed these atoning rituals and made them the vehicles of his forgiveness. The result was, however, that sacrificial worship lost more and more of its original motive and meaning, and acquired the uniform character of an act of obedience which had to be performed as part of the prescribed method of fulfilling the Law. It is true that it remained the great sacrament of reconciliation, but the living fellowship between God and man, which had found expression in the ancient sacrificial concepts of gift, communion and expiation, shrivelled up into a mere correct observance of the legal regulations. Moreover, in so far as the Law in later Judaism was understood one-sidedly as the performance

---

[1] The issue, therefore, in the polemic of the prophets is whether the breaking of the covenant can be healed by sacrifice or whether sacrifice has any meaning only within the context of an intact covenant relationship—not an attempt to replace the cultus by morality. Cf. further ch. VIII. 6. III, pp. 364 ff., below.

[2] Pss. 40.7 f.; 51.18 ff.; 69.31 f.

[3] In later Judaism; cf. II Macc. 3.32 ff.; 12.42 ff.

demanded from men by God, and therefore something that merited God's favour, sacrifice also came to be regarded from this point of view and lost the character of a gift of grace. The obedience which it demonstrated became the thing that mattered; hence side by side with it grew up other acts of obedience of equal value, such as the patient endurance of suffering, the practice of love, piety, prayer and—in scribal circles—the study of the Torah. [1] And since other equally valid methods of atonement beside those of the cult were developed in obedience to the Law, the end of the cultus with the destruction of the Temple could be absorbed without too much dislocation.

Thus it was that *the heart of the cultus was stripped almost unnoticed of its original functions*. It was, so to speak, pushed on to a siding; and once this had happened its fate was sealed. That this was possible must be laid at the door of the change in the priorities of piety which resulted from the influence of the great wars of religion against the Syrians. The present world-order was regarded as lying under final judgment, and the divine world to come was raised to the position of the true goal of the religious life. In such circumstances the sacrificial cultus as the sacrament of the present reality of God, entering into communion with his people in judgment and grace, became a meaningless concept. Instead it became a one-sided expression of human subjection to the strict demand for obedience to a distant deity, and, like the whole of the Law, was degraded from being a precious source of blessing in its own right to a means by which the final realization of man's fervent eschatological hopes and longings could be ensured. Keep the Law perfectly for just one day and the Messiah would appear! What has happened may be described as *an organic combination of two incompatible ideals* in Old Testament piety, namely that of the divine Lordship expressed and actualized in immediate historical reality and guaranteed by a life lived in accordance with the covenant order, and that of a miraculous yonside world of paradisal perfection, in which history is done away. In that the one, however, sank to the level of a means for the attainment of the other, both suffered a serious depreciation. God's rule in the present became a gloomy and irrational tyranny, only supportable because of the vision of the future; and God's hoped-for dominion in the future underwent even more serious degradation

---

[1] Prov. 16.6; Dan. 4.24; Ecclus. 3.3, 30; 18.20; 32.1 ff.; 35.1–7. Cf. O. Schmitz, *Die Opferanschauung des späteren Judentums*, 1910, pp. 55 ff.

in proportion as it was conceived simply as a means of fulfilling men's unsatisfied earthly longings, and set up Jewish world-dominion as the essential feature of salvation in place of the divine perfection.

The effect is substantially the same when, as in the Hellenistic Diaspora, the emphasis is on mystical communion with God rather than on eschatological bliss; it is only the course taken by the devaluation of the sacrificial system which is different. Here men had lost the power of recognizing God's manifestation of his real proximity through the concrete forms of history, and so they resorted to systematic reinterpretation of the sacrificial ordinances, seeing them either as the symbolic expression of eternal truths or as a guide, which had to be understood allegorically, to ascetic purification from the defilements of the physical (Philo). Hence this also became a means of achieving a salvation of a totally different kind, a mystical sinking of the soul in the Deity, which no longer had any need of the mediation of history.

In each case the result was to render sacrifice superfluous, because its original meaning had been lost owing to a change of the greatest consequence in the orientation of piety. The new value attributed to it as a substitute for the old only served to confirm that it was expendable. It is the intercessory function of sacrifice, its significance as a medium of intercourse with God, which men are no longer capable of inwardly making their own. For in the atoning sacrifice, and also in the other sacrifices to which the idea of atonement has been transferred, the essential theme is that the gulf between the angry God and the human sinner can only be bridged by the interposition of an act of reparation; and in that it is God himself who establishes the way in which such an atoning substitute can be offered, he shows himself by this very act the covenant God, who is concerned for the maintenance of the covenant despite all the sin of man. Ancient Israel had a living understanding of God's part in the atonement sacrifice; and that is why the restoration of the Temple worship after the Exile was felt to set the seal on the restoration of God's covenant favour. But the Pharisees had lost the power to discern God's part in the work of cultic atonement; they saw only man's performance and thought that this *per se* atoned for sin and merited the divine forgiveness. In sacrifice the Pharisee drew near to God with just as much confidence because of his piety as he did in any of his other acts of obedience. For the same reason he no longer had any real understanding of the overflowing assurance of salvation of the Psalmists, who had enjoyed so overwhelming an experience of God's sovereign mercy to sinners that they could afford to dispense with sacrifice. Similarly, the Hellenistic mystics did away with the intercessory character of sacrifice in order by interpreting it allegorically to open up the way to the union of the soul with God. *But an effective liberation from the need for sacrifice was not to be attained by either of these methods.* Even after the destruction of the Temple, sacrifice continued to occupy the attention of the devout in the form of the problem of how to achieve complete fulfilment of the obedience demanded by the Law. Its omission from the daily worship of God was just as irrational as had been its earlier centrality. Complete liberation from the institution of sacrifice, without at the same time losing its proper and indispensable effects, could only be attained in that relationship with God which was based on Christ. Moreover it was achieved not by the construction of a new theory of sacrifice, but by *the faith of the primitive congregation in Christ's intercession.* In the laying down of his life God's action for the reconciliation of humanity was triumphantly revealed in the provision of the supreme reparatory act of atonement. Christ as the Substitute for all those threatened by the wrath of God accomplished once for all his priestly service and brought to an end the sacrificial worship of the Old Testament.

Moreover, because this atoning substitution was revealed at the same time as the work of the messianic King sent by God for the setting up of his Kingdom, it brought about *an organic union of both the great motifs of the religious life* which the old covenant had never achieved. The reality of the divine Lordship revealed in history and the consummation of the world to come found their common centre in the person of him who as the Risen Christ would always be present among men and as the Exalted Christ would one day return as their redeemer. The eloquent testimony to this reconciliation of hitherto conflicting themes is the 'figurative application of the Old Testament theology of sacrifice to the death of the mediator between God and man' in the New Testament. [1] Equally removed from rationalizing speculation and from slavish adherence to the details of the cultus, it yet expresses the tension between judgment and mercy which is so conspicuous a feature of Old Testament sacrificial worship in that it both does justice to the majesty of the holy covenant God, and at the same time is continually liberated by that love which

[1] Cf. O. Schmitz, *op. cit.*, pp. 301 ff.

makes atonement for sin and which 'by one offering hath perfected for ever them that are sanctified'. [1]

(c) Prayer

Sacrifice and prayer go extremely closely together, as appears at the outset in the words used for each. *heʿ·tīr*, originally a technical term of sacrificial language, [2] is used in Hebrew to mean 'to pray'. Conversely, *biqqēš ʾet-yhwh*, 'to seek Yahweh', serves as a phrase for 'to sacrifice'. [3] Prayers such as accompanied the act of sacrifice are also preserved in the Psalter; for instance, the supplication of the king going forth to war, [4] prayers at the presentation of vows and thank-offerings, [5] festival liturgies [6] and so on. Even if the present form of these prayers is frequently of no great antiquity, as a type they are as old as sacrifice itself; and because it is a peculiarity of liturgical formulas to hand down and preserve forms fixed in times very different from their own, it is possible to draw conclusions about the early period even from prayers that are quite late.

Hence it is still possible to detect here and there *the traces of primitive elements* in Israelite prayer. Thus the most frequent terms for praying derive from words meaning to call or cry aloud. [7] The use of the verbs *hitpallēl*, strictly 'to make cuts in oneself', and *ḥillā*, 'to stroke', [8] recalls ancient customs of prayer in which the person praying wounded himself in order to attract the attention of the deity, [9] or touched the image or symbol of the God with his hands or lips, [10] though naturally this proves nothing as to whether these particular meanings of the words were still present to the consciousness of Yahweh worshippers in their prayers. Even the custom of stretching out the hands may originally have had magical significance. [11] Whether in some passages a form of incantation can still be detected, it is impossible to decide with certainty. [12] In any case it is

[1]Heb. 10.14.
[2]Cf. Arabic *ʿatara*, 'to sacrifice' and Ex. 8.4, 25; 9.28; 10.17 etc.
[3]Hos. 5.6.
[4]Ps. 20.
[5]For the former cf. Pss. 61; 65: for the latter, Pss. 21; 66; 100; 116; 118; Jonah 2; Jer. 33.11.
[6]Pss. 24; 50; 67; 81; 95.
[7]*qārāʾ bᵉšēm*, Gen. 4.26; 12.8 etc. *qārāʾ ʾel-* Deut. 15.9; I Kings 8.43; Jer. 11.14 etc. *zāʿaq* Judg. 3.9, 15; 6.6 f.; I Sam. 7.8 f.; Hos. 8.2; Micah 3.4, etc.
[8]Ex. 32.11; I Sam. 13.12; I Kings 13.6 etc.
[9]Attested for the cult of Baal, I Kings 18.28.
[10]Ex. 17.16; Hos. 13.2.
[11]Ex. 17.11; cf. the Babylonian prayers linked with the lifting up of the hands.
[12]The examples most often cited are those of the Song of the Well (Num. 21.17f.),

clear that we are here dealing with the rudiments of primitive practice, which no longer possess any significance of their own and emerge mainly on the periphery of the Yahweh religion, until in the end they are completely suppressed by it. An early instance of deliberate mockery at the expense of these striking practices in prayer is to be found in I Kings 18.27 ff.

The tendency here discernible in the Yahweh religion may be seen also in the part played in it by two types of invocation closely related to witchcraft, namely *the curse and the blessing*. In Israel as well as elsewhere there was a very real belief that once a word had been spoken it exerted power in a quasi-material way, irresistibly effective in operation and largely independent of the deity—a belief closely related to the primitive ideas of 'power' in general. The anxious efforts to render harmless the curse which the Gibeonites had pronounced against Israel on account of their massacre at the hands of Saul led to the execution of Saul's descendants, despite the fact that this was in direct contravention of the principle of the Book of the Covenant, which forbade the punishment of the children as expiation for the sins of the fathers. [1] The last charge of David to Solomon to see that the Benjamite Shimei was eventually punished for his curse reveals the tenacity of the belief in the near-automatic operation of a curse, even though it had been forgiven at the time and the person concerned was well aware that it had been undeserved. [2]

In addition, however, to evidence of this kind there are instances in the other direction, which show how Yahweh became Lord over the blessing and the curse and stripped them of their original character. Because the curse is uttered in the name of Yahweh, [3] it is he who carries it out; [4] but equally this means that he has the power to apply the curse to a different object or to make it ineffective. [5] Hence the use of the name of Yahweh in the curse for the purpose of personal vengeance was forbidden at quite an early stage

Joshua's command to the sun and moon (Josh. 10.12) and Elisha's arrow symbolism (II Kings 13.14 ff.), but in all these cases other explanations are more likely; thus in the case of Elisha it is probably a question of effective symbolism of future events by the man of God.

[1] II Sam. 21.

[2] I Kings 2.8 f. Cf. also the need to remove the curse once expressed by a countering blessing, Judg. 17.2.

[3] I Sam. 26.19; II Kings 2.24; Deut. 27.14 ff.; cf. I Sam. 17.43.

[4] Judg. 9.57; Deut. 28.20.

[5] Deut. 30.7; II Sam. 16.12.

and its malicious use made punishable.[1] This opens up the possibility of replacing the curse, which operates by its own intrinsic force, by the prayer for vengeance, which hands over the punishment to the free act of God.[2] By an analogous development the blessing of the man endowed with special power[3] comes to be replaced by intercession,[4] which becomes an especially popular element of the cultus.[5] Here also it is ultimately the will of Yahweh which determines the scope of the blessing, where formerly the tendency had been to ascribe this to the particular intercessor.[6] Just as in the sphere of prayer proper magical practices with their ideas of compulsion were purged away, so the blessing and the curse are subjected to moral conditions. The blessing of Yahweh is promised to Israel solely in the event of their fulfilling his demands, as the blessing and cursing formulas at the end of the Law prove with especial clarity.[7] Moreover, there will be no fulfilment of the blessing pronounced by the unworthy priest.[8]

Thus it is that the character of incantation disappears completely from the prayer of the Old Testament. The three characteristics of incantation are the magical utterance of the name of God, the frequent repetition of the prayer in identical terms, and a special manner of reciting it in a murmured or whispering voice;[9] and the absence of these features is significant for the character of Israelite prayer. Great store was set by the divine name, even to the extent of using it from time to time as a tattoo-mark;[10] but we hear nothing of its being kept secret as an especially efficacious medium of power —quite the opposite, in fact, since the fundamental revelation of Yahweh to Moses consists in the revelation of his name,[11] in order

[1]Ex. 20.7; Deut. 5.11; cf. Pss. 59.13; 109.17; Job 31.30.
[2]Jer. 11.20; 12.3; 15.15 f.; 17.18; 18.19 ff.; Ps. 137.
[3]The Old Testament affords no direct instance of this. Some slight after-effect of the old belief may be seen in the authority of particular intercessors, whose prayers are confidently believed to be granted sooner than those of other men (I Sam. 7.8 f.; 12.19; I Kings 13.6; II Kings 19.4).
[4]Cf. P. A. H. de Boer, 'De Vorbede in het Oude Testament', *OTS* 3, 1943, and F. Hesse, *Die Fürbitte im Alten Testament*, 1951.
[5]I Sam. 1.17; 9.13; II Sam. 6.18; Lev. 9.22 f.; Num. 6.24–26; Deut. 26.15.
[6]Ex. 32.32; I Sam. 15.11; Jer. 15.1; Zech. 3.7; cf. p. 167 above.
[7]Deut. 28; Lev. 26; cf. Ex. 32.33.
[8]Mal. 2.2.
[9]So J. Hempel, *Gebet und Frömmigkeit im AT*, 1922, p. 14.
[10]Isa. 44.5; Zech. 13.6; perhaps also I Kings 20.41.
[11]Ex. 3. The refusal to reveal the name in the case of the angelic manifestations of Gen. 32.30 and Judg. 13.18 emphasizes that the nature of the celestial is incomprehensible to men; there may nevertheless also be a remnant of the name-*tabu*.

that men may use it to call upon him and to remember his dual
nature as both the Judge who punishes and the Lord of compassion,
to whom in particular the poor and oppressed may turn.[1] There is
no mention of any value being attached to frequent repetition of the
prayer, nor of an anxious preoccupation with the exact form of
words, nor of a correct manner of recitation. The normal way of
praying was to speak aloud, and[2] the introduction of stereotyped
formulas[3] was conditioned by the duty of making a confessional
statement on particular occasions.

This exclusion of all irreligious ideas of compulsion from the
practice of prayer is in accordance with Israel's strong sense of the
exalted Lordship of God, and the same sense is expressed in the
gestures which accompany prayer. The acts of kneeling and raising
the hands, followed by the bowing of the face to the ground, correspond to the behaviour of the vassal in the presence of his king, and
symbolize the submission of the supplicant to a will higher than his
own.

The strength and genuineness of the life of prayer in Israel is
attested first by the freedom of its cultic prayers and hymns from
any trace of hollow pathos or high-flown flattery; rather its marks
are a childlike simplicity, sincerity and confidence toward him who
has been their God 'from Egypt until now'.[4] Secondly there is none
of the disparity between the prayer of the cultus and the prayer of the
private individual which is such a notable feature of the prayer
literature of the rest of the ancient world, for instance, that of
Babylonia.[5] Because the official cult is not dominated by lifeless
formal trumpery and degrading incantations, there is no need for
a real and living piety to take refuge in private prayer, but real
adoration and lively religious feeling lend force even to public
worship. The fierce attacks of the great prophets on the formalist
practice of prayer,[6] together with their own example,[7] resulted in
the introduction of the true spirit of prayer even in the cultus. The
practice of the life of prayer was greatly advanced by the Exile, as

[1]Pss. 9.10; 25.16 ff.; 40.18; 70.6, etc.
[2]Cf. I. Sam. 1.12 f.
[3]Deut. 26.13 ff.; 21.7 f.
[4]Cf. by contrast F. Heiler, 'Urteil über die antike Ritualpoesie' (*Das Gebet*, pp. 172 ff.).
[5]Cf. O. Weber, *Die Literatur der Babylonier und Assyrer*, pp. 141 f.
[6]Isa. 1.15; 29.13; Amos 5.23.
[7]I Kings 19.4 ff.; Amos 7.2, 5; Jer. 12.1 ff.; 15.15 ff.; 16.19 ff.; 17.12 ff.; 20.7 ff.

the treasury of prayers in the Psalter bears witness; but this advance was endangered in later Judaism by the inclusion of the cultus in the category of works of obedience. Prayer similarly became an obligatory and meritorious work of the pious; and there were prescribed times,[1] forms,[2] and apparel[3] for prayer to remind him of his duty.

Indicative of the pattern of Old Testament piety is the fact that the dominant motives of prayer never included that of losing oneself, through contemplation, in the divine infinity.[4] There was no room in Israel for mystical prayer; the nature of the Mosaic Yahweh with his mighty personal will effectively prevented the development of that type of prayer which seeks to dissolve the individual I in the unbounded One. Just as the God of the Old Testament is no Being reposing in his own beatitude, but reveals himself as the controlling will of the eternal King, so the pious Israelite is no intoxicated, world-denying mystic revelling in the Beyond, but a warrior, who wrestles even in prayer, and looks for the life of power in communion with his divine Lord. His goal is not the static concept of the *summum bonum*, but the dynamic fact of the βασιλεία τοῦ θεοῦ.[5]

v. *Synthesis*

Taking it all in all it may be said that both as a means of expression and as a sacramental institution the cultus performed a vital and indeed indispensable function in the Yahweh religion. Even if many elements in it were never fully assimilated, yet the overall pattern of the worship of God from the very first took its special stamp from the unique nature of man's relationship with God as the Old Testament understood it. The living relation between belief and cult showed itself in the incessant transformation and extension of cultic forms, revealing the massive power of assimilation inherent in the religion of Yahweh. The expulsion of belief in spirits, 'power' and magic even from the most ancient sacred rites meant that these had been disarmed in their most impregnable strongholds;

[1]Morning and evening prayer, I Chron. 23.30; prayer thrice daily, Dan. 6.11; Ps. 55.18.
[2]The Eighteen Benedictions (*Shemoneh Esreh*) and the *Shema*[6], formed by combining Deut. 6.4–9; 11.13–21 and Num. 15.37–41.
[3]Special tassels on the clothing, called ṣîṣiyyōt, on the basis of Num. 15.37 ff.; Deut. 22.12; and prayer boxes on leather straps, tᵉpillīn, on the basis of Ex. 13.9; Deut. 6.8; 11.18.
[4]Rightly emphasized by Hempel, *op. cit.*, p. 28.
[5]Formulated in this way by F. Heiler, *Das Gebet*, p. 409.

and as the gradual doing away with the sacred objects in the Mosaic period proves, this process was carried out inexorably to its logical conclusion. Equally fundamental was the rejection of the naturalistic conception of God, which found in the cult many useful and congenial ways to intrude itself. In the struggle against the localization of the deity, against Nature mysticism, orgiastic practices and misunderstanding of the meaning of sacrifice, the significance of the cultus as a form in which belief in a spiritual and personal God could be both expressed and lived was safeguarded, and the claim of religion to affect every aspect of the national life upheld.[1] Not until the period of later Judaism, when piety underwent a transformation of the greatest consequence which turned the religion of Yahweh into a religion of observances, was there a threat that the soteriological character of the cultic actions might be obscured by the attempt to comprehend them all in the one-sided classification of works of obedience. This development, however, was not something based on the essential nature of the cult; it was the result of its subjection to the alien standard of legalism.

[1]On the dangers of the cultus cf. ch. II. 2. 1 (b), pp. 46 f., above, and ch. VIII. 6. III (b), pp. 364 f., below.

V

THE NAME OF THE COVENANT GOD

IF THE SAYING *nomina sunt realia* is valid in any context, it is surely that of the divine name in the ancient world. The question, therefore, of what kind of name the God of Israel bore is no idle one, but can be the means of arriving at an important insight into Israel's religious thought.

The special covenant name of the Israelite national God, the name which he, so to speak, subscribed to the charter of the Sinai covenant, is essentially Yahweh. But other designations of the deity are older than this name and have, therefore, a prior claim on our consideration. [1]

I. GENERAL SEMITIC DESIGNATIONS OF GOD

1. One of the oldest general Semitic designations of God is '*ēl*. As applied to Yahweh it is found in the prose writings relatively infrequently and, indeed, seems to be avoided by certain writers altogether. On the other hand, in the purely poetic books of Psalms and Job, it is often employed. That in this, as in other respects, poetry is preserving an older idiom, is shown by the part which the name '*El* plays in the ancient Semitic systems of name-construction. For in Israel, just as in Babylonia and Arabia, the oldest names are formed not with the special name of the individual deity, but with the general component -*el*. [2]

---

[1] A good collection of the relevant material is to be found in A. Murtonen, *A Philological and Literary Treatise on the Old Testament Divine Names* (Studia Orientalia Fennica XVII. 1), 1952.

[2] For Israel, cf. the names in the Genesis narratives, such as Ishmael, Bethuel etc., and the lists of names in Num. 1.7 f., 13. In the case of pre-Israelite Canaan, there are names like Milki-ilu, Rabili, Atanah-ili from the Amarna and Taanach documents; in Babylonia, Ilumma-ila, Ibni-ilu, etc. (cf. H. Ranke, *Early*

The original meaning of this word is uncertain. Competing derivations include: (1) from a stem *'ūl* 'to be strong' [1] or 'in front'; [2] or (2)—and this more probable—from the root *'lh* meaning either 'to be strong, powerful' [3] or 'direction, sphere of control'; [4] or (3) from the root *'l* 'to bind', hence 'binding force'. [5] One can, therefore, choose between 'Mighty', 'Leader' and 'Governor'. It is worth noting that whichever of these meanings we adopt stresses the distance between God and man. In this they are in conformity with a basic characteristic of the Semitic concept of God, namely, that what is of primary importance is not the feeling of kinship with the deity, but fear and trembling in the face of his overwhelming majesty. Another point which it is necessary to remark is that they do not identify the Godhead with any natural object, but describe it as the power which stands behind Nature or the overruling will manifested in it.

If, however, this general designation of the deity was favoured right down to the second millennium as the theophorous component in personal names, whereas it was only later that the particular names of the different Nature deities were introduced into the system of name-formation, this can only mean that the individual person, or even the larger social units of the tribe, the city-state and the nation, did on occasion, in their own special domain, worship simply *the* God, beside whom other gods played but a subordinate role. This indicates, therefore, at the least a monarchic polytheism, and in many cases what amounts in effect to a practical monism with some inkling of a higher unity behind the multiplicity of gods. [6]

In addition to this tendency to exclusiveness, the ancient Semitic use of *'ēl* demonstrates a strong link between the divine activity and the social life of the community. Such names as 'God is merciful', 'God helps', 'God is judge' are extraordinarily frequent and show that we are dealing not merely with some spiritual being of little

---

Babylonian Personal Names, 1905); in South Arabia, IlC-awwas, Jasma'-ilu, etc. (cf. F. Hommel, *Ancient Hebrew Tradition as illustrated by the Monuments*, ET, 1897, pp. 83 ff.).

[1]So e.g. H. Schultz, *OT Theology*[2] II, p. 126 n. 4.
[2]So Th. Nöldeke, *Monatsber. der Berl. Akad. der Wiss.*, 1880, pp. 760 ff.
[3]So A. Dillmann, *AT Theologie*, p. 210.
[4]So J. Hehn, *Die biblische und die babylonische Gottesidee*, 1913, pp. 200 ff.
[5]So O. Procksch, *Die Genesis*[2, 3], p. 439 and in *NKZ* 35, 1924, pp. 20 ff.
[6]This is also attested by the use of the plural *ilani* for the idea of 'divinity' in the Amarna letters.

positive account, but with a deity who draws into the sphere of his concerns the moral and social needs of a people or tribe.

If we compare the role of the ancient Israelite El in the Genesis narratives with the above indications, then the features mentioned stand out with remarkable clarity. In the first place there is evidence in these narratives of a worship of El among the migrant Hebrew tribes of the early period, which—though the narrator himself is scarcely conscious of this—is quite spontaneously opposed to the cult of the Canaanite Baal [1] and thus affords confirmation of the exclusive character of the El-cult to which attention has already been drawn. [2] In the second place, the frequent practice of naming El after one of the patriarchs ('God of Abraham', Gen. 31.53; 'Fear of Isaac', 31.42; 'Mighty One of Jacob', 49.24) or of designating him as 'God of the fathers', or, alternatively, according to the standpoint of the speaker, as 'God of my father', 'God of thy father' and so on, [3] indicates a special association of the deity with the individual leader, such as later parallel phenomena among the Nabataeans and Palmyrenes show to have been a distinctive religious category. [4] This distinctiveness consists in the fact that the deity is not associated with particular cultic sites, but with persons who experienced his first revelation and in whose family he is now worshipped. In this way the god is drawn into the context of the social and the historical—a development not

[1]All the divine names preserved in Genesis include the component '*ēl*, with the sole exception of the *paḥad yiṣḥāq*, Gen. 31.42—a fact which is hardly to be explained as a product of tendentious emendation, since no stress is laid on the opposition to the Canaanite Baal and, in addition, the personal names of the patriarchs, the very foundation-stone of the saga, indicate that their owners were El worshippers. Even Isaac, Jacob and Joseph can be authentically cited as theophorous personal names with the component El, though this was dropped at a later period.

[2]'Exclusive' is used here, of course, in the very relative sense of the special elevation of the protector or tribal god, not in the sense that other gods are rejected or their existence denied. The strict insistence on this kind of exclusiveness is seen also in the refusal of all *connubium* with the Canaanites. The later exaltation of El itself into a personal name points in the same direction (cf. below). It is worth noting that the Ras Shamra documents recognize a certain opposition between El, the supreme god and 'Father of Years', and Baal, the warrior storm-god and King of the gods. While El, admittedly, still retains his hereditary position as supreme god, it is clear that Al'iyan Baal, the 'Conqueror', on whom the great fertility and vegetation myth centres, has already far outstripped him in actual significance. The figure of El, the divine Father, embodies the link with the civilized world at large, whereas it is the particularist development of religion in Canaan that is reflected in Baal.

[3]Gen. 26.24 (J); 28.13 (J); 31.5 (E); 31.29, 42 (JE); 32.10 (J) etc.

[4]For the detection and evaluation of these facts we are indebted to A. Alt in his penetrating study *Der Gott der Väter*, 1929.

to be found, for the most part, in the case of the local divinity proper. The concern and activity of the god is manifested in the destinies of the tribe or of the individual worshipper, not in natural forces, of whatever kind, nor in the rights of possession of particular localities.

2. This distinctive concept of God bound up with the name El is further illuminated by some of the *epithets of the Father-God* used in combination with El. The divine name El Shaddai, which is also known to us from sources outside the patriarchal sagas, probably reflects an ancient connection with the world of Babylonian religion. [1] It may be derived from the Babylonian designation of the deity as *šadū*, 'mountain', i.e., 'Lord' or 'Most High', [2] which as a primitive form is close to *šāday*, [3] and points to the link between the ancient religion of Israel and Mesopotamia. Moreover, in later times, when there was no longer any clear idea of the meaning of the name, [4] the original force of 'exaltedness' seems still to have been deduced from it, as we may conjecture from its use by the poet of the Book of Job and the translation of it in the LXX version of that book by κύριος or παντοκράτωρ.

Just as, in the last instance, the epithet strongly emphasized the unique meaning of *'ēl* for the circle of the worshippers, so it is with the epithet most nearly related to it—*'elyōn*. [5] This denotes the *deity as Most High*, and therefore as apex of the pantheon. Such a pyramidal monarchical structure in polytheism seems to have been well known in certain circles of ancient Canaan. The usage is also attributed to Melchisedek, the priest-king of Jerusalem, while Philo Byblius attests as a name of the god of Byblos (*alias* Gebal) Eliun, who was titled Hypsistos. Significantly, the Creator-concept is in

[1]This name, which is associated with Abraham in the latest source P (Gen. 17.1, *et al.*), is also attested from ancient poetic passages (Gen. 49.25; Num. 24.4, 16) and functions as a theophorous component in the lists of personal names (Num. 1.6, 12, etc.).

[2]Friedrich Delitzsch, *Prolegomena . . . hebr.-aram. Wörterbuch zum AT*, 1886, pp. 95 f.; F. Hommel, *Ancient Hebrew Tradition*, pp. 109 ff.; J. Hehn, *op. cit.*, pp. 265 ff.

[3]The Massoretic pointing *šadday*, which assumes the root to be *šdd* 'to destroy', is only guesswork and does not accord with the usage of the name.

[4]The Greek translators sometimes read *šēdī*, 'my protector God', and sometimes split the word into two parts *še-* and *-day* = 'He that gives sufficiency', θεὸς ἱκανός.

[5]Gen. 14.18 ff.; cf. Num. 24.16, where it is used in conjunction with Shaddai. On the question of the historical evaluation of Gen. 14.18 ff. cf. Gunkel, *Genesis*[3], 1910, pp. 285 ff.

both cases associated with this 'most high god', [1] thus making explicit that distinction of El from a force of Nature which is demonstrable also in other places.

Whereas in the general usage of the earlier period the name Elyon receded considerably in importance, [2] at a later time, when the tendency, either under pressure from external conditions or for propaganda purposes, was to avoid the use of the too specifically Judaistic, it won particular favour. The title commended itself in such circumstances as a convenient means of indicating a kind of half-way stage between Judaism and paganism because of its universality and lack of definition; and by using it instead of anything more nationalistically Israelite, it was possible to establish a link with the loftier heathen concepts of God which was of the greatest convenience especially for the Jewish Diaspora. Elyon, i.e. ὕψιστος, is a favourite term not only with I Esdras, [3] but also in Ben Sira [4] and Daniel [5] and very frequently in Enoch, Jubilees and II (4) Esdras. The polytheistic colour that originally attached to the word is by now completely forgotten, and all that it conveys is the implication of sublimity and omnipotence.

The divine name 'ēl 'ōlām is attested only once for the early period, [6] and this in connection with the cult-site of Beersheba. Most probably to be regarded as the name of the local deity worshipped there and adopted by the Israelites, it may be taken to mean 'God of Ancient Days' or 'God of Eternity'. In either case it signifies the permanence of the deity exalted over the changes and chances of time. Some connection with the time-mysticism of the ancient East is within the bounds of possibility, [7] and this would also explain the appearance of the name

[1]Gen. 14.19: qōnē šāmayim wā'āreṣ. This idea cannot be attested elsewhere in connection with the worship of El; but this is not to say that it is necessarily foreign to it, since it is perfectly in keeping with such conceptions as can be established.

[2]The usage continues to be natural to poetry: cf. I Sam. 2.10 (as emended); II Sam. 22.14; Pss. 21.8; 46.5; Deut. 32.8. Also Pss. 47.3; 50.14; 57.3, etc.

[3]I Esdr. 2.3; 6.31; 8.19, 21; 9.46.

[4]Some 50 times.

[5]Dan. 3.26, 32; 4.21, 29, 31; 5.18, 21; 7.18, 22, 25, 27.

[6]Gen. 21.33. The closest parallel is šmš 'lm, the eternal Shamash, in the gate inscription from Kara-tepe, 9th–8th cent. (Welt des Orient 4, 1949, pp. 272 ff.)

[7]Particularly emphasized by R. Kittel, Die hellenistische Mysterienreligion und das Alte Testament, 1924. According to the late evidence of Damascius the Phoenicians worshipped a god by the name of Χρόνος ἀγήραος, i.e. 'never-aging Time'. According to Philo Byblius the most ancient god of the Phoenicians was Ἧλος, who was also called Chronos. Because of the strong Egyptian influence on Phoenicia Egyptian time-speculations must also be taken into account; from the third

among the nomadic Hebrew tribes before the Occupation. But all the same, under whatever influences the adoption of the name may have come about, it is still significant that it was with the concept of the living power exalted above time that El, worshipped as the supreme Lord, was associated. Here is made explicit the refusal to drag down the deity into the flux of natural phenomena—something which is inevitable in the case of those vegetation and nature gods for whom the mystery of life and death plays such a vital role.

It is evidence of the great antiquity of this particular divine name, that the aspect of the divine Being which it emphasized should recede into the background in the Yahweh religion long before other attributes. [1] In spite of the importance which Beersheba enjoyed as a place of pilgrimage during the most flourishing period of the nation's history, a fact attested by both Amos and Hosea, [2] nothing more is heard of the special name of the God of Beersheba. Men only learnt to value Yahweh as the eternal, immortal God, when they had had brought home to them in the most painful manner the transience of the nation, an experience which caused many to question even the living power of the national God. During and after the Exile, therefore, there are frequent references to the eternal God, whom the stars obey, and before whom this fleeting world cannot but tremble; [3] to the everlasting King, who puts the false gods to shame; [4] to the eternal Governor, exalted over the world and time. [5] With this intense emphasis on the transcendence of God eternity was also naturally included among his attributes.

The rare title, '*ēl r°'ī*, the '*God of seeing*' or '*God of appearance*', [6]

---

millennium onward the festival of the birth of the Sun celebrated the beginning of the New Year as the resurrection of the deity and in the Hymn to the Sun of Amenophis IV we read: 'Thou art the Time of all life, and by Thee all live!' The Babylonian doctrines of the world-cycles may possibly be connected with primitive Indian and Persian speculations on Zrvan, 'Endless Time', as the supreme Lord and Renewer of all things. Nevertheless, the idea expressed in the name *el 'olam* should probably be sought in the unchangeable power and effectiveness of God rather than in relations with any of the foregoing, which it is hard to define with any certainty: cf. E. Jenni, *Das Wort 'Olam im Alten Testament*, 1953, pp. 53 ff.
[1]Whether the phrase '°*bī- 'ad* of Isa. 9.5 belongs to this context is doubtful. The same applies to Ps. 45.7.
[2]Amos 5.5; 8.14; Hos. 4.15.
[3]Isa. 40.28; cf. 60.19; Pss. 90.2; 93.2; 145.13.
[4]Jer. 10.10.
[5]Isa. 26.4; Dan. 4.31; 6.27; 7.14; 12.7: cf. also Ecclus. 18.1; 36.19; II Macc. 1.25; Rest of Esther 13.10; Wisd. 7.26; 17.2 etc.
[6]Gen. 16.13. (German: 'Erscheinungsgott'. Tr.)

acquires a certain importance from its connection with the Baal religion. In the Amarna letters and in some Egyptian texts a *ba'al rᵒ'i* occurs as a Canaanite deity, who enjoyed particular veneration as far afield as Egypt. [1] If it be correct to see here the effect of Canaanite influences on the Ishmaelite tribal god, [2] then the retention of the divine name El—which is shown to be an original element by its connection with the meaning of the name Ishmael—is as noteworthy as the typical emphasis on the deity's care for his worshippers as the distinguishing mark of El. [3]

The name *'ēl 'ᵉlōhē yiśrā'ēl*, which Jacob, according to Gen. 33.20, confers on an altar he has built, is the strongest indication of the relationship between El and his worshipper. Whether the name be translated 'El, God of Israel' or 'El is the God of Israel' is immaterial. The fact is that the appellative has become a personal name. [4] In face of this El all other *'ēlīm* are but usurpers of the name: only the deity who has Israel under his protection can be thought of as really and truly God, the Ruler and Governor.

It is possible that the same significance may attach to the divine name *'ēl bēt-'ēl*, [5] which is likewise ascribed to Jacob. Whether the name is interpreted as a noun clause, 'El is in Bethel', or taken as a simple attributive, 'El Bethel', on the analogy of Baal Peor, etc., the two translations are in any case so close in meaning, that the deity would in this instance be described simply as the protective divinity of Bethel.

3. The singular *'ᵉlōah* [6] never attained to any importance in

[1] Cf. H. Gressmann, *Mose und seine Zeit*, p. 290 n. 5, and *AOT*, p. 96; *ANET*, p. 258.

[2] It should nevertheless be borne in mind that the possibility of a name of such generalized meaning appearing quite spontaneously in independent *milieux* is not to be excluded.

[3] According to M. Noth (*Die israelitischen Personennamen*, 1928, pp. 99 f.) the development of El-worship is another example of the way in which deities which were originally tribal gods, when with their worshippers they entered on a more settled existence at sanctuaries of long standing, occasionally acquired the attributes of the local divinity.

[4] The same process can be attested in Syria in both earlier and later periods. El was the customary personal name of the Father of the Gods in Ras Shamra: cf. O. Eissfeldt, *El im ugaritischen Pantheon*, 1951. There is also evidence of El as a deity in Zendjirli between the ninth and seventh centuries (Chantepie de la Saussaye, *Lehrbuch der Religionsgeschichte*⁴ I, p. 626).

[5] Gen. 35.7.

[6] Like *'ēl*, this may be an independent formation from the stem *'lh*, as the parallel forms in Arabic, Syriac and Aramaic would seem to suggest. For other explanations, cf. J. Hehn, *op. cit.*, p. 210.

itself, but the plural form ' *lōhīm*[1] played a part of the greatest significance. That the word was also plural in meaning is indicated beyond reasonable doubt by the frequent employment with it of the plural of the verb.[2] Yet there is a good deal to be said for the view that ' *lōhīm*, as distinct from *'ēlīm*, was originally used as a so-called 'abstract plural' or 'plural of intensity',[3] serving to expand and reinforce the concept in question, and to elevate the person designated by it to the status of a general representative of his class.[4] In that case, the employment of the word as a true plural in the sense of 'gods' would be secondary. As an 'abstract plural', however, the term corresponds to our word 'Godhead' or 'divinity' and is thus suited to the task of summing up the whole of divine power in a personal unity.

In Israel, however, the employment of ' *lōhīm* in this sense is not the result of a slow process, a gradual unification of the local deities whereby polytheism was eventually overcome.[5] On the contrary, the Amarna letters afford evidence that not only in Babylonia, but in pre-Israelite Palestine also, the plural was in current use in religious thought to express the higher unity subsuming the individual gods and combining in one concept the whole pantheon. Thus the Moon-god Sin, for instance, is designated as *ilani ša ilani*, literally 'the gods of the gods', that is to say, the supreme god. The same plural is used in Syria for a single deity and constructed with the singular of the verb. Indeed, the Canaanite vassals of Pharaoh even went so far as to address their overlord, who had of course long claimed divine status, not merely as *ilia*, 'my god', but, carrying flattery yet further, as *ilania*, literally 'my gods', in the sense of 'my godhead' or 'my supreme god'. We are here presented with a fully naturalized idiom, by which a single divine person is designated by this plural, 'gods', as embodying the totality of divine life. Israel's use of the term ' *lōhīm* to exalt the God of Sinai as supreme

---

[1]Usually explained as the plural of *'ēl*, on the model of the segholate forms, but according to Procksch (*Die Genesis*[2, 3], p. 439) as the plural of ' *lōah*. The derivation from an Arabic stem *'aliha*, 'to be afraid', does not commend itself (cf. E. König, *Theologie des AT*, p. 135).

[2]Cf. Gen. 1.26; 20.13; 35.7; II Sam. 7.23; Ex. 32.4, 8, etc.

[3]Söderblom speaks, though with some reserve, of a plural of 'extension', which would roughly signify a 'very great deal' of something (*Das Werden des Gottesglaubens*, German tr., 1916, p. 301).

[4]Cf. the plurals *b*'*ālīm* and ' *dōnīm* to mean 'lordship', 'lord'; also *q*'*dōšīm*, Prov. 9.10, '*elyōnīm*, Dan. 7.18, etc.

[5]So E. Meyer (*Die Israeliten*, p. 211 note), *et al.*

deity need, therefore, have involved nothing more than the adoption of a form of expression already long established.

In the event ' *elōhīm* became by far the most frequent designation of the divinity. The original meaning of the 'abstract plural' ' *elōhīm* may not have been actually present to the mind of every user of the word; nevertheless, the term differed from '*ēl* in connoting an express emphasis on the exaltedness of God and, for this very reason, came to be preferred in general usage to the plainer word, which lacked the same overtones. The same considerations may also have been responsible for its application to individual supreme deities among the neighbouring peoples. [1] Finally it is used in an extremely generalized sense to mean the 'divine essence' or 'nature'. [2] Side by side with these developments, however, the use of ' *elōhīm* as a true plural, like '*ēlīm*, never dies out. [3]

The concept here considered makes its first appearance in the service of conscious theological reflection and the religious education of the people in the Elohistic source of the Pentateuch. 'That for which Elijah fought in his fearful contest with the Tyrian Baal was the principle: Only One can be God, Yahweh or Baal, and it is Yahweh! This principle was also the basic conviction of the Elohist, and his typical method of emphasizing the fact is his almost exclusive use of ' *elōhīm* for Yahweh.' 'Yahweh is not just one individual '*ēl*, but ' *elōhīm*, the sum of all gods, i.e., Godhead pure and simple, and as such, for Israel at any rate, he rules out all other deities.' [4] The retention of this designation of God, even after the introduction of the name Yahweh in Ex. 3.13 ff., proves with what effect the Elohistic narrator had championed the particular conception of God implicit in his term.

A similar design led the writer of Gen. 1 to use the term *elōhīm* for the Creator God. By choosing this particular name, which as the epitome of all-embracing divine power excludes all other divinity, he was able to protect his cosmogony from any trace of polytheistic thought and at the same time describe the Creator God as the

---

[1] I Kings 11.5 (Astarte); 11.7 (Chemosh and Milcom).
[2] The term is applied to the spirits of the dead, I Sam. 28.13. The angels, however, are also called *benē* ' *elōhīm*, Gen. 6.2, 4; Job 1.6 etc.; here the word *benē* is not to be taken in a genealogical sense, but as an expression connoting 'congruence' or 'belonging together'. Analogous is the use of *rūah* ' *elōhīm* to mean the 'spirit of divinity': Gen. 41.38; Dan. 4.5 f., 15; 5.11.
[3] Ex. 12.12; 18.11; 34.15, etc.
[4] Eichrodt, *Die Quellen der Genesis*, 1916, pp. 108 f.

absolute Ruler and the only Being whose will carries any weight. In fact the term proved of the greatest value in assisting Israel to clarify those concepts of God which distinguished her own faith from that of heathenism.

2. SPECIFICALLY ISRAELITE DESIGNATIONS OF GOD

1. The new understanding of the divine nature which came with Moses is inextricably bound up with a new name for God, *Yahweh*. E (Ex. 3.14) and P (Ex. 6.3) make such a point of this, that in them the crucial divine revelation to Moses culminates in the communication of the new divine name. Henceforward, all proclamations making known some truth about God are associated with this name: it is through her worship of *this* God that Israel is marked out from all other nations. It may indeed seem surprising that there is no thought of an open exposition of the new divine name to the people at large. All they received was simply the message, 'Yahweh, the God of your fathers . . . hath sent me unto you' (E, Ex. 3.15), or alternatively, 'I am Yahweh and I will bring you out' (P, Ex. 6.6). An understanding of the meaning of the name was granted only to the founder of the religion:⁴and in any case it is given almost, so to speak, in parenthesis—the real emphasis falls on the promise of liberation.[1] From this it may be concluded, that in Israel there was less interest in the etymological significance of the divine name than in the concrete content which it conveyed, and which was to be deduced from quite a different source, namely the demonstrations in history of the power of its owner. Nevertheless, it is by no means pointless to inquire what meaning originally lay behind the name Yahweh.

As is well known, the name occurs both *in a longer and in a shorter form*—as the Tetragrammaton *yhwh* and as *yh, yhh*, or *yhw*.[2] For a

[1] Herein lies the element of truth in the assumption that these passages represent a later interpretation: so P. Volz, *Mose*², 1932, p. 58 n. 2; W. R. Arnold, 'The Divine Name in Ex. III. 14' (*JBL* 24, 1905, pp. 107 ff.). Nevertheless, almost all the later treatments of the problem have rightly rejected this view.

[2] This form must certainly have been vocalized as *yāhū*, as is made clear both by the pointing of Israelite personal names, and in particular by the fact that in Assyria in the ninth and eighth centuries it was written Ya-u. The duller, but not very different, pronunciation Yaho may have spread at a later date, and may be assumed for the Egyptian-Aramaic papyri; though even in this latter instance M. Noth, *op. cit.*, p. 104, would read Yahu. Yaho is supported by the pronunciation Ἰαώ, found in the Church Fathers. *yw* on many potsherds and on the Samaria ostraca is simply an abbreviated form of Yahu.

long time controversy has been principally concerned to discover which of these forms should be regarded as the original, and which as the derivative. As far as the tradition of the name within Israel is concerned, the result has been to establish that *both forms of the name go back to the earliest period* and have always been used side by side. On the other hand it can hardly be decided with any certainty, whether the shortened form was current only in the functions in which alone it has come down to us, namely as a component of theophorous personal names and as an exclamatory form—usage which would confine it predominantly to secular idiom [1]—while *yhwh* would have been the official name in the cultus: or alternatively, whether the shorter form was far more widely employed, while the Tetragrammaton ought to be regarded as primarily literary. The latter suggestion is, however, improbable, for the very good reason that the most ancient witness to the longer form, the Mesa stele, would more naturally have used the popular and generally current name of Israel's god, rather than the literary one.

As regards the linguistic relationship of the two names, *the extra-Israelite evidence* has proved of great importance, since it seems to suggest that the shorter form goes back to a period far older than the time of Moses. The component Ya'u or Ya'um is already to be found in Babylonian names of the third millennium, such as Lipušyaum, Yaubani, Addaya, Akiya. Whether these are examples of a divine name in the strict sense, or simply of a loan-word being used as a substitute for such a name, [2] in either case it becomes extremely difficult to maintain that the shorter form was derived from the Tetragrammaton—a view which is perfectly possible linguistically and was for a long time the dominant hypothesis. Indeed the weight of probability is all in favour of the reverse relationship. [3] Seeing

[1] So H. Grimme ('Sind *yhw* and *yhwh* zwei verschiedene Namen und Begriffe?' *Bibl. Zeitschrift* 17, 1925, pp. 29 ff.) and also—at least as regards the later development of Israelite usage—G. R. Driver ('The original form of the name "Yahweh": evidence and conclusions', *ZAW* 46, 1928, pp. 7 ff.). Similarly G. J. Thierry, 'The Pronunciation of the Tetragrammaton', *OTS* 5, 1948, pp. 30 ff. On the other side, A. L. Williams ('Yāhōh', *JTS* 28, 1927, pp. 276 ff.) sees the real name in the shorter form.

[2] The latter view is urged particularly by J. Hehn, *op. cit.*, pp. 222 ff.

[3] The extant evidence will hardly allow of a definite conclusion. M. Noth (*op. cit.*, pp. 108 ff.) argues that the Babylonian name-components Ya-um, Ya-u and Ya should be regarded as totally distinct from the Old Testament name of God, and that the latter is of purely Israelite provenance. Nevertheless, it may be questioned whether the available material makes such a decision possible.

that in the whole internal tradition of Israel[1] and in the one non-Israelite instance of the Mesa stele, however, the full form of the name appears to be characteristic of Israelite religion from the very first, there is much to be said for the conjecture that the expansion of *yh* or *yhw* to *yhwh* is connected with the religious foundation of Moses.

The whole problem would appear in a much clearer light, if we were able to make any definite statement about the change of meaning which accompanied the expansion of the name. This, however, cannot be done, because the original sense of the shorter form remains completely obscure[2]—with the result that the majority of scholars have concluded that the word has no meaning at all.[3] As far as the Tetragrammaton is concerned, Ex. 3.14 at least reveals this much, that to Israelite ears the sound of the name suggested some affinity with the verb *hwh* or *hyh*. The explanation proposed in this passage, which regards the word as an archaic Imperfect Qal form, commends itself as by far the most probable, and in its turn confirms the pronunciation *yahweh*, which at various times has been suspected without good reason as unreliable.[4] Against the name's being a form of the Hiphil is the fact that there is no other known instance of this mood of the root *hwh* or *hyh*. Moreover, Hebrew has other stems, such as *br'* and *'sh* at its disposal to express the meaning 'call into being, create'. Those explanations which see the name as meaning 'He who sends down', in the sense of 'He who hurls down the lightning' or 'causes the wind to blow', involve the use of obsolete or infrequent and secondary meanings of the verbal stem. Hence the most natural interpretation remains that which equates the Tetragrammaton with 'He is', 'He exists', 'He is present'.[5]

If it should be asked, how this meaning accords with the personality and work of Moses, it cannot be denied that it fits remarkably

[1]F. C. Burkitt ('On the name Yahweh', *JBL* 44, 1925, pp. 353 ff.) rightly stresses that the tradition shows no sign of later correction.

[2]J. Hehn (*op. cit.*) makes an attempt at interpretation, but is still unconvincing.

[3]So H. Gunkel, art. 'Jahve', *RGG*[2] III, pp. 9 ff. While F. C. Burkitt (*op. cit.*) assumes a connection with the older form of the verb 'to be', *hyh*, which cannot, however, be more precisely determined, G. R. Driver (*op. cit.*), and likewise A. L. Williams, see the name as derived from a repetitive, semi-ecstatic shout at festivals, comparable to the Greek Ἰαχχος or Εὔιος.

[4]Cf. A. L. Williams, *op. cit.*, pp. 278 ff.; B. D. Eerdmans, 'The Name Yahu', *OTS* 5 (1948, pp. 1 ff.)

[5]Closely related is the formation of the Arabian divine names *Yaġuṭ* and *Ya'ūq* (Wellhausen, *Reste arabischen Heidentums*[2], pp. 19 ff.).

well into the whole situation. There can be no difficulty in under-standing it as a deliberate new formation on the basis of the old form Yahu, with the purpose of expressing *the idea of existence in the divine name.*[1] This is certainly not a matter of Being in the meta-physical sense of aseity, absolute existence, pure self-determination or any other ideas of the same kind. It is concerned with a revelation of the divine will, which God grants to Moses when he entrusts him with the good news, 'I am that I am'—that is to say, I am really and truly present, ready to help and to act, as I have always been. It is possible to speak of the Being of God in very different ways. There are ancient Babylonian names which assert the existence of God in a general sense, such as Baši-ilu and Ibašši-ilu, which mean 'There exists a God'. Only the godless and the fool can say 'There is no God'. The Hebrew Yahweh is distinguished from such cases by fervour of feeling and the dynamic of practical proof. What is stressed is not a general existence at all times and places, but existence here and now. *The emphasis is not on passive, but on active existence.*[2]

When understood in this way, however, this divine name has its particular significance for the historical mission of Moses. What could be of greater importance both for him and for his nation than the conviction of the succouring presence of the God of the Fathers? At a time like that, metaphysical speculation would have been no more helpful than the revelation of some power in nature, were it the Thunder God with his bolts of lightning or the Wind God riding upon the storm. The only thing which could provide the religious basis for a new national entity was the certainty, deeply impressed both on the founder of the religion and on his people, that the deity was demonstrably and immediately present and active.

Furthermore, the new divine name proclaimed by Moses agrees in a remarkable way with the earlier Hebrew designations of God.

[1]So rightly A. van Hoonacker, *Une communauté Judéo-Araméenne à Eléphantine* (Schweich Lectures), 1915, pp. 67–73: 'A modification, an adaptation of the pre-existent name Yahu.'

[2]J. Hänel is, therefore, right to describe the meaning of the explanation of the name given in Ex. 3.14 as 'an underlining of the element of reality', and to draw attention to the similarly constructed sentences in Ex. 33.19; Ezek. 12.25 (*NKZ* 40, 1929, p. 614). A similar view had already been put forward by J. Hehn, *op. cit.*, pp. 215 ff. Nevertheless, the element of constant faithfulness and effective action in power is also inseparable from the name. Cf. further M. Buber, *Königtum Gottes*[2], 1936, pp. 80 ff., and the statements of Th. C. Vriezen, "Ehje 'ašer-'ehje' (*Festschrift für Bertholet*, 1950, pp. 498 ff.) which point in the same direction.

It shares that *opposition to all that is merely naturalistic* and part of the phenomenal world, which is characteristic of the worship of El. Nevertheless, it goes much further than the divine names hitherto in use in its emphasis on the concrete nearness and irruptive reality of God, and contrasts vividly for this reason with their generalized statements on the rule and guidance, the exaltedness and eternity of the divine.

Finally, the thought-content of the name Yahweh fits in well with what is known from other evidence of the essential nature of the Mosaic faith. For this is totally determined by the impact of a God who, at one time inspiring terror and at another bestowing blessing, is at all times *a controlling and effective reality*, establishing his dominion and granting victory by unprecedented demonstrations of power. [1]

This meaning of the name Yahweh, which is so closely bound up with the Sinai revelation, seems still to have been experienced as a living force even in later times. It is true that the shortened form Yahu remained in use alongside the full form Yahweh, in particular in the giving of personal names (where it was still further reduced, when standing at the beginning of the name, to Yĕho or Yo), but also in poetic diction in the abbreviated form *yāh* (Ex. 15.2; Pss. 68.5, 19; 118.5, 17 f., etc.). Nevertheless, the use of the full name was far more extensive. In the circumstances the strong insistence that Israel's God is called Yahweh, or that he will show himself to be Yahweh, [2] may well be an allusion to the promise, implicit in the name Yahweh, that God is near at hand and mighty to control. In much the same way the oft-recurring phrase, 'Ye shall know that I am Yahweh!', which may be uttered as a threat as well as in consolation, [3] in either case is a constant reminder of the *real presence* of God, whether this be to afflict or to bless.

In Deutero-Isaiah, however, the use of the name Yahweh leads in a different direction. This prophet especially evinces a much greater interest in metaphysical statements about God's exaltedness over the universe. Hence for him the name Yahweh is associated with *the concept of eternity* and is emphatically designated as the name

[1]Cf. in this connection ch. VI. 1, pp. 209 f., below.
[2]Hos. 12.6, 10; 13.4.; Deut. 7.9; Mal. 3.6. It is possible that the remarkable phrase, *wᵉ'ānōkī lō'-'ehyeh lākem*, in Hos. 1.9 should be understood as a reference to Ex. 3.14, *'ehyeh šᵉlāḥanī*; cf. Hehn, *op. cit.*, p. 215.
[3]In the former sense, Ezek. 6.13; 7.27; 11.10; 12.16, etc.: in the latter, Ezek. 37.13 f.; 34.30.

of the God who is the First and the Last, before whom no being was formed and after whom nothing will exist.[1] The overpowering experience of God's positive control in the present, which the name connotes, is thereby displaced in favour of an emphasis on the constant immutability of his nature, and the way prepared for the LXX interpretation, which uses the term ὁ ὤν to denote unalterable Being as the chief characteristic of the deity.

2. An expanded form of the name Yahweh was created by combining it with the plural ṣᵉbā'ōt, either in the phrase yhwh 'ᵉlōhē (haṣ)ṣᵉbā'ōt,[2] or in direct juxtaposition: yhwh ṣᵉbā'ōt.[3]

Two facts are of decisive importance for the correct understanding of this epithet: firstly, that it is found in close connection with the sacred Ark;[4] secondly, that it is extremely popular in prophetic diction.[5] The former consideration makes it certain, that the epithet ṣebā'ōt was a favourite designation of God as a warrior, seeing that for a long time the Ark served as a palladium in war.[6] A one-sided emphasis on this datum might encourage one to connect ṣᵉbā'ōt with the armies of Israel, which the Warrior God accompanied into battle; and indeed, the frequent use of ṣᵉbā'ōt for the Israelite hosts,[7] together with the explicit evidence of I Sam. 17.45, might seem to establish the equation beyond dispute. Nevertheless, quite apart from other weaknesses,[8] this explanation does not account for the prophetic usage; for the assumption which it involves, that the meaning of the divine name was transformed and spiritualized by connecting it with the heavenly hosts, comes to grief on two facts. Firstly, the name ṣᵉbā'ōt is never applied to the heavenly hosts;[9] secondly the

[1]Isa. 40.28; 41.4; 43.10 f.; 44.6; 48.12.
[2]With the article: Amos 3.13; 6.14; 9.5 (foll. LXX): more frequently without the article: II Sam. 5.10; I Kings 19.10, 14; Amos 4.13; 5.14 ff.; Jer. 5.14, etc.
[3]Thus in the vast majority of instances.
[4]I Sam. 4.3–5.7 ff.; II Sam. 6.2.
[5]247 out of a total of 278 instances! (E. Kautzsch, 'Zebaoth', HRE XXI, p. 622).
[6]Num. 10.35 f.; Isa 6.4 ff.; I Sam. 4.3 ff., 21 f.; II Sam. 11.11; 15.24 ff. This is also attested by the use of the name in such passages as I Sam. 15.2; 17.45; II Sam. 5.10; 6.18; Ps. 24.7 ff.
[7]Ex. 7.4; 12.41, 51, etc.
[8]I Sam. 17.45 is a fairly late passage, and the mention of the ṣib'ōt yiśrā'ēl, which in addition usually refers to the mass of the people in general, rather than to the military body in particular, is common to passages in the Deuteronomic, Priestly and Psalm literature as well.
[9]Both for the angels and for the stars the consistent usage is the singular, ṣᵉbā' yhwh, Josh. 5.14, or ṣᵉbā' haššāmayim, I Kings 22.19; Ps. 148.2; Dan. 8.10: also Deut. 4.19; 17.3; II Kings 17.16; Jer. 8.2, etc.

prophets use the term as a matter of course, and assume without further explanation that their hearers will be acquainted with the new meaning of the name, despite the fact that the transcendent omnipotence and exaltedness, which for them is connoted by the term Yahweh Ṣeba'ot, is in curious contradiction to his character as leader of Israel's battle-line, and would be bound to give rise to serious misunderstanding. If the prophets could appeal to Yahweh Ṣeba'ot as the Judge exalted both over his own nation and over all the nations to support their threats against Israel, then both for themselves and for their hearers this name must have connoted more than simply the national deity. If the attempt to find a meaning for the name is not to be abandoned altogether, [1] then the only remaining possibility is to assume that *ṣᵉbā'ōt* does not refer to any particular 'hosts', but to all bodies, multitudes, masses in general, the content of all that exists in heaven and in earth [2]—as indeed the LXX translation, κύριος τῶν δυνάμεων, shows them to have understood it. This assumption throws a brilliant light on the prophetic usage of the word; but it also shows that there is a universalist tendency in the older Israelite conception of Yahweh, and proves that the primitive concept of the high God El had not been forgotten. That subsequently the name Yahweh Ṣeba'ot could have been applied to the

[1]So H. Gressmann, *Ursprung der isr.-jüd. Eschatologie*, 1905, pp. 71 ff.; E. Kautzsch, *op. cit.*, p. 626.

[2]So R. Smend, *Lehrbuch der AT Religionsgeschichte²*, pp. 201 ff.; J. Wellhausen, *Kleine Propheten³*, 1898, p. 77: also, on new grounds, J. Hehn, *op. cit.*, pp. 250 ff., who adduces the Assyrian designation of God as *šar kiššati*, 'king of the mass, the fullness, the sum of things'. Cf. also Gen. 2.1; Ps. 103.21. In the case of the Warrior God it is obvious that the dominant thought is that of the destructive forces of nature, and this assumption is confirmed by I Kings 19.14; Isa. 2.12; 29.6; 13.13 and other passages. B. N. Wambacq, *L'Epithète Divine Jahvé Seba'ot*, 1947, would prefer to explain the evidence in terms of a gradual development of the concept, the sense of 'hosts' passing from an original reference to the Israelite battle array to the forces of nature and the nations of the world, but this is hardly convincing. Nearer to the view of the present writer is that of V. Maag, *Jahwäs Heerscharen* (Schweiz. Theol. Umschau, 1950, No. 3–4), 1950: he explains 'hosts' as referring to the mythical forces of nature in the Canaanite spiritual system, which were stripped of their divine power in the time of the Judges, and sees in this an important stage in the conquest of all hostile forces by the omnipotence of Yahweh. An original approach is that of O. Eissfeldt (*Miscellanea Academica Berolinensia*, 1950, pp. 128 ff.), who attempts to arrive at the meaning of the name by interpreting *ṣᵉbā'ōt* as an abstract or intensive plural in the sense of 'might', or adjectivally as 'mighty', and associates it with Yahweh as an attributive term, 'Yahweh, the Mighty One'. Unfortunately there is no instance of such an extension of *ṣābā'* in an intensive plural in the sense which he assigns to it, for the word is only attested elsewhere with the meanings 'army', 'military service', 'forced labour' or 'mass', 'multitude'.

God of the armies of Israel or to the Lord of the stars, especially if the original meaning had fallen into oblivion and precautions were called for to counter the heathen cult of the heavenly bodies, is perfectly understandable. Similarly the use of the word as a cult-name at the sanctuaries of Shiloh and Jerusalem[1] is explained by its connection with the especially sacred cultic object of the Ark.

This still gives no indication of when or under what influences this name expressive of the divine sovereignty came into fashion. It would only be permissible to draw definite conclusions from the fact that it is not found in the Pentateuch or in the Books of Joshua and Judges, if there were no reason to suppose that later redaction might have deleted it: but such a possibility cannot be excluded. [2] Furthermore, the question of whether foreign influence has to be taken into account is still very obscure. [3] In any event, the choice of this particular epithet to express the whole essential character of the Yahwist faith remains of the utmost significance.

3. EPITHETS OF YAHWEH

1. Whereas Ṣeba'ot in later times to a greater and greater extent lost its appellative sense and turned into a proper name (whence the use of σαβαωθ in the LXX), other epithets retained their original meaning. Among these is the term *melek*. [4] The conception and designation of the deity as King are primitive Semitic practice, of which incontestable evidence is afforded by the large number of personal names compounded with *melek* going back to the most ancient period. [5] The fact that one primitive Semitic meaning of the word was 'guide' or 'counsellor' precludes any objection to its use among peoples without the institution of kingship. Hence one would have to have very weighty reasons for denying the ancient Hebrews any acquaintance with this designation of God; and such reasons are

---

[1]I Sam. 1.3, 11; II Sam. 6.18; Isa. 8.18; 31.4 f.; 37.16; Pss. 46.8, 12; 48.9, etc.
[2]Cf. A. Klostermann, *Geschichte des Volkes Israel*, 1896, p. 76.
[3]Hehn, *op. cit.*, appears to have this in mind.
[4]In this connection, cf. A. von Gall, 'Über die Herkunft der Bezeichnung Jahves als König', *Wellhausen-Festschrift*, 1914, pp. 145 ff.; W. Caspari, 'Der Herr ist König', *Christentum und Wissenschaft*, 1928, pp. 23 ff.; O. Eissfeldt, 'Jahve als König', *ZAW* 46, 1928, pp. 81 ff.; M. Buber, *Königtum Gottes*², pp. 49 ff.; G. von Rad, '*melek* und *malkūt* im Alten Testament', *TWNT* I, 1933, pp. 563 ff.; A. Alt, 'Gedanken über das Königtum Jahves', *Kleine Schriften zur Geschichte des Volkes Israel* I, 1953, pp. 345 ff.
[5]The relevant material may be found in W. von Baudissin, art. 'Moloch', *HRE* XIII, pp. 269–303; *Kyrios* III, 1928, pp. 44 ff., 97 ff.

not forthcoming.[1] On the other hand, it is extremely doubtful
whether anything can be said about the distinctive character of any
early Hebrew deity of this name, since there is no mention anywhere
in the Old Testament of the worship of a god Melek in the early
history of Israel, and the worship of Melek which emerges in
Judah in the middle monarchical period is almost certainly a foreign
importation.

A striking feature of the Mosaic conception of God is its *attitude of
reticence toward this designation of the deity*. Num. 23.21, and possibly
also Num. 24.7, 8a; Ex. 15.18; Deut. 33.5, may be cited to prove that
the title of 'king' was already applied to Yahweh in the pre-monarchical period. Furthermore, it is of decisive importance, that the idea
of Yahweh as ruler is attested for the Mosaic period by the divine
throne of the sacred Ark (ch. IV. 2. 11); and according to certain
indications in the Yahwist historical narrative (Gen. 3.22; 6.1 ff.;
11.7; 18.1 ff.) the idea of the heavenly court, which waits on Yahweh's
command, was also well known in the pre-monarchical era.[2] Hence
there is not much force in the argument that Yahweh could only
have been spoken of as King after the introduction of the monarchy
into Israel.[3] From the time of the occupation of Canaan onwards
there is no reason to suppose that the Israelites were not acquainted
with the mythical divine kingship of Canaanite religion.[4] In spite of
all this, however, it is impossible to maintain that the title *melek* was a
distinctive mark of the earliest Yahweh worship. That it occurs so
seldom may be connected with a strong sense that the religious and
political life of Canaan, with its divine kings and its concept of
monarchy, was something alien. A reversal of this attitude only comes
with the period of the kingdom in Israel.

Various observations suggest, that with the introduction of the
monarchy, the title of King for Yahweh also came into favour.
First, there is the specifically Hebrew name of Saul's son Malkišua'
(I Sam. 14.49)—to which should perhaps be added the name of
Jonathan's great-grandson Malki'el (I Chron. 8.35; 9.41, foll.
LXX[B]). Secondly we may cite such a passage as Ps. 24.7–10, a

[1]It is not a valid objection that the majority of Hebrew personal names compounded with *melek* may have been borrowed from the Canaanites, since there
are instances of similar names of genuinely Hebraic formation: e.g., *malkišua'*,
I Sam. 14.49.
[2]Cf. A. Alt, *op. cit.*, pp. 351 f.
[3]Thus von Rad, *op. cit.*, pp. 567 f.
[4]Thus A. Alt, *op. cit.*, pp. 353 f.

poem which must certainly be assigned to the earliest phase of the monarchy and in which the greatest stress is laid on the use of the title King for Yahweh. The fact that we are here dealing with a processional hymn of the Ark suggests that the cult of God the Lord enthroned on the Ark was the context which encouraged the more frequent use of the kingly title. Moreover, the Procession of the Ark was connected with the royal festival on Zion [1]—yet another circumstance favourable to a new attitude toward a term which had hitherto been avoided. It is quite consistent with such a view, that it should be precisely the cultic poems, which provide most of the evidence for the designation of Yahweh as King. In addition to Ps. 24 may be cited Ex. 15.18; Deut. 33.5; Pss. 5.3; 29.10; 48.3; 68.25; 74.12 and 84.4; and it is hardly possible to advance valid objections to a pre-exilic dating for any of these passages. The particular *milieu* in which this usage became established was presumably the priesthood of the capital and the court circle.

All the more striking is the silence of classical prophecy in this connection. Even the oft-quoted verse, Isa. 6.5, cannot detract from the fact that the title of King is not applied to Yahweh in any other passage of this prophet, even where it might have been expected. This would suggest that the Call vision is an example of occasional borrowing from a different complex of ideas, possibly from a festival liturgy in the Temple. [2] Even though in Isa. 30.33 the destruction of the Assyrian is pictured as a sacrifice offered to Yahweh as *melek*, the point of this is simply to contrast the honour due to the true *melek* with the superstitious practices in the valley of Hinnom, in which the *melek*-concept has been distorted into something heathenish. The use of the title in this context (*l·melek* is a better reading than *lammelek*) is, therefore, subservient to a sarcastic polemic against those false Melek-sacrifices, with which a perverted longing for salvation thinks that it can purchase the favour of Yahweh. It is no proof that Isaiah approved this epithet in other connections. As far as Jeremiah is concerned, 8.19 is obviously quoting a despairing cry of the people, not of the prophet himself. On the other hand, it is true that there are extant anonymous weal-prophe-

---

[1]Cf. pp. 123 ff. above.

[2]The conjecture is sometimes put forward, that the use of the title of King here is polemical in intention (cf. Eissfeldt, *op. cit.*, p. 104; Baudissin, *op. cit.*, p. 101). Against this, however, it should be remembered, that the visionary experience is markedly passive in character, and does not therefore lead one to expect any conscious polemic. Ezek. 20.33 f. must be rejected as redactional.

cies, which make use of the title of King.[1] These, however, are not to be regarded as a result of Isaianic prophetic activity. They belong in the context of the priestly policies aimed at national independence, which naturally cultivated the hope that Yahweh as King would interpose his assistance. With these prophecies we are still within the same circle of popular thought, from which, we conjectured earlier, were drawn the exponents of the concept of God as the nation's King. Admittedly, I Sam. 8.7 and 12.12 seem to describe the $n \cdot b \bar{\imath}'im$ as also being supporters of this idea; but it is here enlisted by them only in the service of a polemic against the claims of the earthly monarchy as a tactical manoeuvre. It was possibly favoured in certain circles of the older prophetism for a time, at any rate until they had made their peace with the monarchy;[2] but it is never heard of again.

The critical attitude of classical prophecy to the idea of God as King was doubtless confirmed, and in the eyes of later schools of thought justified, when *the Melek-cult with its child-sacrifices*, whether as a result of Phoenician or of Ammonite influence, invaded Jerusalem in the eighth and seventh centuries. The rapidity with which it was absorbed was almost certainly due to the fact that it found a point of contact in the cult of Yahweh as *melek*, and so was the more easily assimilated into Israelite worship: cf. Micah 6.7; Ezek. 20.25 f. According to II Kings 16.3; 21.6, certain kings were the most zealous promoters of this cult. Hence, with the victory of the partisans of the pure Yahweh worship in the Josianic reform the ancient Israelite concept of God as King came to an end. In the Deuteronomic literature it is proscribed as strictly as in classical prophecy.[3]

This consistent rejection of a divine title common to the whole Semitic world by just those men who were the most earnest champions of pure Yahwist ideas reveals a most marvellous sensitivity to anything which was out of harmony with the character of Israel's faith. In their judgment this threatened to distort the true picture of

[1]Thus Micah 2.13; 4.7; Zeph. 3.15; Jer. 51.57 (46.18; 48.15).
[2]According to the view of A. Bentzen (*Die josianische Reform und ihre Voraussetzungen*, 1926, pp. 58 ff.) the people involved here are the country priests, who might be expected to react against the policies of the priesthood in the capital. Personally, however, I cannot accept this characterization of the later source of the Books of Samuel.
[3]Whether Ex. 19.6, where Israel is described as a 'kingdom of priests', is of Deuteronomic authorship, can hardly be established with certainty. If it is, then this would represent an attempt to rescue the concept of the God-King from its association with the earthly monarchy, and to give it a purely theocratic significance.

God; for the absolute sovereignty of the God whom they served meant something quite different from the arbitrary despotism of the tyrant. In the King-God of the priests and the ruling class they saw *the personal and social element in the relationship between God and man jeopardized* in favour of a purely formal relation to God, which under the forms of outward devotion would only too easily stifle the sense of personal surrender, and drive the God who was available to every Israelite in equal measure into an inaccessible seclusion. However, once the prophetic position, thanks to the Deuteronomic reforming movement, had become the dominant one, the way was open for a new understanding of this divine name which should avoid the dangers of the *melek*-worship of the past and present the real value of the king-concept in a purer form.

In the event it was *Deutero-Isaiah* who by his use of it rehabilitated the title of King as applied to Yahweh. His starting-point was certainly the pre-exilic hymn, but at the same time he broke the ground for an entirely new usage. For it was in accord with his whole preaching that the Kingship of Yahweh acquired the sense of the bringing in of the new age, in which all nations would obey the sceptre of the one universal God. Admittedly, it still has a very particularist ring, when he speaks of the King of Jacob or of Israel (41.21; 44.6), or when the possessive pronoun explicitly stresses God's close connection with his people (43.15). The sense of this connection is also retained in the phrase, 'Thy God reigneth!' (52.7). But such passages are not to be dissociated from the prophet's hope for the whole world: Yahweh proves himself King of Israel, in that by liberating his own people he also effects salvation for all the nations: cf. especially 52.7, 10. This close *association of the title of King with Yahweh's eschatological act of salvation* is peculiarly the achievement of this prophet. [1] The festival of Yahweh's Enthronement, which was celebrated in the second Temple as a result of the impact of Deutero-Isaiah's gospel, [2] brought home to the congregation the new import of the glorification of God as *melek*. [3] Here and there the older usage might still raise its head, [4] but for practical purposes its part was finished. The use of the title of King to connote

[1]This is not to deny, of course, that the idea of God as King at all times evinces 'a propensity to eschatology': cf. Eissfeldt, *op. cit.*, p. 96.
[2]Cf. pp. 127 f. above.
[3]Pss. 47.7 f.; 93.1; 95.3; 96.10; 97.1; 98.6; 99.1.
[4]E.g., Pss. 44.5; 146.10; Obad. 21.

Yahweh's Lordship over the nations became more and more deeply rooted, [1] and came to be the ideal expression for the absolute majesty of God, quite irrespective of who might be regarded as constituting his subjects in any particular instance: cf. notably Ps. 95.3 and Obad. 21. Beyond all question something new has been made of the old concept of God as King, the inherent defects of which have been overcome now that it has been removed from the sphere of the cultus and linked inseparably with the idea of universal religion. Moreover, the emphasis on the use of the kingly title for Yahweh now betokened an inner liberation for the Jewish people, for it was a rebuttal of the pretensions of the 'great king' and lord of this world, under whose earthly rule they had to live. [2] To the growing power of the earthly sovereign was now opposed, almost by way of a slogan, the certainty of a higher dispensation which in the end would triumph. Yahweh's title of King provided a shorthand *expression summing up the assurance of the prophetic faith.*

It should not, however, be overlooked, that this new understanding of God's Kingship underwent yet another creative development. Such passages as Mal. 1.14; Jer. 10.7; Pss. 103.19; 145.11–13 certainly speak of Yahweh's universal Kingdom, and to this extent conform to the line laid down by Deutero-Isaiah. Nevertheless, it is easy to detect in them a quite different note. The divine dominion, embracing the whole world, is seen not so much as a hope, a blessing longed for and expected in the future, but as *a fact of the present moment*—perhaps not perceived by everyone, but none the less real for that. It is this present reality which effectively orders the world here and now; it is to this that man has to bring himself into obedience, and this which is extolled by the confident praises of the pious. As a result of thinking along these lines, the conception was arrived at of *a Kingdom of Yahweh, subsisting from the beginning of time and already established at the Creation.* The idea may be found expressed in passages such as I Chron. 29.11; Dan. 3.33; 4.31, 34, and it was to dominate later Judaism. [3] The compact formula of the Kingdom of God no longer refers simply to one aspect of the divine activity, but

[1] Ps. 22.29; Isa. 24.23; Zech. 14.16 f.
[2] That this concrete historical situation played a great part in encouraging the new idiom is obviously a reasonable assumption; but equally it is to be doubted whether it was the sole cause which evoked it.
[3] E.g., Ps. Sol. 2.30; Ecclus. 51.1; III Macc. 2.2; 5.35; I Enoch 9.4; 81.3; 84.2 etc.: cf. the survey in W. Bousset, *Die Religion des Judentums in späthellenistischen Zeitalter*[3], 1926, p. 313.

comprehends the whole essence of the divine Being. 'His Godhead and his Kingship are co-terminous.'[1]

That Judaism should have used the concept of God's Kingship in this absolute way is not simply to be ascribed to a growing impotence and rigidity in its sense of man's relationship with God, leading to an over-emphasis on the divine omnipotence. Even if this did in fact contribute to the popularity of the title of King, the new use of the title after the Exile ultimately reflects a different need. The problem of reconciling the relationship of God to his world with the religious inheritance handed down from the past had been posed with greater insistence than ever before; and somehow it had to be answered.

II. Another general Semitic designation of God is *ba'al*, '*the Lord*', or 'the master', 'the owner'. Sometimes used as an epithet,[2] sometimes with the force of a proper name,[3] its predominant reference is to the god of a particular locality. Since in this capacity the divinity had no competitors, it was possible to call him simply *habba'al* without defining him more closely.[4]

This designation is nowhere so significant for the religion of the country as in Canaan. All the innumerable pocket states of this area had their divine lord, described as Baal, whom they worshipped as *the owner of the land and the dispenser of its gifts*. Hence the Old Testament makes the worship of the *b'ālīm* the common religious characteristic of all Canaanites without distinction.[5] But because this religious disintegration is such a prominent feature, it should, nevertheless, not be allowed to conceal that, owing to the constantly recurring basic traits which they have in common, these various Baals do become fused into a certain general unity. Especially evident is the naturalistic character of these deities: they have their being in the natural phenomena of their district, in the vegetable and animal life and in the natural resources on which these depend for their growth, springs and rivers, the storm and the heat of the sun. Hence fertility rites, with their physical mimicry of natural processes, play a great part in the cult. Similarly, the Baals are constantly coupled with a female consort, who as goddess of Love and Motherhood is found sometimes as Baalah, at others as Astarte or Asherah.

[1]Cf. Baudissin, *op. cit.*, p. 219.
[2]E.g., Melkart, the Baal of Tyre.
[3]Baal of Sidon, Baal of Heaven: in personal names, Adonibaal, Hannibaal.
[4]Judg. 2.13; 6.25; I Kings 16.31; 18.26, etc.
[5]Judg. 2.11; 3.7; 8.33; 10.6, 10; I Sam. 7.3 f.; 12.10, *et al.*

If this status of the Baal as a *local vegetation deity* immediately calls to mind polydaemonism, yet at a higher level the picture is quite different. Behind the individual Baals stands the impressive figure of a great Lord of Heaven, who throughout Syria from the second millennium onwards was worshipped as the Godhead towering above all local gods. This was the *Ba'alšāmēm*, who not only ruled over the storm in his role as God of Thunder and bestowed fertility, but as both the Lord of the Universe and the compassionate protector of the individual presents the most exalted figure in the Syrian pantheon.[1] From him are derived the features of the sky-god which are associated with Baal in Canaan from the earliest times.[2] His connection with the sun was the natural result of the influence of Egyptian doctrines of sun-worship in the fourteenth century.[3] His importance may be traced from the twelfth century onwards[4] in Phoenician, Palmyrene, Punic, Assyrian and Aramaic dedicatory inscriptions. The exalted majesty of this heavenly Lord also endowed the local Baals, who were quite frequently regarded simply as local expressions of his being, with a spiritual importance which raised them above the level of limited vegetation deities and made them into opponents who were not to be underestimated, when Israel was confronted with the world of Canaanite religion.

Hence, wherever Canaanites and Israelites lived side by side, there was the possibility of a far-reaching approximation of their religions, one of the signs of which was *the adoption of the title Baal by the worshippers of Yahweh*. Just as the *ba'al bᵉrīt* of the Shechemites, a guardian deity of covenants and oaths comparable to Ζεὺς ὅρκιος, could be accommodated to the Israelite outlook in the form of *'ēl bᵉrīt*,[5] so it was possible to take a further step and transfer the name Baal (always, of course, to be understood in its appellative

[1]Cf. W. F. Albright, *From the Stone Age to Christianity*[2], 1946, p. 176. O. Eissfeldt ('Ba'alsamen und Jahve', *ZAW* 16, 1939, pp. 1 ff.) has rightly pointed out the importance of this god for the Baal worship which Yahwism encountered in Canaan, even though he may seem to go too far in questioning the worship of independent local Baal deities.

[2]Attention has been drawn by Gressmann, 'Hadad und Baal', *Baudissin-Festschrift*, 1918, pp. 191 ff., to *ba'alu ina šamē*, the 'Baal in Heaven' of the Amarna letters and of Egyptian texts from the period of Ramses III.

[3]Cf. H. Gressmann, *op. cit.*, pp. 205 ff.

[4]*b'l šmm* occurs in the inscription of Yehimilk from Byblos (R. Dussaud, *Syria* 11, 1930, p. 306; J. Hempel, *ZAW* 48, 1930, p. 310). *b'l šmyn* is found in Aramaic Syria in the inscription of King Zakir of Hamath from the eighth century (*AOT*, pp. 443 f.; *ANET*, pp. 501 f.), etc. Cf. Eissfeldt, *op. cit.*

[5]Judg. 8.33; 9.6, 46.

sense) to Yahweh, worshipped as the Lord of his people. A whole series of Israelite *personal names* compounded with Baal, especially in the families of Saul and David, [1] bears witness to the fact that even out-and-out Yahweh worshippers had no objection to the use of the Canaanite divine name. This has nothing in common with those straightforward changeovers to the worship of Baal, which did also occur here and there, even though it is true that all kinds of forms of thought and worship did come over with the borrowed name. The fact that an extensive amalgamation of the two deities did not take place was due first of all to the instinctive feeling that the national God Yahweh and the nature god Baal, who had no concern with history, were inherently in opposition. With the growing strength of the Israelite element in the country during the period of the Judges, and especially with the national unification under the monarchy, this led to a conscious effort to exalt the national God even in the matter of personal names, so that from the time of David onward names compounded with Yahweh begin to preponderate. Secondly, however, national feeling had always been conscious that *the worship of Baal was something essentially alien.* The deeply religious character of this feeling was uncovered by the prophetic movement, and from the time of Elijah's struggle it left its stamp on the entire nation. The passionate polemic of Hosea, in its condemnation of Canaanite forms of cultus, was also directed at eliminating the name of Baal. [2] The result was that the designation of Yahweh as the Baal of Israel ceased to be harmless, and disappeared from the usage of religious language. [3] In later Judaism this condemnation of the name Baal was explicitly recognized by introducing the reading *bōšet*, 'shame', [4] and the personal names in the Books of Samuel and Kings were altered accordingly. [5] The retention of the older form in Chronicles and the absence of any alteration in the original form of the LXX seem to suggest that this scrupulous

---

[1] Išba'al, son of Saul, II Sam. 2–4; cf. I Chron. 8.33: Meriba'al, son of Jonathan, II Sam. 4.4; cf. I Chron. 8.34: B'elyada', son of David, I Chron. 14.7. Several names formed with Baal are to be found on the ostraca from Samaria of the time of Ahab; cf. the texts in H. Gressmann, 'Die Ausgrabungen in Samaria', *ZAW* 43, 1925, pp. 147 ff.
[2] Hos. 2.10, 15, 19; 13.1; cf. Jer. 2.8; 7.9; 11.13, *et al.*; Zeph. 1.4.
[3] An echo survives in Isa. 54.5.
[4] Jer. 2.24; 11.13, *et al.*
[5] Išbōšet, II Sam. 2–4; Mephibōšet, II Sam. 4.4, *et al.*; Yerubbešet, II Sam. 11.21. The later version of the LXX reads ἡ αἰσχύνη for *ba'al*, e.g., I Kings 18.19, 25—or even ἡ Βάαλ in the sense of ἡ αἰσχύνη, Hos. 2.10, 13.1, *et al.*

avoidance of the sacrilegious divine title cannot be earlier than the second century BC.[1]

III. '*ādōn*,[2] 'Lord', does not belong to the common stock of Semitic divine names, and is current only among the Canaanites and Hebrews. Since, however, it cannot etymologically be derived with certainty from any Hebrew root, it may only have been adopted by the Hebrews in Canaan; and on the whole it may not be a word of Semitic origin. As in Phoenician, so in Hebrew '*ādōn* is not used as a divine name properly so-called, but serves as an epithet,[3] or as a title combined with other divine names, or as a substitute for the theophorous component in personal names.[4] In human social relations the word is used as a courtesy title, indicating in a quite general way that the person to whom one is speaking is of higher status than oneself. Similarly, when it is used of God, it simply has *the force of an ascription or title of honour*, and is not employed to give expression to the idea of the deity as ruler.[5] Hence its predominant use as a form of address in prayer,[6] combined with the first person possessive suffix: '*ᵃdōnī*. The unmodified form is not met with until the post-exilic period, and then only sporadically.[7]

In earlier times, therefore, this name for God is only of limited significance. Nevertheless, the present form of the text, especially in the prophetic books, presents quite a different picture; the suffix form '*ᵃdōnāy* appears frequently throughout, either as a proper divine name or attached to the name Yahweh, even where there is

[1] Thus W. von Baudissin, *Kyrios* III, p. 63.

[2] Cf. especially, W. von Baudissin, *Kyrios* II and III.

[3] Ex. 23.17; 34.23. As a title placed before the divine name in Isa. 1.24; 3.1; 10.16, 33; 19.4.

[4] Phoenician: Adon-esmun, Adon palaṭ; Canaanite: Adoniṣedeq (Josh. 10.3); Hebrew: Adoniram (I Kings 4.6), Adonijah (II Sam. 3.4).

[5] This only occurs when the sphere of God's dominion is explicitly named in an appositional phrase, as in the combination '*ᵃdōn kol-hā'āreṣ*, Josh. 3.11, 13; Micah 4.13; Zech. 4.14; 6.5; Ps. 97.5. Contrary to the opinion of L. Köhler (*Old Testament Theology*, ET, 1957, pp. 30 ff.), therefore, it is not possible to base on the frequent occurrence of this name in the OT the theory that the most striking characteristic of the faith of the OT, and the one mark which alone gives it a certain unity, is the Lordship of Yahweh; moreover, this takes no account of the fact that this idea is a normal part of the general Semitic conception of God.

[6] Thus throughout in the Pentateuch, but also in the Prophets and Psalms: cf. the table in W. von Baudissin, *Kyrios* II, p. 60. In later times this mode of addressing Yahweh became less common and had an archaic touch. The vocalization with long 'a' is an artificial device to distinguish the form of the name reserved for the deity from the secular '*ᵃdōnay*, 'my lord'. Even this plural form is, however, apparently not original, for the normal mode of social address is the singular '*ᵃdōnī*.

[7] Mal. 3.1; Ps. 114.7.

no question of his being either directly or indirectly addressed. This, however, as recent evidence has shown,[1] is the result of a later alteration of the texts, as a consequence of a changed attitude to the name of God. In the last centuries BC the fear of profaning the sacred name Yahweh had already led to the substitution of other names. As a result of a preference for the form of address anciently used in prayer and under the influence of the LXX's consistent rendering of Yahweh by κύριος, *the use of Adonai for Yahweh* now came, though not earlier than the first century BC, to be interpolated even into the sacred Scriptures to a steadily increasing extent. Only the Pentateuch, because of the early recognition of its especially sacred character, and books like Chronicles, which were admitted at a late stage, escaped this treatment. It was possible to adopt the suffix form as a valid proper name, because excessive use had weakened the force of the suffix—a development which can be observed in analogous forms, such as Rabbi. In the process, however, Adonai lost the firm connection with the worshipper, which had originally characterized it, and in the sense of 'Almighty Lord' came to express the idea of the absolute dominion of God over the universe. This marked it off decisively from the κύριος of the LXX, which always retained the connotation of personal belonging, and made it completely subservient to the late Judaistic conception of God, with its emphasis on transcendence and universal authority.

It has occasioned a good deal of surprise that among the numerous names and epithets of Yahweh there should not be one which is related to the covenant and designates him as its Lord. The answer to this question is extraordinarily simple. One of the commonest names of Yahweh is 'the God of Israel'. This name covers everything which might reasonably be expected in a name for the covenant God, for it implies that this God has given himself to Israel for its own, by entering into an especially close relationship with it. This is why it is possible to call upon him in prayer as simply 'my God', 'our God' without particularizing any further. To imagine that the actual word *berît* must somehow be brought into the designation of God is to push the requirement of logical systematization too far. Furthermore, the name of the city-god of Shechem, *El berît* or *Ba'al berît* (Judg. 9), possibly indicates why an explicit mention of the *berît* in a name for Yahweh held no attractions. According to the

---

[1] That this has now been established is due to the work of W. von Baudissin, *op. cit.*

most probable interpretation, this deity was a god of contracts, a kind of Ζεὺς ὅρχιος, who was invoked as guardian of all agreements concluded between man and man. The use of *b'rit* in a divine name would thus have led to a colourless generalization and to a misconception of the real meaning of the word for Israel, neither of which possibilities was of any interest to a member of the people of Yahweh.

The designation of Yahweh as the God of Israel is especially significant for this reason, that it is the only instance of a name connecting Yahweh with a particular earthly entity. Israel's neighbours spoke of the God of the land and the God of the capital. To the Assyrians, for this reason, Yahweh is 'the God of the land of Samaria' (II Kings 17.26 f.; 18.34 f.). But the Israelites themselves never spoke of God thus, even though they valued the land of Canaan with pride as the land of his inheritance. The Baals of Canaan might be differentiated by towns and districts, as for example, the Baal of Ekron (II Kings 1), or of Peor (Num. 25.3) or of Hazor (II Sam. 13.23). But Yahweh was not to be spoken of in this way. He is not the God of Jerusalem, even if there could be no objection to speaking of the Temple as his dwelling-place. Hence this particular divine name stresses the fact that, though Yahweh indeed enters into a personal relation with his people, he is not to be localized at any place on earth in such a way that he can be described as the God of that place. The designation of Yahweh as the God of Dan and Beersheba, denounced by Amos (8.14), is patently a Canaanite practice imported into Israel, and for this reason is condemned by the prophet as apostasy.

Both in the new formation of its own divine names and in the selection it makes of those which it has inherited or which have been imported from without, the faith of Israel demonstrates an unmistakable tendency to emphasize both *the mighty immanence and the exalted transcendence* of the deity. God is conceived as set over against the numerous forces of Nature, but also as summing up their multiplicity in his own *unity*. The lines of development which can be detected in the individual histories of each of the divine names have already made abundantly clear the direction of the forces which shaped them. We are dealing not with the symmetrical growth of a unified basic plan, but with a wealth of tensions, compelling an ever fresh and unique delineation of the knowledge of God. For the divine reality to which this refers is ultimately beyond reason and therefore only to be expressed in contradictory formulations.

VI

THE NATURE OF THE COVENANT GOD

A. AFFIRMATIONS ABOUT THE DIVINE BEING

I. GOD AS PERSONAL

THE STATEMENTS about the Divine Being which are directly connected with the setting up of the covenant may be classified under three heads. The first of these is that the Deity acquires an explicitly personal character. The especially high value attached to the divine Name at an early period, and the nature of its use, were movements in this direction. Indeed, the proclamation of the divine Name is so inseparably connected with the revelation of God himself, that different epochs can actually be distinguished by the mere fact of their using different names for God.[1] Moreover, by his own act of bestowing a name on himself, God chooses to be described as the definable, the distinctive, the individual. In this way the faith of Israel sets its face against both an abstract concept of deity and a nameless 'ground of being'. Both the intellectualist and the mystical misunderstandings of God are rejected.

That this proclamation of the divine Name was treasured as an act whereby God himself came forth from his secret place and offered himself in fellowship is shown by the eagerness with which the divine Name was used, whenever men wished to be assured of his nearness and the reality of his succour. Prayers and oaths, blessing and cursing, battles and victories,[2] all were 'in the name of Yahweh', b·šēm yhwh, that is, they were accompanied by the utterance of his Name and by the assurance that in this way his presence could be summoned

---

[1] As in the E and P strata of the Pentateuch.
[2] Gen. 4.26; 12.8; 13.4 etc.; I Sam. 20.42; II Sam. 6.18; II Kings 2.24; I Sam. 17.45; Ps. 20.8, 6.

to one's aid. After all, did not Yahweh himself declare his presence by the utterance of his Name[1] and consecrate a spot to his worship by indicating it as the place where his Name was named?[2] On the same principle his worshippers are confident that by means of the Name revealed to them they can secure the intervention of God himself and the assistance of his power. For by revealing his Name God has, as it were, made himself over to them; he has opened to them a part of his very being and given them a means of access to himself.

The close relationship apparent here between the Name and the nature of God can only be understood from a knowledge of primitive beliefs about names. For primitive man the name is not merely a means of denoting a person, but is bound up in the closest possible way with that person's very existence, so that it can become in fact a kind of *alter ego*.[3] Hence knowledge of the name is more than an external means of distinguishing one person from another; it is a relation with that person's being. When, therefore, the priests pronounce a blessing over Israel in the Name of Yahweh,[4] it is more than the expression of a wish that they may be blessed. By 'laying the name of Yahweh on the people' they are in fact setting in motion an actual beneficent power.

It is clear that this is coming dangerously close to those beliefs in 'magic' and 'power' which make use of the name to exert compulsion over its owner; and the Old Testament is fully aware of this. However, the supremacy of the divine Person called upon in the Name is ensured by two things. First, he feels no need to keep his Name a secret,[5] but rather expressly communicates it to his worshippers to be used freely.[6] Secondly, he at the same time threatens dire punishment for any misuse of the Name,[7] thus educating men in a truly personal relationship with their God. Consequently we look in vain for any instance of the magical use of the divine Name in the Old Testament. The whole climate of the religion of Yahweh was so

[1] Ex. 33.19; 34.5.
[2] Ex. 20.24.
[3] Cf. Fr. Giesebrecht, *Die alttestamentliche Schätzung des Gottesnamens*, 1901, pp. 68 ff.; B. Jacob, *Im Namen Gottes*, 1903, pp. 72 ff.; W. Heitmüller, *Im Namen Jesu*, 1903, pp. 132 ff., and the works on the history of religion there cited.
[4] Num. 6.24 ff.
[5] Such concealment plays a particularly important part in Egyptian religion, and is found also among the Romans.
[6] Ex. 3.13 ff.
[7] Ex. 20.7.

obviously unfavourable to such a use, that it never had a chance to develop. Only blurred traces, such as are to be found in all religious language, bear witness to the suppression of practices of this kind inherited from the pre-Yahwist period.[1] The assurance that the divine Name constituted a guarantee of Yahweh's presence remained a free gift of grace at the hand of the sovereign God; and this God is beyond the reach of any human pressure and retains his freedom *vis-à-vis* the men who call upon him.

Finally, the constant and emphatic connection of the divine Name with cultic worship[2] shows how vividly men were aware that in the Name of the covenant God they encountered him in person and experienced his activity. Because of this, the Name becomes nothing less than an alternative term for Yahweh himself.[3] The idea that in the Name is comprehended the spiritual and personal activity of Yahweh, that aspect of his being which he turns toward the world, was so much a part of current religious thought, that the Deuteronomic school was able, with the help of this concept, both to establish the reality of Yahweh at the cultic site in the sense of his real presence, and at the same time to avert any physical or sensual interpretation of this fact—an achievement only to be found in Israel.[4]

---

[1] The most usual expression for calling upon Yahweh, *qārā' beśēm yhwh*, may be regarded as a case in point. Taken literally, it means 'to call on Yahweh by means of the Name'; and this, as a substitute for the simpler phrase, *qārā' 'el-yhwh*, might be thought to admit the idea that the Name exerted a compelling power over its owner. Such passages as Isa. 44.5; Zech. 13.6 possibly refer to a practice of tattooing the divine Name, which would suggest that the Name was used in the same way as an amulet. Blessing and cursing in the Name of Yahweh clearly presuppose Yahweh's independence of action (cf. Ps. 129.8; Num. 6.27), since curses and blessings are in general uttered subject to Yahweh's confirming will (Judg. 17.2; Josh. 6.26). Instances such as II Sam. 6.18; II Kings 2.23 f.; Ps. 44.6 are to be understood accordingly. Cf. ch. IV. 2. IV (c), pp. 172 ff. above.

[2] In addition to the frequent expression, *qārā' beśēm yhwh*, meaning 'to pray', reference should also be made to the phrase, 'the profanation of the Name', which occurs several times in the Holiness Code, and to the habit, especially popular in the Psalms, of linking the Name with the verbs for thanking, praising, blessing, honouring and loving.

[3] Cf. Pss. 5.12; 7.18; 9.3, 11; 18.50, etc.; also the various ways in which the divine Name is used, as mentioned in n. 2 above.

[4] Cf. further ch. IX. 1. II (b), pp. 409 f. below. The way is here being prepared for the development by which the Name acquires independent status as a form in which Yahweh reveals and manifests himself, and this will call for our attention later in a different connection: cf. vol. II, ch. XII. The general significance of the divine Name is dealt with in the masterly and comprehensive treatise of O. Grether, *Name und Wort Gottes im AT* (BZAW 64), 1934.

Quite as much as the general fact of his having a name at all, the particular individual names of God, from 'ēl onward, point to the personal character of the God they designate. In this connection it is of great importance to note that these names do not reflect God's activity in Nature, but reveal the deity as closely concerned with regulating the life of his worshippers[1]—and this so forcefully that no other will beside that of God himself is any longer to be taken into consideration. Generally speaking, whenever the content of the divine being is defined in terms of the mysterious forces of Nature, that being is in danger of vagueness or disintegration. The polymorphous quality of Nature leads to a plethora of powerful spirits; the consequence is always polydaemonism or polytheism. On the other hand, wherever a higher unity is recognized in the multiplicity of phenomena, then the various forces are confounded in one universal divine being; Pantheism worships a divine life manifesting itself in all things, and it is with this that it thinks to be at one.

The situation is quite different where God is not encountered in the mysteries of Nature, but where men are compelled to call a halt in the face of a superhuman will when shaping their individual and social lives; where they have to do with a will which demands their submission, not merely in a colourless and general way, but in the concrete details of daily life, in migration and the conduct of war, in lawgiving and tribal brotherhood, in marriage and the family, just as much as in the acquisition of the means of livelihood. A divine will which so expressly makes a human community its goal cannot be conceived as a dark, impersonal power or as an unconscious life-force. It must be thought of by analogy from the demonstrations of the human will, that is to say, as a being which itself thinks, wills and acts after the manner of human personality.

From the time of Moses onwards this understanding of the divine nature is intensified in a way which is significant for the whole classical period of Israelite religion. Both before and after this period the divine activity is experienced with less immediacy, with less of the shattering force of God's consuming presence. The divine power operates more from a distance, and sometimes seems to be reduced to nothing more than a general providential purpose. By contrast, the characteristic note of all those statements concerning the divine operation determined by the Sinai revelation is the fearful dynamic

[1] Cf. A. Alt, Der Gott der Väter, 1930, pp. 46–66.

of the divine demands. The description of God as *'ēl qannā'* (Ex. 20.5; 34.14) exactly hits off this impression.[1]

But even where this precise term is not found, it is nevertheless the idea of the jealous God which determines the whole slant of Mosaic religion, with its passionate striving for Yahweh's sole dominion and the total subjugation of man to his will. In the emergence of all the Israelite men of God from Moses to Ezekiel the fact that there is no escape from the nearness of God is reflected with overwhelming power. Even though recourse to the sword to give effect to Yahweh's will[2] was later replaced by the operation of the word of spiritual power, yet it is still true of the prophets, that their fundamental spiritual attitude was a passionate concern to see that Yahweh's will alone should be of any account. There was to be no compromise of any kind; any infringement was to be avenged without pity. If anything is foreign to such a conception of God, then surely it is the neutral character of deism or the vague worship of a divine providential ordering of the world.

Even, however, where this sense of the immediate reality of the divine presence is weakened, the overriding certainty of God's all-ruling will still makes itself felt in another way. For the existence of God is quite independently retained as the basic assumption of all thinking, as the unshakable cornerstone of man's whole attempt to construct a picture of life and the world. In the thick of the gravest fightings and fears on the subject of God's behaviour, as for instance in Job or Ecclesiastes, his existence remains at all times unquestioned. It is simply beyond dispute.

2. GOD AS SPIRITUAL

The more emphatically this concrete picture of God as personal guarded against any deviation which might regard him as a blind

[1] In all periods of OT religion reference is to be found to the 'jealousy' of Yahweh: cf. Josh. 24.19; Deut. 4.24; 5.9 f.; 6.15; 32.16, 21; Num. 25.11; Isa. 9.6; 37.32; Nahum 1.2; Zeph. 1.18; 3.8; Ezek. 5.13; 16.42; 23.25; 36.5 f.; 38.19; 39.25; Isa. 42.13; 59.17; 63.15; Zech. 1.14; 8.2; Joel 2.18. J. Hänel (*Die Religion der Heiligkeit*, 1931, pp. 49 f., 196 ff.) succeeded in expressing the close connection between this attribute, in which the personhood of God is seen at its most intense, and the concept of holiness, by coining the term *Eiferheiligkeit* (lit. 'jealousy-holiness'), a quality which he regarded as the truly distinctive feature of the Mosaic conception of God. It is impossible not to agree with this contention, but it is equally impossible to limit this feature simply to one single period of Israelite religion. It must be recognized as the basic element in the whole OT idea of God.

[2] Cf. Ex. 32.19 ff., 27 ff.; Num. 25; Deut. 33.9; Josh. 6.16 ff.; Judg. 20 f.; I Sam. 15.32 f.; I Kings 18.40; 19.15 ff.

natural force acting on impulse, the greater, it must be admitted, was *the danger of approximating him too closely to the human*. Quite involuntarily the limitations inherent in human personal life were transferred to the idea of God. In other words, the immanence of God threatened to overshadow his transcendence. This can be seen most clearly in the strongly anthropomorphic and anthropopathic expressions applied to him. It is well known that not only were individual parts of the human body, such as hands, eyes, ears, face and so on, attributed to God,[1] or physical actions such as laughing, smelling and whistling,[2] but that he was spoken of quite ingenuously as experiencing hatred, anger, vengeance, joy, regret and similar human emotions.[3] It would certainly mitigate the total effect of this evidence, if it could all be regarded as nothing but a naïve and childlike manner of expressing spiritual truths, or as a poetic disguise for religious experience; and it is true that both these elements are present, and do have a part to play which must be taken into account. Nevertheless it is equally true that there is here a parallel to the manner in which paganism speaks of its personified natural forces. To hush up what there is in common with heathen ways of thought is merely to gloss over the facts, and to obscure the individuality of Israelite religious faith. An unprejudiced evaluation of the Old Testament's humanizing of the deity leads us to see, however, that in fact it is not the spiritual nature of God which is the foundation of Old Testament faith. It is his personhood—a personhood which is fully alive, and a life which is fully personal, and which is involuntarily thought of in terms of the human personality. There can be no doubt that among the great mass of the people, and especially in the earlier period, the deity was frequently conceived as restricted to physical modes of living and self-manifestation. They understood the anthropomorphic expressions in a quite literal and concrete way, and so managed to acquire a most inadequate conception of the divine supremacy.

It is, however, obvious that this deficiency was not regarded by the leading spirits in Israel as particularly dangerous. It is precisely the prophets who use such an abundance of anthropomorphic and

---

[1] I Sam. 5.11; Ps. 8.4; Isa. 52.10; II Kings 19.16; Num. 11.1; Gen. 3.8; 32.31.

[2] Pss. 2.4; 37.13; Gen. 8.21; Isa. 7.18.

[3] Deut. 16.22; Isa. 61.8; Ex. 22.24; Gen. 9.5; Deut. 32.35; 30.9; Isa. 62.5; Gen. 6.6.

anthropopathic expressions for God's activities, that anyone trained in philosophical thinking cannot but be constantly scandalized. Deutero-Isaiah makes his God scream and pant like a woman in childbirth (42.14). Others do not even shrink from transferring the behaviour of animals to Yahweh—as when Hosea speaks of the beast of prey tearing its victim or of the devouring moth (Hos. 5.14, 12). It is hardly surprising that the anxious formalism of later Judaism and Alexandrian philosophy was unable to come to terms with such boldness of speech, and sought to render it innocuous by means of allegorical interpretation. In this regard, some have even flatly asserted a kind of carelessness on God's part as to the manner in which he is revealed; and indeed, it is patent that those whose task it was to proclaim the divine will regarded it as far less damaging that men should have to grope in the dark on the subject of Yahweh's spiritual nature, than that they should remain unconscious of the personal quality of his behaviour and operations. A doctrine of God as spirit in the philosophical sense will be sought in vain in the pages of the Old Testament. Not until John 4.24 is it possible to declare: 'God is a spirit'.

An examination of the history of religion may, however, provide some indication why there is no mention of God's spiritual nature at the Old Testament stage.[1] For it is demonstrable that in every case where such a dogmatically constructed conception is to be found the immediacy of the religion is weakened, and an effective communion with God obscured. The religion in question either dissolves into a frigid deism or a rationalistic moral philosophy, or else it plunges into pantheistic speculations, and tries to satisfy its properly religious needs with a mysticism of feeling. Only the Christian faith has been able to accommodate the recognition of God's spiritual nature without prejudice to his immediacy in religion, because it has its focus in the person of Jesus, and thus possesses an assurance of the personhood of God which is proof against all misinterpretations. Nevertheless, even Christianity has again and

[1] 'God himself shatters' the spiritualizing 'images and concepts' which men make of him for themselves, in order that he may encounter them in living reality as a person. 'He empties himself, and lays by the form of divinity; he humbles himself and assumes the form of man. He appears to men not as distant conception or lofty idea, not as the Absolute, the Incomprehensible, the Infinite, but as the one who is truly closest to all, as supremely the personal friend or foe of that humanity in which he reveals himself' (W. Vischer, *Zwischen den Zeiten*, 1931, p. 365). On the whole problem cf. F. Michaeli, *Dieu à l'image de l'homme*, 1950.

again been given a great deal of trouble by the dangers associated with this particular aspect of the faith.

It can, therefore, only be regarded as a wise self-limitation on the part of God, that he should have presented himself and caused himself to be understood primarily as personal, while leaving veiled, so to speak, the fact that he was also spiritual. Yet at the same time definite provision was made to counter any excessive deviation in the direction of subjecting God to human limitations. This was achieved primarily through the experience of *the infinite superiority of the divine nature* to all merely human attributes and capacities— an experience which marks every encounter with the divine in the Old Testament. Nowhere, not even in the remarkable familiarity of the descriptions in the patriarchal narratives, is there any trace of that companionable equality of God and man which is so characteristic not only of the Greek stories of the gods, but also of the Indian and many of the Babylonian and Egyptian myths. The plain fact of God's superiority to everything human is brought out so clearly throughout the Old Testament that even many Christians never notice the very definite defects in its picture of God.

Man's experiences of God are indeed so deeply impressive that they absolutely demand the use of imagery for their description; and yet they are of such a quality that they point unmistakably to a *superhuman* personality. God is experienced as the Most High, El Shaddai, Elohim, Yahweh Seba'ot, and at the same time as free from the necessity for any physical satisfactions, because he is the possessor of an inexhaustible life which has no need of human service. In this connection it is interesting to note how emphatically the Deity is felt to be the *living* God. From the first the name Yahweh lays the stress on the immediacy of God's actual operation and on the way in which the practical reality of this operation can constantly be experienced afresh. Furthermore, when a man calls upon God to prove the truth of some assertion, it is his living presence which is brought to mind in the formula *ḥay yhwh* used for the oath. Hence, at a fairly early stage, Yahweh is emphatically designated *'ēl ḥay*; and it is as such that he is constantly extolled in his absolute supremacy.[1] As the Living One he is the source of all life,[2] and demonstrates the reality of his existence, in contrast to that of the

---

[1] Gen. 16.14; Hos. 2.1; I Sam. 17.26, 36; II Kings 19.4, 16; Deut. 5.23; 32.40; Josh. 3.10; Jer. 10.10; 23.36; Pss. 42.3; 84.3.
[2] Jer. 2.13; 17.13; Ps. 36.10; Deut. 30.20.

lifeless, non-existent gods of the heathen,[1] by his incessant and marvellous activity. This contrast between the mighty and imperishable life of God and the illusory life of earth was given conceptual formulation by Isaiah, when he set the menacing powers of this world over against his God as *'ādām* and *bāśār* in the face of him who was *'ēl* and *rūaḥ*.[2]

The possessor of this highest form of life can obviously not be bound by the limitations which circumscribe human personality. Hence it is generally found that, where there is further reflection on this question, there is also an explicit denial of such limitations on the divine being. Elijah's derision at the expense of Baal, who may be sleeping or on a journey or who may have his head full of other affairs, already bears witness to an effort to conceive of the God of Israel as the *fullness of perfection*. This is later expressed in dogmatic form: God does not sleep (Ps. 121.4); he does not have eyes like the eyes of men (Job 10.4 f.), for he is the searcher of hearts and does not depend on outward impressions (I Sam. 16.7; Pss. 44.22; 139.23 f.). Even in the origin stories of Gen. 1–11, which are written so largely at a popular level, the supreme Judge and Lord of mankind shines through the God who walks in the garden, shuts the door of the Ark, and comes down to visit the Babylonian tower. This God, even when he assumes human guise, is nevertheless exalted above all inadequacy or limitation.

In addition, however, to this distinctive character of Israel's general experience of God, in which he is presented as the supreme, the living and the perfect without qualification, there are also *specific reactions against particular limiting or materialistic conceptions of the Deity*, such as might cast doubt on the supramundane quality of his nature.

One such reaction may be studied by examining the forms in which the Deity manifests himself. In various circles within the nation the attempt was begun at an early stage to create forms to express the irruption of God into worldly reality which should do justice to his transcendent spiritual being. The custom of speaking of the *mal'āk Yahweh*, or of the *pānīm*, the *kābōd* and the *šēm* of the Deity, results from a sense of the tension between the immanence and the transcendence of God and from a desire for its resolution.[3]

---

[1] Cf. especially the proof of Yahweh's living reality adduced by Deutero-Isaiah in Isa. 40–43; also Ps. 135.5 ff. and Jer. 10.1–16.
[2] Isa. 31.3. Cf. p. 215 below.
[3] Cf. Vol. II, ch. XII.

Another expression of this sense that the world cannot comprehend God is to be found in *the prohibition of images in the Decalogue*.[1] It can hardly be doubted that this rejection of any formal representation of Yahweh voices a conviction that God, though always close at hand, cannot be adequately presented under any form derived from Nature. Rather, to conjure him up in any form whatever is to misunderstand him completely and to strip him of his real value. Naturally, this is not the expression of a purely idealist conception of God, as if he were pure Thought or Mind, which is the interpretation sometimes put upon the command by those who contest its Mosaic origin. The transcendence of God is not maintained in an abstract fashion or with strict logic even in this instance; but there is a deliberate intention of eliminating the danger that the Deity might be limited to a particular place or made available to man's control in a physical way. It is in keeping with this line of thought that in later times Yahweh's invisibility is actually inferred from his self-revelation at Sinai, even though in that revelation nature-symbolism still plays a very important part (Ex. 20.22; Deut. 4.12, 15–18).

The greatest writers of the Old Testament also championed Yahweh's supremacy over all his creatures, though in a different way. Attention has already been drawn to the preference of both the Elohistic and the Priestly narrators in the Pentateuch for the divine Name Elohim;[2] and in each case this arose from a clear theological insight, which designated Yahweh as the sole occupant of the divine realm. The statement of Isaiah mentioned above, concerning the opposition between flesh and spirit,[3] expresses the same thought with pregnant force. Neither in this case, however, is it a question of God's being 'spirit' in opposition to 'matter', regarded as the principle of the physical and finite. 'Spirit' is the inexhaustible power of the divine life, in which all life takes its origin; and *bāśār* is the life of earth, which is essentially transitory and, like everything earthly and created, exhibits no principle of life in itself. This contrast, however, appears in a new light, when the *rūaḥ* is associated with the ethical factor. Yahweh's divine life, exalted over all created things, rests at its deepest level on moral perfection. The opposition between the

[1]Ex. 20.4. Cf. W. Zimmerli, 'Das zweite Gebot', *Bertholet-Festschrift*, 1950, pp. 550 ff.
[2]Cf. pp. 185 ff. f. above.
[3]Isa. 31.3.

permanent and the transitory world is in the last resort a conflict between the moral will which forms the world and that which is attached to egoistic and material ends.

It is fully consonant with such a clear awareness of the absolute superiority of the personal God that *the prophets* should reveal a sensitive feeling for it. Wherever the habit of conceiving God in human terms might result in a dangerous obscuring of his true character, they also make their protest. It is not anthropomorphisms as such that are important to them in this connection; indeed it is precisely about these that they seem to be least anxious. The spiritual and physical realms are not for them exclusive antinomies; and, for this reason, they go on presenting the trans-physical in physically conceivable forms as the old sagas had done. One has only to read Isaiah's grandiloquent portrayal of Yahweh appearing in judgment (30.27 ff.) to have some idea of the prophets' majestic indifference to this whole question. By contrast, however, when certain anthropopathisms are endangering the purity of the idea of God, their voice is heard in clear condemnation. 'God is not a man that he should lie; neither the son of man that he should repent;' the purpose of both Num. 23.19 and I Sam. 15.29 in making this declaration is to combat the erroneous idea that it is easy to talk God round, and that his threats and promises need not be taken seriously. Again, Hosea protests against the reproach that his God allows himself to be carried away into executing punitive judgment by caprice or passion: 'I will not execute the fierceness of mine anger . . . for I am God and not man; the Holy One in the midst of thee, and I do not come to carry off (the prey) like a roaring lion' (11.9).[1]

Despite such protests, however, the prophets have no desire to imply general disparagement of other ways in which men speak of God. For it is obviously not practicable to portray a personal conscious life in popular speech without having recourse to the common imagery of human psychical experience. The living movement of God's dealings with men disappears when philosophical abstraction dictates the language to be employed. The prophets are concerned to portray the personal God, who woos his people with love, and cannot be indifferent or cold to their rejection of him. Hence they speak frequently and emphatically of his anger and jealousy, his love and sorrow; and it is easy to see that the values which lie hidden in such language can never be abandoned. 'The repentance

[1] Author's reading (Tr.).

of God . . . grows into the assured conviction that human development is not for Him an empty, indifferent spectacle, that it is just
this inner immutability of His being, which excludes that dull,
dead unchangeableness which remains outwardly the same, however
much circumstances may change. . . . His jealousy is meant to
express that He is not an unconscious natural force, which pours
out its fulness in utter indifference, but that human love possesses
real value in his eyes. His fear indicates that He is a God who
sets a definite aim before Him, who constantly keeps the development of the world within the limits of His eternal decrees, and that
His wisdom does not tolerate the self-assertion of short-sighted man.
God's wrath and hatred . . . are standard expressions for the self-
asserting majesty of his living essence.'[1] For this reason, God's
kindness which bestows and blesses life can always stand side by
side with his jealousy, the unchangeableness of the divine decree
with his repentance, God's triumphing over the raging powers of
this world with his fear, his beneficent power with his wrath. To
draw all one's conclusions about the idea of God from the one class
of statements only, without taking into account the other, would be
manifestly mistaken; but it must be admitted that this is a mistake
which Old Testament studies have not always managed to avoid.

This then is the characteristic attitude of the prophets. Their
dominant interest is not speculative thought, but piety; and therefore the only tendencies to limit the Deity which they are determined
to keep at bay are those which might have a detrimental effect on
man's confidence in and reverence for God alone. The man, however,
who has acknowledged him as the Living and the True may conceive
of him in human terms in other respects without coming to harm.

Entirely different motives actuated *the thought of the Priestly school*
in its powerful opposition to that humanizing of God which marked
popular thinking. Here the description of God derives essentially
from the *tabu*-concept, and concentrates on the unapproachable
majesty of the Deity, with the result that a drastic division is made
between the divine reality and everything earthly and profane. The
absolute sovereignty of the Ruler-God, which was equally proclaimed by the prophets, but in the dynamic terms of God's victorious
struggle against the hostile powers, is now the object of peaceful and
static contemplation, which sees it as the dominion of a yonside
world, dwelling in a light to which no man can approach. God's

[1]H. Schultz, *Old Testament Theology*², II, pp. 109 f.

presence is physically perceptible only in the carefully delimited area of the Tabernacle or the Temple, and in the form of the *kābōd*; only in the revelation of his Name does the divine Thou invade the human sphere, and allow himself to be involved with human destinies through the medium of prayer. Moreover, the divine acts of power themselves are effected through mediators of a supernatural kind, angels and messengers of the Most High, except when the effect is produced by a simple word, the least physical thing in our experience, as in the case of the Creation. In the current of Priestly thought, therefore, as this may be discerned primarily in the P stratum of the Pentateuch, but also in Chronicles, the memoirs of Ezra and the cultic poetry, the transcendence of the Godhead is developed with a clarity which either results in a complete silencing of naïve anthropomorphic conceptions of God or at least supplies a powerful corrective.

We cannot, however, ignore that this Priestly language about God promoted the development of conceptual theological thought and laid the foundations for a monotheism defined in abstract terms. Such a development involves the danger of losing that sense of the nearness of God which is part of the endowment of faith, and of sinking into the nothingness of despair in the face of an inaccessible Deity. This danger was overcome, because in the Priestly conception the transcendent God also remained the God of the covenant, whose promises assured to every member of his people direct access to him, and whose law enabled them to discern his life-sustaining and beneficent will in the concrete situations of daily existence. As a result, however, of the tribulations of the Jewish community after the Exile, the force of this affirmation of the law as the revelation of God's personal will was lost, and was replaced either by a formal legalist attitude to the letter of the law or by a morbid escape from the pressure of reality into a world of apocalyptic fantasy. In these circumstances over-emphasis on God as other than and beyond Man became a feeling that the divine was utterly remote, and led to impermissible methods of satisfying religious longings.

This may be seen first of all in the anxious approach of later scribal learning to the evidence of the living, vigorous faith of prophetic times. Nobody any longer knew what to make of the prophets' trenchant statements about a God who was in close contact with every detail of life. It was thought to be owed to the exalted majesty of God to separate him as much as possible from all connection with human modes of being and feeling, and to portray him in the most sublime and abstract manner.[1] This programme was carried out even in the instruction of the ordinary man, when, as a result of the dying out of Hebrew, the Scriptures had to be expounded in Aramaic in the paraphrases called the Targums, or presented to the Diaspora in a Greek translation. These versions preferred to substitute abstracts for the concrete imagery which had been used to describe God.[2] In place of the manifestation of God himself we find God's angel,[3] the holy place[4] or the majesty.[5] New terms for God come into use. It is as if any direct naming involved a profanation of God's sublimity, and that therefore equivalent expressions for him had to be chosen, such as 'the heaven', 'the height',[6] 'the word' (*mēmrā'*), 'the dwelling' (*hašš·kīnā*),[7] 'the power',[8] 'the great majesty'. The most frequent substitute was 'the Name' (*haššēm*).[9]

This aversion from the idea of any natural connection of the world with the real activity of God had its reverse aspect in an exaggerated desire for miracle, and in the practice of crediting the divine Name with magical power. If God should at any time break into this life, then the event must be as inconceivable and disparate from ordinary experience as possible.[10] Moreover, if God's Name is so holy that it may not even be uttered, then superstition attaches to it all the more readily, ascribing to it hidden power which, with certain precautions, can be made to act in one's own interests. Especially is it of service, either written or spoken, against demons and spirits.[11] It was also held that an oath by the secret Name of God was exceptionally effective.[12] Hence the result of what was

[1] Cf. e.g., the version of the Genesis story in the Book of Jubilees.
[2] Cf. LXX of Josh. 4.24; Ex. 15.3.
[3] Cf. LXX of Isa. 9.5; Pss. 8.6; 137.1; Job 20.15: also Jub. 3.1; 12.25; 16.1 ff.; 18.14; 48.13.
[4] Cf. LXX of Ex. 24.10 f.: frequent in the Mishnah.
[5] Cf. LXX of Num. 12.8: also Targ. Onk. of Ex. 3.1; Ecclus. 17.13; Tobit 3.16.
[6] Dan. 4.23; Tobit 4.11: very frequent in the Books of the Maccabees and in the Mishnah —— LXX of Ps. 72.8; Luke 1.78; 24.49; Man. 9.
[7] Frequent in the Targums.
[8] Mk. 14.62.
[9] Especially in the Mishnah.
[10] Cf. II Macc. 3.24 ff.; 5.2 ff.; 10.29; III Macc. 6.18 f. etc.; also the demand of the Pharisees for a sign from heaven, Matt. 12.38 f.
[11] Cf. on this point W. von Baudissin, *Studien zur semit. Religionsgeschichte* I, 1876, pp. 179 ff., and *Kyrios* II, pp. 119 ff., 206 ff.; O. Eissfeldt, 'Jahvename und Zauberwesen', *Zeitschr. für Miss. und Religionswiss.*, 1927, pp. 170 ff.; F. Weber, *System der altsyn. palästin. Theologie*[2], 1897, pp. 85, 257 ff.
[12] Cf. Enoch 69.14 ff.

ostensibly a higher veneration of God was something quite unknown to the Old Testament and previously confined to heathendom—the cultus of the divine Name. It is instructive to note that the religion which is distinguished by the strongest emphasis on the divine transcendence, namely Islam, has also experienced a flourishing cultus of the Name.

Nevertheless, all this is only a tendency within Judaism; and it would be unfair not to recognize that, wherever the Old Testament Scripture still exerts a strong influence (as in many passages of Chronicles and Daniel), something of the vitality and ardour of the old faith still emerges. Moreover, even in Tobit and Ecclesiasticus we encounter a piety fashioned by and large on Old Testament lines, and for which, however prominent may be the role of mediators, a living sense of the relationship of God to the world has not as yet completely disappeared.

3. GOD AS ONE

Israel's recognition that God is One follows a very similar pattern to that of their acknowledgment of him as spiritual in nature. There can be no question at the beginning of the nation's history of any absolute monotheism in the full sense of the word, that is to say, of a realization that apart from Yahweh no gods whatsoever existed. The study of the history of religions shows quite clearly that the level of a religion is not determined by the question whether or not it is acquainted with monotheism. However precious this particular understanding of God may be, it cannot be described as decisive for the truth of a religion. To believe that it can is typical of the rationalistic treatment of religion, which assesses it solely by its quality as an intellectual construction. There are religions which are either monotheistic or very close to monotheism, such as the Egyptian Sun-worship or Islam, which nevertheless in respect of their inner life are inferior to non-monotheistic faiths. Hence for us today the problem of monotheism in the religion of the Old Testament is very far from being such a burning issue as it was for earlier generations, when on the answer to this one question very often depended one's decision about the rightness or otherwise of the Old Testament revelation as a whole.

It is easy enough to show that in ancient Israel the reality of other gods beside Yahweh was still a fact to be reckoned with. The very fact that a particular name was chosen for Israel's own God, however lofty the conception of his nature displayed in the meaning of this name, proves that men felt the need of special nomenclature to distinguish this God of theirs from the other gods, whose existence must therefore have been assumed without question. In addition, however, there are unambiguous statements to this effect. Among the best known is that of Judg. 11.23 f., where Jephthah rejects the claim of the Moabites to a part of the territory east of Jordan on the grounds that only what Chemosh gives to the Moabites and Yahweh to the Israelites can properly be regarded as their just and legal possession. II Kings 3.27 assumes that every people and country has its own protector deity, and that he may prove effective in power against Israel. According to I Sam. 26.19, in a foreign land one must worship the foreign gods. In the face of such passages some may be tempted to fall back on the theory that they represent only the lower, popular outlook, and that the convictions of the religious leaders must be placed more in the foreground of the total picture. Such a suggestion is not totally invalid, at least in so far as these pieces of evidence clearly do not provide the only or the whole story about Yahweh's relation to the gods. They do, however, receive strong support from those hymns which extol Yahweh as the highest and the one without peer among the gods, such as Ex. 15.11; Pss. 89.7; 95.3; 97.9; or which describe his jurisdiction over them, as in Deut. 32.8; Ps. 82.1.

This unreflecting assumption of the existence of many gods is consonant with the fact that nowhere in the earlier Old Testament writings do we find a clear statement of the monotheistic idea. Not until the seventh century does the monotheistic formula appear which describes Yahweh as the true God over all the kingdoms of the earth, the only God, in contrast to whom all 'gods' are nothing (I Kings 8.60; II Kings 19.15, 19; Deut. 4.35; Jer. 2.11; 10.7; 16.20 etc.). Deutero-Isaiah in particular employs this new knowledge with great emphasis in his poetry, and returns to it again and again (41.29; 43.10; 44.8; 45.5, 6, 14, 21 f.; 46.9). The way in which he contrasts Yahweh and the gods of the heathen, and stresses the nothingness of the latter in face of the God of Israel, expresses an exultant joy at a new and overwhelming apprehension of truth, bringing spiritual liberation and furnishing a valuable weapon for the refutation of heathen religion.[1]

[1] On this question cf. B. Balscheit, *Alter und Aufkommen des Monotheismus in der israelitischen Religion* (BZAW 69), 1938. One might possibly be able to derive

But a long journey had to be accomplished before this point could be reached. Moreover, even when it has been reached, it remains true that God's revelation does not tear up the laws of human thought, nor does it short-circuit the working of the human spirit; it provides the material which, when willingly accepted, leads to a clarification and enrichment of human knowledge. Intellectual recognition of God as One presupposes the experience of his activity as also something unique. We have seen that even so early as the religion of the patriarchs there is an emphasis on the exclusiveness of their relation to their El, and thus an ascription of unique value to the tribal deity. It is at the Mosaic stage that the conviction of Yahweh's *oneness* emerges in a really dominant manner. Yet other nations also regarded their God as unique and any infringement of his sovereignty within the nation as dangerous. What gives this belief in Israel its unparalleled importance is first, that *it rules out all rival deities*; secondly, that *it is not restricted to the official cultus*, but is the responsibility of each individual; lastly, that *it is maintained at all periods with such shattering force* that nothing comparable can be observed in the history of any other civilized people.

As far as the first of these points is concerned the principal documentary evidence is the first commandment of the Decalogue (Ex. 20.3, with the corresponding passage in the Book of the Covenant, Ex. 22.19; also Ex. 34.14; Deut. 12.29 ff.; 13.1 ff.). Even those scholars who do not accept the Decalogue as Mosaic grant that this intolerance of all rival deities constituted one of the essential features of Mosaic religion. It runs clearly through all the poetry and narrative, throwing into relief too boldly to be controverted the authority of the divine as comprehending and determining the whole of life. In the reckless energy and self-surrender which characterizes all the leading spirits from Moses onward through the whole succession of the prophets, this power of the divine self-assertion shines forth like light reflected in a mirror. The gravest crisis in the history of the Israelite state was the civil war against the Omrid dynasty in the ninth century, which flared up over the question whether the

---

Albright's view that Moses should already be regarded as a champion of monotheism (*From the Stone Age to Christianity*[2], 1946, p. 207) from a less stringent definition of monotheism; but if the crucial sentence, 'the term "monotheist" means one who teaches the existence of only one God', is to be taken to imply in fact a denial of the existence of other gods, then this is precisely the point which cannot be established from the evidence concerning Moses and the early period of Israel. The same applies to E. Auerbach, *Moses*, pp. 226 and 241.

Tyrian Baal was to exercise sovereign rights in Israel side by side with Yahweh.

It is worth noting in this connection that any disintegration of the Godhead into male and female principles was also firmly excluded. Yahweh never had a female consort; and thus any idea that he needed to be complemented—a fate which befell all the other major Semitic deities—was rejected. It is very significant that in Hebrew there should be no word for 'goddess'; El or Elohim has to serve to denote the heathen goddesses. That even in Israel the effort was made to introduce a Mother-goddess side by side with Yahweh is shown by the protests, prominent both in the cultic reformers and in the prophets, against the *Aštart* or *Aširat* cultus (cf. I Kings 14.23; 15.13; II Kings 18.4; 23.6; Deut. 16.21; Jer. 2.27 etc.). Nevertheless, the erection of a sacred pole, the symbol of the goddess, was always felt to be impermissible, however complaisant may have been the attitude to stone pillars. The Elephantine papyri, which record the worship of a goddess called Anat-Bethel or Anat-Yahu during the sixth century, show how this heathen tendency could prevail, when a Yahweh-worshipping community was cut off from the parent congregation.

If the worship of Yahweh alone was to be maintained without exception, it was vital that no distinction in this respect should be made between the national and the private cultus. The Decalogue and the Book of the Covenant are directed at the individual Israelite. Similarly the Shechemite Twelve Commandments (Deut. 27.15–26) curse the individual who shall be guilty of transgressing them. Since the inclination toward alien gods was especially liable to take the form of magic and the use of images as amulets, the commands against images of false gods and against sorcery must also be taken into account under this head (cf. Ex. 20.4; 22.17; and parallels). Among other peoples there was by contrast a great deal of indulgence toward the divine patrons of the private citizen, so long as respect was always shown to the god of the State.

Finally, so far as the consuming intensity of the demands of faith is concerned, the Sinai revelation and its after-effects remain its abiding witness—a fact which can hardly be paralleled in any other religion. The awfulness of the divine majesty, which can only be worshipped with trembling, here creates a deep impression. The passionate intensity with which the Deity both asserts and imposes his own will burns out of the Mosaic picture of God; and this, by endowing men simultaneously with fear and gratitude, drives them on to champion the claims of God without thought of the consequences.[1]

During the early history of Israel, however, the consuming holiness of God and the experience of his annihilating majesty provided a substitute for the missing monotheistic belief. This was the only way in which the as yet unexplained relationship of Yahweh to other gods could be prevented from becoming a danger to his absolute value for Israel. But with the widening of spiritual horizons and the development of the national culture the knowledge of Yahweh as One could be introduced to round off the picture of God without causing difficulties. It is quite probable that ideas of a monotheistic character may already have dawned on the most advanced spirits; it would be quite easy to credit Moses, for instance, with such ideas without further question, except that we have no tradition to this effect. Moreover, all those who dispute the existence of a lofty conception of God in the early history of Israel should reflect that at the very time when, under Solomon, there was a vast expansion of the cultic side of religion, an author emerges who gives evidence of highly developed religious thought, namely the Yahwist. His sky-god Yahweh guides his own either by dreams, as in the case of Abraham, or, as with Eliezer, by angels; but even when he visits his faithful worshippers in human form, he remains the exalted Lord of the whole earth and Judge of mankind, and is free from any national limitations. He leads Abraham forth from Babylonia and guards him in Egypt. He guides Eliezer and Jacob to the Children of the East, and rescues his people from the house of bondage in the teeth of the rulers of this world. In fact for the Yahwist there is not even such a thing as a serious claimant to rivalry with Yahweh. His whole temper is monotheistic, even though he has not as yet discovered the form of expression to match it; and it is hardly fair to make him responsible for the many utterances of an undeveloped idea of God which came to him with his traditional saga material.

The struggle of Elijah against the Tyrian Baal marks an epoch.[2]

[1] Cf. pp. 207 ff. above; also M. Buber, *Königtum Gottes*[2], p. 92.

[2] According to O. Eissfeldt (*Der Gott Karmel*, 1953) who, in opposition to the hitherto dominant assessment, advances good reasons for seeing in the narrative complex of I Kings 16.29–19.18 'a picture corresponding to historical truth', the deity in question was originally a local mountain-god Karmel, who by the time of Elijah had, however, become identified with the Syrian *Ba'alšāmēm*. About the same time as Eissfeldt, K. Galling adduced religio-historical material which points in the same direction ('Der Gott Karmel und die Ächtung der fremden Götter', *Alt-Festschrift*, 1953, pp. 105 ff.).

The memorable words which have been handed down as uttered by him at the climax of the conflict—'If the LORD be God, follow him; but if Baal, then follow him'—as also the prayer, 'Hear me, O LORD . . . that this people may know that thou LORD art God' (I Kings 18.21, 37) show clearly that more is at stake than merely a trial of strength between two deities over the extent of their respective domains. This outlook, which was still very much alive in Jephthah's words in Judg. 11.24, is here completely superseded. The question is whether Yahweh or Baal is 'God'. Elijah's words embody the certainty, that apart from the God of Israel there are in reality no gods worthy of the name; in other words we are manifestly at the stage of practical monotheism.

In this case it was the struggle against Nature religion which led to a deeper recognition of Yahweh's uniqueness. One hundred years later a similar effect was produced by the need to come to terms with the fact of the great world powers, which were threatening to crush Israel. Now it was Isaiah who, with impressive confidence and faith, proclaimed the nothingness of all the 'gods', whom he could only designate as 'ᵉlilīm, 'nothings' (Isa. 2.8, 18; 10.10; 19.3); and in his grandiose vision he foresaw their complete extermination by Yahweh, as the True God took possession of his world-wide dominion (2.18 f.; 10.4[1]). Isaiah set Yahweh as 'ēl and rūaḥ (31.3) over against every other power, and saw in the future the kingdom of this one and only Lord established over all the nations (2.2–4). This consummation was to convert into hard fact that vision of the King whose glory filled the whole earth, which he had received at the time of his call (6.3).

It is hardly surprising, after this first clear comprehension by the prophets of the universality of God, that instances should be multiplied in which the very names given to the heathen deities deny them any kind of existence. In Jer. 2.5; 10.8; 14.22 they are called hebel, hᵃbālīm, i.e. literally 'breath', and so by extension 'nothing', 'illusion'. In Ps. 31.7 we find hablē šāw'; in Jer. 2.11; 5.7 lō' 'ᵉlōhīm. From now on their images are loaded with scorn and mockery as the work of human hands, maᶜᵃśēh yādayim. šiqqūṣīm 'abomination', and gillūlīm, 'gods of dung', are favourite appellations with Ezekiel and the writers of the Deuteronomic school. Scathing sarcasm at the expense of the manufacture of the idols occurs in Jer. 2.26–28; 10.1–16 (the

---

[1]Following the emendation of Euting and de Lagarde, this refers to the over-throw of Osiris and Beltis by Yahweh; cf. Duhm, *Jesaja*[3], 1914, *ad loc.*

latter certainly not the work of Jeremiah himself) and in Isa. 40.18–20; 41.4–7; and 44.9–20 (the last-named passage again not from Deutero-Isaiah); further instances are Pss. 115 and 135. This often extremely robust polemic is certainly unfair to the loftier heathen ideas of God; but it most decidedly hits off popular pagan religion. Moreover, it should be remembered that the chief concern of the writers was to show their own compatriots the folly and absurdity of idol worship, which in a time of political impotence was threatening to seduce a good many Jews with its external glamour. Deutero-Isaiah produces a particularly high grade of polemic, when he makes men realize the powerlessness of the gods of the hosts of heaven in face of the living onslaught of the power of Yahweh. For Yahweh rules all the stars by his word (Isa. 40.26) and manipulates history from afar, while the world-revolution of which Cyrus is the instrument finds the idols and their worshippers completely helpless (Isa. 41.1 ff., 21 ff.; 43.9 ff.; 44.6 ff. etc.).[1]

This achievement was given permanent confessional form for Judaism in the prayer of the *Sema'*. The first part of this comprises Deut. 6.4–9, and therefore begins with the affirmation: *š*ᵉ*ma' yiśrā'ēl yhwh 'ᵉlōhēnū yhwh 'eḥād*. This statement, which certainly comes from the time of Josiah, has been given various interpretations;[2] but, whichever be the correct one, the text became the basic formula of absolute monotheism. 'This means that the belief that God is One is no longer simply something appertaining to religion, but has also become a part of theology and metaphysics, a most valuable and vital element in the sum of human knowledge. From Ezra onwards to associate God with other *'ᵉlōhīm* becomes steadily less meaningful, and the preference for titles such as "God of Heaven" and "Most High" expresses a conscious cultivation of the monotheistic idea of God.'[3]

[1] Nevertheless Job 31.26–28 still regards the temptation to star-worship as something to be taken seriously by the pious.

[2] Linguistically, it is certainly possible to support the rendering 'Yahweh our God is one single Yahweh'; that is to say, he is not a God who can be split up into various divinities or powers, like the Baals of Tyre, of Hazor and of Shechem etc., but one who unites in himself as a single person everything which Israel thought of as appertaining to God (Dillmann, *Handbuch der AT Theologie*, p. 238). However, the other rendering, 'Yahweh is our God, Yahweh alone!', is also possible. In this case the thought would be concentrated more on the exclusive position of Yahweh vis-à-vis all other deities. C. A. Keller (*Das Wort Oth als Offenbarungszeichen Gottes*, 1946, pp. 117 ff.) has called attention to the importance of the sign wrought in Egypt for the recognition of God's oneness in the Deuteronomic literature.

[3] H. Schultz, *Alttestamentliche Theologie*, p. 505; cf. ET, vol. II, p. 114.

Judaism later evinces a certain effort after fair-minded criticism by seeking to explain the origin of idol-worship. Thus Wisd. 13 and 14 regards the error of those who worship divine powers in fire, wind, air, water or stones as less blameworthy than the worship of images, which is euhemeristically explained in terms of the veneration of the departed or of an absent ruler. On the other hand a new realism in demonology makes itself felt in the idea of the heathen gods as demons, a conception advocated in many apocryphal works[1] and in the LXX version of various biblical passages[2] such as Pss. 95.5; 105.37; Deut. 32.17; Isa. 65.11. This view did once more allow the gods some sort of existence, and in this respect betrays a marked difference between Judaism's general outlook on the world and that of the prophets. Nevertheless, the fundamental monotheistic creed was of course quite safe from any further attacks from this direction.

The development of Old Testament religion shows that the essential factor in the emergence of a vital and moral monotheism was not philosophical speculation, but the experience of God's close and living reality. If monotheistic belief had secured a foothold in Israel prematurely, it would have made no progress, but would have become a pale abstraction devoid of inner force. This has been the fate of all monotheistic conceptions arrived at by speculative methods, from the Aton of Amenophis IV and the Brahman of Indian religion to the Πρῶτον κινοῦν of the Greeks. It was only because their God Yahweh was at hand to dominate the whole of life and to give practical proof of his reality that Israel's picture of God was able to grow, and that her concepts could be expanded without endangering the inward vitality of her religion.

[1]Enoch 19.1; 99.7; Jub. 11.4 f.; 19.28; 22.17.
[2]Instances occur even in the MT at Hos. 12.12 (reading laśśēdīm instead of śᵉwārīm); Deut. 32.17; Ps. 106.37.

VII

THE NATURE OF THE COVENANT GOD
(continued)

B. AFFIRMATIONS ABOUT THE DIVINE ACTIVITY

I. THE POWER OF GOD

FROM THE VERY BEGINNINGS of Israel's religion it is easier for
the observer to detect the main outlines of the divine activity
than those of the divine being. The latter, as we have seen,
remain essentially outlines, and never undergo any more profound
speculative or metaphysical development; but the description of the
divine activity is couched in precise and concrete terms, adapted to
express *the note of personal decision* which marks the Old Testament
revelation of God. It is, in fact, not so much a question of doctrine,
as of expressing the divine will.

Undoubtedly it was Yahweh's warlike activity, affording as it did
sensible experience of his power, which evoked the most powerful
response in ancient Israel. The oldest poetry sings the God of War:
he hurls the Egyptians into the sea;[1] the powers of heaven and earth
enlist in his service, when he sweeps down from Sinai to overthrow
the Canaanites before his people.[2] Campaigns are conducted under
the guidance of his oracle;[3] to him the spoil is devoted.[4] His anger
pursues the guilty man, whose treachery has cheated his people of
their victory, or who has ignored his call to arms,[5] just as his

---

[1]Ex. 15.21.
[2]Judg. 5.20 f.; Josh. 10.11 ff.; I Sam. 7.10; II Kings 3.22; Ex. 23.28; Deut.
7.20.
[3]Judg. 1.1; 20.18, 23; I Sam. 14.37; 23.2; 28.6; 30.8; II Sam. 5.19; Num.
14.40 ff.; 21.2 f.
[4]Josh. 6.17 ff.; I Sam. 15.3; Deut. 13.16 ff.
[5]Josh. 7.16 ff.; I Sam. 14.37 ff.; Judg. 5.23; I Sam. 11.7.

blessing is assured to the doughty fighter.[1] The impression which this experience of God made on the pious is reflected in many of the epithets with which Yahweh is honoured; the God of Israel is praised in hymns as a warrior-hero, powerful and highly exalted, terrible and glorious in holiness, mighty and a doer of wonders.[2] The title 'Yahweh of Hosts' very specially refers to this demonstration of his power in war. The way in which this aspect of the picture of God remained very much alive at all periods is too well known to require substantiation by examples. It is embellished with details drawn from the myth of the struggle with Chaos; and in the colourful language of the prophets it reaches its highest level of intensity.[3]

In so far as it is the fearful, savage and terrifying features of the picture of God, which, generally speaking, are the traits most prominently associated with his power and greatness, it is to a certain extent understandable that many scholars portray the God of ancient Israel as no more than a 'sinister and frightful being, easily provoked to anger', in whom one looks in vain for the characteristics of kindness and concern.[4] Yet it should never be forgotten that the point which was made earlier about the personal nature of God also applies here. The awe-inspiring terribleness of God is not experienced as the incomprehensible rage of a chaotic force, a stupendous irrationality, but as the operation of a self, a personal will. For this reason it possesses an absolute value, regardless of human beings and their desires; and this absolute value blesses mortality even as it terrifies it.[5] This brings out the second point, that the relevant Old Testament evidence is attempting to portray not just some God of 'catastrophic' character, but the divine Lord of his people, who in virtue of the covenant applies his power on Israel's behalf. This is still true, even when he is executing fearful judgment on his own people. Even though man draws near to this God in awe and trembling, there is a lively sense that his character is known to be kind, loyal and ready to succour; and it is this which makes it possible to rejoice in the assertion of his power, even when

[1]Gen. 49.23 ff.; Deut. 33.21; Judg. 5.9, 14 f., 24.
[2]Ex. 15.21, 3, 11; Ps. 24.8.
[3]Cf. the fine description in Hempel, *Gott und Mensch im AT*, pp. 30 ff.; also H. Frederiksson, *Jahve als Krieger*, 1945.
[4]Cf. B. Stade, *Biblische Theologie des AT*, p. 91; H. Gressmann, *Palästinas Erdgeruch in der israelitischen Religion*, 1909, p. 78 *et al.*
[5]Cf. also the remarks below on the subject of God's anger and holiness, pp. 258 ff.; 270 ff.

this takes destructive and terrifying forms. The reason, therefore, why his might as a warrior is emphasized so strongly is not that he is regarded simply as a savage destroyer, but that this is the way in which he gives the most impressive and immediately convincing demonstration of his rightful position as Israel's ruler. The symbols of this rule, the royal throne of the Ark, the rod of God, the oracle of the sacred lot, constitute the most important sacred objects of the Yahweh congregation in Mosaic times; and it is this rule which the multitudes acknowledge, when they gather for his festival to exult in his Kingship.[1]

On closer inspection, therefore, it would seem that Israel's joy at the proofs of Yahweh's might implies, as well as a recognition of all the harshness and destruction and gloomy grandeur, an awareness of the life-giving and creative aspects of his marvellous power. The whole series of miracles by which the life of the nation was preserved during the Wilderness wanderings testifies to this; and similar miracles continue to occupy as natural a place in the later accounts of Yahweh's activity as do his wondrous acts in war.[2] Furthermore, when it comes to describing the bliss of the eschatological golden age, the peaceful pictures of natural prosperity, the mythological colour of which confirms their pre-prophetic origin, play just as important a part even in the earliest references as God's triumphs in battle.[3] In the nature of the case, this aspect of the divine wonder-working power is more strongly emphasized after the entry into Canaan and the experience of living in a highly-developed civilization, and new details are employed to illustrate it; but there is no need to explain it in terms of borrowing from the deities of this culture. It would be more reasonable to ask whether it was not under foreign influence that Israel acquired her eye for the marvels of God's power in the silent regularity of the processes of Nature, the turning of the seasons, the courses of the stars, the emergence of life. Certainly it is possible to point to the fact that the Babylonian Creation myths[4] and the

[1] Num. 23.21; 24.7; Ex. 15.18; Deut. 33.5.
[2] Ex. 15.25; 16.1 ff.; 17.6; Num. 11.31 ff.; 20.11; Judg. 15.18 f.; I Kings 17.2 ff., 8 ff.; 18.34 ff.; II Kings 3.17; 4.16, 34; 20.10; Isa. 38.8.
[3] Cf. Gen. 49.11 f.; Num. 24.6; Deut. 33.13 ff.: also H. Gressmann, *Der Messias*, 1929, pp. 149 ff.
[4] Cf. the traces of Babylonian Creation concepts in Gen. 1, and echoes of the same in the poetic language of Isa. 51.9; Ps. 89.11; Job 9.13; 26.12 and elsewhere: further cf. the points of contact with the Enthronement festival adduced by S. Mowinckel, *Psalmenstudien* II.

Egyptian contemplation of Nature[1] supplied Israelite thought with varied material—possibly through the mediation of Canaanite festivals and cultic hymns[2]—and stimulated it in many ways. But it should not be forgotten, that the most influential assumptions supporting the subjection of the whole natural order to the mighty authority of a divine Lord were attached in the religion of ancient Israel to the covenant God, who not only led his people in war, but also granted them Canaan as the land of their inheritance, and thus was naturally worshipped as the giver of all the blessings of nature and everything that went with the fuller life of civilization.

To show how decisive these basic assumptions were for the Israelite attitude to Nature we need cite no more than the independent form taken by their concept of Creation. In the work of the Yahwist narrator this concept is already marked by a firm exclusion of polytheistic mythological elements, and by a deliberate linking up of Creation with history. The result was that those heathen speculations concerning the mystery of life and death, which must have been known to Israel (cf. the Osiris and Adonis cults, and the resurrection myth of Bel-Marduk) were nevertheless rejected. Instead there was a determination to hold fast to the idea of an immediate dependence of mankind and of the whole Creation on the peremptory, controlling will of Yahweh, the only eternal God; and this leaves hardly any doubt what was really the decisive factor shaping Israel's characteristic belief in the subordination of Nature to the divine *imperium*. It was their experience of Yahweh's control of history, working purposefully toward a goal, and brooking no contradiction of its authority.

Constantly present behind all the testimonies to Yahweh's marvellous power is one particular presupposition, which it is indispensable to keep in mind, if their witness is to be rightly assessed. This power is the power of the God of the covenant. The comparative isolation in which statements about it sometimes appear has to be understood in the light of the characteristic tendency of Israelite

[1] A comparison of what is in this respect the classic text, namely the hymn to Aton (Ranke in *AOT*, pp. 15 ff.; *ANET*, pp. 369 ff.), with Ps. 104 leaves no doubt of the presence of Egyptian influences.

[2] It is obvious that the adoption of the agricultural festivals in Canaan would be favourable to such a process. On the subject of Canaanite influences on the poetry of Israel cf. F. M. Th. Böhl, *Theol. Lit. Blatt*, 1914, cols. 337 ff.; Jirku, *Altorientalischer Kommentar zum Alten Testament*, 1923, pp. 220 ff.; A. Alt, 'Hic murus aheneus esto', *Zeitschrift der Deutschen Morgenländischen Gesellschaft* 86, 1932, pp. 33 ff.; W. von Baudissin, *Adonis und Esmun*, 1911, pp. 385 ff.

THE NATURE OF THE COVENANT GOD

spirituality, which surrenders itself completely to one particular impression or image, and yet at the same time keeps in mind the totality to which this individual aspect belongs and to which it is a witness. This 'impressionistic'[1] quality of Israelite thought should be a warning not to dogmatize on the basis of the apparent isolation of these statements; rather it calls for a careful recapitulation of the basic attitude behind each separate affirmation.

This requirement becomes all the more urgent, when it is realized that the covenant community between Yahweh and Israel found its aptest expression not so much in the attribution of power, which can be paralleled in all religions, as in a whole series of quite different propositions. Pre-eminent among these is that of Yahweh's lovingkindness.

2. THE LOVINGKINDNESS OF GOD (ḥesed Yahweh)

Wherever a bᵉrît governs relations between human beings, the kind of behaviour which is expected in the normal way of those so associated is clearly recognized as ḥesed. David expects ḥesed of Jonathan on the grounds of the covenant existing between them, and Jonathan entreats the same attitude from David in view of his future kingship.[2] It is the brotherly comradeship and loyalty which one party to a covenant must render to the other. Thus ḥesed constitutes 'the proper object of a bᵉrît, and may almost be described as its content. The possibility of the establishment and maintenance of a covenant rests on the presence of ḥesed.'[3] Hence there are frequent instances of ḥesed and bᵉrît being used in zeugma.[4]

Israel's relationship with God, being a covenant fellowship, consequently took over the ideas bound up with this particular legal form of human relationships, even though these were modified by the exalted nature of the divine party to the contract. One particular type of conduct expected from fellowship as an immediate result of the conclusion of the bᵉrît was the duty of loyal mutual service; without the rendering of ḥesed on both sides the maintenance of a

[1] This name was given to the peculiar structure of Israelite spirituality by J. Hempel in his valuable study: 'Die Stellung des AT in der Geschichte des religiösen Bewusstseins als systematisch-theologisches Problem', Altes Testament und Geschichte, 1930, pp. 65 ff.
[2] I Sam. 20.8, 14 f.
[3] Cf. Nelson Glück, Das Wort ḥesed, 1927, p. 13. Cf. also W. F. Lofthouse, 'Ḥen and Ḥesed in the Old Testament', ZAW 51, 1933, pp. 29 ff.; H. J. Stöbe, Bedeutung und Geschichte des Begriffs ḥäsäd (Diss. Münster), 1951; cf. VT 2, 1952, pp. 244 ff.
[4] Deut. 7.9, 12; I Kings 8.23; Ps. 89.29; Isa. 54.10; 55.3 etc. All passages listed in N. Glück, op. cit., p. 13 n. 1.

covenant was in general unthinkable. Hence there was a strong, living conviction in Israel that Yahweh's kindness and readiness to succour was something which could be expected of him in view of his having established the covenant relationship. The redemption from Egypt was early understood as an act of this succouring love,[1] and for all his terrifying power the God of Sinai is also the loving protector, who remains true to his promises and exerts his power for the good of his covenant people. The very first clause in the terms of the covenant is a pledge that he wills to be the God of this people: 'I am Yahweh thy God!' (Ex. 20.2). This is echoed in what he teaches men about himself in order to assure them of a loyalty and love consonant with the covenant relationship,[2] in his leading them mightily through the wilderness, in his forgiving their transgressions.[3] It is this knowledge which enables men to glorify him for his unshakeable benevolence,[4] in face of which all the destructive designs of the enemy and even all demonic powers must give way.[5] In particular, David and his house can count on the divine lovingkindness, because Yahweh has by his promises entered into a special relationship with him.[6] This constancy of the divine succour, based as it is on the covenant community, is given pregnant expression in the frequent collocation of *ḥesed* and *bᵉrît* as two closely related demonstrations of God's favour.[7] Nor does this constancy exclude the punishment of sinners; rather it is evinced precisely in the fact that punishment ,is used to restore the disrupted covenant relationship.[8]

Hence it is to Yahweh's *ḥesed* that men have recourse in difficult situations (Gen. 24.12; I Kings 3.6). The wish that one expresses at parting (II Sam. 15.20) or to those who have been found faithful (II Sam. 2.6) is that they may never cease to experience the divine

---

[1] Cf. Ex. 3.7 ff.
[2] Ex. 20.6; 34.6 f.
[3] Ex. 15.13; Num. 14.18–20; Ex. 32.11 f., 31 f.
[4] Num. 23.8, 19.
[5] Num. 23.21, 23; 24.9; Judg. 5.31.
[6] II Sam. 7.15; 22.51; I Kings 3.6.
[7] In parallelism, II Sam. 7.15 ff.; Pss. 25.10; 89.28, 33 f., 49; cf. Ps. 4; Pss. 106.45; 103.17 f.; Isa. 54.10; 55.3. Compare the collocation of *ḥᵃsîdai* and *kōrᵉtê bᵉrîtî* in Ps. 50.5. In hendiadys with the meaning 'covenant loyalty', Deut. 7.9, 12; I Kings 8.23; Neh. 1.5; 9.32; Dan. 9.4; II Chron. 6.14. The conclusions about the meaning of *ḥesed* which J. Elbogen has drawn from this combination are not tenable, but they derive from correct observation ('ḥsd, Verpflichtung, Verheissung, Bekräftigung', in the *P. Haupt-Festschrift*, 1926, pp. 43 ff.).
[8] Ex. 34.7; Num. 14.20 ff.; II Sam. 7.14 ff.: cf. the context of the account of the establishment of the sanctuary, Ex. 33.5 ff.

faithfulness in the divine community; and indeed, the practice of referring to this faithfulness in gratitude and confidence developed into a stereotyped liturgical formula for use in prayers of petition and thanksgiving: 'O give thanks unto the LORD; for he is good: for his mercy endureth for ever.'[1]

The unbreakable character of the divine disposition of love is beautifully reflected in the description of outstanding and tested human loyalty as *ḥesed 'lōhīm* or *ḥesed yahweh*, that is to say, loving constancy such as Yahweh himself both desires and demonstrates (II Sam. 9.3; I Sam. 20.14). The popular conjunction of *ḥesed* and '*met*, 'truth', has the same significance.[2]

At first sight one might be inclined to place these confident assertions of God's succouring love on a par with the testimonies to be found in other religions to the assistance and lovingkindness of God. Even as early as the ancient Sumerian inscriptions it is clear that care on which one could rely was expected from the deity, and in particular from the god of the city, who was more or less obliged to provide such care in virtue of his position as the city's founder and protector.[3] Among the Babylonian gods, apart from Shamash, it was Marduk who was predominantly extolled for the attributes of justice and compassion. As the son of Ea, the chief magician of the gods, and the one who shared his secret powers, he rose to be the redeemer-god, who could break every evil spell, and whose righteousness and compassion filled every sufferer with confidence.[4] Indeed, the deity himself in his oracles sometimes recalls the help he has vouchsafed on previous occasions and demands confidence in his continued succour.[5]

---

[1] Jer. 33.11 ff.; Pss. 100.5; 106.1; 107.1, 8, 15, 21, 31 etc. It is not, however, satisfactory to render *ḥesed* at this stage by 'mercy', as if it were synonymous with *raḥ*ᵃ*mīm* (J. Ziegler, *Die Liebe Gottes bei den Propheten*, 1930, p. 33).

[2] Gen. 24.27; 32.11; II Sam. 15.20. The two concepts are found again and again in the Pss., sometimes in a more restricted, sometimes in a looser sense: e.g., Pss. 25.10; 40.11 f.; 61.8; 85.11; 89.15. Quite often they are combined with explicit reflection on the actual covenant relationship. '*mūnā* is frequently used instead of '*met*. Collected references in Bertholet, *Bibl. Theol. des AT* II, 1911, p. 244 n. 1.

[3] This is most beautifully expressed in the prayer of Gudea, King of Lagash, to the city goddess, Gatumdug: cf. Thureau-Dangin, *Die sumerischen und akkadischen Königsinschriften*, 1907, pp. 91 ff.; *Les Cylindres de Goudéa*, 1905, pp. 8 ff.

[4] Cf. the picture of this god drawn by Zimmern in *Keilschriften und AT³*, pp. 372 f. One of the fifty names of Marduk is 'Compassionate One, whom it becometh to make alive': cf. J. Hehn, *Hymnen und Gebete an Marduk*, 1906, p. 288; also pp. 325, 328, 336, 372.

[5] Cf. the oracle of the Ishtar of Arbela to Esarhaddon, *AOT*, pp. 281 f. *ANET*, p. 289; comparison with the text of Gen. 15.7 and 26.24 will reveal the similarities in the form of the divine utterance.

In spite, however, of these resemblances in the picture of God, the differences which undoubtedly exist should not be forgotten. In particular it is the association of Yahweh's *ḥesed* with the covenant relationship which gives the divine lovingkindness an incomparably firmer basis. Because in Israel it was possible to speak of one God, whose demands sought jealously and exclusively to shape the whole of life, the succour and lovingkindness of this God were given an internal foundation which will be sought in vain among the Babylonian Nature deities. The element of uncertainty—which with the latter, despite all the fine individual traits, is always present—may be seen first in the fact that it is constantly necessary to take into account that there may be a second and hostile divine purpose, capable of crossing the more gracious intentions of the first.[1] Secondly it should be noted that there is a policy of re-insurance by means of an elaborate system of incantations, which is always available to save men from having to rely on nothing but the unconstrained will of the deity. Conversely, the eradication of mantic and magical practices in Israel argues for the strength of the conviction that on the lovingkindness of this God men can utterly depend. Moreover, in the grateful portrayal of God's leading and redemption of the nation from the time of the patriarchs onwards, a portrayal which plays so great a part in all Israel's historical writing, the scope of the divine love and loyalty is enlarged to cover the whole course of history, revealing the unalterable integrity of that love in a manner to which there is no parallel. Exclusiveness and involvement in history, therefore, characterize the affirmations of ancient Israel on the subject of God's lovingkindness.

The imagery which portrays *God as the Father-Shepherd of his people* also serves to illustrate the kind of divine behaviour implied by the term *ḥesed*. The father-son relationship assumes *ḥesed* as the kind of conduct binding on its members.[2] It is true that in the Semitic idea of fatherhood the element of rule, of ownership and of general authority receives equal emphasis with the element of love. Frequent instances of this may be found in the Babylonian hymns,[3] though the songs of

---

[1] In the oracle mentioned above Ishtar has to influence the will of Aššur in favour of her protégé; there was, of course, no certainty that she would succeed in the case of all the gods.

[2] Cf. Gen. 47.29.

[3] The ruler-god Enlil appears as the 'Father of the land'; cf. S. Langdon, *Sumerian and Babylonian Psalms*, 1909, p. 103. The storm-god Adad receives the title of Father as the mighty and exalted God, *AOT*, p. 249.

lamentation call on the sympathy of the 'compassionate father',[1] and in the beautiful hymn to the moon-god Sin both elements are to be found in the same song of praise.[2] In the Israelite use of the title 'Father' the dominant idea is that of the Creator of all natural existence, for this gives God a legal claim on the worship of his people at the same time as he himself confers on them his own protection.[3] Nevertheless, it is the compassion of the heavenly Father which is invoked when his help is supplicated, and he is confessed as the Father of the fatherless.[4] Under prophetic influence the Deuteronomic teacher of the Law goes a stage further, when he teaches men to see the attitude of a father even in the afflictions which Yahweh sends. God does not merely punish, but by punishing seeks to educate (Deut. 8.5, taken over and given an individual application in Prov. 3.12). The same conception of the title of Father predominates in later Judaism, where there is a marked growth in the use of this designation. In this connection the close association with the idea of Yahweh's Kingship is significant; the concept of God's love is obscured by the emphasis on the power of the divine ruler.[5]

The imagery of the shepherd also describes the lovingkindness of Yahweh as the fulfilment of that association with Israel which he established in the beginning. The office of a shepherd as an image of kingship is of course found throughout the Near East,[6] and is ascribed to gods as well as to kings, often in stereotyped forms. This element of the courtly style always has something of an official stamp, as a result of which the characteristics of love and providential care appear simply to be taken for granted as involved in faithfulness to the kingly calling, and so become quite impersonal

[1] Cf. Hehn, *Hymnen und Gebete an Marduk*, no. 21, p. 365; also no. 14, p. 352.
[2] Cf. *AOT*, p. 241; *ANET*, pp. 385 f.
[3] Ex. 4.22; Num. 11.12; Deut. 32.6, 18; Isa. 64.7; Mal. 3.17. The people's obligations are stressed in Isa. 1.2; 30.1, 9; Deut. 14.1; Isa. 45.9–11; Mal. 1.6; 2.10. The idea that Yahweh is in a special way the father of the king (II Sam. 7.13 ff.; Ps. 2.7) likewise comes under this heading; apropos this element of the courtly style of the ancient East cf. ch. IV. 2. III, pp. 125 above, and ch. XI. 1, pp. 477 ff. below.
[4] Isa. 63.15 f.; Ps. 89.27; 68.6. For a more profound application of this imagery, cf. further below.
[5] Jub. 2.20; 19.29; Apoc. Bar. 78.4; Wisd. 11.10; 14.3; III Macc. 2.21: the idea of a cosmic principle plays a part in Apoc. Mos. 37, 38, 42; Orac. Sib. III. 550, V. 328. Even the Rabbinic designation 'Father in Heaven' refers primarily to the Lord of the world: cf. W. Bousset, *Die Religion des Judentums*[3], pp. 377 f.
[6] Cf. L. Dürr, *Ursprung und Ausbau der isr.-jüd. Heilandserwartung*, 1925, pp. 116 ff.

attributes of the ruler, whether human or divine.[1] In the Old Testament too the title of Shepherd, which remains in use from the earliest to the latest periods,[2] frequently becomes nothing but a platitudinous formula which happens to be suitable for the divine ruler. Nevertheless, the force of personal experience is constantly at work to restore to the *cliché* its original warmth and to endue it with new and vivid colour—a development to be seen at its most striking in Deutero-Isaiah;[3] and the sense of the incomparable greatness of Israel's God invested the knowledge that the nation could call itself 'the people of Yahweh and the sheep of his pasture'[4] with a quite different emotional quality from any attainable in non-Israelite polytheism. Especially significant for the strong feeling of security associated with the thought of Yahweh as shepherd is the tendency to individualize the picture in the language of prayer used privately by the pious; and this feature seems to go back to a fairly early stage.[5]

This relationship of community, in accordance with which God acts toward his people, takes on a new note, when the sin of the nation is seen in all its seriousness as a breach of faith which can never be made good, as something which destroys the bond of fellowship beyond hope of redemption—a perception which dates from the prophetic era. At this point there occurs a transformation of the concept which is absolutely without parallel in the ancient East. The friendship, with the withdrawal of which Yahweh threatens the people (Jer. 16.5), consists of *ḥesed* and *raḥ⁰mîm*, lovingkindness and mercy: its suspension consequently involves the suspension of the covenant community and the delivering up of the people to death. If, in spite of all, Yahweh allows his *ḥesed* to continue in operation toward the sinner, in so far as the latter is penitent, then this restoration approximates to the conception of clemency, or grace. In fact the limitation of *ḥesed* in the old sense is transcended, and its place is frequently taken by the term *raḥ⁰mîm*, mercy, a quite

[1]So it is, for example, with the beautiful phrase about the 'shepherd who gathers those that are scattered', which occurs frequently in Egyptian and Babylonian courtly style from the earliest down to the latest periods: cf. the preamble to the Code of Hammurabi, the boundary-stone inscription of Merodach-Baladan II and Micah 4.6.

[2]Gen. 49.24; Ex. 15.13; Hos. 4.16; Micah 2.12; 4.6 ff.; Zeph. 3.19; Jer. 31.10; Ezek. 34.23; 37.24; Pss. 44.12, 23; 48.15; 74.1; 77.21; 78.52 f. etc.

[3]Isa. 40.11; 49.10; but also Ezek. 34.12 ff.; Ps. 80.2.

[4]Pss. 79.13; 95.7; 100.3.

[5]Gen. 48.15; Pss. 23.1–4; 31.4; 107.41.

238 THE NATURE OF THE COVENANT GOD

spontaneous expression of love, evoked by no kind of obligation; and this now sheds a new light on the whole concept. Nevertheless the prophets intentionally retain the older term in order to emphasize that the greatness of their God shatters all human values; Yahweh's kind of *ḥesed* is proved to be divine precisely because it is made available afresh to the apostate. Thus Yahweh betroths himself to his faithless wife Israel for *ḥesed* and *raḥ°mīm*, which he pays down, as it were, as a purchase price, and which Israel repays with loyalty and knowledge of him (Hos. 2.21). Thus again, according to Jer. 3.12 f., once God's wife Israel has come to see her sin, he takes her back as the *ḥāsīd*, one who has experienced the loving constancy of a covenant far surpassing human standards; indeed he bestows on the wife who has been brought home eternal *ḥesed* (Isa. 54.7 f.).[1] This transformation of the *ḥesed*-concept can be seen also in a unique deepening of the father-image as applied to God. Hosea uses it with new insight, when he describes Yahweh as the father teaching his little child to walk and carrying him in his arms;[2] and so does Jeremiah, when he portrays Yahweh's sorrow over his faithless people as the disappointment of a father, who, in his intense affection, wishes contrary to custom to give his daughter an equal place in the inheritance with his sons, but, when he looks to hear from her the name of father as a sign of her faithful attachment, meets only with gross ingratitude.[3] But Jeremiah goes even further. He sees the father-relationship as an image of an undying love, the kind of love which will take the lost son to its arms again with fervent emotion, whenever that son returns in penitence; and this despite the fact that even the love itself cannot give a reason for the triumph of such compassion over the most justifiable indignation, but is aware of its own behaviour only as an inner but incomprehensible imperative.[4] Because in this way *ḥesed* is granted at large to men who have absolutely no claim upon it, but rather in accordance with the *jus talionis* can expect only to be excluded from fellowship, it is seen to be a gift of grace. What began as a *ḥesed* granted as a matter of course in the *b°rīt* has become, as a result of the thoroughgoing questioning of the old conception, a completely new concept of faithfulness and love. The miraculous quality of this new love is seen to reside not

[1] Cf. further Micah 7.18; Isa. 63.7 f.; Jer. 31.3; Pss. 90.14; 25.6; 40.11 f.; 51.3; 69.14, 17; 86.5.
[2] Hos. 11.1–3.
[3] Jer. 3.19.
[4] Jer. 31.20.

only in the condescension of the exalted God,[1] but also, much more inwardly, in the mystery of a divine will which seeks communion with man. The poet of Deut. 32 was certainly influenced by this profounder prophetic conception, when, in order to express Yahweh's kindnesses to his people, he turned to the tender image of the favourite child,[2] whom the father guards as the apple of his eye; and a comparable figure is to be found in Deut. 1.31. Ps. 103.13 illustrates very beautifully how the prophetic interpretation of the father-image was reflected in the prayer life of the individual.

In addition to this deepening of the concept Judaism saw an enlargement of its scope, in that the divine lovingkindness also came to be regarded as the most profound meaning of the relation between Creator and creature; or, to put it another way, the Creation was included among those relationships based on the idea of community. Thus it is possible to speak of the whole earth's being full of Yahweh's *ḥesed* (Pss. 33.5; 119.64), and to declare that his lovingkindness is over all his works (Pss. 36.7; 89.14; 145.9). In fact the Creation itself is a work of the divine *ḥesed* (Ps. 136.1–9). This universalist conception was always firmly maintained, even though not inconsiderably limited by the definite feeling that the actual world lay under God's anger and judgment.[3] It fitted in admirably with the Jewish belief—given its most forceful expression by the Priestly school—that God was the true Lord of the world, both in actual fact here and now and for all time to come; but in comparison with the prophetic version of the *ḥesed*-concept with its warmth and restless eschatological enthusiasm it had a much more markedly rationalistic character. This contrast already distantly adumbrates a polarity in the Israelite knowledge of God which we shall later recognize in a more precise form.[4]

3. THE RIGHTEOUSNESS OF GOD

One expression of Yahweh's covenant love is his righteousness. Just as the *ḥesed* which God desires from man includes the practice of righteousness—for a correct attitude toward the rights of others is at any rate one important aspect of willingness to take one's part

---

[1] Cf. the hymning of the proofs of Yahweh's *ḥesed* as miracles in Pss. 4.4; 17.7; 31.22; 106.7; 107.8, 15, 21, 31; 136.4.

[2] Deut. 32.10, reading with Marti *yᵉdīdō śāmō* instead of *yᵉlēl yᵉšīmōn* (*Die heilige Schrift des AT⁴*, ed. Kautzsch-Bertholet, p. 319).

[3] Ecclus. 39.22; 50.22–24; Wisd. 11.24–26; II Esd. 8.47.

[4] Cf. chs. VIII and IX.

in community[1] so God shows his favour by doing justice and righteousness.[2]

It is a decided obstacle to any attempt to define the concept of divine righteousness, that the original signification of the root *ṣdq* should be irretrievably lost. The predominant usage of the Old Testament points throughout to the idea of right behaviour or a right disposition, which can be predicated of things, of human beings and of God. The statements about human righteousness obviously cover the widest field, because they refer to social, ethical and religious behaviour; and it is true that in this context the element of the forensic is strongly emphasized, this being the main reference of the verbal stem *ṣdq*. When applied to the conduct of God the concept is narrowed and almost exclusively employed in a forensic sense. God's *ṣᵉdāqā* or *ṣedeq* is his keeping of the law in accordance with the terms of the covenant. But once this point has been made, it is necessary to go on at once to warn the reader against thinking simply of a kind of *iustitia distributiva*, such as is familiar to us from Roman legal thought. In Hebrew thinking there is no such thing as an abstract formal concept which might be classified according to an objective standard, thus presupposing a universal idea of righteousness. E. Kautzsch made an attempt along such lines[3] to discover the point at which all the various meanings of righteousness converged, making at one time the objective norm of truth or the subjective one of uprightness, at another the objective divine command or the subjective conscience, at another even the idea of God or the idea of man the focal point; but such an attempt intrudes conceptions quite foreign to the Hebrew mind, and for which there is no basis in the naïvely realistic thinking of the Israelite. With the insight of genius H. Cremer recognized this[4] and described *ṣdq* as a concept of relation referring to an actual relationship between two persons and implying behaviour which corresponds to, or is true to, the claims arising out of such a relationship. This thesis, even though it may be contested at isolated points, has been strikingly confirmed, as to its major contentions, from the sociological angle by the work of M. Weber[5] and from the psycho-

---

[1]Hos. 10.12; 12.7; Prov. 21.21.
[2]Jer. 9.23; 3.12 f.; Ps. 145.17 ff.
[3]*Die Derivate des Stammes ṣdq im alttestamentlichen Sprachgebrauch*, 1881.
[4]*Die paulinische Rechtfertigungslehre im Zusammenhange ihrer geschichtlichen Voraussetzungen*, 1899.
[5]*Religionssoziologie* III: *Das antike Judentum*.

logical by that of J. Pedersen.[1] The former demonstrated the central significance of the covenant concept for Israelite life and thought, while the latter in his exposition of the primitive basis of Israelite psychology presented in quite a new light the function of the community relationship for the total Israelite understanding of life. Hence what constitutes right conduct naturally depends on the actual circumstances and the demands which arise from them, and not on some universal norm. In particular, in the case of the righteousness of the judge, it is not a question of the impartiality with which a formal standard of justice is applied, but of rightly satisfying those claims which are brought forward as a result of particular concrete relationships; 'justice', *mišpāṭ*, is no abstract thing, but denotes the rights and duties of each party arising out of the particular relation of fellowship in which they find themselves. In this way everyone has his own special *mišpāṭ*: the king, the Deity, the priest, the firstborn son, the Israelites as a group, and so on. The task of righteousness is to render this justice, and the claims which it implies, effective in the proper way, so that the good of all those united in the one community of law may be safeguarded. It should not be forgotten, however, that *mišpāṭ* also frequently denotes the administration of justice or the judicial sentence, and therefore covers both specialist forensic activity and the means of righteousness, as well as its ultimate goal. The protection of the law always implies positive constructive behaviour, aimed at advancing the good of the community; *ṣᵉdāqā* is *iustitia salutifera* (Cremer).[2] Thus the verb *šāpaṭ*, which is often used to describe the practical application of righteousness, primarily refers to 'doing justice', the noblest activity of any ruler, just as the meaning 'to rule' is combined with this on many occasions.[3]

It may therefore be said that in the case of Yahweh his righteousness implies the same kind of right conduct which in Israel upholds the law by means of judicial procedure; the justice appropriate to Israel on her side is determined by her position as the covenant people, in virtue of which she can count on the intervention of the

[1] *Israel* I–II.
[2] This has also been rightly emphasized by E. König, *Theologie des Alten Testaments*[3, 4], pp. 178 ff.
[3] On this point, in addition to Pedersen, *op. cit.*, pp. 336 ff., cf. H. W. Hertzberg, 'Die Entwicklung des Begriffes *mišpāṭ* im AT', *ZAW* 40–41, 1922–23, pp. 256 ff. and 16 ff.; also K. Cramer, *Amos*, 1930, pp. 165 ff., and K. Koch, *Ṣdq im AT* (Diss. Heidelberg), 1953.

divine assistance in any danger which threatens that position. *In the early period of Israel's history* God's righteousness seems only to have been spoken of in connection with his help against outside enemies. Yahweh watches over the 'justice' of his people in that he safeguards their existence by his victories over their foes, and Israel's triumphs in war are therefore proofs of the righteousness of God, *ṣidqōt yhwh*.[1] Even where the actual word is not found, it is obvious that a connection is frequently understood between Yahweh's activity as Judge and the defeat of external enemies, as when Jephthah, in the conflict between the Israelites and the Ammonites, appeals to God's judicial decision (Judg. 11.27), or when David's victory over Absalom is understood as God's upholding of his, David's, *mišpāṭ* (II Sam. 18.31). The execution of Yahweh's righteousness by the tribe of Gad (Deut. 33.21) is also to be understood in this sense.[2]

Within Israel too Yahweh is recognized as the protector of the right against any perversion of justice. Just as Moses' administration and reorganization of justice rests on divine authority (Ex. 18.13 ff.), so the whole law ultimately derives from the divine giving of the law on Sinai. Throughout the ancient world the deity was considered as the guardian of justice; in Babylonia, for example, the Shamash hymns give very fine expression to this conception,[3] and many of the confessions of sin reveal remarkably lofty ideas of the divine righteousness.[4] But the value attached to the covenant law of Israel as a clear and unified expression of the will of God far surpasses these. In the former the character of the gods as personified natural forces made it impossible either to find any unifying principle in their demands or to exclude entirely the notes of arbitrariness and caprice; but the will of Yahweh for the community, because it was not subject to interference from any other, could be made known unequivocally through the covenant law. Moreover, it was precisely the inflexible rigidity with which he demanded obedience which resulted in a growing confidence that the exercise of his own power was controlled by the same standards. Hence in Babylonia, despite a developed science of oracles and omens, we find a terrifying

[1] Judg. 5.11; the idiom remains in the later period, cf. Micah 6.5; I Sam. 12.7.
[2] On the other hand Ex. 9.27, where Yahweh is described by Pharaoh as *ṣaddīq*, must be understood as 'to be in the right', 'to have right on one's side'. An exact parallel is Jer. 12.1, unless the reading should be *ṣādaqtā*.
[3] Cf. A. Ungnad, *Die Religion der Babyloner und Assyrer*, pp. 185 ff.
[4] Cf. the literature listed in ch. III, p. 76 n. 1 above.

uncertainty about the principle of God's dealings with men;[1] but the Israelite is certain that God in his turn will act toward him in accordance with those principles of law with which he himself is well acquainted. Furthermore, there is the history of the nation from the Exodus onward to give him concrete instances of this principle of reciprocity; and this brought with it the possibility of combining these various individual instances to a greater and greater extent into a unified pattern of divine conduct. For all its rigidity the mighty conception of the Deuteronomic scheme of history is simply the logical product of a deeply rooted popular under-standing of *the just judgment of God in the life of the nation*. The strength of this conviction of God's judicial authority is attested by its spontaneous extension to cover the whole earth—a development which may be seen in the stories of the Deluge, the Tower of Babel and the destruction of Sodom.[2] That this emphasis on collective retribution did not, however, cause men to forget the relevance of the divine will to each member of the nation, and that the individual did not hestitate to look to Yahweh to protect his personal rights, is proved by innumerable instances.[3] It is evidence of a truly passionate devotion to the ideal of *God's impartiality in judgment* that at the intercession of a David or an Abraham the suffering of the innocent in the stead of the guilty should be rejected as intolerable, or that David as the responsible party should submit himself to punishment.[4] The whole conception of God in Babylonia made such prayer quite impossible.

If, nevertheless, in these latter cases there is no actual mention of Yahweh's 'righteousness',[5] this is in keeping with the fact that, so long as the minds of the mass of the people were dominated by the conviction that for all their shortcomings they represented a nation pleasing to God, and any danger to their legitimate pretensions was envisaged only in terms of a threat from without, this aspect of God's judicial authority occupied less of their attention than his main-tenance of the rights of the covenant people. It needed the social and political schism of the nation in the Age of Prophecy to cast doubt

[1]Cf. further pp. 260 f. below.
[2]That the title 'Judge of all the earth' in Gen. 18.25 may not be the work of the Yahwist, but of the Deuteronomic narrator, does not affect the present contention.
[3]Cf. e.g. Gen. 16.5; 20.3 ff.; 31.7, 50; I Sam. 24.13 ff.; 25.39; Ex. 22.20–26 etc.
[4]II Sam. 24.17 ff.; Gen. 18.22 ff.
[5]The exception is Gen. 18.25, but this, as already mentioned, may be due to Deuteronomic usage.

on the idea of the covenant people as a unified entity, before a feeling for the righteousness of God as this might reveal itself in the inward life of the people could be awakened.

In the circumstances there would seem to be good grounds for the opinion put forward by some scholars,[1] that in the early period of Israel Yahweh was not conceived as righteous, that is to say, that the idea of righteousness was not the dominant element in Israel's conception of him. In fact it is true that the Israelite of that time *did not make ṣedāqā the focal point of his picture of divine authority*, but only for this reason, that as yet the rights of the covenant people did not seem to him to be threatened from within. But the whole structure of Israelite thought excludes the possibility of its ever attaching decisive importance to a formal concept of *iustitia distributiva*, such as most interests the one-sided outlook of the modern critic. Once this is recognized, a whole series of objections, which Yahweh's habit of acting in the interests of his own people, though taken for granted by the Israelite historians, nevertheless raises in the mind of modern man with his particular attitude to justice, completely disappears. It is true that Yahweh's actions do not always accord with a formal ideal of righteousness, but for the pious Israelite they are inescapably bound up with the fact of Israel's election, which with its goal of a holy people bringing blessing to the whole world is something on a far higher plane than any merely distributive concept of justice.[2]

The emergence of *prophecy* in Israel brought with it a new approach to the question of God's righteousness.[3] The prophets saw it in the light of a situation in which the very existence of the covenant people was jeopardized by the severe strains imposed on its internal organization; and therefore, when they came to describe the attitude of the covenant God to this situation, they found in the concept of righteousness a terminology which their own people could understand, and which would serve to characterize the effects and purposes of the divine intervention. Thus the dowry, which according to Hosea Yahweh will give to his people when they are once more united with him in a new covenant, consists of righteousness and

---

[1] Cf. e.g. B. Stade, *Biblische Theologie des AT*, pp. 88 ff.; R. Smend, *Lehrbuch der AT Religionsgeschichte²*, pp. 105 ff.; W. Cossmann, *Die Entwicklung des Gerichtsgedankens bei den alttestamentlichen Propheten*, 1915, pp. 3 ff.

[2] On this point cf. also p. 285 below.

[3] Cf. F. Nötscher, *Die Gerechtigkeit Gottes bei den vorexilischen Propheten*, 1915.

judgment;[1] and the manner in which he speaks elsewhere of the renewal of his people[2] proves that the prophet does not envisage the purpose of these gifts as the restoration of Israel to its place among the nations, but as *the establishment of those godlike features in its inner life* which befit the character of the covenant people. This is admirably confirmed by *Isaiah*'s picture of the conduct of the Prince of Peace, who establishes his kingdom with judgment and with righteousness (Isa. 9.7) and puts an end to all violence and oppression, so that his people are united in the harmony of a purpose in keeping with the nature of their God (Isa. 11.3–5, 9). The reverse side of this succour which God in his righteousness provides is, of course, the punishment of the covenant-breaker; and this fact is brought out all the more strongly when Isaiah is describing Yahweh's act of redemption in the setting up of his kingdom. Here the prophet gives the concept of righteousness an individual application comparable to his treatment of the idea of holiness,[3] for he connects the happy assurance of Yahweh's intervention on behalf of his people inseparably with *the profoundly serious reality of the judgment* which must threaten the people so favoured.[4] Only so can the congregation, united in faith (28.17) and ruled by the ancient covenant law (1.27), escape the annihilating judgment determined for the whole earth (10.22), and the holy God be known and worshipped as the almighty Lord of all the world (5.15 f.).[5] This close association of God's righteousness with his holiness, of which it is the revelation, bases Yahweh's intervention for the restoration of the covenant people firmly on his position as Lord of the Universe, and in this way frees it from the egoistic limitations of national self-interest, and subordinates it to the world-wide purposes of the divine authority. That nevertheless the fundamental tendency of righteousness is still the

---

[1] Hos. 2.19: there is no sufficient reason to excise this expression, as is often done. The question of the gifts which God is going to bestow on his people does not arise until v. 22.

[2] Hos. 10.12; 12.7.

[3] Cf. p. 279 below.

[4] Cremer speaks in this connection of a 'startling, unexpected experience of God's righteousness', of 'a different aspect of it which had not been taken into men's calculations' (*Paulinische Rechtfertigungslehre*, p. 32).

[5] Isa. 1.27 and 10.22 are often regarded as not genuinely Isaianic: but it is possible to outweigh this not unjustified opinion (10.22 in particular can only be regarded as a fragment that has undergone later revision), when one considers how well the ideas which they contain fit into Isaiah's general outlook. This applies even more emphatically to vv. 5.15 f., the authenticity of which is sometimes contested, but which must originally have followed 2.9.

bringing of salvation may be seen from its relation to faith as the proper human response to its operations (28.16 f.); and in general it may be said that for Isaiah the divine claim culminates in the requirement of faith.

In the period after Isaiah the righteousness of God is still connected with his prosecution of justice within the covenant people; it is to this end that he protects the individual (Jer. 11.20), safeguards the holiness of his ordinances (Jer. 9.23; Zeph. 3.5) and equips the king for his judicial functions (Ps. 72.1). *Jeremiah*, like Isaiah, sees the embodiment of this work of Yahweh in the messianic king (23.6); but by making the king acquire his name, *yhwh ṣidqēnū*, 'The LORD our Righteousness', as a confession of the people's faith, he stresses the mediatory function of the Prince of Peace, who is to endue Israel with the true character of the covenant people both inwardly and outwardly, in the form of piety and of salvation. In other circles during this period we still find the old usage, which sees the fulfilment of Yahweh's righteousness in the victory of Israel over their enemies (Micah 6.5; Deut. 32.4, 36).

It was, however, *Deutero-Isaiah* who first elevated the concept of God's righteousness to the status of the key to the understanding of the whole divine work of salvation by drawing out the full implications of Isaiah's statements. He taught men to see the operation of Yahweh's righteousness in the redemptive acts by which he proposed to restore the covenant people, and to this end he coupled the concept of righteousness with those of God's covenant lovingkindness, loyalty and succour.[1] This righteousness might also take the form of judgment on the heathen[2]—an idea which made it possible to incorporate the older language on the subject. But the decisive element was that of God's gift of salvation, both to Israel and to the Gentile world,[3] through the setting up of the covenant. The response to this on the human side was to be a new state of righteousness, which would include both outward prosperity and a just ordering of public life and of the nation's attitude to God.[4] It is quite in keeping with the unique concept of the covenant charac-

---

[1] Isa. 42.6, 21; 45.8, 13; 46.13; 51.6.
[2] Isa. 41.2, 10 ff.; 58.2; 59.16 f.; 63.1: the three latter passages belong to the appendix to the prophecies of consolation in the Sixteen Chapters, and reflect a changed situation.
[3] Isa. 51.5; cf. 45.24.
[4] Isa. 45.8, 24; 48.18; 51.7; 59.9; 60.17; 61.3, 10 f.; 62.2.

teristic of this prophet,[1] that this righteous dealing on God's part, which was at first purely a product of the covenant relationship, should now be given a universal reference and extended to his attitude to the whole world of which he is Lord. In the light of the eschatological consummation the relation of the Creator to his creatures has, so to speak, been drawn into the sphere of the covenant; and the marvel of God's love is revealed in the fact that he has granted to all men the right to call upon him for aid. At the same time, however, the use of the term *ṣᵉdāqā* to designate this readiness on the part of God to succour his creatures reminds men that what is involved is the perfecting of a fellowship, in which on the one hand man's total failure is made plain, and on the other the continuity of the divine action, God's loyal adherence to an eternal purpose, shines forth in all its splendour. *The maintenance of the fellowship now becomes the justification of the ungodly.* No manner of human effort, but only that righteousness which is the gift of God, can lead to that conduct which is truly in keeping with the covenant. Here too the relationship of legal obligation has become the relationship of grace.

This proclamation of God's righteousness had the most decisive effects on *the piety of later Judaism*, and echoes of it are to be found in many of the Psalms. God's righteousness is constantly extolled as the refuge of those in misery, who can commend their right and their cause, *mišpāṭ* and *rīb*, to the divine Judge.[2] 'Righteousness' and 'mercy' are often found in parallelism,[3] since they both express God's dealings in accordance with the terms of his fellowship. In fact, *this righteousness can even be invoked as a basis for the forgiveness of sins*[4]—a striking testimony to a deeply rooted sense that the righteous God is the same Lord who is ready to maintain the covenant and to grant righteousness to all its members. In his sight every oppressed and suffering member of his covenant has a just cause; even the sinner, when he humbles himself beneath the divine judgment and asks for forgiveness in upright confession of his sin, is justified in looking for absolution and protection from the righteousness of God. For even in his sin he can take his stand on the rock of the covenant

---

[1] Cf. above pp. 61 f.
[2] Pss. 9.5; 35.23 f.; 43.1; 76.10; 94.2; 129.4; 143.1, 3, 11; cf. Mal. 3.20.
[3] Pss. 31.2, cf. 8; 33.5; 36.11; 48.10 f.; 85.11; 89.15; 103.17; 143.11 f.; 145.17.
[4] Pss. 51.16; 143.1, 2; Micah 7.9: the idea is applied negatively in the prayer of Ps. 69.27, where the wish is expressed that the enemy may never attain to the righteousness of God.

fellowship, where grace and forgiveness are to be found, in contrast to all those who shamelessly and wantonly transgress the ordinances of all law, human and divine. The confident expectation which Deutero-Isaiah had taught the nation in his vision of the decisive conclusion to which God was bringing his just cause has now become the attitude of the individual believer, who can in the same way reckon himself among the righteous whom Yahweh will accept. God's eschatological vindication has become the means of resolving the conflict between the destiny of the individual and the course of history.

Deutero-Isaiah's understanding of God, albeit with some modification, may have become the norm for the congregation in so far as God's saving action was seen in his righteousness, but the same cannot be said of *the element of universalism*, which for this prophet was inseparably bound up with the idea of *sᵉdāqā*. In the course of the destructive struggles between the various groups within Judaism men lost sight of this ideal, and only thought of the restoration of the covenant people. Moreover, with regard to the heathen the oppression of a foreign tyranny encouraged men to invoke the divine righteousness for the purpose of punishing the Gentile world.[1] Yet even here the prophetic influence spread and in many of the Psalms was given wonderful expression.[2] This is all the more significant in that most of the latter are cultic hymns, which in a period of particularism imposed by the Law yet perceived that the righteousness of God implied the salvation of the world. Equally remarkable is the way in which the boundaries of God's present and future rule melt into one another, and any mention of a clearly defined break with the present is avoided.[3] The abiding witness of such voices in the cultus was the more precious since *later Judaism* was unable to accept such an attitude. It is true that here and there isolated statements still affirm Yahweh's saving righteousness toward the world as allied to his mercy,[4] just as his righteousness toward Israel goes hand in hand with his lovingkindness.[5] But in step with the gradual transformation of the basis of Jewish piety into a righteousness of works, *the righteousness of God also acquires overwhelmingly the character of iustitia distributiva*, the impartial allocation of reward and

[1] Pss. 9.5; 43.1; 48.11; 76.10; 129.4; Micah 7.9.
[2] Pss. 33.5; 36.11; 96.10, 13; 97.2; 98.2; 145.17.
[3] Cf. pp. 428 f. below.
[4] E.g. II (4) Esd. 11.46.
[5] Enoch 71.3; Jub. 1.6; II (4) Esd. 8.36.

punishment in accordance with the standard of the Law.[1] This means that for the heathen, being sinners without the Law, the only real possibility is God's punitive righteousness;[2] and this state of affairs is not altered by Aqiba's fine saying: 'The world is judged by the measure of God's mercy.'[3] On the other hand an idea to which formerly little attention had been given now gains in importance. This is the conviction of *God's educative righteousness*, which he devotes to his people in his concern that in due season they shall be led into the way of his Law, and not fall like the heathen under his annihilating judgment.[4] It must be admitted, however, that this is only a very limited return to the old concept of *iustitia salutifera*, and still distorted at that in the direction of an impartial weighing-out of each man's deserts.[5]

From what has been said it will be clear that the essence of the original biblical concept of God's righteousness lies neither in the ethical postulate of a moral world-order nor in an ideal of impartial retribution imposed by some inner necessity nor in the personification of the ethical in God. Instead it exalts over all abstract ethical ideas a *loyalty manifested in the concrete relationships of community*. It is true that this is firmly related to the Law as the basis of community, but its meaning is not exhausted in the execution of retributive righteousness. It is rather *a personal quality that transcends all laws and standards*; it bestows permanence on a fellowship which is constantly being shattered on the rock of the Law, because it provides it with the means of mending the broken bond. In doing so it gives men the possibility of ultimately attaining the goal of the Law, namely the glorifying of God's name in willing self-dedication to their brethren. Hence the righteousness of God remains an *essentially religious conception*, which resists any attempt to water it down into ethical ideas; and it only comes properly into its own, when it is combined with the sovereignty of God, as its indispensable effect.

[1] Cf. the list of passages in Couard, *Die religiösen und sittlichen Anschauungen der alttestamentlichen Apokryphen und Pseudepigraphen*, 1907, pp. 43 f.: also A. Bertholet, *Biblische Theologie des AT* II, p. 364, and W. Bousset, *Die Religion des Judentums³*, pp. 385 ff.
[2] Cf. the justification of the punishment of Pharaoh, Wisd. 12.15 ff.
[3] Pirqe Aboth 3.16. The continuation, 'and everything is done according to the multitude of his works', proves conclusively that here, as in Wisd. 12.15, the only idea is one of resignation in the face of resistless and overwhelming Omnipotence.
[4] Cf. Odes of Solomon 3.5; 8.26 and the passages listed by Bousset, *op. cit.*, pp. 385 f.
[5] Cf. Apoc. Baruch 13.1 ff.

4. THE LOVE OF GOD

As distinct from those expressions of the nature of God which are involved in the covenant relationship of rights and duties, and which serve to give definite direction to the working out of the divine purpose of fellowship, God's love belongs to those spontaneous emotional forces which are their own justification, and which establish a personal relation of immediate authority.

The Old Testament possesses a particularly rich vocabulary to express this idea. First and foremost, there is the stem *'hb*; here, the human experience from which the basic meaning is derived is the overwhelming force of passion between men and women,[1] but the stem is used also to denote the attachment that unites blood-relations, the selfless loyalty of friends, and the ties of social life. Nevertheless, it always retains the passionate overtones of complete engagement of the will accompanied by strong emotion. *dbq* and *ḥšq*, 'to cleave to someone in love', are used in a comparable way; by contrast, *rḥm* seems to have become restricted in meaning to one particular aspect of the idea of love, that of compassion toward the helpless, a feeling of kinship closest perhaps to the attitude of a mother toward the child who needs her help.[2] The root *ḥnn*, often employed as a synonym for the last-named, denotes the affection shown by a superior to his inferiors,[3] especially that of the rich man for the poor, while *rṣh* and *ḥpṣ*, which may be terms from the language of sacrifice and court etiquette respectively, lay more stress on the fact of appreciation than on the feeling involved.[4]

In the early period of Israel surprisingly little use was made of this wealth of terminology to describe God's dealings with men.[5] Israel was well aware of Yahweh's affection for his people, which found expression in his saving acts and aroused in the nation exultant enthusiasm and self-surrender; but for the purposes of description the preference was for such terms as 'lovingkindness', 'faithfulness' and 'righteousness', which were rooted in the covenant

[1] Cf. S. of S. 8.6 f.
[2] Cf. *reḥem*, 'womb'.
[3] Cf. W. F. Lofthouse, '*Ḥen* and *Ḥesed* in the Old Testament', *ZAW* 51, 1933, p. 30.
[4] Amos 5.22; Jer. 14.12; Ezek. 43.27; Lev. 7.18; Gen. 33.10; Mal. 1.8; I Sam. 18.22; II Sam. 15.26; 20.11; 24.3; Esth. 6.6; Num. 14.8; Ps. 18.20.
[5] Completely unambiguous references are only to be found in the following passages: to Yahweh's compassion, II Sam. 24.14; Yahweh's gracious affection, Num. 6.25; Gen. 33.5, 11; 43.29. The dating of Ex. 22.26; 33.19; 34.6 cannot be exactly determined, since there has been redaction of the text.

relationship, and those concepts which derived from the uninhibited emotional life tended to be avoided. There was still no reflection on what motive might underlie the divine act of election. A strictly sober-minded approach kept to the facts of what God had actually promised and performed, and refused to allow religious feeling to break out in an excess of emotion[1]—an attitude which was extremely significant in face of the religious eroticism of Canaan.

It was the prophets who first dared to transcend these hitherto absolute limitations under the impact of direct divine self-revelation. It is, moreover, a remarkable fact that the first man to take this step, *Hosea*, was also the one to attain the richest and most profoundly developed understanding of the idea of love in the whole Old Testament. The transition from the idea of the covenant to the conception of the marriage between Yahweh and Israel was made easier by the element of contractual obligation common to both,[2] but it needed the shattering experience of the prophet, whose whole being was committed to Yahweh's service, to make the marriage-bond the supreme demonstration of God's attitude to Israel. However, the application of this parable, which the prophet acquired the right to use only at the price of his own heart's blood, brought out overwhelmingly *the quite irrational power of love as the ultimate basis of the covenant relationship*, and by means of the unique dialectic of the concept of love illuminated the whole complex of the nation's history. The depth and seriousness of Israel's faithlessness, which lay at the root of the people's alienation from God, and which merited the most terrible punishment; the inconceivable condescension of Yahweh and his fidelity to the faithless nation far transcending the categories of human thought; the stand which had to be taken within the nation against the anti-God forces of Nature worship, so corruptive a factor in the nation's history; all this was presented with heart-rending force in the conduct of the husband toward his faithless wife, whom he delivers up to punishment, yet strives to win back, seeking to touch her heart through the pleading of her children. The prophet's use of the imagery of marriage means that for him the relationship of law is largely displaced by a living fellowship of love, which demands the total allegiance of man as the object of that love,

---

[1]There is one instance, and that in the heightened language of a hymn, of the description of the faithful worshippers of Yahweh as 'them that love him', Judg. 5.31. Ex. 20.6 seems to be Deuteronomic in tone.

[2]Cf. J. Ziegler, *Die Liebe Gottes bei den Propheten*, pp. 73 ff.

and can never be satisfied with the formal fulfilment of obligations. Furthermore, the fact that it is declared to be God's will to maintain this fellowship, even when its object is an adulteress or a harlot, clearly demonstrates the inadequacy of all legal categories for the task of describing man's relationship with God; and the necessary consequence of this is that re-casting of the concepts of rights and duties to which allusion has already been made.[1] The danger, however, which threatened from the side of the Canaanite fertility cults, that God's love might be misunderstood in an erotic sense, was warded off by the inseparable association of that love with the nation's experience of its history.[2] The impulsive and compulsive character of merely natural love is replaced by *deliberate direction of the will and readiness for action*, evinced in God's choice of one particular people before all others and his faithfulness to the task of training them. Hence Hosea's picture of the father educating his child is not out of place.[3]

But this demonstration of the way in which the concept of love is worked out in history is far removed from any attempt to reduce the love of God to a rational principle, to turn it into some sort of 'ethical law of the universe'. This is ruled out first by *the strong emphasis on the inexplicable and paradoxical character of God's love*, which is portrayed in terms of the wooing of a wanton—an absolutely grotesque proceeding, flying in the face equally of morality and of justice. Secondly, there is an equally strong and passionate emphasis on the divine anger; for Hosea is outdone by hardly any other prophet in the ferocity of his threats and the savagery of his proclamations of punishment.[4] *The wrath of love* is presented in all its paradoxical

---

[1]Cf. pp. 236 f., 245 f. above. This implies no sort of depreciation or condemnation of the legal aspect of man's relationship to God, but its interpretation in accordance with the dominant fundamental principle of love. Hosea is fully conscious of the Law as the proclamation of the divine will, cf. 4.6 ff.; 8.12 f.; 13.1, and possibly also 6.5 f.; but 'he pulls down the theory of the Covenant, in order to expose God's love as its foundation, and then builds it up again with righteousness, judgment, loving-kindness and faithfulness' (Quell, *TWNT* I, p. 31 = *Love*, p. 18).

[2]Hos. 11.1; 12.10; 13.4, the 'God from the land of Egypt'; 13.5, the guiding through the Wilderness; 4.6; 6.7; 13.1, the making of the covenant; 13.6, the conquest of Canaan; 4.6; 12.14, God's guidance through the prophets; 7.15; 11.7, the strengthening of the nation.

[3]Hos. 11.1, 3, 4.

[4]Cf. the imagery of Yahweh as the moth, the worm riddling the wood, the lion, the leopard, the mother-bear robbed of her young, 5.12–14; 13.7 f., and the frightful slaughter of the land, 9.12, 16; 10.13 f.; 14.1, and its annihilation by death and Sheol, 13.12 ff.

actuality; indeed, so deeply has the prophet entered into its truth, that he sees it as a conflict within the very being of God himself, whom he portrays as suffering and bewildered in the face of the lovelessness of his people (11.8; 6.4). It is true that this conflict ends with the triumph of love (11.9); this irrational power of love is integrated with the divine holiness and seen as its innermost essence. But this means no more than that *the inexplicable mystery of love has been explained in terms of the even greater mystery of personality in God*, and characterized simply as the opposite of all merely human potentialities. Taking the message of the prophet as a whole, it is utterly impossible to rationalize it into a dogmatic statement about the nature of God; it can only be understood as the product of faith, breaking through the *opus alienum* of the divine wrath, to the vision of love as the ultimate and decisive power. For this reason the most appalling outbursts of anger and the expressions of favour toward the new Israel—'I will love them no more' (9.15) and 'I will love them freely' (14.4)—are allowed to stand side by side with no attempt at reconciliation, signifying that on the basis of the prophetic faith at any rate there is no method of reconciling them. The only answer is to flee from the wrathful to the loving God, a proceeding possible only in that unique situation, which the prophets declare to have arrived, where decision is called for in face of the immediate irruption of the great turning-point of history.

This association of the love of God, which Israel has failed to recognize as real and which has therefore turned to wrath, with the expectation of the End is also a feature of *Jeremiah*, the only man to have fully absorbed the preaching of Hosea. Even though the radiant gleams of first love may light up the days that are gone,[1] the present has brought only the dissolution of the bond of love between God and his people;[2] the beloved will be sold into the hands of her enemies,[3] and love has turned into a hate that knows neither compassion nor mercy.[4] Nevertheless, even in the act of condemning, this love—whether it be conceived as the love of a husband or a father—is still the love that woos the nation and suffers as a result of their rejection, not a cold, calculating requital, sealing Israel's fate. This means that it is still possible to hope for the greatest of all mercies, that even the

[1] Jer. 2.2.
[2] Jer. 3.1.
[3] Jer. 11.15; 12.7–9.
[4] Jer. 12.8; 13.14; 16.5; 21.7.

rejected nation may escape the destiny of judgment, if only they can find it in them to say 'Yes' to God's proposal.[1] But the very greatness of the offer is what makes the situation so perilous; for love that seeks the ultimate response, the surrender of the personal will,[2] cannot but destroy those who resist it. Condemnation is always close at hand. Moreover, just because acceptance means the renunciation of all rights of one's own and the clear recognition that one can have no claim or merit in the face of God, there can be no grounds for expecting that a nation which seems to be cursed with an inexplicable tendency to evil will ever make the saving decision. Hence the only possibility, when the present has incurred the judgment of God's wrath, is to fall back on God's creative love, which transcends all human thought, and which despite his anger will attain the goal of grace, a new and inwardly converted Israel.[3]

To the enthusiastic proclamation of this love of God bringing its great work to perfection the prophecies of consolation of *Deutero-Isaiah* are dedicated. He was always finding new terms in which to praise God's inexhaustible redeeming love. Israel, the divorced wife, now degraded to the position of a slave, a dishonoured captive, a childless widow loaded with ignominy, would be brought out of her misery and showered with abundant blessing as a bride beloved, a joyful mother of many children, a princess re-instated in her position of honour.[4] Never was Yahweh's love spoken of with greater tenderness or imagination, especially in the incomparable saying about mother-love.[5] And yet Deutero-Isaiah does not enter so deeply into the incomprehensible, paradoxical quality of the divine love as his predecessors. The imagery of the reclaimed harlot has quite disappeared, and God's repudiation of Israel seems often to be no more than a passing loss of regard;[6] for it is expressly emphasized that there is no legal obstacle to Yahweh's taking Israel back, since no documents of divorce were ever actually executed.[7] There is certainly no obscuring of the prophet's insight into the seriousness of the nation's guilt; sufficient proof of this is to be found in the reproaches inter-

---

[1] Cf. 3.1 ff., 12 ff., 22 ff.; 4.1.
[2] This is the purpose of the *da'at Yahweh*, the knowledge of God, which Jeremiah like Hosea longs to see.
[3] Jer. 31.3 ff., 20, 31 ff.
[4] 40.2; 49.14 ff., 20 ff.; 50.1; 51.17 ff.; 54.1 f., 6 f.; 60.4 ff., 15; 62.4.
[5] 49.15.
[6] 49.14; 50.1; 54.6 f.; 60.15.
[7] 50.1.

spersed throughout the chapters[1] in which the prophet underlines the magnitude of the remission granted to the impenitent people, and urges his compatriots, sunk in the obstinacy of despair, to accept in faith the new offer of divine love. But *the 'rational' features susceptible of popular understanding are those that predominate in his demonstration of God's love*, especially since great force is attached to the aspect of legal relationship in the divine marriage-bond with Israel. Yahweh is the *gō'ēl*, the Redeemer, who is obliged to ransom his near of kin;[2] the wife who has been visited with double the appropriate punishment needs to be appeased and encouraged to enable her to forget her misery;[3] Yahweh's love is the bestowing of a privilege which is bound to work out in the form of Israel's supremacy over other nations.[4] Even if, however, all these features are left out of account in one's interpretation as being truly relevant only to the miraculous eschatological order, the mystery of divine love is still weakened in that it now approximates more closely to the kind of conduct required of man in his communal relationships.

This is even more true in the case of *Ezekiel*. Jeremiah had already in his interpretation made the metaphor of marriage on occasion into more of an instructional parable on the relationship of Yahweh to the two sisters, Israel and Judah;[5] his contemporary now used it entirely in this sense, in order to castigate Israel's idolatry and politics as adultery and prostitution.[6] The emphasis is much more on Yahweh's proprietary rights in Israel than on his love; and the imagery of marriage no longer plays any part in the picture of the day of salvation.[7]

Under the influence of the prophets the idea of love also found its way into the work of *the Deuteronomic doctors of the Law*, but it was here given a particular stamp. In face of the dissolution of the old attachment to traditional law and morality the lawgiver now sought to give binding force once more to the broken pattern of national life by basing it on the love of God and the corresponding self-surrender of love on the part of man. *The Law* is no grievous yoke imposed by a stern tyrant, no rigid juristic system, but *a gift of love*, in which man

[1] 42.18–25; 43.22–27; 45.9–13; 48.1–11; 50.1 f.
[2] 43.3; 49.26; 60.16.
[3] 40.2; 54.6 ff.
[4] 43.4; 49.22 ff.; 52.4 f.; 60.
[5] Jer. 3.6 ff.
[6] Ezek. 16 and 23.
[7] Ezek. 16.60–63 appears not to be original. Cf. p. 61 above, n. 6.

encounters the loving God who has highly favoured him.[1] Yahweh granted the Law that he might train up a people for himself, rejoice in them and endow them with every blessing.[2] That it should be Israel, that nation of so many weaknesses and errors, whom he had chosen for this destiny simply indicates the inconceivable magnitude and power of his love.[3] Here love, the miracle of free affection,[4] is seen to be the basis of the whole relationship of God to man, and it calls for personal surrender as the living heart of any obedience to law;[5] moreover, the expression of this love is laid down for all to see and understand in the covenant regulations. Love is the effective power in the saving stipulations of the covenant; it ensures their success, and bestows itself in blessing[6] on all who keep its 'commandments'[7] and 'walk in its ways'.[8] The idea of love is now united with the rationalist concept of law, as shown by the fact that it can be mentioned in the same breath with the promise made to the Fathers and the ḥesed granted in the bᵉrît.[9] To realize this love, which constitutes as it were the available capital, requires simply the positive act of obedience to the law; and by this means it is possible to establish, within the framework of this world, a holy people of God, separated from the nations. As distinct from the prophetic conception, in which the love of God is pressing forward to a completely new world order, that love is here understood as *the power which upholds the present order*, and which maintains the covenant in the character of a *restauratio*, not a *renovatio omnium*, though men may admittedly violate its terms and thus lose the right to participate in it.[10] Such love shines forth unalterably like the sun in heaven and constitutes the inner strength of the eternal divine order.

As compared with the preaching of the prophets, this interpretation of the love of God has been considerably toned down and is no longer dominated by the eschatological glory; but it is the one which

---

[1] Deut. 4.5–8, 32 ff., 36 f.
[2] 28.63; 30.9 f., 11–14.
[3] 4.37; 7.6 ff.; 10.14 ff.; 23.6.
[4] Note the emphasis on the emotional element in the use of ḥšq, Deut. 7.7; 10.15.
[5] 6.4 f. etc.
[6] 7.13.
[7] Deut. 5.10; 7.9; 11.1; I Kings 3.3.
[8] Deut. 10.12; 11.22; 19.9; 30.16; Josh. 22.5; 23.11.
[9] Deut. 7.8 f., 12 f. The Father-concept should also be mentioned here, in so far as it is bound up with the true education of the people, Deut. 8.5.
[10] Cf. ch. II, pp. 52 ff. above. As 'ēl raḥūm Yahweh holds fast by the covenant oath which he has sworn to the Fathers (Deut. 4.31); his mercy is identical with his covenant loyalty.

was to predominate in *the post-exilic period*. A significant indication is the weakened sense now commonly attaching to the stems '*ḥb* and *rḥm*; often they mean no more than *bḥr*, 'to choose',[1] and are used quite generally of God's protection of the righteous and his putting an end to their time of affliction.[2] Where they are applied to the eschatological demonstration of Yahweh's love, the stress is no longer on the emotional element but on the change in the external situation, so that they almost become synonymous with *šūb š·būt*, 'to bring about a change (sc. for the better)', 'to turn the captivity' of someone.[3] The fact that the adjective *ḥannūn* is frequently found in a standard combination with *raḥūm* to denote Yahweh's attitude of love,[4] and that *raḥ·mīm* appears in almost stereotyped conjunction with *ḥesed*,[5] is probably the result of a strong tendency to bring the divine love into line with the kind of conduct proper to the covenant fellowship.

All the more significant, therefore, is the way in which, in the language of prayer, this *divine love is related to the individual*. Here is a living expression of man's complete dependence on God's mercy; God not only gives men life and preserves them, but even when man has cut himself off from God through his own fault, God's forgiving grace rescues him and does not exclude him for ever from communion—nay, it enables him to discern in the very experience of punishment a purpose directed to his salvation.[6] In this way one of the principal elements in the prophetic proclamation of the love of God became a permanent possession of the congregation.

The period of the encounter with Hellenism, which once more placed Judaism in the context of the great processes of world history, also gave to its statements on the love of God greater breadth and boldness of speech.[7] Israel's favoured position among the nations as the possessor of the divine revelation, which had been given into its keeping by God as a token of his loving election, was now acknowledged with new joy. God loves his Creation more than any man

---

[1] Isa. 48.14 (said of Cyrus); Isa. 14.1; Mal. 1.2.
[2] Ps. 146.8 f.; Prov. 15.9; 22.11; Zech. 1.12; 10.6.
[3] Already to be found in Jer. 30.18; Ezek. 39.25; later Deut. 30.3; Jer. 33.26. Jer. 12.15 sees the bringing home of the exiles as an act of the divine mercy.
[4] Pss. 86.15; 103.8; 111.4; 145.8; Joel 2.13; Jonah 4.2; Neh. 9.17, 31; II Chron. 30.9.
[5] Pss. 25.6; 40.12; 51.3; 69.17; 119.76 f.
[6] In addition to the passages listed in nn. 4 and 5 above cf. also Job 33.19 ff.; 36.15; Lam. 3.22 ff.; Ecclus. 2.5; 4.17–19; 36.1.
[7] On this period cf. E. Stauffer in *TWNT* I, pp. 38 ff. (= *Love*, pp. 32 ff.).

T.O.T.—I

could ever love it, but his especial love is for Israel.[1] The outstanding proof of that love is the gift of the Torah.[2] The intimacy and faithfulness of this love is presented in many different ways, such as the interpretation of the Song of Songs according to which the Beloved, who is ever at hand to help, is God, or the symbolism of the king who has rejected his favourite wife and then takes her back again into favour. Such instances, as well as the avoidance of the Greek ἔρως by the translators of the LXX and their preference for ἀγάπη, indicate a clear sense of the difference between the divine love and any kind of mystical eroticism. The loyalty of a love which will not spare its own from suffering or even from martyrdom points to a fellowship that is an act of the will and must therefore be preserved to the last; but the satisfaction of that love bestows on the faithful a happiness far surpassing any earthly blessing. The increasing use of the name Father in the prayer of devout individuals is the form taken by the expression of this interior relationship with the loving God in the context of personal piety.[3]

Nevertheless, this certainty of God's love was constantly being endangered, as an ever-deepening sense of sin made men incapable of seeing in God's lordship over Israel anything but the threat of retributive justice; and the question which this raised, though it might be posed on the basis of the Old Testament revelation, could only be successfully answered from quite a different direction.

5. THE WRATH OF GOD

As in the case of love, anger is an instance of a spontaneous feeling, suddenly flooding through the life of the soul and taking charge. Being the normal manifestation of a conscious personality defending itself against the attacks of its environment, it signifies, when applied to God, the emphatically personal character of the Deity. Both the multiplicity of expressions used to denote anger in the Old Testament and the frequent allusions to it indicate the powerful influence which this concept had on men's understanding of God. The inward fire of the emotion of anger is described by ḥārōn and ḥēmā; its operation on its environment, when pictured in terms of 'snorting' by rūaḥ and 'ap, of 'foaming' or 'boiling over' by

[1] II (4) Esd. 8.47; Wisd. 11.24; Od. Sol. 18.3 f.; III Macc. 2.10; Tob. 13.10; II (4) Esd. 5.33; 8.30; Apoc. Bar. 78.3.
[2] Pirqe Aboth 3.15; Shab. 88b (Babyl. Talmud).
[3] Ecclus. 4.10 f.; 23.1, 4; 51.10; Enoch 62.11; III Macc. 5.7; 6.8; 7.6; Wisd. 2.16 ff.; Jub. 1.24 f.

'ebrā, za'am, and za'ap, of the breaking forth of something under pressure by qeṣep.

With God, as with men, anger primarily refers to *any sort of displeasure and the venting of that displeasure regardless of its particular causes*. It will not do, therefore, to equate it directly with 'retributive justice';[1] it is rather the simple opposite of God's good pleasure. Hence any misfortune can be regarded as the work of divine wrath, just as undisturbed good fortune is the mark of the divine favour. In particular, any unexpected and terrifying disaster is described as *nega'* or *maggēpā*, a 'blow', a sign of Yahweh's displeasure.[2]

Such ideas of misfortune are a natural part of the picture of the world held by any living religion. But because Israel shared the conception of God common to the whole of the ancient East, she also assumed that the proximate motive of divine anger must be some human transgression, regardless of whether anyone was aware of the transgression or not. This connection between God's anger and human sin is a standard element in the religious beliefs of all civilized peoples among whom the Deity is worshipped as the guardian of justice and keeper of the laws. While, however, this conviction was unable in any other nation to banish men's terror of the capriciousness of the gods, or to rule out the possibility that their anger might always break out against men without the slightest justification, but simply from jealousy or ill-will,[3] in Israel a new factor had entered into their estimate of events with their experience of the God of Sinai. For one thing the dynamic concentration of all events as related to the will of this one God gave new intensity to the traditional religious assessment of misfortune. But in addition, because the purpose of God's dealings was recognized to be the maintenance of the covenant, their experience of the divine wrath was associated increasingly with the idea of *offence against the covenant or its Creator*, and it was *this* which was understood to determine the displeasure of their divine protector. God's wrath is retribution for

[1] So Dillmann, *Handbuch der AT Theologie*, p. 260. Similarly Cremer, *Biblisch-theologisches Wörterbuch*[9], 1902, p, 767.

[2] The two words were synonymous expressions for any kind of misfortune, injury or sickness: cf. Ex. 9.14; I Sam. 6.4; II Sam. 24.21, 25; Num. 14.37; 25.8 f.; Pss. 91.10; 106.29. Especially instructive in this respect is the description of leprosy as *nega'*, a usage which was still retained in periods which no longer associated it with a particular demonstration of Yahweh's anger: cf. Lev. 13.2 f.; 14.3; Deut. 24.8. For an analogous use of *maggēpā* for sudden death, cf. Ezek. 24.16.

[3] The most famous instance is the Babylonian ascription of the Deluge to the anger of Enlil in the Gilgamesh Epic: cf. *AOT*, pp. 178 f.; *ANET*, pp. 94 f.

the sins men have committed. This is made quite clear by the description of God's intervention as vengeance for outrage done to himself or others,[1] or as jealousy,[2] which safeguards the inviolability of the divine nature and operation and annihilates all that opposes it. Strict application of this principle meant that the wrath of God was no longer something incalculable or arbitrary, but came under the heading of legitimate reaction to the transgression of known stipulations.

Nevertheless, ancient Israel never gave this insight the systematic development that would have made every misfortune a punishment for sin. Men retained the simple perception that *evil for which there was no further explanation* was a part of life, and could not be linked up directly with moral judgments. In war 'the sword devoureth one as well as another' (II Sam. 11.25); the reasons for victory or defeat cannot always be discerned; and even the innocent may be surprised by a fearful end, as were, for example, Abner or the house of Eli.[3] Hence even death is not in itself necessarily a punishment inflicted by the divine wrath.[4]

And yet, on the other hand, Israel also spoke of the divine wrath in just those cases where misfortune struck in extraordinary ways or contrary to all expectation. For Amos it is taken for granted that every misfortune is the product of the power of Yahweh's wrath.[5] Both accidental death and extraordinary public calamity are ascribed to God.[6] The only reasonable attitude to incomprehensible misfortune is simply to bow to the divine displeasure.[7] It is important, however, not to overestimate the significance for religion of this linking-up of disaster with the wrath of God; in many cases it is due to nothing more than the vivid style of popular expression, which has substituted the personal action of God for the idea of an impersonal Fate. But wherever there is considerable stress on a personal relationship with God, as for example in the case of David,

---

[1]Micah 5.14; Deut. 32.35, 41, 43; Jer. 11.20; 20.12; Ezek. 25.12 ff.; Lev. 26.25; Num. 31.3; Isa. 34.8; 47.3; 61.2; 63.4; Pss. 94.1; 149.7; cf. Judg. 11.36; II Sam. 4.8; 22.48.
[2]Ex. 20.5; 34.14; Num. 25.11; Josh. 24.19; Deut. 4.24; 6.15; Zeph. 1.18; Ezek. 5.13; 16.42; 23.25; in his dealings with the heathen, Nahum 1.2; Zeph. 3.8; Ezek. 36.5, 6; 38.19; Isa. 42.13; 59.17.
[3]II Sam. 3.33; I Sam. 22.18; cf. Judg. 9.5 and II Sam. 20.10.
[4]On the subject of Gen. 3, cf. below.
[5]Amos 3.6.
[6]Ex. 21.13; 8.15; I Sam. 6.5, cf. v. 9.
[7]II Sam. 15.26; 16.10 ff.

then it is noticeable that the wrath of God never acquires the characteristics of μῆνις, that malicious hatred and envy which bulks so large in the implacability of the Greek and also of the Babylonian deities.[1] Even if it is sometimes unintelligible, *Yahweh's anger has nothing of the Satanic about it*; it remains simply *the manifestation of the displeasure of God's unsearchable greatness*, and as such is far above human conception. Nevertheless, it does also arouse in men the feeling that there must be a higher law, in virtue of which God's mysterious and wonderful power is exempt from assessment in terms of the rationalistic categories of reward and punishment.

Such experiences, therefore, never lead to confusion concerning the clarity or validity of the divine demands, or to doubt that God has guaranteed their meaningfulness. The note of scepticism discernible in the lamentations of the so-called 'Babylonian Job'[2] is unknown in Israel, even though there is no transference of responsibility to demons to ease the strain on faith. Equally significant is the fact that there is no sign of recourse to incantation or magical compulsion to secure protection against the effects of divine anger, such as we find in the religions of the neighbouring civilizations. Even in incomprehensible cases of affliction there is still no impugning of the divine majesty, no distortion of God's nature into a diabolic caricature, against which the use of any and every method would be justified. It is just those episodes in the early stories which might most readily be understood as the product of demonistic ideas, such as Ex. 4.24 ff. and Gen. 32.25 ff., which exhibit most clearly the transforming power of Israel's conception of Yahweh. It is in these passages that the God who punishes, tests and blesses, who acknowledges the act of consecration implicit in circumcision and the force of faithful prayer, emerges from the uncertain half-light of the aetiological[3] and local[4] legends of popular origin. The fact that such dangerously ambiguous situations could be absorbed into the Israelite tradition and interpreted in this way is the best possible

---

[1] Cf. the descriptions of the merciless power of the gods as the venom of scorpions, an inundation in the night, a snare spread out with sinister intent, etc., in M. Jastrow, *Die Religion Babyloniens und Assyriens* II, pp. 49 f.

[2] 'What to man seems good, that to God is evil: And that which in his heart is iniquity, to his God is good. Who is able to know the will of the gods in heaven? The counsel of God, who can understand it?' cf. *AOT*, p. 275; *ANET*, p. 435.

[3] Though many commentators have failed to recognize the fact, Ex. 4.24 ff. is solely concerned with the origin of the practice of infant-circumcision.

[4] The story of Jacob's wrestling with God is a local tradition from Peniel.

testimony to the power of the nation's living conception of God.[1] To talk in this context of despotic caprice or demonic savagery is to underestimate the largeness of Israel's picture of God, and in the interests of a particular developmental scheme to isolate certain of its features, the real meaning of which can only be derived from the whole. Unlike holiness or righteousness, *wrath never forms one of the permanent attributes of the God of Israel*; it can only be understood as, so to speak, a footnote to the will to fellowship of the covenant God.[2]

These considerations apply also in another type of instance which was always felt to present special difficulty. The *inexplicable transgressions* of men who in the light of the rest of their conduct were clearly not to be classed as godless, but who by these acts incurred divine punishment, were attributed to God's wrath. Thus David recognizes the possibility that Saul's implacable persecution of him may be due to the fact that Yahweh has incited the king to entertain his unjust suspicions. Again, David's own numbering of the people, by which he provoked God's punishment, is said to have been carried out at divine instigation, because Yahweh was angry with Israel.[3] Here the offence is clearly a quite incomprehensible exception to the man's normal pattern of conduct in other respects, and is therefore only to be explained in terms of some superhuman power. Moreover, since there was no question of a principle of evil existing independently of God, but it was customary to attribute the causation of all events without exception to the Deity, God was seen at work in this instance also. Doubtless this gave the divine nature something of a demonic character. Nevertheless, it did not make Yahweh into a demon. The strength of the covenant concept is attested by the fact that, even when such experiences are attributed to God, there is no lessening of confidence in the certainty of God's readiness to succour his people. *Supreme power which is sinister in its intentions was no truly*

[1] On Gen. 32.25 ff. cf. the fine commentary of Procksch, *Die Genesis*[2, 3], pp. 195 f., 373 ff.: also K. Elliger in *Zeitschrift für Theologie und Kirche* 48, 1951, pp. 1 ff. On Ex. 4.24 ff. cf. F. M. Th. Böhl, *Exodus*, pp. 107 f.

[2] Marcion's idea of the wrathful God of the Jews is a misunderstanding, but one that constantly reappears, whenever the love of God is exalted into an independent dogmatic proposition, thus glossing over the profound opposition between the absolute authority and power of the Creator and the individual pretensions of the creature.

[3] I Sam. 26.19; II Sam. 24.1. Ex. 4.21; 9.12; Judg. 9.23; and I Sam. 2.25, which are sometimes quoted in this connection, in fact present fewer difficulties, for, although it is due to an evil spirit that men's hearts are hardened or they are led astray, the punishment is clearly related to evil which they have committed earlier.

integral element in the divine nature; and for this reason God's will for Israel never becomes ambiguous. Ultimately the concept to which all events of this kind have to be subordinated is that of misfortune sent by God. The end of the story in each of the cases quoted proves that these ideas did not exclude belief in the divine lovingkindness, but rather included it. At the same time, however, it was impressed upon the pious individual that his own personal destiny, like that of his supreme earthly rulers, had to take second place to the destiny of the nation, and that even Yahweh's subjects enjoyed no privileged exemption from the enigmatic chances of human life and the natural course of things. If this candid acknowledgement of the restriction which the divine majesty imposes even on its own purpose of election is compared with the tortuous artificiality into which Judaism was led in its attempts at theodicy, it is hard not to recognize that the outlook of ancient Israel afforded a basis for a much more realistic conception of God, and one whose perversion into the later Judaistic doctrine of retribution was permanently detrimental.

Yet even in this later period the feeling that the fullness of the divine nature was not to be comprehended in the scope of such purely rationalist categories as reward and punishment was never quite extinguished. God's marvellous majesty was beyond the reach of all human apprehension and could only be rightly honoured by an attitude of wondering adoration. So, for the poet of Job 38–41, the divine wrath against Job is swallowed up in something greater, something transcending all conceiving, the wondrous divine being. Here is 'the *mysterium*, presented in its pure, non-rational form';[1] but though 'its positive value is something solely inherent in itself and quite inexpressible', this value can yet be sensed by men. It should also be remembered that the author of Ecclesiastes, by the relentless use of *reductio ad absurdum*, demolished all attempts to make the divine power manageable by the categories of human reason, and taught men to worship the incomprehensible greatness of God their Creator by humble resignation to the relativity of human existence.

Nevertheless, however far ancient Israel may have been from limiting the divine wrath entirely to the exercise of *retributive justice*, the latter is without doubt its proper and principal sphere of operation. The strong pressure toward a rationally consistent interpretation of God's activity, which is so noticeable a feature of Israelite religion,

[1] Cf. on this point the remarks of R. Otto, *The Idea of the Holy*, ET², 1950, pp. 77 ff. (Pelican ed., 1959, pp. 93 ff.).

tended increasingly to the dominance of this one concept. Hence everything which might be called punishment for sin is regarded as the operation of God's wrath, and the connection between this wrath and retribution or judgment is constantly present in the national consciousness. The licentiousness of the people, their murmuring in the wilderness, their apostasy to Baal Peor, Achan's theft,[1] all bring God's punishment on Israel in practical demonstration of his anger. Yet it is not true, as is often supposed, that the divine displeasure at the sin is only made known in the punishment that ensues, as if God's special visitation were what first aroused men's conscience. On the contrary, it is recognized that the murderer is cursed of God, even though no man's hand may be raised against him (Gen. 4.11 f.). It is possible to say of an act of violence, for which no expiation has been made, that 'Yahweh will punish it' (II Sam. 3.39). Indeed, because it is known that Yahweh judges those offences with which no human judge is concerned, his wrath is feared even before his punishment is made manifest (I Sam. 24.6; II Sam. 12.13; 24.10).[2]

Nevertheless, there are yet other cases where God's wrath requites transgressions of which men are as yet unaware. Especially in times of national disaster men are quick to inquire whether it is the sin of some individual which has brought God's wrath down on the whole nation, since the solidarity of the community makes all equally responsible. In such cases it is vital, where possible, to detect the guilty person and to execute upon him the punishment which God required.[3] Where this was impossible, sacrifice was the proper means of expiation, enjoined upon the congregation by God himself.[4] Again, not only the transgression of the rules of the covenant called forth the wrath of God, but also contempt for the being of God

---

[1] Ex. 32; Num. 11.1; 25.3; Josh. 7.14; Ps. 80.5.

[2] In view of these facts, such statements as 'The guilt of the offender is first made apparent in his downfall', or 'Yahweh judged according to no known set of rules, and the demands which he made upon men were in many cases revealed for the first time . . . in the way in which he reacted to their behaviour', are—at least in this generalized form—untenable(cf. R. Smend, *Lehrbuch der AT Religionsgeschichte²*, p. 108). The same applies to Stade's judgment: 'So long as he (the Israelite) had no misfortune nor a failure of the oracle to tell him that Yahweh was angry, the idea of his own guilt did not occur to him. Only when these things did transpire, did he conclude that because of some transgression on his part he had become displeasing to Yahweh' (*Biblische Theologie des AT*, p. 201).

[3] Josh. 7; I Sam. 14.37 ff.; II Sam. 21.

[4] I Sam. 3.14; 26.19; in addition Num. 17.11; 18.5 (P) may also reflect the earlier point of view.

himself and for the awe and adoration which were his due.[1] Moreover, with regard to the fate of mankind outside Israel, there was a
more and more decided tendency to speak of the judgment of divine
wrath not only as if it applied to those who oppressed Israel or led
her astray,[2] but also as if the non-Israelite would experience the visitation of the divine judge because of his offences against those basic
canons of morality which were valid for all nations.[3]

It is especially important to realize that bound up with this
conception of the divine displeasure as an act of real feeling is the
awareness that in the case of God *there can never be any question of
despotic caprice striking out in blind rage*. It would certainly be a quite
illicit impairing of the original meaning to suggest that the statements about God's anger were nothing but a naïve use of imagery to
express the way in which God steadfastly safeguards his universal
laws. The transformation of God's reaction to sin into the action of
an impersonal order of things, an objectively necessary universal
law such as is implied by philosophical thought, is an idea quite
foreign to the Israelite outlook. The latter speaks not of some un-
moved divine being, but of a mighty dynamic of divine self-determination, which sets man in the presence of a personal will directed
at himself and laying immediate hold on his life. The portrayal of
this experience of God is impressionistically heightened by the use of
colours more appropriate to human, and even to demonic passion;
but this should not be taken to imply that the image of God has
become demonic in character.[4] Hosea was not the first to reject any
association of God's anger with the characteristics of impulse or
caprice;[5] the whole tone in which ancient Israel spoke of Yahweh's
punishing proves that, for all men's humble acknowledgement that
the divine majesty was absolutely free and that its decisions could
not be anticipated by man, there was nevertheless a *sensitive feeling
for the moral basis of punishment*. Thus it is recognized that generally
speaking Yahweh does not at once give free rein to his anger, but
restrains it in order to punish at a time when the righteousness
of his action will be more easily discernible, and even then, by

---

[1]Cf. I Sam. 6.19 f.; II Sam. 6.6 ff.; Ex. 3.5; 19.12 f., 21; 24.2; Gen. 19.26 etc.,
and pp. 270 ff. below, the section on the holiness of God.
[2]Cf. I Sam. 5.6 ff.; 6.3 ff.; Ex. 17.14 ff.; also I Sam. 15.2 f., and in general the
carrying out of the *ḥērem*.
[3]Gen. 6 ff.; 11.1 ff.; 18 f.; Amos 2.1 ff.; Deut. 29.22; Jonah 3.9.
[4]Cf. P. Volz, *Das Dämonische in Jahve*, 1924.
[5]Hos. 11.9.

proclaiming the coming punishment beforehand, shows that he is concerned that men shall understand his authority aright.[1] In Israelite eyes, the fact of collective retribution expresses the righteousness of the punishment, since the social units of the family, the tribe, the city and the nation are collectively responsible for their members; but more than this, the fact that the punishment is limited in accordance with the terms of the divine blessing proves that God's anger is also limited by his graciousness.[2] The way in which the narrator brings out the magnanimity and practical wisdom of Joseph in being able to reform his brothers through the punishment he imposed on them indicates a readiness to recognize the positive value in punishment.[3] In the time of Micah the attempt was made to diminish the force of the prophetic threats by appealing to the idea of Yahweh's patience, which would protect his people from any annihilating punishment.[4] In the same way God's longsuffering is celebrated,[5] and his readiness to have mercy; and Jerachmeel, 'God is merciful', is among the oldest of Hebrew names. Finally, punishment and forgiveness are not mutually exclusive; rather, the penalty once paid is felt to constitute remission, as may be seen in the case of David (II Sam. 12.15 ff.).

In all this the unique feature of the old Israelite attitude is that *God's anger is conceived as operating in individual acts of punishment*. It is something transient; it is his lovingkindness and righteousness which are truly permanent. It is extremely significant (and confirms the meaning of righteousness developed earlier in this chapter) that God's anger is never coupled with his righteousness. Indeed, in later passages the two are explicitly opposed.[6] Particularly pregnant expression is given to the isolated character of the various manifestations of God's wrath by the way in which both the occasions when it breaks forth and when it is turned away are associated with the divine repentance; anger is a sudden change in God's attitude, to which he is driven by man's behaviour.[7] Any idea that Israel begins by labouring under *the permanent wrath of God*, and that only when this

---

[1] I Sam. 15.23 ff.; II Sam. 12.10 ff.; I Kings 21.19 ff.; Amos 7.1–6.
[2] Ex. 20.5 f.; 34.7 f.; Num. 14.18; Deut. 5.9 f.
[3] Gen. 42–44.
[4] Micah 2.7.
[5] Ex. 34.6; Num. 14.18.
[6] Ps. 69.25, 28; Dan. 9.16.
[7] Gen. 6.6 f.; I Sam. 15.11; even the prophets share this popular conception, cf. Amos 7.1–6, and for a dogmatic statement of the principle, Jer. 18.7–10.

burden is lifted does the divine favour come fully into its own, is quite unknown.[1]

Many indications, however, point to the fact that even in the early period of Israel a change in this outlook was imminent. The feeling that, apart from especially grievous misfortunes and extraordinary offences, the nation could rely on the undisturbed good pleasure of God was giving way to anxiety about the possibility of a general state of guilt for which no expiation had been made.[2] *A complete change of attitude*, however, only came about as *a result of the prophetic preaching*. To these messengers of woe, convinced as they were that God was drawing near for judgment, the whole history of the nation constituted one great picture of stiff-necked rebellion against God, which would be revealed here and now as fearful and irreparable guilt and judged as such. On this view the whole of past history was simply a period during which God had been biding his time until the day of final reckoning. All the punishments experienced hitherto were but efforts to purify and educate; but they pointed to the imminent, final manifestation of wrath which, being the outcome of a radical opposition between God and man, would bring with it annihilating judgment.[3] From being a temporary misfortune the wrath of God now became *an inescapable eschatological doom*, and so implied a definitive statement about the divine conduct; the Day of Yahweh becomes a day of wrath.[4] It is obvious that this is something totally different from the world-cycle of mythological thought, typified by the periodic alternation of weal and woe (cf. further ch. X). The doom of wrath is conceived as the result of an inner necessity, and therefore can only be averted by the irrational power of the divine love, or, better still, be transformed into the gateway of a new existence, as happens in the prophetic expectation.[5]

So long, however, as this frankly miraculous transformation had not taken place, the present still lay under the appalling threat of the eschatological terror. Every approaching affliction might be the beginning of the final doom. This now led to the drawing of a

[1] Once more it becomes abundantly clear that the Israelite conception of God is determined not by uncertainty about his exercise of power, but by the clarity of the covenant idea.

[2] Cf. ch. X, pp. 462 f. below.

[3] Cf. pp. 375 ff. below.

[4] Amos 5.18 ff.; Zeph. 1.15; 2.2 f.; Lam. 1.12. The fact that the idea of divine education sometimes led to the weakening of this absolute statement (cf. e.g. Jer. 18.7 ff.) does not affect the present point.

[5] Cf. above on 'The Love of God' and ch. VIII. 6. iii (b), pp. 385 ff. below.

distinction[1] between this punishment in wrath and punishment l·mišpāṭ, that is to say, of a milder and more kindly sort.[2] Nevertheless, the resultant shadow falling across the present did at least act as an incessant reminder of that deep gulf between God and man which the prophets had revealed. Furthermore, the tendencies mentioned earlier now acquired new significance; from being an obscure feeling the guilt-complex now became a frightful reality, from which no one could escape,[3] while life's sorrow and transitoriness were felt to be the direct expression of God's anger.[4] Where these ideas are taken seriously, *the whole of the present world order comes to be regarded as merely preparatory*; God's real world, the world as its Creator intended it to be, is the world to come. To enter into this future world is to be finally redeemed from the wrath which is consuming the old aeon. Since, however, only the sanctified people of God will be worthy of this redemption, to belong to this people is the object of the messianic hope.

Such radical conclusions from the prophetic preaching were not of course arrived at without reservation. It was the times of oppression, when everything seemed to be in jeopardy, which really gave free course to this stream of development, and the channel through which it flowed was Apocalyptic, as a result of which later Judaism became in increasing measure saturated with these ideas.[5] *In post-exilic Judaism* the experience of liberation from exile and the restoration of Jerusalem and its Temple exerted far too powerful an effect in the

[1] Jer. 30.11, cf. 10.24 f.: later applied to the fate of the individual, Pss. 6.2; 38.2.
[2] Strictly the meaning is, 'in keeping with the original state of fellowship and with what is needed to restore it'.
[3] Cf. the echo of Ezekiel's exposition (Ezek. 20) in the penitential prayer of Isa. 59.9 ff. and in Ps. 106. In keeping with this is the strong sense of being steeped in unrecognized sin, which nevertheless is manifest to God, Pss. 19.13; 90.8, as also that of being a sinner simply as a result of one's natural human descent, Pss. 51.7; 58.4; 143.2.
[4] Most strikingly in Ps. 90; cf. also Ps. 102.11 f., 24 f.
[5] For the operation of God's wrath in the Last Judgment, cf. Enoch 55.3; 90.18; 91.7, 9; Orac. Sib. III. 556, 561; IV. 159; V. 508; Ass. Mos. 10.3; Apoc. Baruch I. 12.4: also Jub. 24.28, 30; 36.10; Wisd. 5.20. The recognition of this guilt-complex may be seen in the dominant mood of penitence, which makes the penitential prayer 'symptomatic of the literature of this period' (Bousset), in the doctrine of the evil impulse (already observable as early as Ecclus. 21.11 *et al.*, and given its fullest logical development in II (4) Esdras), in the attribution of responsibility for the sway of sin to Adam (indicated in various passages, e.g., Ecclus. 25.24, and most explicitly stated in II (4) Esdras and Apoc. Baruch), or to the demons (Jub. 5.6 ff.). The conception of death and misfortune as punishments for sin to which the whole human race is doomed is to be found in its most detailed presentation in the apocalypses of II (4) Esdras and Baruch.

other direction for the adoption of this aspect of the prophetic preaching to be a serious possibility. The interpretation laid upon the change in Israel's fortunes by Deutero-Isaiah, namely that this was *the end of the judgment of wrath upon Israel*, only left room for a judgment either on the heathen,[1] or, in connection with the party struggles within the congregation, on the godless.[2] The Temple and its priesthood were signs of the covenant grace of God that would never cease, and in Law and cultus provided the means to the establishment of a righteous nation whose future was guaranteed by the righteousness of God. Hence it was possible in the more peaceful times of Persian and Ptolemaic sovereignty, which were favourable to the full flowering of the life of the congregation, for the prophetic criticism of the present order to be displaced by the assurance of a new way of life, full of missionary zeal and pleasing to God,[3] and for a sure confidence in the Creator and Sustainer of his people to develop in a wealth of testimony to his kindness and pardoning love.[4] This brought with it, however, a revival of the older and more partial conception of the real character of divine wrath, though modified by a belief in individual retribution. *The wrath of God is strictly limited to the sphere of retributive justice*, which metes out reward and punishment to the individual[5]—a narrow rationalization which, because the retribution in question was conceived as limited to this world, led to the most severe conflict and aroused the protests of Job and Ecclesiastes. The emergent uncertainty here discernible was intensified by the gradual diversion of the efforts of the pious in the direction of a righteousness of works; and with the return of the period of crisis, which from the time of the Syrian oppression had come to stay, the way was prepared for that apocalyptic tension which, oscillating between hope and fear, looked to the μέλλουσα ὀργή[6] to pass the final sentence on the present order of things.

[1] Pss. 9.8, 17 f., 20; 44; 56.8; 57.6, 12; 76.8 ff.; 79.6 ff.; 89.39 ff., 47; Micah 7.9 f., 16 ff.

[2] Pss. 5.11; 7.7; 10.1, 12, 15; 11.5 ff.; 28.4; 31.18 f., 24; 94.1 f.; 125.3 ff. etc.

[3] It was this that was responsible for the spread of the Jewish congregation through Galilee and the country east of the Jordan: cf. G. Hölscher, *Palästina in der persischen und griechischen Zeit*, 1903, pp. 34 ff.

[4] Cf. especially Pss. 25.11; 30.6; 32.5; 51; 65.4; 86.5; 103.3; 130; 143; Micah 7.18–20. An exhaustive list may be found in Bertholet, *Bibl. Theologie des AT* II, pp. 238 ff.

[5] Pss. 17.13 f.; 18.21 ff.; 26.9 ff.; 35.4 ff.; 56.8; 59.14; 69.25; 94.1, 23; 95.10 f.; Prov. 11.4; 24.18; Job 4.9; 20.23, 28.

[6] Matt. 3.7.

6. THE HOLINESS OF GOD[1]

Of all the qualities attributed to the divine nature there is one which, in virtue both of the frequency and the emphasis with which it is used, occupies a position of unique importance—namely, that of holiness. Some indication of the significance of this term as a definition of God's nature is given by the fact that it has been found possible to characterize the whole religion of the Old Testament as a 'religion of holiness' (Hänel).

Nevertheless, one might have qualms about such a definition in view of the great part played by this attribute in the religions of the heathen world. It is impossible not to be aware that the use of the terminology of holiness in the Old Testament grew up in the same soil from which sprang those designations of the Deity, similar or identical in form, by which the most various religions describe him as at once inconceivably wonderful and an object of fear and terror. It is this, the experience of a special force or power, which marks out particular places, persons or things as utterly mysterious and different in kind, withdrawing them from the sphere of everyday life and attaching them to a wondrous world of their own, and in this way makes men aware of the sharp distinction between the world of ordinary existence and that of the supremely powerful, worshipful and yet fearful *mysterium*. Moreover, because this separation of the sacred from the profane involves the necessity of definite rites, which must be strictly observed, for regulating the intercourse of ordinary men with this unique power, the concept of holiness acquires overriding importance for the whole province of cultus.

In so far as their meaning can be determined etymologically, the cognate stems in the various languages indicate the holy as *that which is marked off, separated, withdrawn from ordinary use*. Thus the Greek τέμενος from τέμνειν, the Latin sanctus from sancire, the Polynesian *tabu* from *tapa* denote 'to mark', and so 'to distinguish' or 'to separate'. This would suggest that the term qdš, about which there is not a great deal more to be discovered etymologically, should probably be derived from the stem qd, 'to cut', rather than from the

---

[1]On this subject cf.: W. von Baudissin, *Studien zur semitischen Religionsgeschichte* II, 1878; U. Bunzel, *Der Begriff der Heiligkeit im Alten Testament*, 1914, and *qds und seine Derivate in der hebräischen und phönizisch-punischen Literatur*, 1917; A. Fridrichsen, *Hagios-Qadoš*, 1916; J. Hänel, *Die Religion der Heiligkeit*.

stems *qd'* or *qdw*, 'to be pure or bright', which are known to us from the Arabic and Ethiopic.[1]

The concept of holiness as it emerges from this system of ideas, therefore, is that of a *marvellous power*, removed from common life, impersonal and bound up with particular objects. To defend oneself against it, to make use of it for one's own purposes, or simply to pass it on requires the use of particular methods, adapted specifically to the task in hand, rites which must be carried out exactly. When religious worship is directed to individual deities of a personal nature, then this personal element also makes itself felt in the context of the holy. Nevertheless, the original character of the concept continues to exercise its effect, even if to a very different degree.

From this point of view it is perfectly understandable if the statements about holiness in the Old Testament, in so far as they appear to be concerned with the sacred precincts of a holy being and the rites of men's intercourse with him (as, for example, in the case of the Priestly laws relating to purity and holiness), or to be describing the incalculable actions of an impersonal force (as in the stories of the Ark of God[2] or the censers[3]), seem to be of value rather as instances of the basic beliefs common to all Near Eastern religions than as witnesses to the unique Old Testament conception of God. On the other hand it is important to ask whether this Old Testament conception as we know it from other evidence does not present these statements in a rather different light from that in which they would be regarded if taken in isolation.

The first point to which attention should be drawn is that the energy with which, from the time of Moses onwards, the person of the divine Lord concentrates all religious thought and activity upon himself gives even the statements about holiness an essentially different background from that which they possess in the rest of the Near East. One indication of this is that, although in the religions of the other peoples the predicate 'holy' is lavishly applied to the objects, actions and personnel of the cultus, it is only rarely used of the Deity.

[1] Comparison with the equivalent Assyrian term *qudduŝu* has led U. Bunzel (*Der Begriff der Heiligkeit im AT*, pp. 22 ff.) to conclude that the basic meaning is rather that of 'pure, splendid or shining'. This, however, takes no account of the fact that the immediate cultic use of the word in Assyria and Babylonia already has a long history behind it, and cannot therefore be taken as it stands to indicate the original meaning.

[2] I Sam. 5 and 6; II Sam. 6.6 ff.

[3] Num. 16.10 ff., 35; 17.1 ff.

By contrast it is God himself who is primarily designated by the Old Testament as the Holy One.[1] There can be no doubt that this signifies the introduction of *a personal element into the theory of holiness*, which raises it out of the sphere of merely naturalistic power and the cultus of a non-personal reality on to a higher spiritual plane.

Hence the earliest narrative strata apply the term 'holiness' in a sense clearly derived from the divine sovereignty. It may be the site of a theophany,[2] or the people in their encounter with God,[3] or the spoils of war which belong to God,[4] which is termed holy; but in each case that which transfers men or things to the sphere of the holy is the operation of God's own activity.

In keeping with this is the fact that the earliest evidence for Yahweh's being termed the holy God relates to him specifically as the *God of the Ark*.[5] To regard the Ark in this context as simply a cultic object which serves as the medium of an impersonal, naturalistic kind of holiness, is to misunderstand its significance. In fact, from the time of Moses onwards, the Ark in its role as the throne of the invisible God is the forceful physical realization of the presence of the divine Lord,[6] or equivalently of his Name,[7] among his people; and the reckless equation of the Ark with God in the series of narratives in I Sam. 4–6 bears witness to the vividness of this conception in the early period. As the Holy One, God terrifies with his fearful punishments not only the Philistines and their gods, but also the Israelites, and even David his favourite, and by this means ensures that men will bow in awe before his majesty.[8] 'Who is able to stand before the LORD, this holy God?' This confession of the inhabitants of Beth-shemesh[9] strikingly reflects the feeling of the pious Israelite in the presence of the God of the Ark, and demonstrates that holiness is here understood as the awe-inspiring majesty of the unapproachable King, that is to say, as a personal quality, not as the impersonal power inherent in a cultic object and erupting with devastating effect. The equation of God's holiness with his jealousy, expressed in the composite phrase '*lōhīm qᵉdōšīm*

[1] This has been rightly emphasized by Hänel, *op. cit.*, pp. 25 f.
[2] Ex. 3.5; 19.23; Josh. 5.15.
[3] Ex. 19.6, 10, 14; Num. 11.18; Josh. 3.5; 7.13.
[4] Josh. 6.19.
[5] I Sam. 6.20.
[6] Num. 10.35 f.
[7] II Sam. 6.2.
[8] I Sam. 4–6; II Sam. 6.6 f.
[9] I Sam. 6.20.

hū 'ēl qannō' hū of Josh. 24.19, may therefore be regarded as an authentic interpretation.

As Lord of his people Yahweh is also *the terrible warrior*,[1] and the regular use of the Ark as a palladium in war recalls this aspect of his sovereignty. War is service rendered to the holy God, and as such brings men into immediate contact with his destroying power. For this reason it requires from the warrior a keen sense of the fact that he is a consecrated person,[2] as soon as the decision has been taken to 'sanctify' war.[3] The placing of the enemy and all his goods and chattels under the *ḥērem*,[4] and the stringent measures taken against anyone who transgresses the vow, are an emphatic reminder that the goal and purpose of war are not determined by human lust for gain and booty, but by the will of the national God. It is perfectly clear that the primitive restrictions and rituals imposed on the warrior were in this way transformed from objective *tabu*-regulations into acts of reverence and obedience.

The powerful influence of this personal conception of God may, however, be detected not only in the popular, but also in *the priestly and cultic idea of holiness*. The ancient cultic hymns of praise extol the divine redeemer, who demonstrates his power in his marvellous acts, as the Holy One: 'Glorious in holiness, fearful in praises, doing wonders'.[5] In the cultic law it is pre-eminently the divine Name which is given the predicate 'holy';[6] and this makes the personal nature of God, as he has revealed himself to Israel, the focus of all the statements about holiness. 'Holy' describes the character of God as it has been made known to this people; and, as understood in the priestly conception of God, this means *him who is unapproachable because of his complete 'otherness' and perfection when compared with all created things*. This absolute superiority, which nevertheless at the same time is felt to be that supreme value which gives Israel its unique position as the people of God, defines the nature of holiness, as is shown by the stories of destruction visited upon any illicit penetration into the sphere of the divine. Not only is any alien who

---

[1] Ex. 15.3.

[2] I Sam. 21.5–7; II Sam. 11.11; cf. also I Sam. 14.24 ff.

[3] *qiddēš milḥāmā*, 'to declare a holy war', Micah 3.5; Jer. 6.4.

[4] *ḥrm* is probably a primitive Hebrew root equivalent in meaning to the Canaanite root *qdš*.

[5] Ex. 15.11; cf. I Sam. 2.2.

[6] Lev. 20.3; 22.3, 32. The same conception is apparent in those passages which speak of the profanation of the divine Name, Lev. 18.21; 19.12; 21.6.

draws near to the Tabernacle to be put to death,[1] but also the Levites who arrogate to themselves priestly rights,[2] and even those sons of Aaron who offer improper incense offerings,[3] are consumed by the fire of divine wrath. 'Holy' is the epithet deemed fittest to describe *the divine Thou whose nature and operations are summed up in the divine Name*; and for this reason it comes to mean that which is distinctively characteristic of God, that which constitutes his nature. Hence, generally speaking, holiness as such is not confined to the cultus, though naturally for the priests the latter is the proper sphere of its operation. These conclusions make their first appearance in the priestly prophet Ezekiel, for whom Yahweh's vindication of himself as supreme Lord of the world takes the form of his 'sanctifying himself' either in the heathen, or in their sight.[4] In the Priestly law Yahweh reveals himself as the Holy One through the cultic system.[5]

The fact, however, that this God exalted over the whole world, Lord alike of his own people and of all peoples, has become the focus of the concept of holiness is bound to exercise a decisive effect on those sacred cultic regulations and practices which originally derived from quite different sources. Their true importance now resides not just in the fact that they are imbued with holy power, or alternatively serve either to mediate or avert it, but that through them a link with the divine Lord is set up and maintained. *The whole system of tabu is pressed into the service of a loftier idea of God.* The truth of this may be clearly seen in the conscious efforts of the Priestly teachers of the Law to establish as the unifying principle of the cultic legislation its function as the expression of God's absolute authority over the whole life and being of his people.[6] Even the most external ritual, because it is a part of the way of life of the holy people which God has decreed, and therefore witnesses to his rule, acquires a new, personal note which raises it far above the uncertainty and caprice attaching to the naturalistic rituals of holiness. It may be asked

---

[1] Num. 1.51, 53; 3.10, 38.
[2] Num. 16.
[3] Lev. 10.2 f.
[4] Hebrew *niqdāš*, cf. Ezek. 20.41; 28.22, 25; 36.23; 38.16; 39.27.
[5] Ex. 29.43; Lev. 10.3; 22.32. Points of contact with expressions of more general meaning are to be found in Ex. 14.4, 17, where the Priestly narrator uses the related phrase 'to magnify oneself' (RV 'get me honour') to describe the demonstration of Yahweh's divine power in the destruction of Pharaoh. For the close relation between holiness and majesty, cf. Ex. 29.43.
[6] Cf. ch. IV and ch. IX. 1. II b and c, pp. 406 ff.

whether this transformation obtained from the very first, or with equal force at all levels of the national life. Certainly it may be accepted without more ado that the more objective and impersonal concept of holiness had its effect on many rites, especially those connected with the injunctions relating to purity; it was also intensified at various periods and for particular circles in the nation by intermingling with the life of Canaan. Relics of the naturalistic idea of holiness remain ineradicably in the form of belief in holiness as a contagious and transferable force[1] and the habit of distinguishing various degrees of holiness.[2] Whether the pendulum swung to one side or the other depended ultimately on the extent to which the national consciousness at the time was permeated by the idea of God's supreme Lordship. But there can be no doubt that with the Mosaic concept of God and its adoption by the priestly school of thought a new situation had, at least in principle, been created.

In so far as the priestly understanding of holiness stressed the *unapproachable majesty* of God it was largely in agreement with popular ideas. When, therefore, the sense of holiness in heathen, or even quite primitive religions exhibits a very similar kind of reaction to the divine, the temptation is to denigrate the whole system of ideas which conceived God in terms of the holy as something deriving from the pagan Nature religions, and only to allow it the status of revelation after it has been given a new character by the prophets.[3] Nevertheless, to take this view is to depreciate a purely religious phenomenon on the quite unjustifiable ground that nothing can have real religious value until it incorporates the influence of ethical elements. The comparative study of religion has proved that a profound sense of the opposition between the worlds of divine and human existence is one of the fundamental ingredients in any genuine feeling for the nature of deity;[4] and therefore this particular kind of sense of holiness in Israel is not an inferior element in its religion, but a sure sign of its power and reality. Wherever the holy, that is to say the essentially divine, encounters man, its first impact

---

[1] Cf. e.g. Ex. 29.37; 30.26–29; Lev. 6.20 f.; Num. 31.
[2] Cf. the 'Holy of Holies', *qōdeš qŏdāšīm*, Ex. 29.37; 30.29 etc.; Lev. 21.22: also the distinction between priests and people, Lev. 10.3, and between Levites and priests, Num. 4.4–15; 18.3.
[3] Such an assessment is very frequent: cf. Kittel, art. 'Heiligkeit' in *HRE* VII, p. 570; Begrich, art. 'Heilig' in *RGG*[2] II, cols. 1719 f. It persists partly even in Procksch, *TWNT* I, pp. 91 f.
[4] Cf. R. Otto, *The Idea of the Holy*, and W. Hauer, *Die Religionen* I.

must always be that of an overwhelming power, utterly foreign to the creature and repulsing him; there must always be the sense of an abyss, which at one and the same time profoundly terrifies and inescapably attracts.[1] Hence to enquire into the ethical content of this apprehension of the divine majesty is *to ask the wrong question*. What is involved here is a primary component of the religious consciousness which drives every other into the background—the feeling, 'God is near'; and the very fact that the power so encountered is not 'intelligible', but as something totally different in kind falls right outside the scope of our logical and moral categories, is essential if the divine reality is to be truly transcendent.

The uniqueness of the Old Testament definition of holiness lies not in its elevated moral standard, but in the personal quality of the God to which it refers. With the knowledge of the holy, Israel was also granted the knowledge of the divine Thou, a concrete personal will seeking to enlist the life of the nation in its service. This meant that every experience of the divine holiness, were it never so bewildering or terrifying, yet contained within itself an interpretation, and was henceforward equally intractable material either for belief in a sombre and capricious fate or for the degradations of orgiastic frenzy. The consciousness of standing in the presence of the Holy One had nothing primarily to do with ethical motives; it remained a purely religious phenomenon; though by bringing man close to his divine Lord it afforded an impulse to personal decision, even when God's acts of power did not allow of being understood in ethical terms.

For the purpose of making a right evaluation of the function of this experience of holiness, it is as well to remember that it recurs constantly even at the higher levels of prophetism and Christianity. That God is felt to be not simply the loving Father, not even simply the Judge of sin, but by his nature a power before whom the creature cannot stand, by whom man must be annihilated, confirms the eternal reality of 'that sense of God, characteristic of a Luther or a Pascal, which struggles on the edge of an abyss of despair'.[2] A Christianity which had ceased to be aware of this ultimate fact of the opposition between God and his creatures, would have lost that

---

[1] Hänel is therefore absolutely right when he assigns a positive value to the experience of holiness at every stage (*op. cit.*, pp. 23 f., 318), even though he overestimates its significance for the problem of revelation.

[2] Söderblom, *Das Werden des Gottesglaubens*, p. 322.

note of absolute urgency without which the Gospel entrusted to it can never be other than unthinking and superficial.

The unique understanding of the divine being as the wholly other, the fearful and exalted, which has here been described, to a certain extent justifies the equation of *qādōš* with the concepts of exaltedness, terribleness and majesty, so long as care is taken to emphasize the difference of the latter from the notion of moral perfection, which for us is normally included in the idea of holiness. Even so it is difficult to do full justice to the connotation of the word, for the synonyms suggested lack that peculiar element of supramundane, marvellous and compelling power which is what distinguishes *qādōš* from '*addîr*, '*abîr*, *nōrā*' and so on. In addition these synonyms detract from the special character of holiness in the matter of its external manifestation, for which the language of the Old Testament already has a well-established term in the *kābōd*-concept. Originally *kābōd* denoted the phenomenon of dazzling heavenly fire which accompanied a theophany;[1] but as the external mode of manifestation of Yahweh's transcendent majesty[2] it acquired a definite connection with *qōdeš*, the unapproachable divine nature. Sometimes *kābōd* was conceived as an earthly image reflecting the *qōdeš*;[3] sometimes it is the actual brilliance and glory from that other world, the heavenly robe of light in which holiness is clothed, which, though fatal to mortal eyes, must with the triumph of the divine kingdom fill the whole earth.[4] In either case *kābōd* is a cosmic attribute of deity which is morally neutral. Where God's personal nature is involved, the only applicable term is *qōdeš*.

Still less are any of the above-mentioned synonyms tenable, once *the element of moral perfection has been incorporated into the concept of holiness*. The way was prepared for this development by the transformation, associated pre-eminently with the prophets, which established a dynamic relation between the terminology of holiness and the divine Lord of the nation. This meant that the absolute authority inherent in the Holy One now attached to the laws which were proclaimed as his will. The moral and social commandments, as well as those relating to the cultus, now became the irrefragable standards of man's intercourse with the Deity. The description of

[1] Cf. especially Ex. 24.16 f.

[2] '*Kābōd* is the radiant and so phenomenalized weight or power of a being' (M. Buber, *Königtum Gottes*, 1932, p. 214 n. 17).

[3] Cf. I Kings 8.11; Ezek. 1.

[4] Ex. 33.18; Isa. 6.3; 40.5; 60.1 f.

God's chosen people as a holy nation[1] now implied not only the quasi-spatial concept of 'admission to the realm of the mystery', but also the personal theme of 'conduct in keeping with the nature of God'. Psalms 15 and 24.3–6, which have been rightly described as priestly liturgies, show how this personal element became an integral part of the priestly cultic practice; they remind the visitor to the sanctuary that moral requirements are the condition of his access to the holy place. But the moral element permeated the language of holiness even more strongly when the perfect fulfilment of social obligations came to be understood as the conduct truly in keeping with the divine holiness; and to such conduct the actual term 'holy' was now applied. In the so-called Holiness Code (Lev. 17–26) the divine holiness as defined in purely religious terms is combined with the idea of *spotless purity*, which debars and destroys everything impure. The crucial text is Lev. 19.2: 'Ye shall be holy: for I the LORD your God am holy'. The injunctions that follow make it clear that this holiness which is required of the people because of the holy nature of Yahweh implies moral purity and blamelessness; men are to take care to honour father and mother, to avoid lies and deceit, to be innocent of any perversion of justice, to show compassion to the humble and unfortunate, to abominate all adultery and lust, and so forth.[2]

This clear recognition that God the holy is also God the morally perfect is nevertheless manifestly so far removed from the original presuppositions of the priestly conception of God that *the influence of the prophetic movement* must be adduced to explain it. The prophets oppose the mechanical attitude to man's relationship with God which obtained among their contemporaries with their proclamation, made with tremendous incisiveness, of *the holy personal will* of the divine Lord. This will is not concerned to secure the objective performance of all kinds of legal requirements, but binds every individual in the nation exclusively to itself, and therefore ultimately forces on men decisions striking to the very depths of their personal life. And it is the moral sphere which for the prophetic preaching is of decisive significance; it is here that man has to make up his mind with his whole existence at stake, it is here that the contrast between the sinful will of man and the holy will of God is most patent. The ultimate reason for Israel's imminent destruction is

[1] Ex. 19.6; Deut. 7.6; 26.19; Lev. 11.44 ff.; 19.2; 20.7, 26.
[2] Lev. 19.3, 11 ff., 15 ff.; 20.7 ff., 10 ff.

declared to be her rejection of the moral norms; the first and most important part of the worship of God is humble acceptance of Yahweh's moral demands—and for this there can be no substitute. This naturally means that in any picture of the divine nature *the moral will must be in the foreground dominating the whole.* God's hostility to anything blemished or imperfect, his shining purity and integrity, are felt to be the determining force controlling his relationship with his people. Conversely, this was bound to have its effect on the language of holiness, since the perfection of the divine being had already been comprehensively summed up in this very terminology.

The impact of these ideas on traditional language can be observed in *Amos.* The profanation of the holy Name of God, which he pillories in 2.7, is perpetrated at the holy places; but the emphasis is not on the defilement of the actual sacred site, but on the shameless contempt for the holy God evinced by men who are not restrained from unbridled transgression of God's moral ordinance by any thought that it is in this very place that they have called upon his Name. Again, when Yahweh swears by his *qōdeš* that he will put an end to the luxurious habits of the women of Samaria (4.2) in order to punish the shameless oppression of the poor, the contrast between the holy and everything creaturely is experienced as a similar contrast between moral nobility and irresponsible egoism.

Isaiah went even further along these lines, and made the predicate *qādōš* an expression for the moral governance of the world. In the decisive hour of his life, when in the Temple he found himself confronted by his God, he could not but cry out: 'Woe is me! for I am undone';[1] but what overwhelmed him was not that separation from the divine realm which is the common lot of men, but the contradiction between his own sinful nature and that of the Thrice-Holy. The work of cultic expiation wrought upon him gave him the assurance that '*āwōn* and *ḥaṭṭā't,* that is to say, whatever in his personal conduct was an offence against God, was forgiven. But what he learned in the heavenly council concerning the divine decrees gave him the further certainty that his people were equally bound to be destroyed by this holy God who had taken up his dwelling in their midst. The name *qᵉdōš yiśrā'ēl,* which he now carries before him like some standard or oriflamme of his message, though formed on the analogy of similar titles of Yahweh which emphasize his especially

[1] Isa. 6.1 ff.

intimate relationship with his people Israel,[1] from the very fact that
the accent in the use of the word is on *the transcendent moral majesty of God*,
acquires a primary significance of threatening and punishment. The fact
that this God whose holiness is a consuming fire to anything sinful (10.17)
is the God of Israel makes the future of the nation a prospect to terrify
even the most indifferent and hardened offender. That Isaiah's phrase
was a case of a deliberate new formation is indicated by the way in
which it became the crucial point of disagreement between the
prophet and his adversaries, and was felt by them to be intolerable.[2]

How strong an influence Isaiah's understanding of Yahweh's
celestial nature had on his own time may be seen from the evidence
of the prophets who succeeded him. Both in *Habakkuk*[3] and in
Ezekiel[4] the ethical content of the concept is clearly discernible. By
contrast, *Deutero-Isaiah*, as we shall see later, despite an even greater
degree of formal agreement, introduces new elements and makes a
material change in the meaning of the *q˵dōš yiśrā'ēl*. Even more noteworthy in this connection is the characteristic treatment of holiness
in parts of the priestly law, to which reference has already been made.
It is possible that the extraordinarily close affinity with Isaiah's
message should be attributed to the impact of his powerful preaching
on the priestly circle; for his preaching was *one* of the links between
the prophetic and priestly systems of thought, especially in such
points as his description of Yahweh as pre-eminently the kingly
ruler, who in spite of the affliction he has visited upon her yet preserves Zion in the midst of the storms of destruction, or his ingenuous
assumption of God's dwelling in the Temple, thus giving Zion as the
holy mountain an especially sacred status and at any rate a reflected
splendour of the majesty of heaven.[5]

The prophetic re-shaping of the terminology of holiness took a
quite different line in *Hosea*. The prophet who dared, in opposition
to the legalist and institutionalist interpretations of the covenant
relationship, to expound the force behind the divine purpose of
fellowship in all its inconceivable spontaneity as undying love,
recognized in this love the living power which is set in complete

---

[1]Cf. for instance *ṣūr yiśrā'ēl*, II Sam. 23.3; Isa. 30.29; *'˵bīr ya'˵qōb*, Gen. 49.24;
Isa. 49.26; 60.16; Ps. 132.2, 5.
[2]Exluding redactions, the following passages are relevant: 1.4; 5.16, 19, 24;
6.3; 10.17; 29.19; 30.11 f., 15; 31.1; 37.23 (?); cf. 8.13 f.
[3]Hab. 1.12; 3.3.   [4]Ezek. 5.11; 23.38 f.; 28.22, 25; 36.25 ff.; 43.7 f.
[4]Ezek. 5.11; 23.38 f.; 28.22, 25; 36.25 ff.; 43.7 f.
[5]Isa. 6.5; 1.25 f.; 10.16 f., 32 f.; 28.16; 29.7; 30.27 ff.; 8.18; 31.9; 11.9.

contradistinction to every potentiality of the created order. Hence for him love is part of the perfection of Yahweh's nature and a basic element in holiness. In deeply affecting words he portrays this power at the heart of the divine being prevailing not only over the unworthiness of its object, but also over the demand of its own righteous anger for judgment: 'How shall I give thee up, Ephraim? how shall I deliver thee, Israel? . . . Mine heart is turned within me, my compassions are kindled together. I will not execute the fierceness of mine anger, I will not return to destroy Ephraim: for I am God, and not man; the Holy One in the midst of thee'.[1] The mystery of the divine person and his dealings with Israel far surpassing any human understanding is here conceived with marvellous profundity; the narrow limits of legal form are burst asunder, yet there is unswerving insistence on a radical break with sin and on purity of heart as the conditions of any fellowship with the holy God. There can be no playing down the annihilating power of holiness, and the intensity of the threat of judgment in Hosea can hardly be exaggerated. Nevertheless, in the end it is *the incomprehensible creative power of love which marks out Yahweh as the wholly 'other'*, the one whose nature is in complete contrast to that of the created cosmos.

This unique understanding of holiness as the supreme expression of personal life was, however, confined to Hosea. More than in any other writer its influence may perhaps be detected in *Deutero-Isaiah*, for whom the *qᵉdōš yiśrā'ēl* was not only God the Judge, but God the Redeemer. But even if the prophet is fond of emphasizing God's holiness in support of the belief that he will intervene on behalf of his captive people,[2] the deepest mystery of the divine nature is felt to be not that love which passes understanding,[3] but the marvel, equally exalted above the scope of human thought, of God's creative action and the supreme control over the ways and means of redemption that goes with it.[4] Holiness is therefore once more closely related to the royal majesty of Yahweh; it is rather *the marvel of his mode of being*, than that of his personal conduct. There is clearly an approximation here to the priestly conception, though the relation of the Holy One to the world acquires its dynamic entirely from the divine eschatological purpose of redemption.

[1] Hos. 11.8 f.
[2] Isa. 41.14; 43.3; 47.4.
[3] It is precisely in the hymns on God's unfailing love, Isa. 49–55, that there is no reference to his holiness.
[4] Isa. 40.25; 41.20; 43.14 f.; 45.11.

The unique *conflation of the priestly and prophetic lines of thought* here discernible is also characteristic of the succeeding period. Sometimes the language of holiness seems to refer more to the passive and static quality of the divine, that which characterizes Yahweh as the wholly other, the ruler of his people and of the world who is yet quite withdrawn from all the imperfection inherent in the created order; sometimes the reference is rather to the dynamic of his personal conduct, by means of which God the morally perfect drives men to ultimate personal decision and punishes every evil thing with destruction. Attention has already been drawn to the way in which the priestly prophet Ezekiel combines both these elements.[1] The cultic poetry of the Psalter reflects the significance of the priestly terminology of holiness for the piety of the individual, not only in such explicit phrases as 'the Holy One of Israel',[2] 'his holy name'[3] or 'his holy word',[4] but in general in the high value attached to the holy places with their cultic feasts and rituals. The prophetic form of the concept did not, however, fall into oblivion, even though it appears less frequently;[5] its continued effect is indicated in particular by the mention of the holy spirit of God.[6] Nevertheless, it was the priestly usage of the word which predominated[7] and had the decisive influence on the language of the LXX and on the literature of Hellenistic as well as Rabbinic Judaism.

7. THE RELATION OF THE OLD TESTAMENT PICTURE OF GOD
TO THE MORAL NORM

In connection with the foregoing exposition of the nature of the covenant God perhaps *certain major difficulties* which are commonly found to stand in the way of a fair evaluation of Israel's belief in God may be considered in a final summary. These arise from the particular stress laid on certain divine actions and commands which are not in keeping with the moral norm. It is incontestable, for example, that Yahweh occasionally intervenes on behalf of Israel where the latter is not guiltless, as in the case of Abraham's conduct

[1] Cf. pp. 274, 279 above.
[2] Pss. 71.22; 89.19; 22.4.
[3] Pss. 33.21; 99.3; 103.1; 105.3; 106.47; 111.9; 145.21.
[4] Ps. 105.42.
[5] Pss. 78.41; 51.13.
[6] Ps. 51.13; Isa. 63.10.
[7] Cf. further Isa. 29.22 f.; I Chron. 16.10, 35; 29.16; II Chron. 7.20; Ecclus. 36.4.

toward Pharaoh or toward Abimelech (Gen. 12 and 20), or of Jacob's toward Esau (Gen. 27 f.). It is possible to point to Yahweh's savagery in the prosecution of war, the command to annihilate Amalek (Ex. 17.14), the carrying out of the ban, and so on. A favourite example adduced to prove the ascription of immoral conduct directly to Yahweh is that of the theft of Egyptian property which the Israelites committed on God's orders at the time of their escape from Egypt (Ex. 3.22; 11.2; 12.35 f.).

If, without going into each individual example, we begin by trying to form some idea of *their significance as a whole*, the first thing that strikes us is the simple fact that the conviction that Yahweh was by nature moral had not yet permeated and corrected all the ideas without exception which ancient Israel held on the subject of how God acts. It is necessary to remind ourselves once more that Moses' achievement was not a system of thought worked out and excogitated in every detail, but the mediation of a living experience of God, summed up in a few great fundamental concepts, which was to work like leaven in every department of the national life and lead to the growth of new moral ideas. To imagine that as a result all sub-moral conceptions of the Deity in Israel would be eradicated at one blow is patently to look for something contrary to all historical probability and psychological experience. It would be much more sensible, if we take at all seriously the idea of the historical mediation of the Mosaic faith in Israel, to expect to see something of *the struggle of Moses' world of elevated ideas with the world of sub-moral or morally indifferent conceptions*, which clung to Israel from her past just as to any other nation, and were constantly being reinforced by contact with heathenism.

Those narrative elements in which morally undeveloped ideas obscure the picture of God's activity and present it in a light broken by human imperfection ought therefore to be regarded as evidence of this spiritual process.[1] The criticism which the Old Testament narrators themselves apply, if indirectly, to these passages, bears witness clearly enough to the spiritual adjustment here in progress. Their living faith subjects the independence which man usurps by his

---

[1] Cf. Gen. 12.13; 20.2; 26.7; Ex. 1.19, for Yahweh's protection of a lie prompted by dire emergency; Gen. 30 and 31, his intervention to ensure the successs of Jacob's defrauding of Laban; Gen. 27.33, God does not even render ineffective the blessing which has been obtained by fraud. In addition, cf. the theft of Egyptian property mentioned above. The requital of evil by evil is not however relevant in this connection: Judg. 9.23; I Sam. 2.25; Ex. 4.21; 9.12 etc.; I Kings 22.23.

magic, or by his cursing and blessing, to the mighty operation of the one divine Lord, whose will sets bounds to all human words and deeds, and delivers up deceitful conduct to the retribution of a moral pragmatism at the heart of all events.[1] On the other hand, however, *the religious truth implicit in such ethically imperfect elements* should not be forgotten. They remind us that the one God yet reveals himself in different ways in the different periods of human history, and makes different claims on the obedience of his people in accordance with the general spiritual situation, without at the same time qualifying the reality of his fellowship. We should remember the words of Augustine: 'Nor knew I that true inward righteousness, which judgeth not according to convention, but according to the most rightful law of God Almighty, whereby the customs of various regions and times are shaped to fit those regions and times; though the law itself is always and everywhere the same, not one thing at one time and place and another at another. And it was according to this law that Abraham and Isaac and Jacob and Moses and David were righteous, and all those commended by the mouth of God. . . . Is righteousness then various or mutable? No: but the times over which it presides do not all run a like course.'[2]

It is therefore completely wrong-headed to try to fasten a different interpretation on to the stories we have mentioned, or to dispute every unmoral conception of the Deity. Such false apologetic does nothing to improve matters. What is required is to understand that those features which offend us are simply *the concomitants of a tremendous spiritual struggle* which was bound to burst into flame with the introduction into Israel of the religion of Yahweh.

It is a help to clear thinking if these oft-quoted difficulties are classified under different heads. In this way, for instance, it will be seen that many of the dubious features in the ancient history of the nation derive from *an overwhelming sense of the holy majesty of Yahweh as yet unqualified by any sort of ethical reflection*. It has already been noted during the discussion of God's holiness, that in this context for one

---

[1] Cf. A. Weiser, *Religion und Sittlichkeit in der Genesis*, 1928, pp. 52 ff., 62 ff.

[2] 'Non noveram iustitiam veram interiorem non ex consuetudine iudicantem, sed ex lege rectissima dei omnipotentis, qua formarentur mores regionum et dierum pro regionibus et diebus, cum ipsa ubique ac semper esset, non alibi alia nec alias aliter, secundum quam iusti essent Abraham et Isaac et Jacob et Moyses et David et illi omnes laudati ore dei. . . . Numquid iustitia varia est et mutabilis? sed tempora, quibus praesidet, non pariter eunt.' (*Confessions* III 7: the rendering here given has been revised from Pusey's version by the present translator.)

the moral element is to a great extent disregarded and the dominant factor felt to be simply the religious feeling for the awful supremacy of that being who is utterly different from man. The devout individual feels himself here face to face with something non-rational, something which cannot be solved or explained in the categories with which he is acquainted, but which requires simply to be worshipped as the enigma of God's unmediated operation. Something has already been said as to the value of man's being thus struck dumb by the sense of God's immediate proximity.[1] All that needs to be pointed out here is that these experiences in Israel never resulted in any feeling that God's actions were uncertain or incalculable. For these things were not the only things men knew of Yahweh; his kind and moral purposes were just as strongly present to their consciousness, and never lost any of their force from the presence of other purposes which men could not understand. This state of affairs may be most clearly seen in the case of one particular action which was required in Yahweh's name and which seems to us to be immoral—the imposition of the ḥērem in the holy war. How this age-old religious act of renunciation acquired a new meaning by way of the concept of judgment has already been described.[2]

Thus it was that Yahwism never became a religion of the sword as did Islam, despite the fact that the Wars of Yahweh, which gave its title to a whole book of poetry,[3] were the times above all others when men knew themselves closest to the presence of God and were most strongly moved to surrender themselves completely to religious ends. The only possible explanation is that belief in the moral nature of the national God had become so firmly established in the life of the people, that it could not be uprooted even in those times when 'morality appeared to have been put out of commission by naked religious feeling'.[4]

Another way in which in many narratives the religious point of view is put forward to good effect is that in which *the concept of election* determines the opinion of the narrator. This applies in particular to the history of the Patriarchs, but the sympathy of the story-teller for Abel in Gen. 4 and the rejection of Saul in favour of David may also be mentioned. It should scarcely be necessary to refute for the

[1] Cf. pp. 275 f. above.
[2] Cf. ch. IV. 2. IV (a), pp. 136 f.
[3] Cf. Num. 21.14.
[4] Cf. P. Volz, *Mose*[1], p. 47.

hundredth time those crude and unthinking misinterpretations which imagine that immoral conduct is extolled in the stories of the Fathers; for anyone with eyes to see, the framework in which the stories are embedded clearly expresses the writers' serious criticism of the deficiencies of their heroes[1] and the conviction that God was working to educate them. Incomparably more profound is the objection that God in general allows himself to be ruled by a favouritism which is not based on moral excellence, and so makes his love appear to be something arbitrary. This objection, however, if carried to its logical conclusion is really an objection to the whole idea, fundamental to the Old Testament, of God's elective grace. For there can be no escaping the fact that in the Old Testament *divine love is absolutely free and unconditioned in its choices*; it is directed to one man out of thousands and lays hold on him with jealous exclusiveness despite all his deficiencies. What the prophets had to say about the divine love in the highest flights of their preaching is still to be found—in more simple and popular form—as the real and profound meaning at the heart of all those stories about Yahweh's favourites, and can never be separated from the interpretation of Israelite history as the history of the Chosen People.

A third consideration which has to be taken into account in evaluating the morally inadequate statements about Yahweh's activity is *the forcefulness with which every single happening in the world is attributed to God as its sole and ultimate cause*. The constant references to II Sam. 10.16 ff.; 24.1 and similar passages as evidence of God's wrath even against the innocent prove nothing except that the critics in question are incapable of differentiating between a spiritual picture of the universe and a moral judgment.

All these various considerations, however, converge on one conclusion; they witness to the fact that *religious experience precedes moral understanding*. This in its turn confirms the fundamental principle which is definitive for the whole of Israel's knowledge of God; the will of the Deity is known from his acts and manifestations, and not worked out conceptually from any speculations or deductive processes whatsoever.

8. SYNTHESIS

The unique character of the picture of God in ancient Israel is derived in essence from the attempt to hold together the ideas of a

[1] Cf. on this point J. Hänel, *Alttestamentliche Sittlichkeit*, 1924, pp. 11 ff.

divine *power without limitation* and of a divine *act of self-limitation* in the establishment of a *b'rit*—an act whereby God makes himself known as *sovereign and personal will.* The conception of God's power is given its special character by its association with first the idea of the divine *holiness*, that which is annihilating and inaccessible and utterly distinct from every created thing, and secondly the divine *wrath*, God being, in his sovereign freedom, inscrutable to men. Contrasted with this is God's voluntary engagement of his sovereignty to the covenant fellowship with Israel, by virtue of which he grants men to know his *lovingkindness* as Father and Shepherd and demonstrates his *righteousness* by victoriously defending them against their enemies. Since these dealings of God with his people have as their object the establishment of his dominion in the holy land, the divine will is revealed as *power directing history*; and this implies a *fullness of personal life* which not only is different in principle from mere natural forces, but rejects as utterly alien the primitive conceptions of God attaching to the beliefs in spirits, 'power' and magic.

This unique attempt to combine the ideas of the manifest and the hidden God by way of the claim which he made upon men established itself in the succeeding period in opposition to an understanding of the world and of life which had been enriched by foreign elements, and in the process gained in force both in comprehensiveness and profundity. No longer was it simply exceptional incidents and occasions which were seen in the light of the divine presence, but every detail of life was now interpreted with increasing logical consistency in this way. As a result the *wrath of God* was ever more closely connected with his *punitive righteousness* and with *individual retribution*, while his *holiness* was understood as the *perfection of the divine being*, reflected in the Law as the pattern of life for the holy people and annihilating everything which resisted the purposes of that law. That all this was the work not of some impersonal world-order, but of the *will of a personal Lord*, was newly comprehended and expressed in the recognition of *love* as the deepest meaning of election and of *righteousness* as the power educating the pious in the attainment of their own righteous conduct. Holiness was now understood as God's supremacy over the heathen; the idea of him as Father was extended to cover the whole Creation; the concept of love now applied to God's relations with each individual member of the nation; and consequently men came to a new vision of how far-reaching might be the scope of their covenant God in his operations.

This line of thought presented the divine activity as matched to human understanding and attuned to human needs, with the result that the 'absolute' quality of the divine, God's being by nature 'unintelligible', receded in importance. But in the prophetic preaching the superhuman and enigmatic, nay irrational liberty and superiority of God returned in force. This came about not by a revival of the ancient Israelite way of looking at the matter, but by the ascription of a superhuman character even to God's self-involvement. Indeed, *God's sovereignty* appears to be raised to the highest possible power in the proclamation of the *eschatological doom of wrath*, which reveals the ultimate depth of the abyss between God and man and characterizes the whole of this world as a temporary and provisional order incapable of standing in the presence of the Holy One. But this very act of concluding every element of earthly existence in one vast community of guilt, breaking man's link with God and hurling humanity far from his presence, becomes the means whereby *God's voluntary self-involvement* is revealed as something transcending all human standards and shattering all men's categories of retribution. It means that God's *covenant lovingkindness* now becomes the free gift of mercy; his *righteousness* becomes that redeeming activity, which pleads even for the godless and restores not only Israel but the world; his *holiness* acquires its deepest meaning as the moral governance of the universe or the inconceivable power of love which suffers for the sake of the condemned, until it has achieved his salvation. Thus the ultimate secret of the *divine personhood* is manifested as *love concealed in wrath*, redeeming righteousness, the lovingkindness that remains constant despite the instability of the covenant. The antinomies that must for human thought remain for ever insoluble are fused in the amazing truth that God is a living person; but this truth is manifested as a living reality only to the man who can apprehend by faith the breaking into this present aeon of God's new world.

VIII

THE INSTRUMENTS OF THE COVENANT

A. THE CHARISMATIC LEADERS

I. THE FOUNDER OF THE RELIGION

IN THE OPINION of J. Burckhardt the forces at work in the emergence of a religion also determine its whole succeeding history.[1] If this is true, then the figure dominant at the outset of Israelite religion must be of decisive importance for the interpretation of the spiritual mediators of the concept of Yahweh in later times.

Now it is characteristic of Moses that it should be impossible to classify him in any of the ordinary categories applicable to a leader of a nation; he is neither a king, nor a commander of an army, nor a tribal chieftain, nor a priest,[2] nor an inspired seer and medicine man. To some extent he belongs to all these categories; but none of them adequately explains his position. In many respects he gives the impression of exercising kingly authority; he determines the direction of the line of march and appoints its destination; he gives laws and administers justice and orders the external details of the common life of the tribes. But that which is specifically characteristic of a king, prowess in war and leadership in battle, is just what is lacking in Moses. Similarly nothing is heard of his having made any arrangements for a son and successor to inherit his position. His giving of *tōrā*, that is to say his instructions at the sanctuary and the organization of the cultus attributed to him, suggest the priest; but on the other hand his office of supreme judge is not to be regarded simply

---

[1] Cf. *Weltgeschichtliche Betrachtungen*, ed. J. Oeri, 1905, p. 42.
[2] The points which P. Volz (*Mose*[1], p. 100) enumerates as marks of his priestly character are not sufficient to justify this as an exclusive classification. (In the 2nd ed. of his work, pp. 57, 91 ff., 125 f., Volz advances a quite different opinion.) A similar view of Moses as priest may be found in E. Meyer, *Die Israeliten*, p. 72.

as a priestly function, and we are told nothing of his offering sacrifice, a task which seems to have been reserved to Aaron and the Levites, or to specially chosen laymen such as the young men of Ex. 24.5. The seer seems to be suggested by many individual traits, such as the theophanies, his remaining forty days on the mount of God, his delivery of the divine decisions; but there is no tradition in the case of Moses of the one feature especially celebrated in other seers, miraculous foreknowledge of the future or clairvoyant explication of puzzling situations. Attempts have been made to explain him as a medicine man or magician;[1] but even if isolated features can be made to support this view, in particular the various miracle stories, it is manifestly quite inadequate to cover the whole of this man's life work and the traditions that have been connected with him.

For these reasons, and from a perfectly correct feeling that his most important work lay in the field of religion, the title of Prophet has often been conferred on him, in support of which a number of Old Testament passages from the later monarchy may certainly be quoted (Deut. 34.10; 18.15, 18; Hos. 12.14). Nevertheless, it should be noted that the tradition of Israel taken as a whole does not regard Moses as the prophet κατ' ἐξοχήν, but portrays him, in accordance with his various achievements, as intercessor, miracle worker or lawgiver; it is only where there has been time to reflect on the analogy between Moses and prophetism, that he is explicitly displayed as the supreme preacher of the divine will, towering above all the prophets of later days (cf. Ex. 4.16; 7.1; 33.11 and Num. 11.24–30; 12.1–8). It is in keeping with this that Deuteronomy characterizes him as *the mediator between God and his people* (5.24–28).

Justice, then, can never be done to the full historical reality, if the attempt is made to imprison this outstanding figure in any one of the ordinary categories of 'holy men', *homines religiosi*. It is precisely the secret of this man's greatness that he unites in himself gifts not normally found in combination, and is therefore able to work with lasting effect in the most diverse fields. If we ask, however, what is *the master key to the career* of this rarely endowed personality, the common factor which saves it from being a jumble of dissociated elements, the answer lies in *the concrete historical task* which was entrusted to him in the very hour in which he was seized of a new understanding of the whole nature of God. To bring a nation to Yahweh, the mighty Lord, a nation in which his sovereignty could

[1]The view of Beer in his study *Mose*, 1912.

be established and his nature expressed, which furthermore he could forge into an instrument for the execution of his judgment upon the nations and the founding of a new world order[1]—that was the goal which dominated the life of this man whom Yahweh had conquered. To the service of this calling he dedicated all his wealth of gifts and became *the messenger who should proclaim God's will for social, political and cultic life*, whether in the summons to escape from Egypt and in the holy war or in the marvellous redeeming acts of the perilous wandering in the wilderness. Only such personalities as Zoroaster or Mohammed, who were themselves founders of religions, and who likewise closely combined political and national activity with their religious work, can be compared with him; and it is just the fact that it is only such leader-figures who are at all comparable that should warn us not to try to bring Moses down to the level of those more ordinary servants of God or consecrated men whose operations were confined to a restricted sphere.[2]

One thing, however, is clear at the start. This organizer who enjoyed no proper political power, this national leader who boasted no prowess in war, this man who directed the worship of God without ever having received the status of priest, who established and mediated a new understanding of God without any of the credentials of prophetic powers of prediction, this wonder-worker who was yet far above the domain of mere magic, confronts us from the very outset with one ineluctable fact: Israelite religion is not the product of a scrupulously guarded tradition, swollen with the accretions of history, nor does it rest on any sort of organization,

[1] Cf. the view, long predominant in Israel, that Yahweh's battles were the execution of his judgment upon his enemies: Num. 23.22 ff.; 24.8 ff.; 10.35; Judg. 5.20, 23, 31; Gen. 15.16; I Sam. 15.2, 33; Pss. 2; 45.4 ff.; 110 etc. It is possible to argue about how far the dominion of the new world order was thought to extend; but at least there can be no doubt that from the very beginning it was seen as extending beyond Israel, since it clearly applies to the nations overthrown by her.

[2] An enterprising and most effective attempt to present this comprehensive interpretation of the figure of Moses has been made by M. Buber (*Moses*) with complete disregard for prevailing source-criticism. His penetrating religious exposition will always be of value even for those who cannot follow him in his method or in many details. E. Auerbach in his book of the same title has adhered more closely to contemporary scholarship in his attempt to portray Israel's 'mightiest genius'; on occasion his simplifications and strongly rationalistic interpretation do violence to the material, but he has a sound feeling for the untenable nature of most criticism of Moses hitherto. Each of these authors has in his own way made abundantly clear the need for a new understanding of the accounts relating to the first preacher of the faith of Yahweh.

however cleverly or successfully devised, but is *a creation of that spirit which bloweth where it listeth*, and which in mockery of our neat arrangements unites in the richness of marvellously equipped personalities things patently incompatible, in order that it may forward its own mighty and life-giving work. *At the very beginning of Israelite religion we find the charisma*, the special individual endowment of a person; and to such an extent is the whole structure based on it, that without it it would be inconceivable.

1. *That men's relationship with God should be founded on the activity of one specially called and equipped mediator* is of abiding significance for the whole character of their understanding and worship of God. The single historical event in which God encountered the nation becomes what the mediator declared it to be, *the point of alignment for their belief in God*; the redemption from Egypt received its definitive interpretation at the covenant-making on Sinai—and thus became *the foundation and the orientation of all the mutual relations of Yahweh and his people*. It has already been explained[1] how this meant that man's relationship with God was based on revelation in the strict sense of the word—that is to say, on God's imparting of himself through the contingency of historical circumstance—and required submission to the will of God simply as that was made known here and now; and further how this excluded any attempt to base a doctrine of God on general concepts or principles derived from human experience. It was also pointed out that this makes explicit the principle of God's being undetermined by any involvement with Nature. It remains to add here, that the very fact of the emergence of a mediator supplied further confirmation of these basic features of the new relationship with God; for the activity of the mediator was an emphatic reminder of *the distance between God and man*, a distance not in any way lessened for the chosen people. That this was indeed felt to be the significance of the mediator is indicated by the many interpretations of his work along these lines,[2] but also by the sense, which loomed so large in Israel's religion, that Yahweh was terrible and unapproachable, and that to draw near to him without such mediation was to court destruction. The frequent references to the fact that Moses' own intercourse with God was unique precisely

---

[1]Cf. ch. II, The Covenant Relationship, pp. 37 ff.
[2]Ex. 20.18 ff.; 33.5; 33.7 ff.; 34.9; 34.29 ff.; Num. 11.2; 11.25 ff.; 12.2 ff.; 17.27 f.; 21.7; Deut. 5.5, 22 ff. Cf. also the way in which Moses is in general portrayed as an intercessor.

because it was unmediated, and that this constituted the special character of his position,[1] prove that men never ceased to meditate on the gulf between God and man which he had bridged.

2. Moreover, the way in which Moses brought God near to his people became an important model for the future. For it made clear that *the demands of God in the Law,* which strove to order every detail of the national life and to conform it to the mind of God himself, *were those of a personal will.* From thenceforward the legal regulation of the people's conduct was not only raised to the status of a religious obligation, and distinguished definitively from all merely human opinions,[2] but it was also bound up with the type of lawgiving mediated by Moses. In the Torah of Moses, regardless of whether this is held to be simply oral tradition or to have been fixed in writing, is to be found the source of all law, public and private. Deuteronomy may have derived its distinctive form, the presentation of the law as an address from the founder of the religion, from the traditional practice of having a reader of the law at local assemblies,[3] but it was a real dependence which made this established form the most fitting mode of expression. Again, the constantly recurring formula of the Priestly Law—'And the LORD spake unto Moses'— in both early and late passages, bears witness to the feeling that the regulation of cultic life could only be carried out by associating it with the original giver of the Law. This means, however, that from the time of Moses onwards the will of God, as this applied to the nation, was conceived as being *normative for all human relations and remaining ideally the same for ever*; it was his proclamation of this will, and his application of it to the new problems that were arising, which brought about the submission of the people and caused the rule of God to be accepted. The whole intensity of Israel's devotion to the Law, which arises from her knowledge that she is carrying out God's unchanging will, rests ultimately on this foundation.

Combined with this, however, is a renewed sense of *the Word of God* addressed to the will as the true basis of man's association with him; it is from this, and not from any naturalistic or mystical significance it may possess, that every sacred act derives its sanction; and the obedience of the pious comes to the forefront as the only justification of the sacramental. The person of the mediator

[1]Ex. 4.16; 7.1; Num. 11.24–30; 12.1–8; Deut. 5.24, 28.
[2]Cf. chs. III and IV, The Covenant Statutes.
[3]Cf. A. Klostermann, *Der Pentateuch* N.F., 1907.

determined for ever the personal character of man's relations with God.

3. This divine will, which was normative for the whole of life, also indicated the role of the nation in men's relationship with God, giving it on the one hand an undeniable importance, but on the other taking care that this importance should be clearly limited. Because the divine covenant did not embrace simply the Israelites as individuals or the tribes as separate entities, but the people as a whole, it was possible to recognize *the existence of the nation as rooted in the will of God*. National feeling was given an out-and-out religious colouring; under Moses' leadership the tribes learnt that they had a duty of mutual support not, primarily, because they were all Israelites, but because they were all followers of Yahweh. Loyalty to the nation was made an explicitly religious obligation.[1]

There can be no question but that this subordination of the nation to the aims of the theocracy was achieved more easily in an age which knew none but a charismatic leader, and which was learning to make national unity an effective reality under his direction, than in the period in which the Israelite nation-state was emerging. Conflict only broke out in all its fierceness when nationalist ideals were confirmed and given independent validity under a strong monarchy, and Israel awoke with pride to the fact of her national coherence and power. It must, however, have been of the most essential importance for the clashes which at this stage had to come, that the work of the founder of the religion should already have included among its principal features a definite evaluation both of the importance and of the limitations of the nation, and that this should have become the common inheritance of a wide circle.

4. These considerations may have helped to clarify the underlying importance of the activity of the founder and mediator for the whole structure of Israelite faith and worship. But they should not be allowed to obscure the fact that *the continued influence of Moses* was essentially different from that of other great founder-personalities. The revelation of God which Moses mediated did not acquire its final form in his own lifetime; his work only laid the initial foundation. From those beginnings was to develop a permanent intercourse between God and the nation, with all the possibilities which that implied of further self-imparting by God. However highly the

[1]That this does not imply that Yahweh was included among the purely national deities, has already been explained in ch. II: The Covenant Relationship.

Mosaic interpretation of God's will was valued as determining the line of development for all succeeding ages, *it was never accorded the character of a final and definitive communication concerning God's nature and operation*; it pointed categorically to the future. It is significant in this connection that not one saying of the founder of the religion, not one λόγιον of Moses, has been preserved as part of the content of the revelation; there is nothing to compare with the Gathas of Zoroaster or the Suras of Mohammed. Even the transmission of Moses' law was carried out in a spirit of freedom, as the frequent additions, transpositions and expansions of the Book of the Covenant and the various forms of the Decalogue and other basic laws make clear. *An incessant process of expanding and adapting the law* to meet the demands of changing situations was perfectly compatible with loyalty to the religious and social spirit of the Mosaic legislation. Just as little was it supposed that after Moses there would be no need of any further prophetic souls to interpret or reveal the divine will; on the contrary, an abundant provision of new men of God was regarded as the guarantee that Yahweh's favour was still guiding the destinies of his people. The figure of the mediator was never 'improved' into a hagiological portrait, even though devout and thankful minds may have taken a delight in adding a good many decorative—but non-essential—details to the traditional account of his doings. In complete contrast to the case of the Patriarchs, there is no trace of any cultus of his tomb or relics; the tradition lays particular stress on the fact that no man knew his grave. It is this, among other things, which distinguishes him sharply from the ordinary chieftain and medicine-man endowed with power, a well-known figure in the realm of primitive religion, even though certain stories, such as those of the miraculous demonstrations in the presence of Pharaoh, of his prayer prevailing in the battle with the Amalekites, or of the healing of the serpent-bites by means of a wonder-working idol,[1] might seem to suggest such an identification. It is precisely the fact that the powerful fascination of this mysterious personality did not lead popular tradition, always particularly susceptible to phenomena of this kind, to exalt Moses into a wonder-working magician or *tabu*-man which is the most striking testimony to his belonging to a completely different sphere. Moreover, in his case magical power was quite distinct in character from that of the primitive sorcerer, for it was entirely subordinated to the activity of the Deity; hence,

[1] Cf. on this point pp. 112 f. above.

even when similar in external appearance, there was no similarity whatever in significance. Furthermore, the death of the founder of the religion before the conquest of the Promised Land for which he had paved the way seemed to the Israelite historians on reflection to mean that Yahweh's first servant had been sternly recalled by his heavenly Lord, precisely because that Lord wished to crown his work of liberation without him. At no stage is there any mention of a return of Moses in the future such as was envisaged for Zoroaster or Mohammed. The God who sends his servant safeguards his own supreme sovereignty by refusing to associate his work throughout with the person of the mediator. With unconditional authority he recalls him and discharges him from his service at the very moment when, in human eyes, he would seem to have been most indispensable. The work of the founder of the religion seemed after his death to have been scattered to the winds; in fact, it was firmly established on the *charisma*, the free activity of God-inspired personalities— which is to say, on God himself.

2. THE SEERS

Outwardly the Israelite *rō'eh* or *ḥōzeh* seems little different from similar figures in Oriental heathenism. There are indeed men who, as their name indicates, 'see' more than ordinary mortals not only of the future, but in general of anything that is hidden.

This is very well pictured in the case of Balaam, Num. 24.3 f.: 'The man whose (sc. outward) eye is closed . . . which heareth the words of God, which seeth the vision of the Almighty, fallen down and having his eyes open.' We are dealing unmistakably with people who possess the gift of clairvoyance—a well-attested fact not only in ancient, but in the most modern times. The term *'îš 'elōhîm* is applied to such persons in the sense that they are endued with divine power, they have been initiated into the divine realm.[1] Their clairvoyant gift may be manifested outwardly in widely differing physical phenomena; it may be associated with serious ecstatic disturbances of consciousness, as is palpably demonstrated by Balaam, who with eyes closed and only semi-conscious sinks to the ground and is granted visual and auditory revelations; on the other hand, the gift may be exercised in a fully waking state, or even in sleep, by means of clairvoyant dreams, as seems to have been the case with Samuel. According to I Sam. 3 the latter receives his first divine revelation

[1] Cf. Junker, *Prophet und Seher in Israel*, 1927, pp. 77 f.

while sleeping; when Saul comes to him, he knows him already as a result of a revelation vouchsafed the previous day, and he predicts three incidents which are to befall him on his journey, and which come to pass exactly as foretold.

Important and trifling matters alike may be the objects of this miraculous vision. Samuel is ready with information about the asses, and according to the servant is often consulted about such minor details. Nevertheless, he also knows that Saul is destined for the royal crown. Nor is there thought to be anything unworthy in exercising this faculty for a modest fee; while famous seers like Balaam can count on earning considerable wealth.

All these features are to be found in heathenism as well. The Old Testament, with delightful impartiality, is quite confident that the soothsayers of the Philistines are capable of supplying correct information (I Sam. 6.2 ff.), just as it regards Balaam, who comes from Edom, as being inspired by Yahweh himself. The assumption of the Balaam story, that such men occupied an assured and recognized position among Israel's neighbours, is confirmed by the Mesa stele, where the Moabite king tells of a word from Chemosh which encouraged him in his campaign, and also by the inscription of King Zakir of Hamath, from the eighth century BC, where the Aramaic *ḥāzīn*, 'seers', figure in connection with an oracle promising victory. Much the same applies to the Arabic *kahin*, who held the office not of priest, but of seer, and who delivered his information in rhyme. In Babylonia the priestly class of the *maḫḫu* seems to have exercised similar functions.[1]

Once more it becomes apparent that, in regard to form, there is a far-reaching kinship between the religion of ancient Israel and the religious institutions of heathenism. The soil from which Israelite religion springs is the same as that of the other Oriental peoples. But in Israel the form is pressed into the service of quite different ideas and aims; it is filled with new meaning.

The first point to notice is that the work of the Israelite seer is not confined to the petty affairs and concerns in connection with which the people are accustomed to make use of his supernatural knowledge. He has the further task of championing the inheritance

---

[1] Cf. B. Meissner, *Babylonien und Assyrien* II, p. 64. The women who delivered the oracles at the temple of Ishtar in Arbela, of whom we hear in the seventh century, ought most probably to be included in this category of seers, rather than, as many consider, in that of prophets.

of the Mosaic period, and of maintaining in the face of foreign influences the character which the worship of God had acquired as a result of Moses' work. Despite all the similarity of outward form there is here a drastic difference in the content of the seer's awareness of God; together with an enthusiasm for Yahweh, the holy God of the Fathers, whose actions are directed to moral ends, he inherits a great and sacred task of significance in the history of the world.

In the figure of *Deborah* we find a woman for whom the ideas of Mosaic religion are still vigorously alive. According to Judg. 4.4 she was called, in the language of a later time, a 'prophetess', and the text states that men went to her for judgments, clearly in cases where the local judiciary was at a loss and where she, with the authority of a God-inspired seer, was able to give a decision. In the song called after her (Judg. 5) she is accorded the genuinely ancient honorific 'Mother in Israel', which as regards religious authority places her on a par with the priest, who is given the title '*āb*, 'father'. The influence she wields is strong enough to reawaken in the disunited and disintegrated tribes the sense of comradeship under the banner of Yahweh, and to inspire them to do battle for the warrior God hastening to their aid from Sinai. According to Judg. 5.12 she sings the *recruiting song* for the holy war; and Judg. 4.6 shows her also choosing the leader, who can rely on a sufficient following from the tribes because of the esteem in which she is held. The opening of the song composed while the impact of the events was still fresh in men's minds shows that the liberation from Canaanite suzerainty, which she achieved by means of this victory, was used to promote the Yahwist religious ideal: 'Yahweh, when thou wentest forth out of Seir, when thou marchedst out of the field of Edom, the earth trembled, the heavens also dropped, yea, the clouds dropped water. The mountains quaked (RV mg.) at the presence of Yahweh . . . at the presence of Yahweh, the God of Israel!' This Yahweh, *who comes from the south, is quite unmistakably the one known in Israel by his revelation to Moses*, the one who arises from Sinai, not from the sanctuaries of Canaan, to come to the help of his people.

In the political field, as well as in the fields of law and religion, the seer Deborah pursued an extremely successful career. Looking at the matter purely in terms of concrete results, one might be inclined to rate the political success the greatest. Yet the strengthening of the inward sense of nationhood through her religious and judicial activities ought to be regarded as at least equally important. It may be true that without the external victory there could have been no free development of the national character even on the religious side; nevertheless, the quiet and continuous work of the seer in times of peace was also of decisive importance for maintaining the spiritual supremacy of the religion of Yahweh over the Nature religion of Canaan.

It is hardly to be supposed that Deborah was the only instance of a seer of this kind in the period of the Judges. Just as it is perfectly reasonable to assume that there must have been many other able tribal chieftains beside those political leaders who happen to be known to us from the Book of Judges, who worked to secure the supremacy of the Israelite element in Canaan, so it is extremely probable that there was no lack of those charismatic personalities, the seers. Num. 23.23 expresses Israel's triumphant confidence that the nation would never lack men to make known God's will; and for the close of the period of the Judges at any rate this assumption is confirmed by *the figure of Samuel.*

I Sam. 9 pictures him as a seer in a small town in the hill-country of Ephraim. But even in this popular story it is clear that his sphere of influence was much wider than this modest position might suggest. This is shown not only by his exercise of priestly functions in sacrifice, a role which he inherited as having been a member of the sanctuary at Shiloh, but also by his judicial activity, which was closely associated with the priesthood, and enjoyed peculiar authority as a result of the respect due to a seer. To this extent the Deuteronomic presentation in I Sam. 7, which portrays Samuel as a judge, is quite correct, even if the stylized element in the narrative, which makes the seer the uncrowned king of all Israel, must be dismissed as unhistorical. The important part played by Samuel in designating the future king, and the decisive influence which he exercised on the young prophetic movement, can only be explained if his sphere of influence was in fact a wide one. The fact that we are here dealing with one of the outstanding spirits of all Israelite history at the very turning of an epoch should make it perfectly obvious that the seers were a class of quite enormous importance.

The last representative of the old type of seer may well have been *Gad*, who is mentioned in II Sam. 24.11 as David's seer. His being also termed *nābī'* should rather be attributed to the influence of later conceptions, for which all spiritual leaders were to be identified with the n·bi'îm, than taken as a piece of actual historical information. According to I Sam. 22.5 Gad had already been with David when the latter was on the run as an outlaw and placed his clairvoyant abilities at his disposal. In II Sam. 24.11 ff. he champions the older conception of Yahweh as the nation's sole rightful Lord against the monarchy, a significant indication of the general attitude of the seers as a class to the ancient theocratic ideal.

Taken as a whole, these facts would seem to suggest that the seers of ancient Israel owed their markedly individual character to their close connection with the work of the founder of the religion. When the Israelite received from the seer information about hidden matters, and recognized this as part of Yahweh's readiness to help his people, this meant more to him than the momentary lifting of an otherwise all-concealing veil; it was *the continuation and confirmation of an already existing relationship with God*. It is true that the Greek might also receive from the utterance of the Apollonian seer a deep impression of the atoning and succouring power of Apollo the Healer, and be inspired to worship him. But the utterance could never signify for him the stablishing or confirming of an exclusive relationship already enjoyed with this god and no other; it was never possible for him to see in such contact with the deity the working out of a sovereign design which was authoritative for him and his nation. By contrast, because the Israelite seer derived his oracles from the God who had made himself known through Moses from the days of Egypt onwards as the Lord of the national life, the words which he uttered in the name of this God were seen as the continuation of a divine dialogue with the people, the basis and purpose of which was the sovereignty of Yahweh over Israel established once for all. Because Yahweh was the nation's King, he at all times imparted reliable information of his will for them (Num. 23.21–23). Moreover, if this information was ever withheld, this was not due to the caprice of a God who only occasionally condescended to show his favour, but was a certain indication of his displeasure at human faithlessness, and a threat of his judgment (I Sam. 3.1; 28.6). Conversely, a greater abundance of inspired seers was an assurance of the favour of the covenant God (I Sam. 3.19 ff.).

This profound importance which attached to the giving of oracles in virtue of its connection with the work of the mediator was something of which the seers, or at least the leading spirits among them, were fully aware, and which they sought to bring home to the people. The mediation of superior knowledge, which was their province, was no end in itself, but *a means of safeguarding the full force of the sovereign divine will in Israel*. This was not a matter of a vague religious feeling releasing certain special spiritual gifts, such as may be found among other peoples; all these marvellous powers were made to serve a particular purpose, which the Israelite nation had received as part of its religious inheritance.

Connected with this is the *political activity* in the service of their people which is related of the great seers. Just as the founder of the religion had seen the outward progress of the nation as part of the concerns of religion, so the seers were always aware of the need to intervene in political events and to direct them in the name of their God. They became the messengers of Yahweh to his people, when he wished to set himself at their head in the holy war; and by impressing on the nation in their songs and sayings not only its greatness and its obligations, but also the nobility and blessedness of its vocation to Yahweh's service, they awoke the sense of nationhood. Consequently it was in these circles that there arose *the first preachers of a distinctive expectation of salvation*, partly extolling the victorious conquest of the nations, partly the life of paradisal abundance which Yahweh would grant to his faithful people as the reward of battle (cf. especially the sayings of Balaam, Num. 23–24, and the oracle relating to Judah, Gen. 49.8–12). In this way they transferred the timeless mythological hope of salvation common to the ancient East into the realm of historical experience, and made it a religious assurance of an actual future; and furthermore, they thus provided their people with a mirror in which they could see the course of their historical existence reaching out to a higher goal, with the result that they attained to an ever clearer awareness of their historical task and position among the nations of the world. What the possession of the Promised Land had meant for the men of the Mosaic foundation, the hope of the final salvation came to mean for their successors— the mighty forward march to an assured goal in a future belonging wholly to God.[1]

In this situation, *the unique character attaching to the Israelite seer* could not fail to make itself felt more and more *even in the outward manner of its operation*. This was true from the very first with regard to the technical arrangements and devices which bulked so large in

[1] Cf. ch. XI: Fulfilling the Covenant.

the practice of pagan seers. In this respect the Greeks divided the practitioners of soothsaying into two classes; the one sought to disclose the future by various artificial methods, which could be acquired, such as observation of the flight of birds, prognostication by the stars, inspection of the sacrificial victims, the casting of lots, and suchlike; the other relied on an inner enlightenment for the giving of oracles, which could not be learned, but depended on special endowment. Moreover, the value attached to persons genuinely inspired by the god, such as the Pythia, was much higher than that ascribed to the interpreters of dreams, the readers of entrails, and the soothsayers with their uncertain arts. Now it is a striking fact that in Israel *there is to all intents and purposes no trace of the study of omens*,[1] and even the rest of the technical devices are nowhere associated with the ancient seers.[2] Although, for instance, the traditions relating to Samuel are copious and derive from the most various narrators, there is absolutely no mention of his having made use of the customary arts of the soothsayer. Even ecstasy plays no part in his work; a capacity for clairvoyance, dream-visions and auditions are the sources of his superior knowledge. The picture of Balaam seems to suggest that ecstasy as a means of receiving divine utterances was already well known in the early period (Num. 24.1 f.); yet it is worth noting, that neither at that time nor later is there any use of narcotics to induce ecstasy, nor is there any mention of the need for an interpreter of such ecstatic oracles, as

[1] II Sam. 5.24 is a most remarkable incident, which can hardly be included in the present category: cf. Volz, *Biblische Altertümer*, p. 167 n. 1; also Judg. 6.36 ff. The fact that Balaam is spoken of as using nᵉḥāšîm, divination, in Num. 24.1, only serves to dissociate the God of Israel all the more clearly from such heathen practices. Cf. further the thorough investigation by C. A. Keller mentioned at p. 226 note 2.

[2] The oracle of the tᵉrāpîm, which though early proscribed continued popular in private use, is never connected with the seers; the ephod and the Urim are specifically priestly instruments. The use of music to induce ecstasy and of a species of arrow-oracle make their first appearance with Elisha (II Kings 3.15; 13.15 ff.) and may even earlier have been characteristic of the circles of nᵉbî'îm, in which case the possibility of similar aids having been used by the seers can naturally not be ruled out with complete certainty. Divination by means of a cup, which one might have been inclined to include in the repertoire of the Israelite seer in view of the fact that Joseph is portrayed as an interpreter of dreams, is clearly related as an Egyptian practice, and does not justify any direct conclusions about Israelite conditions. In Gen. 15 Abraham appears in some sense as a seer, who looks for guidance from God in the sacrifice and studies the behaviour of the birds; but this is in all probability a half-forgotten relic of Babylonian practice from the pre-Mosaic period, and one which was no longer properly understood, rather than a usage of the narrator's own time. Cf. pp. 112 f. above.

was the case at Delphi, which would seem to suggest that even the ecstatic gave his information in intelligible speech.

This is not to deny, naturally, that now and then *figures similar to the heathen seers and soothsayers* asserted themselves even in Israel. According to I Sam. 28.3 Saul had to take special measures to put down the profession. The fact that in Isaiah and Micah the *qōsēm* is classed on a level with the priest and the prophet (Isa. 3.2; Micah 3.7) may warrant the deduction that the technical soothsayer had become naturalized in the cosmopolitan culture of the later monarchy. But this certainly does not mean that the men whom Israel acknowledged as seers sent by Yahweh did not feel themselves to be very definitely in a class apart from the heathen sort of soothsayer. Num. 23.23, which expressly excludes *naḥaš* and *qesem*, the interpretation of omens and divination on the heathen model, rightly describes the ideal of the spiritual leaders. Men were conscious of being on a more direct and dependable route to the discovery of what God had to tell them.

The reliability of the tradition on this point is further illustrated by the material relating to Moses, which has not preserved one single instance of miraculous foreknowledge on his part, though the temptation to portray him in such a guise was never far away. It was left to a later period to class him among the seers by ascribing to him the Song and Blessing in Deut. 32 and 33. It is not possible to determine with certainty whether Miriam, the sister of Moses, functioned as a seer after the manner of the *rō'īm*, though Num. 12.2 may be evidence that she did. In any event we hear practically nothing of the activity of any seers in the time of Moses.[1] It was only after he had disappeared from the scene, without leaving behind him any successor of equal stature, that there was sufficient scope in Israel for the work of the seer.

3. THE NAZIRITES

The activities of the second group of charismatics, the Nazirites, were of a different kind from those of the seers;[2] and the various Old Testament indications on the subject can only be reconciled by

---

[1]Num. 11.24 is a later study of endowment with *rūaḥ*.

[2]Indeed, it has been suggested that they were not charismatic at all, since in many cases they seem nothing more than a particular manifestation of religious asceticism, characterized by abstention from wine, avoidance of contact with the dead and dedication of the hair of the head. Such a manifestation could be

assuming that during the monarchical period the character of the Nazirite vow was radically altered, a temporary obligation of a predominantly ascetic character, based on priestly rules of abstinence, being substituted for lifelong consecration and dedication to the holy war (cf. Num. 6; also Lev. 10.8 ff. and 21.11). The ancient Nazirite was outwardly distinguished by his streaming locks, the symbol of the complete dedication of his life to the deity.[1] The way in which he served Yahweh was by warring against the nation's enemies as the champion whose daring feats of arms should inspire his compatriots to heroism in battle. The charismatic character of the Nazirite is clearly indicated by the fact that these warlike feats are described as effects of the spirit of Yahweh (Judg. 13.25; 14.6, 19; 15.14). Such descriptions also suggest that the activity of the ancient Nazirite

---

adequately explained as a reaction against the Canaanite civilization. (So von Orelli, HRE XIII, pp. 653 ff.; R. Smend, *Lehrbuch der AT Theologie*, pp. 152 ff., *et al.*) Nevertheless, this interpretation, which is based principally on Amos 2.11 f. and Num. 6, fails to do justice to the older evidence of Judg. 13–15; I Sam. 1; Gen. 49.26 and Deut. 33.16, where the dominant feature is clearly the positive activity of these men specially favoured by God, especially in the holy war against Yahweh's enemies. Even if it is felt that Samuel and Joseph must be left out of account, and that in the case of Samson there is good reason to assume that the original picture has been obscured by the addition of traditions of a different type, this still does not explain how the Nazirite could come to be so completely misrepresented by the older narrators, who were after all much closer to the institution than was Amos. Moreover, if the figure of Samson proves that apart from the custom of leaving the hair uncut the essential feature of the ancient Nazirite was not ascetic practices, but the performance of mighty deeds of war, then the portrayal of the tribe of Joseph as Nazirite acquires real historical significance. (An original connection with the holy war is assumed also by Stade, *Biblische Theologie des AT* I, pp. 132 f., and Sellin, *Beiträge zur isr. und jüd. Religionsgeschichte* II. 1, pp. 127 ff.) That Samuel no longer exhibits Naziritism in its pure form is indisputable; nevertheless, the features of lifelong dedication to Yahweh and of allowing the hair to grow approximate him so closely to the ancient Nazirite, that the absence of warlike activity on his part (cf. however, I Sam. 7.9 ff.) can be attributed simply to his position as a priest. In designating him explicitly as a Nazirite the LXX is guided by a sound intuition. Finally, even Amos 2.11 f., in which Yahweh's awakening of the Nazirites is connected with the conquest of the land, indicates that the ancient military importance of these charismatics was still known to the prophet.

[1]The term *nāzīr* is applied even to the vine on those occasions when its fruit is denied to men, and when therefore it is to be left unpruned (Lev. 25.5, 11). There is no need to discuss in this context whether the determining motive behind this practice was originally a primitive *mana*-type concept of the divine life-force present in the growing hair (so Orelli and others), or simply 'a rejection of the customs of civilized life as part of the worship of the God of battles and of the wilderness' (Sellin, *Geschichte des Volkes Israel*, p. 129). In either case the actual significance of the Nazirite institution is unaffected.

took forms similar to those of the 'battle ecstasy' found among other peoples—notably in the case of the Nordic 'berserker'.[1]

The Nazirite is, however, distinguished from the later prophetic 'men of the spirit' by being essentially a lone wolf: there is no scope here for the formation of any kind of religious group. It was of considerable importance for the spiritual experience of Israel, that right from the start the ecstatic effects of the spirit, as exemplified in their most striking exponents, in no sense entailed a mystical withdrawal, but were seen to be the means whereby mighty works might be done for the nation's God. It is, moreover, understandable, in view of the type of warlike operations in which these dedicated men engaged, that there should only have been scope for their activities during those wilder years which witnessed the conquest of Canaan, and when there was no organized force to undertake the defence of the country. With the emergence of the monarchy they disappear from the scene, or only continue to exist in a drastically modified form.

It is a remarkable fact—and a significant pointer to the strength of the ancient religion of Yahweh—that even the most violent ecstatic experience then known was successfully contained within the framework of that religion and accommodated itself to the pattern of the faith.[2] The miracle of ecstasy never acquired an independent importance, resulting in its being cultivated for its own sake; nor did it lead to a divinization of mere human beings, commemorating the mighty works of men as the focal object of interest. Here as elsewhere the overriding reality was man's firm relationship with a God who called his people to himself, and equipped them with the gifts and resources necessary to maintain their cause against the most powerful foes. Even in face of the dazzling exploits by which the nation was saved in its fiercest trials the concept of the hero remained something alien to its religion. Admiration and amazement were a tribute due to God alone for the way in which he empowered even feeble men by his spirit for the achievement of marvellous deeds.

---

[1] This might incline one to assume that the dedication by the hero's parents is in fact a secondary element added to the original narrative in the form of the childhood stories (Judg. 13 and I Sam. 1) in the interests of edification; in an earlier version the young man may have made a voluntary dedication of himself on reaching manhood (so Smend, op. cit., p. 153, with reference to Amos 2.11). Nevertheless, both forms may have existed side by side from an early stage.

[2] J. Hempel (Altes Testament und Geschichte, p. 58) has also stressed that there is no reason from the purely historical angle which would make this inevitable.

The direct significance of the Nazirites was their contribution to the strengthening of the sense of nationhood and of the religious basis on which that was built. They certainly did not a little to awaken Israel's sense of its distinctive character, and to lay forceful emphasis on the truth that the election of the nation by the jealous God entailed its separation from all things Canaanite. The Nazirites thus became a major factor in keeping the religion of Israel from drifting into a compromise with that of Canaan, and in urging it to assert itself and to develop to the full its unique character. In particular they animated and sustained the religious conception of war, and in this way afforded significant support to the third group of charismatics, the Judges, to whom we must now turn.

4. THE JUDGES

Under this title of 'judges' the book of that name—or more correctly the Deuteronomic redactor of the book—groups together the most diverse figures. He furthermore subordinates them to the quite unhistorical theory that the men and women so designated exercised from time to time over all Israel a rule whose legitimacy derived from divine authorization. In actual fact the stories of the Judges, once disentangled from the schematizing framework of the book, present us with Israelite leaders of very varied types, who exercised a greater or less degree of authority over the nation or merely over sections of it. Some of them have already been noted under the classifications 'seer' and 'Nazirite'. The third type consists of a kind of chieftains or petty princes, who achieved a distinguished political position by their prowess in war, but whose influence nevertheless seldom extended beyond the bounds of their own tribe. It is this third group which will be considered here, as being Judges in the true sense of the word.

It is indeed open to question whether they ought to be included among 'religious' leaders at all, for specifically religious activity is in their case manifestly of secondary importance. The primary motives which brought them to the front were various. It might be a matter of personal vengeance for some wrong which they had suffered, as was certainly the case with Gideon (Judg. 8.18 ff.) and very probably with Barak also (Judg. 5.12); or, as with Othniel (Judg. 3.10) and Ehud (Judg. 3.16 ff.), their work of liberation might be inspired by an outburst of national feeling provoked by enemy oppression; or finally, as in the case of Jephthah (Judg. 11.7 ff.), it might be simply the desire for the position of chieftain which took a hand in their decision. The only exception would be Joshua, in view of the fact that his position as leader of the tribes came to him by the authority of Moses, and that the conquest of Canaan was carried out as an explicitly religious task. The Shechem covenant (Josh. 24), which was solemnly concluded by him at the covenant sanctuary of Gilgal on the basis of the Book of the Covenant, once more made Israel emphatically aware that it constituted a Yahwist confederacy committed to the following of the covenant God, and that its life was subject to this God's jurisdiction.

But Joshua's position as leader was not heritable. Already in his lifetime it seems to have been divided among the local headmen; and after his death even the covenant sanctuary lost its central importance, sinking in the course of time to the status of an Ephraimite tribal holy place. Despite the fact, however, that Joshua's position was something unique, the religious effects of the emergence of political leaders in the ensuing period should not be underestimated. For even these men could not carry out their projects without adopting the slogan 'Yahweh and Israel'. They were forced into this policy not only by the close connection between national and religious freedom, between the concepts of Yahweh and of the nation, but also because the obligation to take part in wars against their common enemies could only be brought home to any considerable proportion of the Israelite clans and tribes, if it was invested with religious authority and subjected them to the sovereignty of the divine will. Hence the consequences of each new struggle for freedom unleashed by these princes or chieftains included not only a revival of national self-awareness among the Israelite peasantry, but also a rekindling of their sense of religious vocation. The mobilization of the host in the service of Yahweh impressed upon those who had become lukewarm and indifferent the fact that on the worship of this God depended the greatness and glory of the nation, and that these could not be shared with any other people. Consequently the coups effected by these tribal heroes not only gave the Israelite minority room to develop freely, but at the same time strengthened their spiritual powers of resistance by awakening and reinforcing their determination to assert their unique religious character. In this sense the dictum of Wellhausen[1] is

---

[1] *Israelitische und jüdische Geschichte*[7], 1914, p. 24 (cf. ET, *Sketch of the History of Israel and Judah*[3], 1891, p. 11).

perfectly correct: 'The camp, the cradle of the nation, was also the earliest sanctuary. There was Israel and there was Yahweh.'

The popular history testifies to this religious quality in the activity of those who, at a superficial assessment, were merely political leaders by linking their emergence with an endowment of the *rūaḥ* of Yahweh (cf. Judg. 6.34; 11.29).[1] Hence even in those figures who, to our way of thinking, are purely 'secular' it is the miraculous power of the spirit which is the real force behind those acts of redemption that preserve the life of the nation. There is no necessary contradiction between this idea and the fact that it was purely natural occasions that brought them to the fore. It was precisely in the unexpected success of their enterprises that the Israelite recognized the activity of a higher power; and by designating this power as *rūaḥ* he made his political leaders the direct servants of the national God and the instruments by which the latter exercised his sovereignty. This close association of political and military activity with the power of the divine Lord, even if it was fully accepted only in certain circles,[2] served again and again to make clear to men the emphatic way in which the whole of life was related to the one Yahweh, and decisively excluded the idea that political life might be isolated as a purely human preserve (cf. the fable of Jotham, Judg. 9). This formed one of the important presuppositions which later enabled the monarchy to win for itself an organic place in the structure of the national life. Again, even where endowment with the spirit played no part, as in the case of Barak, considerable stress is laid on the initiative taken by the God-empowered seer. Not until he has made sure that the divine power residing in her will be placed at the disposal of the covenant confederacy does the temporary tribal leader dare to commence the perilous struggle that is to carry him to the very heights of success. This partnership of seer and judge is probably not to be regarded simply as an isolated phenomenon (cf. later, Samuel and Saul): rather does it indicate a new way in which the frequent and volcanic outbreaks of nationalist fervour were made to subserve the national God. Even in the

---

[1] It is true that the few pieces of definite evidence against assuming that this spirit-endowment was part of the original picture might make one hesitant. Nevertheless, the fact that the same ideas are found in the case of Saul (I Sam. 10.6; 11.6) does not justify Smend (*op. cit.*, p. 62 n. 1) in excluding the relevant passages from the earlier narratives: only Judg. 3.10 comes from a later hand.

[2] This would seem to be implied by the relative paucity of passages directly attesting this belief.

disintegrated nation of the period of the Judges the common bond of the one Yahweh is still strong enough to prevent the individual tribal leaders from being ruled completely by mere tribal vanity, the mark of opposition and enmity. Instead, the effects of this bond reveal the power of that God who seeks to make of Israel a united People of God.

The result is that in many respects these warrior heroes, who often exercised their power only within very restricted limits, are able to furnish the colours for the portrait of the one great Redeemer who is to bring order out of life's chaos and set up Yahweh's rule over the sorely pressed land (cf. further ch. XI: The Fulfilment of the Covenant). If in contradiction of its original character the messianic hope at an early stage incorporated warlike traits in its picture of the Saviour-Prince, this is certainly a consequence of the redemptive acts of the Judges. Conversely, the popular historians decked these heroes in attributes which approximated them to that great Saviour-figure, and presented them as its prototype.[1] That such a stylizing of the figures of the Judges was, generally speaking, possible presupposes that these men were early regarded as instruments of Yahweh's dominion; and thus, despite the limited significance of their actual historical role, they became genuine mediators of the true conception of Yahweh.

5. NABISM

1. *The Basic Characteristics of the Phenomenon*

At the very time when the disorganized charismatic leadership of the nation was beginning to give way to one in which men of princely and regal dignity were confirmed in their position by a method of election and by arrangement with the elders of the people, *a new phenomenon* also emerged among the religious charismatics. This, the earliest form of prophetism, has been given the name of *nabism*. It at once attracted attention, and evoked criticism as well as enthusiasm; and to this day the most various assessments are made of it. Where one detects only heathen frenzy, another sees the stirring of forces belonging to the essence of Yahwism.

(a) *The Phenomenon of Group Ecstasy*

The novel and peculiar feature which immediately strikes one about this earliest prophetic movement is that of group ecstasy. So much at any rate

[1] Cf. ch. XI, pp. 475 f.

is undisputed. But though ecstatic experiences were already familiar among the seers—whole groups of human beings seized with frenzy, and even innocent bystanders drawn into the circle—yet these were things of which the earliest worship of Yahweh knew nothing.[1] Where then are we to find the reasons for this religious phenomenon? On closer inspection the *cultus*[2] at any rate calls for consideration as *the most likely sphere of its emergence*. The passage in which a *ḥebel*, that is to say, a band or troop of prophets, is mentioned for the first time in Israelite history also notes that this band was coming down from the place of sacrifice, and so had probably been taking part there in a sacrificial ceremony (I Sam. 10.5). Furthermore, cultic places are later recorded as sites of the prophetic guilds, e.g., Jericho (II Kings 2.5), Gilgal (II Kings 4.38), Ramah (I Sam. 19.18 ff.). Again, if one were inclined to draw conclusions about Israelite prophets from the activities of the prophets of Baal (I Kings 18.19 ff.), this would be yet another indication of their prominent part in sacrificial ceremonies.

The point has been made—and it is perfectly justified—that the full-scale cult of excitation with the aid of narcotics or physical self-torture was alien to Israelite custom. It is, therefore, perverse to argue from the mention of such things among the Canaanites (I Kings 18.28 f.), or in the degenerate prophetism of a later time (Isa. 28.7), to their importance for the earliest prophetism. On the other hand, there is one well-attested element of Israelite cultic ceremonial which could easily turn into ecstasy, and that is *the sacred dance*. This formed an indispensable part of divine worship. The force and energy with which it was performed were proportional to the seriousness with which the celebrants regarded it as part of their religious duties and the degree to which it provided an outlet for their enthusiasm for the God so worshipped (cf. II Sam. 6.5).[3] It is clear, moreover, that this cultic dance was practised by the *n°bî'îm* with particular abandon, and that music and song played a

---

[1] The isolated instance of the story in Num. 11.23 ff. is no proof to the contrary, since it has plainly been shaped by later views on spirit-possession.

[2] Cf. Duhm, *Israels Propheten*, 1916, pp. 82 f.; Hölscher, *Die Propheten*, 1914, pp. 143 ff.

[3] W. O. E. Oesterley (*The Sacred Dance*, 1923) has pointed out with great force the far-reaching significance of the cultic dance. The widespread existence of prophetic phenomena of an ecstatic kind shows these things to be a universal feature of human life. On this point cf. J. Lindblom, 'Zur Frage des kanaanäischen Ursprungs des altisraelitischen Prophetismus' in *Eissfeldt-Festschrift*, 1958, pp. 89 ff.; also M. Eliade, *Schamanismus und archäische Ekstasetechnik*, 1957.

great part in heightening and enlivening its intensity. The descriptions of similar customs in various other societies, such as those of the guilds of the Therapeutae recounted by Philo, or the dervish dances of both ancient and modern Islam,[1] or the religious hunting dances of the Basuto in Africa, all enable us to form a fair conception of this cultic practice and the way in which its performance can induce a state of frenzy.[2] Here religious feeling is directly at work, fashioning a form of expression through which God's power can be worshipped;[3] and the extent to which the clear conception and conscious understanding of God's nature either controls the form so created or is excluded by it depends entirely on the level to which the religion in question has attained. Moreover, there is plenty of evidence in the Old Testament that *the cultic dance was accompanied by hymnody* (cf. II Sam. 6.5; Isa. 30.29; Pss. 25.6 f.; 118.27 f.), and there would seem to be no reason to except the cultic dance of the prophets from this general pattern,[4] even if we had not the testimony of later generations, who delighted to put their most beautiful hymns into the mouths of the prophets (cf. Ex. 15; Judg. 5; Deut. 32 f.; II Sam. 23.1 ff.). It is a well-known fact, of course, that in frenzy singing passes into staccato invocations or even ends as inarticulate cries; but it makes all the difference, as regards the way in which ecstasy is understood in a particular religion, whether the initial intention of the ecstatic envisages the stage of semi-conscious or unconscious

[1]The adherents of the Islamic poet Djelal-eddin-Rumi (ob. 1273), known as *Mewlewis*, were 'characterized by a dance to the sound of the flute which formed part of their devotional exercises' (H. H. Schæder, art. 'Islam', *RGG*[2] III, col. 418. Cf. also D. S. Margoliouth, art. 'Mawlawiya' in *Enzyklopädie des Islam* III, pp. 486 ff., and the literature there listed).

[2]Cf. Oesterley, *op. cit.*, passim: also J. G. Frazer, *Folklore in the Old Testament*, 1918, vol. I, p. 224; vol. III, p. 277. An interesting study of the development of the cultic dance from the 'joyous leaping' which accompanied the act of homage and the offering of tribute, and which gave expression in violent movement to the intense mood of excitement, may be found in H. Kees, *Der Opfertanz des ägyptischen Königs*, 1912, pp. 110 ff. Also comparable is the manner in which the founder of the Hasidic movement, *Baal shem-tob*, received his revelations; his disciples were accustomed to accompany their devotions with violent movements of the body, which could lead to a kind of trance-state and which are reminiscent of those of the dancing dervishes. These movements are explicitly described as the outpouring from deep inward agitations of the soul, namely *kawwana*, devotion, and *hitlahabut*, enthusiasm.

[3]This, according to Oesterley, *op. cit.*, p. 22, is the original significance of the cultic dance.

[4]R. Hartmann (*Al-Kuschairīs Darstellung des Sūfītums*, 1914, pp. 131 f., 134 ff.) is informative and perceptive on the importance of music and song for the stimulation of ecstasy among the Sūfīs of Islam.

abandonment as an end in itself, or only as the highest means of expressing his praise or invocation of the deity. The rich early development of cultic poetry in Israel gave the most emphatic support to a positive interpretation of the significance of ecstasy.[1]

To this must, however, be added a second factor. The state of ecstasy enabled many *to impart information in the name of Yahweh* in a way which revealed the presence of a higher kind of knowledge. This demonstrated that frenzy was not merely a dissolution of normal consciousness, but an endowment with higher powers. The *nābī'* became the 'proclaimer'[2] *par excellence*, not only as the man who raised the acts of praising and calling upon his God to their highest power, but as the speaker empowered by God to reveal his hidden will. This constituted a further influence raising ecstasy to a higher plane than the merely egoistic one of an intensified experience of God[3] and enabling it to be understood as the loftiest worship of the national God, in virtue of which the *nābī'* becomes the man 'in whom the word of Yahweh is' (I Sam. 28.6; II Sam. 16.23, where 'to seek a word from God' is equivalent to 'to enquire of the prophets'; I Kings 17.24; Hos. 12.11).[4]

[1] H. Junker (*Prophet und Seher in Israel*) has strikingly demonstrated this point.

[2] This is the overwhelmingly probable signification of the word *nabi'*; cf. the discussion in H. Junker, *op. cit.*, pp. 27 f., 36 f., and H. H. Rowley, 'The Nature of Prophecy in the Light of Recent Study' in *The Servant of the Lord*, pp. 96 ff. W. F. Albright (*From the Stone Age to Christianity*, pp. 231 f.), followed by J. Lindblom (*op. cit.*, p. 102) interprets the word as 'the called' or 'the designated one'.

[3] 'The longing for a heightening of vitality in the atmosphere of the divine', Duhm, *Die Propheten*, p. 82.

[4] The absence of any clear distinction between specifically mystical ecstasy and the enthusiasm of the prophet has led to a good deal of misunderstanding of ecstatic nabism. It is of fundamental importance for the understanding of biblical religion to realize that not every ecstatic phenomenon can be regarded without question as the expression of a mystical type of spirituality. This distinction has been stressed in the case of the NT by Bultmann ('Das Problem der Ethik bei Paulus', *ZNW* 23, 1924, p. 134). If a religio-historical parallel to prophetic enthusiasm is required, then a better example would be the shaman of primitive religion rather than the mystics of India or Persia. For this reason it is also incorrect to characterize the ecstasy of the early prophets as a completely passive state, as does J. Köberle (*Die alttestamentliche Offenbarung*, 1908, pp. 113 ff.). Even the prophetic frenzy is dominated by an intention of self-surrender to the God of Israel; and the release of extraordinary spiritual powers in the course of this condition is so well attested even outside Israel, that it becomes quite impermissible to class the *nābī'* simply as an unconscious psychopath. Moreover, there is a third state between those of conscious activity and unconscious passivity, namely one in which the suspension of personal self-awareness is accompanied by a simultaneous sharpening of other mental forces under the guidance and impulse of a dominating will; and it is this which is characteristic of prophetic ecstasy. In more recent discussion on the subject

(b) *The General Religious Character of the Phenomenon*

Once the basic features of the earliest prophetism which have so far been mentioned are properly appreciated, a number of old controversies appear in a new light. Thus the fundamental connection between prophetic ecstasy and regular Israelite cultic practice clearly shows that the much-ventilated question, whether in this instance a Canaanite element foreign to Yahwism may not have forced its way into the religion of Israel, arises only from an unsound approach which attempts to treat the phenomenon in isolation.[1] In this case, however, we are concerned not merely with a feature common to Israel and the culture of Syria and Asia Minor alone, such as would call for an explanation in terms of borrowing. The ecstasy is an epiphenomenon of the cultic dance to be found in cultures of the greatest diversity and completely independent one of another, and as such must be regarded as something which in general is part of the basic endowment of all cultus, and only requires certain conditions to allow of its emergence. We are not dealing with something peculiar to the Nature religions, nor with a Yahwistic element, but with a primary expression of religious feeling, the significance of which is entirely determined by the character of the concrete form of religion in which it occurs. It is, therefore, equally impossible to subsume it under any general religious category, classifying it in terms of such pairs of opposites as 'physical versus moral', or 'psychic versus spiritual', as belonging mostly to the first member of each such pair. The decisive factor in any assessment must rather be its position in the totality of the particular relationship with God; and this may take the most varied forms.

Likewise it is easily demonstrable that group ecstasy, in spite of its fundamental connection with the cultic life of the congregation, affords no grounds for supposing that its exponents are to be regarded as cultic officials. This view has of late found a good deal of

---

of prophetism this point is being grasped more and more clearly: cf. the account by H. H. Rowley, *op. cit.*, pp. 117 ff., and that of O. Eissfeldt, 'The Prophetic Literature' in *The Old Testament and Modern Study*, ed. H. H. Rowley, 1951, pp. 137 ff. But extraordinarily enough this insight is still restricted to the field of classical prophecy.

[1] This point was rightly discerned by H. Junker, *op. cit.*, p. 102. A. Haldar made a start on breaking down this isolation, when he compared Israelite prophetism with kindred phenomena throughout the ancient East (*Associations of Cult Prophets among the Ancient Semites*, 1945, pp. 118 f.).

favour,[1] but it takes all too little account of the charismatic character of the ancient prophetic movement, and supplies a too far-reaching, and therefore untenable, explanation of the frequently attested association of the n·bî'îm with the cult. Consideration of the religio-historical material illustrative of group ecstasy, whether in the mystery-fellowships of primitive peoples, or among the dervishes of Islam, makes clear the unregulated charismatic character of the phenomenon; and this should from the very first have afforded a sufficient warning against any over-stressing of the cultic aspect of prophetism. However little reasonable it may be to dispute the development of a Temple prophecy properly so-called,[2] it is still quite definitely an unjustifiable simplification of the Old Testament material to classify nabism as a whole as a type of sanctuary officials. In particular this involves overlooking *the well-attested type of the wandering prophet*, exemplified in Elijah, but appearing also in the activities of such men as Amos and Ahijah, and indeed even of so early a figure as Samuel, if he can rightly be called a nābî'. The preference of these God-inspired men for sanctuaries as the stage on which to play their part is an obvious and natural one, and in no way entails their association with the cult personnel, any more than the Arabian *kahin* necessarily has to be associated with a sanctuary, despite the fact that he so frequently appears in the role of a priest or guardian of a holy place.[3] How little the appeal to individual passages affords conclusive proof of the cultic function of the n·bî'îm is brought out with especial clarity in the case of Elijah's erection of a Yahweh altar on Carmel.[4] If the illuminating exposition of A. Alt

---

[1] Since S. Mowinckel first presented this thesis in his *Psalmenstudien* III, 1932, pp. 16 ff., serious attempts have been made to establish it by A. R. Johnson (*The Cultic Prophet in Ancient Israel*, 1944), using the indications in the OT, and by A. Haldar (*op. cit.*) and I. Engnell (*The Call of Isaiah*, 1949), through the comparative study of religio-historical material from the Near East. Vital preparatory studies for this work were provided in the two volumes of collected papers, *Myth and Ritual* and *The Labyrinth*, which S. H. Hooke produced in 1933 and 1935 respectively in conjunction with other scholars.

[2] Cf. p. 332 below.

[3] Cf. J. Pedersen, 'The Role played by Inspired Persons among the Israelites and the Arabs', in *Studies in Old Testament Prophecy presented to T. H. Robinson*, ed. H. H. Rowley, 1950, pp. 127 ff. The place of the inspired poet and the speaker of words of power among the Arabian tribesmen should also be noted in this connection, *ibid.*, pp. 136 f.

[4] I Kings 18.17 ff. is an instructive example, which is also used by A. R. Johnson, *op. cit.*, p. 26, in conjunction with other passages, to prove his own argument.

is correct,[1] and this incident does concern the title of Yahweh, the national God, to a frontier zone of the state of Israel recovered from Tyrian possession—an issue decided under the guidance of the prophet by a sign from God—then the part played by the Yahweh altar is clearly one determined by the circumstances, and not just a feature intruded into prominence by a cultic official. The erection of the Yahweh sanctuary is an unmistakable expression of the exclusive sovereignty of the God of Israel over the contested area.

No more, however, is it possible to demonstrate a firm cultic connection in the case of those guilds of n·bī'īm who lived a community life. It is true that their colonies in many instances show a preference for important sanctuaries; on the other hand it is difficult to adduce Jericho (II Kings 2.5) as an example of this, and Samaria, where we meet the four hundred court prophets of Ahab (I Kings 22) seems not to have possessed any Yahweh sanctuary at all.[2] It is equally impermissible to conclude from the frequent mention of prophets and priests as authorities of parallel status for the revelation of the divine will, that these two classes of men occupied similar positions in the social structure. The emphasis laid on the importance of their decisions is equally understandable in terms of an extremely loose connection between the prophets and the sanctuary. Furthermore it should be noted that all thirty passages in which priest and prophet are closely coupled come from Jerusalem or Judah,[3] and it may well be that in this area special conditions obtained, possibly connected with the Deuteronomic reform.

Any discussion of this question must also take into account the ancient Israelite concept of rūaḥ, which is presented as the force inspiring the n·bī'īm.[4] Anyone who seriously considers the suddenness of the onset of this divine power, the precipitancy with which it overmasters the human personality and the absolute control to which it subjects it, cannot but have considerable misgivings about regarding the men who depended on this gift of grace, and who

[1] In the essay 'Das Gottesurteil auf dem Karmel' in the *Festschrift für G. Beer*, 1935, pp. 1 ff.
[2] Cf. A. Alt, *Der Stadtstaat Samaria* (Berichte über die Verhandlungen der sächsischen Akademie der Wissenschaften zu Leipzig, Philol.-hist. Klasse, vol. 101, fasc. 5), 1954.
[3] Cf. A. Jepsen, *Nabi*, 1934, p. 161.
[4] Cf. I Sam. 10.6, 10; 19.23; I Kings 18.12; 22.21, 24; II Kings 2.9 ff., 16; Hos. 9.7 etc.

were guided by it in such unpredictable ways, as cultic officials, and not primarily as charismatics.[1]

If then these mediators of the spirit of Yahweh did in fact contract firm connections with particular sanctuaries, this can hardly be regarded as an obvious norm for their way of life. Rather ought it to be seen as a deviation from their ordinary free mode of living, dictated by peculiar local and historical circumstances which nevertheless still left room for the continued existence of independent prophetic guilds and individual wandering prophets. Any assessment of the relation of the n'bî'îm to the cultus must therefore avoid any rigid preference for one solution to the exclusion of all others: what is needed is an elastic appreciation of the various potentialities of the new phenomenon.

As far as their being alien to the previous character of the ancient Israelite tradition is concerned, there is more than one piece of evidence to suggest that ecstasy was not felt to be a disruptive foreign body in the religion of Yahweh, but a new impulse bestowed by God. Even so incorruptible a critic of the religious practice of his time as Amos brackets the old prophets with the Nazirites as gifts of God, through whom Yahweh demonstrated his especial concern for Israel (2.11);[2] and the same is true of Hosea.[3] And not one of the later prophets in the course of their conflict with the guild-prophets of their day ever dared to do as they did, for instance, with the sacrificial cultus, and stigmatize the rise of the ecstatics as a degenerate Canaanitism,[4] which had nothing in common with the true nature of Yahweh.

It is important, moreover, to note the respects in which the great individual prophets of the later period knew themselves to be at one with the prophetic companies of the past. It was *the struggle against the religion of Canaan* and *the proclamation of the will of Yahweh* which united these men of God who in other ways were so very different. The very dress of the nābî', the hairy mantle,[5] acts as a

---

[1]Cf. pp. 319 f. below.

[2]It is, of course, quite illogical to limit the reference of this saying, as E. Fascher (προφήτης, 1927, p. 125) does, to men like Elijah and Elisha, and to exclude from its scope the bands of the n'bî'îm.

[3]Cf. Hos. 12.11. Hos. 12.14, regarded by many as not a genuine utterance of the prophet, connects the awakening of the prophets with the liberation from Egypt.

[4]Passages such as Hos. 7.14; Jer. 2.8; 23.13 do admittedly deal with syncretistic features of their own day.

[5]I Kings 20.38 ff.; II Kings 1.8; Isa. 20.2.

reminder of the opposition in which the servant of the God of Sinai must always stand to the religion of pagan culture with its flattery of the senses—an opposition which is confirmed by the later alliance with the Rechabites (II Kings 10.15 ff.). Further than this, however, everything that we hear of the most prominent exponents of nabism in the time of Saul and David bears witness to their participation in the national struggle and their jealousy for the purity of the ancient faith of Yahweh.[1] Finally, the activity of the n·bī'īm at the time of the wars of the Northern Kingdom against the Syrians allows us to draw important conclusions concerning the prophetic guilds during the hard days of the Philistine oppression. For it can hardly be denied that the emergence of group ecstasy precisely in that frightful time of crisis was no accident, but the result of an inner logic of events, even if this is not made explicit by the Old Testament narrators.[2] Today as in the past, periods of intense political and social pressure have been especially favourable to the emergence of such movements, because it is only by such explosive manifestations that religious feeling can acquire room to breathe. The kind of parallels that come to mind are the Flagellant movement in the fourteenth century, the Crusades or the rise of the Dervishes in Islam. In much the same way in Israel of the eleventh century BC conditions were ripe for the full development of something which was already potentially present in the regular cultus.

This shows, however, that in the early prophetic communities we are not concerned with a practice of ecstasy having as its goal a mystical union with God. The mystic has always sought for quietude and avoided religious controversy, for he has never found any difficulty in associating himself with the most diverse conceptions of God.[3] If the enthusiasts campaigned for Yahweh, this is by no means an obvious thing to have happened,[4] nor can it be regarded

[1] Cf. II Sam. 7.1 ff.; 12.1 ff.; I Kings 11.29 ff. In addition, the allusions to God's decisions in favour of David (I Sam. 20.14 f.; 22.5; 24.21; 25.30; 26.25; II Sam. 3.9 f., 18; 5.2) may be thought to point to the activity of the n·bī'īm on his behalf.

[2] This connection has constantly been urged in the past, even by exegetes who in other respects differed widely: cf. A. Kuenen, The Prophets and Prophecy in Israel, ET, 1877, pp. 41–44, 552–8; E. Kautzsch, Biblische Theologie des AT, p. 131; E. Sellin, Der alttestamentliche Prophetismus, 1912, p. 12.

[3] Cf., e.g., the mysticism of Islam: 'Sufism is more tolerant than any other regime; prominent Sufis have candidly placed all positive confessions of faith on the same plane', Chantepie de la Saussaye, Lehrbuch der Religionsgeschichte⁴, I, p. 747.

[4] Thus B. Duhm, Die Gottgeweihten in der alttestamentlichen Religion, 1905, p. 28.

more as an accidental consequence of political conflicts. Rather does
it point to the fact that the idea of Yahweh is inimical to all mysticism,
and seeks to subject the most exalted experiences of religious feeling
to the service of the divine Lord. This distinctness from mystical
ecstasy may in general be accurately summed up by designating the
prophetic experience as 'concentration-ecstasy' in opposition to
'fusion-ecstasy'.[1]

This impression is confirmed both by an enquiry into the nature
of the communion with God afforded by ecstasy and by a closer
consideration of the various forms of prophetic activity.

As regards the former, it is striking how strongly a sense of the
unconditional subordination of the prophets to God is brought out
in the Old Testament accounts. It has been suggested[2] that the
nābī' forced himself into the sphere of the divine, this opinion being
based on the use of dance and music as means by which ecstasy was
deliberately induced. The same line of thought regards those prophetic gifts bound up with ecstasy, namely clairvoyance, prediction
and healing, as endowments freely at the disposal and control of
their possessor.[3] It is, however, highly debatable whether such an
account rightly reflects Israelite thinking on the subject. Israel
knows nothing of the prophet's being able thus to gain the mastery
over God and to force his way into the divine world. Ecstasy with
all its consequences derives from a direct irruption of divine power,
namely rūaḥ, which overwhelms a man and takes him prisoner.[4]
External aids may certainly help to prepare a man for this condition,
but as far as religious experience is concerned they are not the true
cause of enthusiasm—they simply place a man in the right disposition to receive the spirit, which is itself absolutely autonomous in
its working and may even come upon particular men of God quite
unexpectedly.[5] Indeed, the Elijah stories rather give the impression
that its operations tend to the enigmatic and capricious, than suggest

[1] Thus J. Lindblom, 'Einige Grundfragen der alttestamentlichen Wissenschaft'
in Festschrift für A. Bertholet, 1950, pp. 325 ff.
[2] B. Duhm, Israels Propheten, p. 81.
[3] Thus A. R. Johnson, op. cit., p. 24.
[4] Special attention should be paid to the terms used to express this, all of which
stress the element of domination in the working of the rūaḥ: pā'am, to push, Judg.
13.25; ṣālaḥ, to rush into, or to be powerfully effective, I Sam. 10.6; 11.6; lābēš, to
put on like a garment, Judg. 6.34; hāyāh 'al, Judg. 11.29.
[5] In ch. XIII A (The Spirit of God) we shall have to discuss the fact that the
Old Testament accounts know nothing of any magical transmission by means of
sacramental rites.

that the spirit is in any way at the prophet's beck and call (cf. II Kings 2.10, 16 ff.). The prophets of whom we hear at a later time, whom familiarity with the miraculous has deprived of their sense of awe and who feel themselves to be autonomous possessors of the spirit (I Kings 22.24; Isa. 28.9; Jer. 23.21, 30 ff.) represent a different type. The fact that the prophet is asked for counsel on account of his special gifts does not mean that he can exercise free control over those gifts. Often enough he is not in a position to give the awaited answer[1]—a sign that he is dependent on the divine power which alone can equip him for his function.

But if, on the one hand, the emphasis is on the autonomous character of the power that causes the ecstasy, on the other, the fact that this power is clearly distinguished from Yahweh himself serves to keep alive a feeling for the distance between God and man, even in the case of this physically striking endowment with divine forces. A comparison with Greek prophecy, which exhibits similar features, brings out points of agreement and disagreement which make this clear. Even paganism possesses *the consciousness of the prophet's unconditional dependence on the God who inspires him*; this comes out clearly in the Greek tragedians.[2] But there is no realization that man is fundamentally different in kind, and that therefore the divine self-disclosure always confronts him as something objective, and not something to which man can be assimilated; for the Greek, the man favoured by God is possessed and filled by God himself. For the Hebrew *nābī'* this is unthinkable. It is not Yahweh, but only his spirit, which enters into man, and even that only for the time being. Thus all divinization of man is excluded. Even the man of God can only have a share in miraculous powers and superhuman knowledge because of the entry into himself of the wondrous living *materia* over which Yahweh alone has ultimate control.

(c) *The Effects of Spirit-possession*

Nevertheless, *the effects of spirit-possession* in many ways recall the pictures drawn for us by ethnologists and students of religion of those individuals in primitive religions who are 'endued with power'.

[1] I Sam. 28.6, 15; Jer. 28.10 f., 12 ff.; 42.4, 7. Cf. the way in which the Arab *'arrafa* waits upon the spirit of revelation (J. Pedersen in *Studies in OT Prophecy*, p. 133).

[2] Cf. E. Fascher, *op. cit.*, pp. 13 ff., 113. This too, moreover, warns us to guard against judging ecstasy over-hastily as a human method of taking possession of the deity.

For unveiling the hidden will of the gods and control over miraculous powers belong to the characteristic effects of 'power' as such. Nor can it be denied that many prophetic narratives, especially from the Elisha-cycle, give the miraculous power and mysterious knowledge of the prophet a kind of independent existence in their own right by presenting them as a quality inherent in him over which he exercises unrestricted control. Nevertheless, we may not leave out of account the constant correctives provided by expressions to the opposite effect, in which Yahweh appears as the Revealer and the Wonder-worker, even though we have to confirm that there has been some intrusion of magical or *mana*-type concepts into the veneration of the prophets as practised in many circles.[1] It is obvious that in such an outlook, not as yet purified by Yahwism, there lay a danger for the operation of the prophetic guilds; but it is equally clear that this danger was overcome by the ensuing subordination of even miraculous powers to the service which Yahweh demanded.

As far as supra-normal knowledge is concerned, one way in which the distinctive character of Yahweh prophecy makes itself felt is that the prophets use a simple and easily understandable form to convey their information.[2] Another, however, is *the strong pre-occupation with national concerns*, which imposes on the divine oracles of the prophets both a permanent form of control in the shape of public opinion and a weighty responsibility.[3] The *n·bī'īm*, just as much as

[1] Cf. on this point G. Fohrer, *Die symbolischen Handlungen der Propheten*, 1953, pp. 70 ff.

[2] Cf. also the remarks on p. pp. 301 f. above.

[3] Naturally this judgment only holds good for the prophetic movement as a whole. As far as the very beginning of nabism is concerned it may be thought better to allow for different possibilities. In fact for the very earliest period we have no direct evidence on the subject of prophetic oracles. Let it be admitted, therefore, without more ado, that it is conceivable, at least among certain groups of *n·bī'īm* and in many popular circles, that too marked a prominence was given to the circumstances of psychic stimulation, and that these were over-valued as manifestations of divine power without reference to the oracles communicated by these means. It is also perfectly natural that there should have been far less restraint on the momentum of mass-ecstasy as this burst forth at its emergence than after it had been gradually disciplined. It should also be noted that the most diverse natures are caught up in such a movement, and hence the most diverse phenomena can result from it in close juxtaposition, ranging from unbridled ferocity to spiritual control of even the most powerful emotion. But it would be just as wrong to rule out the later stage in favour of the earlier (a mistake made by the majority of more recent presentations) as to acknowledge only the existence of the higher form of ecstatic exaltation (an error into which both H. Junker, *Prophet und Seher*, and E. König, *Theologie des A T* [3,4], pp. 55 ff. [3,4], fall). If we cannot share the view that the sole object of ecstatic prophecy was simply religious delirium, we are brought to

the seers, were in this way constantly diverted from the peril of becoming absorbed in the petty daily affairs of individuals, and of making use of these for their own advantage, and were instead linked up with the living concerns of the nation. In conjunction with this *the concept of the national God* was able to develop its capacity of sharpening and purifying the conscience so as to turn the vision and attention of the prophet continually beyond the individual to the future of the nation. The most shining examples of this, in addition to Nathan and Ahijah, are Elijah and Elisha; and II Kings 5.20 ff. gives a striking instance of the sort of figure men imagined that a righteous prophet of Yahweh should be.

It is in this respect also that there is *the most profound distinction between nabism and those figures such as Cassandra who foretell the course of Fate.* There are certainly parallels to be drawn between the Israelite *nābī'*, communicating his *d·bar yhwh*, and the seer of Apollo, from whom a χρησμός may be obtained.[1] This is even more true of a type of prophecy which comes from a date around 1700 BC, and was discovered among the texts from the North Mesopotamian town

---

this conclusion by a consideration of the religio-historical parallels as much as by the observation of what can be learned from the first *n·bī'īm* to occupy positions of importance. Both the Sibyls and Bakides of Greece and the cultic ecstasy which makes its appearance in Byblos and of which we hear from Wen-Amon derive their special importance for the spectators from the communication of oracles. Moreover in Israel it is not only in the ninth century that *the word of Yahweh is in the mouth of the prophetic man of God* (I Kings 17.24), who is sought out at new moon and sabbath (II Kings 4.23), but the *nābī'* is already winning especial esteem in the time of David for the divine oracle which he conveys, as is shown in the cases of Nathan and Ahijah. It can hardly be correct to see in these spiritual leaders a type of 'man of God' quite distinct from the *nābī'*, when it is really only a matter of greater or lesser spiritual significance. (It should be remembered that Elijah includes himself among the *n·bī'īm* as one of them, I Kings 19.14; and in II Kings 2 he is also portrayed as standing in a very close relationship with them.) To do so one would also have to separate the great classical prophets from their less important spiritual cousins, to distinguish Jeremiah, for example, from a prophet like Uriah (Jer. 26.20 ff.), and to construct new categories for them all, which is clearly impracticable. Speaking of the complex character of the nabistic movement, G. Quell (*Wahre und falsche Propheten, Versuch einer Interpretation* (Beiträge zur Förderung christlicher Theologie, 46.1), 1952, p. 139) describes it as a 'chaotic formation' ('inkohärentes Gebilde'); and in actual fact there is no serious objection to thinking of even the many nameless *n·bī'īm* as prophetic men of God, though their judgments may more often have taken the form of aphorisms combined with the hymns to Yahweh the Judge and Redeemer. However, even if one cannot share this assessment of the first stages of nabism, it is impossible to come to any other conclusion about the total phenomenon and its effectiveness.

[1] Cf. E. Fascher, *op. cit.*, p. 150.

of Mari. It is a message from the ministers (whether priestly or lay is uncertain) of the gods Hadad and Dagan, and brings to the king of Mari the divine commands, expressing in energetic language reinforced from time to time by threats the definite requirement that the sovereignty with which he has been entrusted shall be withdrawn. In its outward form this message echoes the tone of Old Testament prophetic oracles.[1] But the distinction, which is already to be observed in the Israelite n‛bî'îm, not just in the great prophets, lies in *the reference of everything to a divine will which applies to a whole people* and creates for it an inwardly coherent history.

This influence of the will of God as revealed in the history of the nation on the oracle-giving of the prophets is apparent even in those periods which afford us no direct evidence of words from God through the prophets. Our assurance of this is the fact that the prophetic enthusiasm, by the very way in which it emerges, is inseparably connected with the praise of the God who is Lord of history (cf. p. 312 above), and this connection is in the course of time increasingly strengthened and extended. Recent study of the Psalms has rightly drawn attention to the original function of the majority of the Psalms as cultic hymns,[2] and has pointed out the taking over of the prophetic idiom in this religious poetry.[3] Steps had already been taken at an early stage to incorporate the n‛bî'îm into the regular cultus, so that through their intercession and the communication of oracles they might work alongside the priests; and in the post-exilic community they were included in the Temple singers; and these facts presuppose a long-standing practice of religious hymnody in their guilds. Furthermore, *the communication of oracles*, which from the very first was of great importance, normally *made use of poetic form*, and exhibits close relationships with the hymn. Just as the oracles of Balaam (Num. 23 f.) and the 'last words of David' (II Sam.

---

[1]On the subject of these interesting evidences of a self-conscious cult prophetism in Mari cf. A. Lods, 'Une Tablette inédite de Mari, intéressante pour l'histoire ancienne du prophetisme sémitique' in *Studies in OT Prophecy*, pp. 103 ff.; and W. von Soden, 'Verkündung des Gotteswillens durch prophetisches Wort in den altbabylonischen Briefen aus Mari' in *Die Welt des Orients* I, 1950, pp. 397 ff.

[2]S. Mowinckel has done so with especial energy in his *Psalmenstudien* III, IV and VI, 1922–23. The form-critical study of the Hexateuch by von Rad, Weiser, Noth and others has thrown new light on the relations between the Psalms and the cultus of the covenant festival: cf. A. Weiser, *Die Psalmen übersetzt und erklärt* (Das Alte Testament Deutsch, 14/15), 1950, pp. 10 ff. (ET in preparation).

[3]Cf. Pss. 2.7–9; 20.7–9; 21.8–13; 32.8 f.; 40.4; 49.4; 50; 75.3–6; 82.2–7; 85.9 ff.; 95.7 ff.; 110 etc.

23.1 ff.) attest this for the earliest period, so also *many weal-prophecies in the prophetic books*, which either derive directly from the *n'bî'îm* or arise partly from the older prophetic preaching, bear witness to it in later times. *The appearance of the classical prophets in the sanctuary as the authoritative purveyors of divine declarations*, which are delivered in poetic form, clearly follows the custom of their predecessors; otherwise Amaziah could never have addressed Amos, when the latter was delivering his message from God in Bethel, without more ado as a professional *nābî'*. Another witness to the prominence given in the prophetic guilds to working through the word, whether this be a message from the national God or a testimony to his acts, is *the Elohist narrative*. Confessedly emanating from prophetic circles, the wealth of poetry in this work not only corroborates anew the practice of nationalist-religious poetry among the *n'bî'îm*, but indicates further that *the recounting of Yahweh's acts in the past* was employed in these circles as an important method of propaganda. The earlier view, that the ancient Israelite narrative books were composed from the sheer joy of writing and were intended for assiduous readers, may be regarded as disproved, now that it can be seen that these books had an overriding practical purpose, the dissemination of particular ideas through the agency of travelling story-tellers. The current assumption of whole schools of narrators can only serve to confirm this; and the detection of the previous stages, through which the composite narrative has passed, makes it clear that the conjecture is justified which traces the practice of sacred history in the prophetic circles back to an extremely early period.

All this points to the fact that the early prophetic movement was determined through and through by the distinctive character of the Yahweh religion as a historical faith, and that in spite of the similarity in outward form it was fundamentally distinct from the parallel phenomena among the non-Israelite peoples. *The powerful interaction of prophecy and history* gave the ecstatic movement a pronounced concern for the service of the nation.

Does this mean that *the vision of the goal of the nation's history* in a final Golden Age had also been opened up at this stage? Here too it is difficult to arrive at any certain conclusion on account of the shortage of direct evidence; and it is therefore understandable that wherever early prophetism has been regarded as the product of an emotional mysticism lacking in moral motive, it has also been denied any expectation of a salvation in the context of history. If this is not the case, however, it is at least possible to discover the same presumptions in favour of the proclamation of a coming Age of Salvation as in the case of the seers.[1] And the available evidence does point throughout in this direction. Both the 'last words of David' (II Sam. 23.1–7) and the promise of Nathan (II Sam. 7.8–16)[2] argue for the acceptance of the ancient hope by the prophets; as regards the later period, the so-called 'royal' hymns of the Psalter, in particular Pss. 2; 45; 110, which portray the king in the lineaments of the eschatological Saviour-Prince and are marked by an entirely prophetic character, prove that in nabism were to be found the promoters and proclaimers of the coming messianic dominion. Moreover, who can have kindled and spread the glowing hope of salvation entertained by the people, to which Amos (5.18) bears witness, if it were not the prophetic bands who summoned men to battle for Yahweh and extolled the greatness of the national God?

Furthermore, a glance at *the related phenomena in the history of religions* shows that it is precisely the ecstatic mass-movement which provides fertile soil for exalted futurist expectations.[3] The forces released in such a situation encourage men to hope for a new and deeper communion with the deity, a mightier manifestation of the divine works of power. The mysticism which strives after the most intimate connection with the Godhead frequently follows in the train of ecstatic movements and reveals their deepest longing—as in the case of the Dionysiac frenzy in Greece, and of the enthusiasm for the Crusades or the Flagellant movement in Germany. On the other hand the Dervish movement in Islam developed its strongest impetus either in conjunction with the Mahdist hope, or more generally with the expectation of a more perfect establishment of the dominion of Allah. Those who stress the similarity between Israelite nabism and related movements in the history of religions ought to be the first to be alive to these spiritual concomitants. It is quite natural that in a religion so voluntaristic in character as that of Israel the yearning for a new divine revelation should be expressed in forms different from those that obtained elsewhere. It was not possible that this should emerge in mystical guise; it was bound to

---

[1] Cf. p. 300 above.
[2] It should not be necessary to emphasize that the working-over of this speech in the style of a later time is no argument against its historicity.
[3] E. Sellin has pointed this out with emphasis (*Der AT Prophetismus*, pp. 15 f.).

take the form of a religio-nationalist expectation. The pattern of any strong futuristic expectation which was to accord with Israel's religious thought was bound to be that of a new alliance with God analogous to those of the Sinai revelation and the conquest of the Promised Land, that is to say, one involving both a renewal of the inward state of God's nation and its outward strengthening by way of victory in war, occasionally expanded and embellished in glowing colours under the influence of the primal concept of Paradise.[1] A new form of this world, a world restored to the splendour of the garden of God, emerged as the goal of redemption from the present crisis; and in the ardour of enthusiasm which informed the prophetic brotherhoods this goal acquired its professional exponents who did not fail to make an impression on the mass of the people at large. The national resurgence under the youthful Saul, and later under David, was carried along and made possible by the force of this hope.[2]

The inner coherence of the expectation of salvation with the essential nature of the prophetic movement may be illuminated from a new angle by going on to examine the second distinctive characteristic of these men endowed with the spirit, and the one which after their supernatural knowledge established their authority —*their wonder-working powers*. It has rightly been pointed out[3] that the operations of the spirit lie first and foremost in the sphere of the miraculous. Because the *nābī'*, seized by the spirit, was drawn into this sphere, he obtained a share in higher powers, which in turn flowed forth from him and enabled him to perform miraculous deeds

[1] For further discussion of this point, cf. ch. XI below.

[2] One would be quite willing to concede at this point that as well as the exponents of an enthusiastic futuristic hope and a yearning for God which soared above space and time nabism also included other currents of thought. These were content with the immediately attainable aims of practical politics, and envisaged the realization of the religious ideal in the sovereignty of a Yahweh cult purified from all Canaanite influences in accordance with the strict and ancient customs of the fathers. After the stabilization of the political situation under a strong monarchy it was these tendencies which became dominant, while the sparks of the eschatological hope continued to glimmer under the ashes, only to burst into flame at the draught of later fierce conflicts. In addition the monarchy as the promoter of the national and religious ideals saw to it that enthusiasm found a new mode of existence in the glorification of the king as the fulfiller of all popular expectations. In spite of all this, however, it remains true that the powerful re-direction of the whole religious mood toward a new and unprecedented futurist form of the relationship with God, such as may be observed in the emergence of the classical prophets, must be regarded as one of the most important effects of nabism.

[3] Cf. Gunkel, *Die Wirkungen des Geistes*, 1899, pp. 9 f., 15 ff., 31.

of succour. In this way he became *the mediator through whom the divine life made its way into a world otherwise sealed against it.* In him men had the evidence of their senses to show what it meant when God visited his people, and they were never tired of recounting the stories of acts of this kind. Undoubtedly this brought with it the acute danger of depending on the miracle-man and of setting in motion a personal cult, such as may be found even today in the popular practice of the East. The Elisha stories in particular give grounds for suspecting this. Taken as a whole, however, the predominant impression given by the miracle stories presents the man of God as *the helper of his people,* not as one who works miracles for effect or as demonstrations of power; and in his prayer to Yahweh they show the limits of his miraculous power (I Kings 17.20; II Kings 4.33). Thus, behind the wonder-working *nābi',* men can discern the directing and succouring hand of his God (cf. I Kings 17.16 ff., 24; II Kings 2.13 ff.; 7.1; 4.1 ff.), even where it is not a matter of contending for Yahweh and his exclusive worship (cf. e.g. I Kings 18.39; 20.28; II Kings 5.8 ff.; 6.15 ff., etc.). In this way, moreover, in the prophets essential ingredients of the longed-for age of salvation become matters of present experience; their existence already affords *a pledge of, and preparation, for the new age,* in which God dwells in the midst of his people and places his miraculous power at their disposal without restriction (cf. Zech. 12.8). All the more must the ordinary man have tended to see in these men the coming of the great final salvation.

Furthermore, the *nābi',* by *the whole outward way of life* which he adopted, was already preaching the discontinuance of the present order, and the irruption of the great new age to come, to wait for which was the only thing that mattered. For despite the scandal so often provoked by their noisy, tempestuous advent, these men, who abandoned ordinary life and lived exclusively for religion, made a deep impression on the mass of the people. By walking out of the circle in which they had lived hitherto, by making palpable, both in their dress and in their living a secluded life in special colonies, their opposition to any kind of comfortable worldliness or cultivation of self-interest, so that they might dedicate themselves utterly to the service of the religious idea, they brought home once more with unmistakable severity to a nation that had become flabby and soft, that 'life is not the highest good', and that there is something greater than earthly progress and the enjoyment and multiplication of worldly goods. What a profound effect *such a protest against the over-valuation of material goods* was able to exert on the religious life of a nation may be seen not only in the monasticism of the Middle Ages and similar ascetic movements, but also in a phenomenon like John the Baptist, who by returning to the manner of life of the earliest prophetism gave palpable emphasis to the words he had to speak. It is true that in certain circumstances the outward change of a way of life may be nothing else than 'running away from the world as fast as your legs will carry you' (Duhm), instead of an interior rising above it. But when a movement is spiritually active in other respects, to look no further than its external practice is to misjudge the force of this symbolic language.

For with this outward separation from the way of life of their contemporaries went *a strong and active influence on their environment.*

According to the narratives of the Elisha-cycle a kind of pastoral concern for individuals among their fellow-countrymen seems to have been practised in prophetic circles. Like the Indian *guru* or the Arabian *sheikh* the prophet was called upon in every kind of crisis and approached for his advice. He is the great intercessor who can intervene decisively even in the circumstances of individual life. But his activity was even more noticeable among the nation at large. It has rightly been pointed out that, in contrast to the more passive attitude of the men of God of the older sort, who apart from the regular gatherings of the people and festivals only exerted themselves to deal with special requests, the religious leaders are now characterized by their taking the offensive in their work, a hitherto unusual trait. We constantly encounter the exponents of nabism intervening energetically in the course of events, and championing the righteous will of their God without thought for personal risk against all hostile powers, right up to the king himself. Suffice it to recall the names of Nathan, Ahijah, Elijah or Micaiah ben Imlah. The profound effect of this proceeding, which stirred the nation to its innermost depths and led to conflicts of unprecedented violence and passion and put the whole existence of the nation to the hazard, is beyond dispute. But only if these effects are considered in the context of the total picture of the movement can we discern the force which determined all these forms in which its life found expression, and which gave to every detail its ultimate meaning—the effort to bring about the unlimited sovereignty of God. All the evidence goes to show that first and foremost *the mighty dynamic of group-ecstasy* in Israel was ultimately at the service of the Lordship of the God revealed in history, however many of its associated phenomena may shift kaleidoscopically through the colours of a naturalistic, sensual, cultic religiosity.

II. The Theological Significance of Nabism

(a) Consequently it is now possible to assign to nabism its place in the religious history of Israel, and to define more closely its distinctive theological significance within the Old Testament revelation. On the one hand nabism can be seen to be *a powerful reaction of the religion of Yahweh against the whole process of the Canaanization of the Israelite spirit*; in other words, it is *a great new surge forward of the revelation of Yahweh in Israel*, such as had not occurred since the time of Moses. The new element which distinguished the movement, the group character of its religious apprehension, empowered it with an intensity and scope of operation such as the individual men of God had never possessed. The nation as a whole is pointed to the categorical demands of its God with an urgency which could not be disregarded; it is called to resolute and conscious self-surrender to the purposes of its God, and confronted with the seriousness of its decision. The major crises of the nation's public life, from the division of the Davidic kingdom to the fall of the Omrid dynasty, were given their religious interpretation by the words and actions of the prophets, and by the violence and profundity of the upheaval which they caused assisted *the attempt to weld the mass of the people into a new religious unity*. If we reflect how acutely the absorption of whole sections of the Canaanite people and the far-reaching amalgamation with Canaanite religion and culture was imperilling the continued existence of Israel's unity as a nation and its fundamental spiritual character, to such an extent that there was imminent danger that these would be merged in the civilization of the Near Eastern world, then we shall see more clearly the scale of this gigantic struggle for the rebirth of the nation on a religious basis.

(b) But this struggle was directed not only against those influences breaking in from without, the Nature religion and the culture that was bound up with it, but also against the perversion of the original character of Yahwism by the national and religious institutions which were being formed in its own bosom. For the age of prophetism was also the period in which new forms of social life of a political and religious nature were either emerging for the first time or were first fully revealing their true character. To the first group belong *the monarchy and the various forms of the social organization of the state* —the administrative district, the bureaucracy, the city as opposed to the province, international alliances both political and commercial—*which were being consolidated in more or less close association with it.* The more powerfully the forms of political life developed and, in conjunction with the political culture of the Near East, laid claim to independent status in the whole life of the nation,[1] the more doubtful became their subordination to the religious and moral standards of the faith of Yahweh. The revolutions, conspiracies and civil wars; the reckless expenditure of the national resources on dynastic ends and unscrupulous power politics; the abuse of their position by the king and his officials in their dealings with the citizens; the commercial exploitation of the distressed condition of the peasantry by the wealthy towns; the one-sided concern for material advantage in relations with neighbouring states; all these phenomena were already on the increase in the period of early prophetism, and all were symptoms of *a gradual dissociation of the political institutions from responsibility to the national God* and the standard of his will. In the prophetic movement, which clashed violently with all these manifestations of deliberate power politics, the religion of Yahweh gave effective expression to its own essentially dominating and exclusive nature in face of these steadily consolidating social institutions. This was achieved partly by insisting that the national struggle for freedom should form part of the service of Yahweh, and eschew egoistic aims (cf. the wars against Amalek, I Sam. 15, and against Aram, I Kings 20.35 ff.), and partly by coming out in open opposition to the autocratic monarchy, if need be even to the point of smashing the instrument of its power (cf. Elijah and Ahab, Elisha and Joram).

As regards the monarchy, moreover, the conflict, whether consciously or unconsciously, becomes *the rejection of a conception of religion diametrically opposed to prophetism,* a conception which sought to confine the faith of Yahweh within the rigid limits of the official religious and cultic system, and so to prevent its effect from reaching the *whole* life of the nation, i.e. to render it ineffective in this respect. From the time of Solomon onwards, even the Israelite king was increasingly surrounded by *the aura of Near Eastern divine kingship.*[2] The combination of primordial *mana*-type concepts of the chieftain

[1] Cf. the fine survey of the life of the Israelite state in Galling, *Die israelitische Staatsverfassung,* 1929.
[2] Cf. below ch. IX, 2, pp. 436 ff.

endowed with 'power'[1] with the attributes of divine sonship claimed by the Great King sought to effect a fundamental alteration in the Israelite idea of the king. This threat to secularize the Yahweh religion found an inexorable opponent in that radical subordination of the whole of life to the Lordship of Yahweh for which the prophets fought—an opponent so ruthless, indeed, that it was prepared to jeopardize the very existence of the nation rather than betray the longed-for kingdom of God to the pretensions of a 'divine kingship'.

This resulted, however, in battle being joined on yet another front with a class now rising to power for the first time, namely *the priesthood*. King and priest were united by a common interest in the stability and continuity of settled forms of community life. Hence for the most part they got on together extremely well, so long as it was a matter of repressing and disciplining those forces in the national life which were incalculable and capricious, and of establishing permanent organization. As in other nations, so also in Israel the priesthood came to power with the rise of the monarchy. Moreover, the king's religious pretensions to being the fount of absolute authority in his role as son of God, and to concentrating the whole life of the nation on the service of himself, could be more easily combined with the religious practice of the priesthood than with that of the prophets. All that the former required was a nominal subjection to the God whom it represented, and a guarantee that the cult would be sumptuously maintained.[2] As a result of this close association with the political power, and a consequent dependence upon it even in the religious sphere, the priesthood came more and more to stand at the opposite pole from the prophetic movement. That the two were thus opposed in principle did not emerge clearly all at once; at first there was still room for co-existence, and each was open to influence from the other. Not for nothing did prophetism share a common origin with the cultus. Nevertheless, *the radicalism of the prophetic attitude to the sovereignty of God* was bound to obstruct the tendencies of the priesthood, especially at the great national sanctuaries. For prophetism, with its unintimidated criticism of the political establishment, and its call to battle against every encroachment of the power of the state on the religious institutions of the people of God, proclaimed the God of Israel as unconditionally independent of all state 'protection' or subservience to the political

---

[1] Cf. Pedersen, *Israel* I–II, pp. 182 ff. and elsewhere.
[2] For further consideration of this point cf. ch. IX.1.II, pp. 402 ff. below.

order. The whole prophetic movement, which on principle subjected all political and national considerations to the sovereign will of the nation's God, inevitably acted as a vociferous protest against any subordination of religion to the programme of the civil power. Hence it was continually recalling the priesthood to a sense of its most important function, that of guardian of the laws and of the Yahweh covenant. That the prophetic struggle did occasionally have an effect on the priesthood may be seen in the measures taken by the Jerusalem High Priest Jehoiada under the influence of the Jehu revolution staged by the prophets (II Kings 11).

Furthermore, in opposition to the veneration of sacred objects and the conception of physically mediated sacramental grace which bulked so large in priestly religious practice, the emergence of prophetism meant that *the idea of the God-dominated individual replaced all technical and impersonal methods of union as the supreme fact of the religious life.* The more it was taken for granted that early prophetism should take part in the cultic practice of sacrifice and the worship of the altar, the more decisively these things became means to one end—the acknowledgment of Yahweh as sole Lord by a personality whose life was completely dependent on God (cf. Elijah on Carmel).

This personal element in man's relationship with God is also implied quite essentially by the emphasis on the prophet as charismatically endowed in contrast to those who were merely religious functionaries.[1] The individual who belongs to the priestly class is committed to the traditional stock-in-trade of the whole system, and so tends to experience relationship with God more as a matter of mastering a whole series of rules and ordinances and institutions, an essentially technical process demanding no readiness for personal decision. It is the latter, however, on which all the emphasis is laid, when it is a question of the individual's experience of the power of the *rūaḥ*. Further to this point, the priest's increasingly pronounced sense of the importance of his office carried with it a growing danger of superficiality in the feeling for the gulf between man and God, and the presumption of a legitimate right on man's part to exercise control over the divine. By contrast, in the case of the prophets the coming and going of the endowment and operations of the spirit ensured that their fundamental feeling should be one of constant dependence on a divine power quite outside human control.

[1] This is not to overlook the gradual diminution of the charismatic element, a point which will be discussed below.

In all these ways the prophetic movement proved itself a powerful counteractive to the particular dangers of priestly supremacy, the tendency to nationalize and monopolize the worship of Yahweh and to identify it with its sensible expression. Hence it formed the most effective instrument in the hand of God for giving renewed force to the basic character of his revelation in the altered circumstances of a settled and politically mature people, and for opposing it to all the other forces in the national life.

III. *The Degeneration of Nabism*

We are afforded negative confirmation of the above summary of nabism's importance in the development of the Yahweh religion to conscious individuality in the midst of an increasingly powerful national culture, when we go on to consider the reasons for the decline and fall of this important movement. For in so doing it will be seen that these reasons consisted essentially in *an assimilation of prophetism to the forms of social culture* with which it ought to have been in conflict.

The strength and distinctive character of the prophetic movement rested in large measure on its charismatic nature. It was its immediate experience of divine power and endowment which gave it the impetus to attack that subtle humanization of the divine-human relationship which sought to turn it into an institution standardized and regulated by the state, and bound up with tradition and custom, popular usage and practice, office and a position of authority. This force of religious spontaneity was, however, jeopardized as soon as we arrive at *the formation of a distinct professional class*, a prophetic guild, such as was already beginning to affect the character of nabism in the time of Elijah. It is quite true that even in this form the power of the exceptional can predominate, and men of very varying backgrounds can be stimulated to break with the past and surrender themselves to new ways of life. In general, however, the more fluid character of the movement, constantly attaching itself to, or dissociating itself from different strata of society, gradually comes to an end, and is replaced by the regular accession of new adherents. Behind this lurks the danger that the exceptional will be transformed into the accepted, that violent decision in favour of something new and hitherto unknown, desiring to set at defiance all established custom, will be replaced by the harmless choice of a new profession. Routine is substituted for charisma, group conformism and the technique of oracle-giving for inner compulsion. The soaring and straining and striving after broad and lofty aims flags, and petty purposes, the egoistic interests of the group and the individual, come to the fore.

This gradual metamorphosis, by which spirit-filled dynamism becomes the businesslike operation of a spiritual trade or mechanism, has already been described often enough. But in so doing little notice has been taken of the fact that what wrought the transformation was, at bottom, *the influence of those religious groups opposed to nabism both in their structure and their spirituality*. Nevertheless, it is in fact in the assimilation of prophetism in character and method to these, its natural enemies, that the real tragedy of the progressive suffocation and ineffectiveness of the whole movement is to be found. To put it theologically, the supreme and exclusive character of the Yahweh religion was more and more sacrificed by those who should have been its champions to *the independent value of the professional religious organization*, which now allied itself to the established guardians of the popular faith. This desertion to the side of the official custodians of the holy took the form, *vis-à-vis* the priesthood, of *a ready acquiescence in the formation of Temple prophecy*. This was incorporated into the regular cultus, and made the prophetic proclamation of the divine will the function of a cultic official, who gave his liturgically pre-scribed message at the point allotted to him in the service. There can be no doubt that this function is directly connected with the long-standing practice of singing the praises of Yahweh in hymns at the cultic festival. Moreover, the watering down of true prophetic utter-ance to a priestly exhortation in the guise of prophecy[1] did not necessarily and in all circumstances constitute a betrayal of genuinely free inspiration, being its secondary effect. For this reason the classical prophets never protested against this form of the activity of the *nābī'*. The real danger lay primarily in something else that went with this, namely *the development of a sense of office and power* which believed itself capable of controlling the divine revelation, and sought to be lord over the Word. This disappearance of the sense of the divine message as something extraneous to man and objective, and which only the man entrusted with it by the sovereign operation of God would dare to proclaim, brought upon nabism its greatest guilt—that of an increasing failure in its principal task, because it was no longer aware of the difference between the Word of God and human wishful

[1] Cf. the Psalm passages listed above at p. 322, n. 3.

thinking. It is manifestly to this point that *the keenest protests of classical prophecy* are directed. When Isaiah is drawing a line between himself and the Temple prophets, the thing that he pillories is their pride in the technical virtuosity with which they control their oracles, even believing that they can give correct guidance when their senses are befuddled with wine (Isa. 28.7, 9).[1] It is against this impudent confidence in their trafficking with the Word of God that Jeremiah also directs his attack in his famous reckoning with the n*bī'īm in the twenty-third chapter of his book. The man who has to do with Yahweh's mighty Word (v. 29) can only undertake his task in fear and trembling, in constant self-judgment (vv. 15, 19), in absolute obedience, in the renunciation of all self-will (vv. 21 f., 32). Those who in presumptuous confidence desire to control Yahweh's Word (v. 18) are wantonly blinding themselves to the nature of their God (vv. 23 f.), and invoking his judgment upon them. In addition to this wrong attitude it is patent that Yahweh's Word is being exploited for human ends (vv. 14, 17, and cf. Jer. 6.13); indeed, it is mixed up with lies, and darkened with obscure dreams (Jer. 5.31; 23.26 f., 32); nor is there any criterion by which it may be distinguished from the desires of national power (Jer. 14.13 ff.; 23.14, 17: similarly Ezek. 13.3, 6 f., 16).[2] With as much seriousness as Jeremiah, and possibly in collaboration with him, Deuteronomy subjects the prophet to the authority of the Word with which he has been entrusted (Deut. 18.20), and threatens him with death, should he add to it anything of his own. In Deut. 13 the exclusive relationship of Yahweh with Israel constitutes the axiomatic standard for the prophetic message, and is not to be questioned simply because the prophet can demonstrate signs and wonders (v. 3). In its ultimate purpose this judgment is in full accord with the statements of Jeremiah establishing Yahweh's saving will as the absolute and supreme tribunal, from the jurisdiction of which no prophet can exempt himself in order to claim an independent authority based on his sense of prophetic office and

[1] The interpretation of this passage which sees in the allusion to their professional conduct a displacement of the real issue by the n*bī'īm themselves (Duhm, Guthe) fails to do justice to the deepest point of contrast between Isaiah and his opponents.

[2] As Johnson (*The Cultic Prophet*, p. 42) has also emphasized, Jeremiah is not denying that the n*bī'īm can utter genuine words from Yahweh; what he is attacking is the abuse of this gift. On the subject of distinguishing false from true prophecy, cf. von Rad, 'Die falschen Propheten', *ZAW* 51, 1933, pp. 109 ff.; K. Harms, *Die falschen Propheten*, 1947; G. Quell, *Wahre und falsche Propheten*, 1952.

power. No wondrous dreams can dispense a man from earnest obedience to the moral will of God (Jer. 13.5 f.).[1]

From another aspect we see the original basis of legitimation purely by charismatic endowment being abandoned in favour of *close association with the monarchy*, and adaptation to its methods and requirements. It is quite true that, in theory, the 'court prophets' no more disown the original task of prophetism than do those of the Temple. The more definitely the gift of prophecy was related from the very first to public concerns, the more readily must the *nābī'* have sought, when opportunity offered, to control the head of the state and to be able to guide him in his undertakings by means of a right discernment of the will of God. The attitude of Elisha, now the king's ally, now his sworn opponent, illustrates the range of possibilities open to the court prophets. It has rightly been stressed that the four hundred prophets of Ahab need not in every instance have been lying prophets.[2] Nevertheless it is true that, in general, when nabism became a highly regarded and regularly consulted political tribunal, it came under *strong pressure from the national will to power* embodied in the monarchy; and the successful maintenance of its own integrity must have become all the more difficult, the more strongly the inflated numbers of the prophetic guild were influenced by their material dependence on the favour of the king, and the more resolutely the latter moved toward Oriental despotism. What men wanted from the prophet was the word of power which would bring about the *šalōm* of people and state without imposing hard and fast limits on political action in the name of Yahweh's moral demands (Jer. 23.17). There was here a real danger that undertakings called for by dynastic interest would be justified by identifying them with Yahweh's holy war, and that ruthless imperialist policies, which could be forwarded only at the cost of the nation's internal well-being, would be exalted as pious zeal for the greatness of the national God. It is food for thought that Ahab, who had been so vigorously opposed by Elijah on account of his internal policies, could always find prophets, quite apart from the four hundred already mentioned, who were prepared to support his warlike schemes (cf. I Kings 20.13, 22, 28), and only reproached him for his inadequate exploitation of his victory. The extent to which

---

[1] So also Fascher, προφήτης , pp. 136 f. Cf. further von Rad, *Das Gottesvolk im Deuteronomium*, pp. 52 ff.; E. L. Ehrlich, *Der Traum im Alten Testament*, pp. 155 ff.
[2] Cf. E. Sellin, *Der AT Prophetismus*, p. 20 n.1.

the original orientation of nabism had been abandoned may be seen even more clearly in the so-called *Royal Psalms*, which extol the accession of the sovereign as the coming of the God-sent Prince of Peace.[1] The fact that these hymns most probably derive from the court prophets suggests that the divinization of the earthly king which is one of their most prominent features may be regarded as indicative of the attitude of certain prophetic circles to the monarchy and its religious pretensions. The eschatological tension, which looked wholly for the succour promised from God, is here very much weakened in favour of an outlook which sees salvation in the contemporary institution of divine kingship. *Here again institutional religion has repressed the proper prophetic concentration on God's coming.* In addition, the strong emphasis on the military function of the ruler helped to attach a disproportionate importance to an aspect of Yahweh worship which, when placed in false isolation, went more than half-way to meet the nationalistic perversion of the Yahweh religion.

This assimilation of prophetism to the professional religious groups was also conducive to a much stronger emphasis than hitherto on *the sensational manifestations of nabism.* Once the *nābi'* had consented to submit his preaching to the supervision of the priests and the wishes of the king, and in so doing to fit in with traditional religious procedure, it was inevitable that the one feature which remained to distinguish him from these other official representatives of religion, namely *the form* in which he gave his oracles, should acquire in his own eyes an exaggerated importance. Ecstasy, both in its milder and more violent forms, had always strongly influenced the opinion of the average Israelite concerning the special character of the prophetic preaching. Sometimes, as commonly happens in the case of the ordinary man, it invested the *nābi'* with the halo of especial sanctity; sometimes, as is frequent enough in circles with a critical or indifferent attitude to religion, it simply gave him the reputation of being insane. As things were now, the greater the similarity between the prophetic utterances and the Word of God as proclaimed by others, the more decisive for the recognition of his special character became the distinctive manner in which the prophet transmitted it. Hence we find *bizarre forms of ecstatic possession* zealously retained and practised in nabist circles. The more striking effects of *rūaḥ* provided evidence in support both of their own opinion of them-

[1] Cf. ch. XI, pp. 472 ff. below.

selves, and of that of the mass of the people; and for this reason also, it is precisely the opponents of the great prophets who are marked by the most sensational possible methods, and ones which cannot always escape the suspicion of owing something to artifice (cf. I Kings 22.10–12; Jer. 28.10 f.; 29.26).

It is quite true that the great prophets themselves did not hesitate on occasion to present their own message in similar ways; and many of their most valuable insights are associated with ecstatic conditions. But taken by and large their attitude to these things is one of marked reserve, and they are a thousand miles from making use of them, as the n‘bî'îm did, as a tool of their trade.[1] The proof of a prophet's genuineness was not for them comprehended in marvellous psychic experiences. They went beyond these epiphenomena of prophetic experience, and sought the authentication of intellectual and spiritual power in their testimonies. By contrast, slavish clinging to the outward form of the abnormal bore witness precisely to the disappearance of any genuine sense of charismatic endowment, and to an attempt to find an external substitute.

Whereas in pre-exilic times the Temple police looked after the disciplining of recalcitrant ecstatics (Jer. 20.1 ff.; 29.26), later generations would not tolerate even the *form* of preaching in independence of the Law, and attempted in various ways to create a substitute. Poetic inspiration and musical gifts are now characterized as the operation of *rūaḥ*, and in particular the Temple prophet's ability to improvise liturgical utterances is prized as demonstrating his prophetic status (cf. Ps. 49.4; I Chron. 15.22, 27;[2] 25.1–3; II Chron. 20.14[3]). At this point the prophet is finally absorbed into the ranks of the Temple officials.

The high value thus set on the outward form of prophetic inspiration is, however, only a symptom of the stagnation which affected the whole vitality of nabism from the time when it became an established profession. The fact that development had been halted in mid-career, and that forces which had hitherto been alive and concerned with the future were being petrified, is most clearly

---

[1] J. Hempel pertinently describes their struggle against the debasement of ecstasy into a technique as a fight to maintain the purity of ecstatic phenomena as revelation (*Altes Testament und Geschichte*, p. 58).

[2] On this passage cf. S. Mowinckel, *Psalmenstudien* III, pp. 17 f.

[3] The reference in this passage is to a levitical Temple singer: in general, the post-exilic cult prophets seem to have been absorbed into the ranks of the levitical singers.

proved by the inability of the movement to adopt new positions, when changing circumstances made this desirable. In the face of the new problems of social cleavage and of nationalist imperialism in world affairs nabism had no advice to offer. On the one hand, its dependence on those who hitherto had provided its daily bread seriously hindered it from taking an independent stand in the matter of social crises (cf. Micah 3.5). On the other, because it had taken such a large part in the secularization of religion, it was—in striking contrast to its greatest exponents such as Elijah—no longer capable of making a clearly defined distinction between national self-preservation and loyalty to Yahweh, and therefore sought to combat the imperialism of the great powers with the latter's own weapons. Israelite world domination was ever more passionately stressed as the focus of all hope, the goal of the ways of God, and the realization of his kingdom. Thus the nation was exalted to an absolute value which had more affinity with heathen thought than with the religion of Yahweh. The question posed by Assyria's triumph over Israel was never grasped. Because the divine rule was equated with the continued existence of the professional religious groups within the framework of the nation, nabism never reached the stage of criticizing, but remained content with a metaphysical justification of the *status quo* which blocked out all vision of the world-wide character of God's sovereignty. If there was to be any chance of an unprejudiced assessment of the real state of affairs, with a resultant new interpretation of God's saving purpose in the form of a purified salvation-hope, then God's calling would have to set his messengers outside their people in a way quite different from any seen hitherto. Only so could they be granted a vision unobscured by any natural ties. And only such a vision would be able to embrace not just the whole truth of the nation's need, but also the whole majesty of the nation's God.

6. CLASSICAL PROPHECY

It may be doubted whether it is possible to fix forward and backward limits for that later phase, in which the prophetic movement reached its climax, as if this phase were an entity in itself which could be understood in isolation from the laws that governed its organic growth. For nabism itself does not suddenly stop dead, but continues its career right into the post-exilic period; nor in so doing does it present one unbroken hostile front to classical prophecy, but gives frequent evidence of friendly contact. Indeed, at times when it was a matter of standing up for the exclusive worship of Yahweh against a syncretistic religious policy on the part of the king, nabism swung into the same battle line. Conversely, we should not fail to recognize that in many respects there was a close connection between the champions of classical prophecy and the older prophetic movement, even though, under the influence of the often embittered struggle between the two groups, it is easy enough to overlook it in one's interpretation.

1. Links with Nabism

Despite Amos' decided disclaimer[1] it cannot be contested that many prophets considered *the professional designation nābī'* as applying to themselves,[2] and *may even have been members of the prophetic guild*.[3] Furthermore, *their outward appearance* was often directly reminiscent of the figure of the *nābī'*, as were their dress, the rough mantle of hair,[4] and the striking symbolic acts by which they sought to attract the attention of the people.[5] Moreover, the giving of oracles in answer to particular enquiries, sometimes even from foreign nationals, the prediction of definite events, and the use of miracles to legitimate their authority remind us of the seer of the ancient type, or of the prophetic soothsayer.[6]

There is, however, more to this affinity than mere external

[1] Amos 7.14. Cf. in this connection H. H. Rowley, 'Was Amos a *Nabi?*' (*Festschrift Otto Eissfeldt*, 1947, pp. 191–5) and n. 3 below.

[2] Isa. 8.3; Hos. 9.7.

[3] In the case of Haggai and Zechariah incorporation into the Temple prophets was something to be taken for granted. Sellin supports the assumption that Hosea was a member of a prophetic group (*Das Zwölfprophetenbuch²,³*, 1929, p. 7). For Zephaniah, cf. W. Caspari, *Die israelitischen Propheten*, 1914, p. 76; G. Gerlemann, *Zephanja textkritisch und literarisch untersucht*, 1942. For Habakkuk, cf. P. Humbert, *Problèmes du livre d'Habacuc*, 1944. For Nahum, cf. A. Haldar, *Studies in the Book of Nahum*, 1947. For Joel, cf. A. S. Kapelrud, *Joel Studies*, 1948. Some recent studies go even further, maintaining that even the great classical prophets must without exception have belonged to the cultic guilds of prophets; notable exponents of this view are S. Mowinckel, *Acta Orientalia* 13, 1935, p. 267, and *JBL* 53, 1934, p. 210, in the case of Jeremiah and Isaiah, and A. Haldar, *op. cit.*, pp. 112 ff. This assumption seems, however, to be too strongly dictated by extra-Israelite analogies, and to fail to do justice to the OT evidence to the contrary. Whether such a saying as that of Amos (7.14) can just be dismissed out of hand by referring the noun-predicate to past time, and translating: 'I was no prophet, nor a prophet's son' (H. H. Rowley, cf. n. 1) would seem very doubtful. A *hāyītī* would in this case seem almost indispensable; it is certainly customary in parallel instances (cf. T. Boman, *Hebrew Thought Compared with Greek*, ET, 1960, pp. 42 f.).

[4] Cf. Isa. 20.2.

[5] Cf. Isa. 20.2 ff.; Amos 5.1 ff.; Jer. 19.10 f.; 27.2; Ezek. 4; 5 etc.

[6] Cf. e.g. Isa. 37.1 ff.; Jer. 37.7 ff.; 42.1 ff.; Isa. 14.28–32; 18; Jer. 27.2 ff. and Isa. 7.7 f., 11; 37.30 ff.; Jer. 28.15 ff.; Ezek. 24.15 ff., 25 ff.

appearance. *Everything about the way in which their revelation was received points in the same direction.* There is the strong sense of compulsion at the moment of entering on their calling, which may even be heightened to a point at which it completely eliminates the normal power of volition.[1] There is the whole form of their preaching, which with its 'Thus saith the LORD' represents the prophet as nothing more than the speaking-tube of a higher power. Both these features are well known to us from the world of nabism. Likewise, there are extensive similarities in the field of the psychic phenomena of their religious experience. In ecstasy, vision and audition the prophet is subjected to the overwhelming influence of the divine realm, into which his calling has thrust him.[2]

Indeed, even *in the very message* which they are sent to deliver the links with nabism can be clearly discerned. A passionate championing of the exclusive worship of Yahweh, which goes hand in hand with an abrupt rejection of foreign influence, constitutes here, as in nabism, a testimony to the authority of that jealous God who demands undivided submission and deliberate decision for his cause. Thus it is that these prophets continue the protest against those petrified social institutions which pretend to a monopoly of religion, and which misuse belief in God by making it into a metaphysical explanation of the temporally conditioned form of the national life. In this opposition to both monarchy and priesthood we see displayed none other than a development of those tendencies in nabism and in its fight for the primacy of an unmediated religion, which had at first been dominant, but which later became more and more ineffectual.[3]

[1] Cf. Amos 7.15; Hos. 1.2; Isa. 8.11; Jer. 1.7; 6.11; 15.17; 20.7, 9; Ezek. 1.28; 3.14 etc.

[2] Cf. Amos 7.1 ff.; 8.1; Isa. 6.1 ff.; 5.9; 22.14; 40.3, 6; Jer. 1.11 ff.; 4.19 ff.; 23.9; 24.1 ff.; Ezek. 1; 3.15; 4.8; 6.11; 8.1 ff.; 21.19; Zech. 1–6 etc. The parapsychical phenomena in the prophetic experience have been closely examined by G. Widengren, *Literary and Psychological Aspects of the Hebrew Prophets*, 1948. Even today many scholars attempt to deny any element of the ecstatic in the case of the classical prophets (cf. K. Cramer, *Amos*, pp. 19 ff.; A. Jepsen, *Nabi*, pp. 215 f.; J. P. Seierstad, *Die Offenbarungserlebnisse der Propheten Amos, Jesaja und Jeremia*, 1946, pp. 156 ff.). This view, however, neither does justice to the evidence, nor can it account for the exalted plane of the prophetic message. Conversely, too great an insistence on the compulsive psychic experiences loses sight of the equally definite differences between the classical prophets and the *neḇī'īm* (cf. H. Gunkel and H. Schmidt, *Die grossen Propheten* (Schriften des AT II.2), 1915; T. H. Robinson, *Prophecy and the Prophets in Ancient Israel*, 1923).

[3] The most impressive statement of these affinities is that of Gunkel (*Die Propheten*, 1917, and *Die grossen Propheten*, pp. xi ff.).

11. *The Distinctive Character of Classical Prophecy*

Nevertheless, despite these far-reaching affinities which might tempt us to see classical prophecy as distinctive only by virtue of the individual greatness of its exponents, it would be wrong to ignore the existence of *certain major common factors* whereby the later prophetic movement can be seen as a coherent whole with an essentially homogeneous basic character distinguishing it from nabism and justifying a synthetic treatment appropriate to its nature and structure. To begin with, classical prophecy presents quite a different picture with regard to the value attached to striking psychic phenomena. Indeed, on the whole we have to acknowledge a marked recession in the ecstatic and visionary element when compared with the early period. As a rule this element is to be found in the account of the prophet's call, but is seldom in evidence in later life. The only exception to this is the prophet Ezekiel; but in his case his whole spiritual life seems to have been particularly predisposed in this direction by the pressure of illness.[1] Of full-scale ecstatic mass-hysteria there is no mention in the case of the classical prophets, just as there is no longer any sign of its having any pronounced influence on the great leaders of the n*bî'îm, such as Elijah and Elisha, even though these were still in close contact with the prophetic bands. Instead, it is the vision which establishes itself as the exclusive means by which the later prophets arrive at a sense of the calling that both raises them above the mass of Yahweh-worshippers and also marks them out as distinct from the n*bî'îm.

Corresponding to the less important role now played by the ecstatic element is the fact that, as time went by, the prophets came increasingly to recognize and make explicit the principle that a habitually heightened state of feeling was only something of very relative significance. Thus Isaiah, in his famous diatribe against the priests and the prophets (28.7 ff.), reveals a clear apprehension that all visionary insight may be deceitful, if serious concern for moral truth is missing. He roundly denies to those prophets who by their intemperance have deprived themselves of the last vestiges of

---

[1]For this reason it is inadmissible to draw conclusions about the character of classical prophecy as a whole, and to make great play with the ecstatic element in elucidating it, simply on the basis of Ezekiel, for he is a unique phenomenon. Of the many discussions of this question that of A. Guillaume, *Prophecy and Divination*, 1938, may be singled out as exhibiting the basic structure of the prophetic faith with reference to a comprehensive survey of the religio-historical material.

judgment any real ability to perceive the revelation of God.[1] Jeremiah stresses even more clearly the utter worthlessness of all dreams and visions in those who have lost their sense of truth and justice.[2] Ezekiel takes the same stand, when he reproaches the prophets who speak the people fair and cover up the grievous offences of the nation with giving lying oracles and deceitful visions.[3]

However, it is not only these abnormal psychic states which recede in importance as instruments of the prophetic ministry. Individual demonstrations of higher knowledge and supernatural power also play a subordinate role, though recourse is certainly had to them in particular cases. *The proper instrument of prophetic activity* is the spoken and, as time goes by, to a greater and greater extent the written word. The sensational individual act comes to be associated in a strictly ancillary capacity with the oral delivery of threats, warnings, exhortations, laments and accusations, and the written dissemination of these in the form of a broadsheet, or a brief oracular saying, or a kind of statement of account between God and his people. In time, also, larger collections of individual oracles were formed. It is in keeping with the decisive importance of the new medium that the prophets now normally exhibit outstanding qualities as orators, and in most cases also as poets. Only in this way can the word be given that full effectiveness which marks it out as the medium *par excellence* of their public activity.

This pre-eminence of the spoken word, however, signifies simply that the work of the prophets had shifted decisively into *the sphere of spiritual and personal understanding*, and was henceforth to restrict itself to that sphere. Consequently, the prophets had no strong organizational backing, nor were they armed with solid political power to give emphasis to their words. If they were to make themselves heard in this situation they needed a spiritual power and inner conviction which would raise the individual above the mass, and give him complete independence. Hence among the prophets we meet men who, even if they still have some outward connection with the prophetic guild, yet have been freed from all the ties of class or professional self-consciousness. They are capable of moving through life in majestic solitude, even when this means—as it meant, for example, for Hosea and Jeremiah—that their whole existence is

[1] Cf. also Isa. 29.9 f. and 30.10.
[2] Cf. Jer. 23.9 ff.
[3] Ezek. 13.

inundated with the most terrible tragedy. It is *their strongly marked individuality*, indeed, which makes them for us the most clearly defined personalities of ancient Israel, and gives all their preaching the stamp of genuineness and inimitable originality. Even where traditional patterns and systems of concepts are employed, everything is molten in the fire of a personal experience of God, and emerges freshly minted. And where we are permitted to see into the moral struggle through which they strive for the interior perfection of their own selves, then the ultimate source of their personal power and character is revealed. It is in their own submission to the existential demands of God that they are made free from all human ties.

This decision to fight exclusively on the battleground of spiritual issues, and the accompanying personal presuppositions of its chief exponents, give the later prophetic movement a character all its own, and allow us to surmise that it differed essentially in the content of its programme from the aims which had satisfied nabism in the past. Had it been a question merely of bringing an energetic influence to bear, or—when circumstances were propitious—of deciding individual political issues by an act of violence; or again of performing this or that marvellous act of succour or punishment, or of elucidating one particular matter by an oracle; in short, of intervening simply as occasion required without framing such guidance of the national life on any coherent principle; then indeed such a transformation of the whole pattern of the conflict would be quite inconceivable. The old method, even where it called men to new decisions or countered a false tendency in the whole community, could yet presuppose a standard current among all, a generally acknowledged ideal picture of the People of God to which appeal could be made at any juncture. The whole attitude of the new 'prophecy of the Word' demonstrates that this situation has fundamentally changed. What stands in the way of Yahweh's supremacy is no longer this or that error or imperfection, but *a perversion of the whole conception of the divine-human relationship*. It is this which obstructs any insight into the questionable character of the prevailing situation, and condemns to ineffectiveness all such attempts as rest content with the removal of individual abuses. What is wanted now is *a new total understanding of the will of Yahweh*, that is to say, an acknowledgment of a reality which embraces and sustains the whole of life, and which men, for all their zealous and self-conscious piety, have lost sight of, hiding it behind the creations of their own spirituality. This revolutionizing of the whole traditional conception of religion, and its denunciation as a monstrous fallacy concealing the true reality of God, calls for a spiritual struggle aimed at ultimate analysis and decision. The only weapon which can fully meet the requirements of such a struggle is the Word; for only this can save men from adulterating their vision of the true goal with the issues of power which govern the conflicts of this world, and so enable them to see the really crucial issues with absolute clarity.

Nevertheless, for all this catalogue of the features that distinguish the later prophetic movement, we have not yet succeeded in specifying the point from which it derives its special significance. If the prophetic condemnation was only engendered and determined by a comparison of the old ideal picture of the theocracy, as this could be deduced from tradition, with the degeneracy of their contemporary situation, all the points so far enumerated would in the end exhibit a merely formal character, and the conflict with popular piety would remain simply a question of providing a new theoretical basis for religious thought and opinion, without making the forward leap to a truly creative religious life. But what constitutes the incomparable and inimitable originality and creative authority of the prophetic preaching is the fact that it derives from *the experience of a new reality*—one that with compelling seriousness and overriding power drives them to utterance, leaving no room for theoretical controversy, but only for testimony to an immediate certitude.

The menacing irruption of a divine reality unperceived by their contemporaries—it is this, to put it in the most general terms, which is the decisively new factor in the phenomenon of classical prophecy, and which, in spite of many close affinities, both separates them fundamentally from the *n·bî'îm*, and at the same time, despite all their individual differences, binds them together in a real unity. It is vital to keep this common factor in view as clearly as possible, if prophetism is not to be misunderstood at crucial points, and its significance sought in the great diversity of new ideas which it produced— a mistake that is made, none the less, in the majority of descriptions of this high-water mark of Old Testament religious history. Only in this way can we arrive at a correct understanding of the structural individuality of Israelite prophetism, a task which, in spite of many preliminary studies, has yet to be tackled in earnest. But it is a problem which must be solved if mistaken opinions, which are particularly numerous in this connection, are to be corrected.

III. *The Religious Structure of Classical Prophecy*
(a) *The New Experience of the Divine Reality*

(α) The prophetic life was lived, and the thought of the prophets developed, under the impact of a new reality which menaced both their own personal life and that of their nation. To establish this fact is to make clear the dominant tendency of the prophetic conception of God and the world.

In their own personal life the prophets experienced this power terrifyingly as the radical overthrow of everything that had held good for them hitherto, an experience to which the accounts of their calling bear eloquent testimony. There is not one of them who did not receive this new certainty of God in such a way that the whole previous pattern of his life, the thoughts and plans by which he had till now regulated his relationship to the world, was not smashed, and replaced by a mighty divine imperative obliging him to undertake something which hitherto he had not even considered as a possibility.[1] And the same revolutionary forces which they saw in their own lives they saw realized also in the life of the nation by this terrible divine fact, driving with irresistible impetus against the totally differently constituted reality of the empirical world, and hurling it out of its path. Their threatening predictions of the end of the nation and people, marked as they are by apodeictic declarations of doom for which in the first instance no further reasons are given, all stem from the same dominating conviction that the present order is menaced at its very roots by the breaking in of a power hostile to it. This means, however, that the prophets could only conceive or describe the divine reality which they beheld as one that was driving onward in mighty events, aiming at the complete upheaval of all existent reality, and shaking both man and the world in their titanic self-assertion. For these men all descriptive phrases which sought to imprison God in the Here and Now, or to portray his sovereignty over the world as a static and inherently stable situation, were bound to appear palpably inadequate. For them it was a matter not of the place of the eternal divine ordinance in the life of men and nations, but of a head-on collision between the divine reality and the empirical world; the very world itself was being imperilled by a power completely independent of it and therefore unrestricted in authority over it. The words which they had to speak

[1] S. Mowinckel (*Die Erkenntnis Gottes bei den alttestamentlichen Propheten*, 1941) has stressed this fundamental significance of the call-experience.

did not concern God as he is, permeating all things, but God as he is to come, summoning all men to answer to himself. In short, the relationship of God and the world presented itself to them primarily as something dynamic, not static.

It is clear that if the prophetic utterances are regarded from this point of view, they all appear in a special light, and that to disregard this is bound to lead to misunderstanding. Surprise has often been expressed over the fact that the prophets manifestly were not concerned to give concrete advice on how the life of the people and nation might be placed on a new footing, or to arrange for better institutions and for the organization of society. Logically, anyone who really sees this as a gap in the prophetic message can only regard those who proclaimed it as dealers in illusions and fantasies. But such a view is in fact nothing more than a complete failure to understand the true structure of prophetic thought. Similarly, it will become clear that the prophetic utterances, when looked at in the right way, are internally consistent with one another; and that though superficially this coherence may be hard to detect, yet it does provide, often quite astonishingly, the reasons for their contradictions.

(β) Let us now try to bring this picture of the new divine reality, which is so terrifyingly menacing the present order, into somewhat clearer focus. An irrational element now thrusts itself to the fore with extraordinary violence, namely *an inconceivable otherness*, totally destructive of everything which penetrates unbidden into its domain. The numinous terribleness, which we find inseparably connected with the experience of God in the Mosaic period, and which indeed is attested for the far wider circle of primitive religions as a basic ingredient in the experience of the divine, here emerges with shattering power. At the time of which we are speaking the religion of Israel had, in the course of its development into a religion tied to a higher cultural level, undergone the same rationalization as is a typical feature of so many popular religions. As a result of deliberate emphasis on, and cultivation of its positive connections with, the secular culture, the numinous reality of the God it worshipped had to an increasing extent been veiled and made ineffective. This is the only possible significance of the secularization of the whilom religion of Israel which has already been described several times in these pages. This process, by which the awful and serious reality that had given Yahwism its distinctive stamp was rendered harmless, was given the lie in terrifying fashion by the God whom the prophets proclaimed, and was shown to be a complete misconception of the divine nature. All the vital interests of the people of Yahweh, which men had been accustomed to regard as holy and guaranteed by God himself—the state and the monarchy, social welfare and victory in war, a respected priesthood and a magnificent Temple worship, prophetic reading of the future and impressive miracles—all collapse in ruins and are thrown aside as of no worth in the face of the reality of the God of Israel, who rends all pretence in pieces.[1] Furthermore, the very means men had employed in the past to make the deity an intimate and vivid reality, the sacred images and symbols, the unshakable institution of the atonement sacrifice, the days of atonement and repentance, the invocation of such comfortable-sounding divine names as Rock of Israel, Redeemer, Mighty One, Shepherd and so on, are now exposed as nothing more than a huge misconception of the real nature of God, good for nothing but destruction. The God whose messengers curse the cultus reveals his total alienation from all human arrangements and schemes by using the holy places as material for frivolous puns,[2] and by twisting the divine names that promise salvation into their opposite.[3] There is no sort of guarantee that can dam this ruinous flood of God's destroying power, or divert it where possible to one's own use. No sacred institutions can render this harmless, or convert it into a positive force of succour. Its nature can be imprisoned in no holy name, nor fettered by any prayers of the devout.[4] Truly, in the face of this all-questioning power every kind of human activity is extinguished, and even the pious cannot but be aware that he has nothing to offer it, and can only bow before its purposes of doom.[5]

(γ) But the revelation of God proclaimed by the prophets does not stop at this non-rational theistic positivism. It combines it extremely closely with a rational element. For even when they use

---

[1] Cf. the *locus classicus*, Isa. 3.1 ff.

[2] Amos 5.5; Hos. 4.15; 5.8; 10.5; Isa. 29.1 ff.

[3] Isa. 1.24; 8.14; 31.4 (this verse should not be understood in the light of what immediately follows it, but as a threat); Hos. 5.12, 14.

[4] This is the explanation of the prophets' complete refusal to use any one particular name to describe Yahweh's nature—it is too rich and many-sided to be covered by a single concept. The only proper divine name is Yahweh. Cf. Baudissin, *Kyrios* III, pp. 200 ff.

[5] This 'attitude of passivity' toward God has been brought out in particular by Hertzberg, *Prophet und Gott*, 1923, pp. 23 ff., 38. That this is not all there is to be said will, however, be seen below.

the most daring images to speak of the savage, destructive power of Yahweh,[1] the prophets leave no doubt whatever that they are not referring to a natural force, impatient of closer definition, nor to an impersonal Destiny, but to *an absolutely personal God*, whose name, Yahweh, turns the alien, unknown power into a will clearly recognizable as personal. It is true that the prophets refuse, when describing the God revealed to them, to coin a new name designed specifically to express the new element in their revelation. They simply keep to the old name, Yahweh. One thing, nevertheless, this does imply quite unmistakably, namely that this is a divine Thou, speaking to man and having dealings with him. It is not simply a force of destiny striding heedlessly over man, but a divine personality which, in the very act of repulsing and rejecting him, yet enters into a genuine relationship, and takes him seriously as a being with a will of his own. What is new here, however, is not the conception in itself, but the way in which it is applied to the new historical situation. That the national God was a personal being was for Israel a basic axiom of faith. Everything men had to say about his redemption and governance of the people as ruler, lawgiver and warrior-god from Egypt onwards was said in the context of this belief. It is true that the equation of Yahweh with the Baal had altered the personality of the God of Israel not inconsiderably from the Mosaic conception; the element of arbitrary caprice typical of a natural force was distorting its proper features. It is for this reason that the fresh emphasis in the prophetic preaching is on the sovereign Lord of Mosaic belief, whose faithfulness and constancy are made known in covenant and law. The deliberate affirmation of the continuity of the divine activity in the history of the nation which may be observed in the prophets is sufficient proof that they had no idea of severing the ties that joined them to their historical inheritance.[2]

[1] Cf. for example Hos. 5.12, 14; 13.7 ff.

[2] Many of the more recent commentaries have gone astray for this very reason, that they have been unable to visualize the new element in the message of the prophets except in contrast with what had obtained before their time; cf. e.g. B. Weiser, *Prophetie des Amos*, 1929, pp. 76 ff. and 301. Since then, however, it has been recognized that the relation of the prophets to tradition is a problem that will have to be worked out afresh. An extreme solution is to be found in the works of Haldar and Kapelrud (see p. 339 n. 3 above), which urge the dependence of the prophets on the tradition of the ancient East; and those of H. S. Nyberg (*Studien zum Hoseabuche*, 1935) and H. Birkeland (*Zum hebräischen Traditionswesen: Die Komposition der prophetischen Bücher des AT*, 1938) which stress the importance of schools of prophetic tradition for the form and content of the prophetic preaching and its propagation. The element of truth in these theses, which would have it

Nevertheless, it was precisely this historical inheritance which was capable of neutralizing, or at least weakening, the terrifying force of the divine threat to human existence—and in popular belief had in fact already done so. It was just because men thought they knew this God so well, that they felt secure in their relationship with him, and believed that they could relax in comfortable confidence: 'It is not he; neither shall evil come upon us' (Jer. 5.12; cf. 6.14). The tension, which became apparent to the prophets, between the personhood of God, which was within men's comprehension, and the menace of his reality, which was not—a conflict unknown in this form to Mosaic religion—was not to be resolved by harmonization. It could only be made tolerable by an understanding which gave full effect to *both elements in a living actuality*.

(δ) On the one hand this numinous terribleness abolished all trace of the merely fatalistic. The divine power does not carry out its assault on the empirical world in the form of some paralysing disaster which man must willy-nilly suffer to ride over him, but which in his innermost self he can ignore. It is something which plants itself inescapably in the path of *each individual human being*, compelling him to adopt a particular attitude toward it, and so creating *a genuine confrontation*. Man can interpose no lower court of appeal between himself and the threat thus addressed to him. The person of the prophet *compels* him to hearken to the accusation, and to make his decision in accordance with it.

That which thus makes itself heard in the prophetic preaching with such compelling power is, moreover, rooted in experience of immediate reality. The prophet knows that he has encountered God himself in the hour of his call. He has been seized by God's hand, commissioned by God's word coming directly to himself. And just as, in his own case, he rejects all mediation through the Spirit or

---

that the message of the prophets was determined by tradition in the most comprehensive manner, can only be accepted after substantial modification; but there have been careful studies of detailed points which have succeeded in arriving at more tenable conclusions, because they have sought to bring out the links between the prophets and the tradition and environment of their people while still giving full recognition to their new and critical attitude. Such are: A. Peter, *Das Echo von Paradieserzählung und Paradiesmythen im AT unter besonderer Berücksichtigung der prophetischen Endzeitschilderungen* (Wurzburg Dissertations), 1947; G. H. Davies, 'The Yahwistic Tradition in the Eighth-century Prophets', in *Studies in OT Prophecy*, 1950, pp. 37 ff.; and L. Černy, *The Day of Yahweh and some relevant Problems*, 1948.

through an angel,[1] so in all the events of world history he sees God himself at work, and knows how to make men directly aware of this through the visual power of intensely realistic language. It is a distinctive characteristic of the speech of the prophets themselves, especially when compared with the many later interpolations, that it never moralizes. It subjects man to the direct impact of the presence of God, and makes him aware, as he goes his own way, of the nearness of Another, who regards him with a searching eye and confronts him with the decisive question of his life. When an Isaiah speaks of the eyes of the divine majesty, which the men of Judah dare to defy (3.8), or pictures the hand of God stretched out threateningly (9.7 ff.), or describes him as stripping the blindfolding from the eyes of Judah (22.8), so that men are compelled to learn to look on him; when Jeremiah gives similar illustrations of the earnest searching and scrutinizing carried out by the divine Lord (5.3; 6.9); all this makes the near presence of Yahweh, and his direct dealing with men in events, so vivid that the anthropomorphic features no longer diminish but intensify its seriousness. When the personhood of God is really taken seriously in this way, it leads to *a stronger and deeper sense of the reality of judgment*, for it makes the divine demand, while of universal application, the concrete concern of each individual.

Conversely, however, there is so vivid an understanding of *the mysterious quality of the divine personhood* as this comes threateningly upon man, so lively a sense of its numinous otherness, that the narrowness and limitation which personal categories tend to introduce are counteracted. In this connection it is worth pointing out once more that the prophets make no attempt to comprehend the divine nature in a name. They feel it as something so inexhaustible and many-sided as to be beyond the reach of any human definition;[2] nor do they even exhibit a preference for the designation 'Lord', which would, nevertheless, in important respects accord well with their picture of God. On the other hand, all their utterances are dominated by *the incomparable greatness of their God*, which lays all

---

[1] The weakening of this sense of immediacy in the later period of prophecy is one clear symptom of its decadence.

[2] The use of the term *qādōš* in Isaiah is only an apparent exception to this rule. What is involved here is not a definition, but a pregnant formulation of an essential difference between God and man which is bound to issue in judgment. This explains the prophet's preference for the word in his sharp encounters with opponents.

human greatness in the dust (Isa. 2.6 ff.), which guides not only Israel but all the nations in their ways (Amos 9.7), and which, filling as it does all heaven and earth, renders futile all human attempts to approach it (Jer. 23.23 f.). Ultimately the basis of all God's actions is that this greatness shall be seen to be supreme in the world of men (Ezekiel passim); and justice can only be done to the infinite wonder of Yahweh's nature when all human understanding of it is confounded (Deutero-Isaiah).

What the terrifying, irresistible power of Yahweh meant to the faith of the earlier period is now, in accordance with a larger vision and understanding of the world, conceived as his exaltedness over the universe, thus giving intelligible form and basis to that which had hitherto been simply accepted as the datum of his numinous otherness. But this served to make the mystery of the divine nature greater, not less. For this Lord of the world is no passive divine Being, no object of silent and absorbing contemplation, but a passionate will which like a consuming fire threatens with annihilation everything hostile to its own nature, and as such can only rightly be apprehended in the experience of its assault on one's own existence. What confronts us here is a resurgence of the primary element in Mosaic religion, only enriched and deepened in content. In the testimony of the prophets to Yahweh's greatness we see the reflection of a divine reality which impressed itself on their consciousness as something quite unique and not comparable to any earthly object. In this respect as in others the Deuteronomic system of thought utters the true coin of the prophetic faith, when it teaches men to regard the union of tiny Israel with the exalted God in a covenant as the immense and continuing enigma of divine grace, bringing men to worship and adore a God far beyond anything they can conceive.

(ε) In this experience of the reality of God as something *numinous and terrible, definable in terms of personality and great to a degree that allows of no competitor*, is to be found the crucial process by which all that was best in the religious heritage which the prophets shared with their people was revived, but at the same time creatively transformed and made truly effective. It is not true to say that the prophets proclaimed hitherto unknown ideas about God.[1] Those isolated passages

---

[1] The efforts of modern theological study to make the prophets intelligible have tended to present them as the harbingers of a new conception of God, proclaiming him now as the Righteous One, now the Holy, the Loving, the Almighty—in a

in which the prophets express their beliefs about God's nature and attributes are precisely not the ones in which we find the distinctive new contribution that marks them off from the earlier period. Rather are these the points at which the links with the past are most obvious, so that it is possible to say that the prophets no more introduced a new doctrine of God than a new ethic.[1] It is quite true that the prophetic preaching did in fact mediate a deepened and purified understanding of God. But this did not come about because they thought themselves bound to smash a false image of God by the proclamation of new and hitherto unknown divine attributes. It was simply that they established the relevance of that new sense of *God's reality* which had come to them to every department of life; in short, that they took God, well understood to be that same God whose special relationship with Israel they had never contested,[2] really

word, to use the well-known formula, of ethical monotheism. These attempts have had much to say on the subject which has certainly been correct and well observed; but on the decisive point they fail to do justice to prophetism, because they are led astray by the idea of a new *doctrine of God*. This leads them involuntarily to mistake the achievement of the prophets for an intellectual achievement, or at least to present it as such, and thus to turn the prophets into religious thinkers, or, if more stress is laid on the intuitive element in their understanding, into religious geniuses. All the various attempts to break down this supposed intellectual achievement into its rational components, and to demonstrate the psychological and intellectual presuppositions that brought it about, from the extremely simple initial efforts of a Wellhausen or a Stade, to the complicated interpretations of a Hölscher or an Allwohn, armed with the methods of modern depth psychology, thus make the mistake of confusing the religious reality which lies behind the words of the prophet with the kind of philosophical idea on which a thinker bases his new conception of the universe. (This is not to say, of course, that these exegetes were entirely without feeling for the mighty creative *mysterium* of which the prophets were so keenly aware; but this was for them rather an incidental phenomenon, possibly the psychological medium of an intellectual process, which, once it had emerged into thought, could be understood by anyone to be inherently convincing.) In order to demonstrate the novelty of the prophetic idea of God it was therefore necessary to write down drastically the pre-prophetic conceptions; but the violence thus done to the facts exposed from the first the inherent weakness of the whole attempt.

[1] On the latter point a greater and greater degree of unanimity has been attained, while the former has often been invested with all the fixity of a dogma. That changes are on the way, however, even in this connection, has been shown by the fundamental questionings of Weiser (*Die Prophetie des Amos*; cf. e.g., pp. 304 ff. and p. 52 n. 1). Cf. also the carefully considered assessment of the old and new elements in the moral teaching of the prophets in N. W. Porteous, 'The basis of the ethical teaching of the prophets', in *Studies in OT Prophecy*, pp. 92 ff.

[2] It is to misunderstand the saying of Amos (9.7) to read into it an attempt to controvert the idea of an act of grace on the part of Yahweh in the Exodus from Egypt; cf. Weiser, *op. cit.*, p. 303.

seriously. This God, his terribleness untempered by religious intermediaries, makes clear in all their ultimate urgency what are the claims of a holy personal will when backed by a majesty beyond the control of any human power. As the only Lord he invades the world of a religion based on national culture, and exposes its anti-God character by revealing its incompatibility with the real world of God.

It is only by way of thus questioning the contemporary situation of the Chosen People at the very deepest level that the prophets arrive at new pronouncements, precisely formulated and clear in conception, concerning the nature and purpose of the God who orders all things.[1] It is in their struggle to arrive at an intelligible interpretation of the divine decrees that they succeed in presenting their testimony to the divine sovereignty in forms free from any adulteration or obscurity caused by alien elements. In these testimonies the knowledge of God is carried further than in the past, but along the same lines; and from consideration of the coming judgment ultimate conclusions are drawn concerning the relationship of God and his people. Furthermore, this concrete character of the implications of the prophetic utterances about God means that it is impossible to abstract a *doctrine of God* from them, and make it stand by itself as the thing of primary importance, without at the same time completely shattering the whole structure of prophetic thought, and forcing it into categories utterly foreign to its nature. Only as statements about the God who is breaking in *now* into the strictly limited world of Israel, and calling that to account, do the prophetic interpretations of the divine nature and purpose possess inherent validity, and only from this point of view can they be understood. If they are wrenched from this basis and falsely objectivized, the result is bound to be serious misunderstanding.

Hence any presentation of the system of prophetic thought in which the main concern is to understand its distinctive structural character must begin from this clear-cut concrete quality, and never lose sight of it for a moment.

(*b*) *The Working out of the Experience of God in the Prophetic System of Thought*

(α) The new sense of the unity of life.

The first point to consider is the way in which, in the preaching of the prophets, the whole of human life is given a new focus of

[1]Cf. ch. VII; also pp. 50 f.; 58 ff.; 216 f.; 224 f.; 236 f.; 244 ff.; 251 ff.; 267 ff.; 278 ff. above.

unity, to which all its individual phenomena are related with concentrated force. It was a mark of the Israelite life of their time that it had lost the spontaneous unity which characterized its primitive stage. Like every more highly developed civilization it had gone on to elaborate the various departments of life independently, but had failed to produce any overriding, completely binding authority to counter these autonomies and their disruptive effects that were such a threat to the nation's sense of unity. Furthermore, even the latter entity, the nation, with the king as its divinized representative head, was no longer capable of providing a single, unifying framework for all the diversity of life as it was being lived, and of thus rooting that life in a strong sense of community. It was itself too drastically divided into hostile camps by the conflicting interests of party, tribe and class, each of which defined the concept of the nation differently, and promised to further its well-being in a different way. This world, at the mercy of centrifugal forces, was invaded by the prophets proclaiming the advent of the Lord of Israel, terrible in power, with the result that the warring hopes and theories of their contemporaries were compelled to give their attention to this one fact, and be assessed by it. And as the terrifying reality of the true God broke through the ranks of religious, cultural and nationalistic idols that had screened it from men's eyes, so all these gods of a day were seen in a new light. They lost the independent importance with which they had been invested, and became henceforward subordinate means to the service of the one personal divine will, which made the very existence of both nation and individual dependent on their relationship to himself. From this point of view all the complex facts of life once more acquired a unified meaning, even if this meaning was at first the much more strongly negative one of judgment, rather than the positive one of salvation. The God whose claim to sovereignty prevails at every point and compels all men to come to terms personally with himself dethrones the partial deities of human society, and ensures that only one question shall retain any importance: How am I to stand in his sight?

We may perhaps see more clearly the distinctive character of the new unity which this proclamation of the reality of God introduced into life by *comparing it with two other possible methods of rescuing this comprehensive unity*. On the one hand it is conceivable that social life which had grown so complicated might be subjected to some kind of *forcible simplification*. Such simplification is commonly planned along the lines of earlier primitive conditions, and achieves the creation of a basic sense of unity by restoring an environment that will incorporate all its members at an equal level of commitment. This method, which by a basic law of religious development normally leads to the formation of puritan sects, was attempted in Israel by the Rechabites, and did in fact succeed in reviving within their particular circle the original unity which the nation as a whole had lost. Jeremiah's recognition of them (Jer. 35) shows that the prophets understood the tendency here at work, and respected the loyalty that went to its realization, even when they could not take part in the movement as a whole.

The other possibility is that of a *totalitarian religious culture*, such as Islam was able to create by developing its system of law as the unifying bond of all its adherents. By accepting the forms of society while subjecting them completely to the laws of religion a genuinely religious social ethic is produced, the medium of which, nevertheless, is law. Such a religion creates no social forms of its own, but adopts the state as its outward form, thus effecting a compulsory unification of life.

Prophetism displays some connection with each of these possible approaches. On the one hand, like the Rechabites, it is sceptical of the value of civilized life, and foresees its destruction. On the other, like Islam, it acknowledges no organization of life as a whole except that which rests on the authority of God's demands. But its distinctive character becomes clear in its refusal to share in romantic dreams of a reversal of history and a revival of the ancient patriarchal ways of life. Instead, it seeks to understand the purpose of the Creator in allowing life to become richer in content. Similarly, it knows nothing of the optimistic, world-affirming attitude of Islamic ethics, with its approving attitude to civilization, and its belief that it is possible by legislation to subordinate the forms of society to the standards of religion. On the contrary, it regards society's wilful hostility to God as so deeply rooted in man's deliberate personal rejection of God that the resultant dualism between God and the world seems to it unresolvable except in terms of a radical judgment on the contemporary situation. In both cases the determining factor is the conviction of the threatening presence of the God of Israel. It is this which compels men to an ultimate decision, probing into the very depths of their being, and refusing to countenance any attempt at an external remedy for Israel's 'hurt', whether this be by the way of simplification or by legal regulation of the national life. Instead, it leads men to reconstruct the whole of life from the very foundations on the basis of individual human wills renewed by the divine mercy.

(β) The divine-human relationship transferred to the individual level.

How did this new vision of the world work out in the sphere of the individual problems of human life? To begin with, new light is thrown on *the sympathetic understanding of the covenant God for each individual member of the covenant community*, with the result that a whole series of religious problems are brought to life which, even if present in earlier periods, were only so in latent and unwakened form beneath the surface of religious consciousness. Taking it by and large, it may be said that in this regard cultural development had prepared the way for the prophetic preaching. The social structure of the nation had been seriously shaken by the disruptive influences of civilization, and the old stable forms of economic life (cf. above) had disintegrated. These factors had the effect of loosening the ties that bound the individual to the collective will; and by compelling him to make choices between opposing decisions called for an attitude of spiritual independence and a sense of the value of his own opinion. Into this spiritual situation now came the prophets, preaching a God who was calling to account not only the nation and its various component groups, but each individual citizen. This preaching, though it certainly was aimed at the nation as a whole, was also bound as a result of concrete circumstances to be especially concerned with the capacity of the individual for judgment and decision; and this all the more because it saw in the communal side of religious practice the supreme temptation to godlessness, bringing the individual under its spell both by the power of custom and tradition, and also by the suggestive effect of its mass display. This meant that unprecedented brutality had to be used if the individual was to be confronted with the decision that would cut him off from his group and his compatriots. *The prophetic preaching created a split within the nation* which separated membership of the true people of God from the mere fact of belonging to Israel, replacing this qualification with one based on the personal assumptions of the individual.

All this penetrating criticism, calling for an urgent decision, helped to transfer the problem to the individual level. And this process was reinforced, and extended into a permanent re-shaping of the divine-human relationship, by *closer definition of the content of the decision required from the individual*, as this emerged from the new experience of the reality of God. For the God who commandeered the prophet, his every thought, his every act of will, and proved himself in his dealings with him a personality with a controlling and re-creating will of his own, had no less a goal in his claim to sovereignty over his people, and sought to bind every member of the nation to himself in an equally exclusive relationship. In other words, his aim was to subjugate them to himself in their thoughts, in their resolves, in short in the very core of their responsible personal life. What raised the individual divine-human relationship to a new plane, making it a full and living reality, was the way in which the prophets carried to its logical conclusion the belief that *man's relations with God were explicitly personal in character*.

At first, indeed, it might have seemed that all human activity *vis-à-vis* God was to be suppressed by the overpowering majesty of Yahweh, and nothing left to man save to bow himself in terror and resign all will of his own. And it is quite true that anyone who sets out to expound the prophets cannot fail to be struck again and again by the insistence with which the initiative is reserved to God alone, and all human activity ruled out. It is possible, in fact, to speak without qualification of *a proper passivity on the part of man in face of the Godhead*;[1] and the best answer that can be made to the divine challenge is seen to be the unconditional surrender of the self to the divine operation, 'waiting upon God', allowing oneself to be led by the hand.[2] Neither on behalf of others nor of himself does the prophet entertain any idea of a speculative or critical attempt to fathom the thoughts of God, or to press one's personal claims. With his consciousness of knowing God's will, and of expounding it rightly to others, goes inevitably the conviction that he can uphold this claim only in so far as he is himself a man dominated by God.[3] In this attitude toward God the fundamental temper of Mosaic religion once more emerges pure and strong. Nevertheless, a merely passive state of submission is not enough; it must be combined with a *conscious autonomy of spiritual action*. The divine power that crushes all things human before it in the dust still shows itself wholly personal in

[1] Cf. Hertzberg, *Prophet und Gott*, pp. 28, 38; Hölscher, *Die Propheten*, p. 250.
[2] Cf. Hos. 4.16; 11.1 ff.; 12.7; Isa. 7.1 ff.; 18.4; 28.12; 30.15 etc.
[3] Cf. the accounts given by various prophets of their calls; also Amos 3.7; Isa. 8.11; Jer. 6.11; 15.16; 17.16; 20.9.

character. For it does not seek from men the submission of senseless automata, nor does it coerce them into slavery; it challenges them to make their own judgments and decisions. The resultant action is not, however, the spontaneous product of the human spirit, verifying its experience by logical or ethical standards intrinsic to itself. It is *personal decision*, a conscious reaction to the proffered revelation, a definite 'Yes' or 'No' to the claims of the divine reality.[1] When Hosea describes the right conduct that God expects from man as love,[2] he charges the individual divine-human relationship with the highest possible spiritual potential by making it a matter of a personal surrender of a kind that leaves no room for impersonal performance. When Isaiah, in the course of his decisive conflicts with the false worship of his own day, expresses the right attitude of the pious man in the term 'faith',[3] he is summing up intense spiritual

[1] It is with regret that one notices in Hertzberg, *op. cit.*, the absence of any reference to the fact that this active aspect of 'believing' and 'waiting upon God' was already present in earlier prophetism. In pointing the contrast with Jeremiah's type of spirituality he seems to have forgotten it. Even if the earlier prophets have left us no reflections on the subject, they possessed the thing itself. This 'activity in passivity' which marked the relationship of the prophets to God has been excellently expounded by S. Mowinckel (*Die Erkenntnis Gottes bei den AT Propheten*) and J. P. Seierstad (*Die Offenbarungserlebnisse der Propheten Amos, Jesaja und Jeremia*, 1946). The former defines the compulsive element in the prophet's acceptance of his call extremely well as a moral imperative arising from an existential relationship of communion between God and man. The latter points to the fixed determination that characterizes the soul of the prophet, and arises from his encounter with the God of judgment and graciousness, evoking a constant readiness to hear and obey. This makes it possible for the prophet to be continually open to fresh experiences of God's witness to himself, thus setting up God's will over the domain of his own free and responsible personal life, and affirming that will and making it his own in the most personal way in his conduct, suffering and prayer. Less convincing is the attempt of A. Heschel (*Die Prophetie. Das prophetische Bewusstsein*, 1936; cf. my review in *Theologie der Gegenwart* 30, 1936, pp. 112 ff.) to describe this active element in terms of the concept of the prophet's sympathy with the divine 'pathos' revealing itself in love and wrath. Moreover, if man's relationship with God is rightly described not as a union of essence, but of feeling and will, then the use of the expressions 'pathos' and 'sympathy', which proceeds from definitely philosophical presuppositions, is likely to weaken the clear-cut distinction which Heschel wants to make between prophecy and other comparable phenomena, and to open the door to mistaken interpretations of a mystical character. It accords better with the nature of prophecy to refer with E. Jacob ('Le Prophétisme israélite d'après les recherches récentes', *Revue d'Histoire et de Philosophie Religieuses* 32, 1952, p. 64) to the biblical concept of the *da'at 'elōhīm*, which is to be understood as a relationship of the most intimate communion, personal and reciprocal in kind. Cf. also A. Guillaume, *op. cit.*, pp. 343 f., who rightly stresses that the act of revelation is the divine answer to man's submission in prayer.

[2] Cf. Hos. 4.1; 6.4, 6; 10.12, and the parable of marriage in chs. 2 and 3.

[3] Cf. Isa. 7.9; 28.16; 30.15.

activity in one immensely meaningful word, which has indeed become, in its sense of the realization of the invisible hand of God, the designation of the central function of religion. The strong emphasis which we find in Hosea and Jeremiah on the 'knowledge of God' [1] does not, according to the generally agreed opinion, equate this *da'at yhwh* with intellectual contemplation or theoretical knowledge of the divine will, but with the act whereby man admits the nature and will of God as these have been revealed into his inmost spiritual self, with the result that that self now seems permeated and conditioned by the essential character of God. Again Amos, even though he has no word for 'ingratitude', is able to make the idea clear enough (2.9–12), and to characterize the essential nature of sin against God as precisely this utter insensitivity to all benefits. But what does all this mean, if not that *the knowledge of God can only be achieved by a real act on the part of man?*—an act, moreover, which is something quite different from mere cerebration, namely a real personal decision and acknowledgment, and not knowledge in the ordinary, neutral sense of the word? In this re-activation of the forces that shape personality, in response to the challenge of the God of the prophets, is to be found a real expansion of the divine-human relationship already existing in ancient Israel.

It was, however, of fundamental importance that this prophetic 'individualism' (if we may for once be permitted to use that misleading word) went hand in hand with a full recognition of the primary importance of *the People of God*. Not for a moment did the prophetic preaching question the fact that God's activity was directed toward a community; and it sought out the individual, and challenged him to decision, as a member of that community. This is also the reason why, when, as in the case of Amos, the soul of the prophet is full to overflowing with the unprecedented horror of the threat to the nation's very existence, there is nevertheless little or no mention of any positive action which the individual as such can take to win the favour of God. [2] It is only when there is some vision of a new existence for the nation beyond the annihilation of the present order, that the

---

[1]Cf. Jer. 2.8; 4.22; 9.5; 22.16; 31.34; Hos. 2.22; 4.1, 6; 5.4; 6.3, 6; 13.4.
[2]Herein lies the truth of Weiser's easily misunderstood remark (*Amos*, p. 306): 'It is characteristic of the light in which Amos looks at man's situation that he makes no serious attempt to indicate any way in which it might be possible to restore the bond between man and God.' It is not that man is regarded as an impotent creature, condemned to mere passivity in face of the fact of God—this

divine imperatives are brought out more strongly. It is thus perfectly clear that for the prophets there can be no isolating the personality, as this is seen from God's angle, from the national community. The personality, once awakened to conscious life, can never become an end in itself, for its relationship with God is attested as true and real just in so far as the person in question devotes himself to the service of his brother. It is this too which gives an intensely practical seriousness to the required decision for or against God, and safeguards it from spiritual trifling or quietistic self-admiration.

At the same time, with the recognition of the individual as an 'I' capable of responsible action in answer to the challenge of the divine 'Thou', we arrive at a unique *understanding of human personality*. This understanding is clearly differentiated both from the whole range of immanentist conceptions, deriving from the data of the spiritual world (the psychological basis of personality), and from the various attempts, deriving from animism, to base its value on some indestructible soul-stuff, which would ascribe to it a share in the actual being of God (the metaphysical basis). *It is only by the act of God that the existence of the human person as a unique entity can be guaranteed;* for only this excludes the possibilities of a false isolation and independence on the one hand, and on the other of disintegration at the hands of a destructive, naturalistic analysis of the idea of the soul.

(γ) The prophetic critique of daily life.

Consideration of the distinctive re-shaping of the divine-human relationship, as so far outlined, also suggests new perspectives on *the prophetic critique of men's ordinary conduct in the world*.

Generally speaking, the special feature of prophetic thought on this subject has been held to be that their preaching starts from the fact of moral judgment;[1] and the distinctive character of their faith is seen as summed up in their recognition that the true divine goal for the universe is that it should be morally ordered[2]—an insight

---

is the sort of timeless world-view which is nothing more than a theorizing construction placed upon the concreteness of the prophetic preaching; it is rather that the prophet is compelled to keep silence on the subject of action by the individual because he sees men as decisively involved in the national community on which the doom of annihilation is to fall.

[1] Cf. Oettli, *Amos und Hosea*, 1901, p. 24, and many others.

[2] Cf. Kittel, *Geschichte des Volkes Israel*[6] II, 1925, pp. 325 f.; H. Schultz, *O T Theology*[2] I, p. 217; Hänel, *Das Erkennen Gottes bei den Schriftpropheten*, 1923, pp. 202 ff., and *Prophetische Offenbarung*, 1926, pp. 10 ff.

which led them to ethical monotheism. This view is, of course, based on perfectly sound observation. Nevertheless, to regard it as the key to the prophetic preaching, and to employ it as such, is open to serious objections. For there is always the danger of laying the stress in the prophetic preaching too one-sidedly on the intensity of its moral demands, and of forgetting in the process that this is only one aspect of a whole which in every aspect is directed by its new sense of the reality of God.[1]

How strongly the prophetic message was dominated by this purely religious sense of immediate contact with the divine may be seen from those *threats and promises for which no moral motive is given*, but which nevertheless cannot be explained away as 'not genuine' by any reasonable standards of criticism.[2] No one could ask for a clearer demonstration that the new divine reality, whose irruption the prophets experience, is not to be expressed in terms of any ethical common denominator.

This is made equally clear by *the content of the moral demands* in the prophets. Any attempt to deduce from this a morality essentially different from that of ancient Israel is doomed to failure. It is true that the moral ideal of the individual was gradually transformed, that the stress came to be laid on the passive virtues of peace and love and the readiness to suffer, and that in the process spiritual and moral values and ideals acquired overriding importance. But this represents a clarification and refinement of the ancient Israelite outlook, not a complete re-orientation of the basic principles of morality. Rather is it true to say that the prophets are aware in their rebukes and exhortations of championing fundamental and generally accepted axioms of morality, which do not first have to be justified to the people. These are *the ancient duties of solidarity and brotherhood* in one's conduct toward a fellow-countryman, as already proclaimed in the ancient books of the Law; and it is these which the prophets now apply to the conditions of their own time, and for the neglect of which they declare God's judgment. The idea that foreign nations are also subject to the moral standard is sometimes regarded as a new element; but it is all too easy to overlook the fact that the validity of moral norms was not restricted to Israel even in the earlier sagas

---

[1]M. Buber, *The Prophetic Faith*, ET, 1949, gives an absorbing exposition of this point.
[2]Cf. Amos 3.12; 5.1–3, 18 ff.; Hos. 5.8 ff.; Isa. 3.1 ff.; 7.20 ff.; 10.27 ff.; 32.9 ff.; Jer. 4.5 ff.; 6.1 ff.; 6.22 ff. etc.

and historical literature. There too, certain fundamental ordinances are binding even on those outside the community. Moreover, where the prophets do advance to what is in principle a universal outlook, the development is due less to their own moral sensibility than to the greatness of the God who drives them in this direction.

Hence the significance of the prophets for the ethical ideas of Israel is to be sought rather in the fact that *they bring the impact of the divine reality directly to bear on the sphere of moral conduct.* What calls forth their fiery indignation is the realization that Israel pays just as little heed to Yahweh's moral demands as to his will in other directions. Men imagine that they can enjoy the protection of his presence, and even indulge in communion with him through the cultus, without bothering themselves about those fundamental laws of the divine Sovereign which intrude into the practice of daily life. 'That the righteous God is to be taken as God seriously and unconditionally',[1] and is not to be treated as a harmless bogeyman for children, is the seminal thought of all prophetic criticism of the moral situation. This is clearly shown by the way in which they speak of the majesty of the moral law. Their argumentation does not revolve round the question of what good is in itself; indeed, the concept of 'the good' appears relatively seldom.[2] Instead, the good is simply what Yahweh commands; and because he commands it, it is of absolute obligation. He would not be the Lord whose passionate will to self-assertion burns like a fire in the soul of the prophet, if any response other than that of unconditional obedience were thinkable in face of his commands. Nor would he be the wholly incomparable, before whom all earthly things must bow themselves even to the dust, were there anything at all other than his will by which human conduct ought to be guided.

If the intensified polemic of the prophetic preaching sometimes gives the impression that Yahweh in his other roles of Creator and King has been almost squeezed out of the picture by the immense emphasis on the force of his ethical purpose, yet this too is a direct result of something lying at the very heart of the prophet's experience. These men had experienced their God as a personal Thou, compelling men to ultimate personal decisions and resolves. Hence *the* sphere *par excellence*, in which, as they saw it, a man's attitude to this new reality of God was to be decided, could only be that realm in

[1] Weiser, *op. cit.*, p. 317.
[2] Cf. Isa. 5.20; Amos 5.14 f.; Micah 3.2; 6.8: also Baudissin, *Kyrios* III, p. 212.

which human will, pressed to an ultimate decision, could fashion its life out of the very foundations of personality and make its surrender with the commitment of a man's whole existence, namely the realm of morality. For the distinctive and exalted quality of the moral will consists precisely in this, that it lays claim to the whole man in existential decision, and makes it impossible to substitute any performance of objective acts for such personal commitment. Hence the struggle to secure acceptance of God's claim to sovereignty, just because it was personal in character, was bound to be predominantly and with especial keenness decided in the field of morality.

In the heat of this conflict, moreover, the prophets found that *the figure of Yahweh as a demanding personal will grew to colossal proportions.* When Amos speaks to his people of Yahweh's righteousness, he indicates the unique scale of God's authority in this connection by elevating the divine purpose of righteousness into a purpose for the whole universe, whose demands are revealed as irrefragable not only to Israel, but to the whole human race. When Hosea confronts his people with the yearning love of Yahweh, he makes the essential nature of the deity something miraculous and exclusive and supernaturally abundant, in order to distinguish it from all human love, and to make known the unique exaltation of the God with whom nothing on earth can be compared. It is well known how successfully Isaiah was able to imbue the ancient, traditional predicate of God, *qādōš*, with the new sense of ethical exaltedness. But the exceptional quality of his achievement lies in the fact that this concept now became wide enough to embrace the absolute otherness of the divine nature, from the angle of his moral perfection as well as from that of his transcendental majesty, and so provided an expression adequate both to the all-surpassing greatness and to the goodness of God. By the time of the later prophets, however, the whole richness of Yahweh's living personality is fully present, as it were in the round, to the prophet's mind; and consequently this kind of exaggeration of one attribute is no longer found. And it is precisely this sense of a divine nature so inexhaustible as to transcend all conception, that safeguards them, while they are warding off the dangers inherent in a nationalistically limited deity, from preaching as a result a bloodless, abstract monotheism, which would certainly do away with the narrowness inseparable from concrete attributes, but only at the cost of watering the Godhead down into a lifeless mental concept. Even where the formal language of monotheism is found, as in Jeremiah and Deutero-Isaiah, it is still linked with the living, inner dynamic of the divine personhood, confirming the divine majesty simply by virtue of its inconceivable inherent richness.

Thus it is that what deepens ethical judgment, and gives it its power of radical penetration, is the force of this new assurance of God. This also explains why, when they are speaking of man's rejection of the will of God, the prophets never 'quote' the Decalogue or the Book of the Covenant as a reliable source-book of threats and punishments, even though fairly clear allusions to these texts are to be found here and there.[1] This fact, which at first sight seems so surprising, is not to be explained externally by literary-critical arguments about the late emergence of the laws. Sufficient explanation is afforded by the internal presuppositions of the prophetic preaching. Such neglect of the categorical imperative of the law is only striking if the starting-point of this preaching is sought in some basic conviction of an ethical character. Once *the primarily religious orientation of their criticism* becomes clear, the fact ceases to be awkward. To the minds of these men the relation between God and man could never be comprehensively covered in the law, with its suggestion that once these requirements had been fulfilled there would be nothing more to do. The distinctive meaning of the divine-human relationship was the surrender of the *whole* man. An appeal to the law would have been quite unsuitable as a means of making this clear to their people. It would have diverted their attention from the main impact of the prophetic demand, and encouraged the heresy that the performance of precisely defined duties would provide a reliable guarantee of God's good pleasure. The God revealed to the prophets was no rigid lawgiver, but a living will, laying hold on life in all its aspects, and insisting on shaping it according to its own design from the very core of personal life outwards. Thus it was that they were able to sit loose to the particular expression of this will to be found in the law, and, for example, to champion, in the teeth of the cultic law, the primacy of the divinely ordained service of one's fellow-man.[2]

(δ) The prophetic attitude to the cultus.

The prophetic attitude to the cultus is not to be understood in terms of a simple either-or of morality or sacrifice, nor are the prophets to

[1] Cf. Hos. 4.2 f.; Jer. 7.9.
[2] Cf. on this point B. Balscheit and W. Eichrodt, *Die soziale Botschaft des AT für die Gegenwart*, 1942, pp. 33 ff.

be characterized as champions of 'ethical religion'. To do so is once again to force these men into too narrow a frame, and to exaggerate the importance of the cultus in their sayings. The well-known passages,[1] for all their pointed antithesis between cultic activity and righteous dealing, do not justify us in conceiving the prophetic ideal as a cultless, moralistic religion.[2] In this context as in the others it is much more to the point to try and understand the prophetic attitude by starting from the divine revelation that determined it. It then at once becomes apparent that the very same factor which sets the moral demands so firmly in the centre of the divine purpose is also the one which is decisive for the devaluation of the cultus, namely *the personal quality of the divine-human relationship*. It is because of their experience of the divine Thou, that the prophets put up such a passionate resistance against anything that tends to depersonalize this relationship and, this is just what happens when the fear of God is misprized in the relations between man and man, and God himself is sought only in the cultus. God becomes an impersonal source of magical power, which can be manipulated with no feeling of reverence whatsoever simply by means of a meticulous routine; for, so far as his will, the core of his personality, is concerned, man by such an attitude declines to recognize the claims of his divine Lord. What the prophets were up against in their fight with the cultus was the mystical approach to the Godhead; and therefore the defiantly volitional quality of the Mosaic religion broke out in them with renewed vigour.

That this, however, should have happened more drastically than ever before is due, at least to a very large extent, to *the degeneration of cultic life in the prophetic period*. The luxuriant growth of cultic practice, the consequence of which was 'a debasement of the religion of Yahweh into a religion of cult',[3] sharply distinguishes the situation in their day from that in the early period of Israel. Bound up with the eager frequenting of holy places both on pilgrimages and at festivals was a tendency to attach increasing importance to sacred objects, a tendency stimulated both from abroad and by influences reviving within Canaan itself. This association of the holy with the sensorily perceptible led to a corresponding passionate yearning for experience

[1] Cf. Amos 4.4; 5.21; Isa. 1.10 ff., 15 ff.; Jer. 7.9 ff., *et al.*
[2] There is even less justification for this if the prototype of this antithesis between righteousness and the cultus is to be found in the proverbial wisdom: cf. Gressmann, 'Die vorexilische Spruchdichtung', *ZAW* 42, 1924, pp. 286 f.
[3] Cf. B. Duhm, *Israels Propheten*, p. 117: also ch. II.2. 1, pp. 45 f. above.

of the divine by means of physical magic. It did not need the considerable admixture of directly heathen elements, in the form of images and symbols of the deity and orgiastic practices, to bring home to those with eyes to see the seriousness of this whole tendency in religion. Even more challenging must it have been to see how even the genuine, orthodox cult of Yahweh was marked by the smug self-confidence of the whole cultic machine and those who operated it.[1] No longer did men tremble before the inconceivable majesty of God, for they fancied that they had power over his power; and consequently the genuine religious feeling of the nation was poisoned. Either it was perverted from the way of interior surrender to that of formal performance and the fulfilling of obligations (Isa. 29.13), or it learned to find its satisfaction in intoxicating communion with the deity. In face of so drastic and decisive a misconception of religion any man who lived by a direct awareness of God was bound to find himself involved in a ferocious conflict over ultimate principles. When they saw how, with the help of the cultus, religion was being falsified at its very heart, they could not help repudiating such a cultus root and branch, and setting up in opposition to its deluding power an obedience to the moral demands of God which could alone afford an infallible touchstone of the right attitude to God's personal will. Hence *the issue was bound to be pushed to the point of a clear 'either-or', if only to deny their opponents any possibility of evasion.* The whole cultic approach to God, with its ideas of merit and its sacramental mysticism, was separated by an unbridgeable gulf from that of humble obedience toward an almighty divine Lord.

The result of the conflict, however, which went far beyond the limitations of its original historical setting, was to achieve a clarification of the principles governing the relation of the cultus to the worship of Yahweh. Those sharp antitheses in which the prophetic polemic at its climactic points so delighted did not contain the doctrine of a cultless worship. Only a complete misunderstanding of both the external and internal situations which gave rise to these sayings could even look for such a message in them. On the subject of what is to be done with the cult as a whole the prophets say nothing. Because, on this subject as on all others, they are dominated

[1] Weiser has given us a striking sketch of this situation as it obtained in Amos' day (*op. cit.*, p. 319); but the passages in Amos (2.8; 4.4 f.; 5.21, 27) may be combined with similar ones from the other prophetic books, which prove that the same antithesis prevailed in the time of his successors; cf. Isa. 28.7, 9, 15, 18; Jer. 8.8; 6.13 f., 19 f.; 5.31 etc.

by the certainty of God's imminent advent, all schemes of organization seem to them poles apart from the concrete demand for absolute
readiness to obey.[1] But the intense fervour which was such an
essential ingredient of their fight for the personal quality of the
divine-human relationship implied an estimate of the cultus which
was bound to deprive it once for all of the status to which it pre-
tended, namely that of being the preferred medium of the knowledge
of God, and of the community's association with him. Henceforward,
the cultus could no longer justify its existence on the grounds that,
as work done for God, it was a good investment, or that it offered
an assured means of access to the living power of God, the success
of which was guaranteed by its intrinsic mechanical effectiveness
regardless of the state of heart of the participant. Yahweh's majesty,
so overwhelmingly proclaimed by the prophets, and the personal
quality of any fellowship with him, excluded both the one and the
other, and subjected the cultus to the standards of spiritual and
personal intercourse with God.[2] Whether as the common act of the
worshipping community in confession and prayer, or as the sacramental mediation of God's blessing, the cultus could now be no more
than the making visible of a personal surrender and acceptance, the
symbol of an *existing* covenant grace, not the basis on which it was
granted. Thus what had been present in embryo in the preaching of
Moses now came to full development. Wherever the spirit of the
prophets remained a living force, the cultus became a symbol, a
poor, stammering one, but a genuine symbol none the less, of man's
awe and will to self-surrender. God's blessing on the cult, and
acceptance of it, no longer rested on man's own merit, but on God's
gracious condescension. Such passages as Isa. 40.16; 43.22 ff.; 52.11;
Pss. 40.7 ff.; 50; 51.18 ff. give vivid expression to this evaluation of

[1]Opinion on the attitude of the prophets to sacrifice has undergone a radical
change in the last decades as a result of the study of the cultus in Israel. The old
position—that it was possible to establish an absolute rejection of the sacrificial
cultus—should still, however, not be entirely abandoned. Cf. e.g. J. P. Hyatt,
Prophetic Religion, 1947, pp. 125 ff. N. Söderblom, however, had already cast
doubt on the idea that the prophets envisaged total abolition of the cultus (*The
Living God*, 1933, pp. 306 f.); and today, when the tendency is to regard every
prophet as a member of a guild of cult prophets, such an idea is naturally even
more out of the question—indeed, there are signs of the opposite danger of dis-
missing the prophetic criticism of the cult as an unimportant trifle. Cf. A. Haldar,
Associations of Cult Prophets, 1945, p. 113, and *Nahum*, add. note 2, pp. 155 f.;
A. Guillaume, *Prophecy and Divination*, pp. 369 ff., where the rigid opposition to
sacrifice in such passages as Hos. 6.6; Amos 5.25 ff. is argued away.

[2]Cf. ch. IV, pp. 99f. above.

the cultus, which had been concealed behind the prophetic polemic;[1] and the further logical step by which the atoning power of the sacrifice was limited to inadvertent transgressions establishes beyond doubt the influence which prophetism's critique of the cult exerted in priestly circles.[2]

This internal victory over the cultic misconception of religion is all the more remarkable, when we consider that the spiritual structure of prophetism might very easily have tended to sheer iconoclasm and to a radicalism divorced from history. Perhaps this is the germ of truth in the view that the prophets were in principle anti-cultic and moralist. It is perfectly true to say that their whole inward temper made it impossible that they should ever have been partisans of the cultus; and indeed, it is in the violence of their opposition to it as it was in their own day, in their scornful denigration which simply disregarded any value it may actually have had, that their fundamental spiritual outlook, which turns its back on the present and reaches out to the God who is to come, makes itself really effective. In a world which was racing to destruction, any attempt at representing God, at 'having God at one's disposal', as a means of escaping judgment and conflict, is, from such a standpoint, objectionable in itself. It is far too cheap a way of enabling man to stand before the God at whose appearing the universe must flee away, and man himself be crushed in the consciousness of his inexpiable guilt. Any attempt to obliterate the gulf between God and man by a presumptuous 'God is on our side' is bound to be felt as treason to the divine majesty; and therefore the cultus, as a means of 'making sure of God', must be branded as arrogance and a lie.[3]

The fact that the possibilities which this implied of a theoretical rejection of any kind of cultus were never realized proves once more, as clearly as can be desired, how completely the prophet allowed his task to be dictated by the concrete situation, and how far removed his preaching was from creating any systematic form of doctrine, the effect of which could only have been to deaden the direct impact of the divine reality which he had experienced.

[1] Cf. the similar view of S. Mowinckel, *Psalmenstudien* VI, pp. 51 ff.; and more recently, V. Schönbächler, *Die Stellung der Psalmen zum alttestamentlichen Opferkult*, 1941.

[2] Cf. Num. 17.6–13 and ch. IV, p. 161 n. 6.

[3] Cf. in this connection the penetrating study of M. Schmidt, *Prophet und Tempel: Eine Studie zum Problem der Gottesnähe im Alten Testament*, 1948.

(ε) The prophetic attitude to the national religion.

The same considerations also apply to the judgment which the prophets in the course of their activity were compelled to pass on the national religion as a whole.

Attempts have constantly been made, on the basis of the violent judgment-sayings in which the prophets sever the tie between the people and their God, to prove that they completely rejected that faith in her election which formed the very foundation of Israel's assurance of God, and united the nation to him in the closest possible way.[1] Such a rejection, however, would only be probable, if this faith had never existed in any form other than the perverted one which was espoused by the opponents of the prophets, and which was no more than a caricature of its original. But if the doctrine of election is understood as expressing a relationship between God and Israel which was rooted in history,[2] and by means of which Israel was rescued from any kind of naturalistic association with God, then it is possible to do unbiased justice to the many prophetic statements concerning the special relationship between Yahweh and Israel,[3] and to derive from them important evidence for the general character of prophetic opinion, as this was shaped by the direct impact of their new assurance of God.

1. Common presuppositions.

The basis common both to the popular faith and to the prophetic preaching is the belief in a self-communication of a previously unknown God to Israel in particular, or in other words the recognition of the fact of revelation. The consequence of this fact is that Israel acquires in very truth a special position among the nations. Even where the word 'election' is not used, the thing itself is implied—as, for example, when the prophets speak of the redemption from Egypt or the gift of the land of Canaan. No prophet ever thought of combating this faith as in any way a false assumption that imposed limits too narrow for the concept of a God exalted above the universe. On the contrary, it is precisely to the condescension of the mighty Lord of the world, as this can be seen in the act of election and the history that stems from it, that the prophets prefer to appeal in their efforts to drive

[1] So—to quote him for the last time!—Weiser, *op. cit.*, pp. 319 f.
[2] Cf. pp. 42 f., 50 f., 348 above.
[3] Cf. Amos 2.10; 3.11 f.; 4.10; 5.21 f.; 9.7; Hos. 2.17; 9.10; 11.1; 12.14; 13.4; Isa. 1.2; Jer. 3.4, 19; 2.2 ff.; Micah 6.4 f.

home the unique importance and value of the nation, and the full seriousness of its responsibility.[1]

Consequently, they do not even shrink from speaking of a *real presence of God in the midst of his people*, made manifest in signs and wonders. The whole of past history is for them filled with such divine manifestations; and so far from finding fault with their people for expecting special acts of God, they regard them as to blame for not taking sufficiently seriously God's real intervention in their destinies, both in the past and in the present, and for seeking instead to safeguard their position with all kinds of earthly assistance. Indeed many of them, and these not by any means the least important, go so far as to give express approval to the association of this real divine presence with a holy place—a belief which plays such a large part in the popular religion. It is this that makes strange bedfellows of Isaiah and Ezekiel; for both emphasize Yahweh's dwelling on Zion,[2] not just for this present time, the fate of which is sealed when Yahweh abandons his earthly dwelling-place, but also for the future, when God's perfect dominion is to find its focus in this place, so bestowing on man a hitherto unattainable communion with his God.[3] It is altogether too easy an expedient to charge Isaiah with an unsuppressed vestige of nationalist particularism, or Ezekiel with sacerdotal narrow-mindedness.[4] It would be far better to recognize that this fact, which is so astonishing to any idealist theory of the religion of the prophets, is a necessary consequence of the distinctively historical character of the revelation, which gives the Here and Now a specific importance; and that the prophet knows of no content of revelation which might be proclaimed as timeless truth (which would indeed be to do away with the strict concept of revelation altogether), but finds revelation only in inseparable association with the historical datum through which it is made. The statement that God spoke to Israel, that is to say, that the real, personal God spoke to the real Israel, present in its historical existence—not that a universal cosmic idea spoke to the human soul—allows men also to place a special emphasis on the historical scene of this revelation, and so to distinguish the real historical dealings of God with his people quite

---

[1] This point is made with especial force by K. Cramer, *Amos*.

[2] Isa. 8.18; 31.9; Ezek. 8–11; cf. Zeph. 3.5.

[3] Isa. 2.2–4; Ezek. 37.26 f.; 43.1 ff.

[4] The various attempts to relieve Isaiah of this incubus by literary-critical methods prove that such reproaches are felt to be out of keeping with the universal outlook which he shows elsewhere.

clearly from any moralistic re-interpretation or mystical sublimation. To insist that God's perfect revelation is connected with Jerusalem, and not with any other place you happen to fancy, or even with no particular place at all, is first to safeguard the personal character of this revelation from the shallowness of syncretism, and secondly to prove, if rightly understood, the absolute sovereignty of God's self-communication—which indeed, by this assertion of its own essentially individual, temporal form, preserves itself from confusion with the general ruck of possible religious ideas. The fetishistic misunderstanding of such a connection was obviously less feared by the prophets than a divorce of the revelation from its historical medium which would assimilate it to the worship of the divinized forces of natural and instinctive life—that peculiarly Near Eastern concept of religion, which was at the time making such powerful inroads in Israel.

2. The prophetic re-shaping of the national religion.

It was this naturalistic conception of God which was also the principal source of danger to the purity of the belief in election, and which opened the way to all kinds of perversions. On the one hand there was the possibility that the cultus would be changed into a relationship of rights and duties, in which the cultic procedure itself, by a kind of foolproof technique, could provide access to the source of divine power. On the other, the covenant concept might be misused to glorify national egoism.[1] The whole difficulty of the prophetic position in the face of this gradual distortion of religious concepts that originally had meant something quite different will be obvious. It was precisely because a common basis of faith united them to their people that they could not safeguard their own conception of God by any sort of clean break that would separate it from that of the nation at large, but were driven to adopt a programme of profound criticism and conflict. Once more it is a question of the prophets' distinctive awareness of God. Because God was present to them as a personal moral will of limitless power and authority, they were bound to think of the communion bestowed by him not primarily as the enjoyment of the bounty of the divine Lord of the land, but as a relationship of worship and loyalty to which all the other relationships of life had to be subordinated. Once the Israelites had become settled landowners, Yahweh, as their God, was bound to acquire

[1] Cf. pp. 45 f., 328 ff. above.

many features which had formerly been alien to him from the old gods of the culture pattern[1]—but wherever there was a vital sense of his character as Lord of the social union, and guide of its destinies, any confusion with the fertility gods was constantly rendered impossible by the force of his own will, shaping the course of history. If therefore it was desired to bring the abundant blessings of civilized life within the domain of the national God, this could only be effected by using the two categories of Creator and Lord of the land. It is a remarkable fact that the first of these is only infrequently used by prophets before Deutero-Isaiah;[2] the special manifestations of God's graciousness toward Israel were too much in the forefront of their minds for the description of his general creative activity to be able to satisfy them. By contrast they made frequent use of the category of Lord of the land in various forms, either portraying him as ruler (Isaiah), or husband (Hosea), or princely lover (Ezekiel). From this point of view natural blessings acquired a quite distinctively religious significance as signs and pledges of divine favour, to which, on the side of the nation, the maintenance of a relationship of worship and loyalty to Yahweh directly corresponds. The classic picture of this correspondence is to be found in Hos. 2.4 ff. Here too the personal quality of the divine-human relationship comes out; the real blessing is that in the enjoyment of prosperity man experiences a relationship with the Lord of the nation, and contact with the will that shapes his destiny.

This barrier against any degeneration into eudaemonism was, in essence, already implicit in the ancient Israelite view of God; but the prophets deepened and strengthened it at various points. Thus, in opposition to any idea of mediation through physical magic, dependent on the scale of man's performance and its strict adherence to certain rules, they describe the access to himself which God grants in the covenant relationship as a *spiritual communication, personal in character*, becoming effectual in faith, love and obedience. In this way any perversion of the divine-human relationship into a legalistic one, based on works, is presented as antithetic to the living force of mutual personal intercourse. At the same time, moreover, the real divine presence guaranteed by the covenant is removed from man's direct possession. The meaning of this presence is not a standing

---

[1] J. Hempel rightly calls attention to this adaptability of the Yahweh religion in *Gott und Mensch im AT*, pp. 38 ff.

[2] Cf. Hos. 8.14; Isa. 29.16.

authorization for man to draw on a stock of divine power, but an encounter with the divine personhood in its word and will. These are presented to man in both Law and prophecy, both of them ways essentially indirect; for only this indirect self-disclosure, requiring from men the resignation and surrender of their own wills, can be worthy of the greatness of such a God, and exclude any idea that man might be able to override God's nature. From another angle, it does away with the godless self-assurance with which Israel imagined she could presume on Yahweh's succouring presence. By allowing men to see clearly the personal pre-conditions of any experience of God's self-communication it frees the covenant relationship from the character of an automatic mechanism of divine self-commitment, which could be relied upon in any and every circumstance.

Another inevitable consequence of this dominating vision of life as something shaped in answer to the challenge of the divine will was to leave the covenant relationship free to pursue its proper goal without being cramped by the aims of egoistic nationalism. Before the consuming fire of a God who prostrates all human majesty the glory of the earthly king grows pale. He becomes a man who is himself in need of grace and forgiveness, whose worth consists in this, that he is permitted to be the first of the servants of his God, but who, as much as anyone else, is dependent on God's indirect self-communication.[1] The goals of the nation's life are not to be determined by an autonomous divine deputy. He, as well as the nation, is called to the service of the exalted Lord of the world; and both are to learn the purpose of election in the realization of a national life dependent upon God. If the ultimate purpose of the covenant is submission to God's sovereignty, then the continuance of the covenant is clearly determined by man's readiness for such submission. Where this readiness is lacking, the inevitable consequence is the abrogation of the doctrine of election in judgment. The ultimate horror of this conclusion, which is necessary to protect God's freedom from being anthropocentrically distorted on the basis of a perverted notion of the covenant, becomes bearable in practice, however, in the contemplation of God's all-surpassing greatness. In that this attitude illuminates God's cosmic purposes, it achieves something which in the Mosaic period was effected by the inexplicable and terrifying power of God's near presence, namely the severance of divine

[1]An idea formulated most clearly in Isa. 11.2 f.

sovereignty from any attempts at human control, even when this was disguised in the religious thought-forms of an earlier time.

On this basis it becomes much easier to understand why the prophets have so little to say about Yahweh's covenant with Israel, and the statutes that went with it. This conception had long become too fixed as a description of a relationship established once for all, a statutory institution, and so no longer did justice to *the vital personal quality of the divine-human relationship*. And this, for the prophets, was the thing that mattered.[1] For them election was only the beginning of permanent intercourse, the reality of which derived from constant fresh decisions for God—a lasting association committing man to obedient attention to a divine will ever calling him to new tasks.[2] For priest and people, on the other hand, election was a matter of firmly established ordinances, placed at man's disposal, and which in certain circumstances might even support man against God. An appeal to the character of the covenant, therefore, offered no protection against a complete misunderstanding of Yahweh. It is precisely those who are most zealous in familiarity with the Law who have no knowledge of Yahweh (Jer. 2.8). Man had learnt how to get his own way by skilful manipulation of the Law; and if the prophets had upheld the value of the covenant statutes, then a quibbling legalistic spirit would have made use of just these statutes to contest the demands made by these 'men of the spirit'. Hence the biting sayings against the scribes skilled in the Law (Isa. 10.1 ff.; Jer. 8.8), who in the consciousness of their learning refuse to countenance the prophetic claims. Similarly, those passages that do conceive the coming salvation in the form of a covenant[3] place all the emphasis on the fact that then outward regulation will have made way for inward readiness to accept God's will, and the fully living quality of intercourse with God will have triumphed over all external legalism of conduct.

(ζ) Sin and judgment.

If this has been a correct description of the positive prophetic ideas on how best to shape both the individual and the collective divine-human relationship in their contemporary situation, then it should be possible to check the accuracy of the picture by reference

[1]Cf. pp. 50 f. above.
[2]Cf. Jer. 2.6, 8.
[3]Jer. 31.31 ff.; Ezek. 34.25; 37.26; Isa. 42.6; 49.8; 54.10; 55.3; 61.8: cf. pp. 58 ff. above.

to the negative side of the prophetic message, namely their *sayings on sin and judgment*. In doing so it is hardly necessary to prove that the prophets, for all that they associate themselves with the moral judgment of their time by their concrete stress on particular sinful actions, yet always return to the personal spiritual attitude from which transgressions of law and morality arise. The conception of the divine-human relationship as something laying claim to the very depths of the whole human personality here makes itself felt by causing sin to be portrayed as at bottom a wanton jeopardization, nay, dissolution of this relationship. Thus Hosea can sum up sin as ingratitude,[1] with its ultimate basis in an antipathy to God's very nature and will.[2] And when he wants in contrast to describe right conduct, then he uses the terms Love, Faithfulness and Knowledge of God[3]—once more the most intimate processes of personal decision. Isaiah describes sin as rebellion against the divine Lord, a rupture of the relationship of *pietas* between a father and his children arising from pride and lack of faith, which will not allow themselves to be set right by the transcendent God.[4] All these attempts to express the matter are repeated and modified in various ways by the other prophets; in Jeremiah, for instance, there is a deepening through tenderness and inwardness, whereas in Ezekiel the lesson is pointedly harsh, as in the parables of chs. 16 and 23. But in every case both the essential elements are found in close association, the concrete and personal quality of the indictment, and the profound spiritual grasp of the nature of sin. In this way both the tabuistic and the juridical-moralistic assessments of sin are overcome: from this standpoint, cultic offences can only be classified as sin, if they are regarded as a refusal of obedience or reverence,[5] and so all the mechanical and impersonal overtones of the idea of infringing a sphere of divine power disappear. Furthermore, individual transgressions of the social or moral law are in this way removed from the realm of the external performance of legally stipulated obligations, and assessed as the expression of a moral or immoral will. In contrast to a false

---

[1] Hos. 2.10 ff., 15; 4.1; 5.4; 9.17; 13.6.
[2] Hos. 6.4, 7; 7.14; 8.11; 9.8; 12.11, 14 f.
[3] Hos. 4.1.
[4] Isa. 1.2, 4; 2.6 ff.; 5.12, 21, 24; 9.8 ff.; 28.1, 10 f., 14, 22 etc.
[5] This is the theme of the fierce rebukes launched against the feeble postponement of the work of rebuilding the Temple (Hag. 1.2 ff.; Zech. 8.9 ff.), or against defective cultic practices (Mal. 1.6 ff.; 2.1 ff.), all of which are very different in tone from the utterances of later Temple prophecy on the subject of Sabbath-breaking (Isa. 56.1 ff.; 58.13 ff.; Jer. 17.19 ff. etc.).

isolation of sinful actions, which conceals from itself the true significance of the spiritual state as a whole, this approach, as distinct from all materialist misconceptions, by preserving the unity of the personal moral will, and defining the concept of guilt in terms of the disturbance, or indeed complete destruction of an absolutely personal divine-human relationship, succeeds in grasping the issue in all its existential seriousness. The ultimate logical conclusion is drawn by Ezekiel in his clear-cut formulation of the moral responsibility of the individual for his own actions. This is something that no one can take away from him, any more than he himself is allowed to be liable for the guilt of another.[1]

If by thus expounding *the personal quality of sin* the prophets are able to bring out its full seriousness, they are equally successful in illuminating *its appalling power and extent*, and so in making it impossible for men to take lightly the task of overcoming it or making reparation for it. They are able to achieve this, because they understand how to bring home most effectively to the consciousness that clouding of the capacity for moral knowledge and that crippling of the will which arise from sin, that is to say, its corrosive effect on the forces of personal life. Isaiah describes the progressive effects of the first wrong decision as a deep sleep sent by God himself, or as his hardening of man's heart for judgment.[2] Jeremiah speaks of the compulsion of the evil *habitus*, which brings to nothing all good intentions, and destroys all hope of conversion.[3] From rejection of God's demands comes rooted hostility to God himself, which no experience of miracle or prophecy can any more do anything to help; and to expiate this by purely human expedients cannot but seem a ludicrous proceeding because it betrays a complete misunderstanding of its true character.

This attitude to the national God is now with increasing severity attributed to the whole people. With a profound and penetrating inspection is now combined a broad sweeping survey, leading to the discovery that *throughout the nation's history this turning away from God has from the very first been present as the woof in the web.* Hosea

---

[1] Cf. Ezek. 18. It is quite true that too much stress on these moral maxims in the direction of the individual's freedom of decision at each separate moment may lead once more to a fragmentation of moral behaviour. But Ezekiel is quite well aware of men's solidarity in corporate guilt (ch. 20), and of the power of the sinful disposition (36.26 ff.).

[2] Cf. Isa. 29.9 f.; 6.9 f.; 28.22; 28.7, 13; 5.18 f.

[3] Cf. Jer. 13.23; cf. 2.24 f.; 6.7; 8.4 ff.

sees the mendacious character of Israel's inmost soul already pre-figured in the patriarch Jacob; from Egypt onwards the nation has tried to escape from God's guidance; the entry into Canaan was synonymous with a falling away from Yahweh[1]—in short, every incident of its history exhibits the nation's ungrateful and rebellious spirit.[2] Their present disobedience is but the working out of a per-manent attitude of mind.[3] Here we see something which in an earlier period was known as the solidarity of corporate guilt transferred from a naturalistic corporeity of common blood to a spiritual kinship deriving from a common anti-God attitude, and acquiring all the more force in the process. The attitude of the people as a whole embraces every individual, and embroils him in the general guilty behaviour. The present too is taken out of its artificial isolation. It loses its appearance of being more or less fortuitous in its moral tone, and becomes the necessary end-product of the whole of preceding history. This does not mean that it has been determined by previous generations, and so may be relieved of the burden of personal responsibility, but rather that what had been the hidden orientation of men's attitude, running through the whole period of Israel's election relationship, and making it into a time of divine patience and tolerance, is in this generation brought to a head and stripped of its camouflage. What stands revealed is man's ultimate basic attitude to God, in that man can be seen to have reacted to God's dealings with him in the same way in the past as in the present; and therefore, what God now does with his people is similarly removed from all the contingency of the actual situation and its historical manifes-tation into a sphere of absolute opposition and conflict between God and man. Judgment becomes the disclosure and inexorable working out of the ultimate radical opposition between God and mankind.

This *power of evil*, unaffected by the procession of the ages, is by many prophets pursued even beyond the borders of Israel *into the Gentile world*. When Amos at the beginning of his book utters his great prophecy of judgment, this is not merely an extension to the nations, on account of their particular sins, of a conviction of Yahweh's punitive visitation which had hitherto been applied only to Israel. Rather, the fact that this conviction goes hand in hand with the announcement that the conflict between Yahweh and Israel is to

[1] Cf. Hos. 12.4, 13; 11.1 f.; 9.10.
[2] Cf. Amos 4.6 ff.; Isa. 9.7 ff.
[3] Cf. Ezek. 20; Jer. 7.24 ff.

be settled once for all elevates the somewhat temporally and historically conditioned execution of God's punishment of the Gentile world into a similar final reckoning—this time with humanity as a whole,[1] whose sins, like those of Israel in particular, have long constituted a rejection of God's demand for obedience. It is true that the prophets do not enter into a discussion of the relations between God and mankind. But by adopting the mythological concepts of the Chaos-monster and its slaying at the hands of the Creator of the universe, and transferring them to the subjugation of tyrant nations and their rulers by Yahweh,[2] they sketch the evil in man in the lineaments of a demonic cosmic power, comprising in itself all that rejects God, and striving with the God of Israel for the dominion of the earth.[3] Looked at in this way, the sin of Israel can be seen for the first time in its full import as a taking sides in a cosmic conflict; the people whom God has chosen enter the struggle against him on the side of the nations whom he despises, and thus logically incur the same fate as has been prepared for the rest.[4] The dualistic world-view which in pre-prophetic Israel was content with the antithesis of the People of God and the nations of the world is now widened and deepened into an opposition between God and sinful humanity as a whole, and thus acquires the moral and personal quality which distinguishes it sharply from all the various kinds of pessimistic world-denial which cannot but remain embedded in naturalist mysticism.

Corresponding to this simultaneous inner deepening and broadening of the concept of sin is the way in which the prophets also carry *the concept of judgment* to its logical conclusion. The more completely they were confronted with the power of sin, not only in their own

---

[1] That this was also looked for outside prophetic circles would seem to follow from the frequent incidental reference to the judgment of the nations in many passages which, however, only treat it as a background to the judgment on Israel: cf. Isa. 3.13; 2.12; 1.2; 28.22. Cf. also ch. X, pp. 458 f. below.

[2] Cf. Isa. 17.12 ff.; 14.12 ff.; Nahum 1 f.; Ezek. 38 f.

[3] Of especial importance in this connection is the mythical figure of the one whom the prophets expected to execute the divine judgment: cf. Isa. 5.26 ff.; 8.9 f.; 14.26 f.; 28.14 ff.; 29.1 ff.; Jer. 4–6; Zeph. 1.2 ff., 14 ff.; Joel 2.1 ff.; Isa. 13. Cf. also the absorbing exposition of the prophetic oracles of disaster in the comprehensive treatise of W. Stärk, 'Zu Hab. 1.5–11. Geschichte oder Mythus?', *ZAW* 51, 1933, pp. 1 ff.

[4] This connection between the sin of Israel and the sin of the world at large is, however, in most cases not explicitly worked out—the exception being Isaiah, who expressly designates *hybris* as the real root of sin both in his own people and in the heathen.

nation but also in the world outside, the less could they be satisfied with individual punitive visitations, such as had been known in the past history of Israel, as a means of enforcing the ultimate demands of Yahweh for absolute obedience. Any nation which went so stubbornly against the will of its God as to make the entire pattern of its life, in the state, in social conditions and in cultic organization, into a conspiracy against Yahweh (cf. Jer. 11.9), a systematic rejection of his exclusive sovereignty, had forfeited the right to exist. Any world which reared itself up in such titanic defiance of the divine Lord of the universe could not but incur his annihilating judgment.[1] This is why the prophets proclaim the ruin of state and monarchy, the dissolution of every system of corporate life, the destruction of the holy places and the cessation of the cultus—in other words, nothing less than the complete annihilation of the nation in its present form. Granted that this message is often proclaimed conditionally, that the opinion of the prophets oscillates from time to time toward the possibility of restoring a state of affairs pleasing to God,[2] yet

[1] Only in Isaiah and Ezekiel do we find a vision that comprises both these acts of Yahweh's judgment, and understands their common inner rationale. In the rest of the prophets it is either one or the other that dominates the horizon. Nevertheless, there can be no doubt that both are equally involved in the logical consequences of the prophetic world-view.

[2] It would in fact have been surprising if now and then some improvement in the nation's conduct or some particularly striking crisis in its fortunes had not fired the prophets with a hope that the people would be fully and freely converted. Thus Isaiah in his early days could still hope for a reformation of the whole body, both head and members (cf. 1.21 ff.; 32.1 ff.); and again during the Assyrian crisis, the meekness of Hezekiah and the humiliation of the war party seemed to open up new prospects (cf. 1.18 ff.; 37.31 ff.). The same was true of Jeremiah at various times (cf. 3.19 ff.; 18.1 ff.; 26.13; 30.18 ff.). This should not, however, deceive us into thinking that the proclamations of disaster were not seriously meant, or that the idea of a purifying judgment can be invoked as an easy way of weakening their force (so Kautzsch, *Biblische Theologie des AT*, pp. 256 ff.). The eschatological hope of salvation does nothing to limit the seriousness of the judgment; on the contrary, it is what gives it its full severity. For this hope looks for a genuine new creation by Yahweh after the old order has been totally destroyed. The 'remnant'—the handful of Isaiah's disciples, the few survivors of the battle, cannot be described as the *nation* purified by judgment in any real sense of the word; in any case, Israel knew only too well from the evidence of her own eyes what the future held in store for any land depopulated by war and deportation. Hence the hope of the prophets is a case of 'hoping, because there is nothing to hope for', and is on quite a different plane from any idea that the nation might after all come out of the judgment fairly cheaply. The prophets' exhortations to the people, which would seem to presuppose that the judgment could be avoided, ought not to be pressed to prove that it was only of an *ad hoc*, not an absolute character. Rather, except for those related simply to particular and passing occasions, or delivered with pedagogic intention (as e.g. Amos 5.4, 14 f.) they

they still leave no doubt that their nation, as it stands, has nothing to expect but merciless destruction. Indeed, the most varied imagery is used to drive home explicitly and forcefully that this is the inevitable and necessary end.[1] Of Israel nothing is to be left but worthless potsherds.[2]

Additional emphasis is given to the inner necessity of this final reckoning between God and people by *the various descriptions of the divine punishment*. The first thing to notice is that, for all their uninhibited use of external disasters to describe the rod of God's wrath—as, for example, natural catastrophes, misfortune in war, or revolution—they nevertheless have a preference for those expressions that are most completely personal. Thus Hosea illustrates Yahweh's punitive measures by the conduct of a man toward his unfaithful wife.[3] Isaiah calls to mind the father whose sons have become disobedient to him, the owner of a vineyard who turns in disgust from his unfruitful property, the master-builder laying his cornerstone on Zion, the smelter purifying his silver, the barber shaving his customer completely bald, the workman who makes whatever use of his tools he pleases.[4] The later prophets in part take over these images, in part add new ones of their own.[5]

The constant theme of all these images is that the divine punishment is a matter of a personal reaction on the part of a dishonoured God who has at last come to the point of destroying from his side the relationship of trust which Israel has already defiled and falsified; and he does this not with the strict and icy indifference of a judge, but with the pain and anger of one whose suit for a personal surrender has been rejected. And because in such a context everything rests on the interior laws of a personal association, the voices of the prophets are eloquent in proclaiming that even the most severe punishment nevertheless results from a moral necessity far

---

testify only to the fact that for the prophets even the inescapable judgment never became just a matter of blind fate. The living quality of the divine-human relationship and the validity of the moral order remained unaffected. Moreover these exhortations tell us nothing of what they thought about the *possibility* of a complete conversion, from the human angle; and their occasional remarks about compulsion to sin suggest a certain scepticism rather than a naïve optimism.

[1] Cf. Isa. 9.7 ff.; 5.25 ff.
[2] Cf. Isa. 30.14, 17; 7.21 ff.; 5.17, 24 etc.; Jer. 19.11.
[3] Cf. Hos. 2.5, 12; 3.3 f.
[4] Cf. Isa. 1.2; 5.1 ff.; 28.16 ff.; 1.25; 7.20; 10.15.
[5] Cf. Jer. 3.19, 22; 2.2, 32.

removed from any kind of caprice. Hosea, by his use of the image of marriage, had made it clear in the most affecting way that the external punishment was simply the inevitable consequence of the preceding inner alienation. Judgment is already involved in man's spontaneous decision to separate himself from God. Guilt and punishment are not totally unrelated things, whose external connection can be brought about in any number of ways; they stand in an extremely close internal relationship.[1] This indissoluble connection between sin and punishment is the point of Isaiah's pun about 'believing firmly' and 'standing firm'; and he identifies the nation's total incomprehension of the prophetic message with that hardness of heart which has been brought about through their own fault, and for which there can be no remedy.[2] The conviction of the rightness of the principle of talion which had been so strongly held in ancient Israel is in this way translated into the inner logical consistency that characterizes the divine dealings with a people who have wantonly severed relations with their God.

(η) The prophetic conception of history.

In the light of the new certainty of God which they enjoyed the prophets were not only able to subject to radical criticism men's most intimate conduct, and the basic attitudes from which this sprang; they were also granted *a new overall perspective*, which for the first time made it possible to question the whole purpose of Israel's historical existence.

First and foremost, their profound comprehension of the opposition between God and man—an opposition finding expression in sin and judgment—was bound to explode any monistic conception of the universe, which might seek to understand it in terms of a self-sufficient and stable unity. The decisive fact about the world situation is that the divine claim to sole sovereignty is resisted by anti-God powers which form a compact power of sin, and which dare to contest God's rights in a titanic act of insolence. The arena in which this struggle is to be decided is history.[3]

The understanding of history that marked the early religion of Israel had already predisposed men to invest it with this crucial

[1] Cf. Hos. 9.15; 10.13; 12.12.
[2] Cf. Isa. 7.9; 28.16; 28.11, 22; 29.9 ff.; 6.10 f.: also Jer. 2.25; 5.3; 6.7, 10, 15; 8.4 ff.; 13.23.
[3] Cf. C. R. North, *The Old Testament Interpretation of History*, 1946; E. Jacob, *La Tradition historique en Israel*, 1946.

character. Even then history had never been a mere succession of natural events, but always the locus of revelation, in which God had demonstrated his grace and power, and man had experienced God's Lordship, now in judgment, now in renewed blessing. And the deeply-rooted belief in retribution ensured that these experiences would be taken with intense seriousness, because it gave men a weighty responsibility in co-operating in the historical process.

While, however, this conception of history created a fruitful tension in national life by endowing men with the capacity for a deeper grasp of historical experience in metaphysical terms, it was nevertheless too limited in its scope to individual incidents to be able to provide a comprehensive interpretation of the whole pattern of life.[1] A faith focused on pledges given in the form of historical facts tended to derive the stimuli of action from a contemplation of the nation's history from the earliest days. But because the great narratives of Israelite history suggested that either with the conquest of Canaan (as in the case of E and P), or with the establishment of the Davidic monarchy (J) the goal and climax of this God-directed history had already been attained, the whole succeeding period came to be regarded as a conservation of something already achieved, and thus lost the forward thrust that marks a movement still striving to reach its goal. From being thought of as a headlong hurrying stream, history had become a land-locked lake, the currents, storms and inundations of which, though they did not allow of stagnation, yet remained confined within a fixed perimeter. How could history any more lead onward, once an ideal divine-human relationship had been realized? All it could do was to work for the preservation of a settled system of life, or for the continual restoration of that system whenever it was disturbed. The early prophetic movement had been marked by violent striving after a new and more complete communion with God; and this enabled it to provide the nation, which was tending to turn in on itself, with a new sense of purpose in its history capable of evoking and harnessing all its powers by virtue of the hope it afforded of complete salvation. But with the establishment of the monarchy everything came to a standstill once more. Men became accustomed to think of the *status quo* as the goal of the nation's history, a goal which no doubt needed improving in detail,

---

[1] J. Hempel has made a stimulating attempt to explain the origins of this outlook in terms of the general pattern of the Israelite psyche (*Altes Testament und Geschichte*, pp. 65 ff.).

but which on the whole was final. In such an atmosphere it was always possible to treat history as the 'supreme test of God',[1] the evidence on which men could base their assurance of him; but it could never truly become the arena of ultimate decisions.

So soon, however, as the whole existing situation was itself jeopardized by a new sense of the reality of God, all this was bound to change. From now on all the events of the past arranged themselves in great connected series, reaching out toward an ultimate supreme decision and reckoning. To the prophets this coming decision was manifestly final, something that would inevitably hale all of present reality before its judgment-seat, and at the same time bear some relation to every item of the past. If hitherto all the events of history had as it were faced backwards into the past, now they must turn about to face the portentous events which the prophets were proclaiming, and which, though they had not yet come to pass, were nevertheless in process of so doing. The picture of the nation's history as a history of sin, that is to say, of decisions taken against God, leading up to a final rejection of the divine claims, and thus bringing to light its true character, suggests straightaway one consequence of this new outlook on the past. It implies not just a new interpretation of history, to provide a theoretical basis for the prophetic preaching, but a totally different conception of its very nature. For the organic interrelation of all its individual elements gives it not just paradigmatic value, but *real significance for the contemporary situation.* It is in history that God's struggle to implement his sovereignty is to reach its consummation, and every separate phase of that struggle has been but a preparation for the final decision. Thus every element acquires its own eternal importance, and at every moment human conduct is subjected to the binding obligation of decision. Nothing is a matter of indifference. Everything throws its weight into one scale or the other, and supplies its own link in the great chain of history, leading on to the *dénouement* of the cosmic drama. Hence the relentless earnestness with which the prophets demand a decision from their contemporaries; hence the frightful threats which Amos hurls against Amaziah, Isaiah against Ahaz, Jeremiah against Zedekiah. Here is Time taken seriously as the once-for-all reality ordained by the Creator, and pressing for decision. The terrifying immediacy of a God so close at hand allows of no reliance on an assured supply of divine favour granted in history,

[1] Cf. J. Hempel, *op. cit.,* p. 34.

no delay in deciding on one's attitude, no clinging to a precedence once bestowed on the people of God. What is required is that men should take sides in the consciousness that this will be a choice of final and absolute importance.

That this does not, however, involve making man and his decision the determining factor in history[1] is ensured by the vision of the exalted Lord of history, the equation of the immanent with the transcendent God. Yahweh's overwhelming majesty is sufficient guarantee that he will attain his goal, God's absolute sovereignty, even in the teeth of man. He is able to overthrow any hostile power. At hand to execute his judgment on his disobedient people stand not only the forces of Nature, but also the mighty nations of the world, all of which are perforce obedient to his nod. Indeed, it is the supreme demonstration of his strength that he can incorporate these hostile powers into his own scheme for history, so that in the very insolence of their resistance to God they are constrained to become the instruments of his decrees. Assyria and Babylon are compelled to serve him by that very impulse of conquest to which they are driven by their insatiable lust for gain or their titanic strivings for supreme power. Their rebellious independence only illuminates more starkly the surpassing power and wisdom of Yahweh, who apportions them their time, and then hurls them back into nothingness.[2] Hence in the very midst of the storms of judgment Yahweh can be regarded as the master-builder who lays on Zion his precious corner-stone (Isa. 28.16), thus bringing the Kingdom of God to completion, even when outwardly everything seems to be shattered in pieces. The God of the universe, whose decree is gone forth over the whole earth (Isa. 14.26), assuredly combines the destinies of all the various nations in one great unity, and guides the tortuous paths of history in accordance with a mysterious and wonderful plan, in order to bring them to the goal which he has ordained.[3] Thus in the very midst of the story of judgment is fulfilled a story of salvation, perceptible only to faith, the end of which is God's new world.

---

[1] This view, which has been brought out by J. Hempel (*op. cit.*, pp. 15 f.), may well apply most of all to the mechanical retribution doctrine of later Judaism.

[2] Cf. Isa. 10.5 ff.; Jer. 27.5 ff.; 25.8 ff.; and Isa. 30.27 ff.; 37.22 ff.; 14.5 ff.; Jer. 25.15 f.; 51.59 ff.: also Isa. 44.24–45.13; 46.9 ff.; Hag. 2.6 ff., 20 ff.; Zech. 2.1 ff. Cf. E. Jenni, *Die politischen Voraussagen der Propheten* (Abhandlungen zur Theologie des Alten und Neuen Testaments 29), 1956.

[3] Cf. Isa. 10.12; 28.23 ff.; 18.7; 45.22 ff.

(θ) Eschatology.

This, however, is as much as to say that this new conception of history is inevitably bound up with *the certainty that history will be finally broken off and abolished in a new age.*

No elaboration is needed to demonstrate how completely this expectation accords with the general structure of the prophetic view of the world. Indeed, it would be impossible even to imagine a theological meaning in the process of history, if the final outcome of God's providential direction were to be found in a conflict between God and man resulting in the total destruction of the empirical world. In fact the markedly dualistic character of this concept of history would be bound to prove irreconcilably contradictory to any belief in God's power and greatness, unless behind the actual state of the world another world were to become discernible, which should correspond perfectly to the will of the Lord of mankind. The prophets' radical critique of the *status quo* rules out any optimistic belief in progress, which might hope that opposition would be gradually overcome; nor can there be any question of God's justifying the existing situation of this world. The contradictions in the world are of such a kind that they cannot be put right by a new way of looking at things, nor could they ever be stepped up to the level of God's demands. In the circumstances any attempt at a theodicy is hopeless; and for this reason no such attempt is ever made by the prophets.[1] Their only resource is to withdraw and throw themselves on God, who has power not only to cause things to pass away, but also to create them anew. In fact the principal proof of the supremacy of his providential government is that he is able, in the midst of the break-up of the old world, to bring about the beginnings of a new development, the nucleus of a new world-order, and to perfect this into a second creation.

Hence to try to see in eschatology an indifferent or inferior appendix to the prophetic system of thought is a fundamental misunderstanding of prophetism.[2] Indeed, so far as the so-called messianic prophecies are concerned—if we are not going to succumb to the temptation to degrade them to the level of merely nationalist popular expectations, which would mean ruling them out altogether as a

[1] The theodicy which some have thought to find in Ezekiel can only very loosely be so described; for what is at issue is not God's Providence, but man's personal responsibility and God's judicial righteousness.

[2] So Gunkel, Volz *et al.*

genuine expression of prophetic thought—our task is to recognize their meaning, the dominant concern behind an outward dress frequently dictated by their period. Careful scrutiny of the relevant passages can, however, show that, while it is true that ancient mythological tradition is often preserved in their language and conceptual content,[1] nevertheless the subordination of this material to the vision of complete divine sovereignty, portrayed by each prophet in his own individual way, makes the old imagery a true interpreter of that great concept of God as Lord over the world and mankind which is the controlling factor in all the prophetic preaching.[2] It is, indeed, only in the eschatological pictures that the message of the prophets is really presented in its completeness, at any rate in so far as it is in them that an answer is given to the difficult questions of world imperialism, the future of the People of God, and the self-assertion of the individual. Nor are these answers given on the basis of an historico-philosophical discussion of earthly possibilities; they spring from confidence in the Creator God, who is bringing his plan for humanity to a victorious conclusion. The mythical features, moreover, which form a striking parallel to the application of the Chaos struggle in the messages of judgment, are here quite indispensable. They are the infallible signs that what is meant by the world of the future, now coming to the birth, is not the end-product of some natural, earthly process, but the creative transformation of the world by the irruption of new divine realities; and it is this which gives the Kingdom of God its quality of being beyond time. This is not to say that the End-history is dissolved in an End-myth.[3] The link with the facts of personality and community which have been moulded in history remains strong and vital. Yahweh's future sovereignty is nothing else than the consummation of his Kingship over Israel. The characteristics of the individual nations give the one great congregation of God, which results from the merging of the peoples, a colour and life which have nothing in common with a world of faery. The community within which the life of the individual is set (the perennial problem of history!) is not dissolved into a multiplicity of blessed individual souls, but brought to its perfection. It is just this close connection with the divine

[1] First pointed out by Gressmann, *Ursprung der isr.-jüd. Eschatologie*, and conclusively established in his posthumous work, *Der Messias*.

[2] On this point cf. Sellin, *Der AT Prophetismus*; Eichrodt, *Die Hoffnung des ewigen Friedens*, 1920.

[3] Rightly rejected by Hempel, *op. cit.*, p. 28.

revelation as manifested in history which elevates this picture of the future far above the level of vague wish-fulfilment, and makes it a disclosure of the goal of God's own operation, to which the present —like all the ages that have gone before—is ministering. Eschatology is to history what fulfilment is to prophecy—justification and interpretation in one.

Moreover, the characterization of this ultimate goal of history as an act of new creation serves at the same time to confirm once for all the prophets' radical criticism of the contemporary situation on the basis of their new sense of the reality of God, and to indicate the impassable gulf fixed between this age and the age to come. The vision of what lies beyond this frontier may certainly enable one to endure the imperfect present, but it does not permit an inert contentment with the given situation. Rather it drives men constantly to inflexible criticism of its imperfections, and to a continual readiness to abandon it and to reach out with all their might toward that enduring order of existence guaranteed by the promises of God.

(c) Synthesis

Looking back, we may describe *the overall spiritual pattern of classical prophecy as that of a dynamic power released by a new sense of the reality of God.* This dynamic, invading Israelite life and thought with overwhelming force, sweeps away all that is stagnant, and unleashes a forward movement which can no longer be restrained, and which, once in full career, pauses for nothing. Here the last and most searching 'settlement' is effected between God and man, and the final sentence of condemnation pronounced on Israel's religion, in so far as this had become merely the product of nationalism and the national culture.[1] Here the critique with which nabism had countered the pretensions of human social institutions to autonomous

---

[1] This applies not only to the prophecies of woe, but also to the exilic and post-exilic weal-prophecies. There is no need to demonstrate that the whole of Deutero-Isaiah is written in the conviction of standing on the threshold of the new age. In addition, the energetic way in which Haggai and Zechariah set about the practical problems of their day, and Malachi's fight against abuses in the community, are far from being attempts to make men feel at home in this world; they must be seen in the light of eschatology. The building of the Temple is to be undertaken and carried through, and the cultus re-established, as an act of faith in the God who is standing at the very doors, ready to bring about the great turning-point of the ages. The newly established Jerusalem community is but a prologue, having meaning not in itself, but as pointing to the coming consummation.

validity, in order to safeguard the rightful sovereignty of God, is brought to completion. But prophecy had more than this to offer. In the lightning of the approaching cosmic storm it saw with quite a new clarity the countenance of the God of Israel. All that had ever been said before about his power, his righteousness, his merciful kindness and holiness now seemed to be swallowed up in the blinding light of a transcendent majesty exalted above all things human. It was, so to speak, withdrawn from the sphere of human relativity, and partook of the absoluteness of a sovereign authority embracing the whole world. In face of this there was no room for the presumptuous confidence that would enlist the covenant God in the service of human ends, and couple him with worldly factors with which he had absolutely nothing in common. In the consuming fire of his judgment he is recognized for what he is—a reality completely other in kind, which, despite its entry into the realm of earthly existence through the acts of election, covenant-making and the historical governance of the nation, is yet in no sense assimilated to this world, but on the contrary subjects this world to its own dominion in order to lead it on to a new and higher way of life. The prophetic world-view progressed beyond the concept of an external, spatial separation between this world and the divine sovereignty—an idea familiar to ancient Israel—to that of the interior, qualitative separation between the nature of man, even Israelite man, and the reality of God which encompasses the whole world. And this reality, controlled as it is by a purposive will concerned to establish a covenant and realize a universal design, is set in an intense antagonism to the reality of this world, with the result that the latter is bound to be smashed against it.

But if this earthly existence is something transient, then all human activity within it, at any rate in so far as it is directed to the realization of human and earthly possibilities, must also lose all value. All human strivings to master the invading chaos are mere foolishness. The only way in which human action can escape from futility, and share in the genesis of the new reality, is as a decision taken in view of the divine advent. It is significant that from the time of Isaiah onwards conduct that is truly in accordance with God's will is included in the category of *rūaḥ*, that is to say, it is a manifest effect of the miraculous divine life, while all that is merely human belongs to the sphere of *bāśār*, the transient and creaturely. Hence a full human life, answering to the purposes of its Creator, is only possible through participation in the miraculous reality of the divine world; and by the same token the ideal of the People of God is also plunged into the sphere of the marvellous, of the *rūaḥ*. The realization of Yahweh's sovereignty is not something empirical and rational, but numinous and pneumatic, and can only be portrayed in that ancient mythical language which befits its nature.[1]

The distinctive quality of the prophetic attitude resides therefore in this; that while it is certainly rooted in that history which is the product of God's operation, it yet feels itself pointed beyond this to a new perfection, in which alone the true sense and meaning of the present is to be fulfilled, and which therefore calls for steadfast endurance in the fierce tension between present and future.

This tension, however, ultimately arises from the following fact. In the case of this new reality, as may by now have become clear, *we are not dealing with a moral or religious idea,* such as might be grasped by a thinker of genius, and then confirmed and expounded in the context of a rationalistic world-view. Granted that such ideas may at first have a revolutionary effect, yet in time they can be given their place in the general system of human thought, and so become common property. But here we are dealing with something quite different, namely with *God himself and his impending visitation of his people.* It is this which is uniquely revolutionary, which cannot be assimilated by the thinking of the average man, and which mocks all attempts to incorporate it into a general theory of the universe. For all that is possible to man in face of God's advent is not to manage or manipulate such a fact by means of rational thought, but simply to choose between comprehension in faith and rejection in unbelief. It is both the strength and weakness of the prophetic message that it can appeal to nothing and nobody save only the revealed will of God himself, which demands obedience by breaking through man's independent thinking, and confronting him with the inexplicable reality of the divine world. Seen from this angle, the tension to which the prophet is subjected is less that of the temporal 'Not yet', than that of the timeless opposition between the traditional religion, which is familiar and comprehensible to natural reason, and that world of God's self-communication which is discernible only to faith; or, to put it another way, between the field of that doctrine of God which is empirically verifiable and attested, on the one hand, and

[1] Cf. R. Otto, 'Prophetische Gotteserfahrung', *Die Christliche Welt* 37, 1923, pp. 437 ff.

revelation on the other; between the known and the unknown; between the God who has come and the God who is yet to come.

It is only if *the real difficulty of this involvement in tension* is grasped, namely that it allows man no rest, no halt for the setting up of secured positions, but only a reaching out in faith toward an as yet unseen Coming One, that we can begin to understand the stress which the prophets lay on their commissioning, endowment and constant guidance by Yahweh. Without such a sense of being held and carried, indeed of being driven and impelled by a higher power, they could never have begun to take their stand on the perilous frontier between the rejected and the newly created People of God, between the foundering world of the present and the emerging world of the future, between this age and the age to come. The prophet is exposed to two threats. On the one side lies the descent into an unhinged fanaticism which no longer has any eyes for the reality of the present; on the other are the temptations either to the violent overthrow of the existing order, on the grounds that a state of affairs so open to radical religious criticism has forfeited its right to exist, or to despairing pessimism in view of the continual pressure of a godless reality.

Both these dangers became acute in the succeeding period, when the prophetic message exercised a decisive influence on religious life without, however, being firmly based on a vivid sense of the complementary truth of God's real government of the world here and now. In apocalyptic the pious sought to escape from a present that had become incomprehensible into the domain of a sterile romanticism of the transcendent which would ensure free play to religious speculation and dreamlike fantasy. In the post-exilic groups of enthusiasts,[1] however, such as the Zealots, we see men driven by their impatience with the tortuous ways of God's providence to try to wrest a more speedy victory for the good cause by the might of their own sword. But this only meant that after every unsuccessful venture the reaction was harder to bear; and consequently in place of faithful reverence for a divine plan which for all its mystery was yet securely guaranteed we find dull resignation or vociferous complaint.

When we reflect that these threats to a healthy religious life followed so hard on the heels of prophecy, our attention is turned to the importance of those stewards of the Israelite understanding of

[1]Cf. Neh. 6.10 ff.; resistance to similar tendencies is already to be discerned in Zech. 2.5 ff.; 4.6.

God who are frequently regarded as at the opposite pole from the prophets. It is true that they were in opposition to prophetism in their championship of the belief that the divine promises and gift of life were permanently accessible to every member of the people of God; but if only one studies the picture as a whole, instead of confining one's attention to certain particular historical situations, they can be seen to provide prophecy with a necessary complement and firm support. We refer to the official ministers of the Yahweh covenant, the king and the priests; and it is to them that we must turn in the next chapter.

IX

THE INSTRUMENTS OF THE COVENANT
(continued)

B. THE OFFICIAL LEADERS

I. THE PRIESTS

1. *The Formation of the Priesthood in the History of Israel*

WITH THE OFFICIAL FUNCTIONARIES of the worship of Yahweh, as opposed to the charismatic leaders, an element is introduced into the Mosaic covenant religion, which is to a certain extent ready-made and independent of it. In the case both of the priesthood and of the monarchy we are dealing with institutions which had already been given fairly rigid form in Israel's environment, and which, for all that many of their features were omitted or modified, were not in essence transformed when they were taken over by the newly-established community. In considering these institutions, therefore, we have to distinguish between this inflexible basic character, which is part of their nature, and the changes which occurred in their forms and functions under the influence of the new religion.

In so far as the priesthood is concerned, however, the account in Ex. 32 might seem to cast doubt on this assessment of the situation. In this story of how the Levites were entrusted with the priestly office the emphasis is quite clearly on their installation *de novo*, as a reward for their proven loyalty, into an office which they had hitherto not possessed. Nevertheless, it would be hasty to conclude from this that the office of priest found its way into the religion of Yahweh simply as an *ad hoc* historical measure of a predominantly charismatic kind. What is really involved is the intrusion of the Levites into this office, and the implied suppression of those who had previously held it. The assumption that the priestly office had already had a place in the Yahweh religion before this incident is in fact rather confirmed than contradicted by Ex. 32; and corroborative evidence is supplied by the fact that the presence of priests among the people is already mentioned before the Sinai revelation,[1] and that Aaron is on one occasion called 'the Levite'—a title which, however, in the passage in question[2] means no more than 'the priest'.

Nevertheless, on the subject of how this priestly office was constituted we are told as good as nothing, and are therefore forced to rely on what we can deduce. One indication is afforded by the close connection attested in the tradition between Moses and the Midianite priest Jethro, an association which extends even to the reorganization of the administration of justice. It would therefore seem highly probable that there were links between the Israelite cultic organization and the ancient traditional institutions of the friendly Midianite tribes. This is confirmed by the references to the priestly oracle of the sacred lot, Urim and Thummim,[3] which in method is reminiscent of the Arabian arrow-oracle. Finally, though often queried, there is the obtrusive fact of the relationship between the Hebrew 'Levi' and the homonymous Minaean term for priest.[4] We must conclude that there is a strong probability that Midianite tradition played a part in determining the form of the Israelite priesthood.

Opinion as to the strength of this influence tends to vary according to how closely it is thought that the Levite priesthood is related to the secular tribe of Levi. But it is precisely on this point that serious difficulties arise. It is true that the OT tradition seems to suggest[5] that the secular tribe, which had disintegrated as a result of some external disaster, voluntarily offered itself for this particular form of religious service, which was then entrusted to it by Moses. But there are strong objections to this version of the facts. In the first place it is hard to conceive of the transfer of even a decimated tribe *en bloc* to the priestly profession, when we remember that the actual circumstances obtaining afforded totally inadequate provision for the maintenance of a large staff of priests.[6] A second and stronger argument against the tradition is that, according to the scheme of twelve tribes

---

[1] Cf. Ex. 19.22, 24.
[2] Cf. Ex. 4.14.
[3] Cf. Deut. 33.8; also I Sam. 14.41; 28.6.
[4] Cf. D. H. Müller, *Denkschriften der Wiener Akademie*, phil. Classe, 37, 1889; J. H. Mordtmann, *Beiträge zur minäischen Epigraphik*, 1897, p. 43; F. Hommel, *Ancient Hebrew Tradition*, pp. 278 f.
[5] Cf. Gen. 49.5–7; 34; Ex. 32.
[6] So Wellhausen, *Prolegomena*, p. 145.

employed in Gen. 49, which comes in fact from the period of the Judges,[1] the secular tribe of Levi must have been in existence after the settlement in Canaan.[2] Even if we bear in mind that such a scheme might be retained in the tradition for some time, even after one or another of the members of the confederation so described was no longer in a position to exercise its full rights,[3] it would seem impossible to reconcile this twelvefold system with a separation of the tribe of Levi so early as the time of Moses. In the circumstances we may well be compelled to disregard completely the idea of an original identity of the tribe of Levi with the religious order of Levites, and to recognize that the two bodies may have entirely different origins. This would certainly leave more room to associate the Levites with the priesthood of Kadesh. Such an association is suggested by Deut. 33.8;[4] and it may be noted that in the tradition Moses' call of the Levites is patently presented as in opposition to the established priesthood represented by Aaron.[5] If proper weight is given to the importance of Kadesh as an ancient cultic centre for a considerable circle of tribes, where oracles were given and justice administered long before the advent of Israel, and if we remember the close connections of Moses with Midian, it does not seem too daring a conjecture to suppose an alliance of Moses with the priestly clans of Kadesh against opposition coming from the ancient Hebrew priesthoods. As a result of this alliance these 'levites', that is to say, priests, were incorporated into the new covenant religion, and entrusted with the care of the covenant sanctuary.[6] The similarity between the word 'levi', which was the title of a functionary, and the name of the tribe,[7]

[1] Cf. M. Noth, *Das System der zwölf Stämme Israels*, pp. 28 ff.

[2] The contention that there never was a secular tribe of Levi at all (cf. E. Sellin, *Geschichte des Volkes Israel*, pp. 41 f.; *Wie wurde Sichem eine Israelitische Stadt?*, 1922, pp. 56 ff.; A. Menes, *Die vorexilischen Gesetze Israels* (BZAW 50), 1928, pp. 2 ff.; Mowinckel, art. 'Levi' in *RGG*[2] III, cols. 1601 f.; B. D. Eerdmans, *De Godsdienst van Israel* I, pp. 61 f.) cannot therefore be sustained.

[3] M. Noth has drawn attention to this point (*op. cit.*, pp. 33 f., 40 ff.).

[4] E. Meyer's attempt to associate the connections of the Levite priesthood with the area inhabited by the secular tribe of Levi (*Die Israeliten*, pp. 78 ff.) is so unconvincing that in fact it acts as an argument for distinguishing the two 'Levis'.

[5] Cf. Ex. 4.13–16; 32; Num. 12.1 ff. and R. Kittel, *Geschichte des Volkes Israel* [5,6] I, pp. 307 f., 373.

[6] This assumption would throw considerable light on their later position within the nation as a whole, when they were a guest tribe whose members were to be found dispersed among the other tribes.

[7] The suggestion has often been made that the tribal name is ultimately identical with Leah: cf. R. Kittel, *op. cit.*, p. 299; Wellhausen, *Prolegomena*, p. 145 ('perhaps a mere patronymic from his mother Leah').

combined with the later success of Aaronic claims to be the legitimate priesthood, undoubtedly made it easier, after the tribe of Levi had disappeared, to identify two bodies which had originally been quite distinct.

Nevertheless, even if we can never be certain on this point, nothing can conceal the fact that the encouragement which a religious fraternity gave to the practice of the new covenant sanctuary meant the introduction into the Mosaic establishment of a vitally important factor. In addition to the charismatic leader-figure and those who may succeed him, there is *a ministry*, charged with the control of stable institutions, the sacrificial cultus—even if as yet a very simple one—at the covenant sanctuary, the manipulation of the oracle of the sacred lot, and all the ritual connected with the Tent and the Ark. In this way, not only were the cultic forms in which the new religion was expressed endowed with the authority of sacred norms, but there was some guarantee that the bond tied by Moses could not easily be severed, and that the new foundation would continue in the face of whatever historical accidents or changes of popular mood the future might bring.[1]

In this matter of the absorption of the ministry into its organism, as in others, the distinctive character of the Yahweh religion continued to make itself felt by causing particular aspects of the professional activity of the priesthood to acquire overriding importance and to develop more strongly than the rest. Pre-eminent among these is *the work of counselling and teaching*, which was already of central importance in the very earliest period. It was based to begin with on the administration of the sacred oracle, which was very specially a part of the priest's duties. In Israel, however, such work was

---

[1]One can only quote here, with complete agreement, the energetic assertion of Noth that the abstract concepts of 'Yahwism' or 'the ideal unity of Israel' are not an adequate description of the bond that united all the Israelite tribes. 'Generally speaking, in considering the situation in question, it is impossible to talk of "religion" without thinking first and foremost of its expression in the setting of particular concrete forms, and of a regulated cultus attached to a particular place. . . . And if we take seriously the realization that for Israel in the earliest period religion without outward cultic forms was unthinkable, then we must logically go on to assume that a religious association of the Israelite tribes could only exist, by and large, under the forms of a common cultus at a common sanctuary. To speak of an ideal or religious "sense of solidarity", or something similar, is to substitute modern Western concepts for ancient Oriental thought, and to overlook the critical importance of stable institutions as both the necessary expression and the pre-condition of any attempt to preserve ideal or religious conceptions' (*op. cit.*, pp. 63 f.).

markedly encouraged by the importance which as a result of the covenant law was attached to a rational interpretation of the will of God. The priest acquired a growing influence as the adviser on the subject of the ritual and ethical requirements for a right worship of Yahweh, on the means of obtaining his favour, and on the method of propitiating an angry God for offences against the law. Thus in the blessing pronounced on Levi in Deut. 33.8–11, a passage which certainly comes from the time of the Judges, the sacrificial ministry is only mentioned last of all, after the giving of oracles and the custody of the *mišpāṭīm* and the *tōrā*, that is to say, the socio-ethical and ritual requirements. The simplicity of the oracle of the sacred lot, which could only answer 'Yes' or 'No' to the questions put to it, and the increasingly thorough exclusion of all other technical devices for making enquiry of the deity, ruled out the possibility that any esoteric priestly science of a mystagogic or magical type might develop. Instead, the prime desideratum of priestly training came to be the ability to put the right questions to the lot in each individual case, which meant in fact the intelligent sorting-out and clarification of the problems presented.[1] In complex cases the element of rational investigation, and the assessment of the situation in terms of the traditional holy law, inevitably played such a large part that the technical oracle—skill in the use of which was one of the chief recommendations of the Levites—greatly declined in importance. Rational instruction on the basis of a knowledge of Yahweh's commands now became the principal and proper source of the respect paid to the order; and the stringent avoidance of orgiastic rites, of the cult of the dead, and of magical healing, which characterized the Israelite cultus, contributed to make ethical and paraenetic counselling of the laity the most important channel of priestly influence.

It is obvious that the right *offering of sacrifices* must have been one of the subjects on which ritual instruction was sought from the priest. Nevertheless, to begin with this side of his activity was less prominent. The reason for this was the fact that the functions of the Levites at the covenant sanctuary had nothing to do with the sacrificial worship of the private individual, but were concerned only with the official sacrificial festivals. The evidence from the time of the Judges and the monarchy suggests that the right of the paterfamilias to exercise the priestly function of offering the sacrifice was uncon-

[1] Cf. on this point the remarks of M. Weber, *Religionssoziologie*, III, pp. 191 ff.

tested for a considerable period, and that there was therefore no need to call in the assistance of a special cultic official. Moreover the decentralization which took place after the entry into Canaan, loosening the bonds between the tribes and frequently allowing the free development of their individual life at the expense of the larger whole, ensured that the special prerogatives of the Levites in the service of the *'ōhel mōʿēd* should not give rise to a complicated sacrificial cultus with a priestly monopoly and an extensive ritual apparatus. The separation of the Tent and the Ark, of the reasons for which we know nothing, and the transference of the Ark from the central cultic site at Gilgal near Shechem to Shiloh, also helped to weaken the importance of the covenant sanctuary. Furthermore, we can see that in many cases tribes or tribal leaders made efforts to set up cultic centres of their own, which should surpass the rest in importance.[1] We hear no more of a compact organization of Levites able to exercise their power from the covenant sanctuary. They were compelled to lead the life of a 'guest tribe', the individual members of which were dispersed among the tribes as *gērim*, clients and sojourners in need of protection, who had to be glad if they were offered a position as domestic chaplain in the house of some well off people, or when one of the larger tribal sanctuaries invited them to be their minister. It is possible that in this situation many gave up the ritual life, and that, even if later on as 'Levites' they formed a strictly separated class, yet they were no longer eligible for the work of the priesthood.[2] Their condition of life seems to have been regulated quite differently in different localities, dwelling-places being allotted to them as metics on certain terms.[3]

Their position was made all the more difficult by the fact that they now had to face competition from many other *more ancient priestly clans*. If the conjecture is correct that Levi originally took up service at the covenant sanctuary in opposition to Aaron, that is, the priestly families of ancient Israel, then the long-standing rivalry between these different candidates for the priestly profession would explain many of the peculiar characteristics of our evidence. In fact both the incorporation of non-Levitical priests into the state cultus by

---

[1]Cf. Judg. 8.24 ff. (Gideon and the ephod at Ophrah); 18.14 ff. (the Danites and Micah's shrine).

[2]Deuteronomy's references to the duty of extending brotherly assistance to the Levites are more easily understood in this context: cf. Deut. 14.27, 29; 16.11, 14. Cf. also M. Weber, *op. cit.*, pp. 183 ff.

[3]Cf. Num. 1.49; 2.33 f.; 35.2 f.; Lev. 25.32 f.; Josh. 14.4.

Jeroboam,[1] and the emergence of the Zadokites (who originally were
definitely non-Levitical) in the time of David, indicate that Levi was
never alone in claiming priestly rights, but was able to win these
prerogatives only gradually and after a struggle. Unfortunately we
can no longer tell how the contest may have swayed first to one side
and then to the other, since the later schematization by which all
priests are included under the heading of the tribe of Levi has badly
blurred the outlines.[2] For the same reason also we are unable to say
from what date Levi got the better of the rival priestly clans. All we
can do is to mention certain factors which brought about this outcome
of the struggle.

In the first place it is obvious that Levi, much more strongly than
the other priestly clans, had preserved *the link with the Mosaic period*,
and had better adapted its practice to the intentions of the founder of
the religion. The whole expansion of priestly instruction in the direction of right exposition and application of the covenant obligations
in a ritual, ethical and social context, gave considerably more weight
in the worship of the Yahweh religion to rational instruction and
simple obedience than to any form of mystical or ecstatic adoration.
Hence the Levitical priests and those influenced by them seem to
have put up a more prolonged resistance than their rivals to the
inroads of Canaanite cultic practices. This is suggested principally by
the imageless character of the cult of the Ark, the outlawing of cultic
unchastity, and the rejection of the cult of the dead and of magic.
For the same reason this group was much quicker to ally itself with
the prophetic reaction against the Canaanization of the Yahweh
religion, as we can tell from the removal of the Omrids in Jerusalem
by the then High Priest. By contrast, the priestly families settled in
Northern Israel seem to have offered less resistance to the under-
mining of the Yahweh religion by Canaanite influences, and so to
have been driven more quickly and violently into opposition to
prophecy.

Beside this firmer adherence to the basic attitudes of the Yahweh
religion, another factor was *the favour of the royal house*, which was

[1] Cf. I Kings 12.31.
[2] Cf. however the concluding sentence of the blessing on Levi (Deut. 33.11):
'Smite through the loins of them that rise up against him, and of them that hate
him, that they rise not again.' Also Num. 16. That the law of the priesthood took
different forms at the different cultic sites is attested not only by the varying codifi-
cations of Deut. and P, but also by the very old description in I Sam. 2.13–16,
which certainly reflects Shilonite law.

shown to the Levites in the time of David, and, after the division of the monarchy, continuously in the Southern kingdom. The influential royal sanctuary in Jerusalem took shape under Levitical direction, and became the stronghold of Levitical ideals; and to this the intrusion of the Zadokites made little difference. The breach with Northern Israel compelled Judah, where Levitical influences had in any case long been at their strongest, to assert its individuality in cultic matters as well; though the removal of the Omrids in the Northern kingdom may have opened up more effective access for Levitical efforts there too under the dynasty of Jehu. In the reforms of Hezekiah and Josiah recognition was given to the best traditions of the Levitical priesthood; and it was also at this period that the monopolistic pretensions of Levi were first given effect, partly by degrading non-Levitical priests, and partly by incorporating them into the Levite genealogy.

The alliance with the monarchy certainly brought about a not inconsiderable *transformation of the Levitical priesthood*. In the first place the cult officials of the State temple found themselves suddenly invested with much *greater power*. This gave them a sensible advantage over their less favoured provincial colleagues, and led to schisms and struggles for supremacy. The dazzling sacrificial feasts of the state sanctuary, with their vast crowds of worshippers, required a numerous clergy, which at quite an early stage was hierarchically organized, and encouraged a richer development of the cultic organization and of the law of the priesthood. Much of what we now find in its later formulation in the Priestly Code must in very early days have been already part of the practice of the state sanctuary.[1] Various passages also indicate that the king himself took the lead in cultic innovations.[2] Small wonder if the local sanctuaries were definitely put in the shade by the cultic centre, and were either deserted, or sought to make themselves more attractive by adapting themselves to Canaanite practices that were still deeply rooted. This conflict between the country priests and the clergy of the capital may have left its mark on many of the ancient narratives,[3] and was a definite hindrance to the religious work of the priesthood.

[1] To this category belongs first and foremost the Code of Holiness (Lev. 17–26), but also the strata underlying the rest of the Priestly Code.
[2] Cf. I Kings 8.22, 64; 9.25; II Chron. 4.1; II Kings 16.14.
[3] Cf. Num. 16 and I Sam. 2.35 f. for the claims of the Zadokites to supremacy, and II Kings 12.4–16; Ex. 32, and Num. 12 for the resistance to these pretensions put up by the country priesthood.

The same applies to the increasing *prominence of the whole apparatus of the cult*, especially that of sacrificial worship, which resulted partly from the interest taken by the kings in the cultus and its outward display, but also from the natural tendency to elaboration characteristic of great cultic centres. The earlier proportion between sacrificial worship and the imparting of *tōrā* was consequently inverted; compared with the lucrative traffic of the Temple the ministry of God's word[1] declined in importance and interest, and as a result the priestly profession lost any really profound influence. That in the process the practice of the great sanctuaries coloured that of the provincial ones is only too natural.

Finally, the priestly families which held office at the great royal sanctuaries attained *a position of growing political power*. The swelling throng of cultic officials dependent on them, their wealth, their influence with the people, their close connections with the government, all made them influential figures in any political conflict; but at the same time their conduct came to be controlled by improper motives. That the priesthood had been thus secularized is amply illustrated by the fact that the prophets, in their fight against the political decisions of the government, were also constantly coming into conflict with the priests.

If credence can be given to certain pieces of evidence in Chronicles,[2] it even seems as if, toward the end of the monarchical period, the priesthood came to oppose the monarchy, and managed to enlarge its power at the expense of the ruler. It is possible to adduce similar developments in the Assyrian kingdom at this time. The position of the king in the cultus and the Temple ritual as conceived by the Jerusalem priesthood may be seen clearly enough from Ezekiel (44.1–3; 45.9–12; 46); and it may be assumed that at the time of Josiah they were not so very far from this ideal. However, the complete disappearance of the monarchy after the Exile left the way clear for the unchallenged supremacy of the priesthood.

The keen opposition of prophetism, and the experience of the Exile, corrected—at least in part—these aberrations from the path of Levitical practice and tradition. The leading spirits of the priesthood came to see *the practice of the Torah*, which was now becoming

---

[1] That something more is meant by this than simply the zealous recording of new regulations, which was a feature of this period as much as of any other (cf. Jer. 8.8; Isa. 10.1; Zeph. 3.4), will be obvious enough from what has been said earlier. Cf. also Hos. 4.6; Isa. 28.7, 9; Jer. 2.8; Ezek. 22.26.

[2] Cf. II Chron. 24.17 ff.; 25.14 ff., 27; 26.16 ff.

more and more a written law, as their most important task. In the person of Ezra the priesthood once more forcefully and successfully fulfilled that guardianship of the divine covenant and its ordinances which had been its duty of old; and in the Law it gave the revived Jerusalem congregation a pattern for its life, which not only enabled it to rise superior to the harshest assaults from without, but also endowed it with an inward power of new growth and unsuspected development. At the same time, however, the work of Ezra imposed severe limits on the priesthood and its influence. In the first place it was itself now bound by the Law and subject to its control. Secondly, with the introduction of the Law a new religious class was called into being, whose members now took their place alongside the priests as the established spokesmen for warning and exhorting the people, namely the scribes. Even though the High Priest, now that the Davidic dynasty was removed, had risen to the position of a Prince of the Church with rights equal to those of the governor—indeed, with the lapsing of the Judaean governorship he attained the secular status of an Ethnarch—yet the scribes were an incarnation of the community's resolve in future to recognize no authority but that of the Law, and even to allow the priesthood only so much influence as was covered by this authority. In the NT period there were at the Temple scribes who received a stipend from the Temple income, and who were fully employed in giving instruction to the priests in the prescribed methods of exercising their office. Thus the very period in which outward control was added to the inward magisterium which they already possessed proved to be the one which subjected the priests to an even harder and stricter authority than that of prophet or king, namely the Law, in which the congregation venerated the Word of God. It may be regarded as an acknowledgment of this new situation, and a return by the priesthood to its noblest task, that not a few from its ranks devoted themselves to the study of the Law, and were numbered among the scribes.[1]

This was all the more important in view of the fact that the priesthood—in the persons of its leading men—had not always been able to cope with the temptations which political position had brought in

---

[1] From now on this tradition never dies out. Even in the Qumran community, which had split with the official cultus, according to the evidence of the rules of the sect (the *Manual of Discipline*) priests played a leading part in the study of the Torah. Even Aaronites seem to have gone over to this opposition movement, made up of the strictest adherents of the Law; for so the frequent mention of them in the *Manual* and the *Damascus Document* would suggest.

its train. The dangerous conflicts of the period of Persian suzerainty had already threatened its standing; and the religious struggles of the second century, and the evil role then played by many of the priests in their support for the Hellenizing party, deprived them of all recognition and of their status as leaders of the congregation. Henceforth the nation found its religious leaders in the teachers of the Law, and from them religious life took its stamp. Consequently, what had always in the past been the most important function of a priest in the Yahweh religion, namely instruction in the Torah, was lost to the priestly class; and the only role that was left to them, that of ministers of the cult, was not enough to maintain their position permanently. Gradually they were felt to be no longer an essential part of the community, and the transition to the cultless era after the destruction of the Temple was accomplished without seriously disrupting the congregation. Not the priesthood, but the keeping of the Law under the guidance of the scribes and Pharisees had become the backbone of the community.

11. *The Religious Structure of the Priesthood*
(a) *General*

Any endeavour to describe the peculiar structural character of the Israelite priesthood has to reckon with two major difficulties. The first lies in the extent of time to be covered, which means bringing to light the constant basic tendencies of the priestly concept of religion from beneath a great diversity of superficial phenomena. The second lies in the complex character of the entity to be described.

As far as the first difficulty is concerned, it is obvious that a single comprehensive systematic assessment cannot investigate every phase of development equally thoroughly, but must inevitably resort to abridgement. The danger that such condensations may result in distorting the proportions of the total picture must always be in the mind of the expositor, and he must be as vigilant as he can to avoid it.

The second difficulty arises from the fact that, as has been mentioned earlier (cf. p. 392 above), the priesthood, unlike the charismatic exponents of Yahwism, does not emerge as a phenomenon deriving exclusively from within the history of Yahwism itself. If that had been so, then the essential character of the soil from which it sprang would have been discernible in every manifestation of its life. But in fact quite the opposite is true; it is the priesthood which imports its own well-marked individuality into the system of the Yahweh religion. However, in coming to terms with the fundamental forces animating the new organism which it is to serve, the priesthood itself is also transformed; and it is vital that any account of its character should bear this process of transformation in mind, and not be misled with regard to the overall character of the whole institution, as this developed within the framework of Yahwism, by striking but isolated phenomena.

It is therefore desirable to begin by calling to mind *some of the distinctive features* of this religious class *which are part of the institution of the priesthood as such,* and setting them beside the particular quality of the Mosaic religion, into the service of which the Israelite priesthood was to enter.[1]

The first point to remember is that the priest was not from the outset the official representative of the religious tradition, but originally emerges as a charismatic, in just the same way as the seer or the prophet. It is as one endued with power that he becomes a leader and counsellor in all kinds of religious activities, and therefore *the indispensable mediator of access to the divine realm,* interpreting the will of God to a wide circle. This implies that *permanent connection with the community in its religious aspect* which is sociologically the distinguishing mark of the priesthood. In general, wherever an unbroken period of historical development results in a higher level of culture, this position leads to *the creation of a sacred tradition,* summarizing the tested and recognized rules for intercourse with the deity. The priest becomes the guardian of this sacred knowledge, of which only he is completely master, and which he exercises on behalf of the community at large. The original close coherence of primitive life means that this knowledge is not limited to the religious sphere in the narrow sense of that word, but covers every department of life, with the result that the priest exerts a decisive influence on the practice of law, on politics, on art and on secular knowledge as well.

The more differentiated, however, becomes the knowledge in his keeping, and the more diversified its influence on the life of the community, the more surely will the original charismatic character of the priest recede into the background, and give way to that of *the*

[1] There has long been a need for a study of the institution of the priesthood from the religio-phenomenological point of view, and this has now been met on a broad basis of comparative study by E. O. James, *The Nature and Function of Priesthood. A Comparative and Anthropological Study,* 1955.

official administrator of given regulations. It is true that a continuing sense of the original function of these servants of God is revealed by the high estimation in which manticism was long held as the principal work of a priest. The recollection died hard that a priest was one especially inspired by God, and that it was to him that the capricious and incalculable divine power disclosed new and unsuspected developments of the religious life in marvellous and totally unpredictable ways. But in proportion as acquired techniques restrict and ultimately replace the incommunicable personal charisma, so the sphere of priestly activity is *dominated by a new spiritual attitude.* The properly creative element recedes, and the conservation of the tradition becomes the overriding principle. *Priestly authority* is no longer based so much on the 'endowment' and spiritual power of the individual, as on his legitimation by the tradition of which he is the loyal servant, and by the religious community which invests him with his official character. Similarly, it is the cultivation of the stock of religious ideas common to all which occupies the centre of men's attention, and the distinctively individual element is pushed into the background. Hence the presentation of religious concepts and feelings has to be conceived in forms and symbols as impressive and widely comprehensible as possible. The effort to objectify the subjective religious experience outweighs the interest in re-shaping the religion from within. In short, the moulding of religion into a visible form, the fashioning of a body for the spiritual content to be preserved, becomes the dominant professional concern of the priest.

The assumption which lies at the root of this whole attitude is the conviction that *outward form is not a matter of indifference* to the interior concerns of religion, but effectively mediates the presence of the divine. *The nature of this mediation* can naturally be conceived in quite different ways. Either the cultus is seen as the form of worship required by God himself, and its fulfilment as the pre-condition which he attaches to the manifestations of his favour—a view which we may typify as the sacramental; or it is used as the most successful technique for releasing higher powers, and as such rests on man's initiative and brings effective pressure to bear on the deity—the sacrificial conception. It may well be that it is rare for either of these approaches to be found pure and unalloyed, and that in general they are combined; yet it is from the predominance of one or the other in the combination that the work of the priesthood derives its tone. In any event, what is decisive for its development is the concept of God involved—the sacrificial view tending to understand him in terms of holy power, the sacramental as personal will.

Even such a very general outline may help us to see more clearly *the significance that the priesthood can come to have in any religion.* On the one hand, from its ranks arise educators of far-reaching influence, whose activities are of decisive importance both for the development of religion as such, and for the impact of religion on secular life. Both the clarification of religious thought by systematic theology, and the shaping of religious practice through the forms of worship, are largely in their hands; and it is from them that poetry, the writing of history, legal and political life all receive their strongest stimulus.

On the other hand, it is also the priesthood that can provide *the most serious obstacles to the development of healthy religious life.* A rapid florescence of the priestly class is precisely what encourages it to separate itself from the community at large, and become a caste, thrusting itself between the secular and religious life of society, and proving instead of a mediator more of a hindrance to direct intercourse with God. The caste's lust for power makes use of its control of worship to bring the congregation into complete dependence on the priest for the satisfaction of its religious needs; and because the cultus is thus compelled to subserve the acquisition of moral and material power, it deteriorates, becoming extensively secularized and losing its religious content. Furthermore, the high value set on tradition turns into a rigid adherence to forms long superseded, stifling any new religious growth; and for this reason the influence of religion on the shaping of public life is either directed along false paths, or completely neutralized.

It is, therefore, *an institution with a very definite personality* which enters the service of the Yahweh religion with the coming of the priesthood.[1] Consequently, it may be assumed from the start that the fundamental concepts of Mosaic religion will be taken up and worked over within this highly-trained professional religious class in ways that are distinctive and in keeping with its whole spiritual

[1] The study of this subject demands that we should take note not only of the historical and legislative traditions of P and Chronicles, but also of the fragments of a history of the Zion sanctuary to be found in Gen. 14; I Sam. 4–6; II Sam. 6; II Kings 11 f.; 22 f.; the so-called Aramaic source for the rebuilding of the Temple (Ezra 4–6); the memoirs of Ezra and Nehemiah; and, with certain limitations because of the strong influence of prophetic ideas, the Book of Deuteronomy. Evidence of prime importance is also provided by cultic poetry, which in hymn and liturgy, and in prayers of thanksgiving and intercession has shaped the ideas fostered in priestly practice for use at religious festivals.

character; and this all the more, because the divine revelation proclaimed by Moses, with its unequivocal simplicity and unprecedented religious impetus, had given cultic life an absolutely distinctive content, which could not possibly be incorporated in the traditional forms as they stood, but directed the conception and conformation of worship along new lines.

The traces of this change within the overall picture of the Israelite cultus have already been discussed in the course of our treatment of the ordinances of the Yahweh covenant.[1] Here the point at issue is the distinctive conception of the divine-human relationship propounded by the Israelite priesthood and underlying their cultic practice. It is, indeed, quite certain that an important historical development took place, which in conjunction with the movement of Israelite spirituality as a whole added new ideas and refashioned the old in more definite and clearer form. But the fact that the specifically priestly spirituality is by and large consistent and pursues a quite definite line of its own in its relations with other spiritual trends, justifies an attempt to present a coherent picture of the total resultant religious attitude—an attitude which, prophetism only excepted, was the most influential of all.

(b) The Distinctive Character of the Priestly Conception of God

We have come to see that one of the controlling basic elements in the Mosaic experience of God was *the awe-inspiring unapproachableness of Yahweh*, which both made his communication of himself into a miracle such as man could only accept with humble gratitude, and safeguarded it from human abuse. Now it was always likely that this fearful repelling power, which marked all Yahweh's revelations, would be understood by priestly ways of thinking in terms of *the concept of tabu*, and what had originally been meant as a personal gesture of warning on the part of a divine Lord be thus associated—or confounded—with the danger zone of a spatially limited, impersonal force. This group of concepts, which was already familiar to the thinking of the great mass of the people, was in fact extremely suited to the task of making the prophetic experience the controlling factor in the basic religious attitude of a far wider circle. In the separation of a sacred enclave and consecrated objects from the sphere of the secular, and in the establishment of definite fasting and purity regulations governing every department of life, all backed

[1] Cf. ch. IV, pp. 98 ff. above.

by the terrifying power of the *tabu*, the priests found an effective method of expressing the inviolability of Yahweh in terms of permanent sensory experience. Thus a large and important sector of priestly religious practice was able to establish a direct connection with Yahweh worship. It is only necessary to call to mind the relevant passages of the Priestly Code in Exodus, Leviticus and Numbers, which certainly go back to extremely early regulations. The comparative study of religions has long been aware of the far-reaching importance of this group of concepts for a conviction both of the reality of God's power, and of the inviolable character of those rules that govern intercourse with it.[1] But in the capacity of a preliminary instructor the system of the *tabu* can also be of service to higher religion by leading men to think of the whole field of law, both moral and social, as rooted in the supernatural, and to invest it with unconditional authority as an expression of the holy. Inseparable from this, certainly, is the constant danger—which threatens every higher conception of God from this side—that the personal element in the concept of God will be weakened, and the holy connected with particular spatial limits; and this can constitute a serious obstacle to the subordination of the whole of life to the sovereignty of the divine will.

In this connection the strong emphasis which the Mosaic preaching laid on the claims of God's sovereignty taught men also to see the *tabu* laws, despite their originally quite different tendency, as the commands of a sovereign personal will, with the result that the impersonal element in these regulations of man's intercourse with God was pushed into the background. On the other hand, the distinctive feature of the *tabu*-concept, the idea of the divine reality as a spatially restricted entity, remained decisive for the whole religious thinking of the priesthood.

This may be seen from the way in which *the unapproachable majesty and otherness of the divine nature* was described. It is presented not as the prophets portrayed it, as the victorious conquest of all God's enemies or rivals in fearful conflict, but as *the strict separation of the uniquely Holy and his people from all other supernatural beings and their domain*. The latter must be shunned as impure; examples of this may be found in the stringent orders for the destruction of heathen cultic sites (Ex. 23.24; Deut. 12.2 f.; 16.21), the outlawing of the swine, a favourite sacrificial animal in other cults, or the frequent

[1] Cf. W. Hauer, *Die Religionen* I, pp. 151 ff.

prohibitions of those mourning customs connected with the worship of the spirits of the dead.[1] It was the Priestly law that most vigorously developed the ideal of the holy people, that is to say, one set apart from all others (cf. Lev. 17–26, and Ezek. 40–48).[2] The more thoroughly this idea of the sharp separation of the divine nature from all that was not God was worked out, the more surely, of course, was it bound to lead to the conception of God's absolute transcendence. Both in relation to the world of men and to the heavenly sphere it seemed that the majesty of the uniquely holy could only be safeguarded by clear separation. The popular notion of *the theophany*, in which the divine being was made visible in human or quasi-human form, and which was in no way repellent to prophetic thought, was avoided by the priestly literature. Yahweh was not perceptible either in the form of an angel or in dreams. In the heavenly sphere too he was unique: 'A God very terrible in the council of the holy ones, and to be feared above all them that are round about him'[3]—none of the sons of God is to be compared with him. This idea was not generally carried to extremes, which would have meant—as actually happens in the case of P, where all the sources are energetically corrected in this respect (cf. Gen. 1.26; 11.7)—the total exclusion of any *mediatory beings* of a divine nature. However, even the concept which did remain prevalent—that of the angel[4]—did not draw God down into this world, but stressed quite unmistakably that there could be no direct access to the Holy One, just as conversely any actual irruption into the earthly sphere was contrary to his nature. Only in the carefully enclosed and consecrated area of Sinai, or of the Tabernacle or the Temple, does God make his presence perceptible to human senses in the phenomenon of his *kabōd*, or in the cloud which acts as its vehicle.[5] But it is precisely this priestly technical term of the *kabōd* which most clearly betrays the effort to play down any sensorily perceptible manifestation of God as far as possible into a mere symbol of his presence. For the light or fire phenomenon in which the divine

---

[1] Cf. Lev. 11.7; Isa. 65.4; 66.17 (Temple prophecy!); Deut. 14.1 f.; 26.14; Lev. 21.1 ff., 11; 19.27 f.; 10.6; Num. 19.14–21: also ch. IV.2. IV (a), pp. 133 f. above.

[2] Israel is presented as a separated people as early as Num. 23.9; cf. also Ex. 19.5 f.; Ps. 16.4 and markedly in Deut.

[3] Cf. Ps. 89.8.

[4] Cf. Ezek. 9.2; I Chron. 21.1, 15 ff.; II Chron. 14.12; 20.22; Zech. 1.8 f.; 3.1 etc.

[5] Cf. Ex. 24.16 f.; 40.34 f.; Lev. 9.23; Num. 14.10; 16.19; 17.7; I Kings 8.10 f.

majesty shows itself is a formless brightness fully in keeping with the strong sense of God's intangibility. And even this pledge of the actual presence of God does nothing to lessen the emphasis on his unapproachableness. Only Moses can enter into it, not the people— and indeed, even Moses is not always in a position to do so; and at its presence the priests in the Temple must suspend their worship.

The divine transcendence is even more heavily underlined when the principal expression of God's self-communication is changed to *the revelation and continuous presence of his Name*. The Deuteronomic literature in particular favours the designation of the Temple as the place where Yahweh sets his Name, or causes it to dwell.[1] Strangely enough, the formula is not found in P, though Lev. 20.3 mentions the profanation of the Name in the same breath with that of the sanctuary, and Num. 6.27 describes the priests in the act of blessing as those who lay God's Name on the Israelites. It should also be noted that God's revelation to Moses is summed up in a new divine Name (Ex. 6.3). These closely related concepts at any rate do nothing to prevent our conjecturing a priestly origin for the more developed theory of God's self-revelation in his Name, even though this may have occurred in other circles at different centres and times. The concept is already suggested by the ancient law of the altar (Ex. 20.24 ff.), and even in the post-Deuteronomic period the idea that the sanctuary is marked out by the Name of God enjoyed considerable favour in priestly circles, as a glance at the language of Chronicles[2] will show. Furthermore, without disregarding the roots of the idea in the high value anciently set on the Name in primitive belief,[3] it is still significant for the tendency of priestly thought that the Name should have been able so effectively to supplant the more concrete manifestations of the deity as the summing-up of the personal attributes and operations of God. Here too there is further evidence of a line of thought we have pursued on previous occasions, in that the personal quality of the divine Thou which is so strongly connoted by the Name *makes it impossible after the manner of mysticism to drag down the divine into an immanent presence in man*. No infinite divine Being draws the seeker after God into its domain, drowning him in

---

[1] Cf. Deut. 12.5, 21; 14.23 f. etc.; I Kings 8.16, 29 etc.

[2] As passages independent of the influence of the Books of Kings, which is here very strong, may be mentioned: I Chron. 22.7, 8, 10, 19; 28.3; 29.16; II Chron. 1.18; 20.8, 9.

[3] Cf. Giesebrecht, *Die AT Schätzung des Gottesnamens*, pp. 68 ff.; J. Pedersen, *Israel* I–II, pp. 245 ff.

itself in blessed union or ecstatic rapture—'*in Gott ein sel'ger Unter-gang*'.[1] Rather the personhood of God confronts the world of men as other in kind, in sharp contrast to any idea of man's being able to share in the divine nature. This Being can be known only through the communication of his Name, by which he summons men to a spiritual and personal intercourse in which, none the less, there must also always be a sense of the permanent and immovable gulf between the two parties.

If this separation of the divine Being from all that is not God leads, in this context, to the use of the divine Name to describe the way in which God exists as a transcendent personality supreme over this world, the Priestly writer finds another equally suitable means of expressing the same idea in *his picture of the Word of Creation*.[2] It is by this means that the Lord of the universe regulates his relationship with our world without in any way becoming involved in its laws, or tied to its order. Here God's transcendence of the material world is set in the sharpest possible contrast to any pantheistic conception of interfusion or evolutionary development. The divine will invades this world in the form of the most super sensory reality our experience can conceive. The Godhead stands over the cosmos in independent fullness of life; but its inaccessible majesty derives from its essential nature of purely transcendent being.

Thus it was that the particular course which priestly thought adopted in assimilating the concepts of the Mosaic revelation led it to confront the divine Being and this world in a way equally removed from any divinization of Nature or humanization of God, and in so doing provided firm pre conditions for a monotheistic understanding.

(c) *The Relations between God and the World*

It is obvious that so emphatically transcendent a conception of God was bound also to colour any description of God's dealings with the world. Here the basis of thinking was the one so forcefully pro-claimed by Moses—*the unconditional sovereignty of the divine Lord over the people whom he had chosen*. The more decisively this divine sovereignty made itself felt in the concrete circumstances of the national life, the more definite was the fact of a real connection between God and the world bound to become; and the more necessary, therefore, was it for priestly thought, in view of the ease with which its strong

---

[1] 'A blessed sinking into God' (Tr.).
[2] Cf. Gen. 1.

emphasis on God's transcendence could be perverted into a complete separation of God from the world, to combine with this emphasis an equally real communication between the divine and human spheres, a genuine incursion of God's power. The need was met by a concept inseparably associated with the Mosaic foundation—that of *the Law*. What has been said above (cf. pp. 402 f.) on the attitude of the priestly mentality to tradition and established order will have made sufficiently clear how ideally this concept accorded with the natural presuppositions of the priesthood. From the very first, therefore, the cultivation and expansion of the traditional covenant law must have found willing supporters in the priests. Moreover, as a serviceable instrument of priestly religious practice, the Law also accorded admirably with the exposition of the priestly concept of God, for it allowed them to present the reality of God's sovereignty without prejudice to the yonside quality of the divine nature. In the Law the will of God becomes concrete and emerges from the transcendence of his personality into the world of the Here and Now. As spiritual power expressing itself in word the Law witnessed both to the fact that God was inaccessible to earthly sense, and to that personal quality of God which the human spirit could comprehend. At the same time it gave the most forceful expression to God's power as Disposer of the whole world. As Lawgiver Israel's God demonstrates his power over the world and man by instructing them in the laws of their own being, and thus keeping them in permanent dependence on himself.

Naturally, *Israel is the principal sphere of the Law's dominion*. With wellnigh crushing force the law of her covenant confronts her with the unconditional character of the divine claims. If the older collections had already deeply impressed on men the irrefragability of the Law, the priestly legislation laid all its emphasis on the majesty of the divine will therein expressed. The imposition of the Law serves to bring out the absolute power of a sovereign who has no need either to seek the agreement of his subjects, or to induce them to keep the law by promises. Even when the thought is of the act of redemption by this sovereign Lord, as in the Exodus from Egypt, it is still emphasized that God has no need of his people. The 'establishment' of the covenant which occasions the founding of the legal order is a resolution of God's independent purpose.[1]

Moreover, by a logical development, the content of the cultic

[1]Cf. Ex. 6.4; 31.16; Gen. 17.7, 19, 21.

law is controlled by the dominating conception that in the sphere of
Israel everything belongs to Yahweh alone, space and time, property
and life. The sacrifices and festivals, the purificatory rites and cultic
ceremonies, all minister to the recognition of this unlimited divine
authority. In everything the Israelite is reminded that his whole life
is dedicated to God, and he is brought to realize that that life must
show outwardly the character proper to the people of Yahweh's own
possession. That this can only be achieved by the most humble
submission to the Holy One is driven home by the all-controlling
concept of atonement, which for P permeates the entire cultus.
Moreover, the very definite insistence on the holiness of the priests,
which is so characteristic of P in contrast to Deuteronomy,[1] underlines the unapproachable exaltedness of the divine Lord, whose
intercourse with men always includes the provision of a screen for
human imperfection.

It has been said that, however much this reverent prostration
before God is to be distinguished from the senseless terror of the
heathen, yet the way in which stress on the divine sovereignty is
carried to extremes in the Law *prevents* the growth of *a proper feeling
for man's communion with God.*[2] This view is dictated, however, by too
particular a comparison with the ingenuous confidence that marks
man's dealings with God in the Book of Genesis, and by too exclusive
attention to the peculiar stamp of priestly thought as found in P.
Certainly the naïve intermingling of the divine and human worlds
which, to the aesthetically inclined spectator, is so delightful a
feature of the old sagas becomes intrinsically impossible to the
priestly mind; after all, it was not for nothing that the priests revised
so large a part of Israel's history and experience of God. But a glance
at the cultic hymns in the Psalter, with their transports of praise
offered to the almighty Lord, or at Chronicles, clinging in faith to
the promises of Yahweh guaranteed by the Law, will suffice to show
that, for all the force and earnestness with which the priestly narrator
draws attention to the gulf between God and man, and resists any
familiarity in human intercourse with him, the joy of being the
possession of this God was not killed, nor was pride in the Law as
the expression of Israel's favoured position lessened. Moreover, even
in P itself it is important not to miss the undertone of enthusiasm
which pervades his work in its adoration of the uniquely exalted

[1] Cf. Lev. 10.7; 21.7; Num. 16.7 etc.
[2] Cf. e.g., Holzinger, *Einleitung in den Hexateuch,* 1893, p. 376.

God. If the basic mood of the Israelite hymns may be described as that of self-forgetful surrender to the fearful and glorious God, springing from the vision of his exaltedness, the attentive reader of Gen. 1 cannot but notice that, for all its architectonic weight and a style like burnished brass, the same mood is by no means foreign to the author of this picture either. And the fact that the Law seeks to make man holy like God himself (Lev. 19.2 *et al.*) means that it ennobles him in the very act of subjecting him to God.

Not only in Israel, but also *in the universe and human race* the Law brings about this subjection of all that exists to God. It is true that the Babylonian priests also saw an important manifestation of the power of God in the fact that the Creator formed the cosmos in a purposeful order, and set its life in fixed paths; and Egyptian hymns too testify that this derivation of the world-order from a mighty creative will was part of an international priestly wisdom. A loving absorption in the marvellous organism of Nature, and in its witness to the power of its divine Creator, forms a link between the religion of Israel and the knowledge of God to be found in the higher religions of paganism. But this conception could only come to full development where it was combined with the recognition that God was a transcendent Being, beside whom no force of Nature could pretend to divine status, and who, moreover, was himself in no danger of degenerating into a kind of vivifying cosmic energy. Only so could the unqualified dependence of the world on God—to the point of conceiving Creation as *ex nihilo*—be safeguarded. Only so could the highest of creatures, man, enter into a permanent relationship with his Creator, and one that should be decisive for his whole life. As the image of God, and lord over his fellow-creatures, he finds that his life is given him to devote to a great task, and that he is commanded to find his own dignity in his very subjection to God. The jubilant echo which Gen. 1 finds in many of the Psalms[1] indicates the liberating effect of the concept of Creation in its monotheistic form, exalting man the more highly, the more absolutely it binds him. In this context even the wonders of Creation can be valued as signs of divine grace,[2] and the deep inner unity between the construction of the cosmos and the redemption of Israel, as being both of them the work of the God who subjects all existence to his saving ordinances, is sung with constant freshness of treatment.

[1] Cf. Pss. 8; 19; 29; 89; 104 etc.
[2] Cf. e.g., Pss. 136.4 ff.; 135.6 f.; 89.2–19.

This presentation of the sovereign power of God acquires its most distinctive form when even *God's relations with the Gentile world* are described in terms of the Law. If the prophets see history as the organic building up of the kingdom of God, carried through in the face of all obstacles, to the priest it is an organized entity, the complexity of which is controlled within boundaries established by God, and thus made serviceable to his purpose. Not only the Israelites, but also the heathen stand within a God-given order which controls their relations with God; it is only within the Noah covenant, which is binding on all men, that the Abraham covenant is set up. All life finds its fulfilment in these mighty and enduring statutes; the task of man is simply to observe the ordinances, and thus obediently to fill the place allotted to him by God. How positive this conception of the relationship between the heathen and God can be is shown by Ezek. 5.6 f., where the attitude of Israel toward the law of Sinai is compared with that of the heathen toward the regulations laid down for them; and an even more striking example is the saying of Malachi (1.11)—who takes his stand on the ground of the Law—that from the rising of the sun to its going down God's name is great among the Gentiles, and in every place a pure offering is made to him.[1] But even such a saying as Deut. 4.19, which is fiercely critical of the worship of paganism, and which ascribes the cult of the host of heaven to an ordinance which God has laid upon the Gentiles, yet sees confirmation of the Gentile world's dependence on Yahweh in the legal authority of the great world rulers.[2] On this way of looking at things it becomes clear why in priestly circles so little attention is paid to the Gentile world. The priestly outlook is too strongly controlled by acceptance of the present world-order as something fixed by divine law, where rights and duties are already apportioned, and everyone has his place to keep. Here too there is a tendency to think rather in terms of Space than of Time. Amid all the transitoriness it is the permanent order, amid all the coming to be and passing away it is the cosmic intelligence, building with proportion and purpose, and constructing enduring, harmonious conditions, on which the eyes of the priest are fixed, and in whose exalted beauty he finds edification. Hence a quite special emphasis is placed on the unshakable continuance of the world-order as once laid down; and

[1] Reverent fear of God's Name is also ascribed to the heathen in Pss. 83.19; 86.9.
[2] Similarly Deut. 32.8 f.

the word '*ōlām*, eternity, is a favourite epithet in the sayings about God's ordering of the universe. His *b'rit* is a *b'rit* '*ōlām*;[1] he wields his sovereignty as an eternal king;[2] the statutes he imposes are eternally valid,[3] but so also are his favour and his promises.[4] The sovereignty of the transcendent God which finds expression in the Law is thus consummated in the fact that its decrees are unaffected by the flux of Time, and possess a force which is eternally binding.

(*d*) *The Place of Man in the World*

(α) Human right conduct

When God's authority over mankind is described in these ways, then judgment of what constitutes righteous conduct in man will move in a similar direction. In this context too priestly thought creates its own distinctive expression, and the difference between it and the prophetic approach is from the outset strikingly noticeable. The difference, however, is not just on the surface, as it might appear to be from the rather one-sided turn given to many of the formulations, especially at the hands of the Priestly stratum of the Pentateuch. Certainly it cannot be said that the priestly attitude to this question is rightly characterized by describing them as men concerned only with external rules, and satisfied simply with the outward observance by the pious of prescribed ordinances, with no demand either for personal surrender or for interior assent to the outward performance.[5]

It has therefore been conceded over and over again, though without any attempt to meet the views of those critics who disagree, that 'the ethic of the prophets is valid even for P',[6] and that, if the moral commands are in the background as far as P is concerned, this is not because they are less important, but because 'they are presupposed throughout, and are only not included in the Law because they are taken for granted'.[7] At the same time it is recognized that in the priestly law we are not moving at a lower moral level than that of the prophets, nor one where the cultus can take the place of moral

[1]Cf. Gen. 9.16; 17.7; Ex. 31.16 f.; Lev. 24.8; Num. 18.19; 25.13; Ps. 105.10. Cf. ch. II, pp. 56 f. above.
[2]Cf. Pss. 29.10; 93.2; 104.31; 145.13; Ex. 15.18.
[3]Cf. Lev. 3.17; 6.11, 15; 7.34, 36; 10.9, 15; 16.29, 31, 34 etc.; Ezek. 46.14.
[4]Cf. Pss. 89.3; 103.17; II Chron. 13.5; 1.9; 6.17; 21.7.
[5]Cf. e.g., as only one among many similar expressions, that of Gunkel (*Genesis*[3], 1910, p. 141): 'P has no sense of personal piety; all that matters to him in religion is objective performance'.
[6]Cf. Kautzsch, *Biblische Theologie des AT*, p. 351.
[7]Cf. Holzinger, *op. cit.*, pp. 384 f.

obligation, but are confronted with a firm basis common to both prophetic and priestly morality.

This fact, however, should not be used to justify the conclusion that there is in general no *difference of principle between the religious thinking of priest and prophet.*[1] What we have to do is rather to define this difference more precisely, and investigate the reason for it. A possible starting-point is provided by the two principal reproaches customarily levelled at the priestly conception of what constitutes right conduct in man. The first points out that in the priestly ideal of piety it is always the act of obedience to the positive injunction which is the prominent feature,[2] with the result that too little significance is attached to man's state of heart, and that genuinely moral conduct arising from free decision is thereby made impossible. The second stresses that the equal status given in the priestly conception of the divine law to ethical and cultic commandments betrays a failure to perceive the principle of the absolute supremacy of the moral order.

So far as the first criticism is concerned, it specifies one characteristic feature of priestly morality, the value of which can only rightly be assessed if we consider the whole of the priestly conception of man's position *vis-à-vis* God. When God's dealings with the world are understood in terms of the establishment of his Law, especial emphasis is naturally bound to fall on the legal organization of national life. *In the Law God's will becomes flesh and blood,* and makes its entry into human history. Here man is directly confronted with his God, and his attitude to the Law therefore acquires immediate religious significance. The man who submits his life to the ordinance of the Law is the one who renders obedience to the demands of God himself. It is this that proves infallibly whether a man is prepared to bow before the majesty of God. The inner disposition, therefore, is not a matter of indifference; but on the other hand neither can it be assessed. Normally, however, right conduct can be taken as the visible, palpable expression of a corresponding state of mind; the hypocrite, if he does not give himself away, has to be left to God. In adopting such an attitude, the priest is very largely in accord with general popular conviction; for the average man the principle that

---

[1] So Eerdmans, *De Godsdienst van Israel* I, p. 188.

[2] An attitude expressed in P, for example, by the use of the favourite formula: *k⁺kōl 'ᵃšer ṣiwwā 'ōtō 'ᵉlōhīm kēn 'āśā,* Gen. 6.22; Ex. 7.6; 12.28, 50; 25.9 etc. Cf. also the insistence on the Torah as the yardstick of all conduct pleasing to God.

normally holds good is that *the righteous, the ones who obey God's commands, are the truly pious.* 'Piety for the Hebrews is no matter of feelings, or of inoffensive formalities; it is a question of proving oneself morally in the sight of the supreme Judge. For God himself is the God of righteousness.'[1] Naturally this may result in mere externalism, content with a kind of bourgeois respectability as its ideal of piety, and deaf to any more exacting claims on its personal life. But it is precisely in Israel that this danger is considerably reduced by the fact that equity and consideration for one's fellow-countrymen are to a great extent matters of law; and this constantly leads to a profoundly personal outlook and self-control.

For the priest, however, it was inevitable that, in giving moral instruction, he should aim at securing *observance of the Law.* To begin with, from the earliest days, when his work was the delivering of oracles, he had been continually concerned with counselling and giving decisions in the concrete cases of practical life; at the same time he maintained a close connection with the practice of civil law in his capacity as a final court of appeal for the settlement of difficult legal points. Furthermore, it was the high value which he attached to the sacred tradition, and his capacity for its systematic codification as a result of his mastery of the art of writing, which led him to undertake the task of transmitting the Law, as occasional pieces of evidence in the OT indicate.[2] Even if, therefore, for lack of OT evidence on the point, there may be some doubt whether he acted as a professional judge, nevertheless both his calling and inclination led him to concern himself intensively with the civil law, and gave him the opportunity to see that the nation was subjected to the will of God by a thoroughgoing implementation of the divine law, and strict obedience to the concrete divine commands. *The Law becomes for him the outward way of life* by which the people of God as a whole acquires a perceptible character through the steady obedience of each individual.

No fair-minded critic, therefore, can consider that the priestly outlook must necessarily be lacking in understanding of that genuine

---

[1] Cf. L. Köhler, *Die hebräische Rechtsgemeinde,* p. 22.

[2] Cf. the conjunction of priests and scribes in II Sam. 8.16–18 and I Kings 4.2 f.; also the laying up of the Decalogue in the Ark, and Samuel's drafting and depositing the law of the kingdom before Yahweh, I Sam. 10.25. Also relevant here are Samuel's activity as a judge, and the authority bestowed on the priests in Deut. 17.8 ff. Deut. 17.18 presupposes the preservation of the Law by the priests; and this can therefore hardly be an innovation of the Josianic period.

morality which goes beyond the outward letter of the law. After all, it is precisely the Priestly writings which take care to preface the introduction of the cultic law with an account of the moral conduct of the patriarchs; and in their abridgement of the nation's history it is all the elements which run counter to their moral ideal which are excluded. Their accounts of the making of the primal covenants are packed with moral content, even if elements of cultic law do also play a considerable part; and the phrase 'to walk with God',[1] used to describe the piety of Noah—and almost as frequently that of Abraham—clearly implies, over and above any individual actions, a consistent orientation of life springing from personal decision.[2]

The really profound distinction, however, between this approach and that of the prophets is to be found in the fact that the moral teaching of the priest is concerned to guide an actually existent people into a particular pattern of life in which the eternal will of God for men is to be given visible form. This means that *the status of morality is described within the limits imposed by an earthly community*, that is to say, it is presented in the form of law. But attention is not explicitly paid to that moral ingredient which must of necessity underlie all else, namely the response of personality. And because this moulding of the people of God according to the possibilities afforded by this world stands, for all its failings, under the shadow of elective grace, it is invested with a value beyond time which can never be endangered by any fluctuations of historical destiny. By contrast everything in the prophetic view revolves round the attitude adopted toward the new reality of God which at this moment *is* endangering the very existence of the nation. In a judgment so radical that it does not even stop at the laws that govern the people of God, for the reason that these because of their involvement with sin are a blasphemy against the Holy One, the only thing that matters is the existential decision of the human 'I'. Any appeal to a sacred law, to the permanence of any system, though it be sanctioned by God himself, would be treachery to that divine claim of sovereignty which is now being promulgated, and which is breaking with the old in order to build the new. Small wonder then if, in comparison with a man's inward attitude to the will of God, any outward rectitude of conduct ceases to have any further value in itself.

[1] Cf. Gen. 6.9; 17.1.
[2] In this connection one is reminded too of the idea of the concept of love as the norm of social ethics in Lev. 19.18: cf. pp. 94 f. above.

(β) Cultic activity

We must start from the same point if we are also to understand *the equal value set on the cultic and moral law* in the priestly system. When the People of God is obliged to develop a distinctive outward form to raise it above the level of its environment and to enable it to confess its faith in the very pattern of its earthly existence, then the mode and manner of its worship can never be a matter of indifference. Just as the body, rightly understood, comes to express the nature of the personality, so *the 'body' that is a form of worship must correspond to the spirit of the faith* which constitutes the vivifying principle of the nation's existence.[1] In fact no one has yet been able to say how Israel could possibly have preserved her religion unharmed without the protective framework of fixed forms of cultic law, the unconditional obligations of which bound the individual Israelites together in community. It is because the priest is concerned not with a sect, but with a People of God, with all the plenitude of its earthly relationships and the forms in which its life finds expression, that the cultic law is for him invested with an authority equal to that of the moral—for indeed, the two things intimately interact.

It is quite easy to show how closely the cultus is involved with the most profound content of Israelite religion. The most important point is not that *cultic forms frequently had the effect of educating men in the moral conduct of life*, though this is easily overlooked. How forcefully, for example, intercession reminds man of his responsibilities in the sight of the righteous God can be seen from a glance at this class of cultic hymns.[2] Especially in those cases where they speak of the divine judgment prepared for the guilty, the vision of Yahweh the incorruptible Judge affords an earnest exhortation to self-examination.[3] In general too the instruction to confess one's sins, a prominent feature, for instance, of Ps. 32, had the effect of making the conscience of the worshipper more sensitive. Again, the priestly instruction given to the visitor to the sanctuary, as we find it for example in Pss. 15 and 24.3–6, provided constant opportunities for impressing on men the moral standards of communal life. Of what development this instruction was susceptible can be seen from Ps. 50, a cultic sermon influenced by prophetic ideas. The vow, too, taken at the decisive turning-points of life, calls to men's remembrance their

[1] Cf. ch. IV, pp. 98 f. above.
[2] No more instances need be cited than e.g. Pss. 5; 7; 17 etc.
[3] Cf. H. Schmidt, *Das Gebet der Angeklagten im Alten Testament* (BZAW 49), 1928.

420   THE INSTRUMENTS OF THE COVENANT

duties toward God;[1] and even the cultic practice of blessing and cursing united religion and morality by subjecting the desire for retaliation to the holy commands of Yahweh.[2]

But even though in these various ways cult and ethic may be inseparably associated, incomparably more important is the manner in which the basic cultic forms are adapted to be the means of expressing the divine-human relationship both of the congregation and of the individual. Especially worthy of attention in this regard is *the part played in worship by the sung and spoken word*. It is in the hymnody and prophecy of the Temple, in prayer and in the pronouncement of blessings, that cultic activity finds its own interpretation. In place of some mystic δρώμενον there is a meaningful reciprocity of word and action, in which the former makes the latter comprehensible, and the latter the former effective. The little that we know for certain of a gradual development of Israelite worship includes not only differentiation and enrichment of the sacrifices and rites in themselves, but also a more abundant use of the word by the introduction of prophecy into the cultus and a more extensive employment of Temple singing. Furthermore the expounding of the ancient festivals in historical terms, thus making them into days commemorating the calling and redemption of the nation, gave the word new importance in the form of the festival ἱερὸς λόγος.[3]

The elevation of worship into the sphere of conscious intelligence and clearly-defined concepts which was effected in these ways is equally clearly discernible in the case of *other cultic acts* which are now *definitely related to the sovereignty of God*, no matter what the roots from which they originally sprang. Thus circumcision is interpreted as an act of purification and dedication, by which is brought about adoption into the community of the purified nation, and at the same time commitment to the keeping of the divine statutes obtaining in this community.[4]

The prescriptions relating to purity, the animistic or manaistic origin of which is often palpable, are given unifying significance by relating them to the holiness of Yahweh, which seeks a people strictly separated from all that is unclean. In this context too we

[1] Cf. the royal vow in Ps. 101, which presents a striking picture of the ideal king: and also ch. IV.2. IV (b), pp. 145 f. above.
[2] Cf. S. Mowinckel, Psalmenstudien V, pp. 134 f., and ch. IV.2.IV (c), pp. 173 f. above.
[3] Cf. ch. IV.2. III, pp. 119 ff. above.
[4] Cf. Gen. 17: also pp. 138 f. above.

should remember the process mentioned above by which the ancient agricultural festivals were linked with the saving acts in history through which Yahweh established his sovereignty. For the rest, reference should be made to the comments on pp. 406 f. above, and the remarks on the cultic ordinances of the covenant in ch. IV.

It is, therefore, when it acts in concert with the moral norms that the cultic law is most powerfully effective in binding the national consciousness to the one divine will. Its vital strength in this respect is brought out most prominently in the testimonies of pilgrims and visitors to the Temple, preserved for us in the Psalter,[1] concerning the experiences vouchsafed to them through the cultus. What is of supreme importance here is not simply the exultation of being numbered among the people of God, and so of being permitted to look for life and protection from the God of Israel; nor again is it merely the potent sense of good fortune generated by a strong feeling of community, or by the tying of the most intimate bonds of friendship as a result of common cultic experience[2]—though the value of all these things should not be underestimated. But its deepest value lies in the fact that here *the firm foundations of the earthly national community in a reality which is living and eternal, the roots of all earthly existence in a redeeming divine grace* which condescends to meet men in these concrete forms, are now brought home to the consciousness with a directness of impact that makes visible the inner organic connection between belief in God and the actions with which he is worshipped.

This subjective effect of the cultus is, moreover, not impaired by the way in which individual elements in it are, on the priestly system, made independent of the spontaneous participation of the congregation, and come to possess meaning and validity in themselves. It is well known that in the Priestly Code the daily burnt offering forms the basic element in worship, and the value of this offering lies simply in its performance, without regard to the presence or participation of the congregation. The private offering, particularly the animal sacrifice with its joyful sacrificial meal, is left to the individual to perform as he may happen to feel inclined, and retreats very much into the background, having clearly lost in significance. Thus *sacrificial worship becomes predominantly an institution regulated by statute,*

[1]Of particular interest in this connection are: Pss. 27.1–6; 42 f.; 84; 122: cf. also 36.11 ff.
[2]Cf. Ps. 55.14 f.

effecting atonement independently of any spontaneous feeling on the part of the individual; and by so doing, it guarantees the presence of God. What is for the most part overlooked, however, is that in this expression of the priestly concept of holiness powerful expression is also given to the absolute supremacy of divine grace. The more emphatically the institution of the cultus is valued as a gift of grace, the more must its basic element be independent of the congregation in order to become a symbol of that sovereign condescension with which God sends down his grace into this particular institution, and exalts it to perpetual effectiveness without regard to the character or conduct of man. Here the fact of a new situation, created by Yahweh's revelation for the benefit of every member of the congregation, in which a promise of free and open access to God's forgiveness and healing is signed and sealed, is made manifest in a concrete institution. To man is left obedience, incorporation into the divinely ordained organism—this being expressed in the payment of a poll-tax for the maintenance of divine worship fixed at the same rate for each individual[1]—and the acceptance in faith of the promise of which he has been thus assured.

A similar stress on the objective basis of the Israelite sense of election is achieved by *the incorporation of prophecy into the Temple worship*, and its gradual transformation into a routine and settled part of the liturgy.[2] This meant that something was introduced as a regular ingredient into the worship of the congregation which had originally sprung unpredictably from a charismatic commission, that is to say, an assurance of his succour on the part of the divinity in person; and as such this gave characteristic expression to the triumphant certainty of Yahweh's faithfulness toward his own people, whenever they turned to him with penitent supplication. This at once calls to mind the promise of grace delivered to the congregation by an Evangelical minister, a resemblance which should warn us against seeing in this feature of the cultus nothing more than a presumptuous attempt on the part of the priest to dispose of the grace of God—even though there may be a very real danger of this perversion.[3]

At this point it may be asked *how this making visible of the divine grace in institutions perceptible and comprehensible to the senses, which is at*

---

[1]Cf. Ex. 30.11 ff.
[2]Cf. Pss. 12.6; 60.8; 75.3 f.; 81.6 ff.; 85.9 ff.; 95.8 ff.
[3]On this subject we shall have something to say later.

present under discussion, can possibly be reconciled with that strong sense of God as utterly inconceivable and exalted far above the sensory world which plays so large a part in priestly thought. Is this not in fact a clear instance of degeneration from Mosaic and prophetic principles to the level of a priestly sacramental mysticism which seeks to make the trans-sensory accessible to the senses? Now there can be no doubt that priestly cultic practice is intensely concerned with the real presence of the deity in the midst of the congregation in its festivals, and consequently there is bound to be a certain tension with the idea of the unapproachable majesty of the covenant God. Nevertheless we should not forget that something of this tension was in fact already present in the Mosaic conception of the jealous God of the covenant. To overcome this difficulty priestly thought makes use of ancillary concepts which are a feature of the conception of God elsewhere in the ancient East, namely the correlative concepts of the original and the copy. The Tabernacle, the prototype of the Temple, with its furnishings, is prepared in accordance with the heavenly model which Moses saw.[1] Use is also made in this connection of the common Eastern idea that every earthly sanctuary is a copy of the heavenly. That this played an enduring part in priestly thinking may be seen from Ezekiel's account of the theophany at the river Chebar, where what appeared to him was not the actual form of the *kᵉbōd yhwh*, but its reflection in the sheet of electrum[2]—a feature patently connected with the sanctuary of the Ark.[3]

The same idea also influences the Chronicler's account of David's preparations for the building of the Temple, where the plan for the sanctuary is ascribed to a writing from the hand of Yahweh.[4] This too accords excellently with the priestly concept of God in that it allows the divine transcendence to be reconciled with the special concern for God's real self-communication in the cult. As copies of the heavenly realities the Temple and its worship act as revealers of divine concepts and effective guardians and mediators of heavenly powers; but all their operations find meaning and unity—and

[1] Cf. Ex. 25.9, 40: also the plan for the building of his temple communicated by God to Gudea of Lagash (in Thureau-Dangin, *Die sum. u. akkad. Königsinschriften*, pp. 95 ff.; cf. *Les Cylindres de Goudéa, Transcription et traduction*, 1905, pp. 12 ff.) and the statue of Gudea from Telloh in A. Jeremias, *Handbuch der altorientalischen Geisteskultur*², 1925, p. 12.

[2] Cf. Ezek. 1.4.

[3] Cf. Procksch, 'Die Berufungsvision Hesekiels', in *Budde-Festschrift* (BZAW 34), 1920, pp. 141 ff.

[4] Cf. I Chron. 28.19.

essential limitation—in the task of establishing God's sovereignty over a holy people. So long as they are employed to express this divine sovereignty, they are safeguarded against abuse in the form of extravagant speculation or debased magic—corruptions which elsewhere attach themselves only too easily to a cultus under priestly control.

But though the equal status accorded to the moral and cultic law by the priests has thus to be understood in the light of their concrete concern to give actual historical existence to the living reality of a holy people, the prophetic criticism of the cult sprang from a contemporary situation in which Israelite religion was being overgrown by a cult which would not be satisfied with this role of an outward means of expression. Instead it desired to be valued for itself, and thus rapidly became a playground for all the demonic forces of a Nature religion, in which the frontier between God and man was displaced, and the sovereignty of God jeopardized. The outcome was bound to be a final conflict between the majesty of God and man's lying misuse of cultic forms, with the equally inevitable result that the cult itself came under judgment. With the earthly institutions of the nation smashed, the cult also fell, and was compelled to share with them that state of waiting upon God's new creation, which is all that remains for those whom his judgment has smitten.

This difference in the fundamental point from which understanding starts is bound also to have a new and forceful impact upon the *attitude* of the priesthood *to the problem of time.*

(γ) Human existence in time (history and eschatology)

When cultic and moral standards are combined in the higher unity of the sovereign and unalterable divine will as expressed in the Law, the value set on the life of the nation in time, that is to say, its historical existence, will be quite different from that which it acquires when the whole concrete institution of the nation is imperilled by the menacing reality of the God of judgment. It is not that history is robbed of its value as the vessel of divine revelation, and replaced by a system of timeless, universal laws. Not only P's outline of history, but also that of Chronicles is dominated by the sense that God does not stand outside history, but actually enters it by means of his self-communication, and fills it with new content. The unveiling of God's work of salvation is a gradual process.

Through the cult of the Tabernacle (P), or the setting-up of the throne of David (Chronicles) the heavenly world is projected into that of earth, and human poverty is flooded with divine power; and in this way the great milestones of human history are made visible. Nevertheless the course of this history is considered not as the prologue to a final decision which, though it may be yet to emerge, is irresistibly approaching, but as *the unfolding of a cosmic order planned for permanence and perfection,* arched over by the rainbow of God's covenant of peace, and proclaiming his Yea to his creation. But even that which is thus unfolded in time is in fact already there from the beginning, because it is already contained in the creative word of the eternal God exalted over all time. A truth which is already permanently existent because it is grounded in the will of God is, by divine arrangement, disclosed in the various stages of the history of the human race, and given effect in particular realities. The institution of the Sabbath at the very moment of Creation, and the construction of the Tabernacle or of the Temple in accordance with a heavenly pattern, are striking examples of this way of thinking; and chronology provided another means of expression well suited to its needs. The carefully calculated architectonic perfection with which the cosmic structure is designed is presented in significant cyclic figures which indicate the manifestation of the Law in the world, and the erection of the house of God at Jerusalem as the pivotal points of world events.[1] The Chronicler's theory gives different expression to this view of history. Here a historical institution of Yahweh's covenant with Israel is no longer recognized; the assumption is that God's election has obtained perpetually from Adam onwards. This view would seem to be related to the philosophical interpretation of the world which also sees truth as something constant and eternal, only revealed more and more in the course of history. Once God's full revelation has been attained, however, all that is to be seen in history is the working out of the permanent ordinances established once for all; gradually all obstacles will be overcome, but no room is left for the occurrence of anything really new.

This basic conception of history is bound to have important effects

[1] P's chronology, as distinct from the later calculations of epochs (cf. p. 469 below), is therefore not to be regarded as a sign of an eschatological approach, as Nöldeke (*Untersuchungen zur Kritik des Alten Testaments*, 1869, p. 111) assumes; on the contrary, it is to be taken as expressing an element of stability in this world. Cf. F. Bork, 'Zur Chronologie der biblischen Urgeschichte', *ZAW* 47, 1929, pp. 206 ff., and A. Jepsen, 'Zur Chronologie des Priesterkodex', *ibid.*, pp. 251 ff.

in each individual case. To begin with, it provides *the basis for a strong constructive element in the presentation of history*. Because in every period what is involved is the same eternally valid divine order, the chronological sequence in the development of individual details becomes unimportant in comparison with their permanent meaning and purpose. The historian will consider it his more pressing concern to piece together this divine order in as complete a cross-section as possible, rather than in a narrative and chronological perspective. Hence earlier and later ingredients have an equal right to be incorporated into the account of the Mosaic giving of the Law, because they each express the same truth. Similar considerations apply to David's arrangements for the building of the Temple,[1] or the portrayal of his sovereignty as exercised over all Israel from the very first.[2]

The study of the past, therefore, is concerned not so much with conveying information about the course and sequence of individual events, as with bringing home to men the legitimate authority with which God has singled out his people, and their place in the total cosmic order. Hence *the external circumstances that accompany the facts of salvation* are arranged primarily in accordance with their usefulness in indicating the value and meaning of this decisive revelation. The central position of Israel in God's plan for history, brought to light in the Sinai revelation, must be made outwardly visible in the multitude of its population, and in the sumptuous magnificence of its sanctuary. Similarly the Jerusalem Temple, the founding of which by David establishes, according to the Chronicler, the definitive organization of the people of God, must be a fame and a marvel to the whole world.[3] That which the deficiencies of the present frequently obscure streams in dazzling brilliance out of the glorious past, and at the same time points to the ideal vision of the future, the realization of which is guaranteed by the eternal and unchanging will of God.

But even the scene of the historian's own time is not exempt from the correcting and standardizing influence of God's fundamentally consistent order. In so far as he can educe the principles of this system, *the narrator will subject even those realities which have not as yet taken shape to the transforming will of God*; and conditions which have so far not been realized in practice can be presented as actually

---

[1] Cf. I Chron. 28.19.
[2] Cf. I Chron. 12.23 ff.
[3] Cf. I Chron. 22.5.

existing in order to give full value to that reality which is the most deeply rooted and assured. The strongly constructive statement of the arrangements for the year of Jubilee,[1] or for the allocation of land to the Levites,[2] ought not to be considered as ordinances actually in force; but for the author in question they are no more a piece of pious poetic licence than was the new project for the sanctuary and the reorganization of the land for the author of Ezek. 43–48. Rather are they the fulfilment of something which actually exists, and which is simply being made more palpable in respect of its meaning and purpose.

It follows that the priestly account of history has to be judged on principles quite different from those that seem desirable to our conception of history-writing. The priestly thinker sees the world differently from the historian of today with his conviction that the empirical is the only kind of account that can be justified, for he sees it as set under the divine imperative with which, sooner or later, it must be shaped to correspond. Hence the empirical is something merely incidental when compared with that eternal ordinance of the Creator which alone is real and a guarantee of reality.

Furthermore, the principal task of divine Providence is *the maintenance and restoration of this order* in the teeth of all the wanton attempts to disturb it perpetrated by those who despise God. Hence the theme of the priestly account of history, whenever we find it describing the events of a period subsequent to the first foundation, is pre-eminently the regularity with which punishment succeeds sin, and the way in which this effects a restoration of the state of affairs that God desires.[3] It is this that enables it to bridge the chasm made in the life of the nation by the Exile, and, with the assistance of the Temple prophecy of Haggai and Zechariah, to present the new set-up of the cultic community in Jerusalem as a *restitutio in integrum*.[4] This assessment of God's guidance of history is also clearly expressed in the cultic hymns and prayers. These extol Yahweh's mighty acts in the establishment of the covenant with his people,[5] or in the maintenance of its monarchy.[6] They supplicate Yahweh to think upon his 'creation' in its present 'abasement'—that is to say, to succour his congregation

[1] Cf. Lev. 25: also pp. 96 f. above.
[2] Cf. Num. 35; Josh. 21.
[3] Cf. I Sam. 4–6; II Sam. 6; II Kings 12; 22; II Chron. 15.8–18; 17.7 ff.; 19.4 ff.; 29 ff.; 34 f.
[4] Cf. Ezra, Nehemiah.
[5] Cf. Pss. 81.2 ff.; 66.5 ff.; 105.8 ff.; 114; 135.8 ff.; 136.10 ff.
[6] Cf. Pss. 9.12 f.; 48.3, 5 ff.; 68; 96.3 ff.; 136.23 f.; 145.11 ff.; 147.13.

stricken by the destruction of the Temple[1]—and entreat him to restore it to favour.[2] This shows that the connection between history and the sovereignty of God which is the crucial factor for prophetic thought is also a vital ingredient in the whole priestly view of the world. Indeed, it is this which at bottom distinguishes Israelite cultic poetry from that of the Babylonians or Egyptians, where we may search in vain for any counterpart to this intense concentration on the coming into being of the Kingdom of God through the self-communication of the Lord of the universe in history.[3] It is true, of course, that this attitude to history only preserves its distinctive character in so far as it is controlled by the divine revelation con-summated in the Law; accordingly priestly thought also finds it particularly easy to combine the vision of God's dominion in Nature with that of his sovereignty over the Gentile world, and to connect his power in Creation with the carrying out of his promise to Israel.[4] In both spheres what is fulfilled is one consistent order. Because, moreover, the God of Israel is thus conceived as identical with the God of the universe,[5] the praise of the Creator acquires a marvellous realism; it is not mere aestheticism, but effective and vital religion. At the same time the recollection of God's exaltation and sovereignty over the whole world has the effect of elevating the idea of his local attachment to the Temple.

This subordination of history to the divine sovereignty as mani-fested in the Law, deeply rooted as it is in priestly thinking, and employed for the understanding of the Mosaic teaching about God, finds its consummation in Ezra and his life-work.[6] Here 'history is related to the Law, and the Law made the formative principle of history' (Schaeder). History illustrates the one abiding fact that God is the righteous and gracious One, and must therefore determine man's will and conduct. The present is related to the past, but in such a way that the complex of tradition, which every fresh genera-

---

[1] Cf. Ps. 74.18 ff.   [2] Cf. *šūbēnū*, Ps. 85.5–8.
[3] Cf. Gunkel, *Einleitung in die Psalmen*, 1928, pp. 46, 78.
[4] Cf. Pss. 89; 65.5, 6 ff.; also the passages listed in n. 1 on p. 413, and the expansion of Jeremiah's promise along the lines of priestly thought in Jer. 33.19–26.
[5] In this connection cf. especially Ps. 24 with its three-member construction.
[6] Cf. on this point, H. H. Schaeder, *Esra der Schreiber*, 1930. Even if Ezra 9 and Neh. 9 are not regarded as Ezra's *ipsissima verba* (though the grounds for such a view do not in fact seem to be adequate) it must be admitted that they are a correct expression of the guiding principles of the man who brought the Jerusalem congregation, in the shape of the Pentateuch, the Magna Carta of its future constitution.

tion makes its own, 'constantly renews man's sense of the norm of the moral life', and so never becomes just an idle metaphysic of history. Obedient fashioning of the present on the sure basis of God's revealed will, and in the spiritual form of the People of the Law, so that the latter ever more fully represents God's kingdom on earth— that is the priestly ideal.

It follows that any *subordination of the present to a great eschatological purpose* involving the ending of this age is bound to be quite alien to the spirit of this whole approach to the world and history. Not only has it no need of such a dissolution of the present in the future; it cannot but feel it to be a flat contradiction. For to the priestly way of thinking the world as it is now is already meaningful as expressing in essence the eternal plan of God. Just as the Creator made this world good in the beginning, so by his ordinances he has preserved it ever since the catastrophe of the Deluge from any recurrence of so drastic a threat to its existence,[1] and has firmly established his dominion over it for all time. Therefore the cultic songs of praise rejoice in the mighty and gracious Ruler of the world, and sing the glory of his eternal kingdom and the wisdom of his laws. There is no trace here of the violent tension imposed on this present life by the vision of the final judgment; it is resolved in the contemplation of the absolutely inviolable, all-embracing sovereign power of the God of the universe, who holds all things in his own hands. It is true that under prophetic influence the hope of Yahweh's ultimate victory over all his enemies finds its way into the hymns, and creates a new and powerful form of the cultic song of praise.[2] But with the inner logic characteristic of the genre the future divine dominion is once more either transformed into a present one, or at least confounded with it.[3] The preaching of the new age by the prophets, and their

---

[1] Cf. Gen. 9.12 ff. The rainbow is here the sign of Yahweh's everlasting ordinance of grace toward the Gentiles, just as circumcision, Passover and the Sabbath are for Israel; cf. the study of C. A. Keller, mentioned in p. 226 n. 2 above.

[2] Cf. Pss. 46; 76, *et al.*

[3] The best examples of this class are the so-called Enthronement Psalms (93; 96; 97; 99), where it is often impossible to tell whether the thought is of Yahweh's eternal kingdom established at the Creation, and continually working itself out in righteous judgment, or of an eschatological setting-up of his throne. To explain this in terms of the prophetic practice of speaking of the hoped-for future as if it were actually present does not, in my opinion, fully meet the case. Ps. 99.6, where the priests Moses, Aaron and Samuel are presented as prototypes of the righteous subjects of the heavenly king, is especially instructive on the subject of this transposition of the eschatological idea of the kingdom into the present. Cf. also Pss. 9.5, 8 f.; 65.6, 9; 113.3 f.; 145.11–13; 146.10; 148.11, 13.

depiction of the full divine sovereignty which would then dawn, may well have had the incidental effect of increasing the stress on the universality of God's kingdom in the priestly hymns as well; in Ps. 66 Yahweh's world-sovereignty is even used to introduce a cultic song of thanksgiving. But the characteristically priestly view is not hereby weakened. It stands with both feet on the solid ground of that earthly reality which, as Ps. 115.16 has it, Yahweh—while reserving the heaven for himself—has given to the children of men; and it is not to be swept off its feet by any longings for a new heaven and a new earth. Another hymn, Ps. 75, which has been enriched with prophetic elements,[1] but which is none the less essentially dictated by a cultic experience,[2] does indeed know of the Day of Yahweh with its judgment of the wicked (vv. 3, 9), but characteristically associates this with Yahweh's continuous judgment (v. 8), and depicts its consummation as the establishing of the pillars of the earth, that is to say, the restoration of eternal ordinances—a metaphor used, significantly enough, by ancient Eastern monarchs to describe their work of government.[3] It was not, therefore, simply a course of action conditioned by his period, but one rooted in the very structure of priestly piety, when Ezra consciously made it his life's work to achieve the elimination of prophetism and its great futurist hope. When the Law was conceived as so exclusively the pivot of the historical process as it was in the building up of the Jerusalem community on the basis of the Torah, the prophetic message, pointing forward to a consummation in the future, was bound to be pushed into the background by the priestly conception of a divine dominion to be actualized on earth. The form which the expectation of salvation took in the work of the Chronicler also remained true to this principle. The emphasis on the everlasting covenant with David, which is peculiar to him, may be termed 'messianic' in a certain sense, inasmuch as it involves the restoration of the Davidic kingdom, and identifies this with the Kingdom of Yahweh, thus exalting its divine character.[4] But here too the day of salvation is presented simply as a working out of eternal decrees; of a 'fundamental break, a dissolution of the present existing God-given order' this expectation knows nothing.[5]

[1]Gunkel calls it a prophetic liturgy (*Die Psalmen übersetzt und erklärt*, p. 327).
[2]Cf. Quell, *Das kultische Problem der Psalmen*, p. 105.
[3]Cf. Gunkel, *loc. cit.*
[4]Cf. II Chron. 9.8; 13.4 ff.; 21.7; 23.3; I Chron. 28.4, 7; 29.23.
[5]Cf. von Rad, *Das Geschichtsbild des Chronisten*, p. 128.

In this deliberate concentration of the content of faith on the truth as once revealed and now setting the standard for all time men found the strength to overcome the practical problems of the present undismayed by any setbacks; and it ought not—as too often happens—to be written off as a dull resignation to the merely practicable, and a farewell to all loftier hopes. In fact the rejection of a tense expectancy of the future final revelation removed a dangerous burden from religious life, and allowed all its energies to be applied to the demands of the contemporary situation. Moreover, to hold fast to the conviction of Yahweh's unbounded sovereignty with unbroken confidence through centuries of political impotence and dependence on pagan world powers, and to stand up for this conviction effectively, hardly called for a lesser faith than did the prophetic promise of the great new era to come. And this all the more that the priestly conception of the Kingdom of God did not simply replace the world-wide character of the prophetic hope with the lesser ideal of a limited particularism, but strenuously championed *the universalist conception*, though only, it must be admitted, in a form in which it could sort with the basic principles of the priestly understanding of the world. The God who chose Israel to be his people, and marked them out by his covenant law, remains at the same time the Creator of the universe, maintaining it by his everlasting decrees, and exercising even over the heathen the authority of a king over his subjects. It is therefore the concept of the free Creation in conjunction with that of the inviolable sovereignty of God which saves religion from being narrowed into a limited particularism; and it is precisely in that experience of God which is mediated by the cult that we find repeated evidence of a strong sense of the world-embracing character of God's dominion, and of the universal purpose of his rule over Israel. Ps. 57 provides a very beautiful instance of this, in which the cultic act of thanksgiving is fashioned into a powerful expression of the universalist conception of God.[1] Similarly in Ps. 66, the liturgy for the offering of a private vow, we find that the first part consists of a striking presentation of God's already existing dominion over the nations, which serves to give special emphasis to the connection between Yahweh's favourable attention to the prayer of the individual and his righteous government of the world at large. The same point may be noted in individual songs of

[1]'The cultic conception heightens experience to the level of the supernatural' (Quell, *op. cit.*, p. 127).

lamentation, where there are frequent references to the Judge of the world.[1] Thus the priestly faith constantly sees the election of Israel against the background of God's universal sovereignty, and makes use of this in its prayer life as a reason for believing that he will hear men's supplications.[2]

What is admittedly lacking in this kind of universalism is *any real application of the idea of God's salvation to the heathen world*. The divine world-order is certainly a saving order to all who come within its compass, inasmuch as it assures to all the divine image and a direct relation to God. But we find only vague indications, which never reach the stage of clear and definite assertions, that the full salvation enjoyed by Israel is promised to all peoples. There are, it is true, the blessings pronounced on the patriarchs, which were handed down at the Israelite sanctuaries, and which witness to the idea that one purpose of the divine election was that God's blessing should work outwards from Israel to all the families of the earth.[3] We may adduce also the vision of salvation in Isa. 61.5, 6, 9, which is thoroughly priestly in character, and according to which Israel as the priestly nation mediates to the Gentiles access to the Holy One. Ezek. 5.5 seems to envisage a mission of Israel to the nations which dwell round about her, and which God has allotted to her in virtue of his having fixed his dwelling-place at the very centre of the world; and this implies some sort of mediatory position. But these embryonic suggestions are never developed. Instead they stand side by side with unmistakable assertions of the permanence of Israel's prerogatives in the divine-human relationship. Even the promises to the patriarchs also include the idea of the military subjugation of the nations.[4] The cult prayers, especially the national lamentations, often express a conviction of Israel's innocence; it is the heathen who deserve God's anger, and Yahweh's honour requires Israel's speedy redemption.[5] Jerusalem's misfortunes are to be understood primarily as visitations for the sins of her forefathers.[6] This certainly should not be dismissed as a commonplace, narrow-minded particularism, for

[1] Cf. Pss. 7.7–9; 56.8; 59.6, 14. Ps. 22.28–32 may belong to the circle of prophetic ideas.

[2] Cf. also the remarks on pp. 413 f. above concerning Yahweh's ordering of the Gentile world.

[3] Cf. Gen. 12.3; 28.14.

[4] Cf. Gen. 22.17; 27.29.

[5] Cf. Pss. 44; 79.6 f., 12; 80; 83.

[6] Cf. Ps. 79.8.

behind it in most instances stands the conception of Israel as the instrument for realizing the sovereignty of God.[1] But this conviction of the eternal validity of God's universal laws, which finds in the divine order represented in Israel as opposed to the chaos of heathenism a value for which there cannot possibly be any substitute, excludes any chance that the Gentiles might participate in God's full revelation except as proselytes. Any change in this attitude was only possible at the cost of completely demolishing the very deepest foundations of priestly thought, namely by doing away with the old covenant, and replacing it with a new—a development which the critical eye of the prophets had foreseen as both necessary and actually willed by God, though without being able to envisage any way to this goal other than that of waiting faithfully for God's appointed hour. It was only when the mediator of a new covenant, sent by God, had called to himself by an eternally effectual sacrifice the new covenant people, and had given them a new way of life in the 'law of perfectness', that the divine ordinance of the old covenant could be laid aside as 'old and waxing aged' (Heb. 8.13); or—to speak more truly—that its deepest aims and purposes could be fully realized, and that which was eternally valid in itself be transferred into a new form, the form of fulfilment.

(e) Synthesis

In contrast to the dynamic of the prophetic world-view the spiritual structure of the priestly faith is patently static in character. The common factor of all its assertions about God and man is to be found in *the concept of permanent order*. The divine Law imposed on the cosmos is both the perfect expression of the divine power in Creation, holding all things in its hands, and the sure guide toward an inviolable unity of all life, in which the meaning and goal of human existence is to find fulfilment. By being incorporated into the priestly spirituality the distinctive character of the Mosaic revelation of God underwent a clearly-marked development, as a result of which essential elements in its content were seen in new forms and in distinctive conjunctions with other ideas. The concept of God was rounded off with the formal recognition of his absoluteness and transcendence— the attributes which decisively distinguish him from the gods of all the naturalistic heathen religions. The claim of unqualified validity for the way of life based on this concept of God escaped being merely

[1] Cf. Ps. 83.17, 19.

arbitrary or contingent, because it was based on a cosmic order fitting both the individual and the nation into a universal system in which the meaning of the world process was revealed. The cultus was developed into a self-contained form expressing the exclusive position of the People of God as this had been firmly established by electing grace; and at the same time it became a way of life for the actual historical nation which was to prove capable of withstanding any attack, even when all political supports had collapsed.

It will at once be clear that the distinctive attitude which this betokens toward the divine revelation vouchsafed to Israel was not without its *deficiencies and dangers*. Development of the concept of God's transcendence can lead to a deistic divorce of God from the world, and weaken the sense of religious immediacy, if not suppress it altogether. Presentation of God's sovereignty in the forms of the Law and of the ordinances of divine Wisdom involves a strong element of rationalism, which no longer recognizes the hidden God, and sets up human postulates in place of his will. Moreover, if the rationality and intelligibility of the world-order are made the decisive criteria of its divine origin, then with the growing realization that the world as it actually is presents irreconcilable contradictions to these claims it becomes inevitable that man's certainty of God will be profoundly disturbed; and this situation is not surmounted by the perilous expedient of theodicy. In ethics this tendency to rationalism finds expression in the harsh individualism of the retributionary theory, which by seeing man's conduct as the arbiter of his fate leaves no room for grace, and makes the numinous and pneumatic element to be found in any genuine divine-human relationship incomprehensible. In the cultus the sacrificial outlook of heathenism, once conquered, threatens to return in more subtle form. Hard on the heels of a crippling of the element of spontaneity in religion follows the degradation of God's ordinances of grace into a mechanical system of priestly techniques; and in place of a reverent obedience, finding in cultic experience the spur to joyful self-surrender, comes the desire to activate the resources of divine power to one's own advantage, and a presumptuous confidence in one's ability to manipulate God's salvation. Concealed in the subordination of history to the Law is the danger of wrapping oneself in a cocoon of eternal verities, and so of cutting oneself off from new and revolutionary realities and insights, with the result that men become encapsuled in an artificial reality, instead of coming to grips with the process of history and mastering it. Finally, the rejection of eschatology all too easily glosses over the unbridgeable gaps and agonizing inconsistencies in the life of Nature and man, and leads to a false optimism, as if a world pleasing to God could possibly emerge from things as they are simply by divine decree. In these circumstances the feeling for the ultimate and decisive questions may be lost; and by ignoring the doubtful quality of even the best human institutions an arrogance is excited toward the whole non-Israelite world which tends to see the basis of Israel's favoured position not in God's unmerited grace but in its own superiority.

Proof that we are not dealing here simply with theoretical possibilities is afforded by the actual instances of all these dangerous developments which may be cited without difficulty from the history of Israel. On the other hand it must be remembered that these developments were not inevitable, in the sense of being part of the essential nature of this particular form of Israelite religion. Rather are they negative developments, and only occur as a result of a crippling of that religious vitality which, at the time when it was originally awakened by the Mosaic gospel, constituted the soul of the priestly theology. It is a disastrous misunderstanding of the priestly type to judge it, as has usually been done in recent scholarship, solely on the basis of those distorted or perverted forms which in common with every other religious type it does exhibit, but which nevertheless do not destroy the value of its real nature. The result has been the loss of any understanding of its particular strength, and of its permanent significance for Old Testament religion, in order to make room for a one-sided glorification of prophetism. In actual fact the priesthood undertook a function just as important for the life of Israel as that fulfilled by the prophets, and one of the greatest importance for preserving and making effective certain indispensable truths in the Israelite understanding of God. While the prophet's vision was constantly fixed on the struggle between the kingdom of God and the kingdom of this world, and because of this dualistic antinomy either found it easy to overlook the relationship of the present world to God, or took a purely negative attitude toward it, the priestly outlook effectively championed the concern of revealed religion with that sole and absolute divine sovereignty which not only has existed from all eternity, but also holds sway here and now over the world and mankind, even where the latter has turned away from God. And not only the origin of the world from a Creator, and the unchangeableness with which that Creator at every moment holds this whole world in his hands and rules it by his laws, but also God's self-affirmation toward the *whole* of mankind, his purpose of giving concrete form to his sacred ordinances for his people in a unity of worship and practical conduct which is to secure the subjection of the world, his mighty and uninterrupted rule in history—all these are indispensable affirmations about the character of the real divine Being; and it was the priesthood which with immense force and consistency gave them their full value.

There are at least two ways, therefore, in which it is wrong to think of the priesthood. It is not simply an enemy of the prophetic preaching, destined to be gradually overpowered. Nor is it just a historically necessary custodian of pregnant but uncomprehended religious material, useful only until the time when that material shall come to maturity and final liberation. Rather is it a form of man's experience of divine revelation which is complementary to that of prophetism, and helps to make the full wealth of that revelation fruitful and effective in Israel not of itself alone, but because it is constantly being completed and fertilized by its opposite number. The religion of the Old Testament only unfolded the richness of its tensions through the interplay of prophecy and priesthood; and this richness was both exalted into a higher unity in the primitive Christian gospel, and also emerged in new forms as a result of its appropriation by Christianity. Ultimately it is the tension between the God who has come and the God who is to come, between the revealed and the hidden God, between the God who has entered into earthly corporality and the God throned in eternal majesty, which, though beyond the scope of human conception, is yet made vividly clear in Christ; and this ambivalence of God's manifestation in the world both keeps human reflection in perpetual turmoil, and yet, when affirmed in faith and obedience, leads men to the divine fullness of the biblical revelation.

2. THE KING

The Israelite monarchy is a very complex phenomenon. It is not enough to see it as the political coping-stone of the nation, the supreme summing-up of its power. To do so is to be sure of failing to understand its conflicts and its destiny. What is far more important is to acquire the capacity to see it as *predominantly a religious institution*.

As such it was far more profoundly involved with the nation's inner-most experience than any element of political life could ever be, and for the same reason was both strongly affected by religious movements and in its turn had its own effect upon them. It was principally Pedersen and Mowinckel who made a start on assessing the monarchy along these lines. Their attention had been drawn to the ancient religious conceptual content of the monarchy by their keen observation of complexes of primitive concepts in Israel, which they then used to throw light on the problem of the king.[1] Since then this question has become more and more the central preoccupation of scholarship, and attempts have been made to clarify the theme of sacral kingship on the broadest possible basis afforded by the comparative study of religions.[2] But grateful though one must be for the conclusions so far arrived at, especially in this field of comparative religion, there are still many individual questions that are hotly debated, and not least the bearing of these conclusions on the understanding of the Israelite monarchy. It is all too easy to underrate the spiritual power of the concept of Yahweh and its transforming effect on traditional material, when a pattern of divine kingship based on myth and cult, and allegedly common to all the civilizations of the ancient East, is used to give a definitive explanation of the Israelite conception of the king. It is not possible to enter here into a discussion that is still proceeding, or to lay down limits for the validity of theses so recently advanced. In the following section only those approaches will be developed which remain decisive for the relationship between the people of the covenant with, on the one hand, its way of life based on the sovereignty of God and the institution of the monarchy on the other.

[1] Cf. Pedersen, *Israel* I–II, pp. 254, 275 f., 306, *et al.*; S. Mowinckel, *Psalmenstudien* II, pp. 299 ff.

[2] Only a selection from the ever-increasing literature on this subject can be given here: S. H. Hooke (ed.), *Myth and Ritual of the Hebrews in Relation to the Cultic Pattern of the Ancient Near East*, 1933, and *The Labyrinth: Further Studies in the Relation between Myth and Ritual in the Ancient World*, 1935; I. Engnell, *Studies in Divine Kingship in the Ancient Near East*, 1943; A. Bentzen, *Messias—Moses redivivus—Menschensohn*, 1948 (ET, *King and Messiah*, 1955); Th. Gaster, *Thespis*, 1950; G. Widengren, *Sakrales Königtum im Alten Testament und im Judentum*, 1955; A. R. Johnson, *Sacral Kingship in Ancient Israel*, 1955. The Eighth International Congress on Comparative Religion, which met in Rome in 1955, made the problem of sacral kingship the central point of its deliberations; cf. the voluminous account in *The Sacral Kingship: Contributions to the Central Theme of the VIIIth International Congress for the History of Religions*, Leiden, 1959, with the copies of the papers and communications there given; also p. 439 n. 1 below.

1. *The Origin of the Monarchy*

There can be no doubt that the monarchy has the same roots as the priestly and prophetic ministries, namely *the office of the primitive chieftain endowed with divine powers*, and exercising both priestly, prophetic and royal functions. The separation of these functions, and their distribution among different individuals, normally took place in the following way. The king appropriated to himself first and foremost the exercise of military power, and of the religious functions retained only the priestly—and that only within definite limits. Nevertheless he kept the character of a religious leader, and it depended largely on the trend of the times and the general spiritual state of the nation to what extent this character made itself felt. Whereas the earliest kings of Babylon claim divine status and honours during their lifetime, and like to describe themselves by the title of High Priest, from the Hammurabi dynasty onwards this aspect retreats into the background, and precedence is taken by the idea of world sovereignty. In the case of the Assyrian kings also it is set aside with the development of military power. Nevertheless the kings liked to retain the aura which went with the ancient religious functions; and so the personal exercise of religious power and activity is replaced by the dogma of the special divine election and commissioning of the sovereign, or even, as had always been the case in Egypt, by that of his having been mysteriously begotten by the deity himself. He is God's son—whether by adoption or descent is immaterial—and as such is pre-eminent over all other religious functionaries.

That such a dogmatic statement of the royal dignity was not in fact simply a hollow theory, a fine-sounding but ineffectual proposition substituted for an actually effective status, is proved by the continued force of the ineradicable primitive experience of the king as the possessor of effective and mysterious divine power. The king remains the person endowed with *mana*, even after the rationalistic structure of civilized polytheistic religion has been reared over the elementary primitive conceptions; and the dogma of his divine sonship is but an alternative expression for this primitive idea of the king's endowment with power. This point has been correctly noted by Pedersen and others. Moreover the incorporation of the king into the cultus ensures that this primitive outlook is preserved; for by this means he becomes either the representative of the deity, as in Babylonia, or incarnate God, as in Egypt, channelling to his people the divine powers without which they cannot live, and by the performance of the ritual at the great annual festivals maintaining the fabric of the cosmic order.[1]

This position of the king was of little significance for the development of religious ideas in the polytheistic religions of the East, unconcerned as they were with history. By and large their conceptual pattern was already complete and fixed when the monarchy appeared on the scene, and their elasticity allowed them to absorb into their system without difficulty the more or less pronounced divinity of the king. The king himself had no ambition to exercise any profound influence on the cultus or the system of religious thought; for him the principal preoccupation was to use religion as a means of upholding the state—if we may ignore exceptions like that of the Egyptian heretic king Ikhnaton. So long as the other protagonists of religion proved of service to this purpose, there was no reason for the king to interfere with their supremacy in their own domain. The possibility of a clash, therefore, only arose when the priesthood advanced claims to political power—which is to say that characteristically enough it was not questions of religion, but of politics which kindled any conflict between the king and the other leaders of religious life.

But this relationship was bound to assume quite another form when it was transferred to a religion like that of Israel, which was eminently concerned with history, and at the same time endowed with a wealth of internal energy. National unity in the form of the 'am yhwh was religious in structure; it was a religious confederacy with considerable independence for its individual members;[2] and this had already posed the question whether the changeover to a nation-state with centralized government by the king and his officials could take place without friction. Certainly the religious character of the monarchy suggested a way in which it might be incorporated into the constitution of the people of God; as servant of the covenant God the king might now be entrusted with the upholding of the divine decrees. But what if the necessities of politics clashed with these decrees, and the building up of the royal power could only be undertaken at the cost of infringing their validity? For the outward constitution of this national community was

[1] Cf. on this point H. Frankfort, *Kingship and the Gods*², 1955; C. J. Gadd, *Ideas of Divine Rule in the Ancient East*, 1948.

[2] Cf. ch. II, pp. 39 f. above.

designed to subserve a divine will which, with its imperious demand
for obedience, subjected every department of life to itself, leaving no
room for any rival human power, and which moreover could count
at all times on champions and advocates totally and resolutely
committed to its cause; and it is clear that the arrival of the monarchy
in such a community would create an atmosphere charged with the
stuff of conflict.

In such circumstances there might well be a temptation to disarm
possible opponents by an even stronger emphasis on the monarchy's
religious character. But when this was effected by a movement in the
direction of the ancient Eastern concept of divine kingship—a very
obvious temptation—then the threatened conflict was bound to
break out in earnest with full violence; for this meant the intrusion
of a man into privileges belonging to God alone, and as such was
felt to be intolerable. On the other hand, when the monarchy sought
to establish its claim to power along the same lines as had the leaders
of the past, that is, on the basis of a charismatic endowment, this
assumed resources of active religious power which there was no
reason to suppose would be found as a matter of course in a hereditary
dynasty. The will of the God of Israel did not just give his people
general rules for their way of life; it assigned them historical tasks,
and required to be understood and interpreted afresh in historical
events. Continuous readiness and adaptability were therefore needed
if justice was to be done to this divine will, and the reins of government were not to be lost to other servants of the covenant God. In
such conditions an outward observance of religious forms was not
enough. In a religion such as this one, which was vital with internal
tensions, everything was taken seriously, and no mere dummy
could last for long. Hence the religious pretensions of the monarchy
were always being weighed in the balance, and it was refused any
assurance from a cultically based dogma of the sovereign's divine
sonship. And if it failed in respect of religious matters, then even
political success could not save it; inexorably it fell from its primacy
in the state.

Hence even a general comparison of the monarchy's natural
qualifications with the demands of Israelite religion suggests that it
can have been no light thing to be king in Israel—indeed, that,
humanly speaking, it was an impossible task; and this was the reason
why not only many individual monarchs, but finally the institution
itself, broke on the insuperable obstacles in its way.

11. *The Ambivalent Assessment of the Monarchy in the Sources*

There is symptomatic value in the fact that from the very first the picture of the Israelite monarchy given in the sources is presented not from one point of view but two. Just as strongly as men felt it to be a political necessity, so they also divined that it was very hard to reconcile with the laws of their religious life. It is a sign of complete failure to understand the basic ideas of Israelite religion to assume that the critical attitude toward the monarchy can only be the product of its later failures, and to imagine that the problem can be solved by assigning the source that displays a critical tendency to a date in the late monarchical period. The relatively late literary provenance of this source has occasioned only a very slight colouring of the problems as they actually were to accord with the preconceptions of its own day; the difficulties were present from the very first, and were felt to be so. They were already implicit in *the contradiction between the genuine Mosaic Yahweh religion and any leadership which was not charismatic.* Up to the time of Saul the charismatic leader was the one who mattered. The way in which the so-called 'judges' emerged, rousing the mass of the people to action, and shaping their political destiny, solely by their own personal initiative and by the hypnotic impression they made, meant that the charisma, which was in any case of decisive importance in the religious field, also dominated the political, and caused it to correspond fully to the internal structure of the Yahweh religion. Consequently the replacement of these sporadic outbursts of power by a settled political institution might be felt from the very first to betray a lack of trust in Yahweh. I Sam. 8.6 f. exactly reflects the impression which must have been dominant in the circles of charismatics. But this was not all; for what came into being with the monarchy was not just a political, but primarily a religious institution. Were the king to claim for himself the same position as that generally accorded him in the Near East, then he would possess the *ius in sacra*, and could set himself up as the infallible expositor of the divine will in opposition to those who had been the agents of the spirit in the past. Because the supreme control would be his, he could reduce them to silence, or at least greatly restrict their freedom of action, even though he himself might not be endowed with that superior spiritual power by which in the past men had recognized the authority of God's representative. As a matter of experience the monarchy always strove to make itself hereditary, and to secure an inalienable authority quite independent of the qualities of the person filling it; was it right to hand over to such an office the ascendancy over the free working of the spirit? The more men were accustomed to see Yahweh's working in the form of unexpected interventions in the course of events, of explosive acts of power shattering in their force, the less they were inclined to acknowledge as the principal champion of the Yahweh religion a man who held office quite without reference to these divine operations.

In these circumstances the old conflict between enthusiasm and official status was bound to break out; but closely related considerations also gave rise to the *fear that the royal power would be abused*. This fear was not excited simply by the prospect of the despotic use of national resources, a prospect which I Sam. 8.10 ff., with a view to stigmatizing the desire for a king as servility of spirit, describes as inevitable; though such servility was indeed an attitude of mind deeply ingrained in the nation, as Jotham's fable in Judg. 9 had testified long since. But behind this those who had hitherto been the nation's religious leaders saw another danger arising, that religion might be used as a means to an end, as just one more horse harnessed to the chariot of dynastic and nationalist designs. The purity of the religious motto—'Yahweh alone'—seemed imperilled, were an absolute monarchy to be able to throw its privileged religious status into the balance; and the example of the Canaanite and Phoenician kings with their self-divinization afforded ample grounds for this point of view.

III. *The Monarchy as a Religious Office in the History of the Covenant People*

How did these conflicts, which were implicit in the nature of the situation, work themselves out in the historical development of the covenant people? As far as we can tell, the seers and the prophets, once they were convinced that the monarchy was politically inevitable, accepted it only on the understanding that it would be definitely charismatic in character. It is immaterial whether, with Procksch, we ascribe Samuel's championing of *Saul* to a first sudden blow against the Philistines, or to the latter's sensational participation in the campaign against the Ammonites;[1] or whether we prefer to assume that he was chosen for a trial period to see if he would retain his new endowment of spirit. What is certain is that the decisive factor in the mind of the ancient historian was the charismatic

[1] Cf. Procksch, *König und Prophet in Israel*, 1924, p. 5.

character of the man, his personal 'enthusiasm'. Under the influence of the spirit of Yahweh he is changed into another man (I Sam. 10.6). The simple farmer's son of Gibeah becomes the leader of the national levy, conscious of his powers and authoritative in command, who drives the arrogant Ammonites back into their desert domain, and dares to strike the first bold blow against the long-standing alien suzerainty of the Philistines. It is not military ability nor the gifts of a statesman, not the setting up of a definite law of the kingdom nor a position of authority in domestic affairs which make the king, but *the proof in his person that he is a man filled with divine power*, and therefore capable of greater things than other men. This emphasis on special capacity, on the special charismatic endowment, is so outstanding that Pedersen was able to make an attempt to explain it in terms of the primitive conception of a beneficent indwelling power or force of soul.[1] The attempt breaks down, however, on the fact that the extant accounts of Saul's prowess as a leader with one voice ascribe it to Yahweh or to Yahweh's spirit, and not to an impersonal force; nor do any traces survive of a popular view behind the accounts which we possess. The unspoken contrast implied by the portrait of Saul is not that between the man endowed with power and the average man, but between the man inspired by God and the ordinary official. Saul shows his suitability for the leadership by making it clear from his near-ecstatic actions, such as the cutting up of the oxen before the Ammonite campaign, and his dictatorial threats to any who refuse to serve, that he is a man seized by the spirit of the prophets, whose whole nature has been changed, and who is now acting under the compulsion of the spirit of Yahweh. The later occasions on which he acts violently on some sudden over-riding impulse serve to prove the same point. As examples we may cite the vow of abstinence taken during the slaughter of the Philis-tines, and intended to heighten the degree of consecration of the warriors to the holy war, and consequently their success; the sudden attack on Gibeon out of zeal for Yahweh; and possibly also, if with some scholars we are to read Saul instead of Jonathan in I Sam. 13.3, the sudden *coup de main* against the Philistine outpost of Gibeah. This older source knows nothing of a political basis for the newly-established monarchy, and we should be chary of recklessly supply-ing the omission. The young king, urged on by the seer Samuel and by his constant contact with the prophetic bands, had at first no

[1] Cf. *Israel* I–II, pp. 184 ff.

other resources than those which the victorious driving-force of his whole nature could supply; and it was this that broke the crippling spell of faint-heartedness which lay on Israel, and swept the nation onward to deeds of unprecedented audacity. Only so was he able to reconcile reluctant elements to the new institution of the kingdom, and to prove that, even though it was of heathen origin and therefore regarded with mistrust, the ancient spirit of Yahweh could still permeate it and make it of service. Moreover this empirical proof was recognized even by those who in the past had been the principal religious charismatics, namely the seers and the prophets. In the title *nāgīd* (meaning probably the man 'proclaimed' or 'designated' by Yahweh[1]), which was the favourite appellation conferred on the new king,[2] and which was invested with a religious aura, the Israelite idea of the kingship, as opposed to the Canaanite *melek* conception, found clear expression.

At the very first attempt, however, it became apparent—and this is the tragedy of Saul's kingship—that monarchy could not be put into practice on this basis. What had been possible in the case of the Judges over a short period and with limited objectives was not enough for a monarchy designed for permanence, and entrusted with solving the critical problems of the nation's destiny. A broader foundation for its existence was needed than the force of a strong personality. As a matter of long-term policy a constitutional basis, arrived at by agreement with those who till now had wielded political power, was indispensable, if the king was to be able to collect his forces and establish his influence in the intervals of peace between his major campaigns, and above all if he was to be allowed to raise a standing army of professional soldiers. The burden of the Philistine war was bound to force even the local chieftains to accept this viewpoint; and by the same token the prophetic party was in the long run unable to obstruct it. It is here that the historical significance of the second account of the election of the king comes in (I Sam. 8; 10; 12). This account, with a certain degree of bias, carefully considers the legal consequences of the monarchy. It is probably correct in saying that Samuel only brought himself to make this concession under the pressure of circumstances; nor can there really be any objection to the statement that he collaborated in drawing up the 'law of the kingdom' (I Sam. 10.25). But a pregnant step had been taken, and

[1]So A. Alt, *Die Staatenbildung der Israeliten in Palästina*, p. 29.
[2]Cf. I Sam. 9.16; 10.1; 13.14.

it remained to be seen whether the official power thus entrusted to the king could be adapted to the needs of the Yahweh religion, or would turn out to be their enemy.[1] The tragedy of Saul is that he failed to unite these two very different aspects of the monarchy. His breach with Samuel gave even the earliest narrators a good deal of food for thought, as is shown by the various attempts to explain it; and efforts to get at the facts of the case are still being made today from a variety of angles. But even if many details have to remain obscure, one deep-seated cause of the estrangement must certainly lie in the transformation of Saul from the charismatic into the official functionary. With the attainment of assured power Saul's method of government changed, and perhaps his character did too. With the same abrupt transformation which can be observed in him in other connections he sought to confirm his power by new religious methods. He acquired the support of the priesthood of Nob with its ephod, and in this way substituted sacramental consecration for personal deeds of power as the basis of his office. Next he sacrificed respect for the ancient law of Yahweh to his own authority in the matter of the ban in the Amalekite war, and thus gave preference to his newly-won political power over the religious rule of service required from the man endued with the spirit. Here human greatness has set itself up against God, and is no longer prepared to spend itself in obedient service. The account in I Sam. 15 is certainly correct when it makes this the point at which Samuel breaks decisively with Saul. The zealot for Yahweh's cause could have nothing more to do with a monarchy which presumed on the power of its office instead of seeking its highest legitimation in selfless effort on behalf of Yahweh's purposes. The institutional sacrificial cultus which Saul uses as his excuse could only serve to draw attention to the gulf which now separated the royal official from the total self-surrender to Yahweh's demands which marked the man possessed by the spirit.

An alteration in the character of Saul is indicated by the way in which his disposition to compulsive action in the service of his idea of Yahweh now breaks out in half-crazy fits of rage and emotionally disturbed behaviour. We hear no more of any mighty deeds similar to those which at the beginning of his reign had put the fear of God into the nation, and made them ready to follow him anywhere. By contrast the story is now one of murderous attempts on David's life,

---

[1] A. Alt (*op. cit.*, p. 34) has impressively demonstrated the shift in the character of the kingdom which this involved, and the inner tension which resulted from it.

of the massacre of the priests of Nob, of outbreaks of fury against his most loyal followers, even against his own son—acts which with cruel clarity betray the disintegration of a mind till now dominated by devotion to a great ideal, and inspired by it to forceful action. It was a disaster for Saul that an official position of power should have fallen to his lot which did not require to be constantly achieved afresh by a supreme effort of spirit and by obedient commitment of his whole personality, but instead clothed him with an authority which deprived him of the compulsion to continually repeated inward decision, and so opened the way to self-sufficient autocracy.

That in spite of this grievous disillusionment the strict Yahweh worshippers of the old school did not totally disown the monarchy is due entirely to *David*. Already during Saul's lifetime the prophets were turning to him, and giving him encouraging words from Yahweh. He was the man they could trust. At the same time he was on excellent terms with the Nob priesthood, who were at once ready to assist him when he was fleeing from Saul. These pointers from David's early days suggest that he already understood that he had to deal with two main representative parties in the religion of Yahweh, which were to a certain extent mutually antagonistic, and that justice must be done to both, and each given its own. This was why as king he succeeded in allying the charismatic and institutional conceptions of religion, and in reconciling both to the monarchy; and as a result he was at the same time able to raise this into a much safer and less vulnerable structure than Saul had done. There can be no doubt that a piety purified by the harsh experiences of his life provided him with the presuppositions indispensable to this work. But equally his actions reveal a breadth of feeling and thought with a capacity for working otherwise incompatible elements in double harness such as few men have possessed. He saw clearly that the priesthood was sociologically related to the monarchy, and consequently indispensable to it, and he therefore decisively associated it with his religious programme. The bringing of the Ark to Jerusalem, where a sanctuary was established for it, and where its attendants were included in the number of his own most important officials and confidants; the zeal with which he himself exercised priestly functions in offering sacrifice, in the cultic dance, in pronouncing blessings, and in the composition and performance of religious poetry; the appointment of his sons to the priesthood; and finally, his design of undertaking the building of a Temple—all point to his fixed purpose of creating a close association between the royal and religious functions. Indeed, in the account of the Chronicler the priesthood claimed him as being absolutely one of themselves. Furthermore, he consolidated his kingdom by making covenants with the elders; he incorporated conquered neighbouring states; he made clever choice of a capital; he organized a standing army; he established a bureaucracy and a court circle—all measures patently governed by a plan of making the constitutional and domestic basis of the monarchy as secure as possible. And yet with all this he still managed to keep the prophetic party on the side of the king! He had prophets about him as his permanent advisers, and fell in with their demands, even when they denied him his dearest wish—to build a magnificent Temple—or remonstrated with him about his sins (II Sam. 12 and 24). There is no reason to doubt that he was sincerely in earnest in setting so high a value on these charismatic representatives of God's will, or indeed, that he felt an inner kinship with them. The so-called Last Words of David in II Sam. 23.1 ff.—and whether they are from his own mouth or not is here quite irrelevant—portray the king as himself a seer inspired by God. The prophets in fact bestow the divine approval on his efforts to stabilize the kingdom, and promise that his dynasty shall endure for ever (II Sam. 7)—a concession one would hardly have thought possible from the charismatics after their disappointment over Saul. The visible blessings which the Davidic kingdom brought to the whole nation overcame men's last doubts whether the monarchy as a permanent institution could be pleasing to God; and the experience of Absalom's rebellion may have played its part by ensuring that even the prophetic party would no longer hold aloof from the manifest advantages of a firmly established dynasty. That for all this men still did not surrender unconditionally to the monarchy is obvious; but David's reign had none the less demonstrated the *possibility* of the office of king within the framework of the Yahweh religion.

David's peculiar achievement, therefore, was that he was able to unite the very diverse religious forces to be found in Israel under the leadership of the monarchy, and at the same time to secure the indispensable constitutional basis which would ensure the effectiveness of the kingly office.

It was a disaster that even his immediate successor, *Solomon*, no longer had the vision to realize how vitally important this religious foundation was for the Israelite kingship. His ideal was the absolutism

of the Egyptian Pharaoh or the king of Tyre, and in pursuit of this
ideal he tried to safeguard the monarch's religious position by the
one-sided expedient of linking it solidly with the sacramental and
cultic wing. The building of the Temple was an act characteristic
of this attitude; and by joining the royal palace to the sanctuary
within a *single* containing wall he provided for all to see a symbol of
the unique position which the king now enjoyed by virtue of a holiness inherent in his office and independent of the holder. By contrast
we do not see the prophetic movement at any point exercising any
considerable influence; and when once in a while we are reminded
of the charismatically endowed king, as for example in the account
of Solomon's dream at Gibeon, it is much more a matter of oracle-
seeking in accordance with priestly practice than of a gift of the spirit
like that of the prophets.

Elements of primitive conceptions were constantly to hand to
help forward this effort to use religion for strengthening the inviolability of the king's position. They upheld his claim to be *by nature*
divine, and on these grounds exempted whatever he did from human
criticism. The withdrawal of the king from contact with the outside
world, now to appear only in a blaze of royal majesty—something
very different from the intimate relations of Saul or David with their
people; the symbolism of the throne with its seven steps, directly
comparing the sovereign with the king of heaven, and presenting
him as belonging to a higher world; all this was bound to foster the
idea of superhuman power, and to attach to the Israelite monarch
that status of a superhuman, semi-divine Being which had long been
accorded to the king in Canaanite thought. Traces of this revival of
primitive religious categories having nothing in common with
Yahwism are already to be found in the time of David; we may cite
the comparison of David to an angel of God (II Sam. 14.17, 20) or
the description of him as a man endued with blessing, which is put
into the mouth of Saul (I Sam. 26.25). Complete expression of the
ancient Eastern concept of the divinized ruler only emerges fully in
the cultic texts written for use at the royal festival, that is to say, the
royal psalms,[1] in which the Israelite king is clothed in the attributes
of a superhuman redeemer with a right to power which is valid
regardless of the opinion of men. However, an intensification of
royal authority along *these* lines was certainly not in keeping with the
ideas of the original Yahwism and its prophetic champions, and was

[1]Cf. pp. 476 f. below, and p. 125 above.

bound to be regarded by them as abandoning the attitude of stead-fast obedience to Yahweh in favour of a position of inviolable human power. For it involved commuting God's personal validation of the king for an objective holiness independent of the conduct of its possessor, and thus adopted an ungenerous attitude toward the claims of God. Hence, in the opinion of the prophets, Solomon's accession saw the kingdom enter on just that road which they had always feared as a dangerous deviation; and if at the end of his reign we find prophetism on the side of the king's enemies, this is only what was to be expected.

It is true that this criticism did not by any means express itself in a radical rejection of the new institution. Even an Ahijah the Shilonite recognized the monarchy as a vital necessity to Israel, and only wished to see on the throne a better protector of Yahweh's people in place of the despot. And in the years that followed this opposition remained concerned with particular cases. For all the prophets' ruthless antagonism to individual monarchs, as seen for example in Elijah, yet they never go so far as to combat the institution as such.

This situation only changes when *the classical prophets* with their profounder understanding of God arrive at a comprehensive critique of the whole life of the nation, and consign everything which cannot stand this test to judgment. Then sentence is passed on the monarchy also: Thou art weighed in the balance and found wanting! The most thoroughgoing controversy with the monarchy is to be found in Hosea—understandably since this is the period when Ephraim was rushing to its doom; for then the veil was torn from the defects of the monarchy for all to see. With fundamental clarity the prophet shows that the primary sin of the kingship, as demonstrated in Saul, is the self-sufficiency of the holders of political power in face of the only real power, that of God:

'All their wickedness is in Gilgal; for there I hated them:
because of the wickedness of their doings, I will drive them out of
    mine house:
I will love them no more; all their princes are revolters.
Ephraim is smitten, their root is dried up . . .
My God will cast them away, because they did not hearken unto
    him.' (Hos. 9.15-17.)

All the later defection was, therefore, already contained in Saul's

T.O.T.—P

act of disobedience in Gilgal (I Sam. 15); the fruit-tree was at that moment already stricken at its root, and condemned to wither.

This insolent self-sufficiency in the face of God's claim to absolute lordship has changed the monarchy from a blessing into a curse on the nation, for it has seduced Israel into turning away from Yahweh, its only helper, and caused it to put its trust in the king—a theme powerfully expounded in Hos. 13.4–11. This is why God, who can tolerate no rivals, has made the monarchy into a scourge of his wrath against the nation: 'I gave thee kings in mine anger, and snatched away princes in my wrath' (13.11, slightly varied from RV: cf. 10.13b–15).

Another development, also implicit in the original transgression, was that whenever the monarchy was confronted by any problem it would always fail to rise to the occasion, and grasp at false expedients. It attempted to cope with the crisis of the moment by playing the game of alliances with the great heathen powers, and by deceitful political manoeuvres (10.4; 8.9; 5.13 f.). The bitterest criticism of this state of affairs is to be found in 10.3 f. To the nation's despairing cry, 'We have no king!', the prophet retorts: 'What use is a king to us? To help us to speak swelling words, and swear false oaths, to conclude alliances, and to break the law.' His complete estrangement from his religious duties had made the sovereign unfit for all his other obligations, and had closed his eyes to those ways of redemption which had God's approval. Instead of becoming the leaders who would guide the nation to an ever deeper understanding of God's will in the changing political situation the kings entangle both themselves and the people in the sin of brutal and self-seeking power politics, knowing no maxim but that of worldly self-aggrandizement by any and every means, and so coming rapidly to disaster.

There can be no sympathy for this totally corrupted institution. No religious consecration can protect it; indeed, even the sacramental holiness with which the despots seek to invest themselves has already lost its power over the people, and become a mere façade: 'In their wickedness they anoint kings, and in their falsehood princes!' This hollow lie of the divinized monarch in fact gives Yahweh even greater reason for vengeance. It is not without significance that Hosea frequently mentions the images in parallelism with the kings (cf. 3.4; 8.4 ff.; 10.1 ff.). Just as, in the case of the idols, men had substituted the worship of an impersonal magical power for the personal relationship with God, so they have tried to titivate a monarchy alienated from God with the glamour of divinity—and both are equally treason to the true worship of Yahweh.

All that remained, therefore, was for the institution to receive the final *coup de grâce*; it was already eaten away within. In Hos. 3.4; 10.7 f., 15 this threat is made with terrible clarity. The beautiful dummy, which could not stand up to the reality of the demands of the God of Israel, is broken in pieces.

The fact that the attitude of this North Israelite man of God is continued in the Judaean prophets shows that it is not permissible to explain Hosea's position as purely the product of his own time. This is Yahwism voicing its fundamental convictions. When Isaiah speaks of the Stem of Jesse (11.1), he is envisaging the destruction of the Davidic dynasty. Jeremiah and Ezekiel look from the monarchy of their own day, for which they can see no future, to a new order established by Yahweh himself, in which the ruler appointed by him will have become a theocratic official very different from the contemporary political and military king (cf. Jer. 23.5 f.; Ezek. 17.22 ff.; 34.23 ff.; and especially 37.24 ff.). This opinion on the part of the prophets was certainly strengthened by the fact that in despots like Ahaz, Manasseh and Jehoiakim they saw on the throne particularly blatant examples of human self-will in hostility to Yahweh. But, on the other hand, neither was there any lack of attractive and pious rulers, such as Hezekiah, Josiah and Jehoiachin. If even such monarchs as these could not alter the prophetic estimate of the monarchy, this can only be because the prophets saw in the whole institution as it had developed a violation of God's unique and exalted sovereignty over Israel. The monarchy was too closely bound up with the whole distorted way of thinking which put its trust in well-filled arsenals, military preparedness, and a policy of adroit alliances, forgetting in the process the supreme Disposer of history, to be able to justify any longer its old claims to religious leadership and precedence. Hence the ruthless champions of Yahweh's greatness worked for the collapse of this inherently untenable position, in order to bring their nation to recognize that absolute claim of sovereignty which belonged rightfully to Yahweh alone.

But not all the parties in the nation which remained true to Yahweh felt it necessary to make such a radical rejection of the kingdom. Instead, the gulf which was more and more manifestly opening between religion and the state led influential groups to attempt, with the help of that ancient ideal of the pre-monarchical period, the covenant people, to resurrect the spiritual conception of a 'holy nation',[1] in which politics had to be completely subordinated to the religious programme. The principal duty of the king was visualized as the superintendence and promotion of the sacred ordinances of the divine covenant, while strict laws were to restrain him from any striving after purely political power.[2] This was the work of an extraordinarily powerful trend from the closing days of the monarchy, supported by the priesthood. Its most influential production was the Book of Deuteronomy, but it can also be seen in the supplements to Ezekiel, and in the Priestly Code. The substitution of the ancient spiritual title *nāśī'*[3] for that of *melek* is the characteristic mark of this attempt to master the new situation by reviving older forms. In the Priestly law the ideal organization of the nation is portrayed as under the leadership of the priesthood, with *n'śī'īm* representing the twelve tribes;[4] broadly speaking, there would be room for the king only as *primus inter pares* in the 'amphictyonic council'. It is true that these attempts at reorganizing the structure of the nation, in which we already seem to hear the ideal of the religious congregation knocking at the door of the nation-state, were unable to postpone the downfall of the kingdom. But they indicated the lines along which after the catastrophe a new way of life might be found for Israel in the form of the people of God.

Even the fiercest criticism, however, should not blind us to all that the monarchy genuinely achieved for the life of the nation. That even the prophets did not refuse to recognize these achievements is proved by the fact that, in most cases, they gave it an important place in their ideal picture of the future. In the event, despite its ultimate breakdown, the monarchy left behind it lasting religious consequences, which it now remains for us to identify.

IV. *The Religious Effects of the Monarchy*

(a) First we must consider the repercussions of men's experience of the monarchy as the supreme religious office on men's *conception of the manner and purpose of God's activity*.

Because of its charismatic character the Yahweh religion tended

[1] Cf. Deut. 7.6; 14.2, 21; 26.19; 28.9. Cf. the expression 'peculiar people', '*am s'gullā* or *naḥ"lā*, 4.20; 7.6; 9.26, 29; 14.2; 26.18.

[2] Cf. Deut. 17.14–20; Ezek. 44.1–3; 45 f.; also ch. III, p. 92.

[3] Cf. Ezek. 44.3; 45.8 f., *et al.*

[4] Cf. Ex. 16.22; 34.31; Num. 1.5–15, 44; 7; 10.14–27; 13.2–15; 17.17, 21; 34.19–28 etc.

to conceive and portray the effective working of God's power as something manifested in convulsive disasters, events quite outside the normal run of things. Just as the charismatic individual felt the divine control come over him from time to time, and therefore regarded it as something exceptional and clearly distinct from the rest of his experience, so the nation experienced God's impact on their destiny, and the revelation of his power, first and foremost in violent catastrophes such as the calamities of Nature or the horrors of war, the uncanny forces of the *tabu*, the startling miracles of the man of God, the mighty deeds of their judges and Nazirites. Of course God's working was also acknowledged in events such as birth and death, sickness, fertility and so on, which were none the less wonderful for being of everyday occurrence; but the characteristic element, so far as the worship of Yahweh was concerned, lay in those acts of God which stood out abruptly from the normal. Even when the divine will proves creative of order and stability, as in the setting up of the Law, it does so in thunder and lightning, in smoke and fire, before which no mortal man can stand except he be a favoured man of God.[1] It has often been pointed out that this conception of God was modified in essential points by the migration to Canaan, and by familiarity with its highly developed civilization. But while this opened men's eyes to the regularity of God's operations in *Nature*—which meant often enough that religion only strayed into naturalistic ideas of God's character—the monarchy was able to exert an incomparably stronger influence on their understanding of God's ordered activity in *history*. The way toward this had been prepared by just that early charismatic conception of the kingly calling which honoured in the monarch the man endowed with the spirit; for this meant that the permanent preoccupations of guarding the state against outside enemies, and of administering justice and keeping peace at home, were bound to be closely associated with the operation of the spirit, thus teaching men to see this as the constructive power at work silently and steadily conserving the moral foundations of the national life. For want of evidence we can only trace this process incompletely; and the abandonment of the charismatic principle, with the switch to a materialist conception of endowment with 'power', may well have retarded it. Yet it is there— as is shown by two major pieces of evidence, which mark the beginning and the end respectively of a line of development. The first is

[1] Cf. Ex. 20.18 ff.

the so-called 'Last Words of David' (II Sam. 23.1–6) from the early monarchical period, in which the inspired royal singer sketches the ideal portrait of the king who rules in the fear of God; the second, from the later monarchy, is the Isaiah prophecy (11.1–9) which pictures the kingly judge as the man graced with the spirit of Yahweh. From such instances it would seem that it was through the monarchy that the operation of the spirit was removed from the sphere of the purely miraculous, and applied to the moral conduct of life in the political, social and ethical fields. Religion infused into the concepts of the state and the Law the power of its own vitality and absolute authority; and by thus taking the values of ethics into its own domain gave them new and effective force.

This applies not only to the manner, but also to the *purpose* of God's activity. The vigorous development and differentiation of community life under the aegis of the monarchy opened men's eyes to the major ends of social righteousness. It was the king who as supreme judge incarnated the judicial majesty of God. It was the king who determined the set of the nation's hopes for an ideal state of society. And it was in their conflict with the idea of the state as represented by the king that the prophets arrived at their understanding of social righteousness as something which was, in the widest sense, a part of that universal divine plan intended to exercise the decisive influence on all earthly affairs, and to settle the destiny of the nation. The more prominently did God's blessing attach to the peaceful activities of the king, and the more disastrous were the effects of his military undertakings and of his strivings after purely political power, the more emphatically did it become clear that the purpose of divine providence, and therefore the goal of the kingdom itself, must be the reign of justice and righteousness; and this not simply in the moral will of the individual, but in the very structure and ordinances of the state. In the picture of the messianic future as drawn by the prophets we can see clearly this transformation in men's understanding of the purposes behind God's operations. Yahweh's part in bringing in the new age is no longer seen as the destruction of the hostile nations in war, but as the building of the kingdom of God by the inward conversion of man, and by the creation of conditions of justice; and therefore even the figure of the Messiah now no longer appears in the guise of the mighty warrior king, but in that of the just judge, or even of the redeemer suffering for his people.[1]

[1] Cf. ch. XI below.

(b) In addition to this significant enrichment of the knowledge of God the monarchy was also responsible for an essential contribution to *the development of the forms of religious life*. Its whole sociological character made it inevitable that it should strive not only to create suitable political institutions, but also to develop equally settled ordinances for religious practice. Its needs called for a permanent method of enquiring from God which could be constantly available for use; and for such a purpose the priestly technique of oracle-giving was without doubt more useful than the intermittent inspiration of the prophet. This explains why we find the ephod held in such high regard from the very first, right from the days of Saul and David. Later the developed oracle technique of the *n·bi'im* is also pressed into the service of the king (cf. I Kings 22). In cases of national calamity the assistance of an established priestly class to conduct and supervise the protective rituals was indispensable. For the education of the people in common basic attitudes, for the cultivation of a unified religious atmosphere—so important for the nation's political awareness—there was need yet again of the work of the priesthood. Furthermore the priestly symbols and cultic rituals were much better adapted to the task of regulating and shaping the religious activities of the laity than the unpredictable declarations of prophet or seer. In short the monarchy resulted in a demand for the priestly conception and practice of religion, which we have already briefly outlined in describing the priesthood.[1] All this meant that institutional religion made great strides. On the one hand this was of advantage in enabling religion to shape the life of the nation, and to give visible form to its relation to the one divine Lord; on the other it brought with it the danger of creating a nationalist particularism, which by giving a false primacy to outward forms would obscure the role of service for which the nation existed, and cripple the universalist forces of religion.

Thus we see the monarchy powerfully promoting a trend inherent in all religion—the tendency to develop and petrify its institutions, and to conceive of itself as a static relationship with ordinances laid down once and for all, a form of human life standardized by laws. This tendency, present from the very first, and represented by the priesthood, was able to work itself out to the full because of the help afforded it by the monarchy. As a result, however, the necessary conditions were created for that fundamental clash of principle

[1]Cf. pp. 398 f. above.

between the static and dynamic understandings of religion which we see fought out in classical prophecy.

At its disappearance from the scene the monarchy left behind it a hierarchy sufficiently firmly established to enable national life to continue after the Exile under the temporary roof of the Church. If we compare the failure in political insight which marked the priesthood after the entry into Canaan and the dissolution of tribal solidarity with its achievement in rebuilding the nation after the annihilation of the state at the Exile, we have an impressive picture of the importance of the monarchy for the shaping of Israel's religious life.

X

COVENANT-BREAKING AND JUDGMENT

I. JUDGMENT AS A GUARANTEE AND RESTORATION OF THE COVENANT

1. The idea of a covenant relationship based on a single free act of divine grace, and bound up with certain conditions, already implies *the possibility of annulment*; and this possibility is something of which men become more and more conscious as greater and greater emphasis is placed on the covenant demands. Just as it is impossible in the case of a covenant between human beings to dismiss the thought of the *'ālā*, the covenant curse on the breaker of the contract,[1] so in the case of the *b'rīt* at Sinai such a curse is found both as a menacing coda to the collections of laws,[2] and in the cultic proclamation of God's covenant stipulations.[3] The force and earnestness with which it was impressed on the people of Israel[4] that these stipulations must never be broken, and that Yahweh would watch jealously to see that they were not, effectively inhibited any complacent feeling of possessing in the covenant a relationship with God that would hold good automatically and as a matter of course. In fact the terrifying possibility that God might himself annul the covenant was explicitly included in the tradition of the Mosaic period;[5] and men were so impressed by the threat of this consequence of disobedience that they did not shrink from enduring

---

[1]Cf. Gen. 31.49 f.; I Sam. 20.16 (omitting *'ōy'bē*) and the instructive treaty of the Assyrian king Assurnirari V (753–745 BC) with Mati'ilu of Agusi, to be found in B. Meissner, *Babylonien und Assyrien* I, 1920, p. 140.

[2]Cf. Lev. 26.14 ff.; Deut. 28.15 ff.

[3]Cf. Deut. 27.15 ff.

[4]Cf. above pp. 75, 209 f., 223, 265 f.

[5]Cf. Ex. 32.10.

the sternest blows to the good estate of the covenant people, whenever a gross breach of the covenant called for expiation.[1]

Nevertheless, their trust in Yahweh's purpose of fellowship as
solemnly declared in the making of the covenant, and their confidence in their own ability to fulfil its terms, were both too strong
to allow of their feeling this possibility as a permanent threat, or one
giving rise to any lasting sense of insecurity. Where the intentions
of the nation were sound, Yahweh's covenant good faith, his *ḥesed*,
would see to it that the continuance of the covenant would not be
imperilled, whatever the offences of individuals.[2] Did he not himself
provide the means of atonement, and help those who were loyal to
discover and punish the guilty who would otherwise have remained
undetected?[3] Hence, though the expectation of God's punitive
intervention was very real, it looked on the whole for *individual divine
acts of punishment*, the aim of which was not an annihilating judgment
that would dissolve the covenant, but rather the maintenance of
that relationship by the removal of disturbing elements.[4]

II. Thus the way was gradually prepared for *a new evaluation of
God's covenant*, in which the possibility of its dissolution was obscured
by the confident conviction that, because God was using this means
to achieve his purpose in history, namely the establishment of his
kingdom, he would therefore not allow this particular manifestation
of his sovereignty to be vitiated, however great man's faithlessness
might be. *The powerful impression made by the position in the world which
Israel attained under David* contributed not a little to this change of
attitude. Here was the dazzling proof of God's benevolence, of his
using the covenant people to extend his own dominion; and the fact
that this turn in the nation's fortunes was very quickly ascribed to
an eternal covenant of God with the house of David[5] shows clearly
how strong was the impact of political success on the conception of
the covenant. This may also have been the starting-point from which
developed that sense of election displayed in the history of the
patriarchs by the great narrators of the Pentateuch, where the
tendency to regard Israel's special position as part of Yahweh's
eternal and unalterable divine purpose is thrown into high relief.[6]

[1] Cf. Ex. 32.25 ff.; Num. 25.1 ff.; Judg. 20 f.; I Sam. 15.17 ff.; I Kings 19.15 ff.
[2] Cf. above ch. VII.2, pp. 232 ff.
[3] Cf. Josh. 7; I Sam. 14.38 ff.; II Sam. 21 etc.: also ch. VII.5, pp. 265 f. above.
[4] Cf. above ch. VII.3, pp. 241 f., and 5, pp. 265 f.
[5] Cf. ch. II, p. 64 above.
[6] Cf. ch. II, pp. 49 f. above.

The emergence of *the dogma of the eternal divine covenant* in the Deuteronomic and Priestly literature[1] is the result of adopting and working out to a logical conclusion just this line of thought, and gives expression to a strong sense both of God's exaltedness and of the stability of his Providence. Consequently all Yahweh's acts of judgment cannot but be regarded purely and simply as passing interventions, conditioned by the needs of the moment, and incapable of endangering the eternal destiny of the people of God. There is no room here for any kind of eschatological expectation of doom.

III. The same tendency is reflected in the increasing consistency with which *the hope of the overthrow and punishment of all Israel's enemies* envisages a final reckoning of Yahweh with the nations on 'his Day'. From the earliest times Yahweh's mighty presence as Lord and Helper had never been experienced more intensely than in the day of battle, which was thus rightly termed 'his day'. It was then that men rejoiced in the consciousness of his unlimited power, putting to flight all those that hated him, and confounding every assault on his sovereignty.[2] The sacred object of the Ark provided empirical support for this sense of having Yahweh in their midst; and the rites by which the war was sanctified also helped to concentrate men's thoughts on the presence of the God of Battles. Hence the holy war belongs pre-eminently to the ages in which men were aware of being in an especially close relationship with the exalted God, and of experiencing his saving presence.

All the more agonizing then must have been the feeling that God was far off, when serious reverses, or a long period of hostile oppression convinced them that Yahweh had turned away from his people in his anger. At such times of crisis, which seemed to cast doubt on all the glory of the covenant, the hopes of all loyal Yahwists were fixed on *a new coming of the covenant God* to his people, in which he would prove himself the invincible Lord, able to put an end once

---

[1] Cf. ch. II, pp. 54 ff. above.

[2] Cf. Num. 10.35 f.; 23.21 f.; 24.7 f.; Judg. 5.1 ff., 4 f., 20 f.; Ex. 15. On this subject of the technical term 'Day of Yahweh' G. Hölscher draws attention to the phrase, frequent in Babylonian incantations, 'terrible day', i.e., the day on which men expected that the god they were invoking would appear to annihilate his enemies (*Die Ursprünge der jüdischen Eschatologie*, 1925, p. 13). It may be therefore that we are dealing with something that was originally 'a fixed concept of Oriental cultic terminology', designating God's appearance in redemption and judgment. Only in Israel is this concept given a new application, in so far as it refers to *God's hoped-for manifestation in history*, and in this way becomes a technical term of

for all to all the powers that threatened his kingdom. The greater the
benefits men had experienced at his hands in the Exodus from Egypt,
in the battles for the conquest of the Promised Land, and in the wars
leading up to the founding of the Davidic kingdom, and the more
menacingly swelled the power of the hostile nations, the higher soared
their expectations of the new dominion he would achieve, and the
more marvellous appeared the time of his ultimate victory. As
Yahweh ṣᵉbā'ōt he led into battle all the forces of heaven and earth;
storm, fire and earthquake went before him as his heralds, the stars
in their courses fought on his side. Not only man, but Nature must
perish at his approach; the nations as far as the ends of the earth
would be crushed before his onslaught, and with them their gods
would be toppled from their thrones, that Israel's God might ascend
the throne of the universe alone. There is not a great deal of direct
evidence of these various features;[1] but a perfectly valid substitute
is provided by the prophetic oracles of doom, in which unmistakable
fragments of the ancient traditional popular hopes remain recognizable in their setting in a new complex.[2] In particular, the
association of the divine judgment with the annihilation of Nature[3]
is certainly not a new creation of the prophets, but derives from the
most ancient conceptions of the part played by the cosmos in man's
destiny. One has only to think of the judgment of the Deluge, and
to compare it with the exactly corresponding element in the picture
of the age of salvation (cf. ch. XI below). Other confirmatory evidence is also supplied by those mythical features interwoven with the
historical expectations, which portray the hostility of the heathen
monarchs as the rebellion of an angelic prince against the divine
Lord of the world,[4] or describe the downfall of the tyrant nations

---

eschatology. L. Černy (*The Day of Yahweh and some relevant Problems*) rightly points
out that, in spite of all kinds of points of contact with non-Israelite conceptions,
this concept retains a quite unique character of its own; but his attempt to derive
the eschatological significance of the term from the cultus labours under the same
difficulties as the cultic explanation of eschatology generally: cf. pp. 497 f. below.

[1] Cf. Deut. 33.17; Num. 24.8 f.; Pss. 29; 82; Ex. 15.10 (cf. 18.11); I Kings
19.11; Judg. 5.20; Isa. 2.18 f.; 10.4 (emended).

[2] For more precise evidence cf. H. Gressmann, *Ursprung der isr.-jüd. Eschatologie*.

[3] Cf. especially Isa. 2.6 ff.; Amos 1.2; Hos. 4.3; Micah 1.4; Jer. 4.23–26;
Nahum 1.3 ff.

[4] Cf. Isa. 14.12 ff.; Ezek. 28.11 ff. Ezek. 38 f., Zech. 14 and Joel 4 seem to have
made use of a myth of an assault by demonic forces against the mountain of God
situated at the mid-point of the earth.

and their rulers in terms of the triumph of the Creator of the universe over the Chaos-monster.[1]

iv. In this ancient Israelite expectation of a doom embracing the Gentile world the universalist element in the Yahweh religion, which in the empirical present was largely restricted and suppressed by the limitations of the actual situation, now attained powerful and uninhibited development. It is not impossible that *foreign influences* may have contributed to this liberation; there is evidence of an expectation of universal doom both in Egypt and Babylonia.[2] However, these latter expectations are connected with the astrological lore of cycles, or make use of the theory of alternating world-ages, in order to glorify a famous ruler whose accession is seen as the long foretold end of an epoch of disaster;[3] the character of the Israelite expectation is quite different. Here the idea of divine wrath working itself out in historical acts is intensified into an eschatological event, and so becomes intimately connected with the consummation of the kingdom of God. In this way futurist expectations are removed from the sphere of myth, and exalted into a historical hope.[4]

v. The result of this is that Yahweh's final reckoning with his enemies is sometimes described as *an execution of his righteous judgment*, and the Day of Yahweh appears as the great day of judgment. Just as Yahweh's acts of power in the past were understood as his judicial proceeding against wickedness and law-breaking,[5] so the idea of moral retribution was associated with the setting up of his sole sovereignty in the future. Thus Ps. 82 describes the deposition of the gods from their thrones as an execution of judgment; and the solemn proclamation in Amos 1 and 2 of the divine sentence passed on the Gentiles presupposes that this way of announcing doom was well known in Israel—otherwise the crushing divine sentence on Israel,

[1]Cf. Isa. 17.12 ff.; Ps. 46; Nahum 1 f.; Hab. 3.4 ff.; Ezek. 32.1 ff.; Isa. 51.9 f.; 27.1. On the problem of Israel's attitude to the nations cf. W. Eichrodt, *Gottes Volk und die Völker*, 1942.

[2]Cf. the Egyptian prophecies in *AOT*, pp. 46 ff. (cf. *ANET*, pp. 441 ff.), the myth of Ira with its related material, and the prophecies of doom, also in *AOT*, pp. 212 ff., 283 f. (= *ANET*, pp. 451 f.): also O. Weber, *Die Literatur der Babylonier und Assyrer*, 1907, pp. 104 ff.

[3]E.g., the prophecy of the priest in the reign of King Snefru, which was composed *c*. 2000 BC to the glory of Amenemhet I (*AOT*, pp. 46 ff.; *ANET*, pp. 444 ff.).

[4]'Myth is the language of belief in the coming of God's dominion at the turning-point of the ages. In the whole compass of the Bible this faith has no other language, not can it have, for it will not cut loose from the origins of its outlook in the Aeon-theology of the ancient East' (W. Stark, *ZAW* 51, 1933, p. 21).

[5]Cf. ch. VII, pp. 242 ff. above.

which comes at the close, would lose all power to convince, for the premisses on which it is based could have been rejected at any time. In general, moreover, the fact that the prophets normally proclaimed judgment on Israel within the framework of a general judgment on the nations,[1] which apparently had already become a fixed stylistic form, makes it almost a certainty that the conclusive revelation of Yahweh's power was being portrayed as the execution of his judgment even in the early period of Israel. But there is nothing strange about this fact, since we have been able to detect the spiritual presuppositions of this picture clearly enough in the influence of the covenant festival on religious concepts.[2] His final judgment on his enemies is the strongest possible testimony that the covenant God will exercise his dominating power to renew the assurance of his covenant fellowship with his people.[3]

Hence the expectation of doom in ancient Israel is genuinely Israelite in character, and there is no need to explain it by deriving it from foreign sources.[4] Characteristic is its close connection with the hope of salvation; the doom of the nations means salvation for Israel. Yahweh's final victory over his enemies consummates the divine sovereignty established in the setting up of the covenant.

2. JUDGMENT AS ABROGATION OF THE COVENANT

1. Even in the pre-prophetic period, however, the way was being opened for *a transformation of this limited vision of the future*. This transformation began in that section of the nation which had the deepest feeling for the shattering seriousness of God's demand for obedience, and therefore expressed the severest condemnation of their own people—that is to say, among the *n·bi'im* and those spiritually akin to them. As the whole Elohistic history shows, it was these circles, which were the ones most profoundly disrupted and disturbed by the Philistine crisis, that kept alive a constant feeling for the terrifying seriousness of judgment as the means by which the holy God protected his covenant from those who despised it; and there-

[1]Cf. Hos. 4.1 ff.; 8.13; 9.9; 12.3, 15; Isa. 1.18 f. (cf. 1.2); 3.13 f.; Micah 1.2–4; 6.1 ff.; Zeph. 3.8; Isa. 51.4 f.; Joel 4.2 ff., Mal. 3.2 ff., 5; Deut. 32.1, 8; Ps. 50.1–4; 96; 98.

[2]Cf. ch. IV.2. III, pp. 122 f. above.

[3]Cf. A. Weiser, *Die Psalmen*[4], 1955, pp. 20 f. on the subject of the festival of covenant renewal.

[4]This has been strikingly pointed out by E. Sellin (*Der AT Prophetismus*, pp. 121 ff.) in opposition to H. Gressmann's derivation from an ancient Oriental myth of world destruction.

fore they were also awake to the danger of falling a prey to that relentless divine vengeance which continually threatened the nation whenever it proved slack or faithless in his service. These men, placed in a decisive epoch, when national life was undergoing both inward and outward changes, were forced by their conflicts with the leaders of the nation to develop their own ideas; and as a result they came to see—much more clearly than did the chief exponents of official religious practice—the danger presented from within to Israel's very existence by the detailed assimilation of its way of life to that of its neighbours, and by its consequent alienation from the purposes that should govern the life of a holy people.[1] Hence it was in these circles that a sense of disquiet arising from the dissolubility of the covenant was kept alive; that the tradition of Yahweh's inexorable proceeding against his own people was fostered;[2] and that strong emphasis was placed on the danger of proximity to the holy covenant God as a reason why intercourse with him took place only through a mediator.[3] Indeed, these men did not even shrink from the risk of Israel's once more losing her outward existence, if inward religious unity could only be attained by political upheaval.[4]

Thus there grew up *a sense of Israel's corporate national guilt* because of its having adopted Canaanite culture and the marks of decadence in cultic and social life that went with it. This sense of guilt could even reach the point of a complete renunciation of the whole contemporary way of life such as we see embodied in the peculiar phenomenon of the Rechabite sects, who returned to a nomadic existence. There can be no doubt that the spiritual effect of these groups was—at least in certain circles—to shake the generally prevailing confidence that, apart from particular misfortunes, the nation was not an object of God's wrath.

This effect was all the more pronounced because of certain features observable even in the popular outlook on life, which provided men with starting-points for a move away from superficial optimism toward a deeper consideration of things. We refer to *the general attitude to the darker side of life*, to death, transitoriness and affliction, in which at quite an early stage a pessimistic streak can be detected, introducing into the dominant note of *joie de vivre* typical

[1] Cf. ch. VIII.5.II, pp. 328 ff. above.
[2] Cf. pp. 457 f. above.
[3] Cf. Ex. 33.3 ff.
[4] Cf. Ahijah the Shilonite, I Kings 11.29 ff.; Elijah and Elisha, I Kings 19.15 ff.; II Kings 8.7 ff.; 9.1 ff.

of a nation conscious of its powers a serious undertone which cannot be ignored. The Yahwist account of the dawn of man's history,[1] with its heart-breaking lament for the curse laid on human existence as a result of a deliberate primal decision against God and the consequent hostile effects of divine punishment, survives as testimony of undeniable significance for the religious feeling of ancient Israel. It is true that, in so far as it was nationalistically conditioned, men's thinking moved along other lines, and was far from drawing all the logical conclusions from this interpretation of human existence. But because there was a complete lack of any systematic harmonization or synthesis, it was possible for an awareness of sin and of a doom of punishment, even though discernible only in the occasional expression of certain moods,[2] to exist side by side with that more permanent current of thought which took account only of the good pleasure of a gracious covenant God. If in addition we remember the social cleavage of the later monarchy, with its pauperization of the masses intensified by political crises, we shall appreciate that, for all the hardening of the dogma of election, the soil was not infertile for the prophetic proclamation of God's judgment on Israel.

II. *This change in the character of the expectation of doom* is apparent in *prophetism* with unambiguous and decisive intensity from the very first.[3] The threat of the coming destruction is not primarily to the heathen, but to the covenant people. Hence, in the terms of the cutting antithesis with which Amos confronts his contemporaries, the day of Yahweh is darkness, not light.[4] Furthermore, both he and his successors are constantly searching for new imagery and new turns of phrase with which to drive home to the hearts and consciences of their hearers *the inevitability of the approaching disaster* as this has been revealed to them in this critical hour by Yahweh himself. The plastic immediacy with which the catastrophe is depicted as already breaking, or broken, over men's heads has led to conjectures that some external enemy actually on the frontier at the time may have been the cause of the prophet's apprehensions;[5] but

---

[1] Cf. Gen. 2–4; parts of 6–9; 11.1–9.

[2] Cf. II Sam. 14.14. J. Köberle (*Sünde und Gnade*, 1905, pp. 59 ff.) very pertinently drew attention to this juxtaposition of dogmatically unsympathetic ideas.

[3] Cf. in this connection W. Cossmann, *Die Entwicklung des Gerichtsgedankens bei den alttestamentlichen Propheten.*

[4] Cf. Amos 5.18.

[5] Cf. J. Wellhausen, *Israelitische und jüdische Geschichte*[7], 1914, p. 104 (ET, p. 82); R. Smend, *Lehrbuch der AT Religionsgeschichte*[2], p. 180, *et al.*

this assumption fails to do justice to the case, for in most instances the mention of Assyria, Egypt or Babylon in the older prophetic threatening oracles is quite incidental. It is rather an immediate certainty of God's wrath, arising from their encounter with their God, and therefore religious in character, which frequently causes them—in defiance of all outward appearances—to speak with such unshakable assurance and conviction of the ruin of all the nation's glory as being visibly at hand. Thus for Amos the corpse of the virgin of Israel is already laid out, and he can raise over her the lamentations for the dead;[1] or with vivid and breathtaking realism he can depict the horror excited by the general mortality, when Yahweh strides through his people as the God of the plague.[2] Hosea gives us unforgettable pictures of invisible, gnawing destruction, or of the cruel, annihilating will of the God of vengeance, in his imagery of the consuming worm, and of the enraged beast of prey thirsting for blood.[3] The most striking examples of this sort in Isaiah and Jeremiah are respectively the poem about Yahweh's giant fist outstretched to strike,[4] and the so-called Scythian songs,[5] which in their visionary power give us a firsthand impression of what it would feel like to be involved in the sudden overthrow of an unheeding Jerusalem. But for preference the prophets employ the imagery of the judicial process, in which the passing of sentence on Israel forms the central point of a world-wide judgment of the nations, and where there can be no appeal from the word of the incorruptible divine judge.[6]

What, however, gives the prophetic message of doom its urgent and irrevocable quality is that it seeks to give an explicit picture of *the final frightful blow* with which Yahweh dispatches his faithless people. Because Israel has been singled out above all other nations for the divine favour, she must also endure a special severity of divine judgment.[7] All the scourges of Nature, all the horrors of war, all the powers of death and the underworld must combine to root out

[1] Cf. Amos 5.1 f.
[2] Cf. Amos 5.16 f.; 6.8 ff.
[3] Cf. Hos. 5.12 ff.; 13.7 f.
[4] Cf. Isa. 9.7 ff.
[5] Cf. Jer. 4.5–31.
[6] Cf. Amos 1.3–2.16; Hos. 4.1 ff.; 8.13; 9.7, 9; 12.3, 15; Isa. 1.2, 18 f.; 3.13 f.; Jer. 1.14 ff.; 25.15 f., 31 ff.; Micah 1.2–4; 6.1 ff.; Zeph. 3.8 ff.; Joel 4.2 ff.; Mal. 3.2 ff., 5.
[7] Cf. Amos 3.1 f.; Isa. 5.1 ff.

the infamous nation from the earth.[1] Yahweh brings his whole world-controlling power to bear to ensure that not one single sinner shall escape him.[2] And the people's hope that in the judgment they will be the remnant who are spared is twisted with bitter mockery into its opposite, and the miserable lot of the remnant is made to testify to the completeness of the destruction.

Moreover the prophets teach men to see the inner necessity of this final reckoning of Yahweh with his people by showing *how deep is the alienation* which separates Israel from her God. Just as, for them, Israel's favoured position, based on God's redemption and election, finds its true meaning in man's trustful surrender of himself to God in faith, love and obedience, and in the way of life which springs from these, so the essential nature of sin lies ultimately in the nation's deliberate turning away from God. This leads to that inner alienation, which makes itself known in contempt for his moral purpose of fellowship, and is for preference characterized as akin to the destruction of those personal relationships based on loyalty, to wit, marriage and betrothal, sonship and duty to a liege lord: in addition, Hosea, Jeremiah and Ezekiel see it in terms of covenant-breaking.[3] The more the whole hideous power and extent of this inner perversion, swelling into a demonic compulsion, a cancer corrupting the whole history of the nation, is disclosed, the more shatteringly can the irremediable character of its breach of faith be brought home to the people, and the more unbreakable is the inner coherence between guilt and punishment shown to be. Israel is placed on a par with the nations; and in the day when Yahweh establishes his universal sovereignty she can look forward not simply to the punishment of the heathen, but primarily to her own condemnation.

This eschatological expectation of doom is so radical and complete that rationalist categories of thought are helpless to counter it; only God's promise of a new Creation, transcending human thinking, can do that. But this very quality makes it the ultimate guarantee against any human abuse of the covenant concept, and enables it to purge the religious interpretation of history of all traces of egoistic wishful thinking. The vital nerve of the prophetic proclamation of

---

[1]Only a few examples from the mass of evidence can be cited here: e.g., Amos 5.3, 16 f.; 7.1 f., 4; 8.8 ff.; Hos. 5.12 ff.; 9.6, 11 ff.; 10.14; 11.6; 13.8 f., 14 ff.; Isa. 3.1 ff., 25 f.; 5.9 ff., 26 ff.; 7.18 ff.; 8.5 ff.; 28.17 ff.; 29.2 ff.; Micah 1.6 ff.; 3.12; Jer. 1.15 f.; 4.5 ff.; 6.22 ff.; 7.30 ff.; 9.9 f., 20 f.; 16.1 ff. etc.
[2]Cf. Amos 9.2 ff.
[3]Cf. ch. VIII.6, pp. 371 f. above, and ch. II, pp. 58 f.

doom is the assertion that 'Yahweh alone shall be exalted in that day'.[1]

III. The truth of this view was sealed and confirmed by the Exile, when Israel as a nation went down into the grave.[2] Gradually the exiles came to accord a general recognition to the prophetic preaching of judgment; but this was deepened and made fruitful by a new approach which prophecy now adopted in speaking to the nation about the judgment of God. Ezekiel awakened and laid hold on men's consciences by pointing out, to those who, under the stunning blows of national disaster, were tending to doubt or even to complete scepticism, the way in which the just retribution of God worked itself out ceaselessly in the life of each individual, and was related to each member of the nation not simply as the threat of a judge, but also as the promise of a redeemer.[3] And as prologue to the hope of the new covenant the prophet set up the goal of a final purifying judgment, in which Yahweh would cleanse his favoured people from all impure elements[4] in order to establish his sovereignty in them. By making *individual retribution* the crucial point, and linking it with the fulfilment of God's sovereignty, the prophetic concept of judgment discovered the form in which it could continue to influence the religion of Judaism.

3. INDIVIDUALIST AND UNIVERSALIST ELEMENTS IN THE EXPECTATION OF JUDGMENT

I. Because at the Exile the nation died, the Return was interpreted as its revival from the grave[5] after doing full penance for its guilt;[6] and this made it possible from thenceforward to regard the prophetic message of judgment and new creation as in essentials fulfilled, and to direct the irrepressible energy of men's hopes to removing the remaining obstacles to the world-wide realization of God's dominion. The understanding of the covenant as an eternal and unalterable relationship of grace could now be revived in all its force;[7] and the restoration of the Temple, by affording a pledge of Yahweh's

[1] Isa. 2.11.
[2] Cf. Ezek. 37.11.
[3] Ezek. 18; cf. 13.9; 14.13 ff.; 33; 34.17 ff.: also W. Eichrodt, *Krisis der Gemeinschaft in Israel*, 1953.
[4] Cf. Ezek. 20.33 ff.
[5] Cf. Ezek. 37.1ff.
[6] Cf. Isa. 40.2; 51.17; 54.8 ff.
[7] Cf. ch. II, pp. 63 ff. above.

unceasing covenant favour,[1] prepared the ground for the community of the Law, which was to find its vocation in the realization of God's sovereignty on earth, and to live in the confidence generated by its own daily experience of his righteousness and loving-kindness.[2] Small wonder that the expectation of doom should now primarily be associated with the abasement of the heathen, and, of course, with the simultaneous glorification of Israel which this implied.[3] As a result, however, there was a danger that the idea of Yahweh's total victory over all hostile powers, which had been propounded with such emphasis by the prophets in their oracles against the nations, would now be sullied and distorted by nationalistic lust for revenge. The acknowledgment of God's majesty certainly remained a principal object of the judgment of the nations;[4] but under the impact of the humiliations and oppressions which the nation had to undergo the Gentiles' rebellion against Yahweh came to be equated with their violation of Israel,[5] their exceeding their authority as the executioners of judgment was charged up as the most grievous of sins,[6] and the injured nation itself was entrusted with the carrying out of retribution[7]—all of which from time to time found ugly expression, as vengeful feelings clamoured for relief.[8] While it is for the most part Israel's enemies and oppressors, those who hinder her restoration, who figure in these expectations, yet hostility to the Gentile world is most intensely expressed in an attitude which lumps all the nations together in a *massa perditionis*, the annihilation of which as a universal eschatological act constitutes the culminating event of the present age.[9]

II. If nevertheless the eschatological expectation of judgment never managed to lose all connection with Israel's own destiny, this must be ascribed to the continuing effect of the prophetic preaching of judgment, which deepened the consciousness of sin, and led men to associate God's vengeance on the heathen with the purgation of the

---

[1]Cf. Ezek. 37.27 f.; 43.1 ff.; Hag. 2.1–9; Zech. 3.9 f.; 4.6 ff.; 6.12 ff.; Joel 4.17 ff.
[2]Cf. ch. VII, pp. 238, 247, 268, and ch. IX.1.II(d), pp. 427 f. above.
[3]Cf. Isa. 63.1 ff.; Hag. 2.21 f.; Zech. 2.1 ff.; Isa. 30.25 f.
[4]Cf. Joel 4.17; Zech. 14.9; Obad. 21.
[5]Cf. Isa. 61.7; Zech. 1.15; Joel 4.2 f.
[6]The beginnings of this attitude can already be detected in Ezek. 25; 27.26; Isa. 47.1 ff.; also Micah 7.7 ff.; Isa. 14.2; Obad. 9 ff.; Joel 4.4 ff.
[7]Cf. Ezek. 25.14; Zech. 9.13 ff.; 10.3 ff.; 12.6; Isa. 11.14; Joel 4.8.
[8]Cf. Isa. 49.26; 66.23 f.; Mal. 3.20 f.; Zech. 14.12 ff.
[9]Cf. Ezek. 38 f. (an appendix added at a later period to Ezekiel's prophecies of salvation); Zech. 12.2 ff.; 14.

people of God. This is clearly brought out both in the Deuteronomic account of history, with its daring condemnation of the whole past of the nation as worthy of death and its teaching that God's unmerited mercy alone is to be regarded as the reason for Israel's existence, and in the Priestly legislation with its dominant concept of atonement. But even in the cultic hymns there is still some tremor of terror at the prospect of Yahweh's great day of judgment, which is to deal with Israel and the Gentiles alike.[1] Furthermore, post-exilic prophecy took care that God's activity as Judge within the covenant people should remain a present reality to each individual,[2] so preserving the hope of salvation from being turned into a false self-confidence. Even though for Israel as a whole the certainty of God's electing and perfecting work remained unimpugned, yet within this circle the distinction between the pious and the sinner[3] continued to form an indispensable part of the expectation of doom; and even for those who were faithful to Yahweh God's judgment was still not meaningless, but constituted a stern method of education.[4]

III. The expectation of doom was therefore well suited to the basically individualist attitude of the post-exilic community. But the older principles underlying the prophetic form of this expectation came to new vigour when, as a result of the period of oppression associated with the Syrian religious persecutions, *Apocalyptic* came to its full powers, and drew the religious system of Judaism within its orbit. Once more the present world was devalued in face of the vision of the coming horror; and static reliance on God's eternal kingdom and its establishment in Israel was rejected in the fervid expectation of a complete upheaval, in which his coming kingdom would finally break through. The conviction of the inescapable nearness of the End gained a new hold over men's feelings,[5] and threw them into a state of tension. This led to the admission of an element originally alien to eschatology, *the ancient doctrine of epochs*, which was really based on the idea of astrological cycles. Nevertheless, in the form in which it is used, for example, in Daniel[6] it is

---

[1] Cf. Ps. 75, and the comments thereon in ch. IX.1.ii(d), p. 430 above. Also Ps. 50; Joel 1.15; 2.11, 14. The references to universal judgment in Ps. 7.7 ff.; 56.8; 59.6, 14 seem to be more a matter of stylistic convention.

[2] Cf. Mal. 1.6 ff.; 2.10 ff., 17 ff.; 3.3, 5, 13 ff.; Zech. 13.2 ff.; Jer. 17.19 ff.

[3] Cf. Zech. 5.1 ff.; Isa. 65.11 ff.; Mal. 3.2 ff., 19 f.

[4] Cf. Hag. 1.4 ff.; Mal. 2.12; 3.3; Zech. 10.9; Isa. 26.1–19; Dan. 9.24.

[5] Cf. Enoch 51.2; Bar. 4.22; II (4) Esd. 4.44 ff.; 5.50 ff.

[6] Cf. Dan. 2 and 7.

subordinated to Israelite historical thinking, and creates a new form
of expression for the religious interpretation of history. In that the
fluctuating history of the world empires is seen as a total scheme
regulated in accordance with a higher plan, better account is taken
both of the essential obedience of world history to law, and of the
independent play of forces within it; and eyes that strain impatiently
for a glimpse of the End are directed to wider developments and
spans of time. Moreover, in this way an even more decisive pre-
eminence is given to the certainty that God's universal plan has
already laid down the outcome of history in the kingdom which
alone is to subject all others to itself, and to last for ever. But it is
also true that men may come to believe that with the help of these
calculations of epochs the secret of God's Providence can be unveiled;
and this notion may replace the certainty of the prophets with an
ill-concealed impatience and lack of confidence which is not satisfied
with trustful reliance on God's intervening at the right moment,
but would like to strive after—or pretend to others to possess—a
secret knowledge, and can never be disabused of its number-mysti-
cism even after repeated disappointments.[1]

Thus it is that a certain clouding of the fundamental prophetic
conception goes hand in hand with its new elaboration. Immense
emphasis is placed on *the irrevocable finality and totality of the approaching
world catastrophe*. Fresh imagery is constantly found to point to the
utter annihilation of the whole cosmos,[2] which is vividly described
in terms of flood or fire.[3] Even the heavenly powers are affected by
this retribution,[4] as here and there the final judgment takes on a
supernatural character.[5] Intensification of the expectation of judgment brings with it the newly emergent concept of resurrection, by
virtue of which even the dead are made to appear before the
judgment-seat of God.[6] This extension of the prophetic picture of

[1] Cf. the various calculations in Daniel (7.25; 8.14; 9.27; 12.7, 11, 12); also
Enoch 18.16; 21.6; 89 f.; II Enoch 33.1; II (4) Esd. 12.11; 14.11; Apoc. Abr. 29 etc.
[2] Cf. Enoch 1.7; 52.9; 83.3 f., 7; 102.2; Jub. 23.18; Or. Sib. III. 82 f.; V. 159,
447, 477 ff.; Ass. Mos. 10.4–6; Test. Lev. 4; II (4) Esd. 8.23; Apoc. Bar. 31.5.
[3] Cf. Enoch 54.7–10; 66; Or. Sib. III. 84 ff.; IV. 160, 172, 175 ff.; V. 155 ff.,
211 ff.
[4] Cf. Isa. 24.21–23; Dan. 4.32; Enoch 10.6, 13; 19.1; 55.4; 64 etc.
[5] Cf. Dan. 7.9 ff.; Enoch 91.15; II (4) Esd. 7.33 ff.
[6] Cf. Dan. 12.2 f.; Isa. 26.19; II Macc. 7; Od. Sol. 3.11 f.; Enoch 51.1–3;
45.1–3; 61.5; 103.8; 104.5; Or. Sib. IV. 180 ff.; II (4) Esd. 7.32 ff., 78 ff.; Apoc.
Bar. 50.2; 51.1 ff.; 85.12 ff. On the provenance of this conception, and its significance for the individual divine-human relationship cf. Vol. III, ch. XXIV of
the present work.

judgment—at least where it obtains in full force—means that the distinction between Israel and the heathen becomes almost meaningless as compared with their common liability to the divine retribution which is threatening all mankind, and thus comes close to the universalism of the early expectation of doom.[1] Meanwhile, however, the effort to exempt Israel as the elect nation from judgment, and so to make doom no more than the reverse side of salvation, is constantly renewed. In this case either judgment becomes in essence simply the annihilation of the Gentiles[2]—in which the Jews take an active part[3]—or else the fate of Israel is completely divorced from the world-judgment, the Messianic kingdom being envisaged as an interim regime until the dissolution of the whole terrestrial order.[4]

Apocalyptic firmly continues to explain the eschatological woes as the consequence of the unbridgeable *gulf between the holy God and the sinful world*. Indeed, the sense of this gulf is even intensified by the agglomeration of the whole power of evil in the figure of the great opponent of God, the *Antichrist,* whose overthrow constitutes the decisive act for the establishing of God's dominion, and the complete disablement of sin.[5] What prophecy had already felt as an opposition in principle is here given form and feature. But at the same time this once more brings with it the danger that hostility to the holy God will be projected on to the heathen world, and away from the circle of the elect nation, with the result that the solidarity of all men in evil may be denied, and the idea of judgment deprived of its keenest pain. It only proved possible to retain the condemnation of this age in unabated intensity when the paradoxical unity of woe and weal, revealed to the prophets in the wrathful love of God, had been experienced as a concrete reality; that is to say, in the Gospel of the New Testament based on the Cross and Resurrection of Jesus Christ.

[1] Cf. II Enoch 39.8; II (4) Esd. 3.33; 7.47, 64 ff., 118 ff.; Apoc. Bar. 14.14; Berakoth 28b; Hagigah 4b ff.
[2] Cf. Enoch 56.7; 90.18; Or. Sib. III. 672 ff., 689 ff.; Test. Jud. 16.18; Ass. Mos. 10.
[3] Cf. Enoch 90.19; 91.12.
[4] Cf. Enoch 93.1–14; 91.11–19; Or. Sib. III. 652 ff.; II (4) Esd. 7.28 f.; 12.34; Apoc. Bar. 30.1; 40.3.
[5] Cf. Dan. 11.36–45; Ass. Mos. 8; Or. Sib. III. 63 ff.; V. 33 f., 214 ff.; II (4) Esd. 5.6 and the NT.

XI

FULFILLING THE COVENANT: THE CONSUMMATION OF GOD'S DOMINION

WE HAVE ALREADY seen how the eschatological expectation fits perfectly into the total pattern of prophetic thought, because it alone is capable of giving an answer to the problem of history—at least if the latter is grasped in its profoundest implications; though conversely a proper expectation of the End proved alien to priestly thinking.[1] Moreover, a preparatory stage of the prophetic eschatology was to be found in the salvation-hope of early Israel,[2] which, though admittedly governed to a large extent by the purely temporal quality of popular hopes,[3] yet had essential traits in common with the prophetic expectation which justify us in according it an eschatological character.[4] Furthermore, eschatology in the form of apocalyptic exercised a decisive influence on the religion of legalistic piety in the post-prophetic period. From all this it is clear that eschatology constitutes an integrating factor in Israelite religion, even though the cultivation of it may have been left to restricted groups within the nation, while others ignored it. The question of its function in the total religious outlook can therefore no longer be shelved by explaining it as a secondary trimming devoid of deeper significance.[5]

[1] Cf. pp. 385 ff. and 424 ff. above.

[2] The very existence of this was long doubted; but it has now been definitely established, principally by the researches of H. Gressmann, collected in his two works, *Der Ursprung der israelitisch-jüdischen Eschatologie* and *Der Messias*.

[3] That is to say, in so far as the ideas of national aggrandizement and military triumph play a part in it.

[4] Cf. pp. 473, 477 f. and 490 f. below.

[5] As a typical expression of this attitude we may quote the following: 'Without doubt the prophets . . . were strongly eschatologically conditioned. But it seems to me that the eschatological tension was something they took over from their

I. THE PRINCIPAL FORMS OF THE OLD TESTAMENT HOPE OF SALVATION

In the period of the Judges and the early monarchy we meet with *two types of salvation-hope*; the one is warlike, and is found in the so-called Balaam sayings,[1] the other is peaceful, and occurs in the oracle relating to Judah in the Blessing of Jacob.[2] In the former Israel's paradisal happiness is painted in eschatological colours,[3] in which the basis and guarantee of this golden peace is the military power of the nation and its God, or alternatively, of its God-appointed leader; in the latter the peaceful kingdom of the saviour, manifested at the end of the line of Judah's rulers, stands in sharp contrast to the tale of battle that is Judah's actual rise to domination.[4] Despite the fundamental difference in these conceptions—a difference emphasized by their differing ideas of who are to be the citizens of the respective kingdoms, the one confined to Israel, the other including the Gentiles in the scheme of salvation—there is yet remarkable agreement in their belief in a return of Paradise as the ultimate goal of God's Providence,[5] and in the appearance of a

---

period, and from popular piety. The highest and most essential element which they provide is precisely not the eschatological, but their grasp on the fact of the present, of the God who reaches down into the present reality of the heart, of the Kingdom of God constructed here and now in faithful human beings' (P. Volz, 'Der heilige Geist in den Gathas des Sarathuschtra' in *Eucharisterion H. Gunkel dargebracht*, 1923, p. 345).

[1] Cf. Num. 23.7–10, 18–24; 24.5–9, 15–18.

[2] Cf. Gen. 49.8–12.

[3] Among these may be included the abnormal fertility of Nature, reminiscent of the garden of Paradise (24.6 f.), the nation, too great to be numbered, living in splendid isolation (23.9 f.), the absence of evil and hardship (23.21), invulnerability to all magic and divination (23.23); cf. A. von Gall, *Zusammensetzung und Herkunft der Bileamperikope in Nu. 22–24*, 1900, pp. 30, 55; W. Eichrodt, *Hoffnung des ewigen Friedens*, pp. 101 ff.; H. Gross, *Die Idee des ewigen und allgemeinen Weltfriedens im alten Orient und im Alten Testament*, 1956, pp. 81, 137, 167 f.

[4] Cf. E. Sellin, *Die Schiloh-Weissagung*, 1908, p. 9. Though it may be true that the Judah oracle received its present shape only in the time of David or Solomon —for it cannot have been possible to speak of the rule of Judah over his brethren before that date—there can nevertheless be no objection to using it to illustrate the expectations of pre-monarchical times, since the whole character of the language presupposes that the Coming One is already a well-known figure. J. Lindblom's attempt ('The political background of the Shiloh-oracle' in *Supplements to Vetus Testamentum*, vol. I, 1953, pp. 78 ff.) to interpret the Shiloh oracle as a political pronunciamento of the Davidic regime would seem to be untenable.

[5] Cf. *Hoffnung des ewigen Friedens*, pp. 102 ff., 114 ff.; H. Gressmann, *Ursprung der Eschatologie*, pp. 208 ff., 287 f.; H. Gross, *op. cit.*, pp. 66 ff.

superhuman ruler-figure.[1] Two notes have been sounded which are to ring on through the whole history of the hope of salvation. Even though the whole content of the futurist expectation does not come into being with them, yet they are of particular importance, because their strongly mythological character testifies that the state of things hoped for is quite different in kind from any transfer of power familiar to us in the ordinary world of our experience. The transformation of Nature, and the divine origin of the expected Saviour, give the coming kingdom a supernatural quality, and therewith a claim to finality.[2]

These unmistakable evidences of the early salvation-hope are corroborated by a series of passages which bear witness to it partly in a different form, partly only by allusion. In view of the bad state of the text any opinion on the passage known as *the Last Words of David*[3] can only be given with considerable reservations. This poem, which in any event is certainly early,[4] seems in vv. 3–4 to compare the future divine ruler to a rising star, rather in the manner of Balaam's fourth oracle;[5] but at the same time it also describes him as an ideal of righteousness and the fear of God. His avoidance of war, which is described in vv. 6 f. more as if it were a divine judgment, links him with the peaceable ruler of Gen. 49, from whom however he is distinguished by the fact that he actively exercises his functions as ruler.

Unique is *the Joseph oracle in the Blessing of Moses*,[6] in which it is the personified tribe that appears as the central figure in a bold expectation of universal dominion characterized at once by military

[1] The differences in the two pictures should however not be disregarded. In particular, the Prince of Peace of Gen. 49 bears a quite distinctive character, in that—strictly interpreted—his activity is not that of a redeemer, but is absorbed in the enjoyment of the paradisal blessings, thus making him more a type than a mediator of the Golden Age.

[2] This point is not affected by the use of mythological attributes in the courtly style of the ancient East; for this too aims ultimately not just at glorifying the king in poetic hyperbole, but at establishing the claim of his rule to absolute value and eternal duration.

[3] Cf. II Sam. 23.1–7.

[4] Cf. O. Procksch, 'Die letzten Worte Davids', in *Alttestamentliche Studien, R. Kittel dargebracht*, 1913, pp. 112 ff.

[5] This exegesis is already suggested by the opening words with their strong sense of mystery, which describe the Coming One as a special manifestation of the inspired prophet, and must therefore amount to something more than a doctrinal presentation of the terms of God's *berīt*, or a somewhat jejune ideal for the reigning monarch. Cf. A. Klostermann, *Der Pentateuch, ad loc.*

[6] Cf. Deut. 33.13 ff.

power and by paradisal abundance. This remarkable modification of the hope of a redeemer points to a closer association with the political hegemony, and thus to the beginnings of its nationalistic perversion. The mythological attributes are here well on the way to being diluted into poetic imagery.[1]

Of more value than this passage, the interpretation of which is not absolutely certain, is the indisputable fact that in the portrayal of the great heroes of the stories of ancient Israel *a series of stereotyped themes* is employed which puts them in the same category as the redeemer and saviour called by God, and miraculously guided and endowed. These themes to some extent give rise to a conventional style.[2] We may note such features as the coming of a new world-era, proclaimed beforehand by a divine messenger or prophet, and ushered in by a child whose origins are either already shrouded in mystery, or else are remarkably humble, whose youth early reveals his uncommon abilities, and who in the prime of his life brings rescue and redemption in a far-reaching dominion described as a time of bliss.[3] These traits, which, it is true, are not all to be found in use on every occasion, but form a kind of symbolic language employed in varying degrees in different contexts,[4] point when taken together to a familiar popular image of the saviour, in which they find their ideal unity. This is confirmed by the discovery of a series of concordant sayings about the redeemer king throughout the Near Eastern world, which can be directly arranged into the scenes of a sacred biography, and prove that in this respect Israel is to a great extent sharing in a common stock of Oriental ideas.[5] Taken purely at its face value this would indeed prove no more than that it was the practice to portray the surmounting of national perils, and the bringing in of better times, in certain stereotyped idioms which formed part of a popular ideal of the redeemer. This ideal only acquires an

[1] The choice of the period to which this oracle ought to be assigned lies between the brief season of Gideon's glory, and the new majesty of the Joseph state after the division of the kingdom. The later period is to be preferred for the reason here stated, but this naturally does not affect the significance of this song of praise for the earlier popular hope.

[2] Cf. Isa. 7.14 with Gen. 16.11 and Judg. 13.3; and on this topic R. Kittel, *Die hellenistische Mysterienreligion und das AT*, pp. 9 ff.

[3] Cf. A. Jeremias, *Das Alte Testament im Lichte des Alten Orients*[4], 1930, pp. 473, 480, 489, 533, 673 ff.; E. Sellin, *Die isr.-jüd. Heilandserwartung*, 1909, pp. 9 f.

[4] Cf. Gen. 30.22; 49.24; Ex. 2.1 ff. etc.; Josh. 10.12–14; Judg. 6.15 f.; 11.1 f., 29; 13.2 ff.; 14.6; 15.14 ff.; I Sam. 1.2 ff.; 7.10; 9.21; 17.46.

[5] Cf. E. Norden, *Die Geburt des Kindes*, 1924; W. Weber, *Der Prophet und sein Gott*, 1925, pp. 80 ff., 119 ff.; on the limits of this similarity, cf. below.

eschatological character when it is not simply attached to this or that historical figure, but as an event in the future constitutes an object of hope and longing. Where this does apply, however, as in the instances first quoted, the fact of a 'heroic style' naturally affords an illustration of the nexus of ideas associated with these prophecies which should not be undervalued.

The hope which finds expression in *the blessings in Genesis* is clothed in different forms. Here, above the level of those benedictions which promise a merely national prosperity, rise others which reach out to the declaration that Israel's role is to be the mediator of blessing to the whole world. This supplies the story of the nation with a goal of absolute value,[1] and expresses a strong sense that all history is working toward a consummation. Moreover, this futurist hope is distinguished from that so far considered by *a distinctive change in the sense of history* underlying it. The future is seen as already implied in the power of the benediction. It is not shaped as something new by the personal, creative intervention of God, but is already actually included in the present, and guaranteed as the unchangeable constitution of the world, unfolded and implemented in virtue of the irresistible force of the blessing. If it is sound to conjecture that these benedictions were cherished and proclaimed in particular at the sanctuaries of Shechem, Bethel, Hebron and Beersheba, and so possessed cultic significance, then we are once more confronted with that distinctively priestly world-view which sees the future as one with the past in an eternal present through the continuing operation of the everlasting divine laws.

This bending back of the eschatological hope on to a reality already potentially given in the present stands out even more clearly in its association with the monarchy. As *the royal Psalms* show,[2] the figure of the Israelite ruler exercised a strong attraction on the popular hope. For with this man, who is adopted by Yahweh as his son,[3] who like an angel of God knows everything that goes on on the earth,[4] who at his anointing has received an indelible character of holiness,[5] and who by virtue of his endowment with the spirit of God can do anything that needs to be done—and always with success[6]—

[1] Cf. Gen. 12.2 f.; 18.18; 22.15–18; 27.27–29; 28.14.
[2] Cf. Pss. 2; 21; 45; 72; 110.
[3] Cf. II Sam. 7.14.
[4] Cf. II Sam. 14.20.
[5] Cf. I Sam. 26.9; II Sam. 1.14.
[6] Cf. I Sam. 10.6 f.

the people are given a leader who sorts with the very highest expectations. Hence on the great festal days of his reign, at his enthronement, at the New Year Festival, the royal marriage, the celebration of victory, he is greeted with songs hailing him as the divine redeemer. Being adopted by Yahweh as his son, he is the representative of the divine universal Lord, and as such is entitled as of right to claim dominion over the nations.[1] He establishes the law of God on earth,[2] and appears to his faithful subjects in the dazzling beauty of an angel from heaven,[3] while he falls upon his enemies in the appearance of terrifying fire[4] such as normally only accompanies a divine epiphany,[5] breaking them in pieces with his weapons and rooting them out from the earth,[6] or else laying them at his feet as his trembling slaves.[7] Hence his throne stands fast for ever, and from it he exercises rule as a divine being, making his sons princes in all lands,[8] while the peoples praise him,[9] and Nature blesses his reign with limitless abundance.[10]

For an explanation of the extravagant honorifics here heaped upon the head of the king scholars have had recourse to *the courtly style of the ancient East*—and rightly so. We are in fact confronted here with stylistic forms common to the East, but associated with Babylon in particular, and belonging to the cult of the divinized monarch.[11] But though these formulas may be understandable enough in a great world power, their application to the king of the pigmy state of Israel is not adequately explained in terms of patriotic

[1] Cf. Ps. 2.7 f.
[2] Cf. Pss. 45.5, 8; 72.1 ff., 12 ff.
[3] Cf. Pss. 45.3; 110.3.
[4] Cf. Ps. 21.10. The text has been heavily glossed, but a study of the context suggests that it may be restored by excising the explanatory marginal gloss *yhwh yᵉballᵉʿēm* and the reduplicated *'ēš* to read: *taṣṣītēmō kᵉtannūr lᵉʿēt pāneykā ūbᵉʾappᵉkā tōʾkᵉlēm*; cf. Gunkel, *ad loc.*
[5] Cf. Isa. 10.16 f.; 29.6; 30.27 ff.; I Kings 19.12; Pss. 18.9; 50.3; 97.3 etc.
[6] Cf. Pss. 2.9; 21.11 ff.; 45.6; 110.5 f.
[7] Cf. Pss. 72.9; 110.1.
[8] Cf. Ps. 45.7, 17.
[9] Cf. Pss. 45.18; 72.17.
[10] Cf. Ps. 72.3, 16.
[11] The most striking example of this is the formula used to describe the extent of the Messianic kingdom—'from sea to sea, and from the River unto the ends of the earth' (Ps. 72.8; cf. Zech. 9.10)—a phrase that can only have been composed in Babylonia. For the only relevant evidence cf. H. Gressmann, *Der Messias*, pp. 1 ff.; also A. R. Johnson, 'The Role of the King in the Jerusalem Cultus' in *The Labyrinth*, pp. 73–111, and the literature listed on p. 437 above.

enthusiasm and political ambition.[1] The latter were certainly not absent in other nations of the Near East, but they produced no comparable phenomena. Such language was made possible only by the belief in election, which awoke the sense of the nation's special mission in the service of the unique God of Israel; the right to universal dominion could therefore be ascribed to the Israelite king as the 'son' of the covenant God without risk of megalomania.[2] As elements in the cultic celebration of the royal festivals[3] the royal psalms proclaim the salvation which Yahweh is going to send through his chosen king.[4] This is the voice *not of an imitation divine kingship, but of a religious conception of the ultimate goal of history*,[5] and as such is intimately bound up with the eschatological hope. What this hope looks for, however, as the future saving act of Yahweh is already, for these hymns, part of present experience in the figure of the king. In him men have before their eyes both the pledge and the beginning of the divine work of salvation.

It was only for this reason, namely that it was a fundamentally eschatological hope that was here conjured up in cultic forms, that this expectation linked with the king was able to survive in full vigour despite frequent disappointment with the individual representatives of the monarchy. In the last resort it rested not on the empirical king and his pretensions to power, but on the saving activity of the covenant God, which even in the days before the monarchy had convinced men that there was an ultimate goal to history. Hence the hope could be transferred without difficulty from father to son, and indeed could be kindled afresh with each king.

In Judah this association of the divine work of salvation with the monarchy took on a distinctive form. Here it was not the individual king, but the dynasty founded by him which was exalted by the prophetic oracles to the status of God's chosen instrument of salvation, and so interpreted as an indispensable component of the people of God.[6] At first this had nothing to do with the eschatological hope,

---

[1] So Gressmann, *op. cit.*, pp. 17, 200 ff., 230.

[2] 'This claim of the Israelite kings to world dominion is not a political reality of history, but an ideal demand of religion' (S. Mowinckel, *Psalmenstudien* III, p. 84).

[3] This applies also to Ps. 45, as S. Mowinckel has shown (*op. cit.*, pp. 96 ff.).

[4] The emphasis throughout is therefore on Yahweh as the agent: cf. Pss. 2.4 ff.; 21.3 ff.; 45.3, 8; 72.1; 110.1 f.

[5] Cf. H. Gross, *Weltherrschaft als religiöse Idee im AT* (Bonner Biblische Beiträge 6), 1953.

[6] Cf. II Sam. 7.11–16.

for men's eyes were clearly fixed simply on the earthly and natural existence of Israel, and there was no thought of a consummation of history. But the leap from this position to the messianic expectation was soon made: in the Judah oracle the bringer of Paradise appears as the last member of the glorious Davidic line. Furthermore, in so far as the divine promise to David was transformed into the establishment of a covenant, regarded as parallel to God's covenant with Israel,[1] *here too we have an understanding of the messianic consummation as the working out of ordinances laid down once for all and now affecting the whole of life*; and it is on the irrevocability of these ordinances that faith is built up.

Nevertheless, side by side with this actualization of salvation in the institution of the monarchy, the properly eschatological hope is also found in every period, looking for the dawn of the age of salvation in a miraculous irruption of Yahweh into the course of history. We have indeed to rely on indirect evidence for this, since nothing has been preserved of the futurist prophecies of the n·bī'îm, in whose circles the expectation of the End was particularly cherished.[2] As circumstantial evidence on this point, however, we may cite that controverting of a clearly definable popular hope which is to be found in Amos.[3] The prophet's contemporaries are waiting for a Day of Yahweh which is to reveal the most magnificent good fortune for Israel, and which therefore they cannot wish into existence quickly or passionately enough. The fact that this was in the prosperous days of Jeroboam II shows that there must have been a living longing for a salvation which even a successful king could not bring about. Our earlier investigations have already shown how the concept of the remnant,[4] which the prophets took over, also voices a salvation-hope, albeit one heralded by signs of a negative character.[5] The futurist visions of the prophets give us abundant information about the content of this longed-for glory, as soon as we observe that they retain many elements of the popular hope, though applying them differently.[6] At the heart of the vision is *the return of Paradise*, in

---

[1]Cf. II Sam. 23.5; Ps. 132; Isa. 55.3; Jer. 33.14–26; Ps. 89.4, 29, 35, 48; II Chron. 7.18; 13.5; 21.7, *et al.* Cf. also ch. II, p. 64 above.

[2]So also Gressmann, *Ursprung der isr.-jüd. Eschatologie*, p. 155: cf. above pp. 323 f.

[3]Amos 5.18, cf. 6.3; 9.10.

[4]Cf. Amos 5.14 f.; Isa. 7.3; also I Kings 19.18; Gen. 45.7 and W. E. Müller, *Die Vorstellung vom Rest im Alten Testament* (Diss. Leipzig), 1939.

[5]Cf. above p. 466; also pp. 378 f.

[6]This theory has been systematically confirmed by Gressmann, *op. cit.*

which not only is an abundance of natural blessings placed without restriction at man's disposal,[1] not only do the beasts lose their fierceness,[2] and the nations beat their weapons into the tools of peace,[3] but the paradisal King also exercises his gentle rule,[4] and a renewed Jerusalem is set on the Mount of God with its stream of life.[5] In this way the central certainty of Israel's faith—'God is in the midst of us' (*yhwh b'qirbēnū*)[6]—will one day be seen in blessed reality. It is probably correct to say that it was the Israelite peasant farmers, worn out by the Syrian wars, whose longing for peace fostered the pattern of this hope, a pattern in such striking contrast to that of the expectations associated with the monarchy.

The attack of the prophetic movement from the eighth century onward was directed against both these forms of the Israelite belief in salvation. The words of consolation in which the message of God's salvation was revealed and which men had loved to hear were now replaced by the certainty of irruptive judgment. 'The Day of Yahweh is darkness and not light!' From this starting-point the prophets remorselessly uncover the feebleness, nay the godlessness of the existing salvation-hope. In one of its forms this turned the golden age into a wish-fulfilment dream of man's material needs by making it an embodiment of sybaritic enjoyment without any longer doing anything to rouse the will to obedient and faithful surrender to the Lord of the new world;[7] in its other form it tried to legitimate the ambitious striving for power, and the uninhibited self-divinization of those who possessed it, by appealing to the benevolence of God's will while wickedly disregarding the fundamental social demands of his covenant. However, by prostrating all human greatness in the

[1]Cf. Amos 9.13 f.; Hos. 2.23 f.; Isa. 7.15; 29.17; 32.15, 20; Joel 4.18; Deut. 32.13; Ezek. 34.26 ff., 36.8 ff., 35 f. etc.

[2]Cf. Hos. 2.20; Isa. 11.6–8; 65.25, and the passages influenced by them: Ezek. 34.25 f.; Isa. 35.9; Lev. 26.6.

[3]Cf. Hos. 2.20; Isa. 2.4; 9.4; Micah 5.9 f.; Zech. 9.10; Pss. 46.10; 76.4.

[4]Cf. Isa. 7.14 ff.; 9.5 f.

[5]Cf. Isa. 2.2; Pss. 48.3; 46.5; Ezek. 40.2; 47.1 ff.; Zech. 14.8, 10.

[6]Cf. Amos 5.14; Isa. 8.8, 10; Ps. 46.4, 6, 8, 12; Micah 3.11: also Num. 23.21.

[7]The celebrated Immanuel passage is to be taken in this sense (Isa. 7.14 ff.). With an ironic twist which makes use of deliberate ambiguity it transforms the popular hope of a return of Paradise into its opposite; for 'milk and honey' may be understood either as the food of the gods, or as the bare sustenance of extreme necessity. Cf. further Gressmann, *Der Messias*, pp. 235 ff.; A. Jeremias, *Das AT im Lichte des Alten Orients*[4], pp. 672 ff.; E. Sellin, *Heilandserwartung*, pp. 25 ff.; also the penetrating argument of R. Kittel, *Die hellenistische Mysterienreligion und das AT*, pp. 1 ff. A different view is put forward by J. J. Stamm, *La Prophétie d'Emmanuel*, 1944.

dust before the divine Judge the prophets made room for the re-creating work of the redeemer. Thus the ingredients of the old picture of hope could be applied in a refined and purified form, in so far as they described God's activity at one and the same time in its cosmic significance and its concrete immanence, namely as a renovation both of the world and of the people. But the emphasis was now laid in a different place, and *the dominating feature in the foreground became the consummation of God's sovereignty.* In face of the centrality of this concept the myth lost its power. Nowhere again do we find the complete picture of Paradise; it has disintegrated into its component parts, and these are used with complete freedom by the prophets, now in one connection, now in another, as they may serve to give form and colour to the prophetic ideas focused on the end of history, or afford means of communicating these ideas in their relations with the people. Thus in Hosea the fragments of the myth are used to invest the new betrothal of Israel to Yahweh with beauty;[1] in Isaiah they form the robe of glory put on by the messianic bringer of righteousness,[2] or provide a colourful illustration of the sovereignty of the God of the universe;[3] and the same may be said of the other prophets.[4]

Consequently the true concern of the prophetic hope can be seen all the more clearly to be the establishment of God's kingdom; and the fact that this hope is an organic part of the prophetic message is shown by the features which patently link it with the prophets' peculiar experience of God and their polemical proclamation of his will.[5] Thus Yahweh's new betrothal with Israel, which as Hosea sees it is to secure for God a people depending on him in pure love,[6] accords perfectly with the whole train of this prophet's thought as he wrestles for his faithless nation, and paints his unique picture of

---

[1] Cf. Hos. 2.16 ff.

[2] Cf. Isa. 9.1 ff.; 11.1 ff. With regard to the political interpretation of Isa. 9.1 ff. by A. Alt ('Isa. 8.23–9.6: Befreiungsnacht und Krönungstag', in the *Bertholet-Festschrift*, 1950, pp. 29 ff.) cf. the pertinent criticism of H. Gross, *op. cit.*, pp. 139 f., and the attractive exegesis of W. Vischer, *Die Immanuel-Botschaft im Rahmen des königlichen Zionsfestes* (Theol. Studien 45), 1956.

[3] Cf. Isa. 2.2 ff.

[4] Cf. Micah 5.1 ff.; Zech. 9.9 f.; Isa. 19.23; 40.3 f.; 41.18 ff.; 43.19 ff.; 49.2; 55.1, 13; 60.13, 19 f. etc.

[5] My own study, *Die Hoffnung des ewigen Friedens*, has helped to demonstrate this inner harmony of the prophetic predictions with the rest of their message. Extremely valuable contributions to this subject may be found in W. Stärk, *Das assyrische Weltreich im Urteil der Propheten*, 1908.

[6] Cf. Hos. 2.21 f.

Yahweh's untiring love. The centre of Isaiah's picture of the future is the rule of justice and righteousness in the moral community of the people and the nations;[1] and this is revealed as the goal of his struggle for the God whom he conceives as the Holy One. Zephaniah follows in his footsteps when he makes the humble, who have renounced all self-reliance, experience the new communion with God and the peace of the nations.[2] Again, the same spirit which we find in the other sayings of Jeremiah breathes through his oracle of the new covenant, which in the face of the nation's breach of the old covenant he fashions as the means whereby the divine law is to be implanted in the hearts and minds of men, and all classes and ages are to rejoice equally in their God.[3] The same central line of religious thinking is continued in Ezekiel and Deutero-Isaiah. The former pictures the transformation of the stony heart into a heart of flesh by the indwelling of God's spirit in man, and then goes on from this inward new creation to the outward one,[4] when Yahweh as the great shepherd of his people brings in the new age of peace in Nature and mankind, and guarantees his gracious presence in the new Temple. Deutero-Isaiah, in his hymns of exultation, is able to give an even more transporting picture of the kingdom of peace and righteousness embracing all nations, exalted over space and time, and unaffected by the destruction of the terrestrial order.[5] In every case there is substantially a common approach, but expressed in varying individual forms; and this inner agreement underlying all outward divergence is proof of the central importance of this eschatological message for the whole of prophecy.[6]

This subordination of all individual features to the overriding principle of the consummation of God's sovereignty comes out especially strikingly in *the figure of the Saviour-King*. In some prophets there is no trace of this,[7] and in others the personal irruption of God himself has thrust it very much into the background.[8] But even where it occupies an important place in the picture of the future it has

[1]Cf. Isa. 9.5 f.; 11.3–5; 2.2–4; 29.20 f.; 32.16 f.
[2]Cf. Zeph. 3.9 ff.
[3]Cf. Jer. 31.31 ff.
[4]Cf. Ezek. 11.19 f.; 36.25 ff.; 37; 17.23 f.; 40 ff.
[5]Cf. Isa. 45.20–25; 51.4–8.
[6]The last-named prophets also give a new eschatological stamp to the covenant concept: cf. ch. II.2.ii, pp. 58 ff. above.
[7]I.e., Hosea, Amos and Zephaniah.
[8]Cf. Jer. 23.5 f. with 30 and 31; Ezek. 17.22 f.; 21.32; 34.23 f.; 37.22, 24 f. in conjunction with chs. 34–37.

undergone important changes. Among the tasks assigned, as a result of his association with the ideal of the king, to the redeemer who was to come at the end of time, one that was retained was his moral and social activity, the execution of righteous judgment on all the evil-doers among his own people, and the bringing of succour to all the oppressed and socially underprivileged. But at the same time this was raised on to a new plane with the emphasis on his function as mediator, through whom complete righteousness was assured to the nation and to each individual in it,[1] and every man guaranteed a new relationship of covenant and peace between himself and his God.[2] Because this mediatorial position was based on voluntary atoning suffering—even to the extent of the surrender of life itself— and achieved its purpose in the interior conquest and transformation of sinners by their acceptance in faith of the intercession made for them,[3] the divine community of the called, perfected in history, finally put paid to all ideas associated with physical magic, and was established as in the fullest sense a personal relation between God and man.[4] With this, moreover, goes the logical rejection of any

[1] Cf. Jer. 23.5 f.

[2] Cf. Isa. 42.6 f.; 49.6, 8.

[3] Cf. Isa. 50.4–9; 53.1–12; an echo of this picture is to be found in Zech. 11.4 ff.; 13.7–9; 11.15 ff.; 12.10–14; cf. O. Procksch, *Die kleinen Propheten nach dem Exil*, 1916, pp. 107 ff.

[4] We shall proceed on the assumption, which there is no need to substantiate in more detail here, that the *'ebed yhwh* of Deutero-Isaiah is indeed to be understood as an individual figure, though neither as a prophet (with Mowinckel), nor as a teacher of Torah (with Duhm *et al.*), but as a royal figure, which has none the less acquired characteristics deriving from other sources. It is noteworthy that H. Gressmann, who had at first looked for a solution along quite different lines, finally (*Der Messias*, pp. 285 ff.) returned to this conception, the original champion of which had been E. Sellin (*Das Rätsel des deuterojesajanischen Buches*, 1908). The same view is taken by I. Engnell ('The Ebed Yahweh Songs and the Suffering Messiah in Deutero-Isaiah', *Bulletin of the John Rylands Library* 31, 1948, pp. 54–93), who sees in the Servant Songs a prophetic proclamation of the coming Messiah deriving from the liturgy of the annual royal festival, and directly connected with the Davidic Messiah of other prophecies—a total conception the formation of which must have been assisted by the myth of the dying and rising God. V. de Leeuw (in *L'Attente du Messie*, ed. B. Rigaux, 1954) also sees in the Servant a royal figure. Bentzen lays less emphasis on the Messianic element, attaching more importance to the influences of a Mosaic expectation, and to the types of the patriarchs and prophets; but he is prepared to understand the Servant as a historical personality (*King and Messiah*, ET, 1955).

In the light of recent discussion it seems doubtful whether the attempts of H. Wheeler Robinson ('The Hebrew Conception of Corporate Personality', in *Werden und Wesen des Alten Testaments* (BZAW 66), ed. J. Hempel, 1936, pp. 49 ff.) and O. Eissfeldt (*Der Gottesknecht bei Deuterojesaja*, 1933) to illuminate the problem by the conception of 'corporate personality', of which we have evidence among

display of military power on the part of the coming Saviour;[1] the execution of judgment on the nations is reserved to God alone.[2] Here the thought of the prophets revives the popular figure of the paradisal King of Peace, though of course subordinating the naturalistic element of paradisal plenty to that reformation of the personal and moral life which the Messiah brings about. The powerful effect of this transformation of the traditional hope of salvation is demonstrated in several passages by the restriction of the saviour-king to

---

primitive peoples, has really taken matters much beyond the point already reached by W. Vischer ('Der Gottesknecht. Ein Beitrag zur Auslegung von Jes. 40–55', *Jahrbuch der Theolog. Schule Bethel*, 1930, pp. 59–115) in his study of the representation of the people by an individual; cf. the excellent surveys of C. R. North (*The Suffering Servant in Deutero-Isaiah*, 1948) and H. H. Rowley (*The Servant of the Lord and other Essays on the Old Testament*, 1952, pp. 1–88). However, while the first-named scholars place the emphasis on the collective understanding of the *'ebed*, and make use of the vagueness of the lines marking off the individual from the group chiefly in order to devalue the individualist features of the figure, the latter see in the prophetic picture a switch, conditioned by the prophet's own times, from the description of Israel as the Servant to the commissioning of an individual—and to this feature of constant oscillation between individual and group is a good deal less relevant. In this connection M. Buber, though rejecting the collective interpretation of the *'ebed*, comes closer to the Corporate Personality theory, when he sees the Servant as a person of many facets, who combines in himself all the struggling, suffering prophets, and who by completing their work not only sets forth the nature of the true Israel, but himself becomes identified with it ('Het Geloof van Israel' in *De Godsdiensten der Wereld*[2], 1948, vol. I, pp. 148 ff., and *The Prophetic Faith*, pp. 217 ff.). Whether the really profound meaning of the mystery of atonement, as understood in the NT, can be grasped along the lines of this solution, which sees the atoning sufferings of the Servant as availing only for the heathen, may properly be doubted.

The separation of Isa. 53 from the rest of the Servant Songs (cf. P. Volz, *Jesaja II, übersetzt und erklärt*, 1932, which gives a valuable review of interpretations up to that time) can hardly be correct. That there are differences from the rest of the book cannot be questioned, but they can be explained along other lines. For an understanding of the suffering king the customs of the Babylonian New Year Festival, in which the king is seen in the role of a penitent, are important (cf. L. Dürr, *Heilandserwartung*, pp. 133 ff.). In the controversy over the relation of the Servant to a historical figure it is of less importance to decide which of the innumerable interpretations has hit upon the right figure, than in what way the connection of this figure with the world of eschatological ideas is to be made clear. On this point the attempt made by R. Kittel (*Geschichte des Volkes Israel* III.1, 1927, pp. 222 ff.) and W. Rudolph (*ZAW* 43, 1925, pp. 90 ff.; and 46, 1928, pp. 156 ff.) to synthetize their views, together with a recollection of the situation underlying the royal psalms, will suggest the right direction in which an answer is to be sought.

[1] Cf. Isa. 9.5 f.; 11.1 ff. (the Prince of Peace); Zech. 9.10; Micah 5.1 ff.; Jer. 23.5 f.; Ezek. 34.23 f.; 37.22, 24 f.

[2] Cf. Isa. 9.3 f.; Zech. 9.1–8; Micah 4.6 ff.; 5.9 ff.; Jer. 23.1–4; 30.16; Ezek. 34.1 ff.; 35.

Israel, while world dominion is reserved for Yahweh alone.[1] In this way nationalistic ambition is deprived of its strongest support, and religious universalism is purified of all alien admixture. But even where the saviour-king continues as world ruler, the peaceful character of his empire witnesses eloquently against those strivings after universal sovereignty which are dominated by nationalism and lust for power.[2]

All these pictures of the future stand in stark opposition to the messianic pretensions of the historical representatives of the monarchy, whom the prophets strip of their aura of divinity in order to direct men's hopes away from them and on to the God-sent redeemer. How, under the impact of their polemic, even the expectation of salvation bound up with the king was changed may be seen from Ps. 72, which hymns the accession of the Judge and Prince of Peace, and teaches men to see in the prayer of the poor for their royal helper the strongest buttress of the monarchy.[3]

Nevertheless, in spite of this theoretical opposition, *from the time of the Exile onwards elements and moods of the popular salvation-hope force their way into the prophetic eschatology.* Partly this was a result of carrying the doctrine of retribution to its logical conclusion,[4] so that it was impossible to conceive of Yahweh's favour apart from a visible reflection of it in outward events—a view which inevitably involved the desire for a glorious position in the world for the restored Israel. Partly it was the influence of the poetic glorification of the great change in Israel's fortunes, as this for example bulks so large in Deutero-Isaiah's incomparably beautiful imagery of the liberation and restoration of the captive and degraded princess Jerusalem,[5] which revived the idea of *Israelite world-sovereignty*, with all the nations as its ministers and all the riches of the nations pouring into its treasury, and gave it a special place in the picture of the

---

[1]So especially Isaiah (9.1–6; cf. 2.2–4), but also Micah, Jeremiah and Ezekiel.

[2]Cf. Zech. 9.9 f.; Isa. 42.1, 4, 6; 49.6 f.; 52.13; 53.12. In Deutero-Isaiah's Book of Consolation traces of the politico-national expectation of salvation (45.14 ff.; 49.22 ff.; 55.4 f.) are still to be found alongside the non-political and universalist (45.20–25; 51.4–6).

[3]Cf. v. 15 (v. 15a, partly following Buhl-Mowinckel, should read: *wîḥî heʿānî wᵉyōdennū wᵉyitten-lō mizzᵉhab šᵉbāʾ*, 'Let the poor live and praise him; and he shall give him better than gold from Sheba').

[4]Cf. Prov. 1.19, 31 ff.; 2.21 f.; 3.33 ff.; Pss. 37; 39; 49; and the speeches of the friends in the Book of Job; on this subject, cf. also Vol. II, pt. 3. ch. XXII.3.II of the present work.

[5]Cf. Isa. 49.14 ff.; 51.17 ff.; 52.1 ff.; 54.1 ff.; 60; 62.

future.[1] When Haggai hails Zerubbabel as Yahweh's chosen redeemer king and world-ruler,[2] he is once more taking up the theme of the old royal hymns, and their association of salvation with the contemporary monarch. Side by side with this threat of a nationalist and particularist narrowness in the concept of salvation goes its *connection with the cult*. It is true that Haggai and Zechariah were exhibiting the genuine prophetic attitude when they looked at the immediately urgent historical tasks in the light of eschatology, and taught men to see the rebuilding of the Temple as an avowal of messianic hope, and the precondition of Yahweh's return in the age of salvation.[3] But to describe the congregation created by this revival as simply being itself the messianic body—as happened in the appendices to Ezekiel[4] —was to give the cultus an absolute significance hitherto unknown. Once more we can clearly detect the transformation of a consummation in the future, which can only be waited for, into a divine ordinance to be carried out in the present. Even those promises to Israel which were originally eschatological in intention, namely that she should be the priestly mediator-people of the age of salvation,[5] the inheritrix of the gracious promises to David,[6] and the guide of the nations to a right knowledge of God,[7] lend themselves all too easily to subordination to this way of thinking which seeks to 'realize' the *eschaton*.

Under the pressure of that cruel fate which seemed always to be frustrating the hopes of the Jewish community, the *passionate longing* with which they strained their eyes *for the End* nevertheless remained alive. After the expectations pinned on Zerubbabel were not fulfilled, the figure of the messianic king faded into the background, and the faith that turned to the future was concentrated entirely on the idea of Yahweh's miraculous irruption; for only if he would assume the sovereignty that was his could the coming age of bliss be assured.

[1] Cf. Isa. 60.4, 10 f., 14, 16; 61.5, 6b; 66.12; Hag. 2.7 ff., and the distinctive motivation of the messianic blessings in Ezekiel: 34.29; 36.20–23, 30, 36 and 36.1–15.

[2] Cf. Hag. 2.21–23; also Zech. 4.1–6, 10–14.

[3] Cf. Hag. 2.4–9, 15 ff.; Zech. 1.16 f.; 2.14 ff.; 4.6 ff.

[4] Ezek. 40–48 may largely come from a later period than the rest of the book; perhaps the line of demarcation ought to be drawn after 43.11a. On this point cf. G. Hölscher, *Hesekiel, der Dichter und das Buch*, 1924, p. 189.

[5] Cf. Isa. 61.6–9. It is in this tradition that Zechariah sees the High Priest as a type and pledge of the Messiah: 3.8–10; 6.9 ff.

[6] Cf. Isa. 55.3 f.

[7] Cf. Zech. 2.14 f.; 8.23; also Isa. 45.14; 19.23. The Servant Songs must have been interpreted of the nation at quite an early stage.

In Malachi, Joel and the Little Apocalypse of Isa. 24–27 we see separate phases—the date of which cannot be exactly determined—of the hope of the End, the last-named certainly taking us down into the Greek period. Here the best thought of the prophets lives on; and though there is no lack of particularist and nationalist tendencies, such as we find expressed in the latter part of the books of Isaiah and Zechariah,[1] in this period either, yet these features only make the power of the universalist hope shine out more brightly.

While, however, the eschatological imagery is already becoming bewilderingly complicated, and betrays an excessive profusion of mythological trappings, *the perfect sovereignty of God*, which is the object of this longing, is mirrored with wonderful clarity in a series of cultic hymns celebrating Yahweh's kingship, and deriving from Deutero-Isaiah's gospel of the king.[2] With enthusiastic confidence the universality of God's dominion is here sung as the fulfilment of the yearning of the cosmos; but at the same time it is transferred from the purely eschatological sphere to the present reality of cultic experience, and so given timeless validity.[3] Here the priestly conception of God's sovereignty, fertilized by the prophetic hope, has found its purest expression.[4]

Up to the Greek period only faint traces are discernible in later Judaism of one particular change in men's view of the world which after that time had a strong influence on the field of eschatological concepts, namely a *thoroughgoing transcendental dualism*. Under foreign, and particularly Persian influences this projected the contradictions of man's earthly life into the world of spirits, and to a greater and greater degree gave the world beyond pre-eminence over this one as the real centre of effective importance.[5] God's work for the setting up of his dominion on earth now becomes a conflict with the devil, to be decided by divine judgment on him and the angelic powers.[6] Even the Messiah as 'Son of Man' acquires a more transcendental character; and the idea of his pre-existence, like that of his purely

[1] Cf. Isa. 65 f.; Zech. 9.11–11.3; 12.1 ff.; 14.1 ff.; also Obad. 15 ff.
[2] Cf. Pss. 93; 96; 97; 99: also pp. 429 f. and 127 f. above.
[3] To call them 'eschatological hymns' is therefore only partly justifiable: cf. p. 429 n. 3 above.
[4] The nearest approach is an oracle like Mal. 1.11.
[5] Cf. on this point: W. Bousset, *Die Religion des Judentums*[3], p. 202 ff.; N. Messel, *Die Einheitlichkeit der jüdischen Eschatologie*, 1915; P. Volz, *Die Eschatologie der jüdischen Gemeinde im neutestamentlichen Zeitalter*, 1934.
[6] Cf. pp. 469 f. above.

temporary sojourn on the earth, now begins to play its part.[1] This process of transcendentalization which, if carried through to its logical conclusion, was bound to lead to a complete spiritualizing of the hope of the End encountered, however, an insuperable obstacle in the concrete concepts associated with the End in the OT scriptures; and it was therefore able to make only partial headway, and that with very varying success in the different classes of society. Hence matters remained in a compromise position, the new ideas being only to a limited extent organically incorporated into the older deposit, which was moreover more tenaciously retained in Palestinian Judaism than in the Diaspora. On the one hand the effect was to broaden the existing eschatological dualism in its cosmic, anthropological and demonological aspects, with a resultant devaluation of hopes which had been exaggeratedly physical in character, and the introduction of valuable new religious ideas, such as the conquest of death through resurrection, and retribution in the world to come.[2] In this way many agonizing enigmas which had persisted in the original hope of the End—as, for example, the repeated postponement of the date of the consummation, and the associated problem of the fate of the righteous—were now resolved, or at least made tolerable. On the other hand the intrusion of transcendental dualism increased the bewildering disorder caused by the juxtaposition of divergent eschatological religious concepts,

[1] The earliest evidence for the conception of the Son of Man as a messianic figure is Dan. 7.13; for the interpretation of the 'saints of the Most High' in v. 27 as meaning the nation undoubtedly represents a reversal of the original sense. The vision passages in Enoch, and the Son of Man vision in II (4) Esd. 13 give the finished portrait of the pre-existent Son of Man, who is hidden in Heaven, and is to come from there to judge the world and to set up the Kingdom of God. There can be no doubt that foreign, and especially Persian influences are here at work. Nevertheless, in Israel too from the very earliest times there is an indigenous conception of the Primal Man (cf. Ezek. 28.12 ff.; Job 15.7 f.; Prov. 8.22 ff. and perhaps Amos 4.12 f.) who, in sharp contrast to the Adam of Gen. 2 f., is a supernatural being, abiding with God even before the creation of the world, and admitted to his counsels; and the importance of this conception should not be underestimated (cf. H. Gunkel, *Schöpfung und Chaos in Urzeit und Endzeit*, 1895, p. 148, and *Genesis*, pp. 33 f.; E. Sellin, *Der AT Prophetismus*, pp. 177 ff.; H. Schmidt, *Der Mythos vom wiederkehrenden König im AT*, 1925, pp. 16 ff., 29). On this whole question cf. H. Gressmann, *Der Ursprung der isr.-jüd. Eschatologie*, pp. 334 ff.; and *Der Messias*, pp. 341 ff.; W. Bousset, *Die Religion des Judentums*³, pp. 262 ff. (with a further list of relevant literature in the note on p. 266), and the works of Reitzenstein; also E. Sjöberg, *Der Menschensohn im äthiopischen Henochbuch* (Acta reg. soc. hum. lit. Lundensis 41), 1946; T. W. Manson, *The Son of Man in Daniel, Enoch and the Gospels*, 1950.

[2] Cf. pp. 469 ff. above.

and so made their clarification and synthetization more difficult. This was accentuated when, as a result of the Maccabean wars, *a new wave of nationalism* swept over every department of life, including the expectation of the End. Already in the immediate post-exilic period the firmly prophetic cast of thought had failed to secure exclusive control of men's minds, but had been accompanied by a revival of popular hopes; now in the time of the Syrian religious persecutions the interests of religion and the nation once more coincided, and so gave new justification to the nationalist and particularist element in eschatology. In spite of the fact that the universalist tenor of the older hope was not denied, and indeed was reinforced by many of the newly adopted ideas such as that of the resurrection of the dead, the main emphasis now fell overwhelmingly on the nationalistic content of the vision of the future. Hence God's sovereignty constantly becomes also the supremacy of Israel in a political sense;[1] in comparison with the good fortune of Israel the salvation of the Gentile world is dismissed very briefly;[2] and it is the natural and material blessings which are of principal interest in the new life.[3] The Messiah concept, awakened to new vigour, is not unaware of the sinless Prince of Peace who takes away all the dark places from the earth,[4] but he is more attractive to men's eyes as the Saviour-Prince, the king of his own land and the dispenser of the messianic blessings, with the result that the old warlike nature of the Messiah is from time to time revived.[5] The song of the great universal judgment of quick and dead, of the new heaven and earth in which righteousness shall dwell, and of the peace of moral perfection in both social and individual life, is but a weaker, subsidiary theme.[6] How strong the nationalist and particularist tendencies in the Jewish hope of salvation had become, how paralysing the accompanying inability to cut away the outward inessentials from the true heart of

[1] Cf. Dan. 2.44; 4.14 ff.; 7.27; Ass. Mos. 10.8 ff.; Enoch 90.30; Jub. 23.30; 32.19 etc.
[2] Cf. Tobit 14.6; Enoch 10.21; 48.4 f.; 90.33 ff.; Or. Sib. III. 616 ff., 716 ff., *et al.*
[3] Cf. Enoch 5; 10.17 ff.; Jub. 23.27 ff.; Or. Sib. III. 743 ff., 772 ff.; V. 275 ff.; Apoc. Bar. 29; 73: also P. Volz, *op. cit.*, pp. 386 ff.
[4] Cf. Pss. Sol. 17.32 ff.; 18.6 ff.; Test. Levi 18; Test. Jud. 24; Enoch 45 ff.; II (4) Esd. 12.31 ff.
[5] Cf. Pss. Sol. 17.21 ff., 30 ff.; II (4) Esd. 13.1 ff., 39 ff.; Apoc. Bar. 35–40; 72–74; Or. Sib. V. 414 ff.; Targ. Pseudo-Jon. on Num. 24.17; Ex. 40.11 (here the Messiah is from the house of Ephraim).
[6] Cf. P. Volz, *op. cit.*, pp. 272 ff., 338 ff., 391 ff.

the matter, the sovereignty of God, is shown clearly enough for Palestinian Judaism by the scenes in the Gospels; while for those conditioned by the Hellenistic world the example of Philo affords eloquent testimony. *Thus at the close of its career the form of the OT hope cries out for a critique and a reconstruction* which will be able to reach out and grasp the unchanging truth hidden under its bewildering diversity, and set this in the very centre where it can dominate all else, while at the same time unifying its struggling contradictions, its resting in a timeless present and its tense waiting for a consummation at the end of history. Both these needs are fully met in the NT confession of Jesus as the Messiah.

2. THE IMPORTANCE OF THE HOPE OF SALVATION FOR THE DOCTRINE OF GOD

Any examination of the development of the OT hope of salvation which is anything more than superficial enables us to see that in this one issue are concentrated all the historical struggles to arrive at a right understanding of the divine revelation—indeed that in many cases the ultimate motives inspiring these struggles emerge here with peculiar clarity, because they are raised to the level of the absolute, final event.

1. First and foremost *the fundamental character of the OT revelation of God is here made unmistakably clear.* For on one point all the various expressions of the hope of salvation are agreed, that they make *a real entry of God into history* the centre of their belief. The danger that threatens from the mythological side, namely that an event conceived as historical may dissolve into frivolous fantasy-formations or magical faery landscapes, is successfully averted by the close association of the hope with the ideas of covenant and election, that is to say, by the relation between the hoped-for consummation and the national community in its concrete earthly actuality. The bliss of Paradise is destined for a nation whose life has been shaped by the demands of the divine will; and whenever doubt has temporarily been cast on this, as in the popular hope of the monarchical period, the ensuing age has brought with it an all the more decisive corrective. Moreover, the conscious awareness that God's sovereignty was the ultimate goal was always able to bid defiance to any intellectual attempts at rarefaction and abstraction, and to see that this particular error, which constitutes a permanent risk whenever there is increased emphasis on the divine transcendence, and which gave especial

trouble in later Judaism as a result of Hellenistic influence, was never able to become a dominant factor. The Israelite hope remained loyal to this earth. It was too full-blooded and alive to find fulfilment in a realm of spirits; what it wanted was a renewal of bodily existence. Furthermore, this meant that any tendency to make the hope too individualist was also avoided. Ever since Jeremiah the relation of the individual to the community had been felt to be a problem, and men had struggled to solve it; and the expectation of the End had by no means been free from this disturbing influence. But the redemption of the individual by absolution and an inner renewal which in the hope of resurrection bursts even the bands of death was always subordinated to the creation of a new people in which the history that had begun here on earth would reach its goal. It is obvious that this concern for the real historicity of the final consummation must have received strong support from the figure of the Messiah. His appearance on earth, and as a man, and his task of kingship imposed a strident veto on any attempt to evaporate eschatology in cosmological speculations, and kept firm hold on a concern for the historical and ethical renewal both of the nation and the world. It was not until later Judaism that men learned to think of a phantasmal manifestation of a heavenly Messiah who retained hardly any connection with the life of this world.

II. In view of this marked insistence that salvation was something concrete and earthly it is of great importance that at the same time *the supramundane character of the messianic kingdom* was also constantly borne in mind. Here the mythical features of the eschatological picture, which for all the process of moral deepening had never been abandoned, play a decisive part. For from the very first they point to the fact that the expected world-order is different in kind from the present one, and this long before the expressions 'the present age' and 'the age to come' had been invented. It is not those in whom power is vested here below who decide the character of the coming kingdom. It comes with the authority of a supramundane, divine reality, leaving human conceptions and calculations trailing far behind. It is therefore not only independent of man's will, but can rise in glory over the most appalling crisis and collapse of this whole world-order. In this way the very diverse products of mythology become the mediators of a spiritual vision which safeguards that absolute qualitative otherness of the historical consummation wrought by the covenant God without which it could not be the work of God at all.

III. Both these things, the historical immanence and the otherness that transcends history, remain united in *the solution* which the eschatological hope provides *of the pressing problems of religion*. From the outset *Israel's position in the Gentile world* was bound to be a major item in the problem of God. Once raised to the status of the peculiar people of a God superior to all others, and aware that this God had reserved his beneficence for Israel alone and used it to give them their paradisal homeland,[1] Israel could never be content to remain just another petty state, but was bound to see its own destiny in relation to that of the Gentile world.[2] The apex of power attained under David seemed for a time to be the realization of their call to be a blessing to the nations; but collision with the world power of the Tigris brought with it a painful conflict between this high-flown sense of vocation and the brutal reality. The prophets were convinced that the victory of the Assyrian and the annihilation of Israel did not make it impossible to believe in the mighty providence of their God, but were rather a new revelation of it. Nevertheless, they were unable to envisage the goal of God's activity as a snapping of all links with history—it could only be a re-establishment of his dominion. Thus Isaiah, at a time when punitive judgment at the hand of Assyria was approaching and seemed likely to bury beneath the wreckage of Judah any possibility of a real kingdom of God in history, found the solution in the marvellous design by which his God would use destruction to create completely new life.[3] He saw this realization of God's sovereignty in powerful images which described the divine 'Nevertheless' with rare clarity and spiritual force in terms of the kingdom of righteousness and peace; and it was this which first gave the prophetic struggle at once its deepest meaning and its justification. Likewise in other passages the prophetic hope of salvation, particularly in its messianic form, by making visible God's universal purposes, provided a solution to the tormenting question, what was to be the fate of God's revelation in face of the rising tide of the world empire—that is to say, it satisfied a concern proper to the religious life. It was only from this starting-point that

---

[1] Cf. the picture which we have, even in the prose writings, of Canaan as the 'land that flows with milk and honey', that is to say, the Paradise land (Ex. 3.8, 17; 13.5; 33.3 etc.), and on this point *Die Hoffnung des ewigen Friedens*, pp. 106 ff.

[2] In addition to the blessings bestowed on the patriarchs cf. that conviction of being the chief of the nations which arouses Amos' sarcasm (6.1).

[3] Cf. Isa. 28.23 ff.; 10.5 ff.; 14.24–27.

the conception of the eternal kingdom of Yahweh, as we find it in the Psalms, became possible.

The same applies to *the problem which arose in connection with the more restricted sphere of the nation's internal life.* The oldest form of the salvation-hope already saw the very closest connection between the glorious future of the nation and its carrying out of the will of God.[1] It was only as fighting God's battle against injustice and violence that the monarchy obtained the co-operation of the nation's religious leaders.[2] But when king and people failed to come up to expectations, then—according to the conviction of his messengers—God was bound himself to create a people well-pleasing to him, in whom his ordinances, for which his prophets had fought so untiringly, would be seen by all the world to be the sources of life and blessing. The whole harsh struggle between national self-seeking and the sovereign divine will could not but end with God's victory in a renewed national life. Hence the Messiah puts an end to the monarchy, whose wars and revolutions had become a curse, with his kingdom of peace which no longer knows anything of war and violence. Instead it seeks its fame not in the growth of nationalist power, to which the life and prosperity of its citizens must be sacrificed, but in the establishment of moral order and social righteousness in which the members of the messianic kingdom, led by the bearer of God's spirit, are united in a harmony of moral purpose.[3] If this picture of the Saviour-King as the loyal and obedient executor of the divine will has importance as an exemplar, certainly the most profound vision of his work in establishing true human community is the one in which, by his voluntary suffering to atone for the congregation of a people disrupted by suicidal egoism, he gathers them into a new unity of humility and worship before the face of the judging and redeeming God.[4]

In this answer to the problem posed by God's irresistible judgment on state and nation there are the beginnings of a solution to the kindred questions of *the relationship of the individual to the community.* The authoritarian control of the Prince of Righteousness in Isaiah

[1] Cf. Num. 23.21 ff.; 24.7.

[2] It is important to note that even in the exaggerated glorification of the king in the royal psalms mentioned earlier the ruler is regarded as the champion of righteousness and truth (Pss. 45.5, 7 f.; 72.1 f., 4, 12 ff.; 110.6), who upholds the cause of God (Ps. 21.8) and executes his will (Pss. 2.6 f., 11; 45.8; 72.1; 110.1 f., 4).

[3] Cf. Isa. 11.1-9; 9.6; Jer. 23.6; Zech. 9.9.

[4] Cf. Isa. 50.4-9, 10; 53.4-6, 11; also the taking over of this idea in Ps. 22.

is given an inward basis in the heart when the individual is brought to religious perfection and liberty by Deutero-Isaiah's Servant of the Lord; for the idea of substitutionary suffering as a means of creating righteousness at once opens up a new dimension both in the relation of the individual to God, and in his relationship with his own community. Both this subject, however, and that of the resurrection of the dead, must be left to a later section.[1]

We have tried to show the central importance of the OT salvation-hope for religion as an answer to those burning problems of faith which concern God's sovereignty over the external destiny of the nation, its internal community life, and the existence of its individual members; and this may also throw new light on the many related questions connected with the origins of this hope.

3. THE ORIGINS OF THE OLD TESTAMENT HOPE OF SALVATION

There are today in essence three lines along which attempts are made to elucidate the origins of the Israelite hope of salvation: the mythical, the national and the cultic.

1. The *mythical elements* which are so marked a feature of the eschatological pictures in the OT, and which can be shown by their frequent lack of organic connection with the historical and national material to have been originally independent and only incorporated at a later date into historical thinking,[2] have in the last decades been illuminated to a surprising extent by the light which has been thrown on the myth system of the ancient East. In almost every case we can now see how these elements of the OT, which seem so strange in their new setting, are linked with the spiritual ideas of the ancient peoples surrounding Israel.[3] It is therefore hardly surprising that constant attempts have been made to find the source of the Israelite hope in ancient Oriental mythology, and more precisely in the

[1] Cf. Vol. III of the present work, ch. XXI–XXIII.

[2] Of these elements the ones which it is principally necessary to take into account are: the peace of the animal creation, the heavenly food of milk and honey, miraculous fertility, the destruction of weapons of war, the supernatural birth of the redeemer, and the divine kingship. All of these can be shown by numerous, and frequently extremely ancient instances to belong to the world of non-Israelite mythology. (Cf. *Die Hoffnung des ewigen Friedens*, pp. 111 ff., 145 ff., 155; H. Usener, *Religionsgeschichtliche Untersuchungen*, 1899, Pt. 3, and 'Milch und Honig' in *Rhein. Museum für Philologie* 57, 1902, pp. 177 ff.; H. Lietzmann, *Der Weltheiland*, 1909, pp. 4, 40 ff.; L. Dürr, *Isr.-jüd. Heilandserwartung*, pp. 74 ff.) H. Gross (*Die Idee des ewigen und allgemeinen Weltfriedens*, 1956) provides a good survey of the greatly increased religio-historical material.

[3] Cf. pp. 474 f. above.

mythological picture of a divine redeemer, quite regardless of whether Babylonia[1] or Egypt[2] or Persia[3] is thought of as the ultimate country of origin. This view is expressed, for example, in such a statement as the following: 'Horus-Osiris-Immanuel-Helios-Aion are members of one and the selfsame series stretching down through centuries and millennia.'[4]

In criticizing this view we must make a clear distinction between the provenance of the mythological material in which the salvation-hope of Israel is clothed and the origin of the hope itself. That the former was not originally native to Israel can today no longer be seriously contested. But this tells us nothing with regard to the second question, which must not be allowed to become confused with the first. Moreover, in answering it we are reminded of the constant necessity for extreme caution by the simple historical fact that in all those religions of the Near East which are fairly well known to us there is not a single instance of unquestionably eschatological thought to be found. Even in Egypt we meet nothing but the myth describing the drama of the gods and the king. Those prophecies that have been discovered which recall the OT messianic predictions can all be shown quite definitely to be *vaticinia post eventum*, made up to honour particular historical rulers.[5] It may well be, therefore, that the historicization of the myth, by which mythological expressions are applied to historical figures, is a regular process, repeated wherever similar spiritual preconditions obtain;[6] and this may be responsible for the kind of 'sacred biography' mentioned earlier.[7] But this does not in any way imply a projection into the future in the sense of a firm *expectation of the End*. For the lore of world-eras, which envisages an almost uniform sequence of alternating periods of woe and weal,[8] is no more than a pseudo-eschatological product of that sort of wish-fulfilment hope and longing for liberation that is in

---

[1]Cf. e.g., A. Jeremias, *Handbuch der altorientalischen Geisteskultur*[2], pp. 313 ff., and *Die ausserbiblische Erlösererwartung*, 1927.

[2]So Norden, *Geburt des Kindes*, and H. Gressmann, *Der Messias*, pp. 415 ff.

[3]So A. von Gall, βασιλεία τοῦ θεοῦ, 1926.

[4]Cf. R. Kittel, *Die hellenistische Mysterienreligion*, p. 65.

[5]This has been irrefutably demonstrated, first by E. Sellin (*Der alttestamentliche Prophetismus*, pp. 234 ff.), and more recently by L. Dürr (*Heilandserwartung*, pp. 1 ff.) and A. von Gall (*op. cit.*, pp. 48 ff.).

[6]So H. Schmidt, *Der Mythos vom wiederkehrenden König im AT*, p. 20.

[7]Cf. pp. 474 f. above.

[8]Cf. A. Jeremias, *op. cit.*, pp. 295 ff.; Chantepie de la Saussaye, *Handbuch der Religionsgeschichte*[4] I, p. 508; P. Hensel, 'Die Lehre vom grossen Weltjahr', in *Erlanger Aufsätze aus ernster Zeit*, 1917, pp. 38 ff.

fact to be found everywhere. The really distinctive marks of eschatology are the very things that are missing: its absolute finality, its interpretation of the meaning of the present, and its qualitative otherness.

It is not until the Hellenistic period that we encounter genuinely futurist hopes which recall the eschatology of the OT. They emerge partly in the form of mysteries, in which the dawn of a new world-era is solemnly marked by the birth of a miraculous divine child (Horus, Aion, Helios), partly in predictions of an astrological type, of which the Sibylline Oracles and the Fourth Eclogue of Vergil are the most important. In the former, however, we are dealing not with eschatological, but with cultic and mystical experiences, the content of which is the change to a new age brought about not in process of history, but by magic. The one fairly loose connection with history is the idea—which may possibly be Iranian in origin, and which in any case is very much in the background—of the sequence of world-ages, each bringing to an end its predecessor. As far as predictions proper are concerned, it has been too hastily assumed that we are in fact dealing here with purely heathen material. The question has rightly been asked,[1] whether we may not have to take serious account of the possibility that these texts have been affected by Judaism, in particular the influential and spiritually active Judaism of Egypt; and whether this is not the real source of the strong note of hope introduced here alone. But even if this possibility has to be dismissed, there still remains a profound difference between this heathen eschatology and that of the Bible, namely that the former is not concerned, as is the latter, with a *consummation of history* to which the whole historical process is directed, and in which it finds its goal.[2] Heathen eschatology stops short at an abrupt, magical transformation having no inner connection with historical life. This is ultimately due to the fact that heathendom, even in its noblest exponents, knows nothing of the God of history who is exalted over all worldly events, and who has appointed an end for the perfecting of this world, just as once upon a time he called it into being.[3]

---

[1] By R. Kittel, *op. cit.*, pp. 61 ff.

[2] So also E. König, *Die messianischen Weissagungen*[2,3], 1925, p. 54.

[3] The only exception is the religion of Zoroaster, which characteristically, like the Mosaic, is a religion of a founder in contrast to the ancient cult religions. Its influence on the religion of later Judaism, which has been referred to above, is hard to confirm in detail; the attempt of A. von Gall (*op. cit.*, pp. 83 ff., 175 ff.) to derive the whole of Jewish eschatology from the Persian is mistaken in its basic premiss.

II. The *cultic derivation* of the salvation-hope [1] would seem to do more justice to its essentially religious character than the mythological. For it starts from the vigorous cultic experience of the festival of Yahweh's enthronement, in which the beneficent power and sovereign authority of God and of his earthly representative were presented with tremendous impact, and the principal content of religious faith thus raised to the level of a present reality. A higher degree of cultural organization, however, led to the dying away of the immediacy and naïveté of vital primitive emotion, so crippling the original force of this cultic experience; and this is said to be the reason why the now unsatisfied longing turned to the future, and projected on to that the values which it could no longer find in the cult, but which it could not do without. In this way the God experienced in the present turns into the Coming One, and the contemporary royal mediator of blessing becomes the future Messiah.

In criticizing this theory we may disregard completely the fact that the significance of the Enthronement festival for religious life, at least in the form assumed, is very much an open question.[2] More important is the observation that in every other case in which we find a dying away of the immediacy of cultic experience in one of the older naturalist religions, the supremacy which has slipped from the official cult is replaced either, in the case of the educated, by a rationalist philosophy of life, or among the masses by the primitive, and never completely extirpated undercurrents of magic, manticism and belief in spirits; but anything comparable to the Israelite eschatological expectation is nowhere to be found. To explain the successful breaking of the general rule in Israel by assuming some special vitality, some indestructible religious buoyancy inherent in this people alone,[3] is patently just to substitute one unknown quantity for another.

If many find it impossible to take this obvious remark seriously, the fundamental reason is that they have not yet understood sufficiently clearly *how essentially different are the dimensions of religious experience* involved in the cultic experience on the one hand, and the eschatological hope on the other. The opposition between these two is reflected in that of the two religious types of priest and prophet.[4]

[1] First advocated in the systematic exposition of S. Mowinckel (*Psalmenstudien* II, 1922), and since frequently adopted.
[2] Cf. pp. 123 ff. above.
[3] So Mowinckel, *op. cit.*, p. 323.
[4] Cf. chs. VIII and IX above.

Neither can be derived from the other, for each is rooted in a distinctive experience of God which dictates its particular development. Influences may be mutual, but they are always forced into line with the particular overall orientation. We encounter a clear instance of this phenomenon in the historical development of the eschatological hope itself.[1] The point may be made clear by looking at the one religion other than that of Israel which has produced an eschatology. For it is surely no accident that it should have been precisely the prophetic founder-religion of Zoroaster which likewise conceived of history not as a cycle or a closed system, but as a pilgrimage through perils and between abysses toward a great goal. Here the whole structure of the religious experience is different from that of cultic activity reposing in an all-sufficient divine present. The latter, when it has been debased by religious individualism, finds its appropriate form in mysticism, which wanders out of history into a supramundane salvation beyond time and remains indifferent to earthly forms of existence. To talk of its 'developing' into an eschatological attitude simply betrays a complete misunderstanding of the underlying religious disposition.

III. Incomparably more realistic is the theory of a *nationalist origin* for the Israelite hope, if only for this reason that, since the national life is a part of the historical process in which God operates, a consummation of the process would seem to come closer to the concerns of this basic religious conviction. In addition there is the fact that political features are present in eschatology from the very first, and that the Messiah seems to have been already regarded as of Davidic descent at quite an early stage. What could be more natural than to see the brilliant era of David as the source of the Israelite messianic hope, with the conflict between the miserable reality after the division of the kingdom and the soaring political pretensions of the ambitious Israelite nation creating the pressure under which currents that had flowed hidden beneath the surface now burst forth and become an inexhaustible spring of high-flown aspirations?[2]

Nevertheless it is impossible, even on this attempt at a solution,

---

[1] Cf. pp. 472 ff. above.

[2] This view, which had already been put forward by R. Smend (*Lehrbuch der AT Religionsgeschichte*[2], pp. 232 f.), P. Volz (*Die vorexilische Jahveprophetie und der Messias*, 1897), K. Marti (*Geschichte der israelitischen Religion*[5], 1907, p. 100) and many others, is also combined in various ways with the mythological theory by the exponents of that view: cf. H. Schmidt, *op. cit.*, and H. Gressmann, *Der Messias*, pp. 200 ff.

to do justice to the facts. It cannot be denied that the supra-national character of the Coming One, who as the bringer of Paradise knows nothing of war or rule by force, does not emerge for the first time as the result of prophetic influence, but was present from the very beginning. This may be concluded not only by arguing back from the ancient features in the prophetic figure of the Messiah, but also from the direct evidence of the Judah oracle, which promises the Peacemaker the obedience of the peoples.

This is strikingly confirmed by the fact that, neither at first nor later where the formative influence is the royal ideal, is the expected bringer of salvation given the titles *melek* or *māšiaḥ*, which alone would have signalized his political derivation. The conception of the eschatological Prince of Peace must therefore stem from another source.[1] This is supported by his close association with the Paradise myth, which as such is non-political and international. In conclusion, therefore, everything can be narrowed down to this one question: How can an eschatological redeemer grow out of a mythical figure?

iv. This question cannot, however, be answered simply on the basis of the Messiah figure. Rather must we turn our attention to *the religious core of the whole salvation-hope.* This is to be found in *the coming of Yahweh to set up his dominion over the world.*[2] This coming of Yahweh was, however, already depicted at quite an early stage as the restoration of Paradise. Just as men had been able to describe the occupation of Canaan as entry into the land of Paradise,[3] so in the fierce struggles of the time of the Judges, during which the very existence of the holy people in Yahweh's inheritance often seems to be imperilled, the restoration and consummation of his dominion in Israel was often sung as the return of the garden of God and its blessedness. We do not know who first gave shape to this bold hope; but it betrays the same overflowing enthusiasm for the way in which God's actions burst all human scales of measurement as do those terrifying pictures of judgment in which the insane fury of Chaos is

---

[1] This is of particular force against Gressmann's attempt to brand the Messiah as a political figure, who would then have to have been borrowed from outside in the form of the world-ruler and paradisal king (*op. cit.*, pp. 272 ff.). To postulate a Canaanite-Amorite Messiah figure, who in turn would have been borrowed from Babylonia or Egypt, is simply a flight into the void.

[2] Prominence has rightly been given to this fact by E. Sellin in *Der alttestamentliche Prophetismus*, pp. 132 ff., 160 ff. Cf. also pp. 459 ff. above.

[3] Cf. p. 492 n. 1 above.

allowed to return for the purpose of destroying Yahweh's enemies. As the oldest evidence shows, it is in the songs in praise of tribe and people that the hope first finds a foothold. The same conjecture may well be valid with regard to the enlistment and triumph songs sung in the holy war; and if so, it may be in the circles of Deborah and her spiritual kinsfolk, the seers and singers, that we ought to look for the sort of people who played a decisive part in the emergence and shaping of the salvation-hope. For it was in these circles that religious enthusiasm, the most fertile soil for great hopes, was a living reality.[1] In any event it must have been a prophetic spirit, and at the same time a poet of God's grace, who first dared to describe *Yahweh's redemptive act as a renewal of the Creation*, and thus made *myth the vesture of a hope rooted in history*.

It is, however, in *the development of this hope* that we really see the transforming power of the Yahweh religion. At first, it may be, the figure of the paradisal king was employed together with the other elements in the picture of Paradise merely as decoration, and was accorded no more significance than the rest of the stage properties. In the Judah oracle, for example, his presence has no other function than to symbolize the abundance of the golden age in a form which everyone can understand. But in the end religious thought, with its distinctively historical cast, could not tolerate such a lay figure of mythology,[2] and pressed it into the service of the jealous God. A pattern was provided by the judges and deliverers in whom ever since Moses men had constantly experienced the helping hand of Yahweh; and in fact the paradisal king seems to have been cast quite early for the role of the champion who would lead the people of Yahweh in the holy war, and procure for them the prize of victory.[3] This transformation is conceivable as early as the time of the Judges, but was doubtless furthered by the monarchy; and certainly the association of the Saviour-Prince with the Davidic dynasty, of which he is seen as the last member, strengthened the link with history. Moreover, from this standpoint the part played by the Judge and Deliverer in the internal affairs of his kingdom could be incorporated into the sphere of activity of the Coming One; and prophecy

[1] Cf. pp. 301 f. and 323 f. above.
[2] The continuing influence of this figure may perhaps be seen in Isaiah's Immanuel; and may also underlie the fact that in the prophets the Saviour-King is never connected with the great wars of the last days and the universal judgment.
[3] Cf. Num. 24.17.

shows how fruitful was this extension.[1] Thus the second important stage in the process of combining the myth and the hope of the End was *the transformation of a mythical symbol into an instrument of the God who shapes the course of history.*

By thus deriving the salvation-hope from an expectation that is primarily religious in character we are now enabled to do full justice to the elements of truth in the nationalist theory. That nationalist colouring was given to the expected bliss cannot altogether be denied. Indeed, this is only natural in that very early period when nation and religion were not as yet two mutually interacting, but independent entities, but rather the nation only existed in virtue of its common religion—or, to quote Wellhausen, was 'but an idea, and as such synonymous with Yahweh'.[2] Just because this is so, however, because it was not the nationalistic instinct which was the all-controlling factor which guided Israel's history from the very first, but rather religious belief which threw a unifying bond around the tribes, it follows that *it is not national feeling but religion which should be seen as the soil in which Israel's bold expectation of the future grew to maturity. It was not because men wished to become a nation, or sought with sorrow a national status that had departed, that they ascribed to Yahweh a restoring action in the future. It was because they knew God, and had made living trial of his sovereign power and his claim to dominion, that in times of crisis they were able to turn their eyes toward a consummation of history that would take the form of the setting up of God's kingdom. It is the man who knows God, who knows God's future.*

4. PREDICTION AND FULFILMENT

It may already have become clear as a result of our discussion of the Israelite salvation-hope so far that OT prophecy, as we have it today, encumbers the problem of its own fulfilment with special difficulties. Many well-trodden ways to an answer to this question have been shown to be no longer open to us; and the tendency is spreading to regard this point, which once provided men with an unshakable foundation, as the most brittle part of the relation between the Old and New Testaments.

[1]On the other hand, the idea that a representative of Yahweh was needed in order to keep the deity from becoming too strongly immanent seems of less importance (cf. Sellin, *op. cit.*, pp. 174, 182). This may be to ascribe too much importance to speculative thought; and it also makes the continuing juxtaposition of Yahweh and his representative not really comprehensible.

[2]Wellhausen, *Israelitische und jüdische Geschichte*[7], p. 37.

1. *The various attempts at a solution*

(a) It will be obvious from the remarks so far made that there can be no question today of reviving the old orthodox view [1] that a complete picture of Christ is foreshadowed in the messianic prophecies. To work out *a prophetic proof* of the truth of the NT Gospel by piecing together from the OT the various traits of the messianic King and the salvation mediated through him, and making them into a coherent picture, would involve insoluble contradictions with the history of OT prediction and its significance within OT prophecy. For the more conscious we are that OT history as a whole is to be seen as an act of God for the bringing in of his Kingdom, the more surely must prediction be subordinated to this action as one of its means, and the more strikingly prominent becomes *the importance of prediction for the historical period in which it makes itself heard.* Just as prophecy as a whole has a mission first and foremost to its contemporaries, to whom it interprets God's will in history, so prediction shares in this task by making the goal of the divine action visible and comprehensible for its own specific world and that world's special concerns. To this end it must adopt a temporal and concrete form, it must enter into the presuppositions, concepts, insights, needs and problems of its own time; and in conjunction with these it will acquire many elements of a temporally and locally limited character, without which it would not speak the language of the period in question. By affording us a more profound insight into precisely this *conditionedness of OT prediction,* by its exact examination of distinctive material of thought and imagery in eschatological language, and the connections of that language with non-Israelite conceptual systems, more recent scholarship has performed a great service to the understanding of revelation. For by enabling us to see with fresh eyes how historical is the character of prediction it gives us an emphatic reminder that the whole of revelation is historical in form, and thus rules out any idea that we might be able to construct a consistent picture of the age of salvation by artificially combining the various individual elements of prediction. Any mechanical transference of OT statements about the coming age of salvation to the Person and Work of Christ is thus shown to be a contradiction of the special character of biblical revelation, which proclaims not a self-

---

[1]On this point cf. L. Diestel, *Geschichte des Alten Testaments in der christlichen Kirche,* 1869; C. von Orelli, *Die alttestamentliche Weissagung von der Vollendung des Gottesreiches,* 1882, pp. 72 ff.

contained dogmatic totality, but a real God becoming manifest in history. Hence other ways must obviously be found of satisfying interest in the significance of prediction for periods beyond its own limited day and age.

(b) Because this insight into the temporal conditioning of prediction at once suggests a distinction between the temporal and transient aspect of the salvation-hope and a timeless aspect that will be universally valid, we may be all too easily tempted to see the real value of this hope in an *increasing inwardness and spiritualization*, and expect in this way to arrive beyond the temporal and historical character at whatever is of permanent importance.[1] But even though the observation that in the prophets the earthly, nationalist and cosmic aspirations yield pride of place to the personal and moral features of the new world is perfectly correct, it does not follow that the former can be set down as the steadily dwindling residuum of a naïve and adulterated popular view which, as prediction developed, would quite obviously make room for the real heart and nerve of the salvation-hope, an 'inward communion with God'. In reality the longing for a renewal of all earthly conditions, both in the actual life of the nation and in the Gentile world around them, always kept its place in Israel's hope of salvation; and the unresolved juxtaposition of nationalist and particularist features and spiritual and universalist ones in the vision of hope in the post-prophetic era warns us against *appealing to historical development* to support a value-judgment which finds the meaning of history in a spiritualization of the Kingdom of God. For at bottom this view is determined by definite ethical and philosophical presuppositions, and no one who does not share them will find the argumentation that proceeds from them convincing.

(c) In view of this difficulty it may be asked whether the deeper truth of prediction ought not to be reduced to *a general readiness to*

---

[1]An instructive example of the working out of this attempt may be found in E. König, *Die messianischen Weissagungen*[2,3], pp. 365 ff. Similarly P. Volz (*Die vorexilische Jahveprophetie und der Messias*, p. 89) sees in the emphasis on the blessings of physical life as the setting of the Israelite salvation-hope a limitation of the OT in comparison with higher religious values. F. Baumgärtel, in his penetrating and on many points illuminating book, *Verheissung. Zur Frage des evangelischen Verständnisses des Alten Testaments*, 1952, identifies this limitation as the decisive line of demarcation between the hopes of the Old and New Testaments (pp. 16 ff., 49 f., 63), and so falls into the danger of spiritualizing the historical form and realistic vision of salvation in the hope of the NT also in a way which is quite inadmissible.

hope which caused the nation to wait for a redemption and a redeemer, and so prepared it for the offer of redemption made fully only in Christ. On this basis all the individual features of prediction have to be dissociated from the question of its fulfilment; the real value resides in the psychological disposition which they evoke—an attitude of responsiveness to God's miracle of new creation, and one not prepared to rest content with the way of life attained in the present.[1] It can hardly be denied that on this conception there is no further point in talking about a 'fulfilment' of OT prediction, for all the internal links between the OT hope and NT reality of salvation have been severed.

(d) And yet, even though we may look for a different solution, this powerful simplification of the bond between prediction and fulfilment may serve as an admonitory reminder on a point of decisive importance. In a search for the fulfilment of individual predictions we can all too easily lose sight of the fact that eschatological thought concentrates on the one great new thing which the future is to bring, namely, *the consummation of God's sovereignty*, however this may be described in individual instances.

To say this is to state a pregnant idea of fundamental importance inseparably linking OT prediction to NT fulfilment. It is not the overcoming of material needs, nor the realization of political ends, which is the decisive factor in the hope of Israel, although both these aspects may have had a powerful effect upon it. But that the God whom Israel knows so well, both from the terms of his covenant and from his historical guidance of the covenant people, should lay all his enemies at his feet, and establish his dominion over all the world—this is at once the inward essence and the outward ideal of

---

[1]This is what the negative assessment of the value of OT prediction by many recent scholars really amounts to: cf. P. Volz, *Jüdische Eschatologie von Daniel bis Akiba*, 1903, p. 9; G. Hölscher, *Die Ursprünge der jüdischen Eschatologie*, 1925. For A. von Gall, who rejects the term 'messianic predictions' (βασιλεία τοῦ θεοῦ, p. 3) the problem of prediction and fulfilment naturally does not exist. In a comprehensive argument based on historical and theological considerations F. Baumgärtel has called for the elimination of OT predictions from the Christian hope, and therewith for the renunciation of the Prediction-Fulfilment pattern as a principle of interpretation in theological debate (*op. cit.*, pp. 28 ff., 75, 132 ff., 137). I myself have also rejected a mechanical application of this scheme in my paper, 'Les Rapports du Nouveau et de l'Ancien Testament', in *Le Problème Biblique dans le Protestantisme*, ed. Jean Boisset, 1955, pp. 109 ff. If this is not done, there is always a danger of over-emphasizing particular prophetic oracles, or of being slavishly bound to the letter of the prediction. But this is by no means to exclude a proper appreciation of biblical prediction and its fulfilment.

OT prediction, and likewise the decisive watchword for the NT fulfilment.[1]

This directly implies, however, *certain definite basic features of the hoped-for salvation* which clearly distinguish its content from that of any other religious hope. Foremost among these is the fact that *redemption is linked to time and history, to space and form*. In striking contrast to the religious philosophy of Greece we are here dealing not with a timeless idea, a new state of the soul, an interpretation of the world which is independent of history, but with *a once for all, decisive event*, by which the situation of mankind is fundamentally altered, and the whole of the future given a new shape. This concrete historical quality of the state of salvation is pregnantly expressed in the figure of the messianic King, which guarantees both the uniqueness and the 'real humanity' of the redemption.

It is this *comprehensive re-shaping* which forms the second basic characteristic of the OT hope. What is involved is neither a private affair of the individual human being, nor a new order realized only in the realm of the spirit; rather is it concerned with the nation and the world of the nations, and with the individual solely as a member of his nation. And this subjection of humanity to the sovereignty of God also implies a renewal of bodily life, in fact of the entire cosmos and its laws.

---

[1] When Baumgärtel singles out this basic idea as the fundamental promise, and sees its content as the divine covenant pledge, 'I am the Lord, your God', we can do no more than agree. Individual predictions must be understood as subserving this fundamental promise. Their significance is not exhausted with the foretelling of a future event, even when they indicate its occurrence correctly (a state of affairs not nearly so infrequent as Baumgärtel seems to think); they also serve, in the context of a particular historical moment, both to illustrate and to explain God's great plan for history and salvation. Prediction is therefore the invaluable method by which the nation is guided along God's paths through the enigmas of history, and it thus retains its inner truth even when it is not literally fulfilled. It is not something that can simply be separated from the fundamental promise as in essence foreign to it; nor can it be described as purely human conjecture, misinterpreting the will of God (cf. Baumgärtel, pp. 32 f.). To deny that it is inspired by God is a serious step; for it not only contradicts the NT understanding, but it also writes off the whole struggle of the prophets against the false predictions of their rivals as a mistake, and thus ultimately throws doubt on the fundamental promise itself. We must therefore go further, and talk about genuine prophecy and its fulfilment, even though in so doing we only seek to remind ourselves that the essential and important thing about it is the fundamental promise— indeed that this is the criterion of its being genuine. As to Baumgärtel's criticisms on the subject of the OT understanding of history and its concept of salvation, which are said to be incompatible with our present views either from the standpoint of scholarship or of religion, cf. my remarks in the essay, 'Ist die typologische Exegese sachgemässe Exegese?', in *TLZ* 81, 1956, pp. 641 ff.

The heart of this all-embracing order, however, is *real communion between God and man*—and this is unthinkable without personal determination of the will. In the covenant relationship the word of God had a decisive place as the supreme expression of the creation of this communion with God, and, by addressing man as an intelligent moral being, and calling him to responsibility, it guaranteed its personal quality. Likewise the consummation of God's sovereignty is unthinkable without the setting up of *a personal communion of will* between God and man. This character of the new divine-human relationship is brought into especial prominence when the perfect fulfilment of the will of God, which in the present is despised, is looked for in the age of salvation, whether it be the messianic King who guarantees this,[1] or God himself who ensures it by renewing men's hearts.[2] Even when not made explicit, however, this forms the obvious underlying presupposition. Its full profundity was grasped when it was spoken of as *realized through suffering*, whether this be the sufferings of divine love for the lost, as in Hosea and Jeremiah,[3] or the suffering of the mediator called by God, as in the Servant of Yahweh in Deutero-Isaiah and the good shepherd in Deutero-Zechariah, or again the suffering of the pious who cleave fast to God through every trial of their faith.[4] Because, contrary to all outward appearance, men here retain their hold on the object of their love and hope, despite the surrender of their own just rights, the will to personal communion is revealed in perfect purity and all-conquering power. The corresponding reality on the negative side is *the elimination of sin* as the decisive cause of separation between God and man,[5] whether this is looked for as the result of a purification proceeding from God, or of the atoning work of the suffering Messiah.[6]

It is this that supplies the profoundest reason for that *renunciation of the present world-order* which forms an increasingly definite feature of the OT hope. The discordances within a world originally created good must make room for the peace of Paradise; but far from

[1] Cf. Isa. 9.6; 11.1 ff.; Jer. 23.6; Zech. 9.10; Ezek. 37.24 and the royal psalms.
[2] Cf. Isa. 2.2 ff.; Jer. 31.31 ff.; Ezek. 36.25 ff.; Isa. 43.22 ff.
[3] Cf. ch. VII.4, pp. 250 ff. above.
[4] Cf. Ps. 22.
[5] Sin is seen as the real cause of all evil in Gen. 3, and in the biblical primal history generally; it is condemned and attacked in the legal organization of the covenant people; and in the sacrificial cultus it is openly recognized as a constantly threatening danger which can only be averted by the covenant favour.
[6] Cf. Ezek. 36.26 ff.; Isa. 53; Zech. 12.10; 13.1.

becoming meaningless within the terms of the eschatological expectations they were experienced as expressions of divine anger and withdrawal[1] which could only be removed by God's judgment and new creation, not by gradual progress.

From this grew up a readiness to resign the method by which the hoped-for salvation was to be brought about wholly into God's hands. The sense that this too is a matter for *God's sovereignty*, and that in the end no human power will be able to obstruct it, constantly creates, through all the stormy doubts and prayers for a final rending of the dark curtain, a willingness to submit to unexpected and bewildering postponements of the hoped-for realization of salvation, and to re-learn the lesson under the impact of new guidance in history. Not for nothing do the weal-predictions proclaim the coming turning-point, and especially its messianic bringer, as a mystery[2] beyond human conception, raised up from the hidden abyss of deity. The singer of the suffering Servant of God passes on his message in full consciousness of the hard paradox of what he is preaching; and when the unheard-of miracle of the divine new creation provides the theme of a whole prophetic book, as in the case of Deutero-Isaiah, this constitutes a serious and decisive rejection of man's whole tendency to 'know better' and to 'interrupt' in his dissatisfaction.[3] The most powerful presentation of this attitude of humble submission to God's decrees, and one in which all protests against his Providence are reduced to silence, is to be found in the Book of Job; here a position is adopted which is decisive for Judaism's whole understanding of God's rule, and which makes it possible to overcome the many disappointments of the hope of salvation.

It is these basic features of the hope which, in spite of the very varied forms in which it was historically expressed, give it *a consistent essential character*, and subordinate it to the one idea of the kingly sovereignty of the covenant God. It is just at this point, moreover, that the question of the fulfilment of this hope comes in. For it is these basic features, inseparably connected with the essence of the OT picture of God, and not any other individual details, which must decide whether the Gospel of the NT has a right to be understood as the real answer to the problem of OT prediction.

[1] Cf. ch. X, pp. 464, 469 f. and ch. VII.5, pp. 267 f. above.
[2] On the subject of the mystery-style of the prophets cf. H. Gunkel, *Die Propheten*, 1917, pp. 125 ff.
[3] Cf. Isa. 42.18 ff.; 44.24 ff.; 45.9 ff.; 46.10 f.; 48.1 ff., 17 f.; 50.10; 55.8 f.

11. *The double relationship of prediction and fulfilment*

(a) As soon as the problem is looked at from this angle, however, it can be seen that there is a distinctive double relationship between the blessings of the NT salvation and the OT hope. It is, of course, impossible to deny that Jesus' redeeming work, considered as the revelation of God's real sovereignty and nearness to his world, is *the fulfilment of essential concerns of OT prediction*, and this in a way which makes it clear that it is by virtue of an inner kinship of spirit that it is in line with the OT and not with any other form of religious hope. Its historical uniqueness combined with all-embracing universality; its basis in a renewal of the life of the will aimed at personal communion with God, and the demonstration that in this fact a new world-order has broken in, putting an end to this age with its apparently irrefragable laws; its concentration of these salvation-blessings in the figure of a mediator and saviour, in whom nevertheless God himself is directly acting and ruling; all these are the essential marks at once of the NT message of redemption and of the OT hope. Furthermore, it may be pointed out that that radical sundering of OT eschatology from mythology, nationalism and cultic experience which our discussions of these various explanations of the origin of the messianic hope[1] have enabled us to demonstrate is paralleled in the relation of the Gospel of Christ to these fields of permanent importance for religion. In its historical career the NT preaching of the Kingdom of God also had to fight against three principal dangers: against mythological thinking, which threatened to dissolve it in speculation, against a nationalism which from the time of Judaism's struggle against the Gentile mission of Paul was constantly menacing the supra-national character of the work of Jesus, and against a cultic narrowness which, in intimate alliance with mysticism, restricted the significance of the kingdom of heaven, which ought to have embraced the whole of history and Nature, to the field of the individual soul, and in the sacramental enjoyment of the divine life forgot the personal relationship of service and loyalty owing from Christ's congregation to its exalted Lord.

(b) And yet, alongside this inward agreement, there persists a *fundamental divergence* between the two things, which cannot be concealed unless one is prepared basically to misunderstand the nature of NT 'fulfilment'. That is to say, the universality of the new Creation, and that ending of the old world-order which is closely

[1] Cf. pp. 494 ff. above.

bound up with it, are not co-terminous with the unique historical fact of the redemption, but as the still invisible goal of the new divine revelation are temporarily postponed. Even though presaged and guaranteed by the Resurrection and the outpouring of the Spirit as already present pledges, they are as yet still linked with the Parousia of Jesus Christ, and so turned into the blessings of hope.

That Jesus' redeeming work had involved this *completely unexpected postponement and rearrangement of the content of the new life promised in prediction* was strongly and painfully felt in the primitive community, but the feeling was overcome in dependence on the OT attitude of faith by a willing recognition of the sovereign authority of the wonderful and only wise God over the actual manner in which salvation was to be realized; and indeed in the end the delay was understood in terms of the love and patience of the divine Lord of the world, 'who willeth that all men should be saved, and come to the knowledge of the truth'.[1] This was supported by a deeper insight into the power of this world, which had been acquired in intimacy with Jesus and in the absorption of his preaching, and which we can see expressed in the apostolic letters. These throw a brilliant light on the suffering of the Redeemer, and the faith of the congregation of his disciples, as the only way in which the world can truly be overcome. The problem which finds its complete solution in the life-work of Jesus is the problem of guilt, and this demonstrates his work as the cardinal point which alone makes it possible for God's renewal of his creation to begin. By the provision of the vicariously suffering mediator, in whom God himself acts both to judge and to forgive in order to win back to himself a human race alienated from him by guilt, a new communion between God and man is achieved; and the characteristic mark of this communion is that it completely disables sin, the real separating force, and thus opens the way to a renewal both of the individual and of the whole world. Here is the realization of one central salvation-blessing of the OT (cf. pp. 505 f. above), but in a way which still withholds from human yearning the other requirements of complete divine sovereignty, namely the ending of the old world-order, and the cosmic new creation, as gifts of salvation to be made visible only at a later date. To know these things as an imminent reality is granted only to the faith which will submit to the authoritative claim of the Crucified and Risen Lord to be the One chosen by God to fulfil the

[1] Cf. I Tim. 2.4.

fundamental promise of the Old Testament. In this way 'fulfilment' is removed from the realm of logical, rationalist knowledge, and made conceivable only to spiritual knowledge, that is, the knowledge accompanied and made possible by a personal decision. The community, which confesses the hidden Kingship of Christ, and takes upon itself as the newly revealed will of God's dominion the extension of that dominion through the herald's cry of his messengers, without any outward means of power or any visible transformation of the world, asserts that *basic characteristic of mystery* which runs through the whole OT expectation of salvation, and denies the right of mere man to lay down, from his knowledge of the prophetic predictions, the lines on which God must work. But this means that it has understood *'fulfilment' not mechanically*, as the solution of a logical calculation, *but organically as the unfolding and unveiling of a mystery of Creation subject to the divine omnipotence*, as a sovereign act of re-shaping, which only now fully brings to light the will of God concealed in prophecy, and is related to all prediction as clear knowledge is related to stammering presentiment.[1]

(c) That this approach does not, however, follow logically and inevitably from knowledge of the OT predictions, but derives from newly acquired personal decision, is clearly shown by the fact that Jesus was rejected by the leaders of the Jewish community. Here, as throughout the history of Israel, the gift of God brings with it the possibility of offence; and this can only be overcome by the resolute performance of an act of faith. But this only reveals from a new angle the truth that *the blessing of salvation is not to be divorced from a personal communion of will between God and man*; and this communion is only perfected in faith without sight.

A glance at the desperate and often mutually contradictory conceptions of the hope of later Judaism, which never made a unified picture, is sufficient to enable us to affirm that the realization of salvation which Jesus offered presented a creative synthesis from a conglomeration of essentially divergent and organically unrelated components;[2] and the undeniable consistency and living force of this synthesis forms an insistent testimony to its truth. But even insight into this fact exempted no one in Judaism from *the decisive*

---

[1] By this more precise statement of some earlier remarks I hope to have cleared up the misconception under which Baumgärtel was labouring, when he used this passage to criticize my conception of 'fulfilment' (cf. *Verheissung*, p. 97).

[2] Cf. pp. 486 f. above.

question, which was whether he was going to ascribe to Jesus the right to make such a synthesis; that is to say, whether he was going to see in his ministry God at work, or only a man, who may have been a genius, but who was also self-willed and inclined to self-divinization. Jesus himself gave those who were oppressed by this question no other help than to point to his complete filial obedience to his heavenly Father, who was to be seen in all his own words and works. Hence it can be said to be his own intention that ultimately recognition or rejection of the 'fulfilment' of OT prophecy in the NT Gospel must proceed from men's attitude to his own person—and without personal decision this is inconceivable.

EXCURSUS

THE PROBLEM OF OLD TESTAMENT THEOLOGY

THE *Theology* of G. von Rad, completed in 1960, presents an attempt to deal with this, the most important of all the tasks confronting OT study, in a way at once so distinctive and so significant that it undoubtedly opens a new phase in the discussion of the problems and methods of OT theology. The following remarks are intended as a preliminary essay in the consideration of the issues there raised. They are not, and could not be, a full assessment of the value of this original and independent outline of OT theology, either as regards its scheme or its treatment of the content; nor can they hope to deal with all the numerous questions to which it calls attention. It provides us with a theologically profound and artistically accomplished handling of the leading concepts and homiletic aims of the biblical writers such as could only be the product of a thorough-going absorption into the whole world of their ideas and beliefs, and forms an extension and completion of the efforts of previous works along the same lines which cannot but be welcomed with real gratitude. Nevertheless, our immediate concern is to bring out the *points de départ* of decisive importance in this reappraisal of the problem of OT theology, and by indicating their distinctive character to use them as a test of our own presentation.

The first point to be considered, then, must be the relationship between the theological expressions of Israel's historical tradition and the facts of Israelite history. The discrepancy between the picture of history constructed by critical study and the salvation-history portrayed in the utterances of OT faith has emerged ever more clearly in the researches of the last hundred years, and has long constituted an urgent problem for the understanding of the message of the OT. In von Rad's preliminary methodological remarks (I, pp. 111 ff.) this rift is wrenched apart with such violence, on the basis of the preceding historical sketch (I, pp. 13 ff.), that it seems impossible henceforward to restore any inner coherence between these two aspects of Israel's history. On this view the OT

narrators, invoking the licence of religious poetry, have dissolved the
true history of Israel; the 'acts of God in history' which they un-
wearyingly repeat (the call of the Patriarchs, the deliverance from
Egypt, the granting of the land of Canaan etc.) are pictures of her
history drawn by Israel in flat contradiction of the facts with the
specific purpose of extolling and glorifying the God of Israel and his
saving work. The formative intention from which this poetry springs
is thus not aesthetic, but the urge of faith to understand, an urge
which convinces itself of the special relationship of God to his people
by drawing a 'salvation-history'. The spurious factuality of this
salvation-history ought not to be confused with historical truth; it
rests on a quite different plane, and possesses a claim to validity only
for the man who is prepared to 'ask the same sort of questions and
accept the same sort of answers'. Anyone who agrees with this conception will have to divorce OT theology completely from the
historico-critical view of Israel's history, and confine it to the presentation of Yahweh's relation to Israel and to the world as this is
variously set forth by the different writers in accordance with their
homiletic purpose, the 'kerygmatic intention' (p. 112). In the circumstances 'reportage', that is to say, the most precise description
possible of these repeated attempts to base the meaning of Israel's
existential situation on Yahweh's acts in history, commends itself
as the best way of arriving at a realistic conception of that daring
enterprise of faith on which Israel embarked again and again in
order to be able to cling, in each new historical predicament, to her
witness to Yahweh and to the salvation-blessings guaranteed by him.

This basic conception of the theological character of the OT historical books enables the author to take their proclamation of Israel
as the people of God, and set over against it the Psalms and the
Wisdom writings as the response of the congregation to the power of
their God thus revealed. In the second volume he can then contrast
this with the message of the Prophets, seen as the radical critique
and reorientation of that faith, and conclude with a synthetizing
discussion of the relationship of the Old and New Testaments.

It is impossible to ignore that in these circumstances any genuine
historical foundation for a confession of faith in Yahweh, the God of
Israel, must always be out of the question. With the critical disintegration of the whole Moses tradition any conceivable historical
origin for the Yahweh faith is completely lacking. Consequently the
emergence of the phenomenon of Yahwism, whose absolutely

distinctive character in comparison with its religious environment even von Rad cannot call in question, has to be ascribed to the chance coalescence of religious ideas springing up here and there; and with this we clearly have to be content, however unsatisfactory and without parallel such an emergence of a religious conception so uniquely penetrating as that of the faith of the OT may seem. Since such an approach must also throw doubt on all the later historical evidence in the OT, one is forced to ask whether a religious testimony which possesses no assured connection with historical reality can be regarded as valid evidence of a historical revelation? Even if one recognizes that there is visible in it an earnest effort to link up faith to some orientation and proof in history, it is hardly possible to avoid characterizing it as a religious philosophy. All this is strongly reminiscent of the trend in NT studies inspired by Bultmann, in which the connection of the kerygma with historical reality has become equally problematical.

This impression is confirmed when we come to the second main point which must be mentioned, namely the question whether what the OT witnesses proclaim allows of being incorporated into a self-contained system of belief. On the ground that the various confessions of faith in Yahweh are sharply distinctive in character the answer given to this question is a decisive 'No'. Indeed, if the testimonies of OT belief do present only a 'number of different and disparate acts of revelation, lacking a definitive focal point' (I, p. 121),[1] then undoubtedly there can be no more talk of any constant factor in God's relations with Israel. The subject of theological study is not a people of God, held together through all the vagaries of the ages by the continuous exercise of divine love, but a selection of theologically important confessions of faith in the God of Israel, organized round the religious concept of the people of God. To describe the confessional content of these has nothing in common with the task of expounding their organic coherence by means of a systematic presentation of Israelite belief; on the contrary, the latter must be rejected as a dangerous process of abstraction which can only lead to the 'bloodless schemata' of a system of religious concepts.

It is all of a piece with this approach that the method adopted in dealing with a third major problem of OT theology, that of the inter-

---

[1] In this connection we would like to ask how, if this is so, the 'reflections of Israel on herself' (I, p. 124) ascribed to various periods can be described as revelation at all?

relation of the two Testaments, should be that of typology. In reviving this very ancient definition of the relationship, however, stringent limitations have been imposed upon it. That the religious utterances of the OT find in the NT and its Christ a corroboration and development of a factual kind is quite definitely not what is recognized as the 'fulfilment' which can bring peace to the continual upheaval of OT faith. Instead the discontinuity of the divine revelations which came to Israel, each historically isolated from the others in a way that no intellectual religious connection could hope to bridge, points to the fact that these un-cohesive 'divine events in history' acquire their ultimate meaning only as prefigurations of the Christ-event. For all this, however, they are to be understood in no instance in their 'static givenness' or mere factuality, but in the distinctive 'leaning' of their occurrence toward a future fulfilment (II, p. 384). Not that there is any method of confirming or establishing this interpretation (II, p. 387). Just as in the OT itself there is already a free, charismatic character about the way in which the typological significance of a particular event of weal or woe is understood (pp. 334 ff.), so in the NT there is no absolute norm for the Christian understanding of the OT; and this would seem to be confirmed by the differing methods of interpretation used by the NT writers. We must therefore give up all idea of a normative interpretation of the OT, and leave everything to the eclectic charismatic freedom of the expositor, who will constantly be establishing new typological connections between the Testaments in a great variety of ways.

The common principle behind these three significant answers to important questions in OT theology only becomes clear, however, when we see in them the effect of *the conviction that the existentialist interpretation of the biblical evidence is the right one*. If what matters in both the Old and New Testaments is the existential understanding of the professing believer, and not the presuppositions or individual content of his belief, then obviously the relation of his convictions to history becomes immaterial. Instead the thing of central importance, as being the proper theme of theology, is the later implementation of his existential interpretation. Similarly, from this point of view, any attempt to draw a unifying line through all the various testimonies is to be rejected as irrelevant, since it could only be a distraction from the main concern, and might obliterate the self-contained character of each individual testimony with regard to structure and content. Finally, in the relationship to the NT, it is the unique form of the individual confession which is the essential factor on which attention must be concentrated, for it is in this that the existential interpretation takes place. The NT 'fulfilment' can then reside only in the reflection of the OT 'type' in the NT act of faith, a process in which the correspondence of the two parts of the existential interpretation can be seen in a great variety of ways, the choice of which must always be left to the charismatic understanding of the expositor.

How does the standpoint of the present *Theology of the OT* compare with that just described? First, the basic assumption that existential illumination constitutes the proper revelatory function of the testimonies of Scripture seems to the present writer quite invalid. It involves an intolerable cramping of the far more comprehensive vision of the biblical preaching, and totally obscures the importance for the faith of the congregation of God's sovereignty in the universe and in the history of mankind. Hence the sacrifices required if this approach is to be carried out without restriction must be rejected as too severe. There must be an absolute refusal to surrender a real historical foundation to the faith of Israel, or to interpret the conflicts between the statements of the OT version of history and that discovered by critical scholarship in a merely negative way as proof of the unimportance of the historical reference of religious statements. This denigration is to be all the more vigorously resisted when it is realized that in the OT we are dealing not with an anti-historical transformation of the course of history into a fairy tale or poem, but with an interpretation of real events inspired by contact with the mysterious Creatorhood of the God who controls history, and from continual experience of his saving action. Such interpretation is able, by means of a one-sided rendering, or one exaggerated in a particular direction, to grasp and represent the true meaning of the event more correctly than could an unobjectionable chronicle of the actual course of history;[1] for it contains a prophetic element, which is something essentially different either from a purely reflective estimate of its own place in the train of events, or from a merely anthropocentric intellectual construction. The link between the testimony of faith and the facts of history is not therefore a topic to be excluded from the scope of OT theology, but calls for continuous

---

[1] This way of looking at the matter does also appear occasionally in von Rad's work (e.g., II, pp. 11 ff.) but without exerting any decisive influence on his fundamental approach.

and careful attention, if the claim of Israel's faith to be founded on facts of history is to be anything more than a mental device for overcoming the problem of history, and lacking, in the last resort, any kind of binding authority.

The verdict against a systematic presentation of the totality of Israel's faith will likewise lose its stringent character, if the variety of the OT testimonies, which must of course be carefully taken into account in its place, is interpreted not as a discontinuity of the revelatory process, but as the result of observing a complex reality from various angles in ways which are in principle concordant one with another. There is in fact no legitimate reason why we should be forbidden to look for an inner agreement in these testimonies of faith which we have so carefully analysed; and in this agreement, despite their great differentiations and internal tensions, certain common basic features emerge which in combination constitute a system of belief which is both unitary in its essential structure and fundamental orientation and also unique in the history of religions. The charge that such a method only arrives at an abstraction is not in fact well conceived. For in the systematic presentation of Israel's faith we are not concerned with framing a system of religious concepts capable of providing a complete all-round 'corpus of doctrine' in the form of a consistent and harmonious intellectual structure. Our purpose is to examine the content for faith of a particular relationship with God, a relationship which has always to be seen as a dynamic process, expressing itself in history in many ways, and fluctuating between periods of rich and profound insight and periods of stunting and impoverishment, but which for all that exhibits a marvellous consistency in fundamental features which marks it out from its religious environment as an entity *sui generis*. That in such a treatment it is often necessary to argue *a posteriori* in order to bring to light a pattern of belief not directly presented as such in the sources is in general nothing unusual or aprioristically questionable. It is simply the method demanded in any scientific description of the content of one's sources—and indeed the one which has to be employed even when concentrating on the kerygmatic intentions of the OT witnesses, as is shown when von Rad is himself led by it to insert an important systematic section ('Die Gesalbten Israels' [The Anointed of Israel], I, pp. 304 ff.). The actual amount of inferential reasoning involved is clearly of secondary importance. However, if misgivings about method do lead one to be content with a number of theologically important confessions of faith in the God of Israel rather than to inquire after the unity that binds them together, then it becomes impossible to make any assured statement about what authoritative force they may have for the Christian congregation. Instead one finds oneself in rather suspicious proximity to L. Köhler, for whom the OT contains only a number of theologically important 'outlooks, ideas and concepts',[1] the varied character of which makes it difficult, if not impossible to speak of any clear relationship between the Old and New Testaments, for the reason that on such a basis there is no means of arriving at an understanding of a distinctive divine reality, revealed in Israel and of binding authority. Such an understanding will only be possible where awareness of a definitive focal point in the OT revelation makes it out of the question to rest content with a number of individual unconnected acts of revelation. If the OT is concerned with the real encounter of God with men at a point in history, an encounter through which a people of God is called into existence, then the focus of its message must be constituted by this concrete relation of fellowship, in which God comes out of his hiddenness and gives himself for man to know. Here is the fountain-head of all further contact with God in history, here is at once the possibility and the criterion of all statements about his will or action. Hence it is in the covenant of God with Israel, taking that term in the developed sense defined on pp. 17 f. above, that there is to be found the point of intersection of all the major lines of the knowledge of God in Israel, just as in the NT this point of intersection lies in the Word's becoming flesh, as being the central saving act by which the NT people of God is founded.

What has been said will already have indicated that the one-sided definition of the relation of the two Testaments in terms of typology is unacceptable to the present writer. However important the connection between type and antitype may be for elucidating the significance not only of many religious expressions, but also of many concrete institutional forms in which the relation between God and man in the OT becomes fixed, and of the worshipping life of those who are the representatives of God's sovereignty, yet by itself it cannot do justice to what the NT understands by 'fulfilment'.[2] In

---

[1] *Old Testament Theology*[2], 1949.

[2] Cf. my essay, 'Ist die typologische Exegese sachgemässe Exegese?' *Vetus Testamentum*, Supplement 4 (Volume du Congrès Strasbourg 1956), 1957, pp. 161 ff.; now also printed in *Probleme alttestamentlicher Hermeneutik*, ed. C. Westmann, 1960, pp. 205 ff.

the latter context the vision of the people of God in both Testaments, and its call to a life of fellowship with God, is bound to lead to a historical realism which leaves far behind the restriction to analogy demanded by the existential understanding.[1] If the proposition, constantly repeated since first expressed by Bultmann, that the OT lies open toward a future is not to remain merely a statement about man, then it can only mean that the OT witnesses experienced God as one who leads men onward to a goal; who in his faithfulness to his work once begun continually overcomes the threats to his saving relationship with Israel by means of judgment and forgiveness; and who guides history toward a consummation in which his purpose of fellowship is to be triumphant. This goal can become ever more richly visible to men as they advance to more profound knowledge of God's nature, not only in its hiddenness, but also in the progressive disclosure of the mystery of his person; but it can never submit to a spiritualization which would take from it its character of a concrete reshaping of the historical world. It is this which gives the so-called 'messianic' prophecy its importance, and its genuine reference to the Christ-event (cf. above, pp. 501 ff.). For it is not simply a prophecy of the 'ideal' (von Rad, II, p. 398), but uses imagery to speak of a real salvation, even if the realization becomes effective only through a sovereign act of reshaping full of the creative richness of God.

We may go further than this, however, and say that in the NT the OT understanding of the world and of man, which springs from the self-disclosure of the divine will in the historical guidance of Israel, finds its deepest aspirations at once confirmed and expanded in a way which can hardly be described by any other name than that of 'fulfilment'. On the one hand the mutual tension existing between the proclamations of priest and prophet and sage is astoundingly resolved in the salvation revealed in Christ. On the other the new irruption of the reality of God in the NT salvation-event, which points to the NT people of God as the legitimate heirs of the old covenant people, overcomes the aimlessness into which later Judaism saw itself led in its attempt to put its OT heritage into practice, and which was inwardly crippling the conduct of its daily life. Hence, though it is undoubtedly true that the Christian community 'recapitulates' the existential experience of Israel (von Rad, II, p. 397), in that it too finds itself on pilgrimage to a final fulfilment, this can

[1] This point is considered occasionally even by von Rad himself: cf. II, pp. 344 ff.

never be an exhaustive description of the inner coherence of the Old and New Testaments, but must be taken in conjunction with the complementary truth of a comprehensive divine new creation in which the OT salvation-history reaches its goal.

The outline which we have here attempted to give of von Rad's definition of the theological problem may afford the reader an introductory insight into the developments taking place today in the field of OT theology, and thus help him to understand the points of agreement and disagreement between the comprehensive treatments under discussion. If at the same time it has also given him some understanding of why it still seems to the present writer, as it did before, that there is one task which OT theology can never abandon, namely that of pressing on from the OT evidence to a system of faith which shall, by virtue of its unified structure and consistent fundamental attitude, present a character unique in the history of religions, then it will have achieved its purpose.

INDEX OF SUBJECTS

Figures in italic refer to footnotes

INDEX OF MODERN AUTHORS

Figures in italic indicate to the pages on which a book or edition is mentioned for the first time

INDEX OF BIBLICAL PASSAGES

Translator's Note. In the German editions of the present work the only passages listed in this Index were those printed in the body of the text. It was felt, however, that this seriously limited the usefulness of the Index as an instrument of study, and therefore a selection of the more important references from the footnotes has been added. Where a passage is cited in the body of the text, the page number is printed in roman type; where it occurs in a footnote, in italic.

In the case of footnote citations it should be remembered that the comment on the passage in question may be found either in the note itself, or in that part of the page to which the note refers.

OLD TESTAMENT

Genesis					
I	186, 410, 413	17.7 ff.	58, *411*	3.13 ff.	186, 187, 189,
I–II	214	18.1 ff.	195		*190, 207*
1.19	*283*	18.5	144	3.17	*492*
1.26	408	18.18	*476*	3.22	283
2 ff.	*464, 488*	18.25	*243*	4.1–7	45
2.2 f.	*133*	20	283	4.16	290, *293*
3	*506*	21	*80*	4.21	*262*
3.22	195	22	150	4.22 f.	68
4	285	22.15 ff.	*476*	4.24 ff.	*138*, 261
4.3 ff.	145	24.12	233	6.3 ff.	187, 409, 411
4.11 f.	264	26.7	*283*	7.1	290, *293*
6–9	*464*	26.24	*234*	9.12	*262*
6.1 ff.	195	27 f.	283	9.27	242
6.6 f.	*266*	27.27 ff.	*476*	11.2	283
6.9	*418*	28.14	*476*	12 f.	*85*
8.21	*142*, 143	28.20 ff.	*145*	12.35 f.	283
9.12 ff.	*429*	30 f.	*283*	13.2	149
11.1 ff.	*464*	31.42 ff.	180	13.5	*492*
11.7	195, 408	32.25 ff.	*174*, 261	15	311
12	283	49	394	15.2	191
12.2 f.	*476*	49.3	148	15.11	221
14.7	*86*	49.8–12	*50*, 301, *473*	15.18	195, 196
15	*302*	49.24	180	16.22	*452*
15.7	*234*	49.26	304	17.14	283
16	*80*			18.13 ff.	242
17	*138*	*Exodus*		19 ff.	123
17.1	*418*	3.7 ff.	*233, 492*	19.5 f.	*40, 197, 408*
				20–23	71

535

APOCRYPHA

NEW TESTAMENT